D0354195

EL MONSTRUO

ALSO BY
JOHN ROSS

Rebellion from the Roots: Indian Uprising in Chiapas (1995)

In Focus Mexico: A Guide to People, Politics, and Culture (1996)

We Came to Play: Writings on Basketball
(editor, with Q.R. Hand Jr.) (1996)

The Annexation of Mexico: From the Aztecs to the IMF (1998)

Tonatiuh's People: A Novel of the Mexican Cataclysm (1999)

The War Against Oblivion: Zapatista Chronicles (2002)

Murdered By Capitalism: A Memoir of 150 Years of
Life & Death on the American Left (2005)

Zapatistas! Making Another World Possible:
Chronicles of Resistance 2000–2006 (2006)

Iraqigirl: Diary of an Iraqi Teenager (conceived and
edited with Elizabeth Wrigley-Field, 2009)

ANTHOLOGIZED IN
Nuclear California (1984)
Fire in the Hearth (1990)
Third World Ha Ha Ha (1995)
The Zapatista Reader (2002)
Puro Border (2003)
Shock & Awe (2003)
Voices of the U.S. Latino Experience (2008)

POETRY CHAPBOOKS
Jam (1974)
12 Songs of Love & Ecocide (1977)
The Psoriasis of Heartbreak (1979)
The Daily Planet (1981)
Running Out of Coastlines (1983)
Heading South (1986)
Whose Bones (1990)
JazzMexico (1996)
Against Amnesia (2002)
Bomba! (2007)

EL MONSTRUO

DREAD AND REDEMPTION IN MEXICO CITY

JOHN ROSS

NATION
BOOKS

New York

Published by Nation Books, A Member of the Perseus Books Group
116 East 16th Street, 8th Floor
New York, NY 10003

Nation Books is a co-publishing venture
of the Nation Institute and the Perseus Books Group.

Books published by Nation Books are available at special discounts for bulk purchases
in the United States by corporations, institutions, and other organizations. For more
information, please contact the Special Markets Department at the Perseus Books
Group, 2300 Chestnut Street, Suite 200, Philadelphia, PA 19103, or call (800) 810-4145,
ext. 5000, or e-mail special.markets@perseusbooks.com.

Designed by Pauline Brown
Typeset in 10-point Palatino by the Perseus Books Group
Jacket author photograph © Marcia Perskie

Library of Congress Cataloging-in-Publication Data
Ross, John, 1938–
El Monstruo : dread and redemption in Mexico City / John Ross.
p. cm.
Includes bibliographical references and index.
ISBN 978-1-56858-424-9 (alk. paper)
1. Mexico City (Mexico)—History. 2. Mexico City (Mexico)—Social conditions.
3. Globalization—Social aspects—Mexico—Mexico City. 4. Globalization—Social
aspects—Mexico—Mexico City. 5. City and town life—Mexico—Mexico City.
6. Mexico City (Mexico)—Politics and government. 7. Mexico City (Mexico)—
Economic conditions. I. Title.
F1386.3.R67 2009
972'.53—dc22
2009037122

10 9 8 7 6 5 4 3 2 1

To the denizens of the Centro Histórico past and present whose iron-willed tenacity and inextinguishable resilience have kept this island afloat in the face of the most monstrous odds for parts of three millennia now.

"The city received me with all the indifference of a great animal—without a caress or even showing me its teeth."
—ERNESTO GUEVARA, "EL CHE"

"The city is not just a geographical or spatial place. It is an essential process of our lives and our history. The city is us and where we come from. To take back the space of the city is to recover for all of us a territory that transcribes our lives."
—CUAUHTÉMOC CÁRDENAS,
FIRST ELECTED MAYOR OF MEXICO CITY

EL MONSTRUO

WELCOME TO EL MONSTRUO

MURDER AT THE HOTEL ISABEL

It is a comfortable room, but drafty throughout the winter months in this mile-high city. I have considered buying an electric heater, but given the state of the wiring, even a small appliance could short-circuit this old hotel, so I make do with sweaters and long johns until the sun grows stronger and spring is upon us again.

Room 102 has grown considerably smaller since I moved in here a quarter of a century ago. True, the 16-foot ceiling has not noticeably dropped, but 102 is now so cluttered with piles of paper that it is difficult to navigate the floor space these days.

One whole wall is lined with five-foot-tall stacks of newspaper clippings. The clippings are largely useless—to get at the files near the bottom of the stacks, I have to deconstruct this jumble of yellowing newsprint. Actually, the last big earthquake (6.2) did the job for me, spilling the contents of these moribund archives a foot deep all over the fraying carpet.

Books, another hurdle, occupy the northwest corner of my cave, but in no particular order. I can never find the titles I am looking for, so I am always scouring the used bookstores down on Donceles Street for titles that I know I have already bought, and the volumes have taken over one of the twin beds where my lovers once slept. There is no room for new lovers now.

When curious visitors wonder why I have stayed in this creepy hotel with all my useless detritus for so many years, I patiently explain that I have become accustomed to the antique furniture that has grown old with me. Despite their great age, the twin beds are still quite firm. The generous cedarwood *ropero* or closet cabinet is positively Porfirian, dating back to the turn of the last century when this old *casona* (mansion) on the corner of Isabel la Católica and República de El Salvador was first converted into a hotel by its French owners. But the *ropero*, which is elegantly stamped with the Isabel's initials fashioned in brass letters, is so stuffed with drafts of old manuscripts that I can't open a door or a drawer without inviting an avalanche.

In addition to the *ropero*, I share the space with a bureau of equal antiquity, a pair of writing desks strewn with the tools of my trade, and a dressing table where Irma Guadarrama used to sit to prepare for the day. I still see her lovely face in the large circular mirror.

Also living here are four tattered armchairs upholstered in brocade with carved, sturdy armrests that groan with age when one sits back on their arthritic springs, their legs as tottery as my own. Indeed, over the years, I have become another piece of hotel furniture.

I do not know who lived in this room before me. When I checked in a week after the great earthquake of 1985, the hotel was deserted and there were no clues, a business card or a forgotten article of clothing or an empty pill bottle, to inform me who the last tenant had been.

One reason Room 102 is so drafty is the large French windows that open onto a cracked balcony. In the winters, the cold air whooshes under the threshold or over the transoms of the splintered wooden doors (the panes are embossed with exquisite floral designs), and in the rainy season, the water pours in both above and below. I don't visit the balcony as much as I once did, ever since a foot-wide chunk of it cracked off the cornice to which it was attached and crashed to the sidewalk. Eliseo, the waiter in the restaurant one floor below, who has been here as long as I have, came running to dust off the startled pedestrians, but no one was seriously crushed.

When I first came here, I could sit for hours staring down the gargoyles and cherubim on the façade of the former National Library across the narrow street or conversing with that intrepid traveler Baron Alexander Von Humboldt, who stands tall in his stone greatcoat in the ex-library's scrubby little garden. But as the old neighborhood began to heal itself from the earthquake, the bumper-to-bumper traffic on Isabel la Católica Street became insufferable and I closed up the French windows and rarely visited the balcony.

Then one day, a young reporter from *Guillotine Magazine* dropped by and told me all about poor Wilfred Ewert, a onetime guest at this hotel, and what happened to him when he stepped out on his balcony on New Year's Eve 1922–1923.

It was a lively period in the life of this neighborhood, here in the heart of the old city and the country that bears its name. The Mexican revolution had finally petered out with the murder of the Great Zapata in 1919 and the streets of the inner city percolated with postrevolutionary insouciance. Cafés and cantinas and a *casa de citas* (whorehouse) or two lined both sides of Isabel la Católica Street.

Two blocks east on the northern corner of the enormous Zócalo plaza, adjacent to the National Palace, President Obregón had commissioned Diego Rivera to daub his first mural on the walls of the National Preparatory School. The Mexican Communist Party had set up shop one block south around the corner, on Mesones Street's flophouse row.

The shooting had died down and adventurous tourists took up residence in the cheap, elegant hotels on the surrounding blocks. D. H. Lawrence and his Frieda took rooms at the Monte Carlo on Uruguay, a stone's throw from the Isabel, and sucked up the postrevolutionary ferment that would soon inform *The Plumed Serpent*, a title that first brought me to Mexico at the end of my teens. While in residence at the Monte Carlo, Lawrence is said to have complained much about the plumbing.

The Centro attracted other young British writers. Stephen Graham lived at the Iturbide on Madero Street and Wilfred Ewert here at the Isabel. The three Englishmen knew each other and sometimes drank in the cramped Bar Isabel downstairs, although Lawrence, who depended largely on Frieda's income to survive, was more of a nodding acquaintance.

Ewert, a dashing lad who had soldiered in the Great War, had just published the hot London novel of 1922, *The Way of Revelation*, which wove the tales of a clutch of "bright young men" through the hell of the battlefield. Although London critics had been kind to the book, the *New York Times* limited its comments to describing *The Way of Revelation* as being "500 oddly printed pages." Just turning 30, Ewert, like Lawrence, was keen to set his new novel in this exotic, explosive land.

Stephen Graham was Wilfred's senior and would outlive him by many years. He had found limited success with several travel books on prerevolutionary Russia. Some critics suggest that he was a spy for the British Intelligence Service. One source, the Spanish writer Javier Marías, speculates that Graham had known young Ewert in London, was wildly jealous of his growing literary reputation, and followed him to Mexico. Another Internet entry infers that Graham was gay, citing an article of his published in 1933, "Dancing Sailors," in which the writer describes gavotting with "nancy men" in a North Woolwich, London, dance hall.

Although the gunfire had quieted in the aftermath of the revolution, Mexicans still owned many guns, which they traditionally fired into the air to bring in the New Year, a tradition that Ewert's friends would soon lament.

Soon after midnight on that fateful evening, Ewert is said to have stepped out on the balcony of Room 53 of the Hotel Isabel, which under the old enumeration of the rooms, if my calculations are on the mark, lay two stories above what the management now numbers as 102, and was struck full in the right eye by a bullet of indistinguishable caliber fired by an unknown hand. He was killed instantly. Stephen Graham, who visited his corpse in the Mexico City morgue, testified that his colleague wore a "puzzled, dismayed look" on his handsome young face.

The dead writer was quickly interred in the British cemetery which, years later, would be dislodged by the construction of the Interior Circuit, the city's first raised roadway. The precise details of the writer's demise are described in a volume that has long since disappeared from public circulation, *The Life & Last Words of Wilfred Ewert*, written soon after his death by, as the reader may have already surmised, the aforementioned Stephen Graham.

Wilfred Ewert was not the only Englishman to have encountered a *bala loca* (crazy bullet) in this neighborhood during the New Year's festivities that year. On January 2, George Stebbins, a Boer war veteran described as being in "the meat business" appears to have been trapped in a *riña* (ruckus) between soldiers outside the Salón Palermo, two streets north on 16th of September Avenue, in which he too caught a fatal slug—the soldiers were said to be arguing about the merits of local bullfighters.

One further coincidence in this sinister skein: On New Year's Day, Carlos Duermas, a reporter for the daily *Excelsior*, who occupied an adjoining room on the third floor of the Isabel where Ewert was encamped, was struck by a speeding car near the Balderas Street newspaper row and left to die in the street.

We know about these remarkable acts of unexplained violence thanks to a dazzling feat of literary fiction, *Negra Espalda del Tiempo* (The Dark Shoulder of Time), authored by the Spanish experimentalist Javier Marías, whose deeply researched version of Ewert's death serves as both digression and a reference point to sustain the Spaniard's argument about literary and real time. Marías envisions literary time as being "the kind of time that hasn't existed yet, the time that awaits us, and also the time that does not await us, the time that does not happen or only happens in a sphere that isn't exactly temporal, a sphere that may only be found in writing and perhaps only in fiction."

While police reports attributed Ewert's unfortunate end to a loose bullet (*bala suelta*) or *bala ciega* (blind bullet) or *bala loca*, Marías is suspicious that this too may be a literary fiction. Bullets fired into the air from the ground, as the police speculated to be the origin of the shot, lose speed as they travel upward, eventually reaching terminal velocity and falling back to earth. In this trajectory, the *bala suelta* etc. has diminished capacity to inflict damage on any target it may encounter by caprice, and injuries so received are rarely fatal ones.

Shooters consulted consider that for the bullet that plugged Wilfred Ewert in the right eye to have hit him at lethal speed, the missile must have been fired at eye level, perhaps from a nearby rooftop—the nearest rooftop position would have been from behind the bowling ball–shaped finials on the roofline of the ex–National Library—or from inside the Hotel Isabel itself, a conclusion that Maestro Marías shares. One more thing: In 2008, there are no balconies to step out onto on the third floor of this hotel.

In short, the author of *The Dark Shoulder of Time* fingers the author of *The Life & Last Words of Wilfred Ewert* for this crime, conjecturing that Stephen Graham, driven by literary jealousy, had snuck into the Isabel under the cover of the tumultuous New Year's Eve commotion, entered Ewert's room on the pretext of having a celebratory draught, and fired the fatal shot into his right eye. There is absolutely no evidence other than the Spaniard's conjectural fiction to support this conclusion.

The death of Wilfred Ewert spawned anxieties among the remaining English writers in the neighborhood. When the Canadian poet Witter Bynner checked into the Isabel several months later, he was assigned the dead writer's room, #53. Lawrence was horrified and convinced Bynner to move around the corner to the Monte Carlo.

Despite Wilfred Ewert's uncommon checkout, in the quarter of a century that I have lived at the Isabel, not many guests have given up the ghost on the premises. Lucas Alamán, a historian and Antonio López de Santa Anna's foreign minister, gasped his last here (pneumonia) June 2, 1853, a plaque affixed to the hotel affirms, but that was before my time when the Isabel was still a private residence.

One morning soon after I moved in, Celia Cruz, the stooped *camarista* who made my bed for 23 years before retiring to become a *vidente* or clairvoyant, found Don Alonso, a Spanish traveling salesman who sold pens and pencils in the provinces, dead in his bed across the glass brick patio from 102. Don Luis, a *Gachupín* like Alonso (although the hotel is owned by a French family, the Spanish have always operated the Isabel), paid for a lonely Mass around the corner at the chapel of San Agustín. Celia and Don Luis and I were the only mourners.

Those who take rooms at the Isabel are a mixed bag: busloads of Costa Ricans on a Mexico City shopping spree and Tabasco farmers in town for an Alcoholics Anonymous jamboree and a few Mennonites in overalls from Chihuahua who have come to the big city to sell their cheese, but most are low-rent European backpackers. During political seasons—a presidential election or a visit from the Zapatistas—North American radicals take up transient residencies. I have run into Naomi Klein in the lobby, and Norman Mailer's son.

Death does not seem to register at the Isabel. So far as I know, no guests (the *camaristas* call them *pasajeros* or passengers) have ever hurled themselves from the third floor of the atrium to the glass brick floor below, a death made for the movies (commercial shoots and pornographic videos are the only movies made here).

No *pasajero* has slipped on the slick marble spiral staircase and plummeted to his or her finale or overdosed on heroin or swallowed a whole bottle of sleeping pills and never woken up. The truth is that I've never seen a body rolled out of the Hotel Isabel, but maybe I'm naïve and the dead get quietly carted down the back stairs through the catacombs of the boiler room to be collected in the street.

This is not to say that ominous things do not take place, but when they do they happen behind locked doors on the upper floors. There are no keyholes through which snoops can pry. Guests mingle in the restaurant and the bar and the lobby, which has recently been redecorated in a style that blends a vaguely Moroccan motif with Don Quijote de la Mancha. Upstairs, the secrets are under lock and key. When I stand across Isabel la Católica Street and look up at the windows staring out on the city, the curtains are always drawn.

Nonetheless, odd unexplained sounds pique one's curiosity: a sharp bump in the middle of the night, a steady tapping on the walls, the rhythmic gasps of disembodied lovers having sex in an empty room three rooms away. Every spring, small birds nestle in the airshaft that separates the bathrooms, cooing mellifluously when I sit down to take a shit. Celia once told me that she had heard an animal thumping in pain in the abandoned elevator shaft and she claimed to have seen ghosts drifting through the back rooms on the fourth floor, which are rarely rented. I don't discount these spirits.

Everywhere in the nooks and crannies of this old hotel, from the roof garden where backpackers form instant communities of lost souls (a marijuana plant was recently found growing in a planter box up there) to the lurid warren of spooky rooms on the third and fourth floors, those who have lived here before still circulate amongst us. Wilfred Ewert drags his suitcase from one haunted room to the next as Stephen Graham stalks him through the darkened hallways. And I never stand out on my balcony anymore, just in case the lost bullet that is looking for us all finally finds me.

BEAT CITY

The high heat of the Mexican Revolution attracted Anglo writers like moths to a dangerous flame. Some burnt up upon arrival. In 1913, Ambrose Bierce, the author of *The Devil's Dictionary*, came to cover the war in the north and never got farther than the border, winding up in a common grave in Ojinaga, Chihuahua. American muckraker John Kenneth Turner exposed the underbelly of the Díaz dictatorship in *México Bárbaro* (1914) and lived to tell the tale. The revolutionary writer and activist John Reed traveled with Villa; his account, *Insurgent Mexico*, rivals his masterpiece *Ten Days That Shook the World*.

Katherine Anne Porter arrived in 1920 on the invitation of Diego Rivera and stayed on for a decade, growing progressively disillusioned with Mexico. The poet Hart Crane committed suicide by jumping into the Gulf of Mexico from the steamship *Orizaba* on his way home to Manhattan after a failed homosexual encounter in Veracruz. The postrevolution brought political writers like Frank Tannenbaum (*The Wind That Swept Mexico*) and Carleton Beals. Anita Brenner's *Idols Behind Altars* reflected the postrevolutionary art buzz. Wilfred Ewert's contemporary, Graham Greene, traipsed *The Lawless Roads*, a piquant travel memoir, and penned a biting attack on priest-baiting in Tabasco, *The Power and the Glory*.

Bruno Traven, said to have been birthed in Chicago but who grew up in Germany and took on the persona of the anarchist Ret Marut, had an office under the name of Hal Croft at Isabel la Católica #43— his 40-odd titles are still treasured here. Paul Bowles, whose writings delve the darknesses of the human soul, was a frequent visitor to Mexico before moving on to Morocco. The Beats were not far behind.

Mexico City's lure as a Mecca for expatriate writers is intergenerational. When I first escaped the New York jazz scene and got on the road with a copy of Kerouac's book of the same name in my backpack, *Downbeat Magazine* carried this revealing note: "John Ross has gone to Mexico to write a novel."

Before they moved on to Tangiers to hang with Bowles, Mexico City was the Beats' first foreign destination. "El Monstruo," as Zapatista spokesperson Subcomandante Marcos has affectionately named this city, was cheap and close by, drugs and booze were plentiful, and the cocktail of Aztec blood and urban grit was good for poetry.

Although he was a veteran of another war (the drug war), William Burroughs, the scion of the St. Louis adding machine fortune and a committed heroin addict, first arrived here with the wave of adventurous young gringos who used their G.I. Bill stipends to enroll at Mexico City College (now the University of the Americas), cruise the pyramids and the cantinas, flirt up the señoritas, and aspire to write the Great American Novel.

By 1951, Burroughs was installed at 210 Orizaba Street, a decaying apartment building in the increasingly seedy Colonia Roma Norte, where he had the notorious misfortune to blow his dear wife

Joan Vollmer's brains out during a purported game of William Tell in which a bottle of mezcal had been substituted for the apple.

The Mexico City cops were hardly fools enough to buy Burroughs's preposterous story that the shooting of his dipso wife was purely accidental. He was dragged off to the Lecumberri Black Palace and housed amongst serious criminals before the eternal *mordida* (or "bite") greased the skids and the author of *Junkie* and *Naked Lunch* was out on bail. Within months, William Burroughs skipped back to El Norte never to return to Mexico.

Orizaba #210 was torn down and rebuilt as condominiums several years ago, but its twin, 212, still stands and has taken on the aura of a Beat shrine. My friend Rocío, who was crashing in the rooftop servant's room, was surprised one morning by a photographer scouting a shoot on the lair of the Beats.

While Burroughs was out on bail, his old Times Square disciple Jack Kerouac came to visit, liked what he saw, got back on the road but returned four times in the next five years to the apartment on Orizaba Street which Burroughs had deeded to a fellow expat junkie Bill Garver.

Jack rented a tiny adobe room up on the roof, the *azotea*, where he assembled the poems that became *Mexico City Blues* (few are actually about Mexico City), dedicated to Allen Ginsberg, and wrote two novels, one in French and unpublished. The other, *Tristessa*, is a highly romanticized version of the life of a 23-year-old Mexico City junkie *puta* goddess he met through Garver and of whom he was hopelessly enamored.

In 1956, the year before the publication of *On the Road* sealed his fate, Jack Kerouac was joined in El Monstruo by Ginsberg, Peter Orlovsky, and Orlovsky's autistic brother Lafcadio. Gregory Corso, my West Village homeboy, came along for the ride. The Beats caroused Garibaldi Plaza where the Mariachis and the prostitutes and the pickpockets mingle, and regularly got bombed at the old Club Bombay on the Eje Central near Tlatelolco. Just a few years ago, Beat Padrino Lawrence Ferlinghetti read from his *La Noche Mexicana* (The Mexican Night), a hallucinatory account of a 1963 bus trip through the countryside, at the Bombay. Lawrence invited me to read with him. The Beat goes on.

On my first trip to Mexico in 1957, I kept running into Beats and Near Beats with whom I had rubbed shoulders back in the Village.

Alex Trocchi, Scotland's resident literary junkie long before Irvine Welsh (*Trainspotting*) claimed the title, was hiding out in Ajijic as was Beat sociologist Ned Polsky. I bumped into the late Steve Schneck (*The Night Clerk*) with whom I had read at the Half Note on Hudson Street, at Pancho Lepe's Beat pension in Puerto Vallarta. The legendary hipster drug smuggler Bryce Wilson ran a Beat hotel in Yelapa.

In the '60s, when we were settled into the Meseta Purépecha Indian territory of Michoacán, Timothy Leary would send us acid once a month from San Miguel de Allende and ask us to record our trips. Margaret Randall arrived in El Monstruo in 1962 and began publishing *El Corno Emplumado* (The Feathered Horn), the first international Beat literary magazine. The *Corno* was shut down and Randall run off in 1969 by the Díaz Ordaz government following the student massacre at Tlatelolco. Nineteen sixty-nine was, in fact, the year the Beat Generation died alongside the railroad tracks in San Miguel de Allende when Neal Cassady, the driver who put the Beats On The Road, woozy from tequila and barbiturates, lay down on the frozen ground in the middle of February and never woke up.

FIRST CONTACT

We descended on El Monstruo from the north, El Norte, the north of El Norte, New York City, the East Village, an airless one-room bathtub-in-the-kitchen apartment on Ninth Street, a few yards from Tompkins Square Park. We were my then-partner Norma, a Beat Queen seven years older than myself, and her daughter Dylan, named for the wild Welsh poet who had once bedded her mother. Before we hooked up, Norma had been the consort of Kerouac's childhood sidekick Henri Cru ("Remi Boncoeur" in *On the Road*). I was 21, an angry "younger Beat poet" (*Climax Magazine*). Norma knew the world a little better than I did and drank to soften her sorrows.

We kited bad checks and flew to Texas, crossed the border at Nuevo Laredo, and meandered around northern Mexico, holing up in a cheap hotel near the bus station in San Luis Potosí. Every day we walked out of the city until we were on country roads. We lay down in fields studded with burros and small herds of goats. The stupendously spiky maguey cactuses that divided the land could have stepped out of Eisenstein's ¡*Qué Viva México!* We wore huaraches.

At night, we sucked up bowlfuls of rich, greasy *birria* and *barbacoa* in the market, and I inhabited the all-night *farmacias* where glittering vials of under-the-counter pharmaceuticals were sold over the counter 25 hours a day. I stocked up on Benzedrine "White Hamburgers" and we caught the long-haul bus to Mexico City. In 1960, it took a whole day to get there from San Luis.

The Monster was more self-contained back then—not every square inch of the surrounding Valley of Mexico had been staked out by the squatters. As the tin-can bus bounced along the outlying avenues in the blue dawnlight, Mexico City looked positively ghostly through the dusty, cracked window.

We disembarked near the heart of the city and collected our trunks full of stolen books and baby clothes and household goods. Hipsters who had blazed this route before warned us that Mexico City *taxistas* would rob us blind. The alternative was the donkey carts that waited by the terminal to transport the sacks that farmers trundled in from the countryside to La Merced market just east of the National Palace. We hired one and rode into the very maw of this monstrous city with a burro as our guide.

We arrived on a crystalline November day, the deep sky a penetrating cobalt blue. Twenty-nine-year-old Carlos Fuentes had just published his first novel, *La Región Más Transparente*, translated as *Where the Air Is Clear* (the title is from an epigram by the elegant 1920s writer Alfonso Reyes), the overwrought adventures of Ixca Cienfuegos. The book, which ignited the Latin boom, was murky, but a mile up in the sky, the air was indeed clear. No one wore *tapabocas* (surgical masks) as we see now on winter mornings when the thermal inversions press the industrial gases close to the earth and it is a chore just to breathe. The natives seemed friendly, and street crime was petty and without violence.

We settled into a threadbare room just off the Alameda Park near Chinatown and a couple of blocks from Bellas Artes, and took Dylan to see 14 Woody Woodpecker ("El Pájaro Loco") cartoons at the Alameda Cinema across from the park, and then went out for Mexican chocolate at Sanborn's House of Blue Tiles, just like Zapata's campesinos had done when they burst into the restaurant to the management's great discomfort in December 1914 at the apogee of the Mexican Revolution.

We wound up staying on a few weeks, eating on the street and gawking at Rivera's striking murals on the walls of public buildings. Then as now, the Zócalo, the great square at the core of the old city, was a vortex of social protest—the railroad strike had been broken and its leaders, along with the Stalinoid muralist David Alfaro Siqueiros, had been packed off to Lecumberri. But there was other trouble brewing.

Norma, who was six months pregnant, felt obligated to visit with the Virgin of Guadalupe, and we rode the bus to the Basilica out in La Villa, in the north of Mexico City. Dozens of pilgrims crawled up the Calzada of the Mysteries on bloody knees, and Norma prayed to the Dark Madonna to protect the child growing in her womb, a plea the Guadalupana did not heed. I wrote poems in the Cuban cafés of the Centro that Fidel and Che, who were already dispatching in Havana, had once inhabited.

> *In the street,*
> *The Mexicans chant*
> *Yanqui Go Home*
> *But I am not a Yanqui*
> *And I have no home.*
> *I come from another country,*
> *The nation of the Beat.*

Although the city was clean, even affable, we wanted desperately to get out beyond the buildings and find some land on a really remote mountainside, build a house, plant some corn, raise some goats, have a few kids. So I stocked up on White Hamburgers and we headed south.

Well, at least as far south as the Southern Terminal. The first-class buses refused to carry our trunks of stolen goods. I jumped up on one and harangued the first-class passengers about their treatment of the Indians and the campesinos. I took off my huarache and shook it at the curious crowd that was gathering. "You see this huarache?" I yelled. "This is why you will not let us on your bus!"

There was nothing else to do except hire a *diablero* who hand-trucked our trunks over to the second-class terminal, and we boarded a lumpy old omnibus that took us over the top of the Sierra of

Chichinautzin to Morelos state, and we just kept moving south (to Oaxaca) and west (Michoacán).

Except for brief ins and outs at Benito Juárez International Airport on my way to and from Latin American hot spots, I evaded Mexico City for the next 25 years. Then on Tuesday, September 19, at 7:19 in the morning, the Monstruo was cruelly punched by an 8.1 grade earthquake that killed as many as 30,000 citizens. I was in Lima, Peru, that morning, working Sendero Luminoso stories, and Sandy Close, my boss at Pacific News Service, asked me to head up to Mexico City to cover the aftermath of the tragedy.

I touched down early morning September 26 and caught a cab through the broken city. The driver couldn't get any closer to the old hotel on Isabel la Católica, where I had overnighted down the years, than the Eje Central, and I had to haul my luggage in from that deserted, fractured avenue through piles of rubble.

Miraculously, the cavernous Hotel Isabel on the corner of República de El Salvador had survived the killer quake with only a long, jagged scar running the length of its brick façade. Despite the fact that there were no guests, Miguel Ángel, the solemn deskman, was in uniform. I paid him 5,000 old pesos, about five bucks, he handed me the key to Room 102, and I am still here sharing my nights with the ghost of Wilfred Ewert.

I

THE BIRTH OF
A MONSTRUO

A t high noon, when viewed from the Observation Deck on the 44th floor of the Latin American Tower, this monster of a city appears inert, a gargantuan stone mass spreading to the four cardinal directions as far as the eye can see—which is not all that far, given the dismal air quality. Some 189 meters below, matchbook cars inch through the Monstruo's clotted veins and pedestrians scuttle here and there like cockroaches when a flick of the kitchen light disturbs their feast.

Who first conceived of this city as a monster?

The metaphor was contemplated as far back as Aztec mythology, when the city was just an island. In the past century, Ernesto P. Uruchurtu, the Iron Regent who ruled the metropolis like it was his own private fiefdom from 1952 to 1966, confessed to the newspaper *Excelsior* that Mexico City had become a *monstruo*. Subcomandante Marcos, the quixotic Zapatista rebel mouthpiece, uses the term endearingly when he refers to the capital.

On a Saturday in the spring of 2008, the Monstruo is bathed in ugly scuzz. The glare up here is blinding and the horizon shrouded by pestilent nicotine-stained smog, drizzling particulates, and lethal, albeit invisible, ozone that registers 115 points on the IMECA scale, short of an environmental "contingency" but which cuts like sandpaper on the back of one's throat.

The colors of this city of stone and concrete are muted by the smog: ochres and brick reds and nuanced shades of gray. Close by, the Alameda, a bouquet of mutant chlorophyll, is the only visible green space—the vast Chapultepec Park to the west has disappeared behind a curtain of particulate.

The west is the direction of the New City. Monolithic *rascacielos* (skyscrapers) stand stiff as tombstones on the Paseo de La Reforma, Lomas de Chapultepec, and high-end Polanco, comfortable districts in which the *gente decente* (decent people) consume daily what it takes to feed the Indian south of Mexico for a year.

According to a plaque posted in the lobby by the World Federation of Great Towers, the Torre Latinoamericana, constructed by an insurance company of the same name, was the fourth-largest skyscraper "below the Tropic of Cancer" when it was inaugurated in 1956 by Uruchurtu. The air was still clear and Mexico City the *región más transparente*, and on most days, you could see where El Monstruo began and ended from up here.

The Latin American Tower's façade is all glass and aluminum, the very essence of 1950s modernism. From its base, the building narrows like a wedding cake in layers, tapering into the spiring sky where it is topped by a tall antenna that looks like it stepped right out of the old RKO logo. If King Kong were still alive, the Latin American Tower could be a knockoff of the Empire State.

The Torre Latinoamericana overlooks the broad, busy avenue once known as San Juan de Letrán, now the Eje Central Lázaro Cárdenas, which sports many bars and entertainment venues, most of them concentrated around Garibaldi Square, the Mariachi hangout a mile north. In 1956, the year the Torre opened its doors, mambo was king and the King of the Mambo, Pérez Prado, held forth at the Teatro Blanquita just across the Eje from the crooning Mariachis.

But by the mid-1980s the Torre Latinoamericana, much like the mambo, had been eclipsed. PEMEX, the nationalized oil monopoly, threw up a 54-story skyscraper that remained the Monstruo's tallest structure until the construction of the Torre Mayor on Reforma in 2003, which topped out at 85 stories. Today, the Latin American Tower retains a certain tacky charm, and for those of us who live in the old quarter, the Centro Histórico, it is an iconic reference point always looming over our shoulders.

THE SHAPE OF THE MONSTER

The contours of El Monstruo are achingly flat, acres of low-slung roofs crowded with clotheslines and antennas, the monotony broken by an occasional church cupola and, to the north, by the high-rise cluster of Tlatelolco with 118 buildings, still Latin America's most grandiose housing complex.

The north is the direction of Mictlán, the land of the dead, from which the natives of this place first came and to which they will return when their time comes. The north is also the direction of the Dark Virgin who, as the myth dictates, revealed herself to the Indians on Tepeyac Hill in 1531. An absurd religious theme park and merry-go-round-like Basilica now occupy the site.

The view to the south is blunted by the effluvia. Although the south of the city includes some of the wealthiest and most charming colonies in the megalopolis (Coyoacán and San Ángel are two), money doesn't buy good air. Nonetheless, on clear, cold winter mornings before the thermal inversion descends, the twin snow-capped volcanoes, Popocatépetl ("The Smoking Mountain") and Iztaccíhuatl ("The Sleeping Lady") are sometimes on the eyeline, and it feels for a quick minute as if one can see forever. According to popular mythology, the rumblings and exhalations of the hyperactive Popo ("Don Goyo" to those who dwell on his flanks) presage social catastrophe.

But such days are few in a city where the air quality is said to murder tens of thousands of inhabitants a year. Air quality in Mexico City is predicated on the number of emission-spewing vehicles creeping through the veins of El Monstruo at any given moment (5 million), the formulation of the gasoline, and the configuration of the Valley of Mexico upon whose floor the city sits. In truth, the Valley of Mexico is not a valley at all but a self-contained basin hemmed in by 8,000-foot peaks with no natural drainage. The surrounding mountains lock in the venomous air and turns respiration into a harrowing adventure.

Many have sought to save the Monster from itself. The late leftist illuminati Heberto Castillo, a brilliant civil engineer, had plans to build giant fans on the hillsides to at least keep the bad air moving.

WHAT LIES BELOW

Here in El Monstruo nothing is what it used to be. The city tears itself down and builds itself up again and again with unnerving frequency. What lies below the street stubs your toes every step you take.

The old city lies at the foot of the Latin American Tower. Indeed, the site upon which the tower rises was once the Emperor Moctezuma's fabled zoo where 300 servants catered to the whims of thousands of specimens the Aztec ruler collected—jaguars and tigers and ocelots seized from the southern jungles, delicate Quetzal birds captured in the cloud forests of what is now Guatemala and Chiapas. One whole palace was set aside for birds of prey. North American bison were reportedly on display, tapirs and lynxes and crocodiles, wild boars and American camels. The Conquistador Bernal Díaz del Castillo, who recorded his Conquest in exacting detail, was repelled by the Emperor's collection of exotic serpents.

The Conquistadores came to steal the gold, the Franciscans to save souls. Just as they had torn down the abominable temples of blood sacrifice to Huitzilopochtli and Tláloc in the Zócalo, the padres destroyed the Emperor's zoo, slaughtered thousands of captive beasts, and cleansed and blessed the site. Father Pedro de Gante was charged with building a convent to bring Indian girls to Jesus Christ—a statue of the good padre suggestively patting an Indian girl on the head can be found today on the pedestrian passage that bears his name just a block away. Some sinners insist the statue is a monument to priestly pedophilia.

The Franciscans retained title to the convent tract for the next 300 years. Then in 1856, in the midst of the War of Reform between liberals and conservatives, President Ignacio Comonfort—an ally of the Zapotec Indian chief justice of the Supreme Court Benito Juárez, who was a strong advocate for confiscating the Church's extensive properties—expropriated the Convent of San Francisco. Hundreds of prisoners were released from the city's hellish lockups, handed sledgehammers, and encouraged to pulverize the church buildings into dust while the municipal band tootled *La Cangrejera* (The Dance of the Crab).

The pretext for this pounding was urban renewal—the widening of what is now Madero Street—but the caper had more to do with the booming real estate market. What had once been the Convent of San Francisco was sold off in lots to the highest bidders. Only the cloister, which was rented out for a number of years to Chiarini's Royal Circus, was kept intact.

If the New City with its high-rise tombstones sprawls west to Chapultepec, the old city crumbles to the east, beyond the Zócalo—the great plaza that is still the political heart of the nation—encircled by the National Palace and the Metropolitan Cathedral, past the great tin-roofed sheds of La Merced, the oldest public market in the Americas; the monumental Congress of the country, and the Benito Juárez International Airport, out by the garbage dumps of Suchiapa, surrounded by miles and miles of squalid, dangerous *colonias* all the way to what's left of Lake Texcoco, draped in impenetrable muck from my vantage point, and from whose primal waters El Monstruo first emerged as Tenochtitlán, a long green island on contemporary maps floating like a crocodile in a landscape of smoking volcanoes.

WHEN THE EARTH MOVES

The Latin American Tower prides itself on being the first skyscraper built in a volcanic zone, one indeed particularly susceptible to killer earthquakes. On the soft, spongy soils of the lake bed, construction bordered on folly, but the skyscraper survived its baptism of fire not a year after it opened for business. The 1957 quake toppled church steeples and sent the golden Angel of Independence hurtling from her perch above the Paseo de La Reforma, but the Torre came through un-scathed. The devastating 8.1 *terremoto* in September 1985 panicked the building's elevator operators, who abandoned their oscillating cars 37 floors above street level but lived to tell the tale.

Although the great quake smashed up the center of the city and killed thousands, the Latin American Tower somehow stood its ground—just across the Eje Central, a popular morning café-and-churros stop collapsed, trapping perhaps 300 victims on their way to work. Indeed, butt up against the Tower are the remains of the Guar-diola Hotel, 20 years after the great shake & bake still a decaying jum-ble of broken walls, an urban ruin whose precise archeological age would be hard to determine without carbon dating.

But even if the Torre Latinoamericana has shrugged off the *ollines* (earth movements in Nahuat), death has visited here on high. Rafael Rivas became the Tower's first suicide in 1962, leaping over the barrier that encloses the 45th-story observation platform without leaving a note—witnesses claim he flew off into the void clutching a half-finished jug of tequila.

Up here, given this elevated scale, human activity is diminished. We are those proverbial ants scurrying across the esplanade of Bellas Artes or protesting two blocks north in front of the Mexican Senate, the *ambulantes* hawking their pirate wares under slashes of red plastic on the side streets, the pedestrians dodging the bumper cars on the Eje, the lovers cuddling on the park benches of the Alameda. The distance and the height flatten out and neutralize the chaos down below.

Up here, humanity's rhythms seem choreographed and predictable from hour to hour and day to day, except, of course, when El Monstruo yawns or turns over in its sleep and the ground opens up in geological paroxysms and the sky falls in and time stands still and the dust drizzles down on the desolate streets below where suddenly no one is moving.

Then the lights go out.

OBSTETRICS

The jagged screech of tectonic plates grinding against each other fills up the void. Gravity is unleashed. The Torre Latinoamericana slides off its foundation and lunges into the darkness. For a nanosecond or maybe millennia the 45-story skyscraper seems to float in space and time. I open my eyes, but the inky blackness is impenetrable. The cityscape has vanished and there is nothing to take its place, no Eje Central, no Alameda, no starry-eyed lovers staring deep into each other's souls on the park benches, no protesters in the Zócalo, no National Palace or La Merced, no smoldering garbage pits out by the missing airport. There is nothing. Nada.

Instead, we are immersed in primal broth. A blind, prehistoric shark curls through the murky waters and disappears into the gloom on the other side of the glass. In one blink, we have leapfrogged back to 50,000,000 BC. The rusting spaceship that was once the Latin American Tower lies submerged far beneath the sea and El Monstruo is still just a gleam in the eye of the Creator.

It has taken us 4,000,000,000 years, give or take a few millennia, to get to this part of the story. The Earth has been scooped out of the cosmos, the magma bubbles and cools, fuses, cracks, combusts all over again until finally it finds its orbit around the sun. The moon dislodges itself from the Mothership to leave space for the oceans. Just yesterday, about 15,000,000 years ago, a hard rain of meteors smashed into the wobbly, percolating planet, further rearranging its pitted surface. One great ball of fire and gases plummeted into the ocean near where the Yucatán peninsula hooks north, displacing the sea and asphyxiating the dinosaurs. Now it is midway through the Paleocene Epoch, "the early dawn," and the oceans cover the Earth. The world is about to be born all over again.

As usual, the planet is seething with internal contradictions. The ocean floor caves in and molten rock forces itself up through the wreckage. Each undersea explosion is more stupendously violent than the one before. Enormous masses of volcanic materials accumulate around the crevasses, spiraling upwards toward the sea's receding surface as the geologic epochs fly by at the speed of light. Finally, the volcanoes poke their conical heads above the waters. It is 25,000,000 years later and we are sailing through the Holocene.

The new volcanoes form a belt across what is becoming Mexico from the Pacific to the Atlantic, paralleling the 19th latitude. The volcanoes that survive are still geologically spry, 12,000-foot peaks like Popocatépetl and his Sleeping Lady, Citlalli (Orizaba, Mexico's tallest peak) and La Malinche that dominate the Altiplano and look down disdainfully upon the urban stain of the Valley of Mexico.

The Holocene melts into the Miocene. The world is still an unquiet place. Volcanoes blow their stack and mountain ranges tear themselves asunder, the broken topography flattening into plateaus and deepening into trenches and depressions. A large sinkhole forms in the west of what is now El Monstruo, about where the ritzy colony of Las Lomas sits today. Groundwater wells up through the porous basalt and the lake system fills in.

The Valley of Mexico, sited on the confluence of four conflictive tectonic plates, is susceptible to monster earthquakes. To the south, the Sierra of Chichinautzin collapses, blocking the valley's natural drainage. The year is 2,000,000 BC and the weather forecast is ominous. Great storms rage, lashing the geography and endlessly rearranging the landscape, rounding out the rough edges, etching in the rivers and streams. It takes a long time for the Artist to sculpt the contours.

THE SEED

And then the storms subside and the stiff winds whipping around the summits bear seeds that take root in the rich volcanic soil, and a few million years later the hillsides are covered with *oyamel* pine forests. The first mammals wander into the Valley of Mexico around 50,000 BC. The mammoths and the mastodons graze on the new grass, grow fat and old and die and leave their bones behind to give us a clue as to who was here first.

Giant sloths, a kind of small horse, jaguars (*ocelotl*) and pumas (*miztli*) and wolves (*cuitlachcóyotl*) roam the primeval forest. *Tochtlis* (rabbits) and wild turkeys (*uexolotl*) scurry through the grasslands. *Cuauhtli* the Eagle circles on the heights and millions of migratory birds—egrets and ducks and Canadian geese—feed upon the lakes below, where the fish are abundant and turtles and frogs and salamanders (*axlotl*) bring life to the muddy banks. Man is the last mammal to intrude in this paradisiacal valley.

Science posits that the descendants of Pithecanthropus Erectus finally navigated the frozen land bridge across the Bering Straits 22,000 years ago at the tail end of the last Ice Age, a time frame that Native Americans debunk, insisting that they have been here since the very beginning.

If the scientists' calculations are accepted, the travelers moved at an extraordinary speed through what are now the three NAFTA countries—the first hunter-gatherers are said to have breached the Valley of Mexico circa 15,000 BC, settling around the lake 8,000 years later.

By then, perhaps 5,000 human beings were enclaved in the confines of the valley. The environment was still a fearsome one, with the big volcanoes spewing fiery lava and their smoke plumes blotting out the sun. Large hungry animals ruled the forests.

THE MATRIX

A thousand years before Jesus Christ, at a time when civilizations were flourishing in China and Mesopotamia and Egypt, the Olmecs, Mexico's mother culture, were installing large mysterious granite heads on the Caribbean coastline of the country. Soon they were exploring the central highlands, and their intrusion into the Valley of Mexico is evidenced in the development of the settlements of Texcoco (600 BC) and Cuicuilco (300 BC). The valley's population had grown to 10,000 in the wake of the Olmecs' visitation.

Cuicuilco, a blazingly green teardrop in the smog-encrusted south of Mexico City, is a poignant example of how the past and the present coexist uneasily here in the abdomen of El Monstruo. Wedged between the *periférico* (ring road) and a mountain range of residential high-rises east of University City, Cuicuilco is accessible through the back door of the National Historical and Anthropological College (ENAH) or by leaping the hedge behind the upscale Plaza Loreto shopping mall owned by Carlos Slim, the world's wealthiest tycoon.

Enthroned on its singular spiral-shaped altar, one sees how the Cuicuilcos saw the world: The alignment of the sun and moon with the surrounding volcanoes and the shore where the lake once washed, was at the hub of their cosmovision.

In 2001, when Slim proposed to throw up a bank of 24-story apartment buildings on Cuicuilco's western edge that would have ruptured this alignment, those who defend what came before rose as one fist. The Zapatistas arrived from Chiapas, snaked their way up the spiral altar, and stared gravely at the construction. In the end, Carlos Slim shaved six stories off his sacrilege, but no one was satisfied.

The cultivation of corn spread slowly in drought-ravaged central Mexico, and it took a few thousand years for *maíz* to make its debut down in the valley. Although the lakes were a natural source of irrigation, pumping the water uphill to plots along the shoreline was beyond the technological know-how of the locals, who after all were new to working the land, and the cycles of drought and flooding set back the development of subsistence agriculture.

CITY OF CORN

Things changed dramatically with the discovery of underground springs at Teotihuacan 45 kilometers north of what is now the Monstruo around 100 BC. Teotihuacan was destined to become the New World's first corn culture and ultimately, because its bounty could feed so many, its largest city.

In the vision of the First Peoples, corn cultivation was tied to the disposition of the gods who governed the movements of the sun and those who brought the rain. To keep them in balance, tens of thousands of indentured laborers were put to work assembling the great Pyramid of the Sun, the centerpiece of the Teotihuacan complex, between 150 and 200 AD, now one of Mexico's most lucrative tourist magnets where thousands of white-clad pilgrims climb to the pinnacle each spring equinox to soak up the cosmic rays. Since 2003, amongst other global encroachments, the Pyramid of the Sun has overlooked a Wal-Mart megastore. And in 2009 the governor of Mexico State, a PRI presidential aspirant, sought to install a light-and-sound show that would convert both pyramids into twin jukeboxes that could be seen from 14 kilometers off.

But the megastore is really just a continuing expression of Teotihuacan's dedication to commerce. With its broad avenues and enclosed citadel, the city that grew to 200,000 souls had housed armies of artisans and a great *tianguis* or bazaar in which tons of agricultural produce changed hands daily.

The downfall of Teotihuacan and the diaspora of its population can be chalked up to the recurring droughts that dried out central Mexico during the early years of the first Christian millennium. When the groundwater gave out under the weight of the population, Teotihuacan's carrying capacity collapsed. The juju of the priestly class (human sacrifice was practiced in moderation) just didn't seem to have much clout in staving off eventual disaster. Barbarians drifted in from the north and picked the old city clean around the edges. By 700 AD, the first corn culture in the Americas had gone belly-up.

GIVING THE CHICHIMECAS A BAD NAME

The barbarians—Chichimecas from the northern deserts given to predatory marauding—would worry the valley dwellers for the next 600 years. But the longer the outlanders hung around, the more acculturated they became. The Xólotl Codex depicts the wanderings of Xólotl and his son Nopaltzin in the valley—in the pictographs, the travelers are sheathed in skins and the villagers clothed in white cottons. In the last frames, Xólotl and Nopaltzin have settled in.

Acculturated Chichimecas settled at the north end of the valley where Tula, Hidalgo, now sprawls. The Toltecs delivered a short-lived civilization that rapidly spread beyond the Valley of Mexico. Having adopted as their central deity a minor Teotihuacan god, the Toltecs carried the cult of Quetzalcóatl, the Plumed Serpent, as far south as the Kingdom of the Mayas.

But the Toltecs too were ravaged by the drought cycles and fresh invasions of Chichimecas from the north. When their civilization disintegrated in the 10th century, the valley fragmented into warring factions for the next 200 years, with power accumulating to Texcoco and Azcapotzalco on opposite side of the lake. With diminishing game, perpetual drought, and perennial warfare, the population of the Valley of Mexico shrank drastically in the 11th and 12th centuries.

Then in the early 1300s, a particularly brutish band of outlanders stomped into the valley. Purported to be originally from an island in the mythical Lake Aztlán in the Pacific northwest state of Nayarit, the "Aztecas," or "Mexicas" as they came to be called, had been on the road for more than 200 years hauling around their blood-drenched butterfly warrior god Huitzilopochtli and savaging the locals on their long march south.

These churlish primitives were rebuffed by every group they approached around the lake. Tezozomoc, the fierce lord of the Azcapotzalcos, told them to just get lost. So, homeless and beat and pissed off by their reception in the valley, they encamped on a desolate island in the middle of Lake Texcoco, and it was there, mired in the slough of despond, that their priests saw the vision of the eagle devouring a serpent in the spiky arms of a nopal cactus that is now imprinted upon the Mexican flag, and the prophecy of the Mexica priests was fulfilled.

Sure, maybe the priests just made it all up to put an end to the difficult journey and establish a common destiny for their people, but whatever the gods had really decided, the travelers were tired and here they would stay.

II

CITY OF FLOWERS
& SMOKING HEARTS

This monster of a megalopolis started small. Mexico-Tenochtitlán (from Mexitl, an alternative name for Huitzilopochtli, and *teno-chtli* or nopal) was little more than a collection of mud and wattle hovels for the first decade of its life. The first solid structure of scale was almost certainly the altar of Huitzilopochtli—the "Hummingbird of the Left Hand" and Lord of the Sun at midday—the altar and later the temple that enclosed it would be rebuilt four times during the reign of the Aztecs. The last remodeling was initiated by the Emperor Ahuitzotl in 1485 and baptized with the blood of 20,000 purportedly willing warriors.

Farther south on the tiny island, the Mexica-Aztecas erected a large wooden figure of Quetzalcóatl, Lord of the Morning Star, to bolster their credentials as the true heirs of the Toltecs—in their endless wanderings, the Mexica-Aztecas had dallied for 40 years of pillage and rapine in the neighborhood of Tula, Hidalgo, the Toltec homeland.

The reader should be cautious. What we know of the Aztecs has been handed down by the European invaders, evangelizing Christians who took a dim view of the Indians' religious practices.

The Aztecs' true history had been written and drawn on cactus papyrus in the venerated codices passed down from one generation to the next, but the Christians did not read cactus and at any rate thought the books to be the devil's work—and burnt them on public pyres to banish Satan and bring the Aztecs to Christ.

During their 234-year walkabout after abandoning Lake Aztlán in 1091, the Aztec-Mexicas' basic unit of social organization had been the *calpullis* or clans—there are thought to have been 15 bands of such hunter-warriors, but most of their titles have been lost forever. In their first years on the island, Mexico-Tenochtitlán was divided into quadrants representing the cardinal directions of Anáhuac, the One True World, and the calpullis assigned to these boroughs whose very names invoked the hopelessness of the place they had chosen to settle: Atzacoalco to the northeast was the Place of the Floods; Cuepopan to the northwest the Place of the Flowers; Zoquiapan in the southeast the Place of the Muddy Waters; and Moyotla to the southwest, the Place of the Flies.

When some calpullis complained about the flies, they were exiled to the neighboring islet of Tlatelolco, which later would become a thriving market for the lakeside communities and the Aztecs' commercial center.

Born rough into an uncaring universe, the Tenochas were a contentious lot, and once they had settled in, the calpullis had difficulty reaching consensus on much more than their devotion to Huitzilopochtli. After years of bitter strife among themselves, the calpulli councils called in their southern neighbors from Culhuacan (later Coyoacán) for whom they had served as mercenaries, to resolve their differences and in 1375, some 50 years after the founding of Mexico-Tenochtitlán, the Culhuacan noble Acamapichtli was anointed emperor.

The enthronement of the foreigner triggered a seismic shift in the once more or less egalitarian Mexica social structure. The chiefs of the calpullis were invited to construct their homes around Acamapichtli's palace just outside the sacred precinct of Huitzilopochtli, and the move demarcated class distinctions between "nobles" and "commoners." The "nobles" indeed reproduced like *tochtlis* (bunnies), and the little *pipiltin*, the children of the royal court, were groomed to be the future rulers of Tenochtitlán.

Within a half century, the Aztecs had evolved from a gaggle of autonomous clans into a highly centralized, top-down, increasingly urbanized society.

The Aztec royal court divvied up power between the warrior and the priestly classes. Warriors were devotees of the Eagle or the Jaguar schools. Although they were largely drawn from the pipiltin, commoners could break into high society by demonstrating exceptional skills on the battlefield—i.e., capturing many sacrificial victims in the Emperor's flower (*xochitl*) wars.

The priests had their own dark academies where they were initiated into the arcane arts and the rituals of prophecy and divination that allowed them to peel back the future and control the present. The Aztecs lived in a constant state of fear about what the gods had in store for them next—earthquakes, drought, flood, hunger (the Mexicas had once subsisted in the wilderness on a diet of poisonous snakes). With their powers to delve into the darkness, the priests enjoyed disproportionate control over emperors and commoners alike.

The sun under which the Tenochas lived, the Fifth Sun, was the Sun of the Ollín or the earthquake. The four previous suns had all been destroyed in cosmic cataclysms. The First Sun, 4-Jaguar, had been eaten by jaguars. The Second, Ehécatl or 4-Wind, had been struck by a magic hurricane that turned the humans into monkeys. The Third Sun, 4-Rain, had been decimated by Tláloc, the deity that governed the rain. The Fourth Sun, 4-Water, had also incurred Tláloc's wrath and all sentient beings had been drowned save one man and one woman who climbed into a tall cypress tree, where they were turned into dogs by Tezcatlipoca, the Lord of the Night, for disobeying his dictates.

Given such antecedents and plunked down in a landscape where volcanoes kept popping off and environmental disaster was always on the horizon, the priests of Mexico-Tenochtitlán were very careful to keep things in place and in balance—that is, the sun up in the sky and the rain, which ruled the agricultural cycles and kept the people fed, abundant.

EVERYTHING IS FORETOLD

Huitzilopochtli was the sun at noon, the most powerful sun. There were other suns, Tonatiuh for one, who represented the sun in its daily journey across the sky and whose glyph is a fat, dripping tongue that looks like it could have been etched into volcanic rock by R. Crumb. But Huitzilopochtli was the maximum solar power at the dead center of the Mexica cosmovision and, as the source of all this cosmic electricity, needed to be constantly satiated with buckets of human blood.

"The Hummingbird of the Left Hand" had a curious genealogy. His mother was Lady Coatlicue, always visualized with a fearsome head topped by faced-off serpents, adorned with a necklace of human hearts, hands, and skulls and girdled by writhing snakes, the ultimate Aztec mom. When his sister Coyolxauhqui, the moon, discovered that Mother Coatlicue was pregnant with the young sun god she flew into an Oedipal rage and tried to stab her. Huitzilopochtli, still in the womb, heard the argument and cut through his mama's belly, a kind of reverse cesarean, to burst into the world (albeit prematurely), where he seized his sister and threw her from a great hill to the earth below. The impact of her fall shattered Coyolxuahqui into a thousand shards, which is why we see the moon in pieces one night at a time.

You could look it up. It's all written on the great eight-ton Moon wheel uncovered in 1979 by workers laying cable under the Metropolitan Cathedral that occupies one corner of the sacred precinct once dominated by the twin temples of Huitzilopochtli and Tláloc.

Tláloc, on the other hand, was a more benign deity, a kind of magician and transformer, who, if displeased, could deny the rain. During the dry season his priests, clad in blue and white robes—the colors of the right-wing PAN Party today—harvested small children for the sacrifice that would welcome in the rainy season.

There were, of course, dozens of other important deities that needed to be assuaged—Xipe Tótec, for example, the Lord of the Springtime, a kind of Ed Gein–ish god whose priests danced in the flayed skins of virgins to fertilize the new corn.

For the Aztec-Mexicas, there were no coincidences; spontaneity had no place. Everything was foretold, controlled by the dispositions of the gods, even the small things relegated to 400 lesser deities or tochtlis ("rabbits") who ensured the success of everything from the fermentation of the octli, corn beer (today called pulque), to the recovery of mothers after childbirth.

Such theology required armies of priests and acolytes, soothsayers hepped up on hallucinogenic mushrooms, the ghastly owl men or búhos who cast malevolent spells, curanderos or healers who knew the secrets (Xipe Tótec was good for the eyes). Within the framework of the Aztec ruling class, the priests exercised a decisive quotient of power, especially in times of war and fearful emperors.

MAKE WAR NOT LOVE

The Tenochas did not have a great sense of public relations. They were surly and warlike and when they invited you over for dinner, the guest was apt to wind up in the cooking pots like the daughter of the Emperor of Culhuacan. When her family showed up for the banquet, the priests were already dancing in her flayed skin—the Aztecas claimed the skinning was justifiable retaliation for the Culhuacanos' penchant of seizing Mexica warriors and dressing them in women's clothes—*chisme* (gossip) that may well have been concocted by Gary Jennings, the supreme Aztec scandal slinger, whose best-selling potboilers exposed millions of unsuspecting travelers to the grisly secrets of the Mexicas.

For the Azteca-Mexicas, the best defense was an offense. Hemmed in by city-states that looked down upon them as savages, the Mexicas' ferocity was their foremost asset. They disemboweled their adversaries and ate them with a passion. They sold wolf tickets to the Azcapotzalcos (Lord Tezozomoc had moved on to Mictlán) and brokered the Triple Alliance with Texcoco and the compact enclave of Tlacopan adjacent to Azcapotzalco, which kept the descendants of Tezozomoc quiescent. But the Triple Alliance, forged under the Emperor Itzcóatl (1428–1440) by the power behind the throne, Tlacaelel, was about as much of an alliance as George Bush's ill-named Iraq War "Coalition of the Willing." Wars were often fought under the banner of the Triple Alliance, but the dominant Mexicas, like the Yanquis, always walked off with the lion's share of the spoils.

Although never designated *tlatoani* (emperor), the conniving Tlacaelel was the father of the Aztec empire. First marching his warriors south, overrunning Coyoacán and Chalco and Xochimilco until the Aztecs were the unquestioned Lords of the Lakes, Tlacaelel reached out beyond the Valley of Mexico to conquer Anáhuac the One True World, of which Mexico-Tenochtitlán was the Beating Heart. For 70 years (the same time span that the once-ruling Institutional Revolutionary Party, or PRI, held power in modern Mexico) until his death at the impossibly old age of 98 in 1494, Tlacaelel guided the fortunes of the Aztec rulers and created unimagined prosperity for the Mexica ruling class.

The system of tribute imposed upon the conquered peoples swelled the storehouses of Tenochtitlán to bursting. Each year, the colonies were forced not only to give up their gold and their harvests, but also to provide at least 20,000 fresh smoking hearts for the Mexica gods. Like the Conquistadores to come, Tlacaelel justified Aztec imperialism by the evangelization of their gods, imposing the worship of Huitzilopochtli over all other belief systems and depriving the peoples under their thrall of the human protein they needed to sustain their own gods. Tlacaelel's genius and the Aztec-Mexica success in building empire was predicated upon the marriage of the military with the priestly classes, and while he lived, the operation ran smoothly.

Every year, tens of thousands of young men, brainwashed into believing the sacrifice of their blood would keep the sun up in the sky, were herded up to Tenochtitlán, lined up at the foot of the great twin temples to Huitzilopochtli and Tláloc and led one by one up the 114 steps to their doom.

At the apex of the altar, four priests would spread-eagle the prospective victim upon the blood-caked killing slab while a fifth would plunge the obsidian *tecpatl* deep into his belly, burrow upwards through the soft flesh, and yank out his still steaming heart, holding it aloft for a fleeting moment for the sun to feast upon the bloody, palpitating organ and then stuffing it through the Hummingbird god's gore-encrusted mouth hole. Then the body was released, rolling down the stone steps to the base of the pyramid, where the butcher boys hacked off its choice parts and tossed the torsos into canoes to be distributed in other temples to feed other gods. The leftovers were thrown to the wild animals in the Emperor's menagerie.

And when the killing was done, the rulers and their rivals sat down together to dine upon the haunches of their freshly butchered warriors behind a curtain woven tight with white flowers so that they could not be seen by the commoners. The flower motif was not merely decorative. The warriors whom they digested had been captured in prearranged wars—"flower wars"—to provide for such feasts of reconciliation between the Aztecas and their enemies. Indeed, the Aztecs were appalled by the wanton waste of the Spanish Conquistadores, who seemed to kill for the sake of killing and left all that good meat out on the battlefield to spoil.

CAUTION!

"*¡Es todo una gran mentira!*" Berta Robledo pounded her little fist on the Formica counter. "It's all a big lie!" We were downing café con leche at La Blanca, the Centro Histórico hangout that has been my kitchen for the past 25 years. I had just come from a lecture by Dr. Eduardo Matos Moctezuma, one of Mexico's most respected investigators who has spent three decades digging through the ruins of the Templo Mayor.

What about human sacrifice?, I asked Dr. Moctezuma during the Q and A. Some Mexicans like my pal Berta, a pediatric nurse and left militant, don't believe the Aztecs practiced human sacrifice.

"It happened," the anthropologist assured me. "There are codices that confirm the practice of human sacrifice."

"What codices?" Berta fumed. "Did he give you any dates for these codices? All these codices these *expertos* are always talking about are all from after the Gachupines came. They made the Mexicas draw them to justify what they did to us and to convert us to Christianity. Don't you understand this, *compañero*?"

"But Dr. Moctezuma said there were codices from before the Spanish came. He's going to send me the dates."

"Sure, sure. I'm sure he will. But it's like asking the Devil if there's a hell or not. It's all a *pinche engaño* [damn scam]. Ay, Don Ross, don't even talk about it to me. I get so mad when I think about it. They murdered millions of us and then they say we were the savages, that we ate our own people! Ha! *¡Basta ya!* Enough!" Berta's little tantrum set her glass to trembling in the saucer.

"What your expertos don't tell you is that the altars of Huitzilopochtli and the others, they were for astronomy. The Aztecs invented astronomy. Don't you know that?"

We sat there in silence, sipping our coffees.

Berta Robledo is short and round and very brown like a lot of people who live here in El Monstruo. When she says "we" she is talking about the Mexicas. "Well. Maybe he will send me the dates. I gave him my email," I said lamely. I felt very much like a dumb gringo.

"Let's not talk about it anymore, OK?" she patted my arm. "Let's talk about what's important. Like how Fecal [a not-so-nice nickname for the president] is privatizing our *petroleo*." Berta is an "Adelita," a brigade of women who emulate the women soldiers in the Mexican revolution and had been sitting in around the Senate. "If I find the dates, that will settle it, no?" I persisted.

Manuel the waiter came over to ask us if we were having a debate. "No!" Berta snapped, "The debate is over."

In the end, I suppose, what people think about themselves is the only history that counts.

TIGHT LITTLE ISLAND

Mexico-Tenochtitlán was a tight little island, approximately 3,000 meters per side. The north-south avenue stretched 3.2 kilometers and the east-to-west road ran 2.9. The Aztec-Mexicas were lake people in a previous life, and they took to the watery element like ducks in a big pond.

Tenochtitlán was so shallow on its western edge that the *calpullis* had waded across from Chapultepec (Grasshopper) Hill on the mainland to the place where they would see the eagle devouring a snake in the arms of a nopal cactus. Almost from the day of the founding of the city on March 25, 1325, in what is now the Plaza de Santo Domingo, the Tenochas went to work expanding their real estate.

The Mexicas' model was the *chinampa* system of the freshwater lakes to the south, the fabled floating islands of the Xochimilcos. Workers built wood frames on the lake bottom, anchored them down with boulders and stones, and filled the frames with mud. Some chinampas were merely landfill to provide additional space for settlement but others were cultivated with tomatoes and chilies and squash, beans, *ajonjolí* (sesame seeds), and purple amaranth. (Corn was grown on the terraced hillsides of the mainland.) *Ahuehuete* trees with long roots were planted at the four corners of the chinampas, eventually attaching them to the lake bottom. Twenty-five thousand hectares of these thriving plots filled with rich lake loam would keep Tenochtitlán fed for generations until population growth outstripped the chinampas' production capacity.

Great cities grow up around ports—estuaries of deep rivers that flow into the interiors of their countries and bays that provide navigable access to the world's oceans. For the Aztecs, the five interlocking lakes—Texcoco, Xochimilco, Chalco, Zumpango, and Xaltocan—were their Liverpool and New York, their Tigris and Euphrates. The Aztecas' mastery of hydraulics gave them the building blocks of urban development. Trenches (*acequias*) were cut into the island, bringing the lake water to the land and creating an intricate network of canals that webbed Tenochtitlán.

Every road and footpath had its parallel canal. Two hundred thousand canoes worked the waterways, ferried freight from the mainland, and served as water taxis and pleasure craft and even garbage scows. Footbridges that swung open like gates to accommodate the canoe traffic were installed along the teeming canals.

Soon after the Tenochas encamped, they discovered freshwater springs, but the increasing needs of the settlers quickly eclipsed their bounty. Under the first Motecuhzoma (1440–1464), with Tlacaelel pulling the strings, the Aztecs resorted to armed diplomacy to bring drinking water from the mainland. Under threat of mayhem, the newly submissive Azcapotzalcos encouraged the Mexicas to build an aqueduct that would bring the precious liquid across the lake to the island. The first aqueduct proved a disaster, splintering under the pressure of the inflow and drowning Tenochtitlán under a wall of water. But Motecuhzoma, the "Great Builder," soon installed new aqueducts, one carrying fresh water from Coyoacán to the southwest and the other from the springs under Grasshopper Hill to the west.

The waters of Texcoco were salty and brackish. Although they bred fish, they also bred mosquitoes. Each rainy season, they flooded into Tenochtitlán and spilled over into the sweet-water lakes farther south. The Great Builder turned to a poet for a solution. Nezahualcóyotl, the "Hungry Coyote" and the Motecuhzoma's half-brother, was the king of Texcoco and an accomplished poet whose bittersweet verses about the transience of the world survive in the translucent translations of Miguel León Portilla.

A renaissance man, Nezahualcóyotl—whose name has been borrowed by the sprawling shantytown that now occupies the land he once ruled—was also a master civil engineer. Beginning in 1442, the Poet King assembled an army of slaves and indentured workers to construct a 9-kilometer-long dike at the southern end of Lake Texcoco. By the time it was completed, the dike had become the largest hydraulic project ever attempted in the Americas up to then.

Yet despite its pharaonic dimensions, Tenochtitlán, which had no natural drainage except back to the lake, regularly flooded—and still does today, despite the installation of the Drenaje Profundo (Deep Drain), a water tunnel of such immense proportions that unlucky workers are sometimes swept off by the tide of black water into the neighboring state of Hidalgo and beyond.

Floods ravaged the island city in 1449, in 1452, and yet again in 1482. Each time, the Aztecs rebuilt their legendary city in exactly the same soggy terrain that the prophecy of their priests had drawn them to in the previous century. The decision to reconstruct Tenochtitlán over and over again in this dangerous geography has had profound resonance for the modern monstrosity we now call Mexico City.

A SHIMMERING MIRAGE

Seen from the mainland, Tenochtitlán seemed a shimmering mirage. Spiring high above the palaces in the city's center, the twin temples of Huitzilopochtli and Tláloc dominated the cityscape, the crowning glory of the sacred precinct, a tract the size of two football fields enclosed by 500-meter-long Snake Walls on all sides—murals of serpents decorated its four façades. The precinct was dotted with 78 separate structures including a sacred Aztec hip ball court (*ulama*), the Tzompantli or skull rack (the Franciscan Bernardino de Sahagún counted 200,000 skulls), religious schools, and dozens of temples to lesser gods in the Aztec pantheon ranging from the gory Xipe Tótec to stern Tezcatlipoca to the 400 bunnies.

Just outside the Snake Walls, from which all roads and canals branched off into the city, the pipiltin built their gleaming white palaces with brilliantly colored flags and feathers fluttering on the balustrades—the second Motecuhzoma's supremely ostentatious palace is now the site of the National Palace from which the Great Tlatoanis of the PRI and the PAN still administrate the affairs of the Mexicas.

The interiors of the palaces were lavishly outfitted, gold-adorned beehives honeycombed with hundreds of rooms where the children of the court and their descendants lived in the lap of Aztec luxury. The fresh water delivered to the island was brought directly to the palace district through a latticework of clay pipes, and each room was equipped with its own steam bath and toilet closet—the sewage outflow discharged the royal wastes onto barges on the canals, which carried the nightsoil to the mainland to be spread on cornfields.

When Cortez and the Conquistadores came in 1520, they were flabbergasted by the sanitary achievements of the Aztecs—the European cities they came from were unspeakable pigsties that incubated deadly plagues and smelled like shit.

The first known map of Tenochtitlán, drawn by two of Cortez's cartographers, shows the four quarters of the island city linked up by a grid that emanates from the Snake Walls. Three avenues of hard-packed dirt broad enough for 20 men to stand abreast spanned the island and connected up with three causeways at strategic points on the lakefront, leading to the mainland on the south, west, and north, facilitating the flow of commerce.

Beyond the palaces of the nobles, the lesser pipiltin built their homes, two-story whitewashed blocks of stone and mud with extravagant roof gardens sown with flowers and fragrant herbs and here and there a shade tree. The barrios of the Indians surrounded the lesser pipiltin. These neighborhoods were not so different from today's working-class barrios, with low-slung structures divided into many small rooms grouped around a common patio. Sections of the city were reserved for artisans working in gold and feathers, jade and other precious stones to embellish the upper classes. Each neighborhood was centered around a temple to ensure religious control, and blood sacrifice was practiced to pay obeisance to the urban deities.

What the *macehualli*, the man in the street, actually thought about such savagery does not seem to be recorded anywhere. They were commoners, slaves and workers and only their backs—and their hearts—counted for the scribes who kept the chronicles. As it always is with the man-made wonders of this world, when it comes to those who carried the stones and pounded them flat or were crushed in the quarrying, we will never know their names.

THE AZTECS COME UNGLUED

Tlacaelel was the glue that held Tenochtitlán together. He had stood behind the throne of five emperors for seven decades, building an empire as great as Alexander's and overseeing the transfer of riches that was Tenochtitlán's glory.

But time trudges on. The first Motecuhzoma passed the scepter in 1464 to Axayácatl, who continued the Mexica building boom and maintained the empire despite rumblings from its distant borders until he was carted off to Mictlán in 1479. Tizoc, his successor, proved such a dud that Tlacaelel had to have him poisoned. Ahuitzotl assumed the throne and raised up the last great temple—the sacrificial victims were lined up for eight miles from the foot of the pyramids to the edge of the city, and it took four days and nights to slaughter them all and feed their hearts to Huitzilopochtli.

Not long after this bloody folderol, Tlacaelel succumbed to old age, and for the first time in 70 years there was no power behind the throne. The new emperor, Motecuhzoma II, the nephew of the Great Builder, was inexperienced and spooked from the start that calamity would destroy the One True World on his watch. The year 1507, when the Mexicas' 52-year fire cycle would be extinguished and the new fire lit, seemed a particularly ominous one.

Motecuhzoma did not curry favor with either his subjects or the gods when he had himself declared a deity. All commoners were banished from the royal court and the pipiltin were forbidden to gaze upon him under penalty of being munched.

These were not good years. Drought ravaged central Mexico and there wasn't much for lunch. Even worse, the mumbo jumbo of the priests didn't have much juice with the gods anymore. The harvests diminished and the natives grew restless.

When Motecuhzoma levied increased tributes of sacrificial victims on the Tlaxcaltecos and the Huejotzingos and the Cholulas, rebellion brewed. Their frustrated representatives came up to Tenochtitlán to plead their case before the Emperor and too often disappeared into the cooking pots.

Still it did not rain. Meteors streaked the heavens. Motecuhzoma's chief soothsayer sleepwalked through the palace, warning everyone to flee. Dwarfs and deformed freaks were seen in the streets of Tenochtitlán, a bad sign. The Emperor was convinced that Quetzalcóatl, the Lord of the Morning Star, who had been run off by the smoking mirror Tezcatlipoca and had sworn to return to take his revenge, was about to appear on the eastern horizon.

Quetzalcóatl's color was white. This sense of impending doom was aggravated when in 1517 flying ships were sighted off the Yucatán and men with white skin came ashore. The white men retreated into the sea but returned in 1518 and again in 1519, a Ce-atl (water) year on the Aztec calendar that was propitious to the Plumed Serpent. Motecuhzoma paced the rooms of his resplendent palace, crying out for forgiveness.

"THE WALLS ARE SPLASHED WITH BLOOD"

The story of the Conquest is an achingly familiar one for the native peoples of the world. The freebooter Hernán Cortez came ashore on Good Friday, April 21, 1519, at the mouth of the Zempoala River just north of what is now Veracruz port. The hostile takeover of Mexico was accompanied by 10 ships, 650 men, 16 horses, packs of fierce mastiffs, and cannons that terrified the Totonaco Indians on the beach into submission.

Fearing that the prophecy had been fulfilled, Motecuhzoma sent envoys bearing priceless golden gifts and pleaded with Cortez/Quetzalcóatl to go back where he came from. This gesture would seal the fate of the Aztec empire. The invader explained to the envoys that he had a sickness that only gold could cure and marched his men uphill straight toward Tenochtitlán.

It is a racist myth to think that 650 Europeans conquered a land of 25 million indigenous people. Rather, having pillaged and browbeaten those whose lands they occupied, it was the Aztecs who had carved out their own tomb. Under the Mafia-esque concept that the enemy of my enemy is my friend, Cortez joined forces with the disaffected rulers of Tlaxcala, Huejotzingo, and Cholula. When the Spaniard marched his army between the two snowcapped volcanoes Popocatépetl and Iztaccíhuatl ("El Paso de Cortez" in the tourist guides), there were 200,000 pissed-off Indian warriors (about the population of Tenochtitlán at the time) under his command.

The Europeans had never seen such magnificent cities as they encountered on the way to Tenochtitlán. Tlaxcala was bigger than Granada, and Cholula was "apt for the Spanish." Now, on November 8, eight months after they had landed on these shores, Cortez's men massed at the foot of the causeway on the Texcoco side of the lake and marveled that the temples of Huitzilopochtli and Tláloc were taller even than the Cathedral of Sevilla.

The rest is all treachery. Despite his exemplary hospitality, Motecuhzoma was taken hostage and induced to give up his gold and embrace Jesus Christ. The Christians were offended by the blood-smeared temples and tried to tear Huitzilopochtli from his perch. Aztec rage boiled over. Leaving a small garrison behind, Cortez retreated from the city to settle some urgent business with the Crown. When he returned the garrison had been overrun and its defenders eviscerated. Motecuhzoma, despised by his own people for consorting with the whites, had been cast aside, and the new *tlatoani*, Cuitláhuac, had laid siege to the Europeans' quarters. The Spaniards' situation looked dire.

On June 30, 1520, the would-be Conquistadores, so loaded down with booty that their horses' bellies dragged against the ground, sought to break out of the island city but were massively bloodied by the Tenochas when they tried to flee on the Tacuba causeway, a night dubbed La Noche Triste (The Night of Sorrow) by the European historians, although the Aztecas partied heartily.

But the Europeans had left a deadly time bomb behind—smallpox bacilli carried into the city by a black slave in Cortez's entourage. When the Spaniards returned in 1521, half the population of Tenochtitlán was dead. The corpses of the Aztecs bloated and swelled in every house. Cuitláhuac had perished in the plague that swept the island and Motecuhzoma's rebellious nephew, Cuauhtémoc, now led the resistance.

But the Conquistadores did not immediately enter Tenochtitlán. Surrounding the island on all sides, Cortez blockaded supplies from entering the city and destroyed the aqueducts, cutting off the water supply. Those who survived inside were reduced, like their ancestors, to eating roots and poisonous snakes.

The white men stormed into Tenochtitlán on August 13, 1521, and pulled down the ghastly temples of Huitzilopochtli and Tláloc that so repelled them. Cuauhtémoc, "the Descending Eagle," was captured in an alley between Tlatelolco and Tepito on the spot where a used hubcap shop was doing business last time I checked.

"All of this happened to us. We saw that in the roads lay our broken lances. The roofs have been stripped from our houses and the walls are splashed with blood," León Portilla translates from Tenochtitlán's handwritten obituary. "Worms crawl through the plazas and the streets. The water runs red in the canals. We beat on the walls of our inheritance and they are a nest of holes. With our shields we defended the city, but not even our gods could sustain us."

DEAD INDIANS

The Indians died and died. They just kept on dying. There was no end to their dying. They died from famine. They died from forced labor.

They died under the great burdens they were forced to carry. They died under the horses of the Conquerors. They died run through by the swords of the invaders or in terror at the sound of their cannons.

They died of sadness because their loved ones had died and they died in shame because they thought their gods had abandoned them. The Christians preached to them that they died because of divine retaliation for being demons and cannibals. They died because they were *pinches indios* and had no souls. They died in the autos-da-fé of the Holy Inquisition. They died garroted by the executioners and their bodies were set afire. They died drawn and quartered by the stallions of the Inquisitors. They died under the protection of Bishop Juan de Zumárraga, the "Protector of the Indians."

They died because their forests died and the raped hillsides collapsed into the lakes from which they drew life and the lakes died with them. They died because their *milpas* (cornfields) were invaded by the herds of cattle that the Spanish had let loose and their lands were confiscated by the Crown and incorporated into vast haciendas. They died because they just got in the way.

They died of European-borne diseases in a biological war the enormity of which had never before or since been recorded in the history of man's cruelty to man. Nineteen killer epidemics ravaged the Indians of Mexico in the first century of conquest, diseases to which white men had built up a measure of immunity: smallpox, typhoid, the plague, cholera, measles, mumps, influenza, pneumonia, the *cocoliz*, a hemorrhaging that caused the victim to dissolve into a bloody pool of pus. All they could give back was syphilis, which covered Europe in oozing sores throughout the 17th and 18th centuries.

The Indians died "in heaps like bedbugs" as Fray Motolinía noted. The Franciscan priest Sahagún buried 10,000 on Tlatelolco and then stopped counting—he had run out of ground in which to bury them anyway. The bodies of the Indians clogged up the canals and were thrown in the lake—you could walk from Tenochtitlán to Tlatelolco on the backs of the dead. In 1545, during a few weeks of winter, 845,000 died of smallpox. The years 1563–1564, 1576, and 1581 were plague years. Fifteen thousand Aztecs, half of the population of Coyoacán, which Cortez had taken as his own private estate, were wiped out in a single fortnight.

On the Holy Thursday morning Hernán Cortez had dropped anchor off Veracruz, April 20, 1519, there are thought to have been

12.5 million to 25 million Indians living within the configurations of what is now Mexico—the numbers are inexact and the count distorted by the imprecision of geographical borders. A hundred years later when the Indians had developed relative immunity to the murderous plagues, the Spanish could find only 1.2 million of them. At a minimum, 11.3 million indigenous peoples were wiped off the face of the earth by the European Conquest.

No matter how you count it, the obliteration of the native peoples of Mexico at the hands of the Spanish invaders is the most devastating act of genocide on the books. Hitler's holocaust—6 million Jews, Gypsies, homosexuals, and Communists—is dwarfed by comparison.

The Indians died and died but they did not go away. They refused to abandon Tenochtitlán and stubbornly survived in their own way. By the time liberation from Spain rolled around in the early 19th century, their numbers were on the rebound. Now, in the new millennium, the Indians of Mexico are approaching their pre-Conquest population, numbering 15 million to 20 million native peoples depending on how you count them.

III

CITY OF PALACES & GHOSTS

I live on the island of Tenochtitlán or at least what has become of it. I rent a room on the corner of Espíritu Santo (Holy Ghost Street, now Isabel la Católica) and San Felipe Neri (now República de El Salvador), two blocks west of the Zócalo. The solid granite west wall of the ex–San Agustín convent faces my balcony. The original Augustinian convent, thought to have been built over an Aztec graveyard, was constructed by involuntary Indian labor during the first decade of the Conquest. On quiet nights, I can sometimes hear the voices of the dead Indians murmuring sadly inside the walls and courtyard of the convent. But perhaps it is only the caretakers complaining about the condition of employment.

Farther down Espíritu Santo Street outside the handsome tezontle tile façade of La Profesa, once an Aztec temple and now the favored church of the very rich for their fancy weddings, I am positive that I hear their voices again, but then it may only be the Nahua beggar lady, her children clustered around her, squatting against the wall amidst the tuxedos and billowing chiffon evening gowns and beribboned classic cars. "*Señor, señor,*" she calls out, "*¿un peso, señor? ¿Para comer, señor?*"

The wedding party saunters up Holy Ghost Street to the extravagant Casino Español, once the Espíritu Santo Hospital, established in 1534 on this site to accommodate the dying Indians. I myself hold a discount card that entitles me to treatment at the Hospital de Jesús, the first such facility built in Mexico, inaugurated by Cortez himself in 1524. There used to be a small statue of the Conquistador in the chapel next door, one of only two anywhere in the land he "discovered"—Cortez was never a popular figure in Tenochtitlán.

As I sit in the quiet anteroom waiting for the doctor to emerge, I again hear the ghosts of Aztecs past, but I suppose it is only the cleaning women dishing up the chisme.

Wherever I stop here in what the travel books dub the "Historic Center of Mexico City," I am confronted by disembodied Indian voices. They are with me each day when I pass by Father Gante's girls' school (now the jewelbox Chapel of Our Lady of Lourdes) and enveloped by the Club de Banqueros (Bankers Club), on my way to pick up the *New York Times* in a building even older than the chapel. The voices are with me when I toddle down Donceles, hearing the screaming and moaning behind the walls of the "House of Demented Women" built, as the tile plaque on its ancient façade tells us, by "the carpenter José Sayago" in 1692 and incorporated into the Hospital of the Divine Savior. I hear these voices when I visit the fifth incarnation of the Templo Mayor, re-created for the tourists in the quadrant just north of the Zócalo where the Aztec dance troupes still twirl and stomp. *Señor, señor. ¿Un peso, señor? ¿Para comer, señor?*

Indeed, I live in a city of ghosts.

ERASING TENOCHTITLÁN

Hernán Cortez's first impulse was to tear down what was left of the island city. Tenochtitlán still harbored, and was surrounded by, hostile Indians who even in their debilitated condition could not be trusted to obey the dictates of the Conquerors. And besides, the climate was not so hot either.

The invaders argued among themselves about what to do with the dubious prize they had wrested from the Aztecs, and many votes were cast for relocating on the mainland. But Cortez was not ready to abandon the city he had conquered. Tenochtitlán had been the hub of an empire, a symbol of absolute power from which the Aztec emperors had ruled all of Mexico and to whom, in turn, all of Mexico paid onerous tribute. The mechanism of control had worked for nearly 200 years and Cortez was reluctant to monkey with it.

Instead, he would build a new Spanish city on the ashes of the old Aztec capital from which New Spain (Nueva España—the name the Crown had assigned to Mexico) would be governed. But given the unhappiness of his neighbors, this new Spanish city would have to be vigilantly defended. To this end, Cortez ordered all two-story buildings within the core of the ex-Tenochtitlán to be leveled, to ward off ambush by the disgruntled natives, and excluded Indians from the Spanish district.

The enclave of the Conquistadores is roughly defined on today's city maps as stretching from the Plaza de Santo Domingo, where the Mexicas are thought to have first seen the Eagle devouring the Snake in the arms of a nopal cactus bush, a dozen blocks south to Izazaga Street and including the now rubbished Aztec sacred precinct, the Plaza Mayor (Zócalo), and the palaces of Motecuhzoma and his predecessors that surrounded it.

The new Spanish city was fortified against the threat of the *Indiada*, the long-expected moment of combustion when the natives would run riot in the streets and murder the whites in their sleep. The new city became a kind of citadel, armed to the teeth to defend itself from the former residents who, despite the depopulation of Tenochtitlán, far outnumbered the newcomers, as Cortez was only too aware.

On all four flanks of the Plaza Mayor and on the surrounding blocks, imposing instruments of colonial governance were raised up by closely watched work gangs of vanquished Indians conscripted to build this new power center of the Spanish Crown. Motecuhzoma's palace would be occupied by the Viceroy who would administer the fortunes of New Spain, a tract conceived of as extending from as far north as Wyoming all the way to the Capitanía of Guatemala. Antonio de Mendoza arrived in 1535 to take the job. The viceroy served at the pleasure of the Council of the Indies, through which the Spanish kings exercised their dominion over the New World.

Catty-corner to the viceroy's palace were the Ayuntamiento or City Hall and the Cabildo (City Council building), which would manage the affairs of the new Spanish city. The proximity of national and municipal authorities arranged virtually next door to each other around the Plaza Mayor continues unto this day and is one of the underlying architectural reasons why governing Mexico City is often confused with governing Mexico the Country.

Other public structures in the core of the new city included, of course, the municipal jail (in the Cabildo) and the Alhóndiga, the city storehouse, bordering the Viga canal (now La Merced market). Commercial people rented space on the ground floor of the Viceroy's palace where European luxury goods and oriental silks ferried from the Philippines by the galleons of the Ñao fleet were on display.

The emissaries of the Crown would govern the Indians and a growing number of Gachupines (Spaniards, literally "spur riders,") just off the boat from Spain to find their fortunes in the New World. The Royal Tribunal stood directly across the Plaza Mayor from the Viceroy's opulent digs. Under the *encomienda*, which governed land ownership, the Indians were obligated to pay hefty tribute to the original Conquistadores, their descendants and, in fact, anyone at all who had sufficient wherewithal to acquire an encomienda.

A system of *caciques*, local Aztec nobles who had curried favor with the new rulers, kept the surviving Indians in check. Lest they revert to the old ways, the natives had to be strictly supervised, and to this end the Holy Inquisition was installed in Santo Domingo plaza to keep close tabs on their religious preferences.

GIVE ME THAT OLD-TIME RELIGION

The Crown flourished under both the temporal authority vested in the viceroy and the spiritual authority of Holy Mother Church and its representative in New Spain, Archbishop Juan de Zumárraga. Beginning in 1527, Zumárraga press-ganged thousands of Indians to build up the first cathedral from the rubble of the smashed altars of Huitzilopochtli and Tláloc, and by 1530 the ex-Aztecs were attending Sunday Mass.

Three missionary orders—first the Franciscans, then the Augustinians and the Dominicans—established an important presence in the new city. The evangelization of the New World offered Holy Mother Church the opportunity of reaping a bumper crop of souls not available since the first Christian century.

By the mid-16th century, the ex-Tenochtitlán was packed with churches (84), monasteries (36), and convents (19). The Indians were conscripted to dig and carry. Great beams fell upon them and crushed their backs. The walls fell in on them and they were buried under tons of boulders. But even as they labored, the former Aztecs chanted and sang much as their fathers and grandfathers had when they raised up the great temples of their own gods under the eagle-eyed overseers of emperors who sought immortality in such edifications.

The new temples were strategically sited on the grounds of the old temples—San Miguel Arcángel, two blocks west of my rooms off Izazaga Street, was once the temple of Ehécatl, the Mexicas' god of the wind—one surviving wall of his temple is on permanent display in the Pino Suárez metro station down below. Everywhere, the altars of the old gods were replaced by Christian saints. The maximum illustration of this process of syncretization, the imposition of Christian deities over the pagan gods, is the charming—if totally apocryphal—tale of the Virgin of Guadalupe.

TONANTZIN

One day in 1530, so the old story goes, "Juan Diego," an Aztec noble whose blood name was Cuauhtlatoatzin, was passing by the Hill of Tepeyac in the north of what is now Mexico City, where the devotees of the Mexica earth mother Tonantzin venerated this gentle goddess. He availed himself of the opportunity to drop by her holy site and pray for the recovery of a sick uncle. But instead of Tonantzin, Cuauhtlatoatzin came face to face with a strange goddess, surrounded by stars and framed by the *pencas* (spikes) of the maguey cactus, who identified herself as a Virgin named María Guadalupe. This strange spectral creature urged the Aztec to intercede for her with Bishop Zumárraga to build her a chapel on Tonantzin's hill.

Dazzled by the visitation, "Juan Diego" went three times to see the Bishop, but being a lowly Indian he was not admitted to the prelate's offices. Returning to the site, he bemoaned his failure: "I am the end, the tail. What more can I do?" "I have an idea," the Virgin encouraged. She picked a bouquet of roses that had miraculously bloomed on the dry, cactus-studded hillside and instructed "Juan Diego" to wrap them in his cactus-fiber cloak (*tilma* or *ayate*) and take them to the Archbishop.

This time, Cuauhtlatoatzin would not take no for an answer. When he was admitted to the Bishop's rooms he spread out the tilma, and there, imprinted upon it, was the image of the Holy Virgin, a little darker than in most representations but unquestionably a miracle, no?

The rest is Her Story. The ayate now hangs framed above the people mover in back of the flower-filled altar of the Basilica of Our Lady of Guadalupe, the most lucrative shrine in Christendom, raking in about 2 billion pesos in an average year.

The Virgin of Guadalupe, "the Brown Madonna," was a cruel trick on the Indians. In reality, She is a carbon copy of the Virgin of Remedios that Cortez and his boys had carried into battle against the Aztecs, only her pigmentation has been purposely darkened. Scientific tests performed extra-officially on the tilma, and the testimony of a restorer called in to repair the fabric, demonstrate beyond the shadow of a doubt that the Virgin had been painted on the cactus-fiber cloak, most probably by a 16th-century Aztec artist known as Marcos—which may explain the fascination the tilma held for his Indian contemporaries.

The apparition of the Brown Madonna would eventually become the cornerstone for the Catholic evangelization of the Americas, but at first the Church fathers were a little leery about its authenticity. Motolinía distrusted the Indian cult that grew up around Guadalupe and thought it dangerously subversive. Zumárraga and Cortez did not consider the Virgin's show-up in America newsworthy enough to note in their diaries. In fact, the Miracle did not merit literary recognition for another 117 years until the publication in Nahuat of the Nican Mopohua in 1647. The Guadalupana did not attract widespread popularity until She was adopted by the white criollos as their Patrona in 1737 during the initial stage of their scuffle for independence from the Crown. Subsequently, the Dark Virgin became an icon of Mexican nationalism and marched into battle with the colonials in the war of liberation from Spain.

Even if the Guadalupana was a trick on the Indians, Her appearance was vindicated by the Church under the doctrine that any lie that brought the savages to Christ was justified, and by 1535, fully 5,000,000 ex-Aztecs and other indigenous peoples had been converted to Catholicism. The spiritual conquest was almost complete. In less than a decade and a half, the Conquerors had seemingly wiped out a belief system that had endured for at least a millennium.

But buried as deep within the Indians' hearts as they were under the floorboards of the churches, the old gods still had some scratch. The annals of the Inquisition are filled with hundreds of instances in which figurines of Aztec deities were built into church altars.

Father Motolinía became choleric when he realized that the Indians he thought were worshipping Jesus Christ on the cross were actually praying to the old gods they had hidden away in plain sight behind the crucifix.

Just how tenaciously the Indians clung to their beliefs is encapsulated in the legend of Cuauhtémoc's bones. After years of excruciating torture by the conquerors hungry for his hidden gold, the last *tlatoani* was hanged from a gibbet in Tabasco state in 1526 by Cortez for plotting rebellion. His bones were gathered up and smuggled north to the Descending Eagle's birthplace in Ixcateopan, Guerrero, where they were stashed under the altar in the village church, a secret that the locals guarded for centuries until a drunken priest spilled the beans to the national daily *Excelsior* in 1971. For 400 years, Cuauhtémoc's devotees had secretly worshipped his bones while they pretended to be attending Sunday Mass.

No, the Indians did not forget what had happened to them. Every day, today included, young Aztecs dance in the Zócalo offering copal incense to the four corners of the earth and invoking the coming of the Sixth Sun. Tenochtitlán is not done with yet.

> *Here is the great city*
> *Of Mexico-Tenochtitlán,*
> *In this place that is renowned,*
> *In this place that is exemplary,*
> *Where the wild cactus fruit grows,*
> *In the middle of the waters,*
> *Where the eagle screeches,*
> *Where the eagle spreads its wings,*
> *Where he tears apart the serpent,*
> *Where the fish swim in the blue waters,*
> *In the yellow waters,*
> *Where the boiling waters are found,*
> *Where feathers drown in the tule fields,*
> *Where we are found,*
> *Where all the peoples of the four directions*
> *Of the world will return.*
> —AZTEC POEM, TRANSLATION BY MIGUEL LEÓN PORTILLA

SILVER CITY

The discovery in 1557 of incalculably rich veins of silver in the colony of Zacatecas, in the Chichimeca territories, set off bells across the Atlantic at the court of Charles V. Between 1560 and 1600, New Spain was the planet's leading producer of the precious metal, and like oil today, silver accounted for two-thirds of the colony's exports. The discovery transformed this island of ghosts into silver city.

Ingots and coins were minted in the Royal Treasury (adjacent to the Cabildo on the south flank of the Plaza Mayor, where the viceroy could keep an eye on them), loaded up on stout wooden wagons, and hauled off downhill by straining mule teams to the port of Veracruz to be transferred to the galleons that came once a year, then shipped across the stormy ocean to replenish the coffers of the Spanish king, now the wealthiest monarch in what was known of the world.

The wagon trains did not deadhead back empty. Piled high with sumptuous European consumer goods, the mule teams lumbered back uphill to the capital to stock the elegant stores and warehouses around the Plaza Mayor that kept the colonials outfitted in the contemporary couture of the civilized world. As the volume increased, the plaza itself devolved into an immense encampment of rough teamsters and hostlers, horses and wagon teams, and the din of commerce was music to the viceroy's ears.

The Conquistadores were horsemen and inlanders. (Cortez hailed from Extremadura on the Portuguese border.) They never bathed anyway and had little use for the Aztec waterworks. The hillside forests across the lakes over on the mainland were clear-cut to provide great house beams and finished timber for the reconstruction of the city. Because the soil was sodden, each structure had to be raised off the ground on wooden struts. What was left of the woodlands was burnt down to charcoal to keep the home fires of the new city cooking.

By 1554, half the land in the Valley of Mexico had already been seized by the conquering class. Ravenous herds of sheep, bovines, and an estimated 200,000 pigs were rooting and rampaging through the lakeside lands leaving no blade of grass untouched. Shorn of vegetation, the hillsides collapsed into the lakes with the first rains and sediment filled in the lake bed. By 1600, a third of the system had been displaced.

Nezahualcóyotl's great dike across Texcoco stood in ruins, and in 1637 a new and unnecessary dike extending from Zumpango cut off most of the inflow from the west and lowered the level of the lake to a mudflat. Despite the damage to the lake system, the ex-Tenochtitlán would endure as an island for another century, until 1789, when the construction of the Desagüe (discharge) de Huehuetoca drained the lakes that had served the Aztecs so well forever.

With the lakes drying up before their eyes and the canals fallen into disrepair, the Europeans broadened the avenues to accommodate foot and vehicle traffic—the widths of the boulevards were no longer measured by the number of men who could stand shoulder to shoulder but by the density of wagon and foot traffic that clogged the roads.

Then as now, El Monstruo had a traffic problem, and then as now, the traffic occasioned environmental consequences. The desiccation of the terrain thickened the thin mountain air with choking swirls of dust and grit kicked up by the incessant comings and goings of the wagon trains. The Cabildo opted to pave the streets, at least in the Spanish core of the ex-Tenochtitlán, and Silver City took on a decidedly European look.

But the capital of New Spain was cursed by Cortez's rash decision to rebuild in this problematic geography. Furious *aguaceros* (downpours) thundered from the skies in the rainy months; the run-off cascaded down the stripped hillsides displacing what was left of the lakes, and the overflow triggered such havoc that all the King's horses and all the King's men could not put the once-upon-a-time Aztec stronghold together again. Year after year, the city flooded out, and in 1607, with the streets under water (the locals had reverted to canoes), the Cabildo hired New Spain's most illustrious engineer, Don Enrico Martínez (actually a German named Eric Martin), to construct an eight-kilometer covered canal that would carry off the excess water all the way to Tula, Hidalgo, at the north end of the valley—Martínez contemplated boring through mountains to rid the city of the overflow. Sixty thousand Indian workers were rounded up and his Desagüe General was begun with huge fanfare, but the money ran out by 1611 and Martínez was forced to abandon the ambitious project.

When, in 1629, monster summer storms once again submerged the city, 30,000 colonists fled the island city for the mainland and stayed away for the next five years. As usual, the Indians drowned in the flood. The Cabildo ordered Martin-Martínez arrested for failing to complete the Desagüe and the engineer was carried off to gaol, where he purportedly was held in a cell standing in water up to his nose.

CITY OF PALACES

Despite the scourges nature inflicted upon the metropolis and the treacherous soils underfoot, by the second half of the 17th century, the Gachupín core of Silver City celebrated a building boom unmatched since the apogee of Tenochtitlán. The ostentatious palaces of silver-rich Condes and Marqueses, their titles purchased for exorbitant sums from the Crown, still dominate the Centro Histórico, only now they are the property of financial royalty. Banamex, owned by Citigroup, occupies two (the Palace of Iturbide and that of the Count of San Mateo de Valparaíso, its corporate headquarters) and Carlos Slim, the world's richest man, owns another (the Palace of the Count of Orizaba, popularly known as the House of Blue Tiles).

The City of Palaces, as the Mexico City tourist bureau now hawks it, grew block by block throughout the 17th century. Between the Church and the Crown and the newly installed merchant class, the core city pushed outward, west to San Juan de Letrán, where the modern pyramid of the Torre Latinoamericana now spires, and south to Salto de Agua (a subway stop on the Pink Line today).

New avenues took shape—El Camino a Chapultepec, in our day the elegant Paseo de La Reforma, ran southwest to Chapultepec Hill, and the Calzada de los Misterios (Mystery Road) led pilgrims north to La Villa and the Basilica of the Virgin of Guadalupe.

The New World's first university was established just off the Plaza Mayor in 1648 on Moneda Street—the National Autonomous University of Mexico (UNAM) still holds title to many colonial buildings in the neighborhood, including the now shuttered bar El Nivel, a wedge in the National Palace walls popular with politicians and poets for 170 years. Pumped up by the silver trade, the Palace of Mining occupied almost a whole block between what is now the Mexican Senate and the gilded General Post Office. *La gente decente* strolled the gardens of the Alameda in the evenings.

By 1700, the ex-Tenochtitlán had only a handful of increasingly dysfunctional canals left—one ran behind the Plaza de Santo Domingo, the site of the city's founding; La Viga flowed in from Lake Texcoco and skirted the Ayuntamiento (you can trace its dry bed on Corregidora Street); a third flowed by the gorgeous Regina Coeli church (two blocks south on Holy Ghost Street and hang a right)—neighbors claim you can still hear the ghost waters gurgling.

The city fathers (there were no mothers) refurbished and expanded the aqueducts, and clean drinking water gushed from fountains in Santo Domingo and Salto de Agua and Las Vizcaínas, allowing the hoi polloi to fill their house jugs to the brim. Public markets sprang up around the fountains, decentralizing commerce.

But the most popular selling floor, at least for white folks, remained the *tianguis* (bazaar) in the Plaza Mayor where grains, *elotes* (new corn), *jitomates* (tomatoes), *calabazas* (squash), *chayotes* (prickly pears), and hard fruit from the countryside were offered alongside baskets of dried fish and slabs of fly-specked meat.

In an effort to muffle the high-decibel uproar of the vendors that engulfed the Plaza Mayor, the Cabildo moved the street sales indoors to the Parian Market and farmers displayed their foodstuffs between racks of oriental silks and European ball gowns to the delight of the shopping class.

Such amenities were not available to those who dwelt in the *inframundo* on the periphery. The Indians continued to shop in Tlatelolco, which was now attached to the former Mexica capital by landfill, but were barred from the Spanish district, except for servants and those who slaved in the *obrajes* or workhouses, weaving rough cloth and turning out cheap pottery. (The Crown had forbidden the manufacture of luxury goods in the colony to eliminate competition with European imports, a stricture that stirred subversives to dream about separation.)

THE MOTHER COUNTRY

While New Spain increasingly concentrated global wealth, accounting for half the world's silver coinage, the Mother Country was showing signs of decline. The Crown sucked up the Mexican silver to feed its many wars with the world, but the defeat of the Spanish Armada in 1588 foretold the future of the Hapsburg dynasty. Like the Aztecs, the Spaniards were overextended, and their empire disintegrated out on the periphery.

The Turks drove off the New Crusaders in the eastern Mediterranean and the Crown's push north into the Protestant lowlands of Europe lost momentum. Silver production in the New World could not keep pace with Spain's mounting debts, and the Bourbons were brought in to salvage what was left. But the Mother Country would never regain its lost glory, and eventually the colony would have more weight than the colonizers.

MÉXICO NEGRO

Out in the countryside, vast swatches of land were left vacant by the genocide of the Indians, and the Spanish quickly incorporated them into the haciendas, grazing their enormous herds on the abandoned tracts where the First Peoples had once tended their *milpas*. So many had expired in the first century of European occupation that the labor force was seriously depleted and new workers desperately needed.

Silver was the fulcrum of the Gachupín Empire, and there were not enough Indians to meet the forced-labor quotas in the mines of Zacatecas.

The first Africans were shanghaied from Angola, Gambia, and the Cape Verde Islands by Portuguese slave traders who measured their cargos not in numbers of people but rather tons of flesh. The Africans who survived the passage (a third did not) were penned up in the slave market in Veracruz port until they were sold. Most were assigned to the silver mines, but house slaves were culled out to serve in the mansions of the capital, and these became a status symbol of newly amassed wealth and social standing. Every Gachupín had to have at least ten.

The Spanish were consumed by their racism, and it poisoned the administration of New Spain and the social ambience in its capital. The Conquistadores had come fresh from the ethnic cleansing of the Motherland, having driven the Blackamoors back to Africa and expelled the Jews. Indeed, Cortez did not much distinguish between infidels and refers to the Aztec temples as *mezquitas*, or mosques, in his diaries of the Conquest.

The Royal chronicler Gonzalo Fernández de Oviedo set the tone: The Indians were "naturally lazy and vicious, melancholy, cowardly, a lying, shiftless people." Their marriages "were not sacrament but sacrilege." They were "adulterers, libidinous, and sodomists." "Their chief desire is to eat, drink, worship the devil, and commit bestial obscenities." "God is going to destroy them soon. Who can deny that the use of gunpowder against these pagan beasts is like lighting incense before the Lord?"

On the other hand, the newly disembarked blacks were industrious, used to hard work, with constitutions not susceptible to European diseases. Black slavery would be the savior of New Spain, a theory espoused by the Bishop of Chiapas, Bartolomé de las Casas, an outspoken defender of the Indians, who championed the wholesale importation of black chattel slaves. By 1650, a total of 150,000 Africans had been kidnapped from their homelands and shipped off to dig in the mines and otherwise serve their new masters in Mexico.

During the 17th and 18th centuries, the Europeans constructed the most pernicious system of apartheid ever to be imposed upon the Americas. Whites and blacks both intermarried with Indians and their offspring blended into new castes—soaring syphilis infection became the mark of the mixing. *Mestizo, mulato, morisco, zambo, castizo, cambujo, zambiago, lobo,* and *coyote* were some of the derogatory names (there were 16 nonwhite castes in all) coined to describe the complexities of skin color in New Spain.

Each was assigned a slot in colonial society, and breaking the taboos could result in being roasted on the bonfires of the Inquisition or mob pummelings. The ever present threat of the Indiada was expanded to take into account all peoples of color. When blacks in Mexico City rose in fury at the beating death of one of their own in 1611, justice moved swiftly. Twenty-nine were hanged in the Plaza Mayor, their heads chopped off and toted around the square on pikes.

Even the criollos, Spanish born in New Spain, were not white enough for the Gachupines. After all, most had been suckled on the milk of dark-skinned mammies.

GACHUPÍN! (An interview with Carlos Diez)

Carlos surveys the nearly empty restaurant, one eye glued to the door watching for customers. With his spotless white bata (jacket), lanky build, and kind features, Carlos could pass for a doctor—but he is not. He is the owner of this place, La Blanca. The Diez children, three brothers and two sisters, have run this cafeteria-style restaurant on Cinco de Mayo Street since their father passed on 10 years ago. When Don Marciano died, the place was closed for a week. I've been eating breakfast and dinner here for 24 years. I don't know where else to eat.

I always sit at the counter and gab with old friends. In the mornings, Armando, a dapper man with a passion for the Chivas football team, brings me an egg, a yogurt, and a café americano. Armando has been waiting here since 1957. He doesn't have to ask what I want anymore. In the evenings, it's usually a Spanish bean soup—caldo gallego or fabada or cocido, specialties of the house. Manuel, who came to work at La Blanca a few years after Armando, talks sports with me. It's Manuel's night off. Carlos gives up on watching the door and comes over to sit down.

"How's the book going?" he wants to know. Carlos has fed me through 10 books now. But El Monstruo is about the city he loves, and he is always giving me leads. I tell him I am working on the section about how Lázaro Cárdenas welcomed the refugees from the Spanish Civil War.

"My father wasn't a refugee. He came to Mexico in 1926 to make his fortune from León in the mountains of northern Spain. My grandparents ran the bar at the airport there. They got all the pilots drunk.

"At first, Don Marciano settled in the port of Veracruz and went to work in a bar. Then he bought his own bar, La Bamba. It went well for him and later he came to Mexico City and bought La Blanca from an Asturian family. That was in 1941. La Blanca was down the street then where the parking garage is now.

"The original La Blanca opened in 1913 during the revolution and was named for a ranch out in Texcoco. The farmers would bring their milk to sell here every day. I have a customer whose mother was born on the Rancho La Blanca—she's 97 now."

Carlos calls over Daniel, one of the greeters, who doubles as the restaurant's resident artist, and Daniel gets a ladder and removes from the wall a picture of the restaurant circa 1951. The joint is packed. "The place was half the size it is today—there was only one counter and you could never get a seat." But tonight you could have any seat in the house. A few regulars loiter at the counter. The tables are empty.

"My father first brought me here when I was six years old. We lived far away in the Colonia Anzures and it was a special treat to come downtown. The streets were always filled with ambulantes *and wandering musicians and military parades and good things to eat."*

Because La Blanca is a block from the Zócalo and not far from Tepito and the Lagunilla market district, the clients are a cross-section of the Centro. Tradespeople and professionals, shop owners, politicians, construction workers, and market sellers sit elbow to elbow. The café con leche—*Carlos buys his coffee beans in Coatepec from the same farmers who supply the famous Parroquia in Veracruz port—has the reputation of being the best in the Centro Histórico.*

"*Presidents would come here with their* camarillas *[coteries] just for the coffee. We've had Echeverría and López Portillo and Carlos Salinas and the regent Carlos Hank González, all the bad guys. Even murderers came for our café. The killer they call the* mataviejitas—*he only killed little old ladies— used to sell chocolate bars here to the kids. He would sit where you're sitting right now. He was the nicest guy in the world, a perfect gentleman.*"

"*I haven't killed any old ladies today,*" *I joke.*

"*Once, we had Sara, the niece of the governor of Jalisco. She was the* novia *[girlfriend] of the famous* narcotraficante *Caro Quintero. He kidnapped her from her home and they ran off together. They wrote* corridos *about her. This place was crawling with her bodyguards.*"

What did Carlos remember about the refugees that Lázaro Cárdenas rescued from Franco during the civil war?

"*Well, we weren't with the refugees. In fact, my father was on the other side. But I knew many refugee kids in school and later at the Mundet, the Spanish community organization here in Mexico City. They were friends. We didn't have any political problems with them. The way the Mexicans saw it we were all* Gachupines *[Spaniards] so we had to stick together.*"

An older couple comes in and Daniel seats them in an island of empty tables. Business is off about 30 percent, Carlos figures. "We lost a lot of our regular customers after the earthquake in 1985. Nothing happened to us here—we didn't even break a glass. But Tepito and Lagunilla were torn up pretty badly and the vendors stopped coming in. We closed for a while and a lot of our old customers never came back.

"*Now we're suffering all over again. They say we're in a recession but the prices just keep going up. I go to buy at the* Centro de Abastos *[food depot] every week and every week everything is up up up—eggs, meat, bananas, you name it. We hardly raised our prices this year but still, the way it is, many of our regulars just can't afford to eat at La Blanca anymore. I can understand it.*

"*But what's really killing us is the demonstrators—your friend López Obrador and his damn marches. They're driving the decent people away. My idea is that they should stop marching to the Zócalo. They should go somewhere else like Los Pinos. Let them bother the president.*"

Carlos knows that I'm a López Obrador fan. He's always needling me about "El Peje" (The Gar), as López Obrador is nicknamed. So I needle him right back.

"So do people still call you a Gachupín?"

"Do people still call me a Gachupín? Ha! Every day! Mexicans never forgive us. There's always someone who comes up to me and talks about Gachupín this and Gachupín that. This guy from Gobernación [the Interior Secretariat] was eating here and we started talking. He didn't like my opinions and he said he was going to put Article 33 on me and have me deported!

"Deported? I was born here. I'm a Chilango *[Mexico City–ite]! I grew up and went to school here in Mexico City! How can he have me deported? Maybe my father was from Spain but I'm not. I'm a Mexican—although sometimes, I'm not so proud of it. . . . "*

RICH CITY, POOR CITY

By the turn of the 18th century, the population of the capital had grown to 100,000 souls: 50,000 Gachupines and criollos, 40,000 castes including Afro Mexicans, and 10,000 Indians—most of the surviving original inhabitants had been pushed out to surrounding slum cities. In the ever widening divide between classes, perhaps 10,000 Spaniards and twice as many criollos monopolized wealth and political power.

Physically, the Monstruo had not grown much in the first fifty years of the silver boom. It occupied 14 square kilometers (Tenochtitlán had measured nine). But instead of building out, the city built itself up. The first cathedral, a squat, granite building, was replaced by a much loftier and ornate version that dominated the skyline every bit as much as Huitzilopochtli and Tláloc had two centuries back down history's highway.

The palaces of the nouveaux riches skyed above the Spanish city. Red roof tiles replaced wooden shingles and the physiognomy of the façades was psychedelically transformed. The ruling class was crazy for baroque, and the great homes and palaces and churches were sculpted with phantasmagoric scrollings, curlicues, spirals, gargoyles, cherubim, nymphs, and muses. Behind the Cathedral, rows of artisan shops crafted gilded figures of the saints, chalices, altarpieces, and vestments laced with gold threads and silver filaments for the priestly class. The city—or at least the white neighborhoods—grew infinitely more extravagant.

But for the black and brown underclass, the drabness of life was unaltered. By the mid-1700s, the Church controlled all banking and credit in New Spain and was by far the biggest landowner, holding at least 150 ecclesiastical buildings in the capital and virtually all of the rental property. With its command post at the Metropolitan Cathedral—the largest Church building in Latin America, financed largely by profits from the slave trade—the high clergy collected rents from the city's poor families, often confined to a single room opening on a grubby courtyard in the Aztec style, a design still traceable in Centro Histórico *vecindades* (slum buildings).

With the arrival of tens of thousands of money-hungry Gachupines, freebooters, thugs, and mountebanks, the scum of Europe, life in El Monstruo grew ugly and boisterous. Drunken louts careened through the narrow alleys, fighting and puking their guts out, and the Indians anesthetized their daily humiliation in the *pulquerías*—public drunkenness in Mexico City was considered the worst in the Western Hemisphere.

Aggressive *ambulantes* (street vendors) wandered about hawking their whatnots at the top of their lungs. A permanent stench wafted from the slaughterhouses, hog pens, and manure piles, choking the capital's inhabitants. Garbage collection left much to be desired. Huge heaps of refuse were burnt in the public plazas, further fouling the air, a taste of the monstrous air quality to come. The constant cacophony of clanging church bells assaulted citizens' ears 24 hours a day.

The Cabildo was hopelessly corrupt and did little to stanch the disintegration of public life. One viceroy, Don Juan Vicente de Güemes Padilla Horcasitas, the second Count of Revillagigedo, made a brave effort to fix the city at the end of the 18th century. From 1789 to 1794, he succeeded in driving the ambulant street vendors out of the Vía Pública (public thoroughfare) and into markets, although they soon filled the streets again. The Count sought to cultivate reason and order amongst the citizenry, an unreasonable goal, and posted street signs and even house numbers, but the chaos could not be controlled.

THE GREAT TUMULT

The immense gap between rich and poor, races and classes, often led to riot. The Great Tumult of 1694, when drought, famine, and flood lashed the city with serial calamity and the castes and the Indians joined forces against the white rulers, was an early warning signal of trouble to come. Indian mobs looted the Alhóndiga, the public granary. When the Spanish troops slaughtered several Indian market women, crowds gathered in the Plaza Mayor. The castes and dissatisfied whites joined in common cause. The rioters burst into the viceroy's palace, which was filled with lavish furniture and hangings, and burnt it to the ground. The rioting, fueled by high-octane alcohol, continued for days until finally the Gachupín solders forced the darker races from the center of the city back into the festering slums.

Again in 1767, the expulsion of the Jesuits precipitated fresh rioting. Big death revisited the capital in 1785 when a virulent resurgence of smallpox wiped out 300,000 in the Valley of Mexico, further exacerbating the misery. Wagons rumbled through the streets, hauling the dead and the drunk alike off to Mictlán.

When the German explorer Baron Alexander Von Humboldt showed up in the capital of New Spain in 1804 (the Baron bunked around the corner from me at Uruguay #80), he counted 100 millionaires within the city limits, more than in any one city on the continent, but he was appalled by the sea of poverty in which the masses were drowning. Thirty thousand nearly naked beggars swarmed through the streets each night, sleeping where they dropped. "This country is divided between those who have everything and those who have nothing," the Bishop of Morelia warned.

The Bourbon dynasty lapsed into stupor and the rumblings from the bottom grew ominous. A failed conspiracy to overthrow the viceroy in 1793 made it clear that the jig was almost up. In 1808, when Napoleon's army marched into Spain, *pintas* (slogans) appeared on the walls of Mexico City: BELOVED COMRADES, FATE HAS PLACED FREEDOM IN OUR HANDS. IF WE DO NOT SHAKE OFF THE SPANISH YOKE NOW, WE WILL BE WRETCHED FOREVER.

HIDALGO'S BELLS

Where and when the war for Mexico's independence began is debated by historians as diligently as theologians anguish over how many angels can hoof on the point of a pin. The markers are many.

On September 16 (remember that date), 1808, seeking to take advantage of Napoleon's invasion of Spain, a group of workers—the *chaquetas* or jackets—from the Gachupín-owned stores spread around the Plaza Mayor penetrated the viceroy's palace chanting *"¡Soberanía Popular!"* ("People's Rule!") and were brutally repelled by the royalist troops.

Francisco Primo Verdad, a *síndico* or member of the Cabildo, was fingered as the instigator and jailed in the calaboose of the archbishop's palace adjacent to the Metropolitan Cathedral. Two weeks later, Primo Verdad ("First Truth") was found dead in his cell of "natural causes." Many thought that Verdad had been poisoned.

Despite the growing enthusiasm of Mexico City's criollos for independence, the fuse for liberation was lit not in the capital but rather 200 miles farther north in the silver mines of Zacatecas and the silver-rich cities of Querétaro and Guanajuato. Anti-royalist conspiracies inspired by the French and Yanqui revolutions multiplied. The clergy was often involved. One such plot clustered around the profligate *cura* (priest) Padre Miguel Hidalgo y Costilla, the ex-rector of San Nicolás University in Valladolid (now Morelia, Michoacán), who had been relieved of his duties for conspicuous gaming, embezzlement, and whoring—the good father fathered three children.

Packed off to the one-horse town of Dolores in the lowlands of central Mexico, he entered into a conspiracy with criollos in Querétaro to overrun the governor's palace and declare Mexico's Independence, but his co-conspirators were snitched out by a Gachupín spy and arrested before the plot came to fruition. Notified of the betrayal, Padre Hidalgo furiously rang the bells of his country church summoning the populace to the town plaza where he harangued them at length. *"¡Viva México!"* the priest bellowed at last: "Let's go kill us some Gachupines!" The date was September 16, 1810—two years to the day after Primo Verdad's rebellion. Two hundred years later, the ringing of the bells and at least the first clause of Hidalgo's *grito* are ritually celebrated each September 16 wherever there are Mexicans.

The soon-to-be-defrocked priest's next act was to throw open the doors of the town's teeming jail, releasing hundreds of Indian and black prisoners. Father Hidalgo hoisted high the banner of the Virgin of Guadalupe and marched the prisoners toward Guanajuato, then Mexico's third-largest city and a bastion of the silver barons, looting and stomping the white burghers along the way without making much distinction between criollos and Gachupines. By the time Hidalgo's mob reached the city's gates they numbered in the thousands and had little difficulty forcing their way into the silver capital. Three hundred whites terrified by the fury of the dusky underclass locked themselves into the town granary and were subsequently torched by a disaffected miner nicknamed "El Pipila," now the brand-name for *tacos de carbón* stands throughout Mexico.

Then Hidalgo's ragtag army set off for the capital behind the standard of the Dark Madonna, utterly convinced that the Guadalupana would protect them against the sabers of the Gachupines.

The prospect of race war terrorized Mexico City. For many criollos, the long-awaited Indiada had come at last, and now it was not just the Indians but also the castes and the blacks. Despite their aspirations for independence from the Crown, the criollos now begged the royalist army for protection against the colored hordes. The bulk of the army was largely born in America of European stock—21,000 out of 23,000 troops were "Americanos" led by crack Gachupín horsemen.

By now, Hidalgo's rebels numbered 100,000, the largest attack force assembled since Cortez marched his Indian confederates up to Tenochtitlán, but the insurgents were armed only with clubs and rocks and their field knives, the weapons of the rural poor, and their abiding belief in the Guadalupana was their only defense. The battle was joined at Las Cruces, 25 kilometers from the center of the city in what is now the westernmost delegation of Cuajimalpa.

At full gallop, the Gachupín horsemen led by the dashing Agustín Iturbide repeatedly rode down Hidalgo's irregulars, trampling and slicing the rebels into rout. The Gachupines were accompanied by their own Virgin, the pale-skinned Virgin of Remedios, whom Cortez had brought with him to Mexico. The slaughter lasted all day and the vultures darkened the sky. By nightfall, the ragged corpses of the black and brown insurgents were strewn like bundles of straw upon the plain. Hidalgo's Virgin of Guadalupe was taken prisoner, her banner annihilated by a Gachupín firing squad.

Hidalgo's "army" fled in disarray. The wild-eyed *cura* headed north and was finally cornered in Chihuahua where the royalists executed him Saudi-style, first before an *escuadrón de fusilamiento* and then by decapitation.

LA GUERRILLA

In death, Father Hidalgo passed on the scepter to a trusted accomplice José María Morelos, a rebel priest from Morelia and a black man who had bought his way out of his caste. He carried papers to prove that he was officially "white." Whereas Hidalgo had acted from his gut hatred of the Gachupines, Morelos was a cool-headed military strategist. He broke down the remnants of the rebel forces into small bands of guerrilleros who would prowl the hot lands of the Pacific coast states of Michoacán, Guerrero, Colima, and Oaxaca for a decade, plundering the Crown's treasuries in these far-flung territories and ruthlessly picking off the Royal Army when challenged. By 1814, the guerrilleros controlled so much territory that Morelos convoked a rebel congress in Apatzingán, Michoacán, in 1814, proclaimed independence, and issued Mexico's first constitution.

A three-day ride east, fear and loathing seethed inside the capital. The race card had driven the criollos into the royalist camp and strengthened the hand of the Church, which chalked up the victory over Hidalgo's "satanic maelstrom" at Las Cruces to the powers of the Virgin of Remedios. Outnumbered by the Indians and the castes in their own bailiwick, the Gachupines and the criollos pumped up the race hysteria and cowed the darker masses into a state of uneasy quiescence.

Meanwhile, in Spain the Monarchy had collapsed before the French invasion and no one was in charge. While Spanish patriots fought a guerrilla war against Bonaparte's troops much like the one Morelos waged against the Royalists in the colony, local juntas constituted themselves as authority, but the criollos unanimously rejected the spurious authorities' attempts to collect the tribute Spain thought due from New Spain.

With the Crown disabled, the criollos elected their own Cabildo and took charge of their own affairs. This moment of independence was short-lived. When the Spanish guerrilla finally forced the French army to retreat—Francisco Goya engraved these atrocities in "The Disasters of War"—the monarchy was restored and clamped down upon the liberationists. A royalist Cabildo evicted the criollos' council. The Crown, bereft of funds to fight its wars, imposed crunching taxation upon the colony and enforced the "consolidation," seizing much of the Church's nonreligious property.

The reaction was to be expected. Young Lucas Alamán, an official in charge of public health at the Ayuntamiento who, as fate would have it, died one floor below me in 1853 on Espíritu Santo Street, now Isabel la Católica, noted that mid-level property owners had been ruined by the decrees of the Crown, which had "awakened in them a desire for emancipation."

While High Society carried on as if everything was coming up roses, attending the theater nightly and indulging in masked balls and sumptuous banquets, the criollos split along class lines. A fifth column opened up inside the capital. Perhaps the principal race traitor was the highborn Leona Vicario. The daughter of a wealthy Gachupín merchant, Vicario carried on a torrid correspondence with her lover Andrés Quintana Roo, a deserter from the royal army who had gone off to join the rebels in 1817. When Leona's family discovered the letters, they had her locked away in a nunnery.

THE MELON OF MEXICO

José María Morelos was cornered and killed in 1815 trying to cut the heavily patrolled road from Veracruz to Mexico City, the lifeline of the capital's commercial class. Leadership of the insurgent forces fell to another black man, Vicente Guerrero, the son of a mule driver from La Montaña in the state that bears his name, still the most impoverished region of Mexico.

Although the rebels were not yet knocking on the gates of power, the Monstruo suffered the trauma of a city under siege. The population ballooned by a quarter as refugees poured in seeking sanctuary from the violence in the countryside. The rural rebellion had cut off food supplies to the capital, and hunger was palpable. The Cabildo went broke and all city services fell into disrepair. Clogged drainage caused the usual flooding. A typhus epidemic swept the city and 20,000 died. Packs of wild dogs commandeered the Plaza Mayor.

By 1820, the criollos were being pressed to decide which side their toast was buttered on. Agustín Iturbide, the Savior of the city, rode off into the outback and colluded with Guerrero in the hot lands of Iguala. Over supper, the two decided upon a formula for independence: Mexico would be first and foremost a Catholic republic; slavery would be abolished; and universal suffrage (except for Indians and the castes) would be guaranteed. Indeed, their respective forces would be combined into the Army of the Three Guarantees. By the time dessert was served, they had decided upon a flag (or so the story goes): red for the rebels, the color of the meat of the watermelon upon which they dined; white for the purity of Christ, the color of the melon's inner rind; and green to symbolize unity, the color of its outer rind.

Thus, on September 27, 1821—300 years and six weeks from the date that Hernán Cortez had crossed the causeway to conquer a dying Tenochtitlán—Agustín Iturbide rode back into the capital and proclaimed Mexico's independence from Spain. Six hundred thousand had perished since Hidalgo had proclaimed "¡Viva México! Let's go kill some Gachupines!," most of them the people the color of the earth.

In contemporary engravings, the crowd assembled to greet the former Gachupín general when he rode through the gates of the city doesn't look particularly enthusiastic. Indeed, in subsequent years, every time a new conqueror would arrive in the capital, they would be met by this same stoic curiosity, as if the people were always asking themselves, "What next?"

IV

CITY OF BETRAYED HOPES

The city, which would continue to be the stage set for the high national drama and epic opportunism that marked the wrenching birth of the Mexican republic, was in ruins. The stench of death permeated every cranny in the capital. A British traveler quoted by Jonathan Kandell in his brilliant 1988 chronicle *La Capital* saw only "citizens in rags with offensive sores."

Crammed into the eastern slums, Indians picked through the enormous, smoldering La Viña dumps scavenging for food. Disease and crime incubated in these neighborhoods. Travelers entering the city from the provinces were invariably victims of strong-arm robbery, and wealthier pedestrians were heisted in broad daylight when they visited Monte de Piedad, the national pawnshop that is still sited on the northwest corner of the Zócalo.

BETRAYAL UPON BETRAYAL

Upon his return to the Monstruo, Iturbide, who had betrayed his Spanish masters, now betrayed the new republic by proclaiming himself to be Emperor of Mexico. Agustín I's subjects were not happy with this arrangement. In 1823 they hauled his ass out of the viceroy's palace and hanged him in the Zócalo. Months after he was strung up, Agustín I's velvet and gold throne, which he had ordered from Paris, arrived in Mexico City—it is still on display at the National Museum of Foreign Invasions in Coyoacán.

The criollos caucused and convened a congress, and in January 1824 promulgated a new constitution proclaiming the United States of Mexico, declaring the capital to be a "federal district" from which "the powers of the republic" would emanate. The 62-page constitution was hawked on the streets of Centro for five *reales*, a bargain.

The first president of the United States of Mexico was one Miguel Félix Fernández, a handsome epileptic from far north Durango who had joined Guerrero's rebels in 1817. With a flair for the dramatic, Félix Fernández took the symbolism-charged nom politique "Guadalupe Victoria."

President Victoria would rule for the next five years, plagued by the craven ambitions of his rivals, the sinister plots of his peers, and daily riots by those he pretended to govern. When a mob, purportedly incited by Guerrero and the U.S. ambassador Poinsett, burnt down the Parian market in 1828, Gachupín fortunes went up in smoke, triggering massive capital flight and depleting the treasury. Mexico would live in perpetual bankruptcy for the next 50 years as median income dropped by a third of its pre-independence level.

As a poetic denouement to the years of toxic race war that had so dominated the national psyche, Vicente Guerrero succeeded Guadalupe Victoria on the throne of Mexico. Between Félix Fernández and the stern Zapotec Indian Benito Juárez in 1857, Mexico would have 41 presidents. Eleven of them were named Antonio López de Santa Anna.

SANTA ANNA'S LEGS

The cortege advanced at a solemn stately step along the northwest fringe of the city. The horse-drawn hearse was followed by phalanxes of dignitaries and mourners. First in line were the commanders-in-chief of the armed forces in full regalia and behind them, in lockstep, the young Cadets of the Heroic Military College. A military band pumped out a patriotic dirge. Groups of uniformed schoolchildren came next, and then the common citizens in their funerary finest.

The somber procession, celebrated September 27, 1842, exactly 21 years to the day after Agustín Iturbide had first ridden into Mexico City, entered the Santa Paola cemetery hard by the Heroic Military

College in Santa María la Redonda (Metro stop San Cosme on the blue line) and mourners lined up around the freshly dug grave. A lengthy funeral oration was pronounced by the president of the Patriotic Junta Ignacio Sierra y Rosso, and General Antonio López de Santa Anna, "the Redeemer of Mexico," was so moved by his words that he could not hold back a tear as the dearly departed was lowered into the earth. The deceased was, indeed, an old friend, his left leg in fact, severed by a French cannonball below the knee four years previously during the short-lived "pastry war."

French warships had come calling at the port of Veracruz in April 1838 under the pretext of collecting damages owed to one M. Remontel, a citizen of their country, whose Mexico City pastry shop had been invaded and trashed by Mexican ruffians—but the subtext of this armed collection call had more to do with a "free trade treaty" France was intent on imposing on the Mexicans than with chocolate éclairs.

General Santa Anna, who had recently assumed the title of "Supreme Dictator of Mexico," rushed from his nearby hacienda at Mango de Claves in his underwear and repelled the incursion, albeit mostly on one leg. The dismembered member was first interred at his Veracruz estate, but when "His Serene Highness" (another title bestowed upon Santa Anna by his grateful supporters) once again assumed the reins of state in 1842, it occurred to him to rebury the leg at Santa Paola with full military honors.

Two years after this extravagant self-celebration, a citizen mob, enraged by the General's looting of the federal treasury, returned to Santa Paola, dug up Santa Anna's leg, and dragged it through the streets before energetically ripping it to shreds in the Plaza Mayor. The irate rabble then broke into the Metropolitan Cathedral and smashed a bust of the Supreme Dictator to smithereens. Despite the public's fury, Antonio López de Santa Anna would be returned two more times to the presidency of Mexico.

One footnote to this cautionary tale: General Santa Anna replaced his missing body part with a cork leg that he was prone to lose in battle. At Cerro Gordo, for example, outside Xalapa on the Veracruz road during the American invasion of 1847, the Illinois Rifles captured the peg leg (it was thought to have been abandoned in a carriage during the Mexicans' mad retreat), and for years it was on display in the War Museum of the Illinois Senate in Springfield—Santa Anna's substitute leg was returned to the country of its birth some years later upon the petition of Mexican dictator Porfirio Díaz but that is another chapter in this chronicle of betrayal.

With an ill-trained, under-armed, highly inept military in which blatant self-interest supplanted the honor of defending the young republic, Mexico was ripe for the picking in the years after independence was declared. The Pastry War was preceded nine years earlier by an invasion of Spaniards that was, once again, beaten back by General Santa Anna in the pestilent swamps of Veracruz and Tamaulipas, where the Crown's emissaries dropped like flies from malaria and yellow fever. In 1835, the British had put in to Veracruz to "offer" the locals a "free trade" pact but were obligated by aggressive disinterest on the part of the Mexicans to haul anchor and sail south.

Each threat would propel López de Santa Anna into a new presidency, but the "Liberator of Mexico" (yet another self-inflicted title) had little talent or interest in administering the affairs of state and rather filled up Mexico City with statues, mostly of himself, and allocated a sizable boodle of public monies to import Swiss guards from the Vatican to protect his imperial person. Fortunately, the man was quickly bored, and when he was done with looting the treasuries under his control retired to Mango de Claves to await new opportunities for plunder.

PINCHES AMERICANOS

Of all the invading armies, the Yanquis were the most annoying. From the first day the Mexican republic was established, Washington coveted the vast, sparsely populated (except for 200,000 native peoples) northern territories of Nueva Galicia that Mexico had inherited from Spain. To further this future annexation, John Quincy Adams dispatched Joel Poinsett, a South Carolina planter, to Mexico City in 1822 as the first American ambassador. The next year, the Yanquis would proclaim the Monroe Doctrine, which declared all of Mexico and the lands to the south to be the Americanos' back patio and warned the Europeans they had best not mess around on this side of the ocean. (Poinsett was also the first American bio-pirate, appropriating the Mexica "Nochebuena" Christmas flower—*cuetlaxochitl* in Aztec—and naming it "poinsettia" after himself.)

The Yanqui ambassador plotted secretly with opponents of Guadalupe Victoria, utilizing the York Rite Masonic Lodge as cover for connivance with Vicente Guerrero, and when exposed had to flee the country to evade arrest. One American scoundrel after another arrived to propose, cajole, and threaten the Mexicans into ceding their northern territories.

The territory of Tejas, 1,200 miles north, was a headache for Mexico City. Mexicans were a minority population in the huge territory now overrun with white slavers—slavery had been outlawed in Mexico under the black president Guerrero in 1829. When Sam Houston proclaimed Texas an independent republic in 1836, Santa Anna jumped on his horse, marshaled an army, and dead-marched the recruits all the way from San Luis Potosí to San Antonio de Béjar, cornering Houston's rat pack of cutthroats, mercenaries, and Indian killers in the old Franciscan mission of El Alamo. Ten days later, Mexican troops annihilated Houston's forces at Goliad, but they lost badly at San Jacinto, where the Supreme Dictator was detained long enough to cut a deal with his captors.

Antonio López de Santa Anna would then travel as a private citizen to Washington and take up residence in Cuba awaiting the call of his American masters. Meanwhile, the White House decreed a blockade of Mexico's Caribbean coast. When expansionist president James Polk saw a window of opportunity in 1845, the Redeemer of Mexico's handlers smuggled him through the American blockade of Veracruz to assume the presidency of Mexico yet again, in anticipation of the impending U.S. invasion.

With his headlights set on the 1848 election, Polk promised the American people "a short war" (where have we heard that one before?) and orchestrated a Gulf of Tonkin–like provocation at Matamoros, drawing Mexican troops across the Río Bravo where they managed to whack a few Americanos. Polk wept at the death of the Yanqui soldiers—"our blood has now fallen on our own soil" (sic)—and organized a five-point invasion of Mexico. The U.S. Navy sailed into San Francisco Bay, and Los Angeles was besieged by Kit Carson and his irregulars in Alta, California. Marines landed at Mazatlán on Mexico's Pacific Coast. Zachary Taylor would swoop south from Tejas, and grizzled old General Winfield Scott landed in Veracruz and followed Cortez's footprints to the Halls of Moctezuma.

Starting out in the spring of 1847, General Scott directed his army to take Tenochtitlán, encountering, as expected, little resistance from the Mexicans. Indeed, like Cortez, Scott forged alliances with disaffected

Mexicans along the route—the "Polkos" rejoiced in the Americano invasion. As the Yankee Doodle Dandies climbed into the *altiplano* (highlands), they sang the popular songs of the day, one of which, "Green Grow the Lilacs Oh," became their signature tune, and forever after they would be known as "greengos."

THE FALL OF TENOCHTITLÁN (REDUX)

Much of Scott's invading force had been recruited from the Mississippi Valley (he himself was a Mississippian), and being as big a bunch of hicks as Cortez's country boys had been when they came this way, they were boggled by the size and spread of Mexican cities—amongst the Southerners who accompanied the Mississippi Rifles were Jefferson Davis and Robert E. Lee. In many ways, the "Mexican" war was a dry run for the U.S. Civil War.

Having routed Santa Anna at Cerro Gordo and absconded with his cork leg, the "greengos" occupied Puebla, Mexico's second-largest city at the time, without firing a shot. Polk had dispatched a negotiator, Nicholas Trist, to dictate the terms of Mexican surrender and when the Americans encamped outside the capital on August 20, Santa Anna was summoned from the city and offered $10,000,000 Yanqui dollars to throw the battle, of which he was paid a $10,000 advance—it was all General Scott had in his petty cash drawer.

Scott entered the capital from the southwest, taking the small village of San Ángel, but met with stiffer resistance than anticipated—even if the fix had been pacted with Santa Anna, his poorly armed troops seemed prepared to lay down their lives to save the republic.

Once the western suburbs had been secured, Scott descended into Coyoacán, Cortez's old fiefdom, and following the course of the Río Churubusco, pinned down two brigades of Mexican defenders inside an old stone convent built syncretically centuries before over an altar to Huitzilopochtli. The nuns were evacuated and the Mexican defenders were joined by a band of Irish-American defectors from Scott's army, the St. Patricks or San Patricios, who were prepared to give up their collective ghost to keep the Protestant heretics from overrunning Catholic Mexico.

With only seven pieces of artillery and little ammunition to defend the Fatherland, the Churubusco convent fell in a day. Twenty-one surviving San Patricios were captured and strung up in the

Plaza de San Jacinto in San Ángel, now one of the Monstruo's ritziest districts.

Zigzagging northwest, Scott's greengos rolled into Mixcoac, easily vanquished the Mexican holdouts at Molino del Rey on September 8, and paused to see what was on Santa Anna's mind before pushing into the heart of the city. The Supreme Dictator's response was not immediately forthcoming, and on the 13th, the Mississippi Rifles swooped down on Chapultepec Castle, once the summer home of the viceroy, where 50 cadets of the Heroic Military College were arrayed in a thin line of defense.

Rather than surrender to the invaders, six of the cadets wrapped themselves in the Mexican flag and flung themselves from the ramparts—"Los Niños Héroes," the Heroic Children, who in death were transformed into obligatory patriotic icons for every tin-plate politico who has come down the pike since. Among the cadets who did not volunteer for patriotic suicide was Miguel Miramón. Remember his name.

THE ULTIMATE HUMILATION

From Chapultepec, it was a straight shot downtown—only six stops on the Pink Line today. Sweeping east down Chapultepec road (later the elegant Paseo de La Reforma), the greengos marched triumphantly on the Centro, but when Scott's boys reached the Alameda they ran into heavy fire. The Ayuntamiento, appalled by Santa Anna's capitulation, had encouraged the citizenry to dig up paving stones and hurl them down upon the invaders from the rooftops. Engravings hanging in the National Museum of Interventions—the ex–Churubusco convent—depict my neighbors pelting the Yanquis with everything they had. The confrontations don't look dissimilar to pitched battles between contemporary protesters storming into the Zócalo and the Granaderos, the capital's riot squad.

The Americanos advanced block by block, occasionally firing on their tormentors. Down Isabel la Católica Street on the corner of Madero, in front of the Profesa church, defenders built barricades out of the paving stones to prevent the greengos' passage into the Plaza Mayor. But the Yanqui firepower was overwhelming, and by nightfall on September 14, two days before the 37th anniversary of Hidalgo's cry of liberation, the Stars & Stripes were waving above the Zócalo, the ultimate humiliation.

THE ANNEXATION OF MEXICO

The Redeemer of Mexico fled to Querétaro and established a spurious government in exile. General Scott's troops set up camp on the Alameda. Trist sat down with Santa Anna's proxies to annex Mexico. The negotiations did not produce immediate gratification. Washington wanted all of Nueva Galicia plus the Isthmus of Oaxaca, the strategic narrow neck of the nation that connects the Pacific to the Gulf. The greengos settled in for a long stay. Soldiers flirted with the señoritas and were adored by the Polkos and despised by everyone else. The first English-language newspaper, the *Daily American Star*, appeared— an ancestor of the much-reviled *The News*. Christmas came and went.

Finally, on February 2, 1848, a puff of white smoke exploded from the Basilica of the Virgin of Guadalupe in the villa just north of the city where Trist and the chief justice of Mexico's Supreme Court, a Santa Anna crony, inked the Treaty of Guadalupe Hidalgo, which ceded the Americanos all the land from the Río Bravo to Wyoming, 13 western states from Iowa all the way to California where gold had just been discovered, 1,572,741 square kilometers, a land grab the size of western Europe and fully 51 percent of Mexico's geographical territory. Mexico got nothing in return. Some "treaty"! Here they call it El Gran Despojo—the Great Robbery.

Nevertheless, it ought to be understood that the land turned over to the Americanos in the Treaty of Guadalupe Hidalgo did not really belong to either Mexico or Washington and in fact had only been in Mexico's hands for a mere 27 years since liberation from Spain. Prior to the Spanish Conquest, this immense stretch of land had "belonged" to native peoples for countless millennia.

The Americanos packed up in the spring of 1848. Polk got his short war and the Democrats were a shoo-in for reelection. But, much as when Lyndon Johnson rammed the Gulf of Tonkin resolution up Congress's arse more than a century later, there were a few dissenting voices against the imperialist "Mexican" war. One was the lanky Republican senator from Illinois who mournfully intoned his condemnation of the adventure. For Abe Lincoln, the taking of the Halls of Moctezuma had been "one of the most unjust wars ever waged by a strong country against a weak one."

THE LACERATED CITY

The Monstruo did not suffer these invasions softly. Internecine feuds between political factions punctuated the foreign aggressions. In July 1841, a conservative rising against the liberal president Bustamante toppled buildings downtown. Back in the 1790s, Viceroy Revillagigedo had prided his administration on paving 23 kilometers of streets and sidewalks. By 1853, so many paving stones had been dug up for so many pitched battles that only six kilometers remained.

The comings and goings of foreign and domestic armies had left the infrastructure in grievous disrepair. The dreams of the Monstruo's various governments of building an effective drainage system were abandoned because the money was spent on wars instead. Floods continued to overwhelm the city from one rainy season to the next. Depleted budgets curtailed garbage collection, and the city's hygiene declined precipitously. The notorious Indian districts in the east of the city were riddled with tuberculosis and cholera. The Indians themselves, animated by the 1847 War of the Castes in the Yucatán, were in an uproar at the government's inattention to their plight.

Each morning, chain gangs of prisoners—those who had not been arbitrarily shot—swept the downtown streets. The crime wave continued unabated. After General Scott's troops abandoned the Alameda, gangs of thieves moved in, records José María Marroqui, the city's first official *cronista* (chronicler), building "caves" out of the downed trees and debris from which they sprang upon unsuspecting pedestrians. The poorly paid police went home after sunset and left the capital for the gangs to pillage.

THE REDEEMER'S LAST STAND

The republic he had so assiduously screwed for a quarter of a century called upon Antonio López de Santa Anna to govern yet again between 1852 and 1854. Washington was happy to see their old collaborator back in the National Palace and offered Santa Anna 15 million Yanqui bucks to sell off southern Arizona and New Mexico. These two swatches of Mexican real estate had not been included in the Treaty of Guadalupe Hidalgo, and the gringos wanted to build a railroad. The so-called Gadsden Purchase is known as the "Theft of La Mesilla" south of the border. His Serene Highness knew a good deal when he saw one, pocketed the change, and retired to Venezuela.

During his final two years of service to the nation, the Redeemer was much concerned with larding the capital with statues of himself and his cronies and renaming streets in their honor. Among his beautification projects was the relocation of an immense bronze equestrian statue of Carlos IV, the "Caballito," created by the Valenciano monument maker Manuel Tolsa in 1804 and plunked down in the middle of the Plaza Mayor.

After liberation, the Caballito had become politically incorrect and was hauled off to the University, which now occupied a full block on the northern flank of the Palacio Nacional. But Santa Anna had just installed a towering bronze likeness of himself in the Plaza de los Voladores across from the southeast corner of the Plaza Mayor (where the Supreme Court is now located), and the neighborhood wasn't big enough for both of them.

In 1853, workmen took down the great doors of the University to move the Caballito to a distant plaza; transit would take 15 days. Meanwhile, the pedestal or *zócalo* upon which the Caballito had been mounted remained at the center of the Plaza Mayor. In fact, that is what the people had taken to calling the place, and the 48,000-square-meter central square remains so named today.

BRAWLING LAWMAKERS

Even as I hunker down here at Isabel la Católica #63 scratching out a chapter on brawling legislators then and now, six blocks north, the small, ornamental Senate chamber on Xicoténcatl between the National Art Museum and the Fru-Fru Travestí (drag) Theater (owned by a former senator) is in an uproar.

The senators of the left FAP coalition have taken over the tribune to prevent the parties of the Right from approving a measure privatizing Mexico's petroleum industry via a *madruguete*, a sneak early-morning vote from which the opponents of the bill would be excluded. At night they sleep in little pup tents arranged around the Senate podium. During the day, they make steamy patriotic speeches invoking the fathers of the republic, many of whom once sat in this hallowed chamber, to an empty gallery. Across town, in the Chamber of Deputies, the tribune has been similarly seized by the leftists and an 18-meter-long banner draped across it announcing that the Mexican Congress has been *clausurado* (closed) until further notice.

The right-wing parties are furious. The leftists have "kidnapped" the legislative process, they seethe. "Kidnapped!" They use that word a lot. With kidnapping by criminal gangs one of the few industries to show a potential for growth, the word is freighted with ominous portent.

Juxtaposed against the historical realities of the various Mexican legislatures, the contemporary rightists' indignation reeks of hypocrisy. Mexico's senates and chambers of deputies have always been repositories of contentiousness, dominated by factions disposed as much to fisticuffs as to reasoned debate. Inhabited by an endless stream of mountebanks, bigots, thieves, embezzlers, and bribe-takers, it would be challenging to violate the dignity of Mexico's legislatures.

The Constitution of 1824 provided for a bicameral legislature. During the first years of the republic, both chambers convened on the ground level of the National Palace, one floor down from where the president ruled. He was always pacing around up there. The distance between the legislative branch and the executive upstairs didn't exactly guarantee much independence for the senators and deputies.

Within the Houses, the ambience was confrontational. Debate between those who championed a loose federation of states and those who favored a strong central authority grew so charged in the Senate, a body in which the states hypothetically had equal representation with the capital, that the solons voted to close it down in 1845—the Senate would not be convened again until 1874 when it moved into its present quarters on Xicoténcatl alley.

The Chamber of Deputies was no less obstreperous. Challenges for duels to the death were periodically issued from the podium. Brawls erupted on the chamber floor. Basically the split was between liberal and conservative concepts of governance. The Conservative Party, founded in 1835 by my former downstairs neighbor Lucas Alamán was imbued with the royalist-Gachupín mindset and heavily financed by the oligarchy and the Catholic Church. The liberal profile was encapsulated by the stone-faced, self-hating Zapotec Indian jurist Benito Juárez, who viewed the Church as the Great Satan and was committed to a ferociously liberal brand of capitalism. Juárez, who passionately despised the deposed Santa Anna (the Serene Highness had once called him "a low-class Indian" when the Zapotec was working his way through law school, waiting tables back home in Oaxaca), was selected the chief justice of the Supreme Court once the ashes of the Redeemer's ruinous years in power had been swept away.

As soon as the Americanos decamped in 1848, the hostilities between the two bands resumed and they fell upon each other with great lust and glee. The Chamber could not contain the bad blood between the two parties, and they dug trenches in the streets and battered each other with paving stones. They formed armies and perpetrated atrocities against rural villages that sided with their rivals. The Conservatives under General Miguel Miramón shot both wounded liberals and the doctors who attended to them. Liberal mobs castrated priests.

EL MONSTRUO MEETS LA REFORMA

The Monstruo was the core of the Mexican melon, and the armies rotated in and out of the capital at a dizzying pace. By 1855, the Liberals had gained the upper hand, and Juárez resumed power and pronounced for a series of "Reform" laws that sharply undercut the prosperity of the Church, among them the confiscation of all Church properties other than places of worship; the virtual defrocking of priests, who were forbidden from sporting clerical garb in public; and the legalization of what the papists still call "sects"—Protestant denominations.

In addition to these cardinal sins, the "Laws of Leyva," named for a Juarista senator who had moved them through Congress, limited the clamor of church bells, an aural plague for a century, to calls to prayer. The Reform Laws were consecrated in Juárez's Constitution of 1857.

The Reforma's impact on the capital was instantaneous and triggered the most significant architectural disruption of the city since the destruction of Tenochtitlán. Former Church property was leveled to make way for new constructions. Centuries-old monasteries and colonial-era churches like the aforementioned San Francisco convent on Plateros (now Madero), once the site of Mocuhtezuma's menagerie and the future home of the Torre Latinoamericana, were demolished under the sledgehammers of hundreds of newly released prisoners. San Agustín, the great domed convent across the street from my balcony, became the secular National Library. The glorious La Merced cloister was reduced to a chapel.

The Church buildings that survived were subdivided and rented out, offering an important increase in the downtown housing stock. The Liberals had not seized the Church's properties as an act of sectarian vengeance—their religion was money. The size of the Monstruo had doubled to 20 square kilometers since liberation, the population had grown from 150,000 to 200,000 (Tenochtitlán levels) from 1833 through 1852, and real estate speculation was rife. The wholesale sell-off of the confiscated buildings would finance Liberal fortunes.

New colonies were established by syndicates of shady land sharks. The proletarian Colonia Guerrero north and west of the Zócalo was chartered, and Tepito, the neighborhood where Cortez had captured Cuauhtémoc, became a thriving commercial zone. But the free market did not much please the Church's old tenants—the Catholics had kept a lid on rents to guarantee a modicum of shelter for the poor. Now the speculators jacked up payments, and in doing so, drove the poor into the Conservative camp.

MIRAMÓN'S MILLIONS

The conservatism of the *capitalinos* was a vestige of criollo-Gachupín reaction and the Laws of the Reform were rejected by a sizable chunk of the citizenry. Juárez and his heretics were pushed out of the capital and General Miramón took the helm of state. The treasury as usual was bare, and Miramón's agents borrowed $10,000,000 USD from European royalists who had their eyes on reestablishing a monarchist system in the Americas.

When Juárez again wrested power from the Conservatives in 1861, he found a promissory note and a thousand pesos in the national treasury.

The stern Zapotec's first order of business was to reinstate the Reform laws. The priests were once again stripped of their vestments. Half the capital's churches were shuttered and all of its 20 nunneries closed down. The incessant clanging of the church bells was silenced. But Miramón and his gang had other mischief on their minds.

The Conservatives were received in Paris like prodigal sons. So thoroughly had they been whipped by Juárez that only with the backing of European monarchists could they ever steal power again from the Indian. The royalists canvassed the backwaters of the old continent looking for a likely candidate to redeem Mexico and reinstate

God's kingdom on earth. Eugénie, bride of Louis Bonaparte, nephew of the first Napoleon, proposed Archduke Maximilian, an unemployed prince and a Hapsburg like the first king of Mexico. Maximilian had recently been betrothed to Carlota, the petite daughter of Leopold of Belgium and the granddaughter of Louis Phillipe. They would make a lovely emperor and empress, don't you think?

The new Bonaparte was fixated on imperial aggrandizement. France had recently expanded its frontiers to West Africa, Indochina, and the Lebanon. A foothold in the Americas was a vital building block of the new empire. His moment came in 1861 when the United States plunged into civil war and was in no position to uphold the pugnacious warnings implicit in the Monroe Doctrine. The pretext would be tax collection, since the Pastry War a French specialty.

METTERNICH'S BLUEPRINT

The Mexican adventure obeyed a blueprint designed by Count Metternich, the Henry Kissinger of his day, at the Council of Europe. The royalists would recoup the Americas by establishing a series of kingdoms extending from Mexico to Tierra del Fuego. Already Dom Pedro, a distant cousin of Maximilian, sat on the throne of Brazil. The Europeans dreamt of a slavocracy that would begin in Virginia and spread throughout the hemisphere, and to this end, they entered into negotiations with the Confederacy.

Napoleon III gathered allies. Britain and Spain were owed vast sums borrowed by Miramón's agents. The tripartite invasion landed in June 1861 at the usual spot. Like Mocuhtezuma begging Cortez/ Quetzalcóatl to go back where he came from, the Indian Juárez sent his emissaries to Veracruz to plead poverty. The English and the Spanish, who had less heart for the invasion, bought the sob story and returned to Europe empty-handed, but France had ulterior motives and set off posthaste for the Halls of Mocuhtezuma.

THE EMPERORS OF MEXICO

The French expedition led by General Achille Bazaine ran into gnarly resistance on Guadalupe Hill just south of the city of Puebla, where Zacapoaxtla Indians, press-ganged into battle (some still wore ropes around their necks) under the command of the Oaxacan Porfirio Díaz and General Ignacio Zaragoza (now a major Mexico City thorough-fare), bravely turned back the frogs, a victory celebrated much more intensely each year in Gringolandia than it is in Mexico, as "El Drinko de Mayo," a sort of national nachos day.

Bonaparte, seriously discombobulated at having his army whomped by savages, immediately dispatched 30,000 additional troops to America, and by the following spring, the French took Puebla without a whoop from the Zacapoaxtlas. In Mexico City, Benito Juárez cleaned out his desk at the National Palace yet again, and on May 31, 1863, having declared his republic to be an "itinerant" one, got in the wind.

When General Bazaine entered the city the next week, Conserva-tives had decked it out in French bunting. The upper classes blew kiss-es from the balconies and the church bells clanged ceaselessly. "Mexi-cans are so strange," Juárez mused on his way north. "For anyone who does not know them and is foolish, their ovations and flattery are intoxicating. First they sweep him off his feet and then they destroy him. . . . "

After being blessed by the Pope on the eve of their departure, Maximilian and Carlota set sail for Mexico, a journey Carlota would commemorate each year well into the 20th century at the loony bin to which she had been committed. The royal couple hardly slept a wink during the voyage—Maximilian worked feverishly on the code of eti-quette for his new court, Carlota futzed with her hair.

But their exhilaration was dampened by a less than enthusiastic reception in Veracruz. The *zopilotes* (turkey buzzards) circling the har-bor hunting dead meat were not a propitious sign. The coach trip up to Mexico City took nearly 30 hours over a stomach-churning road-way, and the archduke reportedly lost his cookies several times.

The Conservatives and the Church hoked up their reception in the capital much as they had for Bazaine's troops, but the masses were more suspicious than curious. When the royal carriage pulled into the Zócalo and deposited Maximilian and Carlota at the National Palace, there was no joyous, spontaneous outburst from the neighbors. What next, the denizens of the Centro Histórico wondered. The cathedral bells rang without mercy.

On the first night in the palace, the Emperors of Mexico were so badly bitten by *chinches* (bedbugs) that they packed up and took ref-uge at Chapultepec Castle, the elegant hideaway of the viceroy out in what is now the Monstruo's largest park, which had been shot up by the Americanos back in '47. The castle at the western edge of the city was far from the surly throngs in the Zócalo, and Maximilian and Carlota paused to take stock of their impossible situation.

A thin ascetic liberal sort and the second Hapsburg to rule over Tenochtitlán, Maximilian entertained a kind of "noble savage" vision of his subjects and knew absolutely zero about Mexico's delicate sociopolitical dynamic. The royals—the Archduke with his mad wife at his side—took it upon themselves to improve the quality of life of their vassals. Public hygiene was a prime concern. The dumping of chamber pots from upper story windows, customarily heralded by the cry of "¡Aguas!," was strictly forbidden.

The Emperor and Empress busied themselves restoring Chapultepec Castle and its groomed gardens to their original splendor and dedicated their efforts to the establishment of a National Art Museum. Maximilian ordered the Chapultepec road widened and paved and landscaped and renamed it the Passage of the Emperors, but he never seemed to notice on his frequent trips between the Castle and the National Palace that the people no longer removed their hats when he passed.

Up there on the lofty heights of Chapultepec, the resentment of the Mexicans below in the city never seemed to dawn on the two addle-brained Europeans. Their courtiers, however, most of whom were Austrians, were impatient at their servants' lack of punctuality, and Kandell notes that the Europeans refused to share the toilets with the "niggers."

THE ITINERANT REPUBLIC

After initial success in driving Juárez's Itinerant Republic all the way to Paso del Norte (Ciudad Juárez) on the U.S. border, the Bonapartists had bogged down. The Zapotec, borrowing a page from Morelos's manual, broke his army into guerrilla bands that bit the invaders on the ass every time they turned around. The moment the French abandoned a town, the Itinerant Republic moved in. Bazaine's army was repeatedly ambushed on the roads as the resistance flowered into a full-flavored guerrilla war.

Things were not so hot on the domestic front either. Maximilian and Carlota quarreled and moved into separate rooms and took lovers.

The Emperor was a liberal and not well disposed to rescinding the Reform Laws, and the Church became estranged and demonized him from the pulpits at Mass. Moreover, Bonaparte kept dunning Maximilian for the money Mexico allegedly owed him from Miramón's scam—but the Emperor knew full well how broke his empire really was and considered it tacky to even bring up the issue of the debt with his ministers.

Then, abruptly, the window closed on this comic operetta. The Americanos' Civil War ended in defeat for the Confederacy and Lincoln sent messages of support and promises of arms to Juárez. Bismarck's Prussia was making belligerent noises on Bonaparte's eastern front, and the Mexican adventure was not prospering. The bottom line told Napoleon III to cut his losses, withdraw the French army, and cover his exposed flank, even if he had once sworn to Maximilian that the troops would never be withdrawn until full conquest was assured.

When Carlota got wind of the double cross, she blew across the Atlantic in a rage, spat in Bonaparte's face, and denounced him to Pope Pius—whom she then accused of trying to poison her with the hot chocolate His Holiness had offered the distraught empress. Fleeing the papal palace, she collapsed on the marble steps and was carried back inside the Pope's quarters, reportedly the first woman to ever spend a night on the premises, an unlikely story.

Maximilian was just as off his rocker. He traveled to Querétaro, hallucinating that the people still loved him there, where he was immediately captured by the Juaristas and marched up Campanas Hill to face a firing squad, a stern warning to the world that Mexico would deal similarly with such foreign invaders. Fusilladed alongside the ersatz Emperor was one Miguel Miramón, the Conservative general who had instigated this mini-holocaust in which 50,000 Mexicans, mostly of color, had perished. The Ten Million Bucks were still outstanding.

EL DANDY & THE TIGER

Maximilian was embalmed, wrapped up mummy-style and shipped back to Vienna. Carlota had been committed. The whole crazy *telenovela* was over at last. But it had left its fingerprints on the city.

Perhaps the most ostentatious emblem of Maximilian's brief reign on the throne of Mocuhtezuma was the beautification of the Passage of the Emperors, immediately rebaptized by Juárez upon his triumphant return to the capital as El Paseo de La Reforma. Neat rows of trees and gardens lined the great avenue, illuminated each evening by European-style gas lamps, a favorite venue for the cutpurses and muggers who roamed the dimly lit boulevard ripping off the upper crust that dared to stroll there. Then as now, crime was an act of class war.

The U.S. State Department is forever counseling its citizens to be wary of El Monstruo. It issues travel advisories and posts warnings on its Web site: Stay away from crowds, do not carry cash, take extreme care around ATM machines, hang on to your wallet if you must travel by metro. Above all, avoid little green "ecological" cabs—the drivers may be in cahoots with gangs of *rateros* (robbers) and will drive you to the nearest bank machine to clear out your account before they kill you. Best to hire your own driver and security personnel—there are dozens listed in the yellow pages.

Mexico City's reputation as Murder City South has endured down the centuries. Between 1860 and 1875, the Mexican capital was billed as the most dangerous metropolis on the planet. With the annual murder rate peaking between 400 and 500 out of a population hovering around 200,000, the odds were 400 to one on not getting out of town alive. So many ex-soldiers of so many ex-armies were freelancing on those mean streets that travelers from the hinterlands often arrived at their hotels stripped buck naked. Upper-class victims were kidnapped in broad daylight. Serial killers stalked prostitutes in the seamy La Merced district.

The police were no help. The city's standard hiring practice for cops was to recruit from the prisons, on the fanciful theory that criminals did a better job of catching crooks. This concept became embedded in the Monstruo's various police agencies and continues to flourish in contemporary Mexico City, where it is never very clear who are the cops and who are the robbers.

Chucho El Roto (Jesús the Dandy) was the most notorious criminal of his time, plotting his sensational capers from his cave in the thieves'-den barrio of Tepito, where crime still continues to pay impressive dividends—and every item ever sold under the counter, from a kilo of cocaine to a 10-inch dildo to a case of hand grenades, is available 24/7 to the shopping public in the alleys of this Mexican Kasbah where vast warehouses of stolen and/or pirated goods are accessible only via sinuous tunnels that wind through dark *vecindades*.

In a neighborhood of world-class ne'er-do-wellers, Chucho El Roto was king. He kidnapped priests and rich matrons, collecting significant ransoms in a style reminiscent of today's *secuestros expres* ("express kidnappings"). He picked the pockets of the wealthy at Mass in the Metropolitan Cathedral, purloined their jewels, and heisted foreign-owned banks. Thrice the Dandy escaped from maximum lockups, and his popularity was such that he was proposed for the Mexican Congress, because he could steal no more than those who already sat there. He stole from the rich and sometimes gave the loot to the poor, a dandified antihero in an era when the city was torn in two by the class divide.

In the aftermath of the great 1985 earthquake, I would sometimes accompany my compa Lalo Miranda to visit *damnificados* (quake victims) whose living conditions were particularly precarious. One afternoon, we encountered an elderly resident huddled amidst the rubble of her Tepito vecinidad, the roof resting upon one wobbly floor beam. Lalo tried to convince the *doña* to temporarily move into the government camps while her hovel was repaired—the building was old enough to qualify as a "historical monument," and the law mandated that it must be restored to the condition it was in before the killer quake. The old woman would not be budged. She told us that her rooms had once been the *escondite* (hideout) of the famous Chucho El Roto and that he would protect her from harm.

Perhaps the most lionized of the gallery of rogues who stalked the Monstruo in the bad old days was another Jesús, Jesús Negrete, the "Tiger of Santa Julia." Romanticized as a Robin Hood in a well-received 2002 film of that name, Negrete was anything but. He stole from the rich and poor alike and kept it all for himself. Unlike the Dandy, "El Tigre" had a taste for blood that was never slaked, killing cops and robbers with equal readiness whenever he smelled a double cross. A highwayman who preyed upon the pilgrims on their way to La Villa to worship the Guadalupana, the Tiger took many lovers. Trapped in a boudoir in Tacubaya, Negrete fled out the back door into the fields beyond, where he was seized by a sudden urge to defecate. Seeking privacy in a nearby *nopalera* (cactus patch), he was captured with his pants down.

¡HAY QUE LLEGAR! (An interview with Don Inocencio Salazar)

Propped up at the counter of La Blanca, Don Inocencio seemed as immobile as a block of aging wood, his little eyes staring out at the busy restaurant with undisguised distrust. Born on December 28 a hundred years ago—his son Mario says 200 years ago—"Don Chencho" was named for his Saint's Day, the Day of the Innocents, Mexico's April Fools' Day. Maybe he was thinking that all this was some kind of joke.

Carlos had ordered the birthday cake, but the candles were another story. We had discussed it for days. A hundred candles (or 200 as Mario kept insisting) would have coated the cake with melting wax and ruined it, so we settled for three candles that spelled out "100." When the cake was set before him, Inocencio stared it down as if he wasn't quite sure what it was meant for. Mario and Don Raimundo encouraged Chencho to blow out the three candles and then they did it for him and everyone around the counter clapped.

Carlos brought a knife from the kitchen and tried to coax the birthday boy into cutting the first slice. Raimundo, who was sitting next to him, guided his hand and the customers began to sing. "Estas son las Mañanitas que cantaba el Rey David" *("These are the Little Mornings that King David sang"), the patrons trilled and croaked the Mexican birthday song. "Today is your Saint's Day and now we are singing them to you."*

Inocencio didn't seem to notice the singing. The truth is that the old man is stone deaf. He hasn't heard a word for 30 years, Mario says—he should know. Mario kept saying we had it wrong: His father was really 200 years old.

Don Inocencio was born on Jesús y María Street a few blocks east when cows still grazed on the Alameda and the Canal La Viga was filled with little cargo boats bringing the victuals to market. Dictators had risen and fallen in his times. The Gachupines had gone back where they came from. Juárez and Madero and Villa and Zapata had ridden through the city with their revolutions.

Carlos passed out the slices of the chocolate cake. The folks at the counter just kept singing. "Despierta mi bien, despierta, mira ya que amaneció/ Ya los pajaritos cantan y la luna se metió." *("Wake up my good man, look it's already dawn/ The birds are singing and the moon has set!") A reporter from* El Universal *approached the old man. What is your secret of long life? he wanted to know. Inocencio looked at him blankly. Mario shouted the question in his ear and Chencho suddenly seemed to get the idea.*

"As José Alfredo says, hay que llegar" ("you have to get there"), the birthday boy rumbled—his voice seemed to come from somewhere behind him, in the bathrooms maybe. "¡Hay que llegar!" José Alfredo is José Alfredo Jiménez, whose rancheros, mostly about perfidious women, make strong men weep in their cervezas. "¡Hay que llegar!"

The old man stared at the half-eaten birthday cake, politely waiting until everyone had gotten his or her piece before he attacked his. "¡Hay que llegar!" He said it again and again as if he were trying to convince himself that indeed he had gotten there. A tear leaked from his little eye and streaked his wood-colored cheek.

What was Chencho remembering? The young girls of the barrio falling into his arms? The elegant, perfidious women? The compas in the cantinas de mala muerte ("of bad death")? The dandies and the bullfighters and El Tigre of Santa Julia? Don Porfirio leaving the city, Madero arriving?

Hay que llegar.

"What does your father remember?" I asked Mario, and Mario grinned in that goofy way that is always followed by peals of unnervingly high-pitched laughter. "What does my father remember? Nada," his son confided, "absolutamente nada. He doesn't remember a thing."

V

CITY OF ORDER & PROGRESS

The golden age of lawlessness all came to a crashing finale with the election of Porfirio Díaz to the presidency in 1876—Díaz, a onetime Juárez confederate, was voted in by a crime-weary electorate on a platform of "order and progress" which he forthwith delivered—in that order.

Benito Juárez's return to power and the restoration of the republic had been a rocky road, beset with troubles not always of his making. The country, as always, was bankrupt and the Mexican psyche exhausted by 50 years of fratricidal violence and grand theft that it wasn't done with yet. When Juárez gave up the ghost in 1872, the liberals split into two camps—those who remained loyal to the Zapotec and those who had attached themselves to Díaz, an ambitious general (a Oaxacan like Juárez, but not an Indian) who made his bones commanding the Zacapoaxtlas at the Battle of Puebla.

Four more years of bloodletting followed Juárez's demise until finally, in 1876, Don Porfirio forcibly overthrew the Restored Republic and displaced Juárez's heir Sebastián Lerdo de Tejada on the throne of Mocuhtezuma, capturing the presidency in a disputed election. He would not relinquish high office for the next 34 years, save for one four-year period when he sublet the National Palace to a proxy president for cosmetic reasons (1880–1884). Don Porfirio ruled Mexico with an iron claw for the longest skein since Tlacaelel ran Tenochtitlán from one end of the 15th century to the next.

Restoring public order was instrumental to Don Porfirio's consolidation of power. Police budgets swelled from 202,000 pesos in 1876 to 919,000 by 1879. The old police force was vetted and new crooks hired on—3,000 cops, one for every 153 citizens, patrolled the streets. Actually, there were two police forces: the beat cops and their superiors, who continued to be controlled by the criminal gangs, and a state intelligence apparatus to weed out potential subversives.

Jesús El Dandy gasped his last at Mexico's Devil's Island, the fort of San Juan Ulloa, amidst the malarial miasma of tropical Veracruz, and the Tiger of Santa Julia was cut down by a firing squad in the patio of the Belén prison.

The Belén jail, once a women's madhouse near the Salto de Agua fountain, was bursting at the seams with 5,000 prisoners in a lockup designed to accommodate hundreds. Tuberculosis was epidemic and everyone had scabies, reported John Kenneth Turner, the U.S. muckraker, in his *Barbarous Mexico,* a volume that exposed the crimes of the Díaz Dictatorship.

Under Díaz's inflexible dictates, uprisings out in the countryside were endemic. Seven million disgruntled mestizos and Indians were enslaved on 834 haciendas owned by the president's cronies but their dissatisfaction was ruthlessly crushed by the brutal Rurales, the rural police, and the Federales, the federal troops. When the unconquered Yaqui nation of Sonora asserted its sovereignty, Díaz dismembered its leaders and sent the remnants of the rebel Indian army to the Yucatán in chains to die under the southern sun on the henequen plantations of his associates. John Kenneth Turner reported that 15,000 prisoners expired each year in the Valle Nacional, the Dictator's Oaxaca prison camps. The so-called Pax Porfiriana was indeed the Peace of the Graveyard.

Under Don Porfi's nephew Félix, police brutality was generalized in the capital. When a deranged citizen, Arnulfo Arroyo, punched Don Porfirio in the back while the President strolled the Alameda in 1908, his battered body, riddled with stab wounds, was found outside police headquarters. There was no human rights commission to complain to.

WHAT'S THE MESSAGE? (An interview with Samuel Soto)

Samuel Soto (not his real name) has his nose buried in a paperback book. El Mayor, or the Major, as everyone calls him around the counter at La Blanca, is a history buff. The book is the memoirs of a count. I can't see which one from where I'm sitting. "What's new, my good Ross?" Samuel asks, never taking his nose out of the book.

Samuel Soto's great-uncle was a captain in the Porfirian army, a faithful servant to the Dictator's every bloodthirsty whim. Later he would serve under Don Porfirio's nephew, Félix, the head of the secret police, when he captured the city armory during what is called the Ten Tragic Days, at the end of which Francisco Madero, the first democratically elected president of Mexico and maybe the last, was overthrown in the National Palace. Samuel is proud of his great-uncle, but he doesn't tell this story to everyone. I heard it from Carlos.

The Major is a cop, an undercover cop. He prowls the Centro pumping his stoolies for information. He has a nose for subversion. He's always asking me about López Obrador's demonstrations. Someone, not Carlos, told me that he had been one of the Halcones *(Hawks) who attacked students on Corpus Christi Day in 1971. Eleven or maybe 40 were killed. Maybe he was, maybe he wasn't. A lot of stories get started around the counter at La Blanca.*

When I've tried to approach the Major about his police work, Samuel gets defensive. "Are you trying to interview me, Ross? I'm not for interviews, least of all from you, mi buen *Ross." I've learned that the best way to interview Samuel Soto is to let him do the talking.*

The Major spots my copy of the Mexico City News. *There is a picture of a bombing in Morelia, Michoacán, on the front page. The bombing took place in the crowded central plaza on Independence Eve and eight people were killed. Chunks of flesh are everywhere in the photo. Drug gangs are suspected.*

"Who do you think did this, Ross?" Samuel asks me, not expecting an answer. "What is the message?"

They say it's the Zetas and La Familia, the two drug gangs fighting over control of Lázaro Cárdenas, Michoacán's biggest port where loads of Colombian cocaine comes through in the containers. But I don't tell this to the Major.

"What's the message, my good Ross? Who did this?" Samuel insists, his long fingers tapping on the counter. The Major knows perfectly well who did the bombing and what the message is. He repeats the question all over again. Samuel Soto is a cop. He is used to grilling suspects. You don't have a conversation with him so much as an interrogation session.

"I'll tell you who did it mi buen Ross." *Samuel points accusingly at the photograph. "It's the government. It's always the government. They want to make the people afraid so that they will think that only the government can protect them. The government. That's who it is, Ross. That's the message."*

Who am I to argue? He's the cop. I'm just a hungry reporter. Manuel comes over with two bananas, one for the Major and the other for me. Both of us take home a banana every night. Bananas have a lot of potassium. They're even good for cops.

THE BLACK PALACE

Don Porfirio enlisted the best minds of his times, the *Científicos*, to design a more "scientific" penitentiary that would "rehabilitate" and not exterminate his prisoners. The Palace of Lecumberri in the east of the city beyond San Lázaro was reconditioned along principles pioneered by the Quakers in Philadelphia. Seven wings of cellblocks spoked off from a central command post and inmates were allocated individual cells, the better to contemplate their repentance.

Lecumberri, thereafter known as the Black Palace, was inaugurated to coincide with the celebration of the centennial of independence in 1910 and soon degenerated into a cruel instrument of state repression. Prisoners were spread-eagled on the bars and tortured, their fingernails torn out by pliers. In "El Apando" (the Punishment Cell), the impertinent revolutionary writer José Revueltas records the jailers' unspeakable brutality, first observed during a stint in Lecumberri for social agitation in the 1930s when he was still a teenager. Revueltas was returned to the Black Palace during the monumental 1968 student strike at the National University.

In 1980, in a symbolic if futile gesture to bury the dead, President José López Portillo closed down the Black Palace and converted the prison into the General Archive of the Nation. When I work there at the long tables set in the aisles of the tiered cellblocks (the documents are stored in the cells), I am visited by Revueltas's insistent voice lashing out at Mexico's still-festering justice system.

THE TRAINS RUN ON TIME

Dictators, so goes the old saw, make the trains run on time. In Porfirio Díaz's case, he first had to lay the tracks—about 20,000 kilometers of them. (He had inherited some 200 kilometers from Juárez.) After 23 years, in 1878 the Veracruz line was finally up and running, cutting travel time to the capital in the rainy season from 30 hours to 12. By 1884, trains were operating between Mexico City and Paso del Norte on the U.S. border, the first economic lifeline between these two not-quite-so-distant-anymore nations and by the turn of the century, six train stations sited at strategic points in the city radiated in all directions on the map of Mexico, among them the Buenavista Station north of the Centro, around which the Colonia Guerrero was settled.

In his eagerness to modernize Mexico, Porfirio Díaz lured the British engineer Weetman Pierson to the Monstruo. Fresh from burrowing tunnels under the Hudson River to Manhattan, Pierson oversaw construction of rail lines between the capital and the Yucatán and across the Isthmus of Oaxaca, linking the Pacific to the modern Caribbean Puerto México (now Coatzalcoalcos). In addition, Pierson finally completed Enrico Martínez's nightmare. The Drenaje General (General Drain) system carried off the city's black waters on a 47-kilometer odyssey north to Hidalgo state that included a 10-kilometer covered tunnel ride through the mountains, to spill the capital's untreated sewage first into the Tula River and then into the Panuco, which carried the Monstruo's shit all the way to the Gulf of Mexico.

The railroads sucked up Mexico's raw materials—mahogany and cedar from the jungles of Chiapas, coffee from the Soconusco on the Guatemalan border, rubber and sisal and sugar from Veracruz and the Yucatán, precious metals from the north—and transported them to the ports of Mexico to ship north to the United States and the Old World an ocean away. As an added bonus, the rail lines provided rapid transit for the Federales when they were needed to quell incipient rebellion out in the countryside.

FRANCHISING MEXICO

The Monstruo grew by leaps and bounds under the Dictator. The population jumped to 400,000 by the turn of the century and 560,000—truly monster-size—on the eve of the revolution 10 years later. Land size sprawled to 33 square kilometers as Mexico City absorbed surrounding villages and haciendas. But what the capital gained in heft, it lost in its independence to govern its own affairs, as Don Porfirio assumed the administration of the federal district.

As the city spread, a public transportation system extended its tentacles in every direction. At first, mule-drawn trams moved the populace to and from outlying districts from terminals located in the Zócalo, but by 1889, steam-driven trains plied 19 routes. Most were conceived to ferry the upper and middle classes in the west of the city to the commercial zones—only two lines extended into the working-class districts on the east of town, and at any rate, fares were so steep workers rarely got to ride. One inventory of the privately owned system lists 19 locomotives, 600 passenger coaches, 3,000 mules, 7,000 workers, and one mule doctor. By 1900, the German Siemans & Company was hanging electric cables and the Anglo-Canadian trolley company phased out the mules.

Díaz had in effect franchised out the country. Trade was brokered by foreign bankers and Pierson, now knighted as Lord Cowdray, was honored by the Porfiriato and granted the Águila Oil Company, later to be incorporated as Royal Dutch Shell. El Águila occupied a private reserve on the Caribbean coast, as did John D. Rockefeller's Standard Oil, operated by James Dougherty. Under Díaz, public services—everything from electricity generation to insane asylums—were auctioned off to the highest bidder.

Although Don Porfirio was wary of the American Gorilla with which he shared a 3,000-kilometer border ("poor Mexico—so far from God and so close to the United States" was his motto), Mexico's ambassador to Washington, Matías Romero, kept a "blue book" of available properties on his desk for potential investors to peruse. The Rockefellers and the Morgans and the Hearsts bought up vast tracts in the north of the country for a song.

UPSTAIRS AT THE JOCKEY CLUB

The House of Blue Tiles, now the flagship of the Sanborn's retail goods and restaurant chain, is the belle dame of commerce in the contemporary center of the city, a handsome colonial *casona* whose most glorious avatar was as the Jockey Club, owned by Don Porfirio's father-in-law, the millionaire Manuel Romero Rubio, where the wheelers and dealers of the epoch carved up the country—a glimpse of the grandeur can still be eyed in the upstairs bar with its glittering chandeliers and ceiling-to-floor mirrors.

Sanborn's, once a big player in the foreign commercial class that included the Palacio de Hierro (French) and the Port of Liverpool (British) department store franchises, was sold in 1985 to corporate cannibal Carlos Slim, son of a Lebanese pushcart vendor, whom *Forbes* magazine ranks as one of the richest pashas on the planet. Although it is dubious that even at the current exchange rate Don Porfirio's fortune could match Slim's, the rich grew immeasurably richer under the Dictator's stewardship. The GNP rose by 350 percent and the price of land boomed. Natural resources appeared to be boundless. Mining concessions tore into the mountains and contaminated the rivers, and primeval forests were decapitated with no rules or regulations whatsoever. Those who profited from this carnage drank every night under the glittering chandeliers upstairs at the Jockey Club.

LIFESTYLES OF THE PORFIRIAN RICH AND POOR

Speculation drove up real estate prices to astronomical levels in the capital. The expansion of the Paseo de La Reforma into a kind of American Champs Élysées with its eclectic array of monumental statues to the Emperor Cuauhtémoc and Christopher Columbus (the only one in Mexico) fueled the growth of adjacent developments on both sides of the boulevard. West and north of Reforma, the Colonias Juárez and Roma, Condesa and Cuauhtémoc were chartered, as were the San Rafael and the Peralvillo (originally a hippodrome or rácetrack operated by the Jockey Club which was eventually moved to the Condesa). Farther to the southwest, Tacuba and Tacubaya were established to accommodate the rich.

Dictatorships are defined by their architects. Don Porfirio's master builders created the ornate gilded Postal Palace and converted the convent of Santa Isabella into the domed, rococo Palace of Bellas Artes, both of which remain emblematic of fin de siècle Porfiriana.

The lifestyles of the Porfirian rich in the new neighborhoods borrowed much from the Old World—men wore bowler hats and women carried parasols. The lady of the house was accommodated by brigades of servants when she pushed her pram up Reforma. English butlers and French valets were de rigueur. Don Porfirio himself imported a master German chef named Bellinghausen, the grandfather of my compadre, the *cronista* Hermann Bellinghausen. Some wealthy families kept riding horses and hired stable masters like a young Indian horseman from neighboring Morelos state named Emiliano Zapata, who got his first taste of the arrogance and racism of Mexico's ruling class and quit to start a revolution.

As the upper crust settled into comfortable new neighborhoods, the center of the city grew dingier. The housing stock deteriorated, with whole families crammed into a single room. Services broke down. Water pipes collapsed and the neighbors had nowhere to bathe except the public baths—the Senorial Baths just down the block from my rooms became a popular gathering place. In his impeccably researched volume *Workers, Neighbors & Citizens*, John Lear asserts that housing segregation by class in Mexico City generated proletarian class cohesiveness that would soon be reflected in the popular movement that overthrew the Dictator.

While the rich seemed always to be on public view, the poor were often hidden away in the rat holes of the city. By 1895, a third of the population was living in vermin-infested *vecindades*. "Five hundred meters from the Paseo de La Reforma, this investigator found conditions that in no city would merit the description of civilization," John Kenneth Turner noted in 1910. In a startling vindication of what Baron Von Humboldt saw fully a century earlier, the American observed: "Two hundred thousand people in this city sleep on the stones each night." (In Von Humboldt's day it had been 30,000.) "People walk the streets all night with all their possessions gathered up in a sack . . . sometimes they walk to the edge of the city and gather in camps around the haciendas . . . in the morning, they walk back into the city looking for work and a scrap of food."

Europeans who visited the city were appalled by the poverty. One writer counted 10,000 prostitutes in the center of the city in 1906, five times the number who plied the streets of Paris. Few cities in the world were "so infested with street vendors," a French traveler noted.

A peso-a-day job could bring 50,000 applicants in from the countryside where the going wage was 35 centavos. The working poor toiled 16 hours a day in the textile mills (Don Porfirio's Dickensian version of the colonial *obrajes*). Other industries that exploited the workforce were the *tabacaleras* and the paper mills on San Felipe Neri, and the *aguardiente* distilleries. The city was awash in alcohol—factory workers were given pulque breaks to temper their dissatisfaction with ill-paid menial labor, and public drunkenness was unmatched in the

Americas. The distribution of pulque and control of central city *pul-querías* was monopolized by the Científicos, a tightly knit elite and Don Porfirio's brain trust. One still gets a whiff of the Porfirian past off the puke-stained *teporochos* (drunks) sleeping it off outside the Pulquería La Risa (The Laugh) around the corner on Mesones Street.

Mesones Street draws its name from the flophouses or *mesones* that were the only alternative of the *pelados* (peeled ones) after Porfirian governor Guillermo Landa y Escandón banned sleeping in the parks. Turner asserts that 25,000 *pelados* slept in the flophouses in the center of the city, which charged three centavos a night to sleep on filthy straw mats, a hundred to a gallery. The *mesones* were unsafe for women, who were often raped in the darkness. Men could have their throats slit over a coin.

Some folks ate well during Don Porfirio's heyday—one Colonia Guerrero slaughterhouse sacrificed 5,000 cows and 8,000 sheep each month, but the poor ate skins and hooves. Dogs and cats and, rumor had it, dead babies from the Children's Hospital were sold as meat. By 1910, the mortality rate in downtown Mexico City was 334 per 10,000, worse than Cairo or Istanbul. The median life span was 31—half of all the babies born each year died. In fact, a third of the city's population passed on to Mictlán annually.

Those who protested these indignities were disappeared in the Dictator's fetid prisons or simply dispatched in accordance with La Ley de Fuga, which gave the cops a license to kill if the suspect was considered a flight risk.

By 1910, Don Porfirio's penchant for "order" had driven class and race disparities to the breaking point.

THE BUBBLE BURSTS

The bubble burst in the Great Depression of 1907, when the bottom fell out of commodity prices. Massive unemployment and labor discontent soared. A score of miners were gunned down by the Arizona Rangers during a strike in the Cananea copper pit owned by Colonel William Green, a predecessor to the Anaconda Copper Company, exciting nationalist fury. When textile workers in the foreign-owned textile mills in Río Blanco, Veracruz, went out on strike, they were mowed down by Don Porfirio's Federales, their bodies laid out on flatcars and fed to the sharks in Veracruz port, reported Turner.

As bloated and senile as the Dictator with his classic walrus mustache and splash of medals splattered across his chest, members of both houses of Congress snoozed in their *curules* (dignitaries' seats), and the bureaucracy, encrusted for four decades in the ministries of government, was immovable. A middle class that Díaz had nurtured suddenly found itself unable to realize its ambitions in a sea of old-boy cronyism.

In Anenecuilco, Morelos, just south of the city, young Emiliano Zapata was elected the guardian of his village lands.

¡NO REELECCIÓN! ¡SUFRAGIO EFECTIVO!

In 1908, nearing 80, the Dictator gave U.S. correspondent James Creelman an ill-advised interview in which he promised he would not stand for another term in 1910. The festivities that erupted after the interview was made public startled the old man and he rescinded his invitation to other candidates to enter the field. But it was too late—Francisco Madero, the strange little scion of a Coahuila mining fortune, a vegetarian who had studied at UC Berkeley and regularly consulted a Ouija board, had announced his candidacy on the No Reelection Ticket. A century later, those who honor the revolution that Madero would usher in still sign their correspondence with the epithet "*¡Sufragio Efectivo! ¡No Reelección!*"

Among Francisco Madero's early supporters were the Flores Magón brothers, Ricardo, Enrique, and Jesús, Oaxaca-born anarchists and agitators. After moving to Mexico City as teenagers, the three immersed themselves in the anti-Porfirista movement. From 1900 to 1902, the brothers published two radical newspapers—*Regeneración* and *El Hijo de Ahuizote*—that were suppressed by the dictatorship, and the Flores Magones fled to Texas where they founded the Mexican Liberal Party in exile and fomented rebellion in northern Mexico, at one point invading Baja California in the company of the legendary Wobbly organizer Joe Hill. Ricardo narrowly escaped assassination by the Dictator's agents on many occasions as he moved from city to city in the North American west. Imprisoned repeatedly by the gringo authorities, Flores Magón was sent to Leavenworth at the height of the 1917 red scare, charged with violating the neutrality act, and seven years later was strangled in that federal prison by guards who are thought to have objected to a Mexican flag he had hung in his cell.

Spurred on from the U.S. by the widely circulated *Regeneración*, Francisco Madero's presidential campaign had surprising support as he barnstormed Mexico. Although his patrician background was not particularly attractive to the laboring classes, dissatisfaction with the Dictator's heavy hand drove workers into Madero's camp. This seemed particularly conspicuous in Mexico City's industrial heart.

On May 1, 1910, just 10 weeks before the election, workers organized the first Mexican commemoration of International Labor Day, to mark the martyrdom of the four Chicago anarchists hanged for the police riot at Haymarket Square in 1886 during the struggle for the eight-hour day. Thousands marched to the National Palace to show Don Porfirio their colors and then turned tail and paraded to the upscale Colonia Roma, where Francisco Madero was staying at his father's mansion, to demonstrate their support. Many workers dressed in frock coats and top hats to mock the Porfirian aristocracy.

Furious at the growing opposition to his rule, Porfirio Díaz rounded up the opposition. Death squads—"La Acordada"—gunned down Madero's supporters. Liberals were hanged from public gibbets, their eyeballs gouged out. Three weeks before the election, Madero himself was locked up in San Luis Potosí, but his keepers were sympathetic and he was allowed to flee to San Antonio, Tejas, from which he issued a call to his compatriots to march on the plazas of their towns and cities on November 20, 1910, and rise up in revolution to overthrow the Dictator.

THE CURSE OF THE CENTENNIAL

That September, Porfirio Díaz invested the government's entire education budget to mark the first hundred years of Mexican independence and celebrate his bogus reelection. A golden angel was mounted atop the towering column of Independence on Reforma. The Lecumberri Black Palace opened for business. Ground was broken for a modern Legislative Palace. Military parades and luminous bouquets of fireworks diverted the masses nightly. Governor Landa y Escandón issued new pants to the poor and advised them to bathe if they intended to attend the festivities. Jonathan Kandell compares the party to the one Ahuitzotl threw for the reconstruction of Huitzilopochtli's temple in 1485 during which 20,000 warriors were sacrificed. But the general jubilation only hastened the Dictator's departure as public anger spread at the profligate dispersal of public moneys.

On September 15, the eve of the Centennial and the crowning glory of the patriotic extravaganza, when Don Porfirio appeared on the Presidential balcony of the National Palace to deliver Hidalgo's traditional Grito of "¡Viva México!" he was answered with cries of "¡Viva Madero!" and the police opened fire on the blasphemers.

The 1910 Centennial has become a touchstone in history here. The Mexican metabolism seems to schedule massive social upheaval on the tenth year of each new century—Hidalgo in 1810, Díaz's fall in 1910. As I write this, a few hundred days away from the bicentennial of independence and the 100th anniversary of the beginning of the Mexican Revolution, Mexicans are peering into the future and wondering what the stars might have in store.

VI

CITY OF THE CANNIBAL REVOLUTION

S himmering like the Blue Mosque of Baghdad in the noontime scuzz, the high-domed Monument of the Revolution dominates the skyline from the foot of Juárez Avenue. The architectural metaphor is congruent with the Mexican view of history as a religion, a source of spiritual enlightenment that is a part of their daily lives. Mexicans are connected to their past, embedded in it. Sometimes I am not even quite sure what tense they are talking to me in, the past one or the present, now or then.

My pilgrimage to the Monument of the Revolution begins at the base of the Torre Latinoamericana on the corner of Madero and the Eje Central Lázaro Cárdenas. The Mexico City street map is dominated by names that salute the heroes of the Patria. There are 787 Juárez streets or avenues listed in the Roji Guide.

It is a Sunday in June and the streets around us are miraculously emptied of automobiles—the leftish mayor, the sainted Marcelo Ebrard, has decreed Sundays to be Bicycle Days, and whole families whiz along Juárez Avenue together. The Monument of the Revolution is dead ahead on the eyeline.

The multitudes move along the crowded Alameda where aproned women are hawking shelled corn, and "living statues"—lithe kids from the misery belt—coat themselves solid with silver body paint to cadge coins from the Sunday strollers. Pamphleteers pass out their screeds in the shell of the alabaster Hemiciclo (semicircle) of Benito Juárez, a traditional platform for political gatherings. The Hemiciclo was emplaced here by Don Porfirio in 1910 to spruce up the Monstruo for the Centennial.

At the end of the Alameda, in Solidarity Plaza where the Regis Hotel crumbled into dust in the Great 1985 earthquake crushing a few hundred guests, the senior citizenry ("La Tercera Edad") dance elegantly synchronized *danzones* delivered up by a well-oiled combo tootling in the bandshell.

Most of those headed toward the Monument have just come from a political rally in the Zócalo and they wear little oil-well hats on their head—the *mitín* was to protest the possible privatization of Mexico's oil industry, expropriated from the Seven Sisters in 1938 by President Lázaro Cárdenas, whose tomb sits just up ahead.

The crowd pauses to cross the river of the Paseo de La Reforma, where Marcelo has closed down some lanes to the displeasure of the motoring class, but the traffic stream is still thick and smelly. The avenue, Don Porfirio's glory, is just as shiny as it must have been back in 1910 when he had it spiffed up for the Centennial, but it is taller, lined by corporate skyscrapers and luxury hotels, another world, the first one.

Having safely forded the boulevard to the western shore, the crowd makes a beeline for the buses parked on the streets around the Monument to the Revolution that will carry them home to the provinces until they are summoned for the next *mitín*. A little girl in a blue ball gown and a tiara with an oil well sprouting out of it stares at the old bearded man in a beret. She will tell the kids in school tomorrow about the strange people she saw in the city. "Come, *mi reina!*" her mother orders and pulls her off to the bus.

I stop to chat with Alejandro outside his hovel in the tent city thrown up by militant teachers on the approach to the Monument to protest the privatization of the nation's pension system—everything is being privatized in 2008. The maestros have been here 11 months now and the encampment seems grubbier every day. How long will the teachers stay? "*¡Hasta la Victoria!*" Alejandro, a revolutionary down to his toes, answers: "Until the Victory!

MONUMENTALIZING THE REVOLUTION

The Monument of the Revolution grows more muscular as one closes in on it. Military figures adorn the four corners of the pillars upon which the cavernous dome rests.

But the monument has not always been reserved for the Revolution. It was begun in 1910, another of Don Porfi's Centennial projects, as the new home of the Chamber of Deputies, whose moth-eaten edifice on Donceles in the old quarter had grown cramped. The Dictator laid the first stone September 23, 1910, less than two months from the date on which Francisco Madero would call upon his compatriots to rise up in revolution and overthrow the Dictator. The scaffolding was thrown up and a spider web of steel beams that would become the dome were in place when all hell broke loose and Don Porfirio had to bid adios.

During nine years of the three or four Mexican revolutions that followed, the Monument was shelled and strafed and sacked but by 1933 it was still standing, and Plutarco Elías Calles, the Jefe Máximo rather than El Presidente, declared that this Porfirian ruin would be excellent real estate upon which to monumentalize the Mexican Revolution. The project was completed by President Lázaro Cárdenas, also a revolutionary general, in 1938, just weeks after he had nationalized Mexico's oil fields. It is hardly surprising that both Cárdenas and Calles are tenants of the Monument, their tombs occupying the two southern pillars.

Venustiano Carranza, the First Chief of the Revolution, with his flowing Boulanger whiskers and creepy little blue-tinted glasses, occupies one of the two northern pillars. Directly across the patio, Don Francisco Madero sleeps the sleep of the just, and around the corner at a side door the remains of the irrepressible Francisco "Pancho" Villa, the Centaur of the North, are said to lurk—although some historians like Paco Taibo II question the authenticity of the DNA of whoever is urned up within. Villa was gunned down by Obregón's agents while out on a Sunday drive in 1923 in Parral de Hidalgo, Chihuahua, to which he had been forcibly retired. His grave was vandalized in 1926 by Texas college kids and the head carried off to Gringolandia. The rest of his body parts were reburied in several places.

There are notable absences in this pantheon of all-stars. Álvaro Obregón, the revolutionary general and ultimately Carranza's successor as president of the republic, for one, but he was Calles's most visceral rival, whom the Jefe Máximo probably had assassinated in San Ángel in 1928, so his noninclusion is comprehensible. But the most glaring omission is the Liberator of the South, Emiliano Zapata, the *caudillo* whose legend outshines all of the luminaries of the Mexican Revolutions put together.

"DO NOT GO DOWN TO THE CITY, MI GENERAL"

In 1979, flush with oil money, President José López Portillo became obsessed with concentrating all of the missing revolutionary leaders under the dome of the Monument. To this end, he ordered the transfer of Zapata's bones from the provincial Plaza of the Southern Revolution at the western edge of Cuautla, Morelos, where the Caudillo was boxed up under a gilded equestrian statue of himself in action. The little plaza is two kilometers up a country road from Anenecuilco, the land for which Zapata fought and died. When word of López Portillo's plans got out, the surviving veterans of the Liberating Army of the South surrounded the plaza to keep the President's agents from removing their general's remains to the capital.

Soon they were joined by farmers' organizations from all over the country. The campesinos were determined to keep Zapata from being carried off to Mexico City where he had always been reviled and betrayed. "No, *mi General*, do not go down to the city! We will protect you here! We won't let them mix your bones with those of your assassin, the vile Carranza!" The *plantón* (sit-in) continued for months.

In the end, López Portillo, who tilted toward the messianic, abandoned his quest; the last time I checked in, the General was still resting in the Plaza of the Southern Revolution and the gilded statue atop his tomb had grown by at least two stories. Those who live around the little plaza swear they can hear the old guerrillero's teeth gnashing at night when he mulls the misery of campesinos in Mexico today.

ZAPATA IN THE CITY

Emiliano Zapata truly despised and distrusted Mexico City. This was not unusual. Like most revolutions, the Mexican Revolution was indeed a war against the capital of the country and the power and wealth concentrated there. The scenario was written long ago in other uprisings. With the countryside in perpetual ruin and their lands stolen by the oligarchs, an enraged peasantry seeks redress and revenge, laying siege to the cities where the rulers live in luxury. The metropolis is reviled as the incubus of corruption, vice, degradation, and greed. Such revolutions are equally an affirmation of the traditional country ways by which the people the color of the earth live their lives.

"Much of the Mexican Revolution was a fight to get out from under the Monstruo," Jack Womack, author of the magnum opus *Zapata and the Mexican Revolution*, wrote in a recent email. "The Mexican Revolution was many things and never added up to just one thing because so much of it was fought to get clear of El Monstruo.

"Zapata's fight was for the local life, to be able to do your own business, to work your own land on your own terms without some asshole lawyer from the capital telling you what you can or can't do with it."

The year 1910 was a high-water mark for the provincials' grievances against the capital. The Centennial hoopla had cost the states their social budgets and they hadn't even been invited to the party. The vast north of the nation was particularly incensed at the center's celebration of its own self-importance and deeply resented the southern-born Díaz, a Oaxacan with acquired big city ways. Like-minded dissent continues to thrive in northern Mexico, where the slogan ¡HAZ PATRIA! ¡MATA UN CHILANGO! ("MAKE THE FATHERLAND! KILL A MEXICO CITY–ITE!") is spray-painted on urban walls. Zapata's revolution was steeped in this sentiment.

Although Morelos, the Liberator's home turf, is just to the south and virtually contiguous with Mexico City, Zapata was the most remote of revolutionary leaders. He kept his distance purposefully and only went down to the Monstruo to do his business, and he left as soon as it was done.

He had tasted Mexico City's class hatred and racism when he was chief groom for Ignacio de la Torre y Mier, Don Porfirio's son-in-law and a Morelos sugar planter, who managed to lure young Emiliano to the Monstruo to toil in his stables, where the stalls of the fine horses were sturdier than the hovels of the campesinos of Anenecuilco. He quit in disgust and came back only when he had an army behind him.

WHAT THE LAND WAS LIKE

Back home in Morelos, Emiliano Zapata was elected village leader, entrusted to recover Anenecuilco's lost lands, granted to the Indians by the Crown in the 17th century. The sugar planters, many of whom were foreigners, had gobbled up the Nahuas' land and water without remorse.

"Land and Water" was in fact the slogan of Madero ally Vicente Leyva's campaign for governor of Morelos in 1909 against Díaz's *gallo* (rooster), Pablo Escandón, the scion of an immensely wealthy criollo family that had first struck it rich in real estate during Juárez's Reform, and also a sugar planter who rarely bothered to visit the tiny state. Zapata aligned Anenecuilco's fortunes with Leyva and Madero. Escandón won by a landslide of course, without ever having to leave El Monstruo. To Zapata, Escandón WAS El Monstruo.

By 1910, 2 percent of all Mexicans owned all the land—save for 70 million hectares held by foreigners with family names like Rockefeller and Hearst and Morgan. One hundred percent of the good farming land in Morelos was occupied by 17 haciendas operated by absentee *patrones* (bosses). The haciendas sucked up all the groundwater, leaving villages like Anenecuilco dry as a bone. The unequal distribution of water continues a century hence. Wealthy Chilangos have overrun Morelos with their golf courses and palatial second homes, leaving the villages just as thirsty as they were in 1910.

Years ago, I rented a large house in Olintepec, a *colonia* that shares ejido land (communal farmland) with Anenecuilco, and was able to see how the land must have looked to Zapata when he rode through these fields. I walked out through the tall sugar cane along the irrigation canals to the Caudillo's humble adobe home, now a museum, on a back street in Anenecuilco, and each young horseman barreling down the country lanes could have been the Caudillo all over again.

But an hour and fifty-five minutes later, when I stepped down off a bus in the belly of the Monstruo, the urban hurly-burly swirling all around me, I always got a whiff of the profound culture shock Emiliano Zapata must have suffered when he was forced to visit this city he so detested.

MADERO'S REVOLUTION

Francisco Madero's call for the revolution to commence November 20, 1910, stirred sparse response. Up in Puebla, Díaz's agents murdered Madero's lieutenant, the revolutionary shoemaker Aquiles Serdán, and his family, two nights before the festivities were slated to kick in. In Morelos, Zapata and the peasant army he had assembled bided their time, waiting to see who would make the first move first.

Mexicans are never on time. Finally, in January, Doroteo Arango AKA Francisco "Pancho" Villa, a popular Chihuahua desperado of Hobsbawmian proportions, and his ruthless cohort Pascual Orozco, declared themselves in revolt and were immediately joined by the Maderista governor of Coahuila, Venustiano Carranza and his "Constitutionalist" Army. Díaz's Federales were beaten back at Ciudad Guerrero, Mal Paso, and Casas Grandes. Villa laid siege to Ciudad Juárez on the border, the vital railhead that linked Mexico City to the United States and was the lifeblood of the country's commercial transactions.

By February 1911, with the synchronicity that sometimes made the Mexican Revolution work, the Zapatistas had advanced to Xochimilco. Workers in the heart of the city suffering from what the Porfirian rag *El Imparcial* tagged *"huelga-manía"* or strike fever, declared seven major strikes that paralyzed the Monstruo in 1910–1911. Demonstrators were emboldened enough to assemble in the Zócalo and shout "Death to the Dictator!" beneath Don Porfirio's balcony by spring. Others menaced his mansion on Cadena Street in the Centro Histórico and were repelled by the gendarmes.

Pablo Escandón fled Mexico for Europe, kvetching to the press that Mexico had fallen into "niggerdom." Don Porfirio's class of people was stunned by this threat to their carefree lives and comforts. Indeed, the leisure class had not changed all that much from when the criollos and Gachupines cowered inside the city as Hidalgo's Indiada advanced on El Monstruo.

After three and a half decades in power, the Dictator remained a figure of adoration in the mansions of La Condesa. For the university students, largely the sons of the ruling class, Don Porfi was the epitome of modernity. To them, Villa and Orozco and Carranza were the Barbarians of the North, Zapata the Attila of the South, and they cast the Dictator as the savior of civilization as they knew it.

But the old man was 81, and it hurt just to keep a stiff upper lip. The medals weighed heavily on his chest. He knew in his heart of hearts what his adorers could not admit—the jig was really up. Ciudad Juárez was days away, even via the modern rail system he had built, and the army's mobility to supply his troops was restricted. Don Porfiriopochtli, as political cartoonists were drawing him now, had, like the Aztecs, expanded his empire to a point where he could no longer defend it.

In May, the Dictator sent his vice president, Francisco León de la Barra, to the north to negotiate an easy exit to his 34 years on the throne of Mocuhtezuma, and on May 24, 1911, having brokered an agreement with Madero that León de la Barra would remain as provisional president for the next six months, the old man set sail from Puerto, México, for Paris, France, aboard the German steamer *Ypringa* with this famous caution: "The wild beasts have been loosed. Let us see who will cage them now."

Wild celebrations broke out in Mexico City as if to underscore the old man's dictum—15,000 workers invaded the Chamber of Deputies and marched on the National Palace, where the Dictator's police opened fire, wounding scores. The offices of the Porfirian mouthpiece *El Imparcial* were set afire. By July, the Monstruo was shut down by a general strike. The wrath of the Mexicans had indeed been loosed, and Madero's intentions to cage it up again would dictate the next phase of Mexico's cannibal revolution.

THE GODS ARE SKEPTICAL

After a discreet pause to make sure the old man was really gone, Francisco Madero started off on the long train ride from Ciudad Juárez to Mexico City in early June. There were many treacheries up ahead and he had plenty of time to consider his options as the train lurched from state to state. As he passed through Zacatecas and Aguascalientes, jubilant mobs overran the train depots waving Mexican flags and shouting "¡Vivas!" until they were hoarse and Madero's train long out of sight.

The presumptive president of Mexico arrived in the capital at Buenavista terminal, the great northern station, on the morning of June 9, and the tumult was overwhelming. Kandell compares it to Juárez's return to rekindle the republic. I stare at the news photographs. People are excited, even exhilarated. They push and jostle for a view of the little Lenin look-alike. But some are more reserved. They stand back from the jubilant throng. They have come more out of curiosity than conviction. Their faces seem to ask, what next?

From Buenavista, Madero rode through the city in a Dupont motorcar, the sidewalks bursting with well-wishers and flag wavers. Many residents of the metropolis were relieved not so much because of the hope the little man brought with him as for the fact that this change of power had taken place with a minimum of damage to themselves and their city.

When Madero entered the old city for the final jog to the National Palace, he mounted a white horse. In the Palacio, he met with León de la Barra and they reaffirmed their bargain—Porfirio's stooge would govern for the next six months while Madero campaigned for presidential elections set for November 2. The two emerged on the president's balcony and "¡Vivas!" erupted from the joyous mob that filled the Zócalo below.

But the old Gods of Tenochtitlán were skeptical about Francisco Madero's grasp on the presidency. At 6:00 that afternoon they rendered their verdict, upstaging his triumphal arrival in the capital with a deadly earthquake that surged out of the Pacific Ocean along the Jalisco coast and wrought havoc throughout that western state, killing 400 in Zapopan and setting off the Volcano of Colima before smashing into the north of Mexico City and leveling Santa María de la Ribera and San Cosme. There were no Richter scales in those days to measure the quake, but an uncounted number of lives were lost in the capital— perhaps hundreds, reported El Imparcial, which published three extras that day but paid scant attention to Madero's arrival, burying the story beneath the fold.

"LIKE EARRINGS FROM THE TREES"

Emiliano Zapata had been in the mob that met Madero's train at Buenavista station. In spite of his disdain for this decadent den of thieves, the Caudillo had ventured down from Morelos to present his case for the lost lands of Anenecuilco. Madero was impressed by Zapata's presence and invited him to dinner at his father's mansion on Berlin Street in the Colonia Roma. The wiry, serious Indian with deep-set eyes that burnt as incandescent as coals offered to demobilize his army if Madero would guarantee the return of the village lands. Francisco Madero was magnanimous and listened politely to the campesino leader and Zapata went home to await his decision. Not a week later, he was summoned back to the city he detested to scotch rumors that his army had risen against the government.

As the weeks dragged by, the outlook for a favorable response grew bleak. Madero was a landowner and an apostle of private property and the propertied class. There had been no communication between Zapata and the man who would be president of Mexico since the June meeting.

On November 2, Francisco Madero was elected in a landslide over 11 unknown rivals, and on the 20th, a full year after he had declared the Mexico Revolution, he was sworn in at the National Palace.

At the same hour, south of the capital, Zapata summoned his campesino army to Ciudad Ayala on the hospital hacienda where he enunciated his agrarian program, the Plan of Ayala. The document made it abundantly clear to the new president that the farmers of Anenecuilco and indeed all of the farmers of Mexico would fight on until they got their land back. "Recognition is withdrawn from Francisco Madero as chief of the Revolution and President of the Republic because he has betrayed the principles and tricked the will of the people, and from now on, the pueblos and citizens who have titles corresponding to the hacienda properties will immediately possess them."

Ten days later, Zapata dug up his guns and went back to fighting his war against the city. "Madero is a liar," he told a reporter. "We will hang him from the highest tree in Chapultepec Park."

As the gods had presaged, President Madero's tenure *en palacio* was an uncertain one. In fact, it was not always clear whether he was the president or merely a prisoner in the palace. Surrounded by political crocodiles who all wanted a piece of him, Madero did not know whose treachery to trust least. He was ostensibly protected by a Porfirian army that he had not dismantled and whose loyalty remained undefined. The President was shielded from these sentinels of the ancien régime by his brother Gustavo, the new secretary of the interior and thought to be the brains behind the throne, not a stout line of defense.

But Madero did see eye to eye with the military on one score—the upstart Indian Zapata must be crushed. To head up this mission, he fingered Victoriano Huerta, a general celebrated for his cruelty during the now-deposed Dictator's Yaqui campaigns. Himself a Nahua Indian from Jalisco, Huerta had risen in the ranks in accordance with his talent for suppressing Indian revolt—putting "savages" on "savages" was a Porfirian ethic. General Huerta warmed quickly to the task and hung the Zapatistas from the trees "like earrings." Village after village was burnt to the ground and the campesinos crammed into cattle cars and shipped north as if Auschwitz were the next stop.

Outside of the Estado Mayor—the Presidential Guard under the command of General Lauro Villar—and the Rurales, the rural police with their quaint charro couture, Madero had few friends in the military, and he was eager for Huerta's attention. But Victoriano Huerta, always drunk and duplicitous, his emotions frozen behind thickly smoked glasses, was not to be trusted. Even his confederates with whom he drank himself into a stupor every night at the Jockey Club were careful not to incur his wrath.

THE PLOT CONGEALS

The Jockey Club was not the only venue where conspirators canoodled. Plots against Madero were hatched at the Café Berger and the Colón on Reforma, the Hotel Imperial, and La Opera, a seedy, expensive restaurant two blocks from the National Palace on Cinco de Mayo Street, still a watering hole for political fixers. The plotters drank at the Bar Ángel across Balderas from the Ciudadela (armory) and ate at the Gambrinus restaurant in the Centro.

At the center of the conspiracy was General Bernardo Reyes, a rakish sort with upturned, heavily waxed mustachios that must have been a burden in battle—Reyes had been Díaz's governor of Nuevo León and was often mentioned as his vice presidential candidate in the flawed 1910 election, but his widespread support amongst the popular classes made him suspect in the eyes of the Científicos, who controlled the doddering Díaz in his dotage, and the General was dispatched to Europe, where he sat out the overthrow of the Dictator. His partner in crime, Félix Díaz, Porfirio's nephew, had directed the secret police. General Manuel Mondragón was another likely suspect.

But the most pertinent plotter operated out of an assassin's nest on the corner of Hidalgo Avenue and Rosales Street, just north of the Alameda and opposite the San Fernando graveyard—the embassy of the United States of North America, where Henry Lane Wilson called the shots for Washington.

A native of Columbus, New Mexico, on the border and as blunt-talking and blustery as the first Yanqui ambassador, the rascally Joel Poinsett, Wilson had previously been President William Howard Taft's envoy to Belgium during the troubles in the so-called "Congo Free State," a wholly owned corporation of King Leopold II, the mad Carlota's brother, who measured his control of the territory in baskets of severed heads. Joseph Conrad wrote a book about it.

In Wilson's skewed vision, Francisco Madero was bad for business. Although Don Porfi had often rued the propinquity of the United States and Mexico's distance from God, Yanqui investors had been unconstrained during his reign and Wilson's job was to make sure that those privileges were extended to his clients by the Dictator's successor.

But not all of the moguls were of one mind. Edward Doheny and his Standard Oil actually bankrolled Madero's campaign, hoping for a better deal than he was getting from Díaz, who had grown chintzy in his old age. Madero managed to piss off both Doheny and his arch-rival Lord Cowdray by slapping a 20 percent export tax on every barrel shipped from Mexican ports.

Cowdray (Weetman Pierson) and his Águila Oil Company had just brought in a gigantic well at Cerro Azul in Tampico, and Doheny had struck a humongous gusher, Potrero I, in the Huasteca. Between 1910 and 1912, Madero's years of influence, the nation's petroleum output increased from 3.5 million barrels to 16 million and Mexico, along with Russia, emerged as the world's number one oil exporter. Then as now, oil was at the heart of this darkness.

General Reyes returned from Europe in late 1911 and just days after Madero's inauguration declared himself in rebellion. The general's defiance proved to be aimed more at the press than the battlefield, and he was quickly captured by loyalist troops in Chihuahua and transferred to the military prison at Santiago Tlatelolco in the capital, scant blocks from the National Palace, whence he would plot for the next 13 months from his cell. Félix Díaz had declared himself in rebellion months before in Veracruz after returning from Cuba, where he had accompanied his uncle into exile, and was not captured until December 1912, when he was locked up in Lecumberri, his uncle's model prison in the east of Mexico City.

Despite the imprisonment of the generals, their armies continued to lay waste to the regions where they had their camps. On the left, Zapata pursued his war against the perfidious president, blowing up Huerta's troop trains as they poured into the state. His fighters had infiltrated the southern suburbs of the city. In the north, Villa and Carranza's Constitutionalist Army were restless and upset with Madero's floundering governance but continued to pledge allegiances.

The signs of urban unrest were palpable inside the city. Francisco Madero had called upon the popular classes to resist the temptation to run riot. Notices were posted in the Zócalo asking working people to preserve law and order. Madero, himself a teetotaler, viewed the poor of Mexico City as a drunken lot and saw his new job as regulating their passion for "sensuality, alcohol, and tobacco."

But the masses had another passion—social justice—and when a Mexican was lynched in Texas in midsummer, there were riots in seven Mexican cities and American tourists were beaten and spat upon in the capital. Rolling strikes paralyzed commerce. The Monstruo was swollen with refugees from the Revolution in the countryside and food was at a premium.

The conspirators plotted in the cafés of the Centro Histórico right under the hapless Madero's nose. The names of the plotters were not so secret. Newsboys yelled them out on every corner of the city: Reyes, Félix Díaz, Mondragón—Huerta's name was still being whispered. The newspapers, with the exception of El Liberal, tarred and feathered the little president without mercy and shamelessly ratcheted up the panic quotient: "Alarming Rumors Circulating! Plot Against Madero!" banner-headlined El Imparcial in October 1912 as the conspiracy matured.

In November, Madero recalled Huerta from Morelos to keep a closer eye on him and replaced him with the incorruptible Felipe Ángeles, who had the respect of all factions. The New Year came and went. In his quarters by the San Fernando cemetery, Henry Lane Wilson was getting impatient at his co-conspirators' procrastination. Francisco Madero was out of touch with reality, the Ambassador admonished, not an outlandish diagnosis, and needed to be immediately confined to a mental institution for "the health of the country."

The coup was fine-tuned February 8, 1913, at the Café Berger. The imprisoned generals' backers would provide the logistical support. Mexico City's largest new car dealer volunteered his entire inventory—148 vehicles—to transport the rebel troops into battle. Madero's ears would be nailed to the National Palace by nightfall.

THE COUP BLOSSOMS

Before dawn on the 9th, the cadet aspirants of the Tlalpan Military College and other army schools marched to the gates of the Tlatelolco prison, threatening mayhem if General Reyes was not released—the general had in fact orchestrated his own escape, even instructing his son to fetch him "fine clean underwear" in case he dirtied himself in battle.

With General Reyes and his waxed mustachios leading the column, the rebels marched due east beyond the San Lázaro railroad station to Lecumberri, where Félix Díaz's release had been cooked up with the warden. The insurrectionists then backtracked to the Centro and headed for the Zócalo. Reyes and Díaz rode full tilt down narrow Moneda Street, the hooves of their horses echoing thunderously in the February dawn. Reyes and his men rounded the corner into the great plaza and threw themselves at the Mariana Door of the palace, demanding Madero's surrender.

Suddenly a pair of shots thudded flatly in the frigid air, and General Reyes slumped askew in his saddle and slid to the paving stones—the shooter is thought to have been Gustavo Madero. The president's chief of staff, Villar, was severely wounded in the subsequent interchange of fire. The day had begun badly for both sides in this fratricidal face-off.

BLOODY SUNDAY

I have lived in this neighborhood for a long time. I know my neighbors. They are a desperately nosy lot. They live for *chisme* (gossip), Mexico City's main power food. They love public spectacles, fires and explosions, bank robberies, car smash-ups, jealous husbands throwing their wives from the upper stories of the hotels around the Zócalo. Because they live in the political heart of the city and the nation, they get to see a lot of history happen. Not all of it is pretty.

Shaken by the sudden death of General Reyes, Félix Díaz herded his cadets to the west side of the Zócalo, where they set up their artillery under the overhanging portals. Ammunition had been smuggled into the Hotel Majestic upstairs for the assault on the palace.

Out of all the side streets that feed into the great plaza, the neighbors came to see what the fuss was about, some carrying white flags to show they took no sides. By mid-morning, there were thousands milling on the *plancha* (floor) of the Zócalo, which was then a maze of gardens with real trees, not the flat Tiananmen-like space it is today.

Without warning, both sides opened up, trapping the civilians in the crossfire, and the fiesta of blood began. A rain of bullets fell upon the plaza. The trees were ripped to shreds by Gatling guns. Old people and children were cut in two. "One woman, shot in the stomach, cries out to the Saints," a German journalist telegraphed Berlin, "The corpses are piled up like cordwood." Red Cross workers darted through the carnage and were sliced in half by charging horsemen swinging sharp-edged swords.

The death toll for Bloody Sunday was calculated to be 300 to 500 civilians, and a thousand more were treated at Juárez Hospital. The Mexican Revolution, which up until February 9, 1913, had been fought somewhere else, had finally come to El Monstruo.

JUDAS KISS

Francisco Madero was not inside the Palace when General Reyes attacked. He had spent a fitful night with his family at Chapultepec Castle, still the presidential residence. When Gustavo telephoned to communicate that the government was under attack, the president bravely prepared to make his stand in the Zócalo. His advisers strongly urged Madero to reconsider, but when they perceived the depths of the little man's determination, they all, led by General Victoriano Huerta, swore their loyalty and agreed to accompany him from the Castle to the Palace.

With 800 troops and six cannons, the "March of Loyalty" proceeded down Reforma—the march is still commemorated each February 9 to ratify the military's uneasy subservience to the president. Madero was gratified by the few brave citizens who turned out along the route to shout "¡*Vivas!*" In front of Bellas Artes, shots rang out and the President was hustled to safety inside the Daguerre photo studios on San Francisco Street right by Father Gante's ex-convent at the mouth of the old quarter.

A courier arrived to inform Madero that General Villar was incapacitated by his wounds and he had no chief of staff. Victoriano Huerta sprang to the president's side. "I will protect you, Señor Presidente," he pledged. The two embraced. It was the worst mistake that Francisco Madero, who made many mistakes, ever made.

TEN TRAGIC DAYS

So began the Decena Trágica, the Ten Tragic Days, when the Mexican Revolution came to my neighborhood.

Buffeted by the firepower of the defenders of the National Palace, Félix Díaz retreated from the Zócalo 20 blocks to the southwest to the Ciudadela, a thickly fortified stone armory, now the National Photography Center. Back then, however, it was packed with weaponry: 85,000 rifles, 20 million rounds of ammunition, and 5,000 grenades, quite enough for a prolonged campaign.

Díaz emplaced his heavy artillery and fired in the direction of the National Palace. Both sides engaged in a long-range firefight, their missiles often dropping dismally short of their targets and smashing into slum apartment buildings between the two forts. The neighbors ran from their rooms and often died in the street when they were riddled by errant machine-gun fire. Díaz's cannons drew a bead on the crumbling, overcrowded Belén prison five blocks to the east and blew big holes in the old walls. Those who did not die escaped, and many joined Díaz's rebels at the Ciudadela.

Some 350 troops are thought to have been killed in the bombardments that night, and another 600 civilians lost their lives. Kandell qualifies the carnage as the most impressive destruction of Mexico City since Cortez dismantled Tenochtitlán. Yet even amidst the acrid smoke and screams of pain, the neighbors on the streets around the Ciudadela set up their grease-caked *fritanga* stands—after all, even traitors to the Patria have to eat.

José Juan Tablada, a prosperous Porfirian writer living in an elegant Japanese-style house he had constructed in Coyoacán, a municipality in the federal district but not yet a part of the city and 11 kilometers from the heat of the action, could hear the cannonades rumble in the cold night air. That morning his phone had chimed and a banker friend advised him that it had finally begun: "General Reyes and General Díaz have gone to the palacio." Then the phone went dead. The lights flickered on and off and died. Coyoacán went dark.

The cannonades continued all week. On Wednesday, Tablada observed families gathered at the Xochimilco train depot with all their belongings on their backs. By Sunday, he had packed up his own family and bought steamer tickets to Europe.

Meanwhile, in the heart of the city, life had gone kaplooey. Monday morning dawned in freezing February fog. Sunday had been a day of wild catharsis for the denizens of the city's center—while the bombs burst, looters had emptied the shops in the old quarter and along the Alameda.

Charred bodies were splayed at the bottom of bullet-pocked walls, and some intrepid souls ventured out and turned them over to see if they were a relative. Others were just "insanely curious" to know the grisly details, as one writer bemoans—curiosity was a leading cause of death during the Ten Tragic Days. Just sticking your nose out the front door was dangerous. There were rebel snipers up in the church towers and the loyalists had taken the roofs of nearby government buildings.

As the day warmed up, the killing began anew. Both sides tore up paving stones and dug trenches in the streets just like when the greengos came this way. Loyalist forces attacked from the Alameda, driving up Luis Moya Street one block south toward rebel positions. The buildings in between had all been knocked down, creating a ghastly stage set for urban warfare. Fire engines clanged frantically, racing to put down a house fire.

At night, the blocks between the Alameda and the Ciudadela were a no-man's land. Shadows moved through the rubble, ghostly bands of armed men of whom no one asked any questions.

On Tuesday, General Huerta, commanding the government troops in place of the wounded Villar, again went on the offensive, using the Alameda as his springboard. The Rurales, Madero's most trusted units, in their garish charro gear (they have recently been re-created to patrol the Alameda on horseback, a tourist gimmick), charged up Avenida Balderas intent on capturing the YMCA building that flanks the Ciudadela to the east. Dozens of civilians were mowed down by the Rurales' exuberance.

Díaz's forces counterattacked, launching rockets north across the Alameda and taking out a corner of San Hipólito Church hard by the

U.S. Embassy. Henry Lane Wilson was truly indignant. He picked up the phone and angrily called Madero in the National Palace, threatening to land U.S. troops unless the President provided protection for the alleged 50,000 Americanos trapped in the capital.

The stench of putrefaction saturated the core city on Wednesday. The carcasses of bloated horses, their entrails eaten out by rats, lay in the middle of the streets, stiff forelegs extended. Food was running out and there was no coal to cook it on anyway. Fathers dashed out to find bread and never came home. Although stores and banks were shuttered, empty trolley cars continued to roll eerily through the city.

On the battlefront, Huerta once again threw his troops at the YMCA. Díaz retaliated by taking the police building on the corner of Victoria and Revillagigedo, a block from the Metropolitan Theater, the closest they had come to the old quarter since Bloody Sunday.

Madero was bivouacked in the National Palace—he had sent his family off to the Japanese embassy for their safety. On Wednesday afternoon, Wilson, accompanied by the German and Spanish ambassadors, risked a *bala ciega* and motored to the Palacio to demand protection for their nationals. Wilson again threatened U.S. intervention. (He had somehow forgotten to tell Taft of this detail.) Madero offered to have the Yanqui embassy moved temporarily to Tacubaya, farther west, a safer zone, and angrily dismissed the diplomats.

The ambassadors then drove over to the Ciudadela and struck a deal with Díaz. Foreigners would fly the flags of their countries from their windows and balconies, a strategy that may in fact have made them even more inviting targets. Meanwhile, the residents in the central city took advantage of the chaos to settle old scores with their neighbors. The collateral damage increased as tenants and landlords who had hated each other for years slit each other's throats. But for the most part, the residents of the Centro did not play favorites or take sides the way they had for or against Don Porfirio. Now they were caught between two military forces neither of which much valued their safety.

By Thursday morning, Huerta had not yet launched what he kept promising would be the "final assault" on the Ciudadela, and some were beginning to wonder if he was recycling Santa Anna. In the last days, the loyalists had suffered 200 casualties and Díaz only 18. Something was fishy here, even if Madero did not want to smell it.

Despite the President's chronic state of denial, Victoriano Huerta had, in fact, been in direct communication with Félix Díaz. He presented his terms to Díaz: (A) Madero will fall within a week and (B) Huerta, not Díaz, will be the next president of Mexico. (Remember these scenarios.) The Dictator's nephew was enraged by Huerta's double cross.

The fighting had spread to the elegant homes just south of the Ciudadela where all the streets are named for European cities and countries. Madero's father's mansion between Berlin and Liverpool was torched by a pro-Díaz *turba* (mob). The rebels advanced up Reforma as far as the statue of Christopher Columbus. In the old quarter, a grenade was thrown at the central door of the National Palace, killing a soldier. Machine-gun fire was heard on Isabel la Católica—the hotel's façade was reportedly shot up. Díaz's troops still held the YMCA.

Friday was the day to burn the dead. The half-eaten corpses were collected and doused with gasoline out by the Balbuena military camps east of the train depot.

Remember the Zapatistas? They were watching this Grand Guignol from Xochimilco and wondering if was the right moment to hit the local gunpowder factory. Zapata still had not committed to Madero's defense.

Although the radius of the hostilities was spreading, by Saturday there were few standing structures to take down. The Chinese clock on Bucareli, a gift from the Emperor for Don Porfi's Centennial, was left dangling crazily from its pedestal.

An ominous lull came over the city on Sunday, a week after the terrible massacre in the Zócalo. The cannons were suddenly silenced and sightseers reclaimed the streets of the Centro to inspect the damage. The undeclared truce held the entire day and there was speculation that negotiations were at last under way.

On Sunday afternoon, Madero abruptly left for Cuernavaca— some suspected he was seeking a deal with Zapata. But his mission was even stickier—he had gone to bring Felipe Ángeles back to the Palace to stand between himself and an increasingly erratic Huerta.

(A)

On Monday morning, February 18, when he arrived at the National Palace, Interior Secretary Gustavo Madero was confronted by a much-drunker-than-usual Huerta. The exasperated Gustavo accused the general of plotting against his brother. Why had Huerta waited so long to attack the Ciudadela? The drunken general grew defensive and swore that the "final assault" would begin at 3:00 p.m. that very afternoon. Taking the YMCA was the key to his plan. The heads of Félix Díaz and Miguel Mondragón would hang in the National Palace by nightfall! He invited Gustavo out for breakfast at the Gambrinus, and while at table casually asked if he could look at his guest's pistol. Gustavo stupidly handed over his gun and General Huerta got the drop on him. "Now you are my prisoner," Huerta sneered.

Huerta moved swiftly, ordering the arrest of Ángeles, Madero's personal guardian. The door to the President's office was now unguarded. Next Huerta instructed General Aureliano Blanquet of the 29th Brigade to arrest Madero's whole cabinet. A platoon was dispatched to the National Palace on the pretext of "protecting the President" but was repelled by Madero's loyalists. Three were killed in the second courtyard of the Palace. Madero commanded his Rurales to secure the building, but time had run out. Blanquet burst into the inner office and took Francisco Madero and his vice president Pino Suárez prisoner without resistance. By late afternoon, it was all over. The bronze bells of the Metropolitan Cathedral sent up a joyous clamor.

That evening, Henry Lane Wilson invited the ambassadors over for cigars and fine cognac. Huerta and Díaz dropped by to deliver an ultimatum. Madero must resign. "We invite all revolutionaries to cease hostilities." The diplomats sat in the Sala de Fumar and exhaled. The Embassy Pact, which recognized the legitimacy of Madero's overthrow, was brokered by one William Buckley, the lawyer for the Texas Oil Company and father of the late enfant terrible of the American Right. The ambassadors softly clinked their snifters to seal the deal.

Terror stalked the streets on Wednesday the 19th. Ad hoc firing squads lined up suspected Maderistas. Huerta had Gustavo Madero transferred to the Ciudadela where Félix Díaz's boys had a go at him. Accusing Gustavo of shooting General Reyes, they gouged out his one good eye. As Gustavo flailed blindly, they stomped him to death. Church bells pealed joyously.

Interned in the military barracks in the National Palace, Francisco Madero is ordered to resign. A pen is put in his hand. He refuses. He cannot. He has been elected president by the Mexican people and he will not betray their trust. He would rather die.

But Francisco Madero was hedging his bets, hoping to negotiate safe conduct to Cuba where he had been promised asylum by Cuban ambassador Márquez Sterling. Only with such guarantees will he weigh resignation.

Huerta and Wilson were perplexed. What to do with this little *pendejo*? In exile, he will only agitate and scheme to return. In prison, he would only incite more mischief. Besides he had already broken out of prison once. The liquidation of Francisco Madero for "the health of the republic" was the only viable alternative.

In the streets of the Centro, Francisco Madero was already a dead man. They had murdered his brother. Now they would murder him. It was only a matter of when. And then what? What next?

(B)

General Blanquet designated his lieutenants Francisco Cárdenas and Rafael Pimienta to do the job. They were instructed to drive Madero and Pino Suárez to Lecumberri Prison. The two were not to get there alive. The cover story, which the Porfirian press will run in lockstep the next morning, will be that the convoy had been ambushed by Maderistas intent on rescuing the president and the vice president, and they had both been killed in the skirmish.

The convoy drives through the dark, fear-ridden streets and pulls to a stop in front of the Black Palace, an ominous structure even in broad daylight. The signal is given to drive around to the vehicle entrance at the back wall. The cars pull to a halt behind the prison and both men are roughly pushed out and told to run, but there is nowhere to run. They are blinded by the blazing headlights. Madero and Pino Suárez are both shot in the back—La Ley de Fuga—and their bodies displayed in the prison morgue for the press.

At the embassy that night, Henry Lane Wilson hosted a George Washington birthday party for the diplomatic corps and the champagne flowed like the mighty Orinoco. The ambassador and Huerta and Díaz excused themselves from the party, disappeared into Wilson's office for an hour, and fixed it up between them. Victoriano Huerta will become President of Mexico and Félix Díaz will get to name the cabinet but will not participate in government. The diplomats raised their glasses to the future of this benighted republic.

So the Ten Tragic Days were done with, although there would be many more. Madero, Pino Suárez, and perhaps 10,000 were dead and the city in a ruinous state from which it would not emerge for a decade.

The Decena Trágica was indeed the only moment in nine years of barbaric bloodshed that the Revolution would touch Mexico City and the lives of its citizens with such a devastating hand—but it was quite enough. A hundred years later, when I lean over the counter at La Blanca and ask Don Raimundo, whose father was "a revolutionary of the white cloth" (a Zapatista), whether the Revolution will ever come again, he shudders visibly. "Señor Ross, I hope it won't. I really hope not."

THE CANNIBAL BANQUET

Madero's murder and Huerta's power grab set the table for the next course of the cannibal banquet that was the Mexican Revolution. Zapata's Liberating Army of the South and the northern armies were united against the new dictator, at least in purpose if not always in action. But distrust was the coin of the realm. The patrician Carranza bridled at the low-born Villa's insistence upon being treated as an equal and the unruliness of his troops, who were prone to massacring Chinese coolie workers and transforming nunneries into whorehouses.

The third party in the northern triumvirate was Álvaro Obregón, a rugged young Sonoran farmer who had struck it rich with a garbanzo bean harvester and presided over the Liga Garbancera in his native Navajoa. Elected mayor in 1909, he declared for Madero and fought on the Chihuahua front the next year against Díaz's Federales. By 1913, Obregón was the ranking Constitutionalist commander in the northwest. An instinctive military strategist, Obregón early on divined how machine guns would change the battlefield.

On March 26, a little more than a month after Madero and his vice president were executed, the three generals promulgated the Plan de Guadalupe, rejecting the legitimacy of the Huerta government, and resumed the war against Mexico City.

Although he fancied himself a provisional president (a "vote" was set for October), Victoriano Huerta acted just like a military dictator. One problem with this job description is that military dictators need to have an army, and his was falling apart. The military's Porfirian discipline had been rent asunder by the divide between those officers who sided with Díaz and those who chose to stand with the late president.

Huerta resolved to revamp the army and raise troop levels to 200,000 (about the current size of the Mexican Armed Forces) to meet the threat from the Barbarians of the North.

Huerta's recruitment techniques were less than professional. The "Leva," which press-ganged the poor of Mexico City and surrounding Mexico state into the army against their will, stirred fear and loathing. Huerta's agents "recruited" after bullfights and in the saloons along Mesones Street. Any young or not so young male who could not prove gainful employment was caught up in the draft. Fathers treated their kids to a movie matinee and were dragged off when the show got out. Mourners at funerals and wedding guests were not exempt.

The "volunteers" were concentrated at Buenavista terminal and shipped north to confront the Constitutionalists without training and sometimes without a weapon. In Morelos, Huerta ordered that captured Zapatistas be railroaded to Chihuahua to fight the Villistas. It wasn't a perfect strategy. The forcibly recruited deserted in droves, swelling the ranks of Villa's Dorados ("golden ones"—his crack troops) and Carranza's Constitutionalist Army.

General Huerta basked in a modicum of adulation among the middle and upper classes during the first months of his regime. In times of turbulence, the *gente decente* tend to turn to an *hombre fuerte* strongman with a *mano dura* (hard hand) who would not hesitate to use the Ley de Fuga against those who threaten the sanctity of private property. The monied classes had admired this quality in Don Porfirio and now found it in General Huerta. Uneducated and brutish, the gorilla Huerta was championed by the students of the national university, whose privileges he would defend. Masses were celebrated in the Basilica in thanksgiving for his deliverance. The church bells never stopped bonging.

But Huerta's dipsomaniacal excursions did not inspire confidence or respect. His behavior became more erratic as the rebel armies advanced on the capital. The Provisional President issued draconian edicts and the opposition disappeared. Threats were carried out. General Belisario Domínguez, a Maderista deputy from Chiapas, was murdered on the street that now bears his name in back of the Senate.

In October, Huerta called an election to rubber-stamp his presidency, but a record low turnout moved him to cancel the results. Instead he dissolved Congress and just proclaimed himself the new *tlatoani*.

LA CASA

The capital's fledgling trade union movement—textile workers, streetcar drivers and mechanics, printers, and electricians—had been cautiously enthusiastic about Madero even though he did not espouse their class aspirations, but they were less impressed by his assassin. The House of the Workers, later the House of World Workers (La Casa del Obrero Mundial), opened its doors in September 1912 as a sort of coordinating body for crafts workers. Among its activities, the Casa offered classes for working people so that they might develop new skills to improve their bargaining power. Founded by Spanish and Mexican anarchists unattached to any of the revolutionary factions, La Casa del Obrero Mundial offered "cerebral dynamite"—or so read the sign outside their first headquarters in working-class Tepito.

As anarchists, the Casa rejected the electoral option in favor of "direct action," i.e., fomenting strikes in vital industries, but nonetheless struck an uneasy alliance with the bloody Huerta, who was in desperate need of friends. With the coup leader's blessing, 25,000 workers marched into the Zócalo on May 1, 1913, waving black and red flags.

But the corrupted elections that fall and the Casa's insistent demands for the eight-hour day frayed relations with the usurper and the following May 1 there was no march—in fact, all demonstrations by workers were forbidden. Huerta ordered the Casa del Obrero Mundial closed and its leaders went underground as the General's brief hold on power began to unravel.

THE COLOSSUS OF THE NORTH

There had been a seismic shift at Washington's embassy across the street from the San Fernando graveyard. Woodrow Wilson, a liberal Democrat, had won the hotly contested 1912 U.S. election from Taft and Teddy Roosevelt. Class war issues had been paramount. But although the Colossus of the North had changed the décor, it had not changed its spots. The object of U.S. policy toward Mexico was, as always, domination—only Wilson, the former president of Princeton University, called it "Mexico's integration into the universal commercial world." The Democratic President had a terminal case of White Man's Burden and was determined to teach the Mexicans what "democracy" meant. Wilson's ambassador to Great Britain, Walter Page, put it in a nutshell: "We'll make them vote down there and if they don't do it right, we'll go down there and make them vote again."

Victoriano Huerta was resistant to such improvements.

Indeed, the drunken general now found himself being courted by Washington's enemies. The Germans were interested in keeping Mexico, a major oil producer, neutral in the coming war—they would later offer Carranza the return of Texas, New Mexico, Arizona, and California should the Kaiser emerge victorious. When Wilson's War Department notified him that a German arms shipment was on its way to Mexico, the American president ordered the Navy into action.

Back in 1914, the Monroe Doctrine still stood for something. The Caribbean was an American lake and gunboats replaced diplomacy. Wilson put a Naval blockade on Mexico's Gulf Coast to prevent the German arms from being landed—the munitions were later off-loaded at Puerto México and, to the chagrin of the Americanos, turned out to have been purchased by Huerta's agents in New Orleans.

In April, Woodrow Wilson won war powers from Congress to send in the Marines. "Green Grow the Lilacs Oh!" An exploratory force came ashore in Tampico and when a sailor was arrested, Wilson had his Gulf of Tonkin moment. The Yanks steamed into Veracruz port April 23 and attacked the customs house, losing 17 Marines in the assault, a number that caused the U.S. President to pause before marching uphill to the Halls of Mocuhtezuma.

Conspicuous indignation at this unspeakable act of Yanqui aggression was instantaneous. Anti-U.S. riots roiled Mexican cities. The U.S. Consul was taken hostage in Monterrey and a mob gathered on the Alameda near the embassy, which had been reinforced by Mexico City police. The demonstrators burnt the Stars & Stripes and marched off down Reforma, stoning U.S. businesses on the way. A statue of George Washington, a gift from Washington on the occasion of Don Porfirio's catastrophic Centennial fiesta, was atomized by the enraged demonstrators.

The American president's bonehead play unified the fractious revolutionary forces against the invaders. Huerta, smelling a way out of the increasingly sticky corner in which he was crouched, called for a united front against Wilson's treachery, but the Constitutionalists and Villa were not interested and the Zapatistas would never join forces with the butcher Huerta even against the hated Americanos. The decision of the three revolutionary generals not to find common cause with a drunken dictator spelled the end for Huerta and pumped new life into the Mexican Revolution.

With his army disintegrating and the country going to hell in a handbasket, Victoriano Huerta cut his losses, grabbed as much precious metal left in the national treasury as possible and hotfooted it to Puerto, México, where he caught the next *Ypringa* out for Paris, France, to join Don Porfirio and hopefully locate a moneybags to finance further counterrevolution. The wretched Huerta returned to the Mexican border in 1915 and was arrested in El Paso for violating the U.S. Neutrality Act. Locked up in the Fort Hood stockade, the old fool died of cirrhosis of the liver only a stone's throw away from the country he had all but wrecked.

THE RACE FOR MEXICO CITY

By the spring of 1914, Mexico was already in ruins. Half a million were dead and the dying had only begun. Few farmers felt safe enough to plant that spring, ensuring famine in the fall. On June 27, in the Balkan capital of Sarajevo half a planet away, an alleged Croatian nationalist plugged Archduke Francis Ferdinand and World War I was up and running.

With Huerta on the lam, the race was on for Mexico City. In late June, Villa and his Dorados took Zacatecas, just a train ride away from the capital. But Carranza, who controlled the rail lines farther north, knew that he could not contain the Villistas if they reached Mexico City first and refused to send him any coal or trains, purposely stalling Villa's push on the Federal District. Meanwhile, the First Chief's Constitutionalist confederate Obregón swept down from the northwest, taking Tepic and Guadalajara.

That spring, Zapata had an epiphany. Although the Caudillo hated Mexico City in the deepest whorls of his soul, he had to begrudgingly concede that the power to win back Anenecuilco's land—and by that measure all the lost lands of Mexico's farmers—resided in El Monstruo. No matter who eventually won control of the capital, no one else but he and his rebel army were ever going to make it right.

All through June, the Zapatistas infiltrated the southern sections of the city, riding the dusty track over the Sierra of Chichinautzin, down the steep switchbacks into Milpa Alta. I traveled this back way into the Monstruo with 1,111 new Zapatistas in 1997. At every crossroad, villagers came with *atole* and tamales to feed the Chiapa-necos, "the children of Zapata," just as they had fed the Liberating Army of the South 80 years before.

Encamped in Milpa Alta (high field) in early July 1914, the General paused and looked down upon the metropolis spreading before him. What was he thinking? Womack ventures a guess: "(For Zapata) the Monstruo was much worse than Cuernavaca or Cuautla . . . (Mexico City) was a huge goddamned Babylon, the capital of the whole coun-try's swindlers and chiselers and thieves. . . . If he brought his army into that city for more than a few days, it would go to ruin—alcohol, whores, casinos! The farmers would go into protection rackets! Just total corruption!

"And militarily, he had no machine gun units and no artillery to speak of to challenge Obregón. Urban warfare wasn't an option. They were rural guerrilla fighters—they didn't know the city. Morally and militarily, it just wouldn't be worth it."

But Womack suggests that Zapata had another alternative: neu-tralizing El Monstruo without actually taking it. His troops then com-manded the main Mexican Light & Power plant and the Xochimilco aqueduct, and he had the wherewithal to cripple and drown the hated capital. "He had the power to destroy the Monster, but he turned away." In the end, Zapata had decided that as much as he personally wanted to flatten the capital, the country needed it—indeed, without Mexico City Anenecuilco could never get its lands back.

The Liberating Army of the South retreated back to the hills of Morelos.

WHAT NEXT?

On August 16, just north of Mexico City at Teloloapan in Mexico state, Álvaro Obregón signed off on surrender papers and Huerta's stand-in, Francisco Carbajal, turned over control of the federal army to the Constitutionalists. Four days later, Obregón and the First Chief Carranza rode 12 kilometers through the city in a covered town car. The curbs were lined with citizens thanking the saints that they had not been caught up in crossfire this time around. Unlike Madero's arrival three years previous, which had played second fiddle to an earth-quake, the coming of Carranza was big news. If you missed it live you could catch Carranza's grand entry into the capital at the Salón

Rojo newsreel theater opposite the Alameda—the war in Europe got second billing.

Although the mood in the Monstruo was celebratory, the coming weeks brought grim revelations. The decaying cadavers of Madero supporters who had been disappeared by Huerta's Secret Police were found in cemeteries in Azcapotzalco and Tlalpan and out in Chapultepec Park in the Panteón Dolores.

There were hundreds, maybe thousands, the price the Chilangos had paid for their silence at and tacit approval of Huerta's "hard hand."

General Obregón chastised the capitalinos. They had stood by silently and allowed Madero, their constitutionally elected president, to be overthrown and assassinated, and did nothing when the mad Huerta had spread his poison throughout the city. The Monstruo would pay for it.

Heriberto Jara, a Madero aide, was appointed governor of the Federal District. His first act was to hit the locals where it hurt. Jara slapped a curfew on the cantinas. From now on, working hours would be 9:00 a.m. to 7:00 p.m. and the *pulquerías* would close down by noon.

THE SOVEREIGN CONVENTION

The Constitutionalists controlled the capital but they did not control the country. No one controlled the country. Out in the countryside it was everyone on everyone: Zapatistas on Carranzistas, Obregonistas on Villistas, freelancers on them all. Anarchy reigned. Drunken officers took what they wanted at the point of a pistol. Regional *caciques* (rural bosses) were carving up the republic into personal fiefdoms. Each army had its own worthless currency.

Like Huerta, Obregón and Carranza sought to win labor's backing and the Casa del Obrero Mundial was reopened at a new location: the hoity-toity Santa Brígida's church on San Juan de Letrán. In redecorating the premises, workers desecrated the altar and carried off the pews. Obregón was a committed Jacobin who appropriated churches and jailed 116 priests—his health department later verified that 49 of them were suffering from venereal diseases.

With La Casa del Obrero Mundial back in business, a wave of strikes shut down the city. The Mexican Electricity Workers Union (SME) turned off the lights on the Anglo-Canadian Light & Power

Company and the streetcar workers walked out, inciting urban chaos. Restaurant workers, espousing direct action, took over the upscale Café Inglés near the Zócalo. Dressed in rough work clothes, they occupied all the tables drinking cups of tea 24/7 to the disgust of the café's upper-class clientele.

Somehow order had to be pulled from this orgy of self-interest. Carranza and Obregón resolved to call a Sovereign National Democratic Convention of all revolutionary forces to elect a president and write a constitution that reflected the new social realities of Mexico.

The hotels around the Legislative Palace on Donceles Street where the delegates to the Convention would stay were at full occupancy. But when the Convention was called to order October 1, 1914, there were alarming absences. Villa had sent no delegates. Zapata had refused to travel to the hated capital to meet with "those bastards." In an effort to entice the two to attend, the Convention pulled up its tents and moved to the central Mexican city of Aguascalientes, where it reconvened October 10. The two missing *caudillos* remained no-shows but their delegates registered in such great number that they in fact overwhelmed the Carranzistas.

Expecting to be named president of the Convention, the First Chief was rebuffed and a general agreeable to Zapata and Villa, Eulalio Gutiérrez, was installed. Hoisted by his own petard, Venustiano Carranza walked, out, moving the Constitutionalist government to the port of Veracruz, from which Wilson's Marines had never advanced and whence they were now disembarking. The Stars & Stripes were finally lowered over Fort San Juan Ulloa on November 23.

THE INDIADA COMES AGAIN

On November 24, even as the remnants of the First Chief's army were abandoning Mexico City, Villa's Division of the North entered the capital from the north and the first Zapatista units moved in from the south. The Monstruo was in a frenzy. Attila the Hun and the new Chichimecas were at the gates of the city. Every crime committed within the city limits was attributed to the rebels—kidnappings, hold-ups, homicides, cattle rustling. Jin Chao, a Chinese merchant, was mortally wounded by "a Zapatista bullet."

Phalanxes of police guarded the embassies. "An imprudent joke by one of the drivers caused the jitney passengers to panic" (*El Liberal*).

These bloodthirsty savages will rape your daughter and kill your dog! The criollos and the Gachupines had similarly pissed in their pants when Hidalgo's hordes marched on the city. The Aztecs probably felt the same way about Cortez and his goons.

Having endured the Decena Trágica, the capitalinos feared the worst. Panic buying emptied out the stores. When, in November, Delavan's comet passed over Mexico City, the Chilangos of El Monstruo fled in terror to Chapultepec Park. Newspapers featured prominent advertisements for nerve pills.

From the way Womack tells it, the Zapatistas' entrance into Mexico City was kind of like a bedtime story: "The farmers wandered the streets like lost children, knocking on doors for bread." They poured into Sanborn's, then located a few doors down from the Jockey Club (House of Blue Tiles), about where the Librería Madero does business now, hunkered down on the counter stools in their white pajamas and fearsome sombreros, and ordered hot chocolate.

The classic Casasola photographs of that celebrated encounter are revealing. The campesinos are solemn and unshaven. The white-aproned, long-skirted waitresses hold their distance, regarding the rough-hewn Indian farmers with a blend of urban curiosity and stark terror.

These moments in the Revolution in late November and early December 1914, perhaps its apogee, are the most mythologized. When a fire engine barrels by, sirens blaring, the Zapatistas, thinking it a Carranza war machine, open fire, purportedly killing 12 heroic *bomberos* (firefighters). Or did it really happen that way? Did the Zapatistas really butcher the animals at the Chapultepec Park zoo? Or burn down Tablada's Japanese home in Coyoacán?

Against his better judgment, Zapata took the train down to the capital on November 26, checked into a cheap hotel near the San Lázaro train station, refused to talk to reporters except to snarl that the Monstruo was a hellish place to live, and got back on the train to Cuautla. Villa, who was already waiting for the campesino general in the city (he had requisitioned a mansion on Liverpool Street where Huerta had once bedded down) sent emissaries up to Zapata's General Headquarters in Tlaltizapan and tried to coax the Caudillo into returning. Zapata was reluctant. He had made his decision in July not to risk his army in that Sodom and Gomorrah but at last relented—he would go no farther than Xochimilco, and then only for a few days to meet with General Villa.

Several days later, Emiliano Zapata set off at his own pace on horseback, stepping down the switchbacks of the Chichinautzin. His brother Eufemio, Amador Salazar—a cousin and trusted lieutenant—his infant son Nicolás, and at least one of his wives came along for the ride.

The two rebel leaders met for the first time December 14 in Xochimilco in a rustic schoolhouse. Xochimilco, "the place of the flowers" in Nahuat, now a *delegación* or borough of Mexico City, is still largely rural.

Villa drove down from the center of the city in a motorcar. He was dressed in military jodhpurs and wore a pith helmet. Over six feet tall, broad-shouldered and paunchy and as white-complexioned as a gringo, the Centaur of the North didn't even seem to come from the same planet as the Attila of the South, let alone the same country. Zapata, a small man lean as a blade, was duded out in tight silver-studded charro pants, a lavender shirt, a short black jerkin and his trademark floppy sombrero, a veritable cowboy dandy.

For an hour, the two men sat in sullen silence upstairs in the schoolhouse while their aides made small talk. Finally, Zapata could no longer contain himself: "Carranza is an *hijo de puta* [son of a whore]!" he spat, and the ice was broken. The two cursed the First Chief with gusto. Zapata sent out for cognac. Villa, a militant teetotaler, was scandalized.

They went outside and sprawled under a tall ahuehuete tree—its long roots tie the *chinampas* or floating islands of Xochimilco to the lake bottom—and swapped war stories. The afternoon grew cool, and the two rebel leaders returned to the schoolhouse and laid out their cards. Zapata needed artillery to take out the Carranzistas up in Puebla. Villa agreed to supply him—the weaponry would seal their alliance. They shook hands but did not embrace.

The next morning Zapata rode to the National Palace with Villa and they posed for the press in the president's office. In one portrait, Villa sits in the President's chair, his thick elbows plunked down in the carved armrests. Zapata stands a little to the right behind the throne. He looks like he doesn't trust anyone in the room.

The Caudillo's business in the accursed city was done, and he pulled out of the capital to direct the Puebla campaign. But the artillery Villa had promised never arrived, and there was no alliance.

VILLA'S REIGN OF TERROR

Francisco Villa despised the capital as much as Zapata did, observes his Viennese biographer Friedrich Katz. The Chihuahuan blamed the *capitalinos* for doing nothing to prevent Madero's untimely demise. To make his point, Villa ordered the name of San Francisco Street, the Centro's main thoroughfare, changed to honor the slain president and personally stood on a ladder to install the new signage. The street has been named for Madero ever since.

Meanwhile the Centaur of the North's Dorados rampaged through the city. Villa's lieutenant Tomás Urbina oversaw the pillage from a railcar parked at Buenavista station. Prominent businessmen were snatched from their mansions and held for ransom—at least two kidnap victims were stashed in the basement of Villa's digs on Liverpool Street, Katz reports. Justice was arbitrary. Executions of political rivals were held at night and carried out in secret.

When David Berlanga, a delegate to the Convention, tried to prevent two Villista officers from walking out of Sylvain's restaurant without paying up, they shot him dead. Villa himself played the lout, shooting up the lobby of the Hotel Palacios when a cashier he had taken a fancy to rejected his advances. Shoot-outs on the streets of the inner city were not infrequent. "An Enemy of the Revolution Is Gunned Down in the Street" headlined the newspaper *La Convención* December 28, 1914. Katz counts a hundred corpses among the victims of Villa's reign of terror.

Feuding between the Villistas and the Zapatistas who lingered in the capital grew ugly. Villa himself was accused of taking a potshot at Eulalio Gutiérrez, the president of the Convention, which, despite the fireworks, continued to meet day after day on Donceles Street. Gutiérrez left town and a homicidal tussle for the presidency of the Convention ensued.

On December 15, Villista thugs murdered Paulino Martínez, the spokesperson for Zapata's representatives to the body. The Caudillo had had enough and ordered his troops to pull out of the city, leaving Manuel Palafox in charge of the Zapatista offices at the Hotel Cosmos at San Juan de Letrán #11 ("the leading international hotel in Mexico—with two telephones"). ¡*Ya basta!*

Emiliano Zapata is known to have come down to Mexico City one more time, in May after Palafox was displaced as the head of the

Convention. Zapatista troops advanced into Churubusco and Magdalena Contreras, even seizing the center of Coyoacán, demanding that Palafox be reinstated. But by then the Convention was a hollow shell riddled by intrigue and had lost its grip on the metropolis. It was the Caudillo's final foray into the Monster he feared and despised. After that, Zapata seemed to lose all interest in the city he had been at war with all his life.

THE REVOLUTION BIDS FAREWELL TO EL MONSTRUO

Nineteen fifteen staggered in. El Monstruo was grievously wounded, clutching its belly to keep its guts from falling out. The core of the city had been sacked and torched by the rebel armies. The Decena Trágica had left a gaping hole from the Alameda to the Ciudadela. The burnt-out storefronts on Balderas stood like broken teeth on Desolation Row.

By January, Villa too had lost interest in the capital and, homesick for the wide-open spaces of the north, pulled his troops out of the capital. After rioters stormed the floor of the Convention demanding food, the delegates themselves sought refuge in Cuernavaca, and Carranza's Constitutionalists under Obregón's command cautiously slipped back into the city. The First Chief elected to remain in Veracruz pending the outcome of the immediate future.

Álvaro Obregón had as little use for the Monstruo as Villa and Zapata. It was not a strategic stronghold anymore in a war that had moved elsewhere, and it would require enormous troop deployments to retain. He would stay long enough to secure supply lines to the Constitutionalist troops in Veracruz. During this short interregnum, the Sonoran flashed a steely hand in managing the affairs of the devastated capital. Eighty-six ice cream vendors whose contaminated wares had sickened hundreds were rounded up and forced to consume their toxic product in public—33 died, according to the English-language *Mexican Herald*. On March 19, 1915, Carranza ordered Obregón to abandon El Monstruo and confront Villa's retreating troops.

THE YEAR OF THE RATS

Ironically, the farther the Revolution moved from Mexico City, the more degrading the quality of life in the capital became. The failure of the harvest in the countryside the previous fall triggered widespread hunger in the city that winter. Prices skyrocketed for what little food was available. After decades of relative price stability under the Dictator's iron claw, inflation leaped 145 percent and a *bolillo* of bread, 2 centavos before the Revolution, now cost 25. Corn, the staple of Mexican life, soared from 8 pesos the sack to 200. "Everything has gotten so expensive with this revolution," the hungry sang to the tune of Pancho Villa's signature *La Cucaracha*: "Milk is sold by the ounce and coal by the grain and cockroaches are much admired in this sad nation."

Mobs of women carrying empty baskets broke into San Juan market, La Lagunilla, and La Merced and seized the floor of the Convention. A child was trampled to death during a food handout at the Palace of Mining. Hunger was so palpable that the U.S. Red Cross set up soup kitchens. Rumors steamed through the city that the Jews were speculating with food prices, and Jewish shops on Correo Mayor Street were stoned and burnt. Trees were chopped down on the Alameda for firewood.

Factories were shut down and their workers indefinitely furloughed. Yet another general strike on May 1 left the city without water or electricity for a week. Unemployed bankers sold loose cigarettes on Avenida Balderas to survive. Despite the declaration of martial law, public mayhem was unstanchable. Opposing bands of revolutionaries continued to kill each other with passion. At one hacienda just outside Mexico City, the servants murdered the administrators and emptied out the grain storehouse.

Crime peaked. *Rateros* (strong-arm thieves) ruled the street. But the four-legged rats were even more numerous—a Federal District health advisory counted one rat for every man, woman, and child left alive in "Ratopolis." With the rats came the plague. A typhus epidemic in the last months of 1915 took 20,000 lives. Death wagons collected the bodies from the *vecindades* in the mornings—2,100 died in December alone.

Among those dumped into a common grave in the ravines of the Panteón Dolores was José Guadalupe Posada, the maestro of the *calaveras*, the dancing skeletons, whose macabre, mordant renderings depicted the rich and poor alike as grinning skulls and shambling bones. Posada reserved special venom for the political class whose wheedling ambitions the cartoonist considered to be responsible for the bone heap that is called the Mexican Revolution.

On August 20, the First Chief felt confident enough of Constitutionalist control of the city and moved back into the National Palace. Three hundred thousand anxious Chilangos lined the route from Tlalnepantla in the northeast suburbs to the Zócalo, praying that Carranza would salve their suffering. The typhus epidemic was Carranza's first test as a public administrator. Movie theaters and churches were shut down to thwart the spread of the plague. Health teams were sent out into the slum neighborhoods to bathe and barber suspected carriers. Carranzista health czar General José Miranda called for "a health dictatorship." A special sanitary police took the field. All pets were shot on sight.

THE COMMUNE OF MORELOS

While the hated capital writhed in pain, Zapata's Morelos was flourishing. The Constitutionalists' obsession with Villa had given the Liberator of the South a free hand to consolidate control over the tiny state's cities and municipalities. When his peasant army laid siege to the state capital Cuernavaca, the desperate burghers and bourgeois fled back to the capital like well-heeled rats.

Nineteen fifteen was the year of Agrarian Reform in Morelos. The campesinos took the Plan of Ayala to heart and divvied up the haciendas. Anenecuilco got its fields back. For once, the farmers enjoyed the fruits of their own harvests. It was the year of the Comuna of Morelos, when the people took matters in their own hands and everyone had enough to eat. Indeed, Zapata's people ate a lot better than their cousins in the wretched capital.

A THOUSAND MILES NORTH

Villa's tattered division had retreated to the border with Obregón dogging its heels. The two armies collided again in October at Agua Prieta in the middle of the Sonora-Arizona desert. Obregón's hard-eyed lieutenant Plutarco Elías Calles conspired with General Frederick Funston, commander of the U.S. troops in that desolate stretch of border, and arranged to have his troops transported along the northern edge of the dividing line to surprise the Villistas who were massing to the west. Funston nullified the Dorados' terrifying nighttime charges by illuminating the battlefield with blazing klieg lights.

Villa's horsemen were raked with unrelenting Gatling gun fire when they rode on the Obregonist positions, their mutilated corpses grotesquely draped on the barbed wire Calles had strung up to bollix their charges.

Bloodied but still breathing, the Centaur of the North hobbled east through the deep desert into his native Chihuahua. He would never forgive the Yanquis for their perfidy.

On January 14, 1916, Francisco Villa retaliated at Santa Ysabel in the Chihuahua sierra, where his unconditionals swarmed over a passenger train, executing 16 U.S. mining company engineers. When the U.S. muckraker Lincoln Steffens stepped into the American Club a thousand miles south in the capital that afternoon, he found his compatriots popping champagne corks. Why were the cold-blooded murders of American citizens being celebrated by the gringo business leaders and industrialists? Because, as one of the celebrants explained, now Wilson would be forced to intervene and protect their ranches and mining companies that Carranza was threatening to nationalize.

Then, on March 8, Villa stabbed the Americanos in the eye once again at Columbus, New Mexico, Wilson's hometown, attacking the military garrison there with 80 riders and setting Main Street ablaze. Seventeen U.S. citizens were killed, but Villa lost upwards of 70 men. Eighty years later, I visited the scene of the crime and found the townspeople still smarting from the assault—the first and only land invasion of the United States since its own revolution.

Locals had taken up a petition to have the name of Pancho Villa State Park scratched and a statue of the old bandido was universally reviled. I spoke with Margaret Epps, the 86-year-old retired postmistress, who still had nightmares about Villa's incursion—she was just a little girl delivering milk on her father's wagon when the Mexicans rode in. Now she sat in her rocker on the front porch and sized up every Mexican-looking traveler trudging up the narrow dirt path from the border that skirted her house. "Any one of them could be Pancho Villa coming back this way again," she snorted suspiciously.

Villa's audacity bore instant fruit. Wilson commanded General Black Jack (black because most of his troops were African Americans) Pershing to mount a "punitive expedition" into Mexico. When the Yanquis failed to inform him of the invasion, the First Chief blew a gasket and openly consorted with the Germans, as evidenced in the infamous Zimmerman telegram intercepted by British Intelligence in

1917, in which the German foreign secretary offered the return of the territories lost to Washington in the Treaty of Guadalupe Hidalgo if Carranza would enter the coming war on the Kaiser's behalf.

For 18 infuriatingly frustrating months from May 1916 to January 1918, Pershing chased Villa through Chihuahua—he even called in air strikes. But the Centaur of the North was protected and hidden by his people and the hated Yanquis rebuffed by the hostility of the Chihuahuans everywhere they turned. Although Pancho Villa was America's Most Wanted criminal, with a $5,000 reward on his head on the posters at U.S. post offices, his stock with the popular classes, always high, took off, and many corridos, the mark of true antihero status, were sung:

> Los soldados cansados en la sierra
> Buscando a Villa que no podían hallar
> Cuando luego pasó en un avión
> Y desde arriba comienza a saludar
> (The tired soldiers were in the sierra/ looking for that Villa they couldn't find/ when he passed overhead in an airplane/ and waved down at them from above.)

With World War raging on the Continent and the United States about to plunge into the fray, Woodrow Wilson was in no mood to continue this fruitless pursuit, and Pershing, then holed up at the Colonia Dublin, a Mormon outpost on the Mexican side of the Chihuahua border, withdrew to U.S. territory. Three months later, American lads were falling on the fields of Flanders, and Wilson and the gringos forgot all about Villa and Mexico.

Capitalinos followed Pershing's follies in the newspapers and at the newsreels. These unusual events were happening so far away from Mexico City that they seemed to be taking place in a foreign country—which, to some extent, they were. Geographically, culturally, and temperamentally, the enormous divide between north and south makes Mexico two countries.

LABOR PAINS

Although the Revolution would never again be fought in the capital, 1916 wasn't a much better year than 1915. It began with riots when the banks refused to redeem the worthless currencies issued by the three revolutionary armies—220,000,000 pesos had been put in circulation with zero to back them up between 1913 and 1916.

Labor flexed its muscles. With the encouragement of the Carranzistas, workers signed up with the House of the World Workers and later the CROM (Mexican Regional Workers Confederation), under the direction of Luis N. Morones, and launched a series of strikes that intermittently paralyzed the city. In September 1915, soon after his return to the capital, the First Chief had expropriated the Jockey Club, symbol of so much Porfirian and Huertista intrigue, and turned it over to Obrero Mundial. The elegant House of Blue Tiles, now the flagship of Carlos Slim's Sanborn's chain, became strike central.

During the strike wave of 1915–1916, railroad workers and butchers, department store employees, electricians, and shoemakers walked out to put teeth in their demands for "a nine-hour day." "Walked out" is a sort of misnomer. In Mexico, striking workers drape red and black flags over the façades of their places of employment and take over the means of production, living on the premises until the beef is resolved.

In 1915 and again in 1916, trolley car workers shut down the municipal transportation system and the capital reverted to mules. The Mexican Electricity Workers Union (SME) struck Mexican Light & Power three times in 1916, and telephone workers took on Ericsson, both foreign-owned enterprises.

A general strike was called for May 1, 1916, but was short-lived when Morones caved in to the government's wage offer before thousands of furious workers at the Abreu Theater in the heart of the Centro. Nonetheless, worker resentment lingered, and at the end of July, electricity workers cut off all power, shutting down production, transportation, and commerce in the Monstruo. Thousands gathered on the Alameda chanting "¡Huelga! ¡Huelga!" ("Strike!"). Carranza, who had himself officially elected president in May, took umbrage and, citing Pershing's invasion of Mexico as a security concern, declared martial law. The military went into the streets. The First Chief's secret police hounded labor organizers and radicals. La Casa was evicted from the House of Blue Tiles and dissolved. Strikers were jailed for treason or shot on the spot. One news photo from September shows *la gente decente* daintily picking their way around a handful of dead workers on what looks like the Alameda.

Under draconian pressure from the regime, the labor movement split. Those who stood with Carranza, like the CROMista Morones and Obrero Mundialista Gerardo Murrillo, AKA Doctor Atl, formed Red Battalions and volunteered to fight the Zapatistas in Morelos.

PACIFYING THE WILD BEASTS

The Carranza government was a revolutionary government, but the First Chief was no revolutionary. Under his Huerta-like edicts, public order was enforced and bullfights, dance halls, and *pulquerías* were closed down. Still, his innate pragmatism informed him that he had to pacify—and co-opt—the populace before the Revolution proved to be uncontainable. Food packets were passed out to the poor in the eastern slums of the city. *Cocinas económicas*—"popular kitchens," where the unemployed could eat for a pittance—were inaugurated in working-class colonias. Corn was planted on the banks of the Grand Sewage Canal.

A Confiscation Commission was established and the mansions of the mighty—the Científico Limantour and the Creels, who owned a chunk of Chihuahua the size of the kingdom of Belgium—were seized and subdivided to provide housing for the underclass. Rents were suspended and stipends distributed to the unemployed. By the end of 1916, the worst had passed.

Neighbors sifted through the rubble of the Decena Trágica, sorted out the bricks, and started to rebuild. Movie theaters reopened and new ones multiplied like multiplexes. Chaplin was king at the Palacio Chino with its ersatz oriental décor. Entrepreneurs invited Artur Rubenstein and Anna Pavlova to perform in Mexico City in 1916–1917. Hotels were resurrected. The Isabel cautiously reopened for business and tourism picked up.

A BOLSHEVIK CONSTITUTION

A Constitutional Revolution needs a constitution, and Carranza began to prepare for a Constitutional Convention, set for December 1916. Despite his disdain for the First Chief, Zapata insisted that his word be heard in the new Magna Carta. To underscore their determination, Zapatistas blew up the pumping station in Xochimilco that fall, cutting off the city's water supply. A thousand rebels advanced into the Ajusco, a mountainous zone in the south of the Federal District now incorporated in the Monstruo, and occupied Milpa Alta. White-clad guerrilleros raided into San Ángel just eight kilometers from the National Palace.

The Constitutional Convention was gaveled to order on December 16 in Querétaro, the old mining capital 200 kilometers north of Mexico City. The Juarista Carranza had drawn up an improved edition of the Zapotec's 1857 Constitution, which enshrined the primacy of private property. As two years earlier in the Convention, Carranza arrogantly thought he could just dictate the document but quickly lost control to younger, more radical delegates. The writing of Mexico's new constitution synchronized in real time with the Russian Revolution, and the Marxian fervor of that social upheaval emboldened its framers. Agrarian reform was guaranteed, the precepts of Zapata's Plan de Ayala encrypted in the text of Article 27 in the hope of assuaging the chronically discontent Liberator of the South to at last lay down his arms.

The right of communal property, the *ejido* (literally, the "land outside of town"), was affirmed and confiscation of foreign land holdings incited. Foreigners could not own the Mexican subsoil, i.e., oil fields and mines. Indeed, Article 33 threatened that they could be kicked out of the country if the president deemed their presence "inconvenient." Article 123 in the 1917 Constitution embedded the eight-hour day and the right to form unions and collectively bargain; it was almost Bolshevik in its defense of the industrial proletariat.

The document was even more radically anti-clerical than Juárez's, nationalizing all church properties including the churches themselves, barring the Catholic Church from running parochial schools, and, once again, stripping priests and nuns of their clerical garb—but there were no stated prohibitions on bell-ringing.

Woodrow Wilson decried Mexico's new constitution as "an attack on civilization and democracy." Carranza's response? Mexico's Bolshevik Constitution was promulgated January 1, 1918, the day Pershing's *expedición punitiva* completed its evacuation from Chihuahua.

As is often the case with such documents drawn up in the heat of the revolution, the glorious words were dead on the page before the Constitution was even printed. Agrarian reform? Carranza distributed only three tracts of land, one in Iztapalapa, now a delegation of the Monstruo, and then suspended the *reparto* (handing out of land). Strikes were brutally suppressed. Once the Constitution had been ratified, Carranza felt unconstrained in ruthlessly exterminating his opponents. General Pablo González was commissioned to Morelos, and the slaughter began in earnest.

THE KISS OF DEATH

The Spanish influenza epidemic of 1918–1919 mowed down the wretched of the earth. Ill fed and ill prepared to resist its scythe, a third of humanity succumbed as the epidemic leaped oceans and borders.

The Spanish Flu probably arrived in Mexico in October 1918, at Tampico on the Gulf, and before it had played out by the next spring, a half-million more Mexicans had died.

Marching faster than any invading army ever had, the epidemic reached the Halls of Mocuhtezuma by December. That month, deaths tallied 4,329 inside the city, three times the previous month. Fully 23,000—more than in the terrible typhus plague of 1915, were carried off to Mictlán. The death wagons plied their mournful route in the dawn, picking the corpses out of the gutters to be dumped into common graves or incinerated in the gardens of Balbuena.

By March, the Spanish flu had spread south of the city and planted its kiss of death on Morelos's feverish lips, and Zapata's Liberating Army of the South lost more fighters to the epidemic than it had to all the troops that Madero and Huerta and Carranza had sicced on it for the last eight years. The villagers, the sea in which the rebels swam, were emptied out. Carranza saw a window of opportunity and instructed Pablo González to move in for the kill.

"AND SO OUR GENERAL FELL ..."

All that winter and spring, Colonel Jesús Guajardo, a González agent, had been sending couriers to Tlaltizapan, pretending that he was prepared to defect from the government forces and offering the Liberating Army of the South or what remained of it guns and ammunition. Zapata, whose troops were reduced to boiling weeds for food, met face to face with Guajardo in early April and the traitor offered him a cargo of badly needed bullets. To seal the arrangement, Guajardo threw in a tall sorrel mare, the Golden Ace. Zapata, a lover of horseflesh, was disarmed. The transfer would be made April 10 at the Hacienda Chinameca at the southern end of the Cuautla valley.

Zapata rode down with 200 men but kept them outside the hacienda walls until mid-afternoon. Womack quotes a young aide who tells us what happened next: "Ten of us followed the General as he had ordered. The rest stayed outside under the trees, resting in the shade with their carbines stacked. Three times the bugle sounded the honor call, and as the last note died, as our General-in-Chief reached the threshold of the door, at point-blank range, without giving him a chance to draw his pistols, Guajardo's soldiers fired two volleys and our unforgettable General Zapata fell, never to rise again."

Emiliano Zapata's riddled body was dragged back up the valley to Cuautla by his assassins and thrown down in the town square. A crowd gathered and many refused to believe it was really him. No, he had a scar here, a birthmark there. One night in Huautla down by the Guerrero border, old-timers told me the real Zapata had sent his body double to Chinameca and escaped to Acapulco where he caught a freighter to Arabia, never to return until he was an old man hobbling on two canes, and when he saw what had happened to his people, he was so lacerated he lay down and died.

Zapata's death set off widespread jubilation amongst the Carranzistas down in the capital he so despised, but it had been reported so many times before that many Chilangos did not trust the news. They gathered around the newspaper kiosks and gravely studied the big black newspaper headlines and did not believe what they read. Even when the Caudillo's bullet-pocked death clothes were exhibited in Mexico City by an enterprising entrepreneur, there were many who would never believe it.

The immeasurably sad truth was that the Mexican Revolution really did die that fateful afternoon on the doorstep of the Hacienda Chinameca, although it has lurched around like an untidy zombie ever since.

THE COUP DE GRACE

By 1920, the Revolution was consuming its own tail as if it were a masochistic scorpion. Venustiano Carranza, like all dictators good, bad, or indifferent, refused to get out of the way. Although Obregón thought he had a lock on the 1920 election, the First Chief chose a flunky instead, and when the Sonoran put a move on the National Palace, Carranza packed up 60 boxcars of archives and ingots of gold and transferred the Constitutionalist government to Veracruz, from which he had once ruled.

The First Chief got as far as the Sierra Negra of Puebla, where railroad workers loyal to Obregón derailed his train. Carranza set out on foot, taking refuge in Totonaco Indian villages until he was cornered in a dirt-floor *choza* in Tlaxcalancingo May 21 and shot by an undeclared hand. It wasn't the last shot to be fired, but it was the coup de grace for the Mexican Revolution.

Ten years had careened by since Madero called upon the Mexican people to go to the plazas of their towns and cities and rise up against the Dictator. The bookkeeping is messy, but it is generally accepted that a million Mexicans expired in this fratricidal bloodbath, more than in the fall of Tenochtitlán and the War of Independence taken together. Brothers murdered brothers and fathers their own sons. Another million were forced into exile. Whole communities just picked up and vanished across the border.

Ruthless *caciques* still terrorized Oaxaca, the Huasteca, San Luis Potosí, and Michoacán. The countryside could not feed itself, let alone the city. The industrial plant had collapsed and the nation was $750 million USD in debt. Yet between 1910 and 1920, the oil barons had upped production from 12 million to 63.8 million barrels annually, and U.S. tycoons owned a billion-dollar piece of Mexico, an unfathomable sum back then.

How was it in the Revolution, children asked their elders? Grandfathers handed down the horror stories, the tales of deprivation and despair, and they passed from one generation to the next. Sometimes, the old men picked up guitars and played for them the sad corridos the *jodidos*—"screwed ones"—sang before their misery:

> *Haganos de cuenta*
> *Que fuimos basura.*
> *Vino el remolino*
> *Y nos alevantó.*
> *(They told us/ We were garbage/ The whirlwind came/ And carried us away.)*

VII

CITY OF ARTISTS
& ASSASSINS

Álvaro Obregón was faced with a fundamental dilemma: how to convince 8 million Mexicans that 10 years of revolutionary sacrifice and slaughter had improved the lives of anyone other than the generals who had harvested the spoils of this devastating war?

When rulers have a problem with history, their reflexes are to simply rewrite it. This is really a question of format—how best to sell it to the victims.

VASCONCELOS'S WALLS

Painting walls was a Mexican art even before the people had a name—ancient caves from one end of the country to the other are enlivened with prehistoric glyphs. The Toltecs embellished the walls of their short-lived empire with painted images of the gods. The Mayas decorated the chambers of their dead emperors with messages to the future. The Aztecs daubed the snake wall that fortified their sacred precinct with fantastic serpents. The messages advertised on these rough canvases often depicted the gods' predilection for the peoples who had painted them and the peoples' heroic supremacy over their hapless enemies.

Obregón needed walls to get the message out. He would turn them into billboards for the revolution. José Vasconcelos, his secretary of public education, had those walls.

Vasconcelos, like Juárez and Díaz and the Flores Magón brothers, was a transplanted Oaxacan. When he was a young man, his well-born family had shipped him to the capital to receive a proper education at the National University and in 1909 he made his political debut as a spokesperson for the Ateneo youth movement, which opposed the Científico agenda of Díaz's education minister, Justo Sierra.

Vasconcelos soon joined Francisco Madero's "No Reelection" campaign. A fluent English speaker, he traveled the country with the candidate to handle the questions of the British and American correspondents. During Huerta's brief stint in the National Palace, Vasconcelos took refuge north of the border and later aligned himself with Obregón in the power struggle with Carranza.

His loyalties were rewarded when he was chosen as the rector of his alma mater in 1921—Vasconcelos's mystical motto *Por Mi Raza, Habla el Espíritu* (For My Race, the Spirit Speaks) still adorns university stationary. Vasconcelos was also a lucid spokesperson for autonomy for the university, the largest and oldest in the Americas, then spread over dozens of buildings just north of the Zócalo. Autonomy was finally achieved after students mobilized around Vasconcelos during the 1929 election campaign.

Armed with Obregón's largesse, the secretary of education contracted a trio of hotshot young muralists to stipple the walls of public buildings with revolutionary icons: Diego Rivera, just back from Paris; the stern and doctrinaire Marxist David Alfaro Siqueiros; and José Clemente Orozco, an explosive visionary. Of the three, Rivera was physically and temperamentally the most prominent. Over six feet tall and close to 300 pounds, with bulging frog eyes (his beloved Frida referred to him endearingly as *mi sapo*—my toad), Diego would cast a ham-fisted shadow over Mexican art for half a century.

EL SAPO

Born into wealth in Guanajuato, an old silver city known for its well-preserved mummies, as a student at the National University, Diego Rivera had attended classes in the same buildings upon whose walls he would be contracted to celebrate the inconclusive revolution. Dur-

ing his student days, Diego had haunted the print shop of José Guadalupe Posada on Guatemala Street at the back of the Cathedral and
befriended the political cartoonist, whose mordant images of dancing *calacas* (skeletons) lampooned the politicos who had engineered
the revolutionary bloodletting. But Rivera had missed the revolution,
having passed up the Decena Trágica and other sordid butchery for
the cafés of Saint-Germain on the left bank in Paris, where he sometimes hobnobbed with the likes of Pablo Picasso. Upon his return,
Rivera more than made up for playing hooky from the Revolution,
eventually covering two and a half miles of wall space with his radical
vision.

Installed at the National Preparatory School on San Ildefonso alley by Vasconcelos in 1923, Rivera's initial murals were not met with
much enthusiasm. The Prepa Nacional was a bastion of criollo conservatism, the playpen of privileged youth. Students threw fruit and
spat upon the hulking artist precariously balanced up on the scaffolding. Undaunted by the daily barrage of insults and overripe tomatoes,
Rivera soldiered on, his faith in the revolution enriched with every
brushstroke.

From the National Prepa, Diego picked up paints and brushes and
moved the art show two blocks north on Argentina Street to Vasconcelos's Secretariat of Public Education (SEP), a vast colonial complex
that incorporated the ex–Royal Customs House and the Convent of
the Incarnation. Rivera was given a free hand to monumentalize the
revolution on the walls of two three-tiered inner patios, an enormous
canvas upon which to paint his revisionist version of Mexico's less
than glorious history.

In the SEP murals and later those in the National Palace, Rivera
would depict Aztec civilization as a benevolent and orderly society—
all evidence of blood sacrifice was expunged, and emperors whom
some considered to be little better than swamp Nazis, gloriously lionized. Similarly, the downtrodden campesinos and their righteous
indignation at the cruelties of the Gachupines and Porfirian *hacenderos*
were idealized as the vanguard of the revolution. The red flags and
outsize fists of the urban proletariat radiate from these walls like the
bonfires of redemption.

But such masterful mythification of the underclass often operated on the opposite edge of reality. The grinding lives of Mexico's
threadbare indigenous communities marooned in the distant deserts

and sierras were hardly heroic, and their aggrandizement on the walls of the Monstruo mocked their exclusion. Even in the most lustrous panels, the great Mexican muralists are tainted by a relentless—and racist—paternalism. Dressed up in their authentic Indian duds, Diego and Frida often appeared to be on their way to a costume party.

REDS

Convoked by Siqueiros, Rivera and his comrades formed the Union of Revolutionary Painters, Sculptors, and Engravers to promote their vision of public art—its members would paint for the people and not for the salons of wealthy patrons. (The smoking of marijuana was also encouraged in the bylaws.) The union soon affiliated with the Mexican Communist Party (PCM), and the artists contributed to the party's then clandestine newspaper *El Machete*, printed in the back room of PCM offices around the corner on Mesones Street.

The Mexican Communist Party, founded in 1919, would take two years to come out of the closet. Its early leaders and intellectuals like Valentín Campa and José Revueltas were relentlessly persecuted and imprisoned. Rivera, larger than life and even than his heroic murals, adroitly manipulated the Marxist party and hogged the radical spotlight for himself. El Sapo, feared and beloved by the presidents he served, seemed immune from such persecution.

BOHEMIAN NIGHTS

The postrevolutionary ferment attracted adventurous leftists and incurable romantics to Mexico City. Over the next decade, slews of revolutionary tourists would trek through the Halls of Mocuhtezuma enlivening the local art stew. D. H. Lawrence arrived in 1922 and feverishly scratched out *The Plumed Serpent* around the corner at the Monte Carlo on Uruguay—Wilfred Ewert and his suspected killer Stephen Graham followed his footsteps later in the year. Tina Modotti, an Italian-born, San Francisco North Beach–raised beauty with a blooming Hollywood silent screen career before her, arrived the next year with her young husband, Robo, who suddenly up and died of smallpox. She returned in 1925 with the brilliant photographer Edward Weston in tow and they opened a studio in Tacubaya that was soon a hub of creative spirits. Hart Crane, Katherine Anne Porter, and B. Traven all migrated south to sniff the postrevolutionary flowers. Sergei Eisenstein, the formidable Soviet director, would arrive at the end of the decade, bankrolled by California muckraker Upton Sinclair, to shoot the never completed ¡*Viva México!* before Stalin summoned him home.

When these international bohemians looked at the Mexican Revolution, they often viewed it through the distorted lens Rivera peered through.

The cross-pollination offered the Monstruo a heady mix of art and political fantasy. Weston shot famous nudes of Modotti sunning herself on the roof of the Tacubaya studio (the Mexican government would later use them as evidence of her involvement with a pornography ring). Master photographer Manuel Álvarez Bravo dropped by to encourage Modotti's enthusiasm for photography, and she was assigned by Anita Brenner to shoot for her classic volume of Mexican memorabilia, *Idols Behind Altars*. Diego courted the young crippled art student Frida Kahlo in Modotti and Weston's rooms—Kahlo's spine had been nearly severed in a trolley car accident while on her way to art school one block over on Bolívar Street.

Weston, with Modotti's encouragement, also shot classic nudes of the "indigenous" poet-flapper Nahui Ollin, who lived in a state of tumultuous free love with the surrealist painter Doctor Atl (Dr. Water) in the old convent adjacent to La Merced market. Ollin, who had a penchant for sexual scandal, was in fact the nom d'art of Carmen Mondragón, the daughter of General Manuel Mondragón, Félix Díaz's confederate who had stomped Gustavo Madero to death in the Ciudadela.

Dr. Atl had briefly served as secretary of Obrero Mundial before the threat of jail convinced him of Carranza's wisdom and he went off to Morelos with the Red Battalions to fight the great Zapata. Toward the end of his life, Gerardo Murrillo, Atl's Christian name, would become Mexico's most venomous Nazi.

In addition to his bizarre politics, Dr. Atl was also a dedicated vulcanologist who worshipped at the skirts of Popocatépetl, the subject of many of his paintings. Indeed, Doctor Atl's temper was as volcanic as his passion, and his and Nahui's tempestuous hijinks resonated throughout Mexico City café society.

One venue where those who had come from the far corners of the earth to bask in the flame of the revolution mingled with the Monstruo's most inflammable artistes was the Café de Nadie (Café of No One) on Álvaro Obregón Avenue in the Condesa district, where the Estridentistas (Strident Ones) burst forth nightly—*estridentismo*, whose texts were grounded in urban grit and derived much from the Italian futurists, was "a gesture, an interruption," proclaimed Manuel Maples Arce, one of the founders of this obscure school, which would see an uptick of attention thanks to enfant terrible Roberto Bolaño's *The Savage Detectives*.

Álvaro Obregón, the broad tree-lined boulevard named for the postrevolutionary *tlatoani*, is still a good street for poetry. La Casa del Poeta is housed in the once-upon-a-time home of Ramón López Velarde (1856–1921), a Vasconcelos protégé whose *Suave Patria* (Smooth Fatherland) was hailed as the maximum expression of postrevolutionary poetry.

The Monstruo was in fact loaded with hot young postrevolutionary poets—Xavier Villaurrutia and his lover Salvador Novo, a callow Octavio Paz and his cohort Elías Nandino, the romantic Tabasqueño Carlos Pellicer, all cavorted in the cafés and cantinas of Bohemian city.

In addition to poets and painters, the international effervescence brought a road show of the Roaring '20s to the Mexican capital. Charles Lindbergh flew in solo from New York to inaugurate Mexico City's first international airport in the Balbuena Gardens. The American political commentator Will Rogers admired Rivera's work in person, and Al Jolson in blackface held forth on the silver screen at the Rialto.

BUCARELI STREET

Bucareli Street is a pleasant amble spoking off from the Paseo de La Reforma just before it hooks south and west. When the execrable Santa Anna ordered the great equestrian statue of Carlos IV to be removed from the national university, he deposited it at the mouth of Bucareli Street, named for a long-demised viceroy. Following the revolution, the Palacio Covián on the fifth block of this avenue was designated as the headquarters of the interior secretariat, where, amongst other matters, the internal security of Mexico was zealously protected.

Having recast the Revolution in monumental proportions, Obregón's next task was to smooth over the wounded sensitivities of his immediate neighbor to the north at the indignities the Revolution had wreaked upon U.S. properties and pride. Diplomatic relations with Washington had been broken off after Woodrow Wilson invaded in 1914, and Obregón dedicated a great deal of his presidency to restoring them. Only then could Mexico begin to borrow money again from the international banking community.

Oil was still at the heart of the darkness. Under Carranza's constitution, foreigners could no longer own a piece of Mexico's subsoil, a stipulation the Seven Sisters, who argued that Díaz had given them their holdings in perpetuity, took to court with mixed results. Guided by William Buckley's pop, the National Association for the Protection of American Rights in Mexico was chartered and lobbied the U.S. Congress for nothing less than a declaration of war if U.S. citizens' property rights were not guaranteed.

To manifest his admiration for Washington, Obregón traveled to the U.S. capital in a private rail car at the height of Prohibition and enticed the unfortunate Warren Harding aboard for cocktails. Similarly, when a bankers' commission headed by J. P. Morgan's Thomas Lamont arrived in Mexico to chat about the country's $750,000 foreign debt, Obregón plied them with liquor and filled their rooms at the Grand Hotel with jeroboams of champagne. "Mexico is a free country," the Mexican president pointed out.

In late 1923, Mexican diplomats sat down with their U.S. counterparts at the old Covián Palace on Bucareli Street a block from the Ciudadela, and when they emerged in 1924, the Bucareli Agreement was a fact. Big Oil's ownership of its Mexican fields was intact. Álvaro Obregón had given away the house. Washington and Mexico City renewed diplomatic relations.

One of the first initiatives of the new U.S. ambassador, James Sheffield, a dour Yalie ideologically cut from the same cloth as Poinsett and Wilson, was to introduce American football to Mexico in order to teach the lads at the National University "the fundamentals of American sportsmanship."

POSTREVOLUTIONARY TRAFFIC JAM

Although the Mexican Revolution had been fought against the capital and what it stood for, by 1925 Mexico City dominated the country of which it was the center more than it ever had. Political power radiated from the Monstruo, where all government institutions were concentrated and all decisions were taken. All news was made in the capital and distributed to the provinces. Two-thirds of all commercial goods available in Mexico—refrigerators, cars, etc.—were bought and sold in Mexico City. Despite his agrarian roots, Obregón was on total disconnect with the farmers for whom the Revolution ostensibly had been fought, and minimal land was distributed to the landless.

Álvaro Obregón's vision was urban and modernizing, manifesting itself in the erection of large public buildings. Prerevolutionary projects that had been left unfinished in the turmoil were topped off. The Palace of Bellas Artes opened to the public. Ditto the Mexico City International Airport. The Bank of Mexico rose stolidly at the foot of the Alameda. The architecture was streamlined, functional, and anti-Porfirian—gone was the gilded fin de siècle froufrou.

Under the agile direction of young Manuel Gómez Morín, a Vasconcelos protégé, the Bank of Mexico imposed a semblance of solvency, restoring the fickle faith of foreign investors, and Yanqui dollars began to return to the economy.

The Revolution had left the city's infrastructure in shambles. Insurgentes Avenue, the lengthiest in the Americas, running from north to south through the midsection of the Monstruo, was still mostly unpaved. Heavily trafficked streets were mined with potholes big enough to swallow a Model T. A third of the traffic in the city was still horse or mule drawn—"animal traction" in the Monstruo's traffic regulations.

But the automobile was in the ascendancy. Ford had opened its first assembly plant in Latin America in Cuautitlán in 1925, and the narrow streets of the Monster were clotted with gas-spewing jalopies, 10,781 of them according to a 1921 census. There were few traffic lights to regulate the flow—one was posted at the corner of San Juan de Letrán and Juárez Avenue. It is still the slowest light in town.

Obregón's span in office encapsulated this phenomenon. Whereas he rode to his inauguration in a horse-drawn carriage, his successor Calles would be chauffeured in a Lincoln Town Car.

By 1921, the Federal District—Mexico City and 14 adjacent municipalities—was home to 906,000 Mexicans, 67 percent of whom (619,000) resided in Mexico City proper. Within Mexico City, the metropolis was divided into eight quadrants—about a fifth of the city's population (116,033) lived in the first quadrant—La Primera Cuadra, or Centro Histórico as it is called today.

The wealthy had continued to migrate west. Lomas de Chapulte-pec, more popularly dubbed Chapultepec Heights, with its large homes and clipped lawns, housed the affluent, both native and *extran-jeros* (literally "strangers"). The stunted middle class had spread south of San Juan de Letrán settling into the *colonias* Doctores—where all the street names were those of doctors—Navarte, and Del Valle. Working people moved into new colonies in the north of the city on either side of the Calzada de Los Misterios that led to the "Villa," the complex surrounding the Basilica.

Capitalinos were overwhelmingly renters—only 10 percent actu-ally owned property, and money-grubbing landlord associations con-trolled the housing market. In the aftermath of the revolution, Morones had organized Renters' Leagues, but as the CROM boss grew into a full-bodied *cacique*, he lost interest in the plight of the working people. In 1922, the newborn Communist Party organized a huge citywide rent strike. Fifty thousand renters, led by working-class women, with-held their rent for May and June, underscoring that proletarian unity, which had peaked during the revolution, was still alive and kicking.

Faced with resistance by central city residents, developers specu-lated on the land outside the city limits. Not only were the spaces be-tween the colonias filling in, but the vacant land between Mexico City and the neighboring municipalities was disappearing as the entities merged. The Federal District was knitting itself together into a 14-mile-wide *mancha urbana* or urban stain. The Monstruo grew corpulent.

AN UNCUDDLY CAUDILLO

As was synonymous with succession, Obregón was reluctant to relin-quish his hold on the National Palace, giving the *Dedazo*—pointing the Big Finger—to his fellow Sonoran Plutarco Elías Calles to serve as his proxy. This upset still another Sonoran general, Adolfo De la Huerta, who rose in rebellion in 1923–1924. De la Huerta's revolt was predi-cated on the widespread perception that Obregón and his Bucareli Agreement had leased Mexico to the gringos. The fledgling Mexican Air Force, equipped by the United States, was enlisted to bomb De la Huerta's positions, and another 10,000 were sacrificed on the altar of the Revolution

Plutarco Elías Calles was a decidedly uncuddly caudillo. His conversational dexterity was punctuated by ominous silences and his obsidian eyes drilled right to the marrow of his respondents. He didn't so much stimulate trust as elicit fearful obedience.

Calles was unpopular in certain sectors from the first minutes of his mandate—a deranged woman named Jáuregui took a potshot at the new president following his investiture in the Chamber of Deputies February 5, 1925. The new U.S. Ambassador Sheffield was not inclined to mix socially with the new president, whom he disqualified as an "Indian." "There is very little white blood in Calles's cabinet," the ambassador telegraphed his superiors at the State Department.

Plutarco Elías Calles was obsessed with putting back on track the Revolution that Obregón had derailed by caving in to the gringos on Bucareli Street. Upon taking office, he cancelled all oil leases doled out by Don Porfirio in perpetuity, obligating the Anglo-American-Dutch owners (Royal Dutch Shell now owned Cowdray's Águila) to reapply for 50-year leases, a turnaround that really annoyed Sheffield. Buckley père, over at the National Association for the Defense of American Rights in Mexico, went ballistic, and the war drums pounded in Congress. When in April 1925, CROM boss Morones's goons broke into the U.S. Embassy across the street from the San Fernando cemetery, they discovered hundreds of cables contemplating intervention.

CATHOLIC BLOOD

Where Plutarco Elías Calles, the self-styled *Jefe Máximo* or "Maximum Chief," acquired his taste for the blood of Catholics confuses even his biographer Enrique Krauze. His fathers and grandfathers had all been churchgoers and were each buried in sanctified ground. Yet Calles's hatred for Jesus Christ and those who practiced the religion that bore his name was patent, a stance that put the Jefe Máximo at odds with nine out of every 10 Mexicans if Church figures are to be taken seriously.

Perhaps the source of the Sonoran's scorn for the Christian faith can be ascribed to peer pressure—his comrades-in-arms had embraced Freemasonry and his protégé Lázaro Cárdenas was an initiate. But anticlericalism was rooted as deeply in the Mexican spiritual dynamic as was the adoration of the Virgin of Guadalupe. Masonic mischief tracks back to Poinsett's connivance with Vicente Guerrero in the York Rite temple. Juárez's Reforma embedded laicism in the 1857 Constitution—19th-century anticlerics earned the quaint nomenclature "Jacobins."

Madero's spiritualist baggage was an early expression of the Revolution's anti-Church tilt. Villa sodomized nuns. Carranza's contribution to the debate were Articles 3 and 130 of his 1917 Magna Carta, mandating a lay education and nationalizing the Roman Catholic's real estate in Mexico. While Obregón jailed priests and had them tested for V.D., Calles thirsted for Catholic blood.

When in early 1925 the Maximum Chief got wind of rumors that Mexico City Archbishop José Mora y del Río, the most powerful churchman in the republic, was holding secret meetings with the oil barons, he sicced Morones's CROM boys on the Papists. Under the banner of the made-up Mexican Apostolic Catholic Church, the CROMistas invaded parish churches, disrupting Sunday Mass during February 1926. A priest was pulled down from the pulpit in the Santísima, the ancient (1567) gothic leviathan five blocks east of the National Palace on Moneda Street, during Mass on February 6.

The "schismatics" struck next at La Soledad in the skirts of La Merced market, the city's seventh-oldest church and a house of worship with profoundly popular roots—"Next to Lupita [the Guadalupana], Chole [Soledad] is our favorite," is a motto in the Merced. So when CROMista "Padre" Luis Monge began to read the "Socialist Catechism" ("Hail Socialism! Great shall be the fruit of your doctrinal wisdom!") from the garish altar, he was nearly lynched by an infuriated mob of 300 women. The Mexico City police waded in with flailing truncheons. The fire trucks were called and the *bomberos* washed the flock from the pews and out of La Soledad—one would-be worshipper was reportedly killed in the melee. The takeovers by the apostates spread into wealthier parishes—two women were murdered in the upscale Roma when Morones's boys attacked Sacred Family, the colony's most beloved church.

EL TURCO INVOKES ARMAGEDDON

The scowling Caudillo had acquired a new nickname in the popular argot, "El Turco," for his perceived cruelties. Calles's crackdown was indeed freighted with horrific excesses. In Tabasco, his loyal ally Governor Tomás Garrido Canabal barred all but married priests from saying Mass. Religious place names like Vera Cruz (True Cross) and Corpus Cristi (Body of Christ) were laicized into one word. The Calles Law promulgated in June 1926 decreed five-year prison sentences for priests who dared to wear their vestments in public.

Archbishop Mora y del Río was taken before a court and charged with violating Article 3 of the Constitution, which made it a felony for the Roman Catholic Church to run parochial schools. The schools were shut down and the teaching nuns pushed into the street. Mora y del Río retaliated by excommunicating those responsible for the school closings. The papal nuncio was expelled from Mexico after he laid the cornerstone at a Cristo Rey (Christ the King) shrine in Guanajuato.

An appalled Pope Pius XI responded by suspending all ecclesiastical services in Mexico, a strike of priests and nuns, if you will. The faithful were shocked by the sudden unavailability of the body and blood of Jesus Christ, and the more militant formed leagues and declared boycotts of Mexico City's movie theaters and department stores to shame wealthier Catholics into backing their demands that the Church-run schools be reopened.

Then Calles cut off the debate by ordering the Roman Catholic Church out of business no later than July 31.

As Armageddon closed in, the city's houses of worship overflowed with *creyentes* (believers) seeking the Holy Sacraments. Thousands gathered in the courtyard of the Metropolitan Cathedral. Calles could see them from his rooms in the National Palace on the east side of the Zócalo: young girls in billowy white confirmation gowns lining up to pledge allegiance to God; hundreds of squalling arm babies crying out to be baptized; desperate couples frantic to be wed in the eyes of God before it was too late. On July 29, when a photographer's flash bulb exploded with a loud pop, the 3,000 faithful wedged inside the Cathedral panicked—57 were taken to hospital (*El Universal*).

As the deadline approached, the devout prayed day and night and resolved not to abandon their churches. In Rome, Pius joined them in a 24-hour prayer vigil. But El Turco was unyielding, and rather than risk a bloodbath, the priests coaxed their adamant flocks into peacefully retiring. The churches were then turned over to "neighborhood committees" and padlocked. Morones and the CROMs celebrated the expulsion of the Catholics from the churches of Mexico City with a truculent rally in the Zócalo.

"¡VIVA CRISTO REY!"

Although the evacuation had been bloodless, bloodshed was inevitable. The religious war quickly spread from the city to the countryside. Farmers picked up the gun and reopened the churches the government had ordered shut up. Unified by bloodcurdling cries of "¡Viva Cristo Rey!" the farmers formed armed bands and were soon fighting a decentralized war of the flea against the Federales that Calles had rushed in from the capital to quell the rebellion.

Unspeakable barbarities were reported. Rural schoolteachers were accused of being Bolshevik agents and burnt alive by the Cristeros. A federal general had a soldier who wore a crucifix into battle shot on the spot. The carnage continued for three years through 1929, dumping another 25,000 lives into the charnel pit of the Revolution. Agricultural production declined 38 percent and families went hungry. Two hundred thousand were forced to flee the region.

In the old photos, in their white cotton pajamas, with their bandaleros slung across their chests and brandishing their mausers, the Christ-the-Kingers are dead ringers for Zapata's farmers. There were commonalities in their struggles—Zapata's followers were Guadalupanas too. The Cristero War had profound agrarian roots. Obregón's—and later Calles's—inattention to the countryside and the suspension of the reparto fanned the flames of rebellion.

Zapata's war had been a war on the capital, a war in fact on the very notion of the city itself; the Cristeros too took up arms against the "Centro," where, they thought, all power was concentrated in the hands of the few and the Jews owned all the money. Mexico City was Sodom and Gomorrah rolled into one under the thumb of the anti-Christ Calles.

"AN OCTOPUS SUCKING THE BLOOD OF THE WORKING CLASS"

Much as the Revolution had, the Cristiada kept its distance from the Monstruo. The bloody war was a rural phenomenon fought on far-off battlefields. In the city, the church bells were thankfully silenced for once. Working-class Chilangos discovered they were more Guadalupanas than Roman Catholics, devotees of their National Mother, and didn't need the clerical class to guide them to spiritual enlightenment. But many were disaffected because, with the churches closed down and the priests dispersed, the feast days of the saints were no longer celebrated. Calles's substitution of workers' fiestas did not convince the masses.

Just in case the believers did not buy the Turco's line, Morones's *porras*, a kind of anti-religious police, weeded out the "cultists." *El Universal* describes a raid on the apartment of Señora Ayala de Vargas (Arquitectos #30, Colonia Morelos) where 33 señoras, señoritas, and señores were taken into custody for "practicing diverse acts of the Catholic cult." A printing press was found on the premises.

The scandal sheets loved Luis N. Morones and his 10 pinkie rings. Fabled orgies at his Tlalpan villa sold newspapers. Photos of Morones driving around town in his white-walled Packard crammed full of half-nude floozies filled the front pages. Morones's exploits echoed those of the notorious gray car gang that marauded through El Monstruo during the revolution, and whose homocidal adventures were engraved on Mexican popular culture in the celebrated 1919 silent film *El Automóvil Gris*.

Luis N. Morones had been appointed Labor Czar by President Carranza and charged with keeping the industrial proletariat quiet way back in the middle of the third Mexican revolution. He had indeed perverted the CROM into a kind of protection racket, offering labor peace to the bosses for a piece of the action. "Protection contracts" are still being negotiated by corruption-ridden unions here. In 1924, Calles had the chutzpah to make this gangster his secretary of the economy.

One did not mess with Morones. When the comedian Roberto "El Panzón" Soto did a Morones schtick at the Teatro Lírico, 50 "riflemen" were needed to protect him, according to an overheated *Time* magazine reporter. "Morones is an octopus sucking the blood of the working class, vulturing and gorging on the dupes that elected him," the uncredited correspondent quotes an Obregonist deputy.

LA SOMBRA DEL CAUDILLO

Poor Álvaro Obregón thought he had cut a deal with Calles to leapfrog presidencies, and the 1928 nomination should have been his—but the Maximum Chief was hedging. When Obregón's deputies modified the "No Reelection" Constitution in 1926 to legitimize reelection, El Turco bit his tongue, but his mouthpiece Morones did not. At the

May 1, 1927, International Labor Day rally in the Zócalo, the Aztecs' answer to Al Capone warned Obregón that his health might be endangered if he chose to run.

Things started to get real murky in a hurry. In October, a revolt of Obregonist generals in the military police was crushed. Three were killed at the Police Academy shooting school. Twenty-six generals grouped around former Obregonista Mexico City governor Francisco Serrano were driven out of the city to a lonely promontory at Tres Marías, Morelos, and executed. No mention is made of this in the newspapers I have read.

Three years later, the Mexican Revolution's most prominent journalist, Martín Luis Guzmán, wrote a novel based on these events, *La Sombra del Caudillo* (The Shadow of the Strongman). The novel was never published in Mexico. In 1960, director Julio Bracho made a movie based on Guzmán's novel. The movie was banned from Mexican screens for the next 30 years.

If Álvaro Obregón still had not gotten the message, more mayhem was in the pipeline. In November, on his way to the bullfights at the Plaza México, a carload of Morones's goons tossed a bomb at the candidate's car—he survived and sped off through Chapultepec Park.

The next day, two brothers, Miguel Agustín and Humberto Pro, both Jesuit priests, were accused of the attack by Calles's jut-jawed police chief, Roberto Cruz. The Pros were summarily convicted by a kangaroo court and put up against the wall at the Balbuena police barracks November 23. The papers did not seem to question the frame-up. Seventy years later, Pope John Paul II beatified the brothers Pro during a visit to Mexico City—the Jesuit Miguel Agustín Pro Human Rights Center remains one of the most active in Mexico.

THE ECLIPSE OF ALVARO OBREGÓN

The Maximum Chief's little shop of horrors did not deter Obregón from his single-minded goal of reelection, and with no serious opposition he swept the July 2 presidential balloting. A fortnight later, on July 17, while celebrating at La Bombilla, his favorite San Ángel beer garden near the monument to his dead right arm, a humble street cartoonist sketched the president-elect as he caroused with his *compinches*. Emboldened, José de León Toral approached Obregón's table and showed the sketch to the once and future finance minister Aaron Sáenz. When

Sáenz leaned over to alert Obregón to the cartoonist's talents, Toral pulled a pistol from under his sketch pad and put five slugs into the president-elect's back. The strains of *El Limoncito* (The Little Lemon Tree) performed by the Bombilla house orchestra muffled the shots as Obregón crumpled to the floor.

In the chaos that followed, Toral was beaten bloody and almost throttled to death by Obregón's compinches before the police hustled him off for "questioning." With his face severely rearranged, Toral insisted to the beat reporters that he had plugged the president to bring God's kingdom to earth. He claimed to have been driven to the deed by the mesmerizing influence of the mysterious Madre Conchita, a Capuchin nun at whose shuttered Colonia Guerrero Daughters of Mary convent he attended underground Catholic Mass. Toral was prone to shouting "¡Viva Cristo Rey!" at inconvenient moments.

But there was something fishy about the assassin's story. Obregón had been a bully, but it was Calles, his archrival, who had wielded the big club. Some saw Morones's bejeweled pinkie in the soup, and El Capone was forced to resign as Calles's secretary of the economy.

The true identity of whoever held the hand that pulled the trigger went to the grave with Toral. On November 28, 1928, the killer cartoonist was convicted of the heinous crime in a San Ángel courtroom, and he was executed at dawn the following February 28. Unrepentant, Toral sucked down his last cigarette—a Faro, the slim-jim cheapos that were then the smoke of choice—and faced the firing squad still hollering "¡Viva Cristo Rey!" The term *chupando Faros* has since become Chilango slang for giving up the ghost.

THE REAL CHILANGOS

The Monstruo was aflame with intrigue. The *nota roja* ("red note," sensational tidbits) of passion killings, disassembled corpses, political assassination, and other crimes of perversity dominated the headlines. Every morning, the Chilangos gathered around the kiosks to devour the latest scandal.

The criminal peccadilloes of Mexico City's rich and famous, venal politicians, and celebrity rapists provided cheap entertainment. *El Sol de México, Ovaciones, El Universal,* and *Excelsior* opened a window to a fantasy city that the *jodidos* could vicariously climb through. But that Mexico City wasn't the real one.

For that undefined constituency called the *pueblo*, the real Chilangos (the word derives from Ixachitlán, the American continent or the exotic chilies of the Valley of Mexico, combined with Tenango, place) lived in the barrios and the colonias, *chismando* over the counter at Don Pepe's corner *estanquillo* or haggling over the price of *maciza* at the neighborhood mercado. The real Chilangolandia was found inside the *cubiletes* and *conchas* at Doña Cuca's Panadería and playing *cascarita* (pick-up soccer) in the street. Chilangolandia Real was in the *desmadres* (brawls) at the cantinas "of bad death" and the neighborhood *nicho* to the Virgencita and in the *carpas*, street tents, where the *cómicos* mocked the politicians and bored, heavy women in rhinestone G-strings gyrated for the working stiffs.

Mexico City was—and is—a patchwork of such neighborhoods, of *manzanas* (blocks) grouped into *barrios*, usually with common connections either by *oficio* (profession) or hometown. Barrios are old and traditional. *Colonias* pull together the barrios into a specific stretch of real estate delineated by land speculators and developers, although occasionally they are formed by popular demand when squatters just sit on land until they embarrass the city into providing services.

In March 1928, the Mexican Congress provided some administrative relief for this colorful muddle. The 14 municipalities which, along with Mexico City, comprised the Federal District were dissolved and became delegations of the City of Mexico.

The eight sectors of what was formerly known as Mexico City became the Cuauhtémoc delegation, which was eventually split into three delegations (Venustiano Carranza, Benito Juárez, Cuauhtémoc). Azcapotzalco and La Villa of Guadalupe were the two northernmost demarcations; Coyoacán and San Ángel and rural Xochimilco, Magdalena Contreras, Tláhuac, and Milpa Alta subdivided the south of the city. Cuajimalpa and later Álvaro Obregón and Miguel Hidalgo spread into the west. Iztacalco and Iztapalapa covered the eastern flanks of the city all the way to the shores of the vanished Lake Texcoco.

Designated by the Constitution of 1824, the Federal District would now be identical to Mexico City and governed by the newly created Department of the Federal District. Instead of a governor, El Monstruo was now to be ruled by a "regent," a kind of throwback to its Gachupín past, who would be appointed by the President of the Republic, whoever that was going to be.

The battle for political control of Mexico City had been struck. To many, it was as much a battle to control the country of which the city had been designated the capital. Indeed, to many Chilangos, the two had become one and the same.

GAMBUSINO! (An interview with Don Alfredo, an urban gold miner)

Don Alfredo stopped coming in for breakfast. He told Armando, the morning counter man, that from now on he was going to live on fresh fruit and that La Blanca cooked with too much grease.

A few weeks later, I bumped into Alfredo on his way to early Mass at La Profesa. He told me all about the fresh fruit. I pointed out that La Blanca's menu offered papaya and melon, pineapple and bananas. The house yogurt was the best in town. Don Alfredo took me up on it and returned to the counter for breakfast.

If the truth be told, Alfredo's hiatus had less to do with fresh fruit than the fact that one of his customers was looking for him. Something about a watch.

"Buenos días, compañero Alfredo."

"Buenos días, Señor Juan. *How did you wake up this morning?" I told him about my new book,* El Monstruo, *and Alfredo agreed to an exclusive interview. This is his story.*

"I was born in La Villa near the Basílica. I was half an orphan and never knew my father. Our circumstances were humble and my mother and two sisters had many needs. I had to abandon school when I was 12 and got a job watching cars in the market near the Basílica. I loved to watch the processions of the pilgrims. They would carry colorful banners of the Holy Virgin and always hired Mariachis to accompany them. They seemed so happy.

"But I have to confess to you that I doubted the Miracle of the Guadalupana. I didn't believe in the tilma. I think she was an invention of the Gachupines. The Españoles invented Her to dominate us and take away our religion."

"But Alfredo, you still go to Mass. . . . "

"Well, yes, I do. Just in case.

"My first real job was at an insurance company in the Torre Latinoamericana. You looked down on the whole city and you felt so above it all. But when I came down for lunch or at night, the streets would be swarming with people and it was if I had returned to earth.

"I always liked gold and watches and I started hanging around the jewelry stores in the Zócalo. The Monte de Piedad [national pawnshop] has *the best selection. I began to buy and sell small items and pretty soon I had regular clients and it became my business. But I was not like those coyotes that stand around Monte de Piedad and try to trick you into buying your pawn ticket. Those fellows are low class. I appraise fine jewelry and watches and buy them for a good price and sell them for more.*

"My clients have money. I can go to Polanco or Lomas and sell a piece. The Jews are the toughest bargainers. They set a price and they refuse to budge. I suppose that's how they got so rich. But I have poor customers too— the poor have always put their little money into gold to protect them against the devaluation of the Mexican peso.

"A Rolex Daytona series chronometer, 18 karats, I can sell for 60,000 pesos. I can show you one if you wish. It is a very slender watch. Paul Newman had one that was valued at 450,000 U.S. dollars. But Rolexes are not the best watches. For me, the Patek Philippe, a fine Swiss watch, is the maximum expression of watchmaking. You can't get one for less than a million pesos. Only collectors will have them. The Piaget is another terrific Swiss watch.

"I have never knowingly bought or sold a stolen watch. My reputation is worth more than that. I make it a point to stay away from Tepito—it's my taboo. Have you ever heard of the Rolex gang? They would stand in traffic with a gun and force drivers to hand over their watches. Sure, you can get a cheap Swiss watch in Tepito, but I would advise you not to go looking for trouble.

"I call myself a gambusino, *an urban gambusino, a gold miner in the metropolis. Gambusinos look for gold in natural places, in rivers and in old mines. My mine is the city—you can find gold in the Monte de Piedad and on the streets in certain districts. You never know where you will encounter gold in this city.*

"Bueno amigo John, I have to go. I have a customer waiting for me in Ecatepec. I think it will be a good outcome. Buen provecho *and have a nice day."*

"Igualmente, Don Alfredo."

EL MAXIMATO

The shadow of the Caudillo so shrouded the Obregón hit that the Jefe Máximo abandoned any intention of serving out the dead president-elect's term. Instead Calles would appoint four proxies over the next five years to manage the presidency, but there was never any question as to who was running the show. While his puppets dispatched the orders from the National Palace, the Maximum Chief continued to rule from a large stucco California-style home on a corner lot in the Colonia Anzures. The real power during the Maximato, as this dark episode in Mexican politics is dubbed, belonged to the man "who lived in front."

Interior Minister Emilio Portes Gil, a member of El Turco's inner sanctum, was appointed interim president and charged with conducting the nation's affairs for the next 14 months while re-do elections were arranged. Portes Gil was a cautious man, fine-tuned to the whims of his boss, who by 1928 was veering sharply to the right.

"THE GREAT PARTY OF THE NATIONAL REVOLUTION"

In September, Calles delivered his final Informe, or State of the Union message, to a joint session of Congress and called for the formation of a state party, the Party of the National Revolution (PNR), an initiative that would stamp the Jefe Máximo's political legacy.

The time of the Caudillo was done with, the Caudillo concluded. Now the country needed to build institutions. The institution Calles proposed was a big tent party that would draw from all political expressions—in 1928, Krauze estimates, 8,000 regional parties and political associations crowded the landscape. Calles was not an inclusive man by nature, but he had few options short of killing all the regional *caciques* who had designs on state power, a strategy that would only invite fresh civil war.

The Maximum Chief's proposal for the formation of what *Time* magazine's overwrought correspondent always referred to as "The Great Party of the National Revolution" was received with spirited applause. One of the most enthusiastic endorsers was new U.S. ambassador Dwight Morrow, the dour Sheffield's replacement, who had so endeared himself to Calles by facilitating an end to the Cristero mess that the Jefe Máximo had forgotten all about who owned the oil fields. In a flagrant breach of diplomatic etiquette, Morrow rose from his seat in the official guest section of the Chamber of Deputies to lead the cheers for the new party, "an explicit signal that Washington would totally support Mexican authoritarianism," writes historian Sergio Aguayo of the occasion.

No matter what the initials of the state party would be—PNR, PRM, and ultimately PRI—the United States would look favorably on one-party rule south of the border for the next seven decades, the longest-running political dynasty in the known universe.

FILM NOIR

The film noir that colored political life in the capital grew more noir-ish with each shift in the name tags at the top. Calles, who developed an affinity for fascism on a presidential junket through Germany, had turned violently anti-Communist and anti-Semitic; Portes Gil, attuned to the Maximum Chief's moods, followed right behind. The newly arrived Soviet ambassador to Mexico was welcomed with a deportation order. Suspicious foreigners were tailed everywhere in the city by government agents.

By the late 1920s, Mexico City had become a nexus for Latin American political exiles and the internationalist ferment percolated in the cafés and cantinas of the Centro. Among them were César Augusto Sandino, the leader of the Nicaraguan resistance to United Fruit's hegemony, who sought asylum here after the U.S. Marines put a price on his head, and Julio Antonio Mella, the fiery Cuban student leader who had fled the island after dictator Gerardo Machado issued orders for his detention.

Mella and Tina Modotti were both on staff at *El Machete*. They had first met at Mexico City rallies in support of the doomed anarchists Sacco and Vanzetti—who themselves had spent a year in Mexico on the lam from Wilson's World War I conscription.

Julio Antonio, who chaired the "internationalist" section of the Cuban Communist Party, was a striking young man, a hypnotic speaker and natural leader, and he and Modotti were soon living together at the Zamora Apartments on Abraham González Street near the Secretariat of the Interior. Modotti, the consummate revolutionary tourist, was planning to relocate from Mexico to the Soviet Union.

On the night of January 10, 1929, Modotti left work at the *Machete* offices on Mesones and joined Mella and an unidentified Cuban in a café on the corner of Isabel la Católica and República de El Salvador, close by the Hotel Isabel. The threesome moved on to La India bar one block west on Bolívar where after a few rounds, the unidentified Cubano suddenly remembered he had other business to attend to. Tina and Julio Antonio decided to brave the frigid night air and walk the

10 blocks back to their apartment. The time was approximately 1:30 in the morning.

Twenty minutes later, on the corner of Abraham González and Morales streets, a pair of shots burst out and Mella fell mortally wounded to the pavement. When the police arrived, Modotti gave them a false name but newspaper reporters recognized her and questioned her closely. "Sensational Crime! American Implicated!" *El Universal* headlined in big bold accusatory type the morning after.

Modotti was held at the police barracks on Victoria Street as a material witness until Rivera magically appeared and paid her bail. Tina was warned not to leave the country until the investigation had run its course.

Somehow Rivera arranged for Mella's corpse to be released to his custody, and the young revolutionary was mourned at an in-house wake at the *Machete* offices on Mesones Street. The next day, Diego and his comrades hoisted up the coffin, swathed in a red flag, and marched down Isabel la Católica Street—passing right under my balcony—and through the Centro Histórico down Reforma all the way to the Dolores Cemetery in a distant corner of Chapultepec Park. Julio Antonio Mella was laid to rest with a rousing chorus of the Internationale.

Whodunnit?

The dictator Machado and his agent(s) in Mexico (i.e., the Cuban Modotti refused to identify) were the number one suspects for the job. But they were not the only applicants. The Cuban Communist Party had not been happy with Mella's "Internationalist" section. Rivera himself had just returned from Cuba. Mella's alleged interest in Leon Trotsky had stirred irritation in PCM circles.

The scandal sheets hinted that the killing had been a crime of passion. Vittorio Vidale, a Stalinist hit man who was smitten with La Modotti, is sometimes mentioned as a possible third party. So was El Sapo, who had seduced young Modotti and in whose murals she sometimes appeared.

Curiously, the only solid evidence of a love triangle—or rectangle as the case may be—is a Rivera panel, "In the Ciudadela," on the third tier of the second patio of the Secretariat of Public Education on Argentina Street. In the right-hand corner facing the mural, Modotti is depicted holding a gun belt and gazing adoringly upward at a beatific Mella. Behind Mella and to his left is a sinister, stubbly-faced figure in a black fedora, Vittorio Vidale, staring balefully at the back of Mella's skull.

Just as curious is the date of the panel—1929—when virtually every fresco of the more than 120 that adorn the walls of the SEP were finished in 1928. Was Rivera working from real life?

A year later, Modotti was again dragged through the mud. Tina, who had just concluded her "first revolutionary photography exhibit" across the street at the National Library, was "invited"—in the wake of an assassination attempt on newly inaugurated president Ortiz Rubio—to leave Mexico under the provisions of Article 33, which orders the deportation of "inconvenient" foreigners. Hounded by the Mexican secret service, she went into hiding. With the help of Vidale, Tina made her way to the Soviet Union. Having safely reached Moscow, she threw her camera in the river and never took another picture again, throwing herself into Stalin's service and running Soviet relief efforts in heroic Spain. After the Spanish Civil War ended in calamity, Modotti and Vidale were allowed to return to Mexico, where, in February 1942, Tina died of congestive heart failure after stepping into a cab downstairs on Isabel la Católica Street. Rivera accused Vidale of killing her.

SEEING RED

Calles's red hunters kept the commies on the run throughout the Maximato. Wracked by schisms, the party purged troublemakers like Rivera for multiple deviations. When El Sapo heard that he had been expunged, he wrecked the Mesones Street offices and took an ax to the press that cranked out *El Machete*. Later, the painter would be re-admitted and re-expelled, this time for making eyes at Stalin's nemesis Trotsky.

The PCM was forced underground in 1930 after the murder of 17 militants during a labor riot, emerging briefly on November 7, 1931, when cadre seized the microphones of Radio Station XEW, "The Voice of Latin America from Mexico," then broadcasting from the balcony of the Olympic Theater on 16th of September Avenue, to send out birthday greetings to their Soviet comrades.

But Calles's crackdown cost the party dearly. In 1929 José Revueltas, still a boy, and 31 other militants were sent to the Islas Marías, Mexico's Robben Island, where Revueltas would write his stunning prison memoir *Walls of Water*. With his billy-goat beard and Coke-bottle glasses, Pepe Revueltas was a seminal figure on the Mexican Left. Expelled by the PCM and the Popular Socialists, both of which he had helped found, Revueltas was a hard-drinking iconoclast who did not fit in any ideological pigeonhole. The Díaz Ordaz government would accuse him of being the "intellectual author" of the 1968 student strike that ended in massacre and cage him up in Lecumberri, his final stretch in the clink. Broke but unbroken, Pepe sucked down his final Faro in 1976, the year the Black Palace was closed down.

THE COSMIC CANDIDATE

The presidential elections of 1929 were the first to be orchestrated by the PNR and they set the style for generations to come. El Jefe Máximo's boy was Pascual "El Nopalito" Ortiz Rubio, former governor of Michoacán. In the opposite corner was José Vasconcelos, Obregón's education secretary, who had provided Rivera with the necessary walls.

By 1929, Vasconcelos had grown disillusioned with the Revolution, which he labeled "a spectacular tragedy," and the interminable stream of caudillos that ran it like a family business ("the Revolutionary Family") disgusted him. During Calles's onerous regime, Vasconcelos's *La Raza Cósmica* (The Cosmic Race, 1925), an embarrassingly racist tract that defined the Mexican Raza as the fusion of the indigenous and the European with heavy emphasis on the European side of the equation, earned him a following with rightist intellectuals.

Vasconcelos's politics bordered on the mystical, and he pandered to the bourgeois elite, intellectuals and bankers like Manuel Gómez Morín. Society women thought him a matinee idol. As a former rector of the National University, Vasconcelos had the overwhelming support of its privileged students—a base Calles tried to undercut by ordering Portes Gil to grant the university its long-sought autonomy.

Vasconcelos's meetings were cultist events, often accompanied by a piano recital and the singing of the Vasconcelos Hymn. Calles and the other Sonorans were the butt of his jabs. "If you are an animal/ Vote for Pascual/ But if your ideas are true/ Vote for Vasconcelos," one jingle rang. Mexican civilization ended where the meat-eaters began, the candidate sneered, a not-so-veiled reference to Calles's Sonora, a leading cattle-producing state.

After the meetings, Vasconcelos's brain trust would gather in the Chinese cafés around Dolores Street, Mexico City's one-block Chinatown, where the restaurants were plastered with Vasconcelos signs—until Luis Morones's boys started breaking windows.

The Cosmic Candidate kicked off his campaign in the capital with a big rally in Santo Domingo Plaza in the heart of the university district, the exact place where the first Mexicas had spotted the first Eagle devouring the first Snake in the arms of the first nopal cactus bush. Vasconcelos cast himself as the new Quetzalcóatl come to save the Raza Cósmica from the evil *caudillos*.

The trouble began after the rally. Two Vasconcelos supporters were cut down by Calles's fascoid "Gold Shirts" on Topilejo Street in the Merced. A third, Germán del Campo, was killed at a meeting in the university district. Vasconcelos's rallies were sprayed by machine-gun fire and he was attacked viciously in the press ("his only supporters are homosexuals, the bourgeoisie, and feminists").

In July, boosted by wholesale ballot-box stuffing, Ortiz Rubio won the election with 99 percent of the vote. A crushed Vasconcelos emulated his maestro Madero and called upon his compatriots to start the revolution all over again, but the country wasn't really all that interested in yet more bloodshed. Disillusioned, Vasconcelos sought self-exile in the United States.

The cosmic candidate's 1929 campaign was in many ways a dress rehearsal for the founding of the National Action or PAN party 10 years later—Gómez Morín and many of the same players would be involved. But more pertinently, '29 was a trial run for the political juggernaut that would eventually become known as the PRI, whose domination of Mexico's electoral machinery would soon be the envy of the continent's dictators.

NOT DEAD YET

By February 1930, Mexico City was in the throes of a political gang war. On the 5th, Ortiz Rubio was inaugurated at the National Stadium in the Colonia Roma, his speech carried to the nation on the golden waves of XEW for the first time ever. From the Roma, the new president drove back to the National Palace for the traditional *balconazo*. No one had taken a shot at him yet.

Upon leaving the palace, Ortiz Rubio's wife called to him to ride with her, but he declined because he feared he would be a target in an open-top car and instead jumped into the passenger seat of a covered Ford sedan. Young Daniel Flores shadowed the car for a block before he plugged the new president. Ortiz Rubio was critically wounded but survived the assassination attempt. Flores was portrayed as a stereotypical Catholic nutcase à la Toral. He was found murdered in his cell at Lecumberri a year later.

MARTES NEGRO

Black Tuesday, October 24, 1929, stimulated mild curiosity on Mexico City's own dysfunctional Bolsa de Valores. "Tremendous Panic in NY Stock Market—Thousands Ruined!" *El Universal* commiserated. "Haggard investors scan the ticker," reads the photo caption on the English-language page. While Wall Street brokers swan-dived from the upper stories of lower Manhattan, an anonymous financial wizard told *Universal* that the Crash would have little impact on Mexico because its money markets had been in the toilet for 15 years.

But of course the forecast proved overly rosy.

U.S. corporations doing business in Mexico stopped doing business. North American insurance companies with huge holdings in Mexican financial institutions went belly-up. Trade decreased by two-thirds—65 percent of Mexico's exports were destined for a moribund U.S. market. By 1932, half the Mexican workforce wasn't working.

Meanwhile, as jobs dried up in the United States, undocumented workers were rounded up by U.S. Labor Department agents and shipped back to the border in cattle cars. Perhaps a million Mexicans were forcibly repatriated between 1929 and 1935. Mexico could not provide for the returnees, many of whom had spent decades working on The Other Side and no longer thought they were Mexicans.

Times were tough and getting tougher. Even the cribs on Cuauhtimotzin Street in Tepito were full of empty beds, and the *putas* were singing the blues. Unlike their counterparts in the north, Mexican bankers did not throw themselves out of skyscraper windows, only because there were no skyscrapers—even in the Centro, the tallest buildings were only six to eight stories, and the rest of the city operated at street level.

Ambassador Morrow, a former Wall Streeter himself, negotiated a rescheduling of Mexico's foreign debt, but even with a diminished burden Ortiz Rubio could not meet his obligations without taking bread out of the mouth of Mexico's hungry, and he suspended payments. Calles, who spent most of his days in Cuernavaca playing cards with his *compinche* Morones, was incredulous. Morrow was a trusted colleague and Ortiz Rubio's failure to pay up discredited Mexico's honor. The Jefe Máximo started making noises about forcibly removing the president from the National Palace. Before the dispute evolved into a military coup, Ortiz Rubio stepped down.

A third flunky, Abelardo Rodríguez, the only Mexican president ever to have been born in the United States (Arizona), was appointed to fill out Ortiz Rubio's term until the 1934 elections came round. The Mexican Revolution, like the Mexican economy, had hit rock bottom.

VIII

CITY & COUNTRY

O nce in my largely misspent youth, I signed up on a volunteer crew installing drinking water systems in the Meseta Purépecha in the mountains of the western central state of Michoacán. It was backbreaking work but the job had its rewards. In the spring of 1961, ex-president Lázaro Cárdenas, whom the Purépechas always spoke of as the "Tata" (father), visited the high mountain town of Santa Cruz Tanaco to inaugurate one of our systems. The moment was a festive one. After the Tata had turned over a few shovelfuls of dirt to cover the new pipes that would bring the *itzu* (water) to Tanaco, lunch was served.

The farmers had sacrificed a sheep in Tata Lázaro's honor and the *barbacoa* smelled terrific. Someone brought the former president a plate, and a big chair was dragged out of the town hall to accommodate him. But Lázaro would not sit in it. Instead, he squatted on the ground with the Indians so he could better hear what they had to tell him.

Lázaro Cárdenas was no longer president and he could do little about the miserable price they were getting for their corn or the wood poachers who were devastating their forests, but he was a fine listener. The Purépechas filled up his big ears for hours with their stories of flagrant exploitation and injustice. Their trust was poignant.

My friend Santiago Bravo, a frontline defender of Tanaco's forests, would travel up to the Monstruo upon occasion to ask the ex-president's counsel. The capital made little sense to Santiago. The traffic intimidated him and public transit was a puzzle he could never solve. But he knew the route to Lázaro's large house on Andes Street in the posh *colonia* Lomas de Chapultepec, where he would await his turn in the outside patio with dozens of other campesinos from all over Mexico who had come up to Mexico City to tell the Tata their troubles. No Mexican president before or since has matched Lázaro Cárdenas's rapport with the people he governed.

TATA LÁZARO'S BIG EARS

But back in 1933, Cárdenas's curriculum vitae did not look so historic. As Calles's fourth-in-line flunky he was expected to follow the dictates of "the man who lived in front." Like many Revolutionary generals once the fighting had ended, Cárdenas, a mestizo from Michoacán, accumulated political power, serving as both governor and senator from his home state.

During the heady days of the Revolution, young Lázaro had ridden with Calles in the genocidal campaign against the Yaquis, driven off Villa at Agua Prieta, and been active in Morelos against Zapata. Militarily the Jefe Máximo's second in command, Lázaro Cárdenas was expected to follow orders. So when Calles pointed the big finger at him, designating Lázaro as Abelardo Rodríguez's replacement, he silently complied.

Under the rules of the game as designed by Calles and the PNR, Cárdenas was assured of the presidency. Although he had no announced opposition, Lázaro set out to listen to those he would soon govern, and the journey changed the course of Mexican history and rescued the Revolution.

For seven months, the Tata traveled from border to border and coast to coast on trains and single-engine planes, in motorcars and open trucks and a few times on a three-wheeled motorcycle. He clocked hundreds of miles in canoes and on foot. He rode horseback over the hump of the isthmus through the Mixtec mountains of Oaxaca. In all, Cárdenas traveled 55,000 miles to the remotest sierras and most distant deserts to listen to the poorest Mexicans in the land. This remarkable journey shaped Lázaro Cárdenas's presidency and altered the body politic of the nation in ways from which it has still not quite recovered.

Fifty-five years after this epic adventure, I would accompany the son of the Tata, Cuauhtémoc Cárdenas, in his own quest for the presidency of Mexico. Everywhere we traveled on a route that replicated his father's journey, the old-timers would speak about the time Lázaro had visited—they often knew the exact date—and reached out to the son to touch his hand. And wherever we meandered through 31 states and the Federal District, Cuauhtémoc carried with him his father's notes from the 1933 campaign.

MEIN KAMPF

Lázaro Cárdenas and Franklin Delano Roosevelt were Depression presidents. They shared a hard time and it enhanced them both. Perhaps no two U.S. and Mexican presidents, with the exception of Lincoln and Juárez, had ever been on the same wavelength.

Much as in Roosevelt's USA, where union organizing and working-class struggle challenged big capital on every front, from auto manufacturing to ocean liners, Cárdenas was immediately confronted with intense labor unrest—642 strikes troubled the waters in 1936–1937 alone. Striking electricity workers, garbage men, teachers, tram drivers, and telephone workers put a big hurt on the Monstruo. The telephone strike, which tied up service for three months, particularly irritated the pashas of industry and commerce.

Up in Cuernavaca, Jefe Máximo Calles took up their cause and commanded Lázaro to crush the strikers. But no strikebreakers were called in and no strike-ending injunctions were sought, and President Cárdenas declined to intervene. Despite Calles's threat to dislodge him, Lázaro could not be moved. Labor's power had to be balanced off against that of the bosses, he argued. The president's role was as a rector between the social classes, to blunt the inequities between them, a dangerously Bolshevik hypothesis.

Calles and Morones only grew more shrill. By April 1935, Lázaro Cárdenas had had enough and dispatched the presidential military group under his command up to Cuernavaca to roust the Jefe Máximo from a sound sleep and put both him and his sidekick Morones on the first plane to California. Calles flew into exile in his pajamas, clutching a copy of Hitler's *Mein Kampf*.

OUT OF TOWN

Now free to govern the country as he saw fit, Lázaro moved out of Chapultepec Castle with its lofty vistas of the city, from whose roost Maximilian and Carlota once ruled, and established the presidential residence closer to the ground, at Los Pinos on the southwest fringe of the great park—but he didn't really sleep there all that much.

Like Emiliano Zapata, Lázaro Cárdenas shared the vision that Mexico City was not really the country that takes its name. In the six years of his presidency, Tata Lázaro would spend a third of his time away from the capital, out in the countryside consorting with campesinos at the expense of the city.

The resumption of Zapata's *reparto*—the distribution of arable land to the landless—that had been suspended by Obregón, was Cárdenas's driving concern in his first two years in office. Between 1936 and late 1937, Cárdenas would hand out 50,000,000 acres to poor farmers. At the beginning of the Revolution in 1910, only 2 percent of all Mexicans possessed the land. When Cárdenas was done, a third of the people were landowners, and the Mexican Revolution in whose name so much campesino blood had been drained, finally began to make sense.

PROLETARIAN CITY

In the cities, Lázaro's leftist slant was assailed by those who still clung to their old Gachupín-criollo convictions. For the Church and the moneyed classes, the Dictatorship of the Proletariat was practically on the doorstep. Some historians claim that the attentions Tata Lázaro lavished on the countryside alienated Mexico City dwellers, but for the masses of the Monstruo the reparto reinforced a connection. Urban as the metropolis is, its denizens are only a generation or two removed from the countryside. No matter what *colonia* of the Monster they now reside in, Santa Cruz Tanaco or Juchitán, Oaxaca, or Tehuacán, Puebla, remain their *patria chica* or "little fatherland."

The ties of the urban proletariat to the agrarian lives of their grandfathers are still firm ones in Chilangolandia. In 2007, a group of "ecological campesinos" whose slogan is *No Hay País Sin Maíz* (We Have No Country Without Corn) began sowing *maíz* in the planter boxes outside the big hotels in the Centro and down Reforma Boulevard. As the spindly stalks sprouted new cobs (*elotes*), Chilangos would stop and gently stroke the new corn and even talk to it. If you look deep enough, inside every Chilango you will find a campesino.

Lázaro Cárdenas's presidency forged a unity of purpose between city and country that has never really been replicated. The Monstruo was (and still is) Cardenista territory. Working people filled out the marches and rallies and spread the word at Red Saturday Nights at Bellas Artes. In 1934, the Mexican Communist Party (PCM) came out of hiding and, finding the Left in power, lined up with Lázaro, joined his administration, and flourished. By the time Cárdenas left office in 1940, the PCM had a whopping 30,000 members on the books, but its ranks shrank abruptly when Rivera prevailed upon the president to grant asylum from Stalin's hit squads to Leon Trotsky.

During Cárdenas's six-year term, the Monster's population finally topped a million—1,229,576 living in 14 delegations and 71 *colonias* in 1940. How to house the new Chilangos was a challenge. With a decaying housing stock that counted little more than half a million units, the workers lived cheek by jowl in the center and east of the city, where the population density was 7,490 residents per square kilometer. The Other Half lived out in spacious Lomas or Polanco, islands of wealth surrounded by a sea of poverty.

Nine out of every 10 Chilangos were renters, and the tenants' movement was formidable. But when tenants organized rent strikes, landlords responded by calling a tax strike. The result was that the city lost revenue and no new housing was being built. The Cardenista city government circumvented this standoff by investing in public housing.

"The poor and the working class must have housing, not just as a criterion of civilization but as a natural right. New housing will be small but hygienic, and comfortable enough for workers to enjoy their families in an atmosphere of tranquility," the Department of the Federal District declared in 1935. "We recognize that the Revolution is not complete while our poor and working-class citizens continue to live in an infrahuman manner."

In 1936, Mexico City created its first planning commission, zoning the metropolitan area for residential, commercial, and industrial use. Urban sprawl had been so relentless that the capital's green space was drying up. The once extensive forest of Coyoacán, Los Viveros, was now entirely hemmed in by concrete, and auto emissions were browning the leaves.

The number of vehicles in the capital almost doubled between 1930 and 1940, from 19,000 to 35,000 fume-spewing motorcars. Streets were widened to accommodate the thickening flow. San Juan de Letrán became a central artery and Tlalpan Avenue was broadened to ease the traffic flow in and out of the city.

By the 1930s, the Mexican highway system had begun to tie the city and the country in a tighter knot. Fleets of buses plied routes between the Monstruo and the provinces. Long-distance phone service narrowed the space between the farm and the capital. So did the airwaves.

NOCHES CHILANGAS

XEW was the flagship station of the Azcárraga clan. Like Tenochtitlán, XEW started small. Soon-to-be communications tycoon Emilio Azcárraga Milmo's mom sewed the curtains for the station's 50,000-watt studios on Ayuntamiento Street near the Balderas newspaper row.

Among the station's early luminaries were the romantic crooner Agustín Lara, "El Flaco" (The Thin Man); "El Charro Cantor" (The Cowboy Singer) Jorge Negrete; and Francisco Gabilondo, the immortal "Cri-Cri" whose kids' songs remain just as viable today among the kindergarten set. I just heard a vendor hawking Cri-Cri DVDs on the metro this morning.

Each program day began and ended with the Mexico City Typical Police Orchestra intoning the National Anthem. Poets Xavier Villaurrutia and Salvador Novo wrote jingles for XEW. When Azcárraga discovered there weren't enough radios in Mexico to bring his sponsors' messages to the public, he began manufacturing radios and selling them on the installment plan.

But although XEW wedded the Monstruo with the country, its metropolitan megalomania heavily favored the Big City. Even today, Azcárraga Inc., now doing business as Televisa—the most colossal communications conglomerate in Latin America, with near dictatorial powers in Mexico—broadcasts Mexico City traffic and weather reports to the far reaches of the nation as if Coahuila or the Yucatán really cared about traffic delays on the Periférico.

As the stars flocked to the golden microphones of XEW, cafés and nightspots thrumming with artists and their groupies sprang up on surrounding streets. Novo and his circle held forth at the old Café Paris on Cinco de Mayo, now the Café Pagoda where I eat *comida corrida* maybe thrice a week in one of the old leather booths from which no doubt Chilango bards once rhapsodized. El Nivel, a bar scratched into the Moneda Street wall of the National Palace, was El Flaco Lara's favorite watering hole. On the streets of the Centro, organ grinders whose horribly out-of-tune *cilindrinos* were a relic from Porfirio's Centennial, cranked out nostalgic melodies.

The capital's café society spread past the inner city. Rivera and Kahlo set the pace for the cultural life of San Ángel and Coyoacán. The art deco Frontón (jai alai arena) on one side of the new equally art deco Monument of the Revolution drew throngs of gamblers. Tango parlors, reanimated by the martyrdom of Carlos Gardel, added international flavor to the Chilango nights.

¡NO PASARÁN!

The Spanish Civil War exploded two weeks after the infamous 1936 Berlin Olympics (Hitler had given Franco the go-ahead at the Games) and Madrid was under siege from the Generalísimo's Mongols. On the Mexican side of the water, the Loyalist cause was championed in Proletarian City and Mexicans joined the International Brigades— Siqueiros returned a captain and Modotti ran the Reds' Red Cross. With Franco's hordes at the gates of the Spanish capital, President Cárdenas ordered that supplies be shipped to the heroic defenders of the city. The Cárdenas government was one of the few that sent arms to the loyalist government. *¡No Pasarán!*

In 1937, Tata Lázaro opened Mexico's doors to refugees from Franco's terror, and 30,000 Spanish Republicans found sanctuary on Mexican shores. Five hundred orphans, "Los Niños de Morelia," were personally adopted by the president and farmed out to families in Michoacán. Refugee families settled in the capital and eventually went into business and grew new roots. Today, restaurants all over the Centro Histórico like La Blanca offer *fabada* and *caldo gallego* and *paella* on their daily menus.

But Cárdenas's right-wing opposition, including many of Gachupín ancestry who sided with Franco, was not happy with the newcomers, whom they labeled "communist infiltrators." For the rightists, their arrival only confirmed Cárdenas's intentions to establish the Dictatorship of the Proletariat.

"TOO MANY EMPTY SEATS" (An interview with Don Raimundo Vargas)

"I was born in the state of Mexico in 1933. My jefe [father] was a campesino and a revolutionary of the white calzón [peasant pants]—that is, he was a Zapatista. He fought for the land and for freedom. But we never got any land.

"We came to the city in 1937 when Lázaro Cárdenas was the president. As you know from history, Cárdenas expropriated the oil from the Gachupines and he asked the common people to go to Bellas Artes and donate a peso or what they could. We were very, very poor, but my father was only too glad to give for the Mexican cause. He always said that Lázaro Cárdenas fought for the good of the pueblo.

"My jefe was a jornalero [day laborer] and he worked in the obra [construction project] in Polanco and the Cuauhtémoc building homes for the ricos. He worked in the University City and helped build the rectory and the swimming pool for the 1954 Pan American Games. I had three sisters and one other brother, and my father would take us on the streetcar to show us what he had built. He was proud of his work.

"We lived in the Santa María Ribera. It was a colonia for the rich but there were poor families there in the vecindades. We lived in one room— there were seven of us. There was a shower in the patio with a sheet of plastic around it. The water came out when you pulled a chain. Naturally, it was only cold water.

"I went to school on Marina Nacional where the PEMEX [national oil company] is now. I was good at baseball. I had a curve ball that the catcher could not catch. It was during the war and there was a lot of work in the factories. Our team was sponsored by the Águila Tire Company and we played in Williams Park near the Euskadi tire factory. We were part of the Industrial League. I left school in the sixth year but continued to pitch for the Águilas for 23 years.

"I went to work with my father in construction. I was only 17 when I got married to a girl who lived in the same vecindad. I still have the same señora and we still live in Santa María Ribera, although in a much bigger place. Later, I went to work with the Filter Queen. They sell auto parts. I had a little *scooter and I went up and down Tlalpan delivering them. After 43 years I retired and gave them the scooter back.*

"I voted for the PRI every year. Alemán was my best president. When Uruchurtu was the regent, the city was like Paris. Those were my golden days. I saw Cantinflas in the carpa *that was at Arcos de Belén. There were great singers then. Pedro Vargas and Pedro Infante had shows on XEW. They were the idols of the people. I remember seeing Pedro Infante and María Félix in* Todos Los Pobres *at the Ciné Latino on Reforma. The values of the* pueblo *were just much better then. There just wasn't so much corruption.*

"Gustavo Díaz Ordaz ruined the city. Mexico City began to fall apart after 1968 when the students were killed in Tlatelolco. I just stopped voting for the PRI after that, but now I go with El Peje.

"I remember the first time I ate at La Blanca. I looked in the window. I only had 20 pesos for the whole week and I thought I couldn't afford it. But I came in anyway and ordered a café con leche *and a* concha *[a type of sweet bread] and it only cost me five pesos. So I started to come in every day. That was in 1978. I only have missed one day since, when we had the earthquake. But a lot of the customers have passed on. There are too many empty seats here now."*

"PRESIDENT CÁRDENAS! GENERAL OF THE AMERICAS!"

Mexico's oil continued to muddy the diplomatic waters. Although worldwide depression had greatly reduced the flow from Mexico, the Seven Sisters had hundreds of millions of Yanqui dollars invested in the Caribbean coast oil fields whose ownership they continued to insist had been awarded to them in perpetuity.

Then in 1936, oil workers unionized and went out on strike for a living wage, but the oil companies wouldn't budge. The dispute went to arbitration and Mexico's labor court awarded the workers 26,000,000 pesos in unpaid wages. "We won't pay, we can't pay," the magnates responded, pleading poverty.

Two years elapsed while the judgment was appealed to higher tribunals. Finally, in March 1938, Mexico's Supreme Court found the oil companies to be in contempt. A showdown loomed.

March 18 did not begin as a history-making day. Holy Week was coming up and Chilangos traditionally abandon the sweltering city for the beach. Lupe Vélez, "The Mexican Spitfire," was starring in *Sandunga* at the Alameda Cinema. In News of the World, the International

Brigades were pulling out of Teruel as Franco's dark legions pushed across the Elba. I was seven days old.

At 10 o'clock that evening, President Lázaro Cárdenas spoke to the nation from the National Palace via the transmitters of XEW. Millions gathered around their radios as the president's words crackled through the ether: "Tonight I speak to our *pueblo*. I want to talk about our petroleum but even more about our dignity, the dignity of Mexico, which the foreigners make fun of." The refusal of the *extranjeros* to obey the judgments of Mexican courts left Lázaro no option but to suspend their concessions. Mexico's oil would belong to the nation from here on out. A state-run corporation would be framed to administer the industry.

Washington's response to the daring expropriation was cautious. World war was on the horizon and Roosevelt could not afford to drive Mexico into the arms of the Axis powers. Cárdenas had shrewdly divined that his Good Neighbor Roosevelt's hands were tied. Later he would confess to historian Frank Tannenbaum that expropriation had been a gamble and he was lucky to have had a Roosevelt in the White House. The Tata's defiance of the Seven Sisters stirred an outburst of national pride that transcended Mexico's borders. Farther south in Chile, poet Pablo Neruda hailed "President Cárdenas, General of the Americas."

LÁZARO'S PEOPLE

Working-class Chilangos celebrated the expropriation on Sunday the 23rd with a monster march and rally in the Zócalo. For five hours the President stood on the balcony of the Palace saluting the enormous outpouring of humanity that swelled below. Contingents of union members marched into the great plaza trundling coffins that bore the names of the Seven Sisters and waving banners demanding that Article 33 be applied to their representatives and the *extranjeros* kicked out of Mexico. The clothing workers had taken out a full-page ad in the morning *Universal* that encapsulated the mood: "INDEPENDENCE!" it read: "HIDALGO 1810. CÁRDENAS 1938." For once, the church bells pealed in solidarity with El Pueblo. A 15-meter-long banner hung from the Cathedral's façade demanding an end to "Capitalist Oppression."

How many workers pushed their way into the Zócalo and its surrounding streets that Sunday? Having spent the last 25 years of my life attending rallies in what is officially known as the "Plaza of the Constitution," I've earned an MBA in Zocalology. The entire space, including the plaza floor or *plancha*, the roadway that surrounds it, and the *portales* or covered area on the west and south side of the humongous space, measures 48,000 square meters. When six citizens are wedged into one square meter, they cannot raise their arms to wave or clap. In the newspaper photos of the event, those packed into the Zócalo on Sunday, March 23, to celebrate the expropriation of Mexican oil, have their arms pinned to their sides and are unable to clap. Yet despite the crush, the people, dressed in their Depression-era best, do not seem out of sorts. They lean into each other easily, as if they were family. All eyes are lasered in on the balcony where Lázaro is speaking. "There are no spectators here—everyone is a participant," *El Universal* observed.

"We Mexicans do not want something for nothing," the president affirmed. "We will pay our debts." Lázaro called for a national *colecta* to raise $350 million Yanqui dollars to indemnify the oil barons. He was confident that the goal would be achieved. "We are a generous people."

I read of these momentous events in a dimly lit chapel at the Lerdo de Tejada library just around the corner on Salvador Street. The pages of *El Universal* are yellowing and torn, some seamed together by paper tape. They have been turned by many hands, returned to many times by Lázaro's people, to marvel at this unique moment of national unity in a city and country that is so often fractured by race and class conflict.

LA COLECTA

The Colecta would be a lesson in national coalescence. The Bank of Mexico created an account to receive the citizens' donations. Every day, the newspapers ran lists of the donors. Many pledge to contribute a day's wages. Ángel Contreras brings 25 pesos *en efectivo* to the bank at the foot of the Alameda. The Senate kicks in 50,000 pesos. Adolfo and Felipe Peña, ages four and two, break open their piggy bank and donate 2 pesos and 71 centavos. The Panadería Calvin pledges 20 pesos, the indigenous teachers of Pequetzen in the Huasteca, a month's wages. The Masons make a substantial contribution. The "Colonia Israelita" (Jewish community) is generous. The Lebanese merchant

José Slim, whose son Carlos is now the world's richest tycoon, kicks in 5,000 pesos. Ángel Armenta, working in Chatsworth, California, mails in one American dollar. Another *bracero*, Vidal Rábago of San Francisco, is good for $100 USD. The prisoners of the Lecumberri Black Palace send 49 pesos 15 centavos. Prisoners in the Morelia Penitentiary forgo food all day and pass along the food allocation.

Every evening, José Siurob, the chief of the Federal District Department, leads members of the "Committee for National Economic Redemption" in a torchlight march from the Theater of the People in the Abelardo Rodríguez public market through the barrios of the Centro collecting money and issuing *bonos*, shares in the new oil company.

A week into the Colecta, with similar drives sprouting up in provincial cities all over the country, Doña Amalia Solórzano, Lázaro's activist spouse, and her sisters in the *comité femenino* bring the crusade to Bellas Artes. The señoras from Coyoacán and San Ángel line up on the esplanade to contribute their jewelry. Petra González, 86, takes off her gold wedding ring, plunks it down on the counter, and collapses into Doña Amalia's arms in tears. A large Italian man barges through the line and hands over an expensive watch.

From 10 a.m. to 5 p.m. every day, the *amas de casa* (housewives) line up to donate their favorite kitchen knives and cooking pots. Nahua Indians from Tlalmanalco in Mexico state bring chickens and pigs, the merchants of La Merced, turkeys. One woman leaves her wedding gown, another a canary in a cage, still another a basket of eggs. This rare moment of national unity has never been repeated.

PARTY TIME

Riding the mood of the masses, President Cárdenas moved expeditiously in the political sphere to consolidate the national revolution. Two weeks later, at its national convention in Mexico City, Calles's state party, the Party of the National Revolution (PNR), was shapeshifted into the Party of the Mexican Revolution (PRM). Revolutionary nationalism would be the new/old party's ideology. Its structure was a sort of united front modeled on what the COMINTERN was then advancing to confront—the threat of fascism—indeed, U.S. Communist Party bigwig Earl Browder traveled to Mexico in 1937 to preach the politics of United Front.

The party Cárdenas envisioned would give equal weight to certain class-based constituencies: the "popular sector" (essentially government workers, but the term came to include small business and the middle class, renters and street vendors) and the urban and rural proletariat. Farmers' voices would be heard through the National Confederation of Campesinos (CNC). Unionized workers were spoken for by the Confederation of Mexican Labor (CTM) and the firebrand Marxist Vicente Lombardo Toledano, whom Cárdenas had substituted for the exiled Morones and his CROM, to voice the demands of the laboring classes.

Toledano's marathon speeches earned him the sobriquet of "Yo-Yo Man," so often did he use the first-person singular *yo*—one observer counted 64 *yo*'s in a single speech.

Such excesses of red rhetoric were an easy target for the actors and satirists who worked the neighborhood *carpas*, tent shows that moved from colonia to colonia providing cheap entertainment for the working class. Mario Moreno was a roustabout and sometimes comedian with the Carpa Ofelia, which often set up in Arcos de Belén near the old city jail. Moreno's character, Cantinflas, was a fast-talking *pelado* from the bottom bowge of Mexico's economic Hell who used his wit to foil the boss and win the girl and the esteem of his neighbors. The origin of his nickname was obscure but popular etymologists note that the word *cantina* is embedded in it.

One of Cantinflas's specialties was political double talk, manic parodies of the leftish *chorros* (endless streams) that so saturated the Cárdenas government's public pronouncements. Cantinflas's schtick took on a life of its own—*cantinflesco* describes the way the nation's politicians often babble.

In every presidential election from Cárdenas's day forward, thousands of ballots are cast with Cantinflas's name written in, as a protest against the mediocrity of the candidates posted by the ruling party and its surrogates.

PASSING THE BATON

In 1940, Cárdenas broke the skein of strongmen who resisted turning over power and handed off the baton to a designated successor. Lázaro, who was still a young man at 46, had a difficult decision before him. His inclinations were to keep the country on a leftward tilt but he sensed that if he pushed further left, the country could fracture. Unity was essential. World war was coming, and Mexico would inevitably be pulled in to protect Roosevelt's southern flank. Cárdenas's longtime comrade-in-arms Francisco Mujica, a left-wing general from Michoacán, was agitating for the job, but the Dedazo went to another revolutionary general, Manuel Ávila Camacho, a political personality so distinct from the anticleric Cárdenas that he even bragged about attending Mass.

The Right consolidated in anticipation of the 1940 presidential elections. The National Action Party or PAN was founded under the tutelage of Manuel Gómez Morín and other veterans of the failed Vasconcelos campaign (but not Vasconcelos) to challenge the "Bolshevik" aspirations of Cárdenas's followers, who in the eyes of the right wing sought to "sovietize" Mexico. More action-oriented than the stuffy PANistas were the Sinarquistas, fascist brownshirts who championed Adolph Hitler and the Nazification of Mexico. The archly Catholic, anti-Semitic Sinarquistas' roots were in the Cristero War.

The candidate of the Right, Division General Juan Andreu Almazán, a onetime Huertista and accomplished aviator, waged what many observers adjudged a winning campaign—he may even have won Mexico City, but we will never know. Despite Lázaro Cárdenas's democratic pretensions, Election Day, July 7, 1940—and every Election Day from now on—was 1910 and 1929 all over again. The official tally gave Ávila Camacho 2,000,000 votes to Almazán's 15,000. One of the latter votes was that of Diego Rivera, who saw "the mask of fascism" behind Cárdenas's mask of socialism.

Gangs of Morones clones roamed the city to keep Almazán's supporters from voting—a *casilla* (voting booth) in upscale Coyoacán was raked with Thompson machine-gun fire. The Almazanistas responded in kind. When PRM candidate Ávila Camacho went to his polling place to cast a ballot, all the election officials were wearing buttons advertising their support for his rival. After shots were fired into the casilla where Tata Lázaro intended to vote in the Los Pinos neighborhood, the then-president decided not to vote at all. Gunfights erupted around the Caballito in the traffic circle of Bucareli and Reforma and 30 were reported killed in postelectoral strife.

Whatever the final count was in the city, the PRM's questionable showing in the capital was a clear sign that the days of the proletarian city were numbered. On the final day Lázaro Cárdenas occupied the

National Palace, federal agents broke down the door at Mexican Communist Party headquarters during a central committee meeting and hauled a dozen Reds off to prison.

THE END OF THE LINE FOR LEON

The high walled *casona* off Río Churubusco Avenue is perfectly preserved. There are even hutches out in the garden where Trotsky fed his beloved bunnies. Inside the creaky old house, it is like he just died a month ago. An empty roll of toilet paper hangs askew by Trotsky's toilet, waiting for someone to replace it. In the office, before the world map where the Catalán Ramón Mercader (if that was really the name of the Stalinist agent) stabbed the ice ax into Trotsky's brain, the carpet looks like it has been freshly scrubbed of bloodstains.

Rivera had convinced Cárdenas to offer poor Lev Davidovich asylum in Mexico over the furious objections of the PCM who rejected Trotsky as a traitor. The Stalinoid Siqueiros confronted El Sapo, who had been readmitted to the party, and he was expelled again.

At first, the Riveras were only too pleased to have Mr. and Mrs. Trotsky as house guests, probably just to piss off Siqueiros, but when Leon proved a Sancho who was schtupping Frida on the side, Diego grew choleric and their little united front fell apart fast.

In 1939, the year of the Stalin-Hitler pact, the Trotskys moved over to the fortresslike home on Churubusco just a few blocks north of Frida's famed Blue House. The new lodgings proved pregnable. On May 23, Siqueiros and 20 assassins, reportedly including Vittorio Vidale, Modotti's lover, assaulted the premises with machine guns but failed to take out Trotsky. A young American disciple was killed and his body thrown out of a fast-moving car in the heavily forested Ajusco.

But Stalin was a persistent assassin. Mercader, posing as a Belgian writer, wormed his way into the old revolutionary's confidence and on August 20 plunged the *pitón*, a small hatchet used by mountain climbers on Popocatépetl, into the back of his head.

The assassination of Leon Trotsky, shaded as the picture was with colorful Reds, blazing artistic geniuses, and sleazy hangers-on, would have made a great mural, but somehow Rivera never got around to painting it.

IX

CITY OF MIRACLES
& HYPE

A cross the Rio Bravo, on December 7, 1941, one week after Manuel Ávila Camacho assumed the presidency of Mexico, millions gathered around their radios to bear witness to President Roosevelt's elegantly parsed indignation at the Japanese bombardment of Pearl Harbor. The United States retaliated forthwith, declaring world war on the Axis powers in Europe and the Pacific. Roosevelt's call for national unity against the evil enemies stirred even the hardest hearts to action.

Mexico signed up right away, rounding up its tiny Japanese community, mostly farmers along the Chiapas coast, and locking them down in a Mexico City immigration detention center in the Colonia Santa María Ribera, where they would spend the remainder of the war.

Yet Mexico did not immediately enter World War II. The resolution of indemnization payouts to U.S. oil companies for the expropriation of their properties was pending. Only when agreement was signed off in early 1942 to the tune of $365 million USD did Mexico commit. That May, following the sinking of the Mexican tanker *Potrero del Llano* by a German U-boat in the eastern Caribbean, the Aztec nation finally went to war.

UNCLE SAM WANTS YOU!

The North American Commission for Economic Cooperation, a precursor of NAFTA, was created in 1942, and Mexico committed to supplying the United States with much-needed war materials—copper for bombs and cables, graphite and bauxite for munitions stockpiles. Mexican oil would fuel the Yanqui war machine. Despite endemic hunger out in the countryside, Mexicans grew foodstuffs to feed the G.I.s, produced cotton for uniforms and leather for boots to shoe the troops. Mexican war posters show a map of the Aztec nation with a dozen arrows all pointing north. World War II was a turning point for the Mexican economy. Whereas the United States bought 65 percent of all Mexico's exports prior to Pearl Harbor, now trade was up to 90 percent.

Mexico City was a strategic rail center for shipping raw materials and manufactured goods north to the border or down to Veracruz for sea transport to the United States. Factories and warehouses were clustered in the north of the city in what eventually would become the Vallejo industrial park. Spurred on by the war effort, between 1940 and 1945 the number of industrial operations in the Mexican capital zoomed 230 percent—at the end of World War II, the city was host to 9,974 factories, over 6,000 more than in 1940.

The industrial plant was zoned by sectors: Manufacturing was concentrated in the northwest corner of the city and factories that emitted noxious vapors and foul-smelling chemicals were confined to the northeast. Farther east, extending into Mexico state, were the brick works. Sand was mined in Tacubaya and Cuajimalpa in the southwest. Construction materials, cement and gypsum, were manufactured in the southeast of the city. Heavy equipment and repair barns lined the avenues around La Villa and the basilica of the Guadalupana.

The war industry changed the way the Monstruo sounded and smelled. Factory whistles made such a racket that anti-noise regulations were promulgated in 1943. There were no laws yet that dealt with the bad air and environmental blight with which World War II–driven industrialization would curse the city.

Only four years had elapsed since Cárdenas's heroic expropriation of U.S. oil properties, but Mexico had become a slavish subsidiary of the North American war industry, providing Washington with everything from bombs to hamburgers to cannon fodder.

Now 300,000 braceros streamed north "to win the war for the *pinches gringos*," as my old pal Don Marcelino García, a Purépecha Indian campesino from Michoacán, always boasted. The *braceros*, many of whom had been booted out by U.S. authorities back in the Depression, filled in for the G.I. Joes and Janes who had gone off to war, picking crops and toiling in the canneries of California. Don Marsa worked on the *traque*, hammering down railroad ties from Oakland all the way to Montana.

Promised citizenship, 250,000 Mexicans and undocumented Mexican-Americans joined the U.S. military—more than a thousand were killed and 1,500 awarded Purple Hearts—but when those who survived returned home they were not hailed as heroes. One Texas funeral home refused to bury a young Mexican who had given his life for his new country.

Even Lázaro Cárdenas himself signed up. Appointed secretary of defense by Ávila Camacho in 1943, Tata Lázaro took up his post in Baja California, where he directed Mexican surveillance operations against possible Japanese incursions for the North American Defense Commission, which operated under U.S. command. In a volume analyzing how World War II irrevocably altered bilateral relations, Howard Cline, a State Department historian notes: "It came as a shock for most Mexicans to find themselves fighting alongside the soldiers of the United States rather than against them."

LA BLANCA GOES TO WAR (An interview with the author of *El Monstruo*, John Ross)

"Don Ray is my guarura, *my protector. This really happened to me. I was sitting at the counter one day reading the newspaper and these three young guys came up behind me and asked me if there was anything about Israel in the news. It was a weird question to ask, but well, there was. It was during the first Intifada and the Israeli Defense Force had killed 31 Palestinians that very day. I told them that was the news. That the Israeli soldiers were killers.*

"Well, it turned out that they were Israeli soldiers and that was why they wanted to know if there was anything in the paper. They started to shout and threaten me. Don Manolo, a corpulent old Gachupín who is related to Carlos's family in Leon, was the greeter, and he came over and told them not to bother his customers and that they should leave. So the Israeli soldiers went outside and milled around, waiting for me to come out.

"Don Ray, who was sitting across the counter, saw the whole thing and he volunteered to be my guarura and walk me home. Raymundo is 76 years old and short and sort of chubby. He doesn't exactly fit the description of a bodyguard.

"We waited for a while and when we didn't see the Israelis any longer, we made a dash for it. The soldiers caught up with us when we crossed Cinco de Mayo. They were going to beat me up. Don Ray stepped in front of me and shook his finger at them. 'Why do you come here to make trouble? Go home to Israel and leave us alone!' he told the soldiers. 'You should be ashamed of yourselves!'

"The Israelis were young and very muscular but the sight of this little old guy, a Mexican grandfather (actually, a great-grandfather), must have touched their sense of shame, and they backed down and went home to their hotel. Ever since then, Don Raymundo has been known as my guarura around La Blanca.

"I could have used Don Ray a few years later when I was attacked by the organ grinders. Organ grinders are really a vicious lot.

"Here I was sitting at the counter minding my own business and kidding around with Don Armando, the morning man, and they showed up outside La Blanca playing their damn cilindrino. Now maybe the organs sounded good when Don Porfirio was still alive but they are all out of tune now. No one knows how to prepare the perforated paper scrolls that make them work anymore. There was only one maestro up in Puebla who could perforate them, and he died. In other words, they make a big racket.

"The way the organ grinders work is this: One guy lugs around the instrument on his back—they are very heavy. When they get to a restaurant or a bar, his partner will crank out the 'music.' The lugger then goes inside and passes the hat for 'la música.' They wear a sort of military uniform— actually they look more like sanitation workers.

"Anyway, the guy who passed the hat came into La Blanca and walked around the counter asking the customers to 'cooperate' for la música. When he got to me, I was really steaming. 'What música are you talking about?' I demanded. 'This isn't música—this is torture! No! I have no money for your música.'

"Of course, when I left, the organ grinders rushed me and started screaming about how could I say they didn't play música. One guy even took a poke at me. Nothing happened really except that he knocked my beret off. I picked it up and dusted it off and they marched off down Cinco de Mayo to hassle the customers at the Café Popular.

"You should never give any coins to the organ grinders in the Centro Histórico. They are a vicious bunch."

VEERING RIGHT AT THE SPEED OF LIGHT

The advance of the right in the capital was not to be denied. The old Gachupín-criollo element had persevered through the Cárdenas years and now did business as the Federation of Organizations to Defend the Middle Class and other kindred fronts. Given the political climate, Ávila Camacho, who did not at all share Lázaro's leftward leanings, undertook the dismantlement of the popular gains of his predecessor's presidency. "Socialist education" was the first to be sacrificed. After 40,000 irate rightists demonstrated in front of Bellas Artes in 1943, Ávila's secretary of education revised the textbooks, blacklisting any reference to socialism.

Red-baiting was all the rage. Interior Secretary Miguel Alemán hounded the Mexican Communist Party into submission and castrated Vicente Lombardo Toledano's "Marxist" leadership of the CTM, promoting a Mexico state milkman, Fidel Velázquez, to his job in 1942.

On the agrarian front, Ávila Camacho froze the *reparto*, handing out minimal acreage during his six years in office. One predictable result: Between 1940 and 1950 landlessness swelled by 74 percent, driving the campesinos up to Mexico City where their cheap labor (*mano de obra barata*) was crucially needed as industrialization heated up.

THE FLOOD THAT NEVER ENDED

Farmers flocked to the Monstruo mostly from the surrounding states of Mexico and Morelos, Puebla, Michoacán, Guanajuato, Querétaro, Tlaxcala, Veracruz, and Hidalgo; the latter lost a quarter of its census between 1940 and 1950 to Mexico City migration. Mexico City's population, 1.7 million at the beginning of the world war, would swell to 3.5 million at the end of the decade, growing an average 5 percent each year for the next quarter of a century.

Since Tenochtitlán times, El Monstruo has always been a magnet, its population expanding from decade to decade through both good and bad times depending upon conditions in the countryside. Immigration to the capital between 1930 and 1940 when agrarian reform was preeminent had totaled about 350,000. Between 1940 and 1950, that number almost tripled to 900,000, and because most of the newcomers were young men and young women in their procreative prime, the number of Chilangos grew exponentially. So did the problem of providing city services.

Many of the newcomers came directly to the Centro, but there was no place for them to live. It was, as they say in real estate circles, a landlord's market, and newcomers were gouged without remorse. Renters' organizations, first organized by Morones's CROM back in the '20s, asserted their clout and joined the PRM's "popular sector" en masse—the CNOP, the National Coordinating Body of Popular Organizations, put the screws to Ávila Camacho, and on July 24, 1942, soon after Mexico entered the war, the President proclaimed a rent freeze on city housing that would last well into the 1990s.

Speculators in the private sector, deprived of a profit motive, stopped building housing and the federal government assumed the burden, constructing a dozen *multifamiliares*—in the U.S. they would be called projects—distributed outside of the center city to ease the downtown crunch.

Water, always scarce in this drought-ridden region, was at a premium. The springs in Xochimilco had given out and aquifers were drying up. The precious liquid was now being piped in from the central Mexican Río Lerma system 100 kilometers distant from the capital. Most city dwellings had no running water—only a quarter of the housing stock had inside plumbing, and water was drawn from public faucets in the patios of the *vecindades* much as it had been drawn from the fountains at Salto de Agua during the Colonia. Public faucets provided a lively venue for socialization in an increasingly compartmentalized urban environment.

Meanwhile, most of the city's 42 small rivers had been paved over and their meager flow directed into the Monstruo's distribution network. The outflow was still an intractable quandary. Extension of the Drenaje General sucked in the black waters from the south of the city, but the system was inadequate for the volumes it moved. Foul smells and diseases lurked along the banks of the Gran Canal as the sewage wended its way toward Hidalgo. The 1946–1952 report of the Department of the Federal District lays blame for the poor health of the residents in the slum-ridden east side of the city on woeful facilities to handle the sewage outflow.

In the rainy season, floods continued to plague the Monster. In one photo dated 1952, a dozen men in sombreros float down 16th of September Street on a raft, waving to the camera in front of the German tool emporium Boker's, near the corner of Isabel la Católica. The water that day was reportedly three meters deep in the Zócalo.

World War II had much the same impact on Mexico City as it did on U.S. cities. Both nations turned urban and industrialized, depleting the rural population and relegating it to the ranks of nostalgia. As the urban centers filled up, city planners grappled to catch up. Traffic in Mexico City, for example, overwhelmed the center's narrow streets. Between 1940 and 1950, the number of vehicles grew as rapidly as the population—from 41,000 to 78,000, about 3,000 additional cars and trucks a year. For the first time, the Monstruo had a parking problem.

OF MIRACLES AND HYPE

The flood of humanity into the maw of the Monster quickened under Ávila Camacho's successor, Miguel Alemán who took the reins of state with an unprecedented half-billion Yanqui dollars in foreign reserves, the spoils of World War II industrial growth. The new president, whose impresarial genius was hailed by private enterprise, parlayed the boodle into what he would soon be hyping as the "Mexican Miracle."

The cornerstone of Alemán's strategy for success was "product substitution," by which high tariff walls were erected to protect Mexican knock-offs of U.S. consumer goods—Mexican-made products like toothpaste and instant coffee, most of them of vastly inferior quality, dominated the market.

Boosted by increased production, the capital's industrial corridors expanded to the limits of the city as Mexico state entities like Tlalnepantla rushed in to close the gap. Although product substitution kept U.S. consumer goods out of Mexico, North American investors were warmly welcomed—foreigners could own 49 percent of all Mexican business but in reality controlled 100 percent through the ruse of *prestanombres* or Mexican "name-lenders." By 1946, transnationals like Johnson & Johnson and Nestlé had opened subsidiaries in Mexico City, hiding behind prestanombres. Not 10 years after Lázaro Cárdenas had nationalized Mexican petroleum, foreign investors could own enterprises outright under special conditions deemed in the national interest.

MISTER AMIGO

Miguel Alemán's thumping 1946 electoral victory was achieved without major fraud. "Mister Amigo," as his backers in Washington had taken to calling the young, business-oriented president, faced marginal opposition. Only Máximo Ávila Camacho, Manuel's ambitious brother, grew bellicose at Alemán's selection and locked himself in the bathroom of his San Ángel mansion, where he purportedly committed suicide by gunshot.

Miguel Alemán wasted no time in putting his personal imprimatur on national politics. At a special PRM conclave January 18, 1946, in the capital, Ávila Camacho launched Alemán as the party's presidential candidate, and the two proposed a significant change in nomenclature: The Party of the Mexican Revolution would heretofore be known as the Party of the Institutional Revolution or PRI. It was time to "institutionalize" the revolution to avoid the *broncas* (scuffling) between power groups that inevitably broke out at the end of every *sexenio* (six-year term).

The corporate structure of the new-in-name party was revised to include the business sector. The military was relegated to the sidelines and peaced off with a factory system that would manufacture equipment and uniforms for the Mexican Armed Forces. Indeed, by 1946, the "business class" was dominated by the scions of the generals, the *cachorros* (cubs) of the Revolution—Alemán was one himself.

The PRI, like the PRM, was one big happy revolutionary family. The new party controlled Big Labor, the rural sectors, both houses of the Mexican Congress, all of the nation's governors, and the Department of the Federal District. In its first electoral outing in July 1946, the PRI registered a *carro completo* (full car), taking all the seats in the Senate (where no opposition party member would sit until 1988), and all but seven token seats in the Chamber of Deputies in addition to Alemán's runaway victory in the presidential race. The consolidation of the PRI and its domination of the capital and the country beyond offered unprecedented opportunities to fleece the Mexicans.

Alemán and his cronies are often referenced as "Ali Baba & the 40 Thieves." During his *sexenio* they amassed considerable fortunes in Mexico City real estate, construction, and industry. Ali Babaman's personal playground was Acapulco, the nascent Pacific Coast resort where he had important holdings and whose hotel zone figured prominently in his portfolio—the coastal highway he built with public funds to ease transit between his various properties still retains the family name. Acapulco soon became Mexico's Número Uno tourist destination.

The suave, congenial president was forever pictured in the PRI-controlled press swinging a five iron on the greens of the resort's many golf courses. While at home at Los Pinos up in Mexico City, Miguel Alemán loved to play at the Hipódromo de las Américas, the capital's premier racetrack, and his presidential functions were as likely to be recorded in the Sociales sections of the daily newspaper, where the frivolities of the celebrity class were hyped, as they were to be found on the political pages.

Mister Amigo's entrepreneurial aura brought Hollywood to the deluxe hotels like the Reforma and the Del Prado—Johnny "Tarzan" Weissmuller and Lupe Vélez, "The Mexican Spitfire" had a spectacular slugfest at the latter. Orson Wells and Rita Hayworth were seen nightly at the Leda and Ciro's, a knock-off of the Beverly Hills dinery. The lifestyles of the rich & famous were the subtext of Alemán's rule.

In 1948, a new technology was added to the *farándula* (party industry) when Alemán granted radio kingpin Emilio "El Tigre" Azcárraga Mexico's first television license, which the tycoon grew into Latin America's most powerful communications conglomerate. Upon stepping down from the presidency in 1952, Ali Babaman would be rewarded with a 25 percent share of Telesistema Mexicano, later Tele-visa, where he and his son would retain a seat on the board of directors for the next 50 years. The newly minted PRI winked blithely at such payoffs.

"A BULWARK AGAINST THE RED MENACE"

On March 3, 1947, Harry Truman became the first U.S. president ever to set foot in the Monstruo. His mission was a double-edged one: to enlist Mister Amigo's support for the soon-to-be formed Organization of American States, a bulwark against Communist intrusion in the Americas, and to return a fraying Mexican flag that General Winfield Scott's "greengos" had seized at Chapultepec Castle on their way to the Zócalo in September 1846. Soon after, Miguel Alemán was invited to Washington to address a joint session of Congress, a historic first for a Mexican president. Truman even sent his presidential plane, *The Sacred Cow*, to Mexico City to fetch his good neighbor. In his address to the U.S. solons, Mister Amigo espoused his self-named Alemán Doctrine, a pledge to exterminate the Commie rats before they could infect the Americas.

During the Alemán years and those of his successor, Adolfo Ruiz Cortines, anti-Communism ruled with all the force of a state religion. In point of fact, it was a religion. The Roman Catholic hierarchy posted huge billboards across the length and breadth of the land advertising *"¡Cristianismo Sí! ¡Comunismo No!"* When you knocked on a neighbor's door, you were apt to be greeted by a sticker that informed THIS IS A HOME OF DECENT PEOPLE. WE DON'T ACCEPT COMMUNIST OR PROTESTANT PROPAGANDA.

Although the Mexican Communist Party had blindly endorsed Alemán's candidacy in a misplaced gesture to curry favor with the newfangled PRI, the Communists would be constantly suppressed, their public meetings broken up by the president's personal SWAT squad, the Granaderos, a police force he inherited from Lázaro Cárdenas. The tools of the Alemán repression were the "Social Dissolution" laws, which made virtually any criticism of the government and the PRI that ran it a crime against nature, and the Federal Security Directorate (DFS), destined to become the most "savage detectives" in all of Latin America.

THE INTERNATIONAL COMMUNIST CONSPIRACY COMES TO EL MONSTRUO

The understanding between Truman and Alemán gave U.S. intelligence agencies a free hand in Mexico City to root out the dread Red rodents. By 1948, the year it was chartered, the CIA was operating out of offices at Melchor Ocampo #252 in the Condesa Colony, according to muckraking journalist Manuel Buendía, later to be assassinated by the DFS. "The Pan American News Agency," a Company front, was run by none other than Watergate bungler E. Howard Hunt from Río de la Plata #148 in the Cuauhtémoc. In his autobiography, Hunt boasts of planting Red-baiting exposés in the only-too-pliant Mexican press.

Pet targets of Washington surveillance were members of the U.S. Communist Party who had fled their homeland as Joe McCarthy's bonfires raged—the ACGMC (American Communist Group in Mexico City) was still functioning in 1968 when dissident spook Philip Agee had a desk at the U.S. embassy.

Among those U.S. Communists, fellow travelers, and just plain pinkos run to ground by U.S. and Mexican Red hunters was Morton Sobell, wanted as a material witness in the treason trial of Ethel and Julius Rosenberg, who was arrested upon touching down at Mexico City's brand-new Benito Juárez International Airport August 15, 1950, and immediately returned to the United States in chains.

Another was Gus Hall, a frontline Smith Act defendant who had jumped bail and fled south of the border—Hall would always claim that he swam across the Río Bravo. The soon-to-be perpetual Communist Party USA candidate for president was rudely awakened in his Mexico City motel room October 8, 1951, by Mexican cops wielding big flashlights and was trussed up, driven 800 miles to the border at Nuevo Laredo, and turned over to the FBI at midspan on the international bridge.

In a memoir written for the government daily *El Nacional*, Diana Anhalt, a daughter of the Bronx who had fled the Red Scare with her parents in 1952, recalled her arrival in El Monstruo. Mike (Misha) and Belle Zykofsky checked into the Sandra's Court motel in downtown Mexico City with all their worldly possessions—jazz records, two oil paintings they couldn't bear to leave behind, Uncle Herman's typewriter, and *The Settlement Cookbook* ("I don't know why—Belle never cooked in the Bronx"), plus their two daughters, ages eight and five. "I brought my ice skates," remembered Diana. "I didn't know where I was." A baker's boy bicycling by with a basket of fresh bread balanced on his head was her first taste of life in the Mexican capital.

U.S. Communists escaped to Mexico (a) because you did not need a passport to cross the border (the Truman State Department denied Commies passports anyway) and (b) because it was cheap. The Zykofskys were small fish. Albert Maltz, Ring Lardner Jr., and Dalton Trumbo, three of the Hollywood Ten indicted on suspicion of subliminally embedding pro-Red sentiments in Tinseltown celluloids, were the stars of the show—Anhalt comments that Maltz's cocktail parties attracted PRI bigwigs.

The black American painter Elizabeth Catlett found sanctuary in Cuernavaca, as did deported *National Guardian* editor Cedric Belfrage. The wondrous experimental composer Conlon Nancarrow, who had fought in Spain, was another refugee, along with Vanderbilt heir Frederick Vanderbilt Fields, the "Red Millionaire."

But for Anhalt, who was enrolled at the private American School, a creation of the U.S. embassy, politics were a forbidden topic of conversation. Anyone could be a spy—a schoolmate, the postman, the cleaning woman. The ACGMC surveillance group spied on the refugee community's barbecues and softball games. But most of the time, Diana recalls, the American Reds were left to their own devices, except when the Mexican government needed a scapegoat to pin unrest upon, such as when National University students commandeered city buses to protest a fare hike in 1959.

By 1981, with the coast a bit clearer, Misha and Belle, now in their 60s, returned to the Home of the Tree and the Land of the Grave. Diana stayed on and became a Chilango for life.

ALI BABAMAN'S BOOM TIMES

The Alemán years were boom times for the Monstruo. The national GNP grew by at least 6 percent each year, in some years 9 percent. Mexico City GNP grew at twice that pace. Under Ali Babaman, the capital prospered and modernized—five times as much as the total investment in all of Mexico's municipalities taken together was sunk into the capital's infrastructure.

Of the nation's 63,000 factories, 12,000 were concentrated in the Federal District, and a second wave of bedraggled campesinos streamed in from the undercapitalized countryside to man and woman them. Twelve percent of the newcomers were from as far afield as the southern states of Guerrero and Oaxaca. With more than 3,000,000 Chilangos registered in the 1950 census, the Monstruo now accounted for 40 percent of the national population. The land area they occupied spread like an ominous ink blot—14,650 square hectares, 26 percent more than when World War II kicked in. Three hundred "proletarian" *colonias*—i.e., not yet hooked up to city services—drew 80 percent of their residents from 34 of the 111 poorest municipalities in the country, according to the National Commission on the Minimum Wage.

Faced with housing this horde of poverty-stricken newcomers, Alemán and his Ali Baba brother Bernardo Quintana, founder of the ICA Corporation, the nation's most powerful construction enterprise, launched a blitz that rivaled the postwar U.S. housing boom. State workers moved into housing built by the Social Security Institute (IMSS) at a half-dozen Mexico City complexes or *unidades*. Ground was broken for ICA-built middle- and upper-middle-class tracts northwest of the city in Naucalpan.

Ciudad Satélite was constructed on hacienda land that had been snapped up by Miguel Alemán father and son for pennies and then resold at a comfortable profit to prospective tenants. Satélite would be a new concept in suburban living, only 20 minutes from downtown Mexico City and its network of freeways, the main trunk of which was the Miguel Alemán Viaduct, the infamous "ditch" that bisects the capital from east to west. Three soaring, shiny, tapered towers designed by master Mexican architects Luis Barragán and Mathias Goeritz were installed to complement Satélite's visionary future.

Today, the towers are virtually obliterated by freeway ramps and giant billboards, and the quickest way to get to downtown Mexico from Satélite City would probably be to walk across the roofs of the automobiles enmeshed bumper to bumper on the access freeways.

SQUATTING IN THE LAIR OF THE HUNGRY COYOTE

The impoverished migrants streaming in from surrounding states found living space where they could take it. Typically, the *paracaidistas* (parachuters) landed on tracts whose titles were never clear. The first squatters would get a discount on their lots to lure other newcomers to buy in. If the squatters were not immediately evicted, the settlers would agitate for city services and regularization of their plots, which were most often the property of others. A generation could elapse before a proletarian colonia was regularized, and by then, the land was theirs by default.

In 1941, a group of *colonos* of unspecified origins set up camp on the desiccated bed of what had once been Lake Texcoco along the extreme eastern edge of the Monstruo, where the city was planning a new airport. The swirling dust and blinding salt grit that blew off this inhospitable tract did not deter these novice Chilangos. They fashioned their hovels from strewn garbage, rusted tin, and cardboard and clustered together for safety.

By 1949, when Alemán ceded jurisdiction of the land to the Mexico state municipality of Chimalhuacán, the Union of Colonos counted 2,000 souls camped out there on the venomous lake bed. By 1952 there were 40,000 of them, and eight years later in 1960, 80,000. A new municipality was created and took the name Ciudad Nezahualcóyotl after the hungry coyote poet-king who had ruled these lands when there was a lake and something could still be harvested on it.

Neza just grew and grew. Unconscionable speculators sold off lots without advising prospective buyers that there were no services. They took out display ads in the newspapers to hawk subdivisions named "Beautiful Hills" (there are no hills in Neza) and La Joyita ("Little Jewel") for 250 pesos down, and no questions asked.

John Womack, then a Harvard student fresh out of Norman, Oklahoma, took one look at Ciudad Nezahualcóyotl and realized that government agrarian programs inspired by Emiliano Zapata and Lázaro Cárdenas, created to keep farmers on the land, had been abject flops.

In 2008, Ciudad Neza, "the world's largest slum" (*New York Times*) had 2.8 million residents and was the eighth-largest megalopolis in Mexico, one of six cities with million-plus populations that ring the Monstruo to form the Metropolitan Area. Population density is 100,000 residents to a square mile.

When you Google in, you encounter an impossibly compact flat landscape of one-story homes stretching endlessly into the horizon. Only half of Neza's 750 streets are paved. Eight hundred youth gangs reportedly roam them. Instead of the names of presidents and patriotic heroes to whom the streets of Mexican cities are usually consecrated, the thoroughfares of Ciudad Nezahualcóyotl have handles like "Damp Buzzard" and "Bed of Stones" streets. Sixty years down history's highway, this is what's left of Alemán's "Mexican Miracle."

STRIPPING BACK THE MIRACULOUS

The Mexican economy is shaped like a pyramid with an exceptionally broad base and a tiny, fenced-in flat top to prevent leakage down below, observed the historian Daniel Cosio Villegas (born just down the street at Isabel la Católica #97). Because of its peculiar construction, there is no trickle down.

During the postwar boom times, Alemán and his Ali Babas did their damnedest not to let the poor spoil their party. Although the PRI needed to keep the poor poor in order to build its electoral clientele, when not needed to cast a ballot, the underclass was permanently excluded from the Mexican Miracle and kept hidden away behind the glitter and gloss, out in the devastated countryside and the crumbling slums of the misery belt surrounding El Monstruo. If an intrepid artist dared to strip back the glitz and reveal the rot underneath, the regime often struck back in spades.

One of those who put his art on the line was Luis Buñuel, the Spanish filmmaker self-exiled from Franco's terror who during the 1940s turned out a remarkable series of low-budget Mexican movies. Although his work like *The Andalusian Dog*, with its razor-across-the-eyeball motif, is soaked in surrealism, Buñuel's Mexican masterpiece *Los Olvidados* (The Forgotten Ones) draws more upon the Italian neorealists—Buñuel was known to be particularly impressed by Vittorio de Sica's *Shoeshine*.

The disclaimer at the front end of *Los Olvidados*, played against a montage of the New York, London, and Paris skylines, tells the story: "Behind the wealth of the cities are poverty-stricken homes where poorly fed children are doomed to criminality. . . . Mexico City, that large modern city, is no exception."

In the opening scene, El Jaibo, just released from juvenile detention, beats a rival to death with a rock in the shadow of an unfinished skyscraper. The symbolism was not subtle. The final scene, where Pedro's dead, crumpled body is slung over the back of a burro and thrown out on the slum's rubbish heap, is a damning indictment of Ali Babaman's "Miracle."

The Mexican president fumed at Buñuel's ingratitude in exposing the nation's underdevelopment and glaring inequities for the world to see and ordered deportation papers drawn up to ship the moviemaker home to Franco's torture chambers. But *Los Olvidados* won Buñuel the best director award at Cannes in 1951 and Alemán's threat to have him deported was retracted.

Gabriel Vargas's "La Familia Burrón" was the flip side of Buñuel's evocation of inner-city poverty. The popular comic strip illustrated the lot of an underclass family living in a crowded downtown *vecindad* on "Cuaja Alley." On the surface, the Burrones resembled Dagwood and Blondie ("Lorenzo & Pepita") but represented the mirror opposite of the Bumsteads' middle-class suburban existence and Dagwood's shameful servility to his boss, Mister Dithers. Regino Burrón had no fixed profession. He seemed to spend a lot of his day in the neighborhood *pulquería*. Vargas's characters walk around in patched pants and a state of perpetual inebriation, three bubbles hovering above their skulls.

Many scenes take place in bottle-strewn back alleys. Regino's ne'er-do-well brother is always on the lam from the *chotas* (cops). On the other hand, Doña Borola Burrón is a working-class feminist whose ingenuity saves the day again and again. The strip, which is played out on the battleground of tenement living and flapping clotheslines, pokes unmerciful fun at the middle class and its Mexican Miracle. Because "La Familia Burrón" was the most popular comic strip in the city, Gabriel Vargas was insulated from political retaliation.

THE DREAM FACTORY

The harsh realities of life on the ground floor of the Mexican Miracle were tempered by the country's burgeoning film industry. The Churubusco Studios opened their gates in 1945, a start-up financed by radio kingpin Emilio Azcárraga and RKO Pictures. Heavily subsidized by the Alemán administration, Churubusco quickly became the Mecca of Mexican moviedom.

Under the direction of former Hollywood extra Emilio "El Indio" Fernández (his mother was reportedly a Kikapú), the Churubusco studios cranked out an unending parade of black-and-white potboilers, often starring the imperious María Félix, whose beauty was exemplary but whose acting talents amounted to slapping around her boyfriends at least once a movie. In *Río Escondido* (Hidden River, 1947) Félix plays a rural schoolteacher who, hounded by a *cacique* (rural boss), goes to the National Palace to plead her case with the president, where she faints in the waiting room and romance, as usual, takes over. Félix was often teamed with Pedro Infante, a drop-dead handsome devil of a singing *charro* (cowboy)— their *Todos los Pobres* (All the Poor) converted Infante into an idol of the underclass.

But the genius of this epoch, which cinema fetishists enshrine as the Golden Age of Mexican movies, was the man behind the camera, Gabriel Figueroa, whose oeuvre of 150 black-and-white films created a universe of shadow and light, striking illumination, and penetrating camera angles that far excelled the plots of Fernández's potboilers. An equally sinister black-and-white aura also permeates the hard-boiled crime sagas of Juan Orol that focus on the underbelly of the Mexico City *hampa* or criminal world.

The Golden Age lasted no longer than a decade. The industry grew greedy and its moviemaking shoddy and the big stars moved on, some to Hollywood. Today you can still observe the three great hulls of the dilapidated Churubusco dream factory from the elevated tracks of the Blue Line between the Metro stops Ermita and General Anaya (Coyoacán), a forlorn monument to an era when the fantasies up on the silver screen softened the daily grind for millions of Mexicans mired in the mud of Alemán's miracle.

MEXICO CITY IN BLACK AND WHITE

The contrast between the top and the bottom of the Mexican Miracle was black and white. Indeed, the contradiction was framed in those opposites. If the movies, with notable exceptions like *Los Olvidados*, represented the dream world, two remarkable photographers stalked the city's streets from the 1940s on, and their legacy shows best what life looked like in black and white at the bottom of the Milagro Mexicano. Taken together, Nacho López and Héctor García were Mexico's Weegees, documenting the grim underbelly of El Monstruo for newspapers and magazines, and their works tell us more about "social dissolution" than a ton of words can ever replicate.

García was a newspaper photographer for *Novedades* and other Mexico City dailies when getting the front-page money shot was what mattered most. His specialty was labor strife and social struggle, and his lens put a brutally damaged face on the Mexican repression. Héctor had been a bracero during World War II, and his work was Exhibit A of what cruelties flowered behind Mister Amigo's amiable mask. He was often handcuffed and hauled off in the Police *julias* (paddy wagons) for his efforts. *Obrero Asesinado* (Dead Worker) is his signature portrait.

García's suicidal dedication to capturing the forces of repression in the act was balanced by a fondness for the chorus girls at the Teatro Blanquita, and his exclusive shot of 1950s Pachuco king Tin Tan naked in the shower is still a stunner.

Nacho López worked for weekly magazines like *Siempre* and *Mañana* and had more time to select and organize what he photographed. His many thematic series, like photo novels of the grotesque, zoomed in on El Monstruo's hellish delegation lockups on the weekends, filled with abused wives, drunken husbands, and drug-addled children. The profile of the poverty in which most of the city's population was trapped was the stuff of López's work: two upturned beseeching hands thrust through the food slot of a solitary confinement cell at Lecumberri, a grizzled campesino studying a stained shard of newspaper, the hard brown faces of workers at a railroad union rally in the Zócalo in 1959.

But Nacho's work had a playful and poetic side. The series in which he persuaded a girlfriend with an amazing hourglass figure sheathed in a '50s "New Look" frock to sashay down San Juan de Letrán while sharply dressed young studs shouted *piropos* (example: "Oh Mama, so many curves and me without brakes"), set against a background of rising skyscrapers, is a pertinent text for those misogynist, modernizing times.

"I LOVE MY CUSTOMERS BUT SOMETIMES THEY DRIVE ME NUTS" (An interview with Armando Peñalosa, the morning man)

"Most of my customers go for the Pumas or América. I'm a fanático *for the Chivas Coloradas. Everyone knows it and they all rib me. But I'm the waiter down here. I'm in charge at this end of the counter and I always win."*

Armando poured out cafés con leche *for three burly construction guys and darted off to the kitchen for their eggs. Armando is the consummate morning man. This is how he does the* café con leche: *He brings you a glass of hot milk and a little cup of espresso. The trick is flipping the cup into the milk without spilling a drop. Armando never spills a drop.*

Armando grew up in the Centro but now he lives far away in Toluca and has to get up at 3:00 a.m. to be here by 6:30 when La Blanca opens. There are three shifts of customers in the morning, he explains. First, the early birds who can't sleep and the market workers in the Lagunilla. Then the office workers and shopkeepers who have to be in by eight or nine and the politicos *and union bigshots who come in together and sit at the tables. The third shift is the tourists and the* jubilados *(retired people) who get up late and don't have to be anywhere really. The* jubilados *will sit at the counter all morning.*

"I came to work at La Blanca in 1957. My brother Chucho was already working here. We were kids from the neighborhood and Don Marciano gave us jobs. We lived in La Lagunilla, the Obrera, the Colonia Morelos [Tepito]. Everything was bien bonito down here back then. There was a lot of movement in the Centro. My customers were boxers and futbolistas and politicos. The PRIista Tulio Hernández would come in with the actress Silvia Pinal on his arm. Cuauhtémoc Cárdenas, the son of the general, would come in with his two sons and sit at my counter."

Armando gives me the wait sign. Two middle-aged women wanted their check. Alfredo, who may or may not deal in hot watches, wanted to know where his papaya was. The Doctor, a dentist, sat down and started bossing everyone around.

Armando serves breakfast all morning and then the first round of comida corrida, the three-course lunch. When he goes home at three, Manuel takes over his spot.

"I used to go and play pool when I got off—pool and dominoes are my weaknesses. I played at ¡Yo Chamaco! on Allende and the Mariscal on San Juan de Letrán and upstairs at Kid Azteca's on 16th of September. I played the champ Cardón up there and he spotted me 25 points and still I couldn't beat him.

"Kid Azteca wasn't really the owner but he came in every afternoon. The Kid fought over 200 fights and he didn't have a mark on him. He was always well dressed and alert even in his 90s, not like the Chango [Monkey] Casanova who you used to see lying in the gutter in Tepito.

"The best fighters came from Tepito. We had great little champions back then: Raúl 'El Raton' [The Mouse] Macías and Rubén 'Púas' [Barbed Wire] Olivares and Carlos 'Cañas' [Cane Legs] Zárate. They all came in here. Those were good times.

"I wouldn't get home until after midnight and the Mrs. put her foot down. After the earthquake, it got dangerous around here with all the rateros *[two-legged* ratas*] running around. She had relatives in Toluca and we moved out there."* Armando smiled to himself ruefully. The good times would never come again. But still times are okay.

The morning man scooped up the empty plates and cups, magically balancing them on his forearm, and walked toward the kitchen. The Doctor wanted his check. Toño the dishwasher taunted him about the Chivas. The tourists started to filter in. They wanted hot cakes. No, they wanted corn flakes. No wait, what are these "chilaquiles"? They had Armando making *the fabled 40* vueltas *(turns). Every time one ordered something, the next one changed their order.*

"*I love my customers,*" Armando sighed as he wiped off the counter. "*But sometimes they drive me nuts.*"

¡CANTINFLAS PRESIDENTE!

Miguel Alemán's reelection seemed assured, but perhaps spooked by the memory of Obregón's messy finale when he sought to return to high office, Ali Babaman bowed out in favor of his compadre and fellow Veracruzano Adolfo Ruiz Cortines. An older, immaculately bow-tied gentleman, Ruiz Cortines had, as they say, *una cola que se pisa*—a tail he kept tripping on. In 1914 as a young customs officer, he had collaborated with Woodrow Wilson's Marines when they occupied the port of Veracruz to teach Mexicans about democracy, a talking point that his rival, General Miguel Henríquez, a flamboyant nationalist, made much of.

General Henríquez, who ran on a ticket cobbled together from tiny civic parties, was conjectured to be a stalking horse for Lázaro Cárdenas's return to Los Pinos, and although he did have the ex-president's support early on in the campaign, Henríquez's opportunistic overtures to the anti-Cárdenas Right and a rally to woo Catholic fanatics at the Basilica of the Virgin of Guadalupe dissuaded the atheist Lázaro from endorsing his fellow general.

With the PRI steamroller building an impressive head of vapor, Henríquez's candidacy (the first anti-PRI campaign) was flattened 74 percent to 15 percent—the PAN, which ran a presidential candidate for the first time, wound up with the remaining one percent. But many consider the real winner to have been Mario Moreno, AKA Cantinflas, who is believed to have taken a third of the national vote, his numbers swelled by women, who for the first time in four decades of "revolutionary" governments, were finally permitted to cast a ballot.

Much as the Vasconcelistas and Almazanistas before them, the Henriquistas were convinced they had been robbed. A July 7, 1952, rally at the Juárez monument on the Alameda was broken up by motorized police, and Granaderos were assigned to put a lid on post-electoral agitation. Six were killed and 524 arrested in the *zipizapi* (pitched battle) that evolved as gunshots and tear gas filled Madero Street and Gante Alley, even reaching Isabel la Católica.

MISTER AMIGO BIDS ADIOS

Miguel Alemán would remain a continuing presence in Mexican politics for more than a decade after he moved out of Los Pinos, always lending his considerable influence to whichever current in power best represented the interests of his Donald Trump–like empire.

Mister Amigo's final gift to the nation whose destiny he had mutated irrevocably was University City, a sprawling campus built on volcanic rock in the Pedregal district in the extreme south of the capital. Inaugurated in 1954, Ciudad Universitaria transferred the bulk of the 22,000-strong UNAM student body away from the multiple colonial buildings in the Centro that the university had occupied for three centuries. Although a number of preparatory schools or *prepas* remained downtown, the move altered forever the nature of the Centro Histórico as a student quarter.

The sparkling new campus was indeed an artful wedding of Le Corbusier and Vasconcelos's "Raza Cósmica," the ancient and the sleek. Mexico's elite artists contributed monumental murals, among them Siqueiros's vision of the future, with giant arms pointing to the horizon ("El Rocco," a dope-smoking anarchist artist, altered the mural during the 1999 student strike and, like Siqueiros, was imprisoned), and Juan O'Gorman's phantasmagoric mosaic that fills the façade of the University library. Ciudad Universitaria is internationally celebrated and was designated part of the Patrimony of Man & Woman Kind by the United Nations in 2003.

Miguel Alemán topped off this eighth wonder of the world with an appropriate pièce de résistance: a grotesque, 20-foot-tall statue of himself, clad in a white toga, that was installed at the portals of the University. Rioting students disfigured and burnt this tasteless pile of kitsch during disturbances in 1965 and the next year hacked it down from its perch. Like Pancho Villa, Mister Amigo's head was separated from his body.

X

URUCHURTU'S CITY

pon assuming the presidency, Adolfo Ruiz Cortines named a new chief of government to head the Department of the Federal District, then a cabinet-level position. The Mexico City Mayor, or "Regent," as he was quaintly titled, was then considered the third most powerful position in the political hierarchy, bested only by the President himself and the secretary of the interior.

In fact, Ernesto P. Uruchurtu (the name is a Basque one) had been Alemán's interior secretary and the most hard-nosed anti-Communist in his cabinet. In addition, the new regent had managed Almazán's 1940 campaign and appealed to the city's Old Guard, the upper-middle-class Gachupín-criollo strain that had been so offended by Cárdenas's Dictatorship of the Proletariat.

Ernesto P. Uruchurtu succeeded an Ali Babaman crony, Fernando Casas Alemán (no relation), a corrupt playboy most noted for his ravishing 15-year-old Chiapas farm girl mistress, Irma Serrano, "La Tigresa," later a terrible ranchera singer and the consort of equally bad presidents, later yet a senator of the republic, and still today the owner of the Fru-Fru drag queen theater on Donceles.

Uruchurtu, whose chiseled profile was drawn weekly by political cartoonist Abel Quezada in *Siempre* magazine to resemble a reasonable facsimile of Dick Tracy, made it abundantly clear that he would abide no social protest. Permits would have to be obtained in order to

211

exercise free speech rights. "The streets belong to the government and the government allows the people to use them in the way it sees fit," he decreed.

FRIDA AND DIEGO RISE UP TO RED HEAVEN

The Red-under-every-bed psychosis peaked between 1950 and 1954. The Soviet Union had obtained the atomic bomb and us mid-century children learned to duck and cover. South of the border, the FBI kept a close eye on U.S. Reds, and the Mexican Communist Party had melted into the underground, frozen in the labyrinth of the Cold War. Uruchurtu, a virulent anti-Communist, had just been named regent of Mexico City. It was not a good time for the Mexican Left. Then Frida Kahlo died on July 13, 1954.

Kahlo, who in her final years was given to drawing iconic portraits of Joe Stalin, had been in hideous pain for months and was cruelly addicted to morphine. Her leg was amputated in early 1954 and Diego pushed her wheelchair when they went to demonstrations now—their final outing had been to the U.S. embassy a week before her death to protest the CIA's overthrow of the Arbenz government in Guatemala. Uruchurtu's Granaderos had driven off the protesters.

Diego was determined to render honors to his wife under the rotunda of Bellas Artes, but the authorities were nervous about what this grief-stricken, aging wild boy might be planning.

El Sapo had been buffeted by too many years in the eye of the social maelstrom. In truth, he had become an eccentric sort of society painter, accepting generous sums to paint murals that were no longer as socially relevant as when John D.'s grandson Nelson was ripping out his head of Lenin in Rockefeller Center ("I paint what I see," said Rivera, to quote an E.B. White poem).

Rivera was commissioned by the Del Prado Hotel to do what is arguably his most popular creation. "A Dream of Sunday on the Alameda" depicts dozens of Mexico's most malicious malefactors and a few unlucky heroes posed before the downtown park. Later, after the 1985 earthquake, which rendered the hotel uninhabitable, the mural moved across the street into its own museum.

When the painter signed off on the masterpiece, he added a typical Riveran flourish: "*¡Dios No Existe!*"—"God Does Not Exist!" Bishops bellowed blasphemy from the pulpits and menacing crowds of

Catholics gathered outside the Del Prado. The management prevailed upon Diego to rectify it, and so, escorted by burly *guaruras*, Rivera erased his words, perhaps a measure of his weariness with the art wars.

Undaunted by the government's reluctance, Diego, accompanied by luminaries of the Mexican art world and the keepers of the Socialist flame, wheeled Frida's coffin into Bellas Artes. He worried that Frida was not dead, that she would awake in her own grave. One by one, the invitees took their place before her bier.

Suddenly, Arturo García, one of the "Fridos," her coterie of once-young student admirers, pulled out a red flag with a large hammer and sickle emblazoned upon it and draped it over Frida. Andrés Iduarte, Ruiz Cortines's Bellas Artes director, frantically grabbed for the flag before the Speed Graphics recorded the subversion for posterity. But just then, ex-president Lázaro Cárdenas arrived to take his place as an honor guard and Iduarte could do nothing to prevent the yellow press from getting a front-page shot of the commie fest at Bellas Artes. The director was fired the next day.

Diego went downhill fast after Frida was gone, his insides rotting with cancer. More out of pity than as a reward for his past misdeeds, he was invited to rejoin the Mexican Communist Party before his death in 1957 and is probably frog-eyeing us now from his perch up in socialist heaven.

In 2007, Felipe Calderón, the right-wing, dubiously elected president of this benighted republic, came to Bellas Artes to inaugurate an extravagant centennial exhibit of Frida Kahlo's work. Outraged by the right-winger's appropriation of Kahlo, hundreds of women greeted him with justifiable revulsion. "Frida Kahlo belonged to the Left," they shouted. "Free Frida! Free Frida!" Calderón had to be escorted to a side door by the military.

THE IRON REGENT

Ernesto P. Uruchurtu was the Monstruo's Chief of Government for 14 years, from 1952 to 1966, serving three Mexican presidents through two and a fraction sexenios, the longest-running public official since Porfirio Díaz, whom he resembled in his dictatorial style and class orientation. In a nutshell, Uruchurtu was a racist, xenophobic, puritanical tyrant who hounded "illegal aliens," mistrusted Jews, and waxed nostalgic about the good old days when Porfirian order prevailed and the *cilindrinos* were still in tune. He was also a strident defender of the city against the ravages of urban blight.

During his near decade and a half as Mexico City's "Iron Regent," Uruchurtu waged war on urban blight and endorsed slow growth and fiscal conservatism. Backed by the middle class and their uppers, he fought against the phantom of megalopolis and was, in fact, the first mayor to address the city as "a monster," in an exclusive interview with *Excelsior*. The capital was becoming "a monstrosity," he railed, damning "metropolitan giganticism" and "macrocephalic development." Uruchurtu was a closet preservationist who defended the Centro Histórico against the contamination of modern utilitarian architecture and who cultivated his inner-city base by extending rent control. But as Mexico globalized, Uruchurtu would pay the price.

Uruchurtu reserved particular spleen for the dark-skinned newcomers from the provinces, whom he accused of turning Mexico City into "a toilet" and who brought with them "no culture or material possessions." "Why must we accept these invasions of millions whom we receive blindly without even knowing their true origins?" (*sic*).

The Iron Regent waged an unrelenting war against squatters newly arrived from the countryside, whose encampments he considered an eyesore; his Granaderos demolished them with brutal relish. *Ambulantes* were swept off downtown streets and their merchandise stolen. Protesting police brutality got you a whipping and landed you behind the *rejas* (bars) for 48 hours. Beggars were removed by force from the old quarter, loaded up into dump trucks, and driven to the edge of the city. Uruchurtu carried out a pogrom against gays.

And the Iron Regent waged war against the night. New high-powered street lighting illuminated even the darkest hours. The vice squad rounded up the ladies of the evening and packed them off in the *julias*. Cantina closing time was moved up three hours to 1:00 a.m. Public drunkenness got you a night in the *bote*. The Iron Regent crusaded against pornography, raiding newspaper kiosks and confiscating girly magazines. Movies were censored at the behest of the Mexican Legion of Decency and grind houses like the Venus Theater, where the groans of the onanists drowned out the cheesy soundtracks, were shut down.

But despite Uruchurtu's war on the night, Mexico City's thriving demimonde refused to die. Hundreds of *giros negros* ("black turns"—seamy enterprises) continued to flourish on the back streets of the

Centro so long as they coughed up the *mordidas* or "bites" that Uru's inspectors put on the management.

Tin Tan, the Pachuco titan, teamed with the midget Tun Tun at Margo Su's Teatro Blanquita. They were often paired with the exotic Tongolele, an ersatz Polynesian dancer born Yolanda Montes in San Francisco, California, who recklessly flung herself about on a great skin drum.

Across San Juan de Letrán from the Mariachi stronghold of Plaza Garibaldi, the Blanquita was a popular working-class venue. Mambo king Dámaso Pérez Prado—"Cara de Foca" (sealface), who boasted that he had invented the Cubano devil dance, smuggled it out of Havana, and made the mambo Mexico's problem—was often featured on the marquee. The story goes that Prado was once bounced from Mexico under Article 33 for converting Mexico's national anthem into a mambo but received a last-minute reprieve from Miguel Alemán.

Old Sealface's Mambos #5 and #8, punctuated by Prado's primordial grunts ("¡UUUAAAHHHHHHHH!") made Mexico into Mambo Central. The Monstruo often found itself enshrined in the Cuban's music: *Mambo del Ruletero* reverberated from every collective cab in the city. Later, during the student troubles, Prado composed a mambo in solidarity with the strikers at the UNAM, and when students at the National Polytechnic Institute complained, Cara de Foca gave them the *Mambo del Poli*.

This reporter tagged along behind a joyous throng that accompanied the Mambo King to his final *pachanga* in 1989. Laid out in a plush white coffin on a bed of white gladiolas in a white tuxedo, Cara de Foca looked resplendent. The pallbearers mamboed him all the way to graveside in the French cemetery, his powerful 16-piece band awakening the dead with an uproarious rendition of what else but *¡Qué Rico Mambo!* ¡UUUAAAHHHHH!

THE CUBANO COLONY

Dámaso Pérez Prado was emblematic of the Cuban colony that had settled into the Centro from San Juan de Letrán westward to Balderas and Bucareli, few vestiges of which survive today outside of the checkerboard-floored Café Havana, now a hangout more for creepy government agents (the Secretariat of the Interior is right down the block) than for the Cubano community.

Cubans had found safe haven in Mexico City from political persecution on the island for the better part of the century—José Martí preceded Julio Antonio Mella to these shores in the 1870s. Renting a small room on Moneda Street adjacent to the National Palace, Martí published his screeds against tyranny in a number of Mexico City periodicals. When Porfirio Díaz raised an army and declared himself against the Juarista government of Lerdo de Tejada in 1876, Martí was forced to flee for his life to Guatemala.

Among the bright lights in the Cuban colony during Pérez Prado's heyday were such popular figures as Chacumbele, a handsome Cuban singing idol contracted by the Mexico City Tigres, one of the Monstruo's two *beisbol* teams, to dance atop its dugout at the old Social Security ballpark on Cuauhtémoc Avenue. Snazzy little Cuban fighters like "Mantequilla" (Butter) Nápoles and Ultiminio Ramos (who answered Bob Dylan's question about who killed Davey Moore) dazzled the fans at the crumbling Coliseo on Perú Street.

In the middle of the '50s, la Colonia Cubana would acquire enhanced notoriety with the arrival of a handful of soon-to-be distinguished revolutionaries.

DR. GUEVARA'S CATS

On September 21, 1954, three months after the Arbenz government was toppled by the CIA, a young Argentinean doctor who had been working in the Guatemalan health ministry, and his fresh-faced traveling companion Julio Cáceres, AKA "El Patojo" (The Kid), crossed into Mexico at Tapachula, Chiapas. A week later, Ernesto Guevara de la Serna, not yet Che, arrived in Mexico City and took a room around the corner on Bolívar Street. "The City received me with all the indifference of a great animal—without a caress or even showing me its teeth," Guevara noted in his diary.

The two friends were virtually penniless but somehow acquired cheap cameras and plied the Alameda and Chapultepec Park shooting portraits of tourists and *quinceañeras* (girls' Sweet 15 birthday fetes) to keep them in Vitamin T (tacos, tostados, and tamales). A fortuitous encounter with the director of the Argentina News Agency, an old family friend, landed Guevara an assignment to cover the March 1955 Pan American Games.

Ernesto also doubled as an allergy researcher at General Hospital. Because his investigation involved cat brains, Dr. Guevara organized hunting parties, scouring the allies of the Centro Histórico for feral felines.

LA ANTILLA

Mexico City at mid-century was teeming with Latin American political refugees. Young Guevara sucked up *maté* with Argentinean compatriots and drank rum with Puerto Rican nationalists. Followers of independence leader Don Pedro Albizu Campos had just shot up the U.S. Congress and tried to take out Truman and were holed up in the city. Peruvian activists from Haya de la Torre's proscribed APRA Party had come here in exile. Refugees from the deposed Arbenz regime set up camp. The ebullient Cuban colony slapped dominoes in the cafés of the Centro with Spanish Republicans.

Che was introduced to a group of Cubans who had risen up at the Moncada Barracks on July 26, 1953, the feast day of Santiago in the city of the same name, when the dictator Batista's soldiers were too drunk to notice. The Cubanos conspired in smoky rooms in the Imperial Building on Article 123 street or on the benches outside La Antilla, a small grocery store on the corner of Emparán Street and Tomás Flores just behind the art deco National Lottery Building in the Colonia Tabacalera (tobacco-workers colony), then run by María Antonia González, a Cuban patriot, and her Mexican husband, the wrestler Avelino Palomo, AKA "El Medrano."

La Antilla is long gone, but Pedro Álvaro, who dishes out tacos of cow brains on the corner, remembers growing up with tropical music pulsating from the bodega. The Cubanos lounged on the benches out front, smoking little black cigars and plotting.

Like many young political travelers, Dr. Guevara was rudderless, halfheartedly saving his precious pesos for cheap passage to Europe and eventually the Soviet Union. His pal El Patojo was working as a night watchman at the Economic Cultural Fund, and some nights Guevara would spread his sleeping bag between the aisles and read Marx and Lenin and Mao until first light.

Che's Peruvian lover Hilda Gadea arrived in Mexico City and he moved into the tiny apartment she rented on Río Rhin in the

Cuauhtémoc. On May 1, 1955, they joined the yearly International Labor Day march to the Zócalo: "(It was) very sad. The march was like a funeral," he laments in his diary. "The Mexican Revolution is dead and no one bothered to tell us."

That June, Guevara touched bases with 22-year-old Raúl Castro through María Antonia, and learned that his big brother Fidel, the leader of the Moncada uprising, would soon be arriving in Mexico City to organize an expedition and reignite the aborted Cuban Revolution.

Ernesto Guevara and Fidel Castro met for the first time at La Antilla in July—in his farewell letter to Fidel April 11, 1965, before his departure from Cuba for parts unknown, El Che would recall the meeting at the little Cuban bodega on Emparán Street.

The two Castros and the young Argentinean medic spent many hours discussing the possibilities of revolution at Hilda's chairless apartment on Río Rhin, and after one of Fidel's marathon four-hour discourses, El Che was persuaded to throw in with the July 26 Movement—to Hilda's enormous displeasure. She was then pregnant with Guevara's first child.

Fidel spent much of that summer huddling with potential recruits who had begun to trickle into Mexico City. Juan Almeida, who had been Fidel's lieutenant at Moncada, arrived, as did Camilo Cienfuegos a little later. In the afternoons, the elder Castro would schmooze with the hugely bearded Spanish Republican poet León Felipe at the Café Sorrento opposite the Alameda. One photo shows the two with yawning holes in their upturned shoes.

Fidel traveled to the United States that fall to raise funds for the expedition while the recruits trained under the tutelage of El Medrano and a comrade wrestler, Arsacio Venegas. The workouts included rowing in Chapultepec Park Lake and forced hikes from one end of Insurgentes Avenue to the other—16 kilometers along the longest known avenue in the Americas. They climbed Chiquihuite Hill rising above the eastern slums, and Che took on the volcano Popocatépetl but suffered an asthma attack a quarter of the way up—Guevara was desperate to conceal his asthma from his comrades for fear he would be disqualified from the upcoming Cuban Revolution.

The winter of 1956 was rainy and cold, recalls Paco Ignacio Taibo II, whose biography of El Che informs this narrative. Fidel returned from a successful fundraising trip in the United States. More Cubans arrived from Miami, San Francisco, and Costa Rica. Guevara and one unnamed Mexican were the only non-Cubans on the team.

Arsacio Venegas rented a gym on Bucareli where the trainee revolutionists practiced karate and learned how to climb walls. On the weekends, they traveled to a hunting club in Texcoco to take target practice. Fidel had begun to assemble an arsenal through the good offices of "El Cuate," a friendly gun dealer with a shop at Revillagigedo #47 in the heart of the Cuban neighborhood. The Castro brothers rented a basement in the Centro and several safe houses to park their guns and recruits. In May, Che and a dozen Cubans moved onto a secluded ranch in Chalco, beyond the airport east of the city, where under the tutelage of Alberto Bayo, a Communist commandant in the Spanish Civil War, they practiced techniques of sabotage.

Like Mella before him, Fidel had a price on his head. The Cuban dictator Fulgencio Batista reportedly was offering $10,000 USD, good money at the time, to take him out. On June 5, 1956, Fidel and six others were busted at a safe house in Copilco near the University City. A dozen more co-conspirators were rounded up lounging on the benches outside La Antilla. When the cops hit the ranch in Chalco, El Che was up in a tree. Hilda and their brand-new baby daughter Hilda Beatriz were dragged in, and Mexican agents advised Che they would be tortured if he did not spill the beans.

The anti-Communist press had a field day. Guevara was described as a Soviet agent, and as was automatic in these situations, the Soviet ambassador was asked to leave. The Red-baiting was so charged that the Cubans were pressed to divulge the true nature of their project to the Mexican people and took out disclaimers in both *Excelsior* and *El Universal* assuring their hosts that they were planning to overthrow the Batista government, not Ruiz Cortines.

The would-be revolutionaries were concentrated at the Miguel Schultz Immigration Detention Center in the Santa María Ribera colonia. Fidel, the leader, wore a suit every day, notes Taibo. Hilda came with the baby, and she and Che picnicked in the patio. Although Guevara's diaries do not mention that he was tortured during captivity, Arturo "El Negro" Durazo, later to become the capital's most blatantly criminal police chief, bragged that Fidel and Che receive so many *calentamientos* ("warming ups" with electric shocks) that "the wax ran from their ears."

Fidel was questioned closely by a young army captain, Fernando Gutiérrez Barrios, soon to head up the fearsome Federal Security Directorate. Gutiérrez Barrios warned the Cuban leader that there was a *soplón* (stool pigeon) in their ranks. Interrogations continued into July.

Then, abruptly, the pressure receded. Ex-president Cárdenas had called upon Ruiz Cortines and pleaded the Fidelistas' case—the Cuban Revolution would later recognize Tata Lázaro as one of its heroes. Gutiérrez Barrios suggested that freedom could be obtained if the appropriate palms were greased and finally, after 57 days behind bars, the prisoners were released—but with one caveat: Everyone had to be out of the country in 10 days' time. From then on, the Cubans were fugitives in Mexico.

SAILING INTO HISTORY

El Che went underground—well, really overground, taking a rooftop room in the Colonia Navarte from which he rarely emerged. Fidel was feverishly trying to book transport. El Cuate knew of a yacht owned by the American Robert Erickson and named for his grandma, that lay abandoned in the tiny Veracruz port of Tuxpan. The deal went down and shipwrights were hired to patch up the 62-foot boat to make it minimally seaworthy.

September and October passed with no word from Fidel, who was seeking to coordinate the sea landing with a revolt by urban cadre. Frank País, who was organizing the uprising in Havana, flew into Mexico City for consultations.

Then in mid-November, orders were issued for the volunteers to assemble near Tuxpan by the morning of the 24th. El Che left in a hurry, grabbing a bus from the San Lázaro terminal down to Veracruz. Friends who came to clean out his rooftop room later recalled that they found a copy of *Das Kapital* open on the bed and Guevara's asthma inhaler, a misstep that El Che would later rue.

And so in late November 1956, on a dark and stormy night, 82 revolutionaries crammed between the gunnels of the old eel pot that still bore the sobriquet of Erickson's grandma, sailed out into history. Their departure was hardly a secret. They would be met in Cuba by 35,000 of Batista's crack troops; only 12 rebels would survive to make their way into the Sierra Maestra and launch a revolution that would change Latin America forever.

URUCHURTU'S FLOWERS

While the Cuban Revolution was blossoming right under his nose, Ernesto P. Uruchurtu, the Iron Regent, was busily planting flowers. Great beds of tulips and gladioli, irises and dahlias, daffodils, daisies, and lilies decorated the median strips of Reforma and Insurgentes and the other major thoroughfares of the capital. The traffic circles or *glorietas* were ablaze with posies and the Condesa and the Roma similarly adorned. Chapultepec Park was tidied up and the Monstruo's green spaces pruned and attended to.

When, on June 28, 1957, a 5.8 earthquake rattled the city and toppled the heavily gilded Angel of Independence from her 100-foot-high perch above Reforma, wrenching her gleaming head from her naked torso, Chava Flores, the insouciant troubadour of Chilangolandia in the 1950s, poked fun at Uruchurtu's zeal for floriculture. It was lucky for the Regent that the Angel fell to the right rather than the left, Chava sang, because if she had tumbled to the left, she would have crushed Uruchurtu's precious gladioli. *"No es justo Uruchurtu, no es justo"* (it's not fair), warbled Flores, an outspoken foe of the Iron Regent's beautification program.

THE MONSTRUO GROWS UP AND DOWN

By 1956, the Monstruo was not only spreading across state lines but growing vertically as well. The crowning of the 45-story Torre Latinoamerican, "the tallest building in Latin America" and the first skyscraper ever to be erected in an earthquake zone, was hailed in the Mexico City press as the dawn of the age of the *rascacielos*. Up until then, most tall buildings in the metropolis, like El Nacional across the street from the Torre and several of the more deluxe hotels down Reforma, maxed out at 12 stories.

But while the Monster was reaching for the sky, it was also sinking in the spongy subsoil of the vanished lake upon which Tenochtitlán was founded. From 1948 through 1954, Mexico City sank 30 centimeters, twice what it had slipped the previous six years. The geologic and hydrological implications of this slippage were profound. With 4.8 million souls in residence (1960 census), the Monstruo could hardly slake everyone's thirst. As the aquifers were sucked dry, the city settled into the lake strata. Meanwhile the Lerma river system, from which the capital was now drawing most of its water, was increasingly tainted with industrial wastes from the many plants along its banks.

Nineteen fifty-six was also the year PEMEX, the national petroleum corporation established by Lázaro Cárdenas, inaugurated a giant refinery out in Azcapotzalco in the north of the city named after the date the Great Man had expropriated the oil from its Anglo-American owners. The "18th of March" refinery would soon put the lie to Carlos Fuentes's first novel to be published the next year, *Where the Air Is Clear*, and damage the lungs of millions of Chilangos for generations until it was finally shut down in 1989.

Contamination readings at the ecological park that has been salvaged from the ruins of the refinery indicate a clear and present danger to the health of all who dare to tread the grass. By the late 1980s, Fuentes was living in London and Madrid and publishing *Cristóbal Nonato*, a cautionary tale about a fetus who refuses to emerge from the womb because of Mexico City's ghastly air.

"NO ES JUSTO URUCHURTU"

Ernesto P. Uruchurtu's modus operandi was all licenses and permits and *multas* (fines). Nothing moved in the city unless it had permission to do so, and permits for everything—driving a cab, renting a market stall, playing an organ in the street, or burying a grandmother—could be obtained by bribing city inspectors. The *mordida* was the grease that kept Uruchurtu's city moving. It still is. In 2007, Transparency International's Mexico City office estimated that 24,000,000 pesos in "small bites" lard palms each year.

Uru's war on street vendors was legendary. The Iron Regent singled out the areas around the public markets as being particularly unsightly. Hundreds, no thousands, of *ambulantes* had set up shop around the crumbling Merced and Lagunilla markets in the old quarter. Uruchurtu sent in the Granaderos and ran off the unlicensed sellers with maximum brutality, reduced the old markets to rubble, and rebuilt them to accommodate 50,000 *puestos* or spaces to be doled out for a price. The scheme paid off handsomely for the city inspectors, but the reorganization did not really work very well. Within a week the ambulantes were encamped around La Merced, Lagunilla, Jamaica, and La Viga, the major markets in the inner city, all over again. Kasbahs of *jodidos* bloomed, offering blemished vegetables and suspect meat, merchandise that had "fallen off the back of a truck," and pirate goods fabricated in a Tepito basement sweatshop (talk about "product substitution").

But inside the gleaming new markets, things were different—the prices, for instance. "I do not think I have ever before seen two onions that are worth three pesos," Salvador Novo, the city's official *cronista*, wrote in the weekly supplement *México en la Cultura*, and Chava Flores, who never missed an opportunity to excoriate Ernesto P. Uruchurtu for uprooting his favorite taco stand to plant flowers, lyrically expounded, "*Los mercados son retenuevos* (the markets are super new)/ *por 20 pesos los dan dos aguacates* (for 20 pesos you get two avocados)/ *no es justo, no es justo, Señor Uruchurtu.*"

"WITH A NEEDLE IN MY HAND" (An interview with Don Juanito López)

Don Juanito López is a tailor. So was my grandfather Solomon. Tailoring was one of the first trades that got organized here in Mexico City—the Great Circle of Tailors was a member organization of the Casa del Obrero Mundial, whose secretary, Luis Méndez, was himself a tailor. Don Juanito's father was a guild member and he still has some of the pamphlets promoting the Great Circle in his shop.

Juanito maintains a workshop in an office building on Isabel la Católica around the corner from La Blanca and drops in just about every weeknight. He was good enough to tell his story for El Monstruo.

"I came to the city from Cholula, Puebla, in 1957, the year the Angel fell down, to join my father who was a tailor and went to work as his apprentice— I did his composturas *[mending]. We had a place in the* taller *[workshop] of Señora Carmelita Martínez in San Ángel. She made specialty charro suits for Jorge Negrete and Pedro Infante, the singing cowboys. They both had programs on XEW and were very popular.*

"Actually, we did suits for many different kinds of entertainers, especially Pérez Prado, the king of the mambo, and his entire orchestra. We also made suits for the Cuban singer Bienvenido Granda and the singing group Los Crooners. A handmade suit cost you 275 pesos in those days.

"The Pachuco style was popularized by the dancer Tin Tan. It was a Spanish cut—the jackets were very long and the pants flared at the top and were pegged at the cuffs. You wore them with a long, gold keychain. The Pachuco style used a lot of cloth and was the most expensive suit we made

in those days—the super-extras were the top of the line and made from pure cashmere."

I tell Don Juanito, "When I was growing up in New York, the Pachuco style or zoot suits were popular with musicians. I think I was 14 when I saved up to buy two pairs of pegged pants—one was powder blue with white saddle stitching on the side seams, and the other was rust brown. I wore them with my stepfather's long suede jacket. My mother hated them, so I had to sneak them out of the house and dress in the hallway. She called them my hoodlum pants."

"Yes, the zoot suit had a bad reputation. But it was just one of many styles we sold. Tailoring is an art. You have to learn the tricks of the trade. The Great Circle of Tailors gave classes to teach the apprentices, but I never went. The truth is that I never wanted to be a tailor. I wanted to be a baker or a farmer. I was fortunate, I suppose, that my father was a master tailor and showed me his art and I was a good learner—most maestros will never show you their secrets.

"In a taller, one tailor will only work on pants, another on suit jackets and another on overcoats. Everyone had their specialty. You become an expert at what you do. You attract customers and they will always come to you because you know their measurements and their favorite styles.

"In the '60s, we got the Italian cuts—short jackets with three buttons and straight pants. The styles changed from decade to decade. In the '70s, the shoulders were wide. We did a white suit for none other than James Brown, who was a big hit in Mexico. I'll never forget delivering his suit to the Del Prado Hotel. James Brown was an excellent dancer and the cuffs had to be just right so he wouldn't get tripped up. 'Mister Brown,' I said, 'here is your suit and here is our card. If there is any problem, please call us.' James Brown reached into his pocket and pulled out a hundred-dollar bill. ¡Guao! That was big money in those days. I didn't know what to say.

"Everything was made to measure. We made suits from scratch. What killed the art of tailoring was the hippies. Everything was a protest—even the way you dressed. The músicos didn't wear suits anymore. There was a big rock and roll show at Avándaro in the Bravo Valley in 1971 and the musicians all wore jeans and torn shirts. They made a very poor impression. After that, everyone went casual. A businessman would go to the office in jeans—they stopped wearing suits and ties.

"Now my clients are mostly businessmen who have been coming to me for a long time. They used to buy four or five suits a year, and now they buy one suit every five years. Many have retired or died.

"In the '90s, I was doing Hugo Boss and Brioni for Japanese executives at Mitsubishi and Panasonic. It would take me 25 days to make a suit from beginning to end. I had three assistants and could charge up to 10,000 pesos [$1,000 USD]. But I don't have any assistants now. When I began in this business, tailors were artisans. These kids today can't even sew a button on straight.

"What I'm afraid of is that my eyes are not as sharp as they used to be. I have a hard time just threading a needle now. A tailor loses his sight and he loses his business. I'm 62 and I don't know how long I have. They'll probably find me dead in my shop with a needle in my hand."

"AN EXTREME LEFTIST"

Adolfo Ruiz Cortines's *sexenio* came to a natural end in 1958 amidst soaring inflation and labor unrest. Finance Minister Antonio Ortiz Mena was prominently mentioned as his successor. The PAN, pleased with Ernesto P. Uruchurtu's iron rule, which had sustained the privileged classes in all their Porfirian glory during the past six years, offered the regent its presidential nomination, but Uru had no interest in the presidency and refused to bolt the PRI.

In a surprise twist, when Ruiz Cortines whirled in the presidential swivel chair and pointed the big finger (Dedazo), the designated pinch hitter was not Ortiz Mena but Ruiz Cortines's *tocayo* (they shared the same first name) Adolfo López Mateos, the labor secretary. López Mateos, who had been Vasconcelos's campaign manager in 1929, was considered the most left-wing member of his predecessor's cabinet, once declaring "I am an extreme leftist within the Constitution." The new president's leftist credentials would soon be sorely tested.

López Mateos was cognizant that the PRI's domination of the capital rested on the continued presence of Ernesto P. Uruchurtu in local government, and he reappointed the Iron Regent to a second six-year term—Uru's second sexenio would be a bumpier ride.

ENOUGH OF THE MEXICAN MIRACLE

By 1956, the laboring classes had had quite enough of the Mexican Miracle. Peso devaluation in 1954 failed to slow out-of-control cost-of-living hikes that had cut workers' buying power by a third. The city's primary school teachers were having a rough time feeding and clothing their families. The National Education Workers Union (SNTE), the largest labor organization in Latin America with 1.3 million members, was run however by labor aristocrats who paid no mind to the deprivations the maestros faced on a daily basis.

Othón Salazar, a young Communist firebrand, had gained a following in the SNTE's Section 9 on Belisario Domínguez Street not far from the Secretariat of Public Education (SEP). Salazar agitated for a living wage and convoked the Revolutionary Teachers Movement (MRM). The maestros marched on the SEP, and when the government shined them on, a strike was called that shut down grade schools all over the city. Othón Salazar urged rural teachers—many of them like himself graduates of the radical Normal training schools instigated by Lázaro Cárdenas to spread socialist education throughout the land— to march up to Mexico City in solidarity.

Thousands of ragged country maestros and their families camped around the SEP's elegant offices on Argentina Street where Rivera had once muralized the walls, hung up swatches of plastic to keep off the cold and the rain, and cooked their food on sidewalk campfires. The slap slap of tortillas could be heard all the way to Uruchurtu's City Hall offices across the Zócalo.

The Iron Regent was seriously displeased by this unruly spectacle and the Granaderos were called upon to administer the usual *santa madriza* (holy beating). Salazar was dragged off to Lecumberri and charged with violating Sections 145 and 145B of the Mexican Constitution, which defined the crime of "social dissolution." The SNTE bosses yanked his teaching credential.

At the end of the 1980s, I hopped a bus out to Alcozauca, Guerrero, a Mixtec-Amuzgo village in the dirt-poor Montaña region, Othón Salazar's birthplace. He was then in his second term as mayor—the only Communist mayor in all Mexico. The Maestro spoke in long florid sentences laced with strings of Marxist-Leninist argot as if he was addressing the masses. There was no one else in the room. He was still fuming about Lecumberri and the Granaderos and Uruchurtu and his damned flowers.

THE MUMMY

Fidel Velázquez was Mexico's czar of all labor czars for half a century. As Supreme Chief of the Mexican Confederation of Labor (CTM), he had the ear of eight presidents and a seat at the table of power from 1952 to his death at age 97 in 1997. During Velázquez's long reign, the CTM ruled Mexican labor and year after year delivered the necessary votes to sustain the PRI's death grip on the nation's jugular vein. Indeed, workers' jobs were conditioned on their voting for the PRI. Each May 1st, Velázquez commanded armies of PRI workers who passed under the balconies of the National Palace to offer their obeisance to the Presidente for all his blessings.

Although Don Fidel would threaten a general strike every few years, the job actions always dissolved before the workers could hit the bricks. The main job of the CTM was precisely the reverse—to keep workers from striking. Following the Morones model, Don Fidel and the Mexican Confederation of Labor were experts at enforcing "protection" contracts that granted the bosses labor peace for a piece of the take.

Fidel was a fountain of anti-Communist slime, spreading his venom throughout the Mexican labor movement. He had come to the pinnacle of power as Alemán's replacement for Lombardo Toledano and never forgot that his toast was buttered on the bosses' side. The CTM organized unions at individual shops and not once went after a whole industry, keeping the workers isolated and divided. Members often had no idea who the officials of their union were. In case of rebellion, Velázquez had a doctorate in Goonsterism and would send in the *golpeadores* (hitters) to "educate" dissidents.

Don Fi's longevity earned him the pet name "La Momia." He did, in fact, look sort of like a mummy, his crinkled skin flapping in folds from his turkey neck. Velázquez's Monday morning press conferences at the CTM were mandatory for novice reporters when I first came here. The problem was that very few of us could understand what he was saying anymore. Two veterans of these séances would hold their mini-recorders up to the Mummy's cracked lips to catch the drift. Then we would adjourn to the press room where they would decipher the message and translate it for us rookies.

Believe it or not, Fidel Velázquez still lives. Today, he stands guard outside the CTM headquarters on Vallarta Street adjacent to the Monument of the Revolution, staring out on a desolate traffic circle, 16 feet tall in his bronze suit, replicated right up to his Ray-Bans from behind which he continues to size up his allies and his adversaries, and probably hankering for one of those foot-long Havanas he always had clenched between his teeth. The last time I visited Don Fidel, a *teporo-cho* (Chilango for drunk) was passed out at his feet.

TIME OF THE CHARROS

Fidel Velázquez was not the original *charro*. That dubious honor falls to Jesús Díaz de León, who seized leadership of the railroad workers union in 1948 and dressed in the silver-studded pants, flowery charro shirts, and sequined sombreros of an ornamental horseman. The tag "charro" has been applied to every labor faker since. But while Brother Díaz de León dressed up like Pedro Infante, railroad workers toiled under perilous conditions for less than 400 pesos a month and lived in ragged colonies of abandoned freight cars on the wrong side of the tracks.

What stung the train men most was how they had been betrayed by the Mexican Revolution. Railroad workers had been the first to join the Revolution, rising up against their Yanqui and British bosses in a surge of revolutionary nationalism even before Porfirio was overthrown. Under Cárdenas, the workers had actually been entrusted with collectively running the national railroad system, but after a series of deadly train wrecks, Ferrocarriles Nacionales was returned to government administration.

Agitation against the charro union bosses mounted through 1958. Spurred by Demetrio Vallejo, a fireplug-size motor-mouthed Communist, and perpetual political prisoner Valentín Campa, a founder of the PCM, the railroad workers staged wildcat stoppages, four hours one day, six the next. In September, the rail workers and striking teachers joined forces in a mammoth Zócalo rally. Molotov cocktails were tossed at the National Palace. Students torched hijacked city buses and the firemen were called out to wash the protesters off the square.

López Mateos, the former labor secretary, called for negotiations— Vallejo was demanding a 100 percent raise that would put the railroad men on a par with other ill-paid public employees. When the talks broke down, a strike was called for Semana Santa (Holy Week) 1959, when Chilangos abandon the capital like lemmings and rail travel peaks.

The showdown came March 25, the second day of the strike. "Extreme Leftist" President López Mateos sent in the military to commandeer the trains. Soldiers marauded through rail workers' colonies in Nonoalco and Azcapotzalco—2,000 were arrested. Vallejo and Campa were marched off to Lecumberri for the next 16 years, charged with social dissolution and stripped of their union membership. Fidel Velázquez fired up a cheroot just in from Havana.

In September 1960, the muralist David Alfaro Siqueiros and Filomeno Mata, the son of a revolutionary journalist, were fingered for supporting the strikers and dragged off to the Black Palace on similar charges. Siqueiros converted his cell into a studio and would spend the next four years painting for his fellow social dissolutionists.

URUCHURTU IN GRIDLOCK

In 1960, for the first time, the census conceded what Mexican demographers had long surmised—more Mexicans now lived in cities than out in the countryside. Nearly 5 million out of 33 million citizens claimed home addresses in the Mexico City Metropolitan Area.

Although the Monster's growth actually slowed between 1950 and 1960 to 4.9 percent annually (it had been 5.4 percent from 1940 to 1950), it would pick up again in the '60s (5.1 percent). The Centro, due at least in part to the Iron Regent's unwelcome mat, was no longer the first destination of the hordes of *jodidos* from the campo. The newcomers settled into the northern industrial delegations, clustering together according to their hometowns. Like the 159 Purépecha Indian heads of family from Tzintzuntzan ("Place of the Hummingbird") on the shores of Lake Pátzcuaro in Michoacán who settled in Colonia Gustavo Madero from 1950 through 1970, many were indigenous peoples.

Uruchurtu's beloved Centro lived in perpetual gridlock. Eight thousand buses clotted the streets, idling in five-mile-an-hour-traffic (as fast as a pedestrian walks) and disgorging their killer effluvia. The 1960 vehicle census topped out at 234,000, three times the 1950 figure of 72,000. As families dug in and found shelter and steady work, the next step up in social mobility was to buy a car. By 1970, it would be twice as bad, and so on exponentially, and it is not over with yet.

The destination for most of these vehicles was the downtown shopping districts—major department stores like Liverpool and the Palacio de Hierro lined the streets south of the Zócalo. Now 72 separate bus routes had their terminals in the Centro, with boarding stations around the Plaza of the Constitution—in stark contrast to his horticulturally oriented first term, Uruchurtu ripped out the Zócalo's gardens to accommodate the bus companies and transformed the plaza into a vast concrete desert comparable only to Beijing's Tiananmen.

The Alianza de Camioneros (Bus Alliance) was Uruchurtu's moneybags. Formed in the 1920s to run urban bus transport after the routes were expropriated from the Canadian and British who held the franchises, the Alianza was composed mostly of the *permisarios* (those who owned permits) and some owner-operators. By the 1950s, the Alianza had a hammerlock on Mexico City public transportation. Photographs peering east down Cinco de Mayo Street show wall-to-wall gridlock with hundreds of buses—kids hanging on to their tails and passengers spilling out the doors—lined up all the way to the Zócalo.

For the bus companies, the solution was simply to widen the streets. Quaint Guatemala and Tacuba Streets were proposed for *amplificación* over the objections of preservationists who also had Uruchurtu's ear. Another proposal that would soon gain traction was to go underground—but the idea of gouging out a subway in the unstable lake soils seemed then to be folly.

Uruchurtu disregarded the Metro plan. He was a fan of surface transportation, having laid out 374 kilometers of new streets during his lengthy tenancy at City Hall. Another 1,377 had been paved for the first time. Fixing the streets put people to work, the contractors made out like bandits, and the PRI's ranks swelled.

One of the Iron Regent's more prodigious projects was the construction of a ring road or *periférico* that would allow traffic to circle the city rather than driving through its narrow streets to reach a destination. The stupendous 20-lane freeway (a second story was added in 2002) remains one of the world's most wondrous monuments to vehicular congestion.

When Chava Flores first discovered the Periférico, he could not figure out how to reach the other side and called out to a pedestrian on the opposite bank for instructions. "How do I cross over?" Chava sang. "I don't know," the pedestrian shouted back. "I was born on this side. I've never been over there."

A NEW TENANT MOVES IN

Just about every third apartment in the city's 547,471 residential structures took in a new tenant in the 1950s: the Telly. From Tlalpan to La Villa and Venustiano Carranza to Cuajimalpa, TV antennas blanketed the rooftops, a dense maze of skeletal rods that must have been disorienting for the pigeons.

Families gathered around the small, blinking screens, hypnotized by Emilio Azcárraga's Telesistema Mexicano. The programming was heavily larded with U.S. cartoons. "Speedy" González, the fast-moving Mexican mouse, was a favorite of Zapatista Subcomandante Marcos, then still a rug rat in Tampico, Tamaulipas.

Much as in the United States, wrestling was the toast of early Mexican television. El Santo, who began his grappling career as the rudest of the *rudos* (bad guys), was transmogrified into the ultimate good guy. El Enmascarado de Plata (Silver Mask—opponents had to rip his mask off to emerge victorious) tussled with villains like the Blue Demon, Tarzan López, and Wolf Ruvinskis at the Coliseo or the Arena México in the Colony of the Doctors. El Santo soon became a celluloid hero battling for justice and the little guy against fedora-wearing crooks, extraterrestrials, and bloodthirsty mummies.

Ernesto P. Uruchurtu was not a wrestling fan. He thought the spectacle demeaning and phony, and tried repeatedly to close down the arenas. The wrestlers got uppity and demanded a bigger piece of the purse under threat of forming a union. Azcárraga cancelled TV coverage at the arenas and staged his own cards at Telesistema's studios near Balderas. Among the scabs were Doctor Asesino and later "The Nurse of Doctor Asesino," Irma González, Mexico's first woman wrestler and the idol of teenage girls throughout the city.

Even without the TV exposure, Mexico City wrestling, a sort of urban passion play, survived the fast-buck '50s and still pulls in the proletarians at neighborhood arenas out in the delegations as well as on Sunday afternoons at the venerable Coliseo, where overheated fanatics are herded into cages to keep them from leaping out of the balcony into the ring.

¡PATRIA O MUERTE! ¡VENCEREMOS!

The triumph of the Cuban Revolution in January 1959 was a thunderclap that resonated throughout Latin America, and Mexico City, where the plot was first hatched, was no exception. The *barbudos'* taking of Havana on New Year's day was diligently followed, most of all on Emparán Street where the Fidelistas gathered around María Antonia's short-wave radio. "*¡Cuba Sí! ¡Yanqui No!*" posters were plastered all over the walls of University City. For once, the Mexican Left, battered by years of anti-Communist slander, had something to cheer about.

Lázaro Cárdenas, "General of the Americas," was summoned to Havana for the first postrevolutionary marking of Fidel's July 26 strike on the Moncada barracks and officially designated a hero of the Revolution for having utilized his good offices to spring Che and Fidel from the slammer. When, in April 1961, CIA-armed, -trained, and -financed *gusanos* (worms) sailed into the Bay of the Pigs and were captured at Playa Girón by the waiting Fidelistas, Cárdenas tried to fly off to the island in solidarity with the Revolution, but López Mateos, "the extreme leftist," had his plane grounded.

At a hastily called rally in the Zócalo the next day, the Tata climbed onto the roof of a parked car and pronounced the Revolution's signature slogan "*¡Patria o Muerte! ¡Venceremos!*" Tens of thousands swore their solidarity with the Cubans and Cárdenas flew off to Havana that evening. López Mateos backed off and did not order Lázaro's plane shot down.

THE KENNEDYS MEET THE MONSTRUO

After the Playa Girón *fracaso* (which his administration had inherited from the Dulles brothers), John Fitzgerald Kennedy resorted to spreading long green around the Americas. The Alliance for Progress, designed to counter the social ambitions of the Cuban Revolution, was floated to coax holdouts to break with the rebels. JFK set out on a Latin American junket to sell his strategy. Mexico City was the first stop.

When on June 30, 1962, with Jackie on his arm, America's heartthrob president drove in from the airport, the city's boulevards were lined with well-wishers waving the Star Spangled Banner and very few protesters— López Mateos's tough-as-nails interior minister Gustavo Díaz Ordaz, a certifiable anti-Communist paranoid schizophrenic, ordered the ¡Cuba Sí's! to be forcibly removed from the welcoming throngs.

Although the young Yanqui President hardly spoke the lingo ("Viva to Mexico" was his contribution), Jackie, form-fitted into a shocking pink frock and matching chapeau, was fluent. The American royal couple, he in a tuxedo and she in a pale blue chiffon evening gown, her luxuriant hair swept back in the ultimate '60s coif, were hosted at a state dinner by the equally debonair Adolfo López Mateos. JFK and the Mexican President were both charmers and babe magnets.

As the defender of the "Free World," Kennedy plucked the anti-Communist heartstrings of right-wing Mexico City elites. But the masses were equally attracted to JFK, the first Roman Catholic ever to occupy the Casa Blanca. After his assassination 17 months later, it was not unusual to find JFK rugs and portraits and other Kennedy kitsch in Mexican homes. Schools all over the country were named for the dead gringo president.

THE SWINGING SIXTIES

Jack and Jackie's popularity was symptomatic of the wave of optimism that washed over the pre-Vietnam '60s when the U.S. product was still a saleable item here. Rock and roll crashed the border with Bill Haley and the *Cometas*. Elvis flicks ignited youth riots at the Cine de Las Américas. Long-haired Tijuana rocker Javier Bátiz packed them in at the Café Ruser in the hot Zona Rosa, an 18-block enclave extending from Reforma opposite the new U.S. embassy to Insurgentes where the Swinging Sixties vibes palpitated.

Once the lair of Porfirian swells, the neighborhood was still sprinkled with tea salons and objet d'art emporiums, but by the early 1960s the Pink Zone was a brash, glitzy venue jammed with go-go girl bars. One had to be seen at Bellinghausen's or the Jacarandas Supper Club to get one's name in the social columns

Although El Monstruo was awash with U.S. spin-offs—all the *chavos* wore Levis, the *chavas* not yet—the Germanic influence held sway on the highway. Volkswagen opened its first auto plant in the New World just outside Puebla in 1964 and began cranking out its beloved "Vochitos" (Beetles). The Vocho was an affordable little car and soon became part of the Mexican family. Its popularity changed Mexican car culture forever. Green "ecological" bug taxis are still ubiquitous in Mexico City—"*express*" kidnappers find them perfect for their business needs, because once lodged in the passenger seat behind the driver, the intended victim cannot get away.

THE PERFECT DICTATORSHIP

The skyline of the Monster continued to spiral upward. The city's modern Medical Center, the largest in the Americas with 23 specialty hospitals, opened for business in 1963.

On November 20 that year, the day consecrated to the Mexican Revolution and just 10 days before he was to be sworn in as López Mateos's successor, Gustavo Díaz Ordaz inaugurated the PRI's new national bunker, 12-story twin towers that glared down on the city from behind tinted windows, plus the truly monstrous Plutarco Elías Calles auditorium—a gilded Calles stands guard at the gate. The complex continues to occupy an entire block on North Insurgentes, walled off from the rest of the world by a formidable 10-foot-tall stainless steel and recently electrified fence.

In keeping with the imperial nature of the enterprise whose initials it bears, The PRI's new digs were designed by an architect who claimed lineal descent from Mocuhtezuma. Then as now, the PRI headquarters dominated the flat (but lively) Colonia Guerrero much as the party dominated Mexico's political landscape.

By 1964, the Institutional Revolutionary Party owned 200 percent of Mexico. The PRI owned the Mexican flag (the party's colors) and it owned all its national symbols—the Eagle and the Serpent and the Nopal Bush. It owned Mexico's history from Cuauhtémoc to Cortez to Calles and Carranza and Lázaro Cárdenas. It owned its workers (the CTM) and it owned its farmers (the CNC) and it owned the land they farmed—the *ejido* was PRI government property. The PRI owned the government, both houses of Congress, every governor, and the Federal District, AKA El Monstruo. It owned the state apparatus, the government bureaucracy, the electoral machinery, the press and the radio and the TV. It owned the culture (Bellas Artes, the Ballet Folklórico) and it owned the budget and it owned the oil.

Mexico was a one-party state, and that party would outlive even the Soviet Communist Party—both had about 3 million members in 1960—to become the longest-ruling political dynasty in the known universe. Whoever crossed the PRI was crushed or co-opted or worse, ignored. Carlos Madrazo sought to reform the PRI and Díaz Ordaz fired him forthwith, and the next thing you knew, he was dead in a mysterious plane crash up in Monterrey.

For those who went along with the game, the PRI provided protection from cradle to grave, but if you doubted, you couldn't get a birth certificate or a job or even permission to be buried in the municipal boneyard.

In 1964, the PRI was at the apogee of its powers and behaved with all the blind arrogance that height implies. Mind you, this was a couple of decades before the snobby Hispanoid novelist Mario Vargas Llosa branded the PRI "the Perfect Dictatorship."

Today, although the Perfect Dictatorship has been out of power for eight years, the twin PRI towers at Insurgentes North #59 still inspire dread for all those who dare to pass that way.

XI

CITY OF DREAD
& REDEMPTION

lthough he had taken as his mistress the tempestuous "Tigresa," Irma Serrano, Gustavo Díaz Ordaz matched up poorly to the dashing López Mateos. A bucktoothed, squinty-eyed nerd, the new president had an unfortunate simianesque gap between his nostrils and his upper lip that earned him the nickname El Chango (The Monkey)—legend has it that *Ovaciones* was once punished for switching captions on pictures of the President and a monkey at the Chapultepec Park Zoo.

As López Mateos's interior minister, El Chango had been the architect of the repressive karma that became part of his "extreme leftist" predecessor's résumé. Díaz Ordaz had gone after Vallejo, Campa, Siqueiros, and Othón Salazar. The assassination of Zapata lieutenant Rubén Jaramillo and his family in 1963 during a land struggle in Morelos state was ultimately trackable back to Díaz Ordaz.

Gustavo Díaz Ordaz and Ernesto P. Uruchurtu both incubated anti-Communist phobias, and the Chango reappointed the Iron Regent to an unprecedented third term. But there were sharp distinctions in their personal agendas and most of all, to whom they were indebted.

In López Mateos's final year in the wheelhouse, a fast-modernizing Mexico had been awarded the 1968 Olympic Games, the first "developing" nation to be so cursed. The games presented Díaz Ordaz with a gold-medal opportunity to trot out the Mexican Miracle on the world stage. The Miracle, though, was showing signs of wear and tear and needed to be touched up with fresh gloss to impress the first world, of which Díaz Ordaz aspired to be a member. Soaring skyscrapers and luxury hotels, fast-moving highways, and a world-class public transportation system were priorities.

ICA, Ali Babaman's old partner Bernardo Quintana's construction empire, would build the Olympic infrastructure. The dream of the Metro was revived. Uruchurtu dug in his heels, however. The Metro would wreck his beloved Centro, and moreover his beloved balanced budgets.

As the mayor of the Monstruo for 14 years, Uruchurtu had always run million-dollar surpluses. One reason for this windfall was that he didn't have to provide for mass transportation—the Alianza de Camioneros had privatized all the costs.

THE SETUP

The rift between Díaz Ordaz and Ernesto Uruchurtu got gnarlier and gnarlier. The President's press team planted stories in the PRI rags blaming the regent for everything from the high price of chicken at La Merced to the abysmal performance of the national football team.

Next came the setup.

Before dawn on September 12, 1966, Uru sicced his Granaderos on a squatters' camp in Santa Úrsula south of the Centro in the Tlalpan delegation, where the enormous Azteca Stadium would soon be built by Televisa to accommodate its soccer team, Club América. City tractors mowed down the tent city and drove the sleepy *jodidos* out into the open where sadistic Granaderos applied the usual *santa madriza*.

It was the sort of brutality with which the Iron Regent had "beautified" the city for 14 years. Only this time there were hostile witnesses. Díaz Ordaz's leaders in the Chamber of Deputies appeared with the *prensa vendida* (sellout press) in tow. Later that morning in the lower house, the witnesses would call upon their fellow PRI deputies to remove "the bulldozer mayor" from office. Just then, a band of disheveled squatters was ushered into the chamber snarling "*¡Muere Uruchurtu!*" (That Uruchurtu should die!). The orchestrated deployment of the *jodidos* was a classic PRI maneuver to rid itself of politicos who had outlived their usefulness. The Iron Regent caught the drift and cashed in his chips before the day was done.

THE MONSTRUO & THE METRO

Díaz Ordaz appointed a crony, General Alfonso Corona del Rosal, to replace Uruchurtu. Contracts with ICA to construct the first line of the Mexico City Metro were inked the next week, although the big dig did not begin until June 1967. Uruchurtu's intransigence had delayed construction long enough so that the Metro would not be up and running for the '68 Olympics but would be soon after, to accommodate the rush of tourists who were expected to descend upon the Monstruo in the post-Games flush.

Uruchurtu fought the Monster and lost. Obsessed with stanching the monstrousness of the megalopolis, the Iron Regent failed utterly. In his 14 years at the helm, the city had mushroomed from 3,000,000 to nearly 7,000,000 souls and was still growing at a 5.1 percent clip.

Most newcomers were the sons and daughters of the *campo*. With the *reparto* fried, there wasn't enough land to divide up, and a campesino with four sons sent three off to the capital to find their way in the world. Television "invited" them up to the big city and they went to work in the *obra*. One cousin brought another. Some came to finish school. Young women found work as domestic servants, the much-maligned *chachas* of middle- and upper-class matrons. New arrivals with less than five years in the Federal District accounted for half its births. Two-thirds of the new workers were functionally illiterate and half worked for the minimum wage. Many were the very dark-skinned Indians that Uruchurtu had sworn to repel.

Despite his commitment to slow growth, his job proved to be an impossible one—he was dealing with a force of nature. Providing water, transportation, housing, health care, drainage, parking, and other social amenities for this mob of humanity was an insurmountable task. When Uru had first been appointed regent, Mexico City was a relatively small and manageable city where the air was transparent. Now it was neck and neck with São Paolo in the doomsday race to be the most crowded and contaminated urban entity in the Americas.

Ernesto P. Uruchurtu did, however, exact a measure of revenge for his unceremonious dumping. For the next three years, Mexico City would be mired in construction chaos as Díaz Ordaz and the

ICA engineers tore up downtown to install the first line of the underground Metropolitan Collective Transit System. The 14th modern Olympic Games would be celebrated amidst the mud and litter of unfinished construction.

TLATELOLCO

With just 900,000 residential spaces, ranging from cardboard shacks out by the airport to the mansions of Chapultepec Heights, to shelter 7,000,000 sentient human beings, there wasn't enough housing to go around. Indeed, the residents of posh enclaves like Lomas, Pedregal, Polanco, San Ángel, and Coyoacán lived in a separate city from the slum dwellers of the eastern and northern neighborhoods and the deteriorating, down-at-the-heels Centro.

It had been Uruchurtu's dream that the Centro would continue to be a place where Chilangos lived and worked. By the time he threw in the towel, 60 percent of those who worked in the center of town still lived there, a story that owed its success to the completion of the Tlatelolco-Nonoalco housing complex, slated to be the largest in Latin America.

Inaugurated in November 1964, the vast housing development replaced acres of dingy slums and railroad yards on what had once been the site of the Aztecs' market island. Back then, Tlatelolco had been the lair of Lord Tezcatlipoca, the god of the night. Once the citadel of the last emperor Cuauhtémoc, Tlatelolco encompassed important ruins, and the housing development combined the millennial with the cutting edge. Architect Mario Pani integrated the remains of the old temples and ball courts with sleek 14-story towers, many of them grouped around the Plaza of Three Cultures (Aztec, European, the PRI) in a 1960s futuristic vision of urban shelter. The 148 structures were honeycombed with 15,000 apartments housing 75,000 residents, many of them government bureaucrats who shuffled papers in the various secretariats within walking distance of their new homes.

The inauguration of Tlatelolco was a sign of hope that social progress was still possible under the thumb of the Perfect Dictatorship. Instead, four years later, Tlatelolco would become a symbol of the state repression that awaited those who demanded a bigger slice of a Mexico where not even the Virgin of Guadalupe could conjure up miracles anymore.

THE ALARM CLOCK

It wasn't as if the signs of social unrest had never been posted along the road to 1968. The labor troubles of the late '50s were a clear warning bell that the Mexican Miracle was not working *milagros* down at the grassroots. The slaughter of Rubén Jaramillo and his family in 1962 was a rude indicator of just how the all-powerful PRI government would respond to social agitation. On May 23 that year, Jaramillo, the last surviving lieutenant of Emiliano Zapata, was eating lunch at his home in Tlaquiltenango, Morelos, when the house was surrounded by 60 state and federal troops. Ruben, his pregnant wife and three children were thrown into army trucks and driven to a nearby archeological site where they were executed with Thompson machine guns.

Gustavo Díaz Ordaz further displayed his hard hand in breaking a doctors' strike in 1965 after 8,000 medics walked off the job at five city hospitals including the new Medical Center—doctors at public hospitals were so underpaid they had to double as cabdrivers in their off hours. Díaz Ordaz was inflexible, and the doctors were forced to back to work under threat of being summarily fired.

University campuses were restive. The military were mobilized to break a 1965 student strike at San Nicolás University in Morelia and again at the Sonora State University in 1967. The alarm clocks rang loud at the UNAM. Between 1952 and the mid-1960s, the student body had quadrupled from 22,000 to 85,000 and the battle for a place in University City triggered troubles.

The rumbling out in what sociologist Guillermo Bonfil termed México Profundo (Deep Mexico), where campesinos had been diminished to second-class-citizen status, was unmistakable. The murder of Rubén Jaramillo begged an answer. At dawn on September 23, 1965, a band of "subversives" led by rural schoolteacher Arturo Gámiz attacked an army fort in Ciudad Madero in the Sierra Maestra of Chihuahua— the similarities to Fidel Castro's assault on the Moncada Barracks could not be blurred. Although all 15 rebels were killed, the date would soon be embedded in the name of the September 23rd Communist League, Mexico's most active urban guerrilla in the 1970s.

In the southern state of Guerrero, another rural maestro, Genaro Vázquez, picked up the gun in 1963. Operating in the mountains that surround the provincial capital of Chilpancingo, Vázquez's Revolutionary National Civic Association (ACNAR) kidnapped the rector of the state university. After a 1967 massacre at a rural school in Atoyac on that state's Costa Grande (Long Coast), Lucio Cabañas, another rural teacher (rural teachers were often graduates of radicalized Normal schools), rose up in the coastal sierra, and his Party of the Poor would carry on a seven-year guerrilla war against the *mal gobierno* (bad government).

Despite the loud ring of the social *despertador* (alarm clock), Gustavo Díaz Ordaz's vision had tunneled in on the coming Olympic Games and he didn't seem to hear the din.

OLYMPIC FEVER

The Olympic Games are big business. Since the advent of the modern Games in 1896, they have had less to do with athletic excellence than with cashing in on the glory and glamour that accompanies the Olympics. The '68 games, the first ever to be staged in what was then designated the "third world," were sold to an unsuspecting Mexican people as an investment in the nation's future—but only those at the top of the power ladder had shares in the bonanza.

Díaz Ordaz sank a cool $200,000,000 USD (billions in today's dollars) in the party. Even before the first race was run, the big winner was Quintana's ICA Corporation. The Olympic Village rose above the ancient altar of Cuicuilco in the south of the city. ICA's Olympic Stadium in University City would host the outside events, its Palace of Sports the indoor competitions. An Olympic pool was built next to the Secretariat of Defense in the city's west. The new Periférico (ring road), dubbed the "Route of Friendship," would hook up events at distant venues, such as boating at Cuemanco in the Xochimilco delegation and weight lifting at the Sports Palace.

Spanking-new hotels like the El Camino Real (ICA) were confected. "We will welcome our visitors with flowers from the airport to the Zócalo," Díaz Ordaz gushed, sounding suspiciously like Uruchurtu. A cultural Olympics would garnish the platter: Leonard Bernstein and Duke Ellington (his *Mexican Suite* was created for the occasion) would headline. Museums and galleries polished up their expositions—a spectacular light show to dazzle the tourists was to be staged for the Pyramid of the Sun at ancient Teotihuacan.

Comparison to Porfirio Díaz's ill-fated Centennial bash was unavoidable.

COLD WAR OLYMPICS

Much like London (1948), Helsinki (1952), Melbourne (1956), Rome (1960), and Tokyo (1964), Mexico '68 was a Cold War Olympics. The Free World and the Other One confronted each other on the playing fields, at the Olympic Village, in the luxury hotel lobbies, and in the inner sanctums of the embassies. American agents trolled the Eastern Bloc and Cuban delegations for defectors. The Central Intelligence Agency and the KGB both brought high-powered surveillance teams to the Games.

The U.S. Embassy in Mexico City was Washington's most extravagant diplomatic outpost in the world. Hundreds of agents had spied on Iron Curtain embassies for years—film of Lee Harvey Oswald when he visited both the Soviet and Cuban embassies in September 1963 are just one example of how closely Uncle was watching. But the Soviet Union and its proxies were not to be outdone, and both sides in the Cold War were in place at Mexico '68. Indeed, the town filled up with so many spies that the Games could have been slugged "The Spook Olympics."

One player in the spy competition was Philip Agee, a veteran CIA operator in Latin America and Africa who worked under the cover of "cultural attaché" to justify his desk at the embassy on Reforma. Agee reported to Winston Scott, longtime station chief in Mexico City and a compadre of ex-president López Mateos, who had been the best man at Scott's wedding. Agee was assigned to work the University, where he would keep a sharp eye out for student troublemakers under the pretext of selling the wonders of the U.S. space program. He even set up a mock-up of a NASA Jupiter rocket to flack Yanqui technological superiority on that turbulent campus.

Universities all over the planet were drunk with youthful ferment in the spring of 1968. In upper Manhattan, students overran the president's office and shut down Columbia. In Prague, young people rose up against the Soviet monolith and dared to dance in the streets. Danny the Red was building barricades on the left bank of the Seine. Student rioters and left-wing union members embraced and came within a hair of driving Charles de Gaulle from power. The assassinations of Martin Luther King in Memphis in April and Bobby Kennedy in Los Angeles in June electrified race and class tensions north of the border.

In the Global South, another assassination had galvanized social upheaval—the execution of El Che by CIA-trained gorillas in the Bolivian jungle. Indeed, 1968 really ignited on October 8, 1967, in a makeshift army morgue in La Higuera, Bolivia.

HOW IT BEGINS

Trivial circumstances can trigger significant rebellions if the chemistry is right. A perceived slight, a fight, an "incident of transit," even a song sung out of tune, can be the tipping point that spills the slagheap of accumulated grievances into the street. As a matter of course, police and military overreaction will aggravate the situation and transform these accidental outbursts into a revolt against authority.

In July 1968, it was a lunchtime tiff between high school students at two *vocas* (vocational schools) in the Insituto Politécnico Nacional system and Prepa 9 in the UNAM network of secondary schools. Who knows who started it? The bad feelings between the two systems really were grounded in class: UNAM students were presumed to be children of privilege, and the Poli system had been created by Cárdenas to train the kids of the working class for state industry and technology.

The three schools were clustered around the Ciudadela, and the *zafarrancho* spread up and down Balderas Street. Street kids unattached to either of the schools jumped in, and when shop owners complained about looting, 200 Granaderos joined the fray, chasing the Poli kids back to the *vocas*, forcing the gates, and dragging the rebels off to the police wagons by their hair.

The blocks around the Ciudadela seethed with fury for two days, stirring memories of the Ten Tragic Days that had unfolded in these same neighborhoods 55 years earlier. The speed of the escalation was an instructive measure of the bad gas seeping out of the bottom of the Mexican Miracle.

On July 26, a march of Polytechnic students from the Ciudadela to the IPN's main campus in the Casco de Santo Tomás (Azcapotzalco delegation) crossed paths on Juárez Avenue with leftists out celebrating the 15th anniversary of the beginning of the Cuban Revolution. Portraits of the late Che were prominently displayed. Both marches joined forces for a rally at the Juárez monument on the Alameda and then, chanting "¡Zócalo! ¡Zócalo!" moved down Madero into the old quarter in the direction of the great plaza.

Three blocks farther east, between Isabel la Católica and Palma, the demonstrators ran into a wall of Granaderos. The *zipizapi* raged for hours, the cops pumping out tear gas, the kids armed with bottles and rocks pulled from the rubble of Metro construction. A dozen buses were hijacked and torched in the Zócalo. When the rosy-fingered dawn rose in the east, two or seven students had been killed in the melee, depending upon whom you believed.

Government agents busted down the door at the Communist Party headquarters and hauled a handful of Reds off to Lecumberri for fomenting subversion and "social dissolution." The truth of the matter was more diffuse. By 1968, the PCM was impotent and the Communists were incapable of provoking anything more revolutionary than a lecture on democratic centralism. The bust did however buff up the Party's cred, and it would grow disproportionately in the coming months.

The PCM did not stand alone in the dock of the accused: Various Trotskyist groups were also cited by El Universal as accessories to the crime. The imaginary Soviet-Cuban plot to disrupt the 14th International Olympic Games and drag Mexico's good name through the mud dominated the *prensa vendida*.

The arrest of three foreign students (two Americans and one Chilean) headed to a Soviet youth conclave in Bulgaria added heft to the fanciful plot. According to Luis Echeverría, Díaz Ordaz's interior secretary, the government had been forced to step in "to protect the autonomy of the UNAM from foreign agitation."

LA PRENSA VENDIDA

One had only to browse the headlines hanging off the downtown newspaper kiosks to appreciate Díaz Ordaz's lock on the capital's dozen daily newspapers. *Excelsior* parroted the Chango's line and was owned by the corrupt Rodrigo de Llano whose own reporters contemplated assassinating him. *El Universal* and *Ovaciones* (its afternoon edition) grew fat on PRI government publicity. *La Prensa* sold government lies and the *nota roja* (sensationalist tidbits). *El Sol de México* and *El Heraldo* were owned by Díaz Ordaz compadres Gabriel Alarcón and Mario Vázquez Raña (Mexican head of the International Olympic Committee). Rómulo O'Farrill's *Novedades* was on the government payroll and his English-language *The News* was overseen by the U.S. Embassy.

On the electronic side, Televisa, with its prime-time hatchet man Jacobo Zabludovsky spreading the lies, was El Chango's most animated cheerleader. Television and radio, where Díaz Ordaz disciples dominated the dial, accounted for 98 percent of all Mexicans' primary news sources.

Such lockstep "journalism" underscored the old I. F. Stone notion that what wasn't in the story was the real story, and millions of Mexicans learned to read and listen between the lines to get the news.

The *prensa vendida* had been preaching anti-Communism to the masses long before E. Howard Hunt ran the CIA's media operation here. Soviet plots had been a staple of their repertoire from Calles's time. Now they had the Cubans to kick around. The '68 Olympics were ready-made to reaffirm the for-sale press's servility to the PRI government's propaganda.

One mechanism for keeping the press in line: the government-controlled PIPSA newsprint monopoly—only those daily blats that repeated the Chango's garbage got some. Paid PRI government publicity was doled out in accordance with the media's allegiance. Reporters were bribed by those they covered—the weekly *sobre* (envelope) supplemented the news gatherers' meager salaries (some reporters had to sell advertising to survive). Political columnists were character assassins who wielded their pens for the highest bidder. The "newspapers" ran *gacetillas*, PRI government press releases, as front-page "news." Because the capital's papers were distributed throughout the country, the lies were disseminated to the four corners of Mexico.

There were exceptions. *México en la Cultura*, a weekly supplement to *Excelsior* edited by Fernando Benítez and a cuddly cub reporter named Carlos Monsiváis, told it like it was with élan. *El Día* infrequently shined a feeble light under this bushel basket of darkness. *Política*, the only left weekly newsmagazine on the rack, edited by Manuel Marcué Pardiñas, was a valuable tool for understanding the country back in the 1960s, until Pardiñas and his associate Victor Rico

Galán were dragged off to Lecumberri. Mario Meléndez's *Por Qué?* and *Por Esto!* were sensationally pro-Cuban; they carried news of incipient guerrilla movements throughout Mexico and would soon become the bible of the 1968 student movement.

EL BAZUKAZO

The actors in this incipient rebellion were often kids with Molotov cocktails from the three historic *prepas* north of the National Palace in the old University zone. After more buses were burnt in the Zócalo on July 29, Corona del Rosal petitioned Díaz Ordaz for federal troops to quell the students. From that date on, army tanks would be parked in the Zócalo.

The street clashes that night lasted well past midnight when hundreds of students barricaded themselves behind the great door of Prepa 3 on San Ildefonso alley where Rivera had painted his first murals. General José Hernández Toledo, commander of the federal Olympic Battalion, ordered his troops to storm the colonial building. At 1:10 a.m., July 30, a bazooka was set up on the esplanade and fired at the huge oak door, tearing it from its hinges; 347 young people were handcuffed and trucked off to languish in Lecumberri.

The *bazukazo* was a watershed. Tens of thousands of Mexicans had passed through the Great Door on their way to a university education. The invasion of Prepa 3 had been the most egregious violation of university autonomy since its creation in 1929. Academics were stunned. UNAM rector Javier Barros Sierra suspended classes and students shut down Polytechnic. The Mexican flag flew at half-mast on both campuses.

On August 1, Rector Barros joined arms with leaders of the university community, serious men in neat beards and dark suits, for a march from Ciudad Universitaria to the Zócalo. Perhaps 80,000 students and faculty members lined up behind them. The marchers got as far north on Insurgentes Avenue as the Plaza México, the city's bullring. Tanks were rolling, and the rector would not risk a bloodbath. But the people of the city were beginning to take sides. Many residents of the nearby Miguel Alemán *multifamiliar* stood on the balconies of their apartments and applauded the valor of the *universitarios*.

¡HUELGA!

The posture of Rector Barros lent gravitas to what had begun as a street brawl. A student strike council was formed from the two school systems. The National Council of the Strike (CNH) numbered 206 representatives from 138 schools and faculties including the vocas and the prepas. Their list of demands, or *pliego petitorio*, called for the firing of Mexico City police chief Luis Cueto and the immediate release of all political prisoners—in addition to hundreds of students rounded up since July 23, the strikers demanded freedom for the all-but-forgotten Demetrio Vallejo and Valentín Campa, whom Díaz Ordaz himself had sent to prison nine years earlier. The students also demanded the abrogation of Constitutional Articles 145 and 145B, which defined the crime of "social dissolution."

Curiously, not one of the students' original demands addressed the quality of higher education or overcrowding of classrooms, and most were stand-ins for expressions of extreme disaffection with the authoritarian rule of the PRI and the President of the Republic. The 1968 student rebellion was only marginally about academic freedom. Changing Mexico was its real demand.

At the enormous August 13 march, the CNH's debut on the streets of the city, 150,000 students and supporters from both the UNAM and Poli and about half that many likenesses of El Che filled Reforma from gutter to gutter on the 13-kilometer route from the Anthropology Museum in Chapultepec Park to the Zócalo. The school yells of "*¡Goya Goya Cachun Cachun!*" alternated with "*¡Cachi Cachi Porra Politécnico Gloria!*" and both schools teamed up in unison chants of solidarity with the beleaguered comrades in Vietnam: "*Ho Ho Ho Chi Minh/ ¡Díaz Ordaz Chin Chin Chin!*"

On the eve of the big march, the President had offered a conciliatory gesture: "My hand is extended." But the students would have none of it. "Dead students cannot shake the hand of the president," they yodeled. "The extended hand has a gun in it!" "There are powder burns on the president's hand!" The strikers congregated under the Presidential Balcony of the National Palace and demanded that El Chango come out and debate them. A large papier-mâché gorilla was set afire.

The uprising was now in its third week and growing exponentially from march to march. The Olympic Games were due to open October 12, just two months hence on Díaz Ordaz's calendar.

"YOUR CHILDREN ARE CALLING OUT TO YOU!"

Communist Cuba's prints were all over the plot to disrupt Mexico '68 if you could believe the *prensa vendida*. The multiple images of Che displayed at the August 13 demonstration were further evidence of a brazen conspiracy against the Patria. The students were "willing dupes of Soviet expansionism" (Vázquez Raña's *El Sol de Mexico*). The students were ingrates for turning against a government that provided them with a free education. "Fathers of families, control your children!" ordered Secretary of Defense Marcelino García Barragán.

But the kids were out of control.

Students went into the neighborhoods and spread their cause in face-to-face encounters with civil society to combat the toxic Red-baiting of the Díaz Ordaz press. They stood on street corners and handed out leaflets that invited, "Mexicans, wake up! *¡Tus hijos están llamando!* Your children are calling out to you!" They held lightning meetings in public markets and shook cans for coins on the buses. They sat down with their elders and explained the *pliego petitorio*.

Many parents joined the strikers on the one-month anniversary of the movement August 27. The march from the Anthropology Museum to the Centro was so long that its head reached the Zócalo before its tail had left Chapultepec Park, perhaps 250,000 participants in all.

The mood was all exhilaration and bravado. "If you can't find me, *mamá*, come down to the Procu's [District Attorney's] office!" hand-lettered signs mocked. The spirit of libertarianism reigned—"It Is Prohibited to Prohibit!"—and inevitably *"Haz el Amor y No la Guerra."* More militant messages abounded: "We Don't Want Your Fucking Olympics! We Want a Revolution!"

The sound systems blasted the international youth anthems of the Beatles, the Stones, and Bob Dylan. Creedence Clearwater and Cassius Clay, who had just taken the name Muhammad Ali, were icons of Mexico's 1968 student uprising. The gringo war against the heroic people of Vietnam was a popular target of outrage, and a dozen tanks were parked outside the U.S. embassy to discourage attack.

Throughout the day, the police and military had stayed discreetly out of sight and the marchers dispersed in the Zócalo without incident. Several thousand students voted to establish a *plantón* (sit-in) in the center of the great plaza under the flagpole to await Díaz Ordaz's September 1 State of the Union message (Informe) to the nation.

The soldiers attacked the encampment just after midnight. General Hernández read an order declaring the occupation illegal, and the Olympic Battalion, wielding unsheathed bayonets, pushed the strikers out—but not before they had run up a red-and-black strike flag on the monumental flagpole in the dead center of the Zócalo. It was still flying the next morning, when soldiers pulled it down and burnt it.

The desecration of the flagpole was tantamount to treason, Televisa's mouthpiece Jacobo Zabludovsky blathered on the evening news. The regent Corona del Rosal called for a day of *desagravio* to remove this stain on the national honor. Sanitation workers and government bureaucrats were ordered to gather in the Zócalo. The government bureaucrats did not want to be there. Many had children among the marchers. Murmurs turned into a chant: "We Are Sheep! Baaah Baaah! We Are Sheep!"

The soldiers immediately put an end to the meeting, firing live ammunition over the heads of the "sheep." By a startling torque of fate, paratrooper-fusiliers under the command of General Bernardo Reyes, nephew of the Ten Tragic Days' General Reyes, opened fire on the Hotel Majestic on the western flank of the plaza. The shadow of another Bloody Sunday hovered over the Zócalo.

BAD MEXICANS

Little by little, the mask of the Mexican Miracle was being ripped away to reveal the ugly authoritarianism of the PRI *gobierno* that festered underneath.

September, with its cluster of patriotic celebrations, is the month of the Patria. Public buildings are swaddled in red, green, and white bunting. Much like the Niños Héroes who jumped from the balustrades of Chapultepec Castle rather than submit to the Yanqui invaders in 1846, politicians wrap themselves in the flag. Even the *putas* in the red-light La Merced district wave little Mexican flags to attract patriotic customers.

On September 1, Gustavo Díaz Ordaz delivered his Informe to Congress as mandated by the Constitution. In 1968, the day of the Informe was still the maximum moment of obeisance to the imperial presidency in the PRI's repertoire. The whole nation was glued to the tube to audit El Chango's ultimatum to the students.

The strikers were "sabotaging the functioning of the city" and would face the dire consequences of their acts if they did not desist immediately. They were "bad Mexicans" who worshipped "foreign heroes alien to our essence," shouting slogans from struggles "alien to our own." Disruption of the Olympics would damage Mexico's international credit ratings and constituted an attack on the stability of the nation. This was his final warning.

At the conclusion of El Chango's rant, the entire Congress, overwhelmingly controlled by the PRI, rose to its feet as one and clapped for 10 solid minutes. The National Hymn was intoned, the one about the cannon's roar and the "soldier in the heart of each Son of God."

MISTER ROBLES'S TORTAS

Despite the president's threats, the tide was turning against him. His tirade had been so out of sync with the realities of what the student movement was all about that only the PRI and the old Gachupín-criollo reactionaries bought into it. Everyday folks, like Mister Robles, expressed their solidarity.

The proprietor of a hole-in-the-wall *torta* shop at the end of the Alameda, Mister Robles would pack up two immense baskets of *tortas* or sandwiches (ham and cheese) at noon each day and hand them out in the UNAM faculties, where the strikers were living in shifts, and out on the "islands," the greensward extending from the Rectory to the Humanities Tower that was the center of campus life.

The students' invitation to their elders to join the struggle had resonance. During the silent march September 13, strike leader Gustavo Gordillo spotted his father, a doctor who had been forced back to work by Díaz Ordaz during the abortive 1965 strike, standing on the curb on the corner of Bucareli Street, vigorously applauding the marchers. "My dad had always been distant and cold," Gordillo remembered in a recent *Nexus* magazine piece. Now he threw his arm around his son's shoulder and joined the march to the Zócalo.

"I PLAY FOR MYSELF" (An interview with Oscar the Vampire)

"El Vampiro" is playing sax by the Bankers Club on 16th of September Avenue. I can hear him a block away. He has a unique sound—big romantic swoops. He plays up and down the octaves a little like John Coltrane. Oscar likes to

play in front of the Bankers Club. He does a jazz version of the Internationale just for the bankers. But the cops hassle him there.

When I get to the Bankers Club, two beat cops are closing in on him. "Oscar," I suggest, "let's go out for lunch." He accepts the invitation, we settle into a corner table at La Blanca, and the Vampire riffs.

"I play in the street. Some people hate it and they will say they have a sick person in the house and ask me to get lost. Still, most people like what I'm doing. But not the cops.

"When I first started out after the earthquake in 1985, I played down in the Metro. It's risky because the platforms are narrow and you can get pushed onto the tracks. You have to keep moving from car to car. There's a lot of extortion. The Metro lines are organized by the mafias and you can get beat up if you play on the wrong train.

"I played on the buses too, but it's not really my thing. You jump up and play two tunes and out. You have to ask the people for money and then give the driver his cut. In the street, people will drop a coin in the case. There's no problem. I can play as long as I like. I play what I like to play. I've built up a big repertoire. I'll play a blues, a march, a corrido, a jazz song and keep switching them around."

Musicians have played on the streets of this city since it was Tenochtitlán. The Tenochas pounded on their teponaztles (drums). In colonial times, there were the estudiantinas (stringed groups singing very loudly mostly in bars). The tribunes played trumpets and told the news. Don Porfirio brought in the cilindrinos (organ grinders). The troubadours and the corridistas took over in the revolution. Now you have bandas de guerra (country marching bands) and the acordeonistas.

"I consider myself a public servant. Street musicians perform a public service and should be subsidized by the city. It's obvious. The police don't understand this. They move us around from street to street like we were criminals. The cops think we are delinquents because we stand in one place too long. It's gotten worse since Carlos Slim bought up the Centro Histórico. The cops don't understand that we're histórico too.

"They treat us like second-class citizens. I'm disobedient. They take you down to the delegation and you have to pay a fine to get your horn back. Even now, when there is a government of the Left in charge, we are persecuted by the police.

"When I first started out as a street musician, I was more of a Communist and I played at all the marches. Now I'm some species of anarchist and I play wherever I choose to play. I like the sound in the Centro Histórico. The walls *are made out of stone and they give you back an echo. The acoustics on Cinco del Mayo are really great, but the* pinche policía *are on my case there. The plaza in front of Bellas Artes—if you play there, automatically you go to jail. The Beethoven statue on the Alameda is still a free speech space and I've been playing a lot under the Caballito, the horse statue in front of the Art Museum.*

"When you hear me, I'm just part of the urban soundscape. Sometimes, I can really get into a groove with the auto horns and sirens or when a march comes along. The important thing is to find your place and play inside it.

"I have a real problem playing around other musicians. On Gante, there's a violin player here, another sax player there, huapangueros, *and African drummers and the blind* cumbia *band. I can't hear myself there—particularly when I play the flute, which needs its own space. It's frustrating.*

"The worst are the organ grinders. They bust into your space and fuck up the mood. They're nothing but a mafia. The cops let them play everywhere. They come into your scene and demand money for la música. *It's just a racket.*

"Who am I playing for? I'm playing in public but bueno, *I'm really playing for myself."*

THE SILENT MARCH

The strike council sessions were all-night psychodramas. Trots, Stalinists, socialists, anarchists, nihilists, and Maoistas (Adolfo Orive, founder of the Maoist Proletarian Line, had just returned from Paris, giving rise to rumors that French riot-trainers were in town) haggled about everything from the purity of their respective ideologies to the projected renaming of city streets—should Circunvalación, which bisects both Tepito and La Merced, be renamed "Mick Jagger" or "John & Yoko" Avenue?

No one was really in charge—the leaders were named El Búho (Eduardo del Valle) and El Pino (Salvador Martínez de la Roca), Tita Avendaño, Roberto Escudero, Heberto Castillo, Raúl Álvarez Garín, Gilberto Guevara Niebla, Luis Cabeza de Vaca, and Luis González de Alba, among many others, but no one really led—and some that had were already dead. The strikers counted 32 *muertos* by the end of September.

By some strike council members' estimates, 400,000 followed the now-familiar route from the park to the Zócalo on September 13, almost double the size of the demonstration just two weeks earlier at the end of August. The movement was reaching critical mass. The more wild-eyed CNH representatives argued that cancellation of the Olympics was within reach.

The September 13 march was enveloped in a monstrous silence. Activists taped up their mouths or wore gauze *tapabocas*. A few masochistic souls actually sewed up their lips. The *prensa vendida* and the government Red-baiters interpreted every chant as another link in the chain of subversion that extended all the way to the Kremlin, and so the marchers said nothing and let their shoes do the talking.

Instead of the emblematic posters of Che, the students carried likenesses of Padre Hidalgo. Independence Day was less than 48 hours away, and they wanted to prove that they were Mexicans. In the Zócalo, hundreds of thousands sang the National Anthem, reclaiming its stirring strophes from the PRI *gobierno*. Suddenly, the bells of the Cathedral began to clang. Could it be that the strikers had supporters even within the bosom of Holy Mother Church?

On the eve of Independence Day two nights later, the students held their own Grito down in University City. Heberto Castillo, the voice of the progressive professors, shouted out the "*¡Viva Méxicos!*" The parallel Grito pissed off El Chango no end. He was the President. He was the only one allowed to give the Grito around here!

TÍO SAM IS ALARMED

The Olympic torch had been lit in Athens on August 24 and was due to arrive in Veracruz at the end of September, whence it would follow the Conquistadores' route uphill to the Halls of Mocuhtezuma. Genuine alarm was sounded in Washington. Ambassador Fulton Freeman met with Díaz Ordaz to express concerns about the safety of U.S. athletes and tourists. CIA director Richard Helms flew into the capital for a hush-hush huddle with station chief Winston Scott and Interior Secretary Echeverría.

Philip Agee was ordered to dismantle his mock-up of a Jupiter rocket. In his *Inside the Company: CIA Diary*, the veteran spook, who would quit the intelligence agency after the massacre, confesses that he had assets inside the CNH who reported on the strikers' deliberations—the meetings were open, if impenetrably dense. Each morning, Agee would compile a synopsis and deliver it to Echeverría's desk.

With three weeks left before the October 12 due date, Gustavo Díaz Ordaz was urged by a nervous Avery Brundage, president of the International Olympic Committee, to close down the protests or risk cancellation. The Olympic tradition was at stake.

IN THE TOILET

On September 18, under cover of darkness, 10,000 troops of the Olympic Battalion, with General José Hernández Toledo in command, moved into Ciudad Universitaria accompanied by light tanks and water cannons. The National Strike Committee was in session in the Faculty of Medicine auditorium. The troops surrounded the building, arresting 557 students. The soldiers divided up the campus in four quadrants and secured the facilities, driving out the strikers who were occupying them, and then formed dragnets to capture the "agitators," i.e., anything that moved. Over a thousand were arrested on the UNAM campus and in raids around the city. By morning, virtually the entire leadership of the National Strike Council was lodged in adjoining cellblocks at the Black Palace, charged with "rebellion," "sabotage," "sedition," "criminal association," "attacking the means of communication," and of course "social dissolution."

One striker who would escape the dragnet down at the University was Alcira Soust Scaffo, a rangy, blazingly red-headed Uruguayan poet who had lived in Mexico without papers for 20 years, supporting herself by running errands and typing dissertations for professors in the Philosophy & Letters faculty. When Díaz Ordaz's troops invaded the Tower of Humanities, Alcira locked herself inside a toilet stall on the sixth floor and squatted down, diligently doubling her long legs so they could not be spotted under the stall door. She would stay in there for the next three weeks, dining on toilet paper to survive.

The military captured the main IPN (Polytechnic) campus at Zacatenco in the Casco de Santo Tomás on the 23rd. Unlike at UNAM, the soldiers met with stiff resistance—one student was gunned down by a "Son of God" while painting a wall slogan.

LA NOCHE DE TLATELOLCO

After 62 days of combat. El Chango had broken the strike. Avery Brundage put away his worry beads. Although there were still pockets of resistance around the city, the students and their allies had been beaten back by superior firepower and their own youthful ingenuousness. What was left of the strike council had entered into backdoor negotiations with Regent Corona del Rosal—the government's point man was a PRI hack, Jorge de la Vega.

On the same day the UNAM had fallen, undercover elements of the Estado Mayor, Díaz Ordaz's elite military guard, gratuitously machine-gunned Voca 7 in the Tlatelolco housing complex just blocks from downtown. No one was hurt but enraged parents and tenants rained garbage down on the intruders from the rooftops.

Sensing an imminent sell-out, diehards called for a meeting on October 2 in Tlatelolco's Plaza of Three Cultures, where they knew they had support. From Tlatelolco, the plan was to march to the Casco de Santo Tomás and confront the troops occupying the IPN.

Eight thousand troops and police, most hidden away down side streets, ringed the housing complex, ready to repel any move on the IPN. The disappointing turnout—about 6,000, many of them Tlatelolco tenants—milled about on the plaza floor. Florencio López Osuna, a second-string strike leader, was speaking from the third-floor landing of the Chihuahua building. It was the usual *rollo* about the Chango and political prisoners, and few of the demonstrators paid it any mind. Vendors plied the crowd, hawking *paletas* (popsicles) and *chescos* (soft drinks) and Mario Meléndez's strident weekly *¿Por Qué?*

At exactly 18:10, as dusk settled in over the gathering, writes the eminent cronista Elena Poniatowska, an unmarked helicopter that had been circling the plaza dropped two flares. It was the signal. The night of Tlatelolco had begun.

Snipers wearing one white glove emerged from the Chihuahua building and fired into the mass below. The gunfire rained down on the plaza and seemed to deliberately target members of the Olympic Battalion—General Hernández Toledo himself was shot in the ass. Members of the Olympic Battalion, many of them reportedly indigenous solders brought in from the countryside to counter this urban rebellion, opened up on the building's façade, destroying gas lines and setting apartments on fire.

Hundreds of students, housewives, old people, and children were caught in the crossfire. Those trying to flee this bloody rat trap were shoved back into the line of fire by the troops and police who had cordoned off the Plaza of Three Cultures. Several demonstrators managed to break through the cordon and dashed for the ancient Santiago church amidst the well-cared-for Aztec ruins and pounded upon the locked doors begging for protection. The priest refused to open them.

The pools of blood grew and grew. Hundreds of abandoned shoes were scattered all over the bloody plaza floor. The gunfire continued for 40 minutes.

How many were killed in that eternity? Thirty, estimated *Excelsior* the next morning, all of them Cuban agitators assigned by Moscow to derail the Mexican Olympics. *El Universal* cited 17 dead. How did they die? "At 18:13, Boris Greenhouse received a bullet in the neck fired from a helicopter into Apartment #501."

The true number of those killed at Tlatelolco varied wildly in reportage, and 40 years later, a final accounting is still pending. According to Raúl Álvarez Garín, the best count is 325, taken by a *Manchester Guardian* reporter who was buried under a corpse heap on the second-floor landing of the Chihuahua building and who later tracked the dead at morgues and hospitals and police and military lockups around the city.

More than 2,000 were arrested, stripped down to their underwear and held in the pens at Military Camp #1 on the western fringe of the city. During the days the students were penned up before being transferred to Lecumberri, the corpses of those who had been massacred in Tlatelolco were incinerated at the camp. The sweet, nauseating stench of their dead comrades' burning flesh filled their nostrils, and some began to sing the National Anthem, only when they came to the part about "the soldier in the heart of each Son of God," they substituted the word "assassin" for "soldier."

News of the massacre ran big the morning after in the *prensa vendida*, only of course it wasn't identified as a "massacre." *Excelsior* charged the snipers had been recruited from the Spartacists and the Fourth International. A cache of weapons discovered in a Chihuahua apartment building was allegedly traced to a Soviet bloc country. *El Universal* photographed "a defiant student wielding an ax."

By the second day, the killings slipped beneath the fold. Tlatelolco was "calm"—the real story was out at the Villa Olímpica, "a vigorous expression of the young people of the world" (*El Universal*). By the fourth day, Tlatelolco had been reduced to "a lamentable incident," and by October 12, the day the 14th modern Olympic Games opened for business, what exactly happened at Tlatelolco had disappeared from public discourse.

WHODUNNIT?

I have asked that question before in this book. It is unavoidable when it comes to Mexican justice.

In papers prepared for his memoirs and obtained by Julio Scherer, Mexico's savviest journalist and the founder of the immensely valuable *Proceso* magazine, Díaz Ordaz's secretary of defense, General Marcelino García Barragán, answers several pertinent questions. The shooters with the white gloves were members of the Estado Mayor under the command of General Luis Gutiérrez Oropeza. They were installed in vacant Chihuahua building apartments prior to October 2—tenants were forcibly evicted to ensure they would be available. The white-gloved officers had been ordered to fire on the Olympic Battalion to provoke the deadly barrage that gutted the carcass of the student strike movement "to save Mexico from a Soviet takeover," Oropeza himself would later write in defense of Díaz Ordaz.

Did Gustavo Díaz Ordaz really believe this bullshit about "a Soviet takeover"? Had 25 years of anti-Communist venom so sickened the souls of Mexico's rulers that they killed their own young to perpetuate the lie?

LET THE GAMES BEGIN

According to Philip Agee, on October 3 Brundage, who had pressured Díaz Ordaz to curtail the protests or face cancellation, summoned the International Olympic Committee to an emergency session. Now the question was whether the games could proceed after the geyser of blood uncapped by the Mexican hosts. Cancellation of Mexico '68 was defeated by a single vote.

On October 12, the day the indigenous peoples of Americas discovered Christopher Columbus and his gang of hired killers, the games began under heavy security measures at ICA's Olympic stadium adjacent to the University City. Thousands of doves were released into the cobalt blue sky. What happened on the night of Tlatelolco was not a topic for discussion. It was the classic *"Aquí no pasa nada, Señor"* with which the PRI always covered up its crimes. *"¡México! ¡México!"*

the hometown fans mindlessly repeated to exorcise the shame of what their country had done to its young.

When U.S. sprinters Tommy Smith and John Carlos, who finished one-three in the 200-meter dash, took their places on the winners' platform, they each raised a gloved fist in a black power salute to protest the racist hypocrisy of their government and were immediately stripped of their medals, evicted from the Olympic Village, and asked to leave Mexico. Both were persecuted for years for their heroic gesture. Once I had the opportunity to ask Carlos if the Tlatelolco massacre had figured into their protest. "We didn't even know about what happened there," he told me.

DOS DE OCTUBRE ¡NO SE OLVIDE!

Each October 2, students still march in Mexico City. DOS DE OCTUBRE ¡NO SE OLVIDE!, they write on the walls with spray cans: "The second of October—do not forget it!" But for years after that first October 2, what happened at Tlatelolco was erased from official memory.

Then, on the 10th anniversary of the massacre, students began again to march and to remember the unforgettable, and now each year, new buried memories are dug up.

Now, past the 40th anniversary of those dreadful days, those who were there have grown old in the struggle and the details have begun to blur. But whether or not there is anyone left who will remember what really happened in the Plaza of Three Cultures on October 2, 1968, Mexico the city and Mexico the country could never be the same again.

XII

CITY OF DENIAL & SHAME

The Monstruo woke up with a monstrous hangover (*la cruda*), put on its shoes, went about its business, and crawled back into bed each night as if nothing had changed only everyone knew that it had.

Aquí no pasa nada, Señor.

Fidel Velázquez's workers marched listlessly beneath Díaz Ordaz's balcony each May 1st. El Chango delivered his penultimate Informe in September and the clowns in Congress stood and clapped for the mandatory 10 minutes. The lame-duck president uttered the time-honored Grito on Independence eve, presided over the anniversary of Madero's revolution on November 20, and marked the day of Carranza's Constitution on February 5, but everyone was just going through the motions.

The tourists came as anticipated and overlooked the anguish etched into the faces of the natives. They donned silly sombreros and went to the bullfights and day-tripped to Teotihuacan for the light show, chugged down margaritas in the Zona Rosa, and visited the monumental National Anthropology Museum out in Chapultepec Park, but they too were just going through the motions.

The sweeping, modernesque Anthropology Museum designed by Pedro Ramírez Vázquez was a priceless repository of Aztec and Mayan deities but ignored their living, breathing descendants tucked away in the distant sierras and remote deserts of the republic. Tourists stepped carefully around the Indian women who sold gewgaws out on the esplanade of Ramírez Vázquez's museum as if they didn't exist.

Aquí no pasa nada, Señor.

PRI RIP

Behind the tinted windows up in the towers at Insurgentes #59, burly men in tinted eyewear looked down upon the capital of the country that they still thought they ruled and colluded to avoid la cruda reality. General Alfonso Martínez Domínguez, president of the Institutional Revolutionary Party, had designs on Los Pinos, but in the end Díaz Ordaz settled on his interior secretary, Luis Echeverría, who had served him as a loyal yes man during his turbulent *sexenio*. Charges against Echeverría—for being the highest-ranking civilian to have signed off on the massacre at Tlatelolco—brought by the special prosecutor for political crimes, between 2004 and 2006, were never sustained in court because of doubts as to the statute of limitations and the definition of genocide. No Mexican president in or out of office has ever been charged with a crime.

Forewarned by General Martínez Domínguez that Echeverría secretly harbored dangerously left-wing ideas, the Chango almost rescinded his Dedazo, and in the few years left him in this mortal coil, lived to regret his choice. To paper over predictable conflict within the highest echelons of the PRI, Echeverría designated Martínez Domínguez as regent of Mexico City.

Luis Echeverría could not deny that he had a credibility problem. He could sense the chill in the hearts of those who lined the streets as he drove to the inauguration ceremony out at the National Auditorium in Chapultepec Park. No one believed in the president or the party he represented anymore although most were cowed into acquiescence by their homicidal tendencies. Rius (Eduardo del Río), the underground comix genius whose *Supermachos* and *Los Agachados* were the spiritual texts for the post-Tlatelolco generation, now drew the party's initials as RIP.

LEFTWARD HO!

No sooner had the balding Echeverría slipped on the red, white, and green presidential sash than he began to move left with alarming dexterity, formulating a cabinet of eager young party activists such as Porfirio Muñoz Ledo (Labor) and Augusto Gómez Villanueva (Agriculture)—his interior minister, Mario Moya Palencia, had previously served as director of the government's cinematography bureaucracy.

Echeverría invited disaffected leftists on board, many only too willing to put Tlatelolco behind them and compromise their consciences for a plump sinecure in the cultural sections of the government. David Alfaro Siqueiros, jailed and castigated by Díaz Ordaz and López Mateos for sympathizing with the railroad workers, signed on, and by the end of the administration, poet laureate Octavio Paz, who had resigned as ambassador to India after the October 2 bloodbath, had his own glossy monthly magazine, *Vuelta*, generously padded with paid government propaganda.

In 1970, Lázaro Cárdenas, his heart atomized by the massacre of the students, passed on to Mictlán out in the Mixteca mountains of Oaxaca where he had retreated seeking solace from the storm he had been at the center of for much of the century, and Echeverría got it in to his big head that he was the Tata's reincarnation. Like Cárdenas, he cultivated the loyalties of the long-neglected campesinos and traveled ceaselessly to spread government largesse, doling out expanses of unplowable land to the dismayed farmers. When glad-handing campesinos in the south of the country, Echeverría invariably donned the local *guayabera*, the Cuban-derived linen shirt that was emblematic of the region. On northern junkets, he costumed himself in expensive leather jackets.

The lights were never extinguished at the National Palace, where the new president put in 20-hour days—many of them filled with impassioned monologues to animate members of his cabinet. José López Portillo, Echeverría's finance minister and eventual successor, marveled in his memoirs that the president never even took time out to piss. On trips to the countryside, JLP confessed he nearly peed his pants trying to keep up with the hyperactive *presidente*.

THIRD WORLD HAHAHA

Luis Echeverría posed as an indefatigable champion of the third world, strengthening south-south ties just as fervently as Díaz Ordaz had looked to Washington as his savior. The Mexican president flew to Cuba and embraced Fidel, gifting the Comandante with a trademark guayabera, and visited Mao's China, returning with a pair of pandas for the Chapultepec Zoo. Despite the Monster's toxic air quality, Ling Ling became the first of her race to breed outside of her homeland.

Echeverría would load up the presidential jet with left-wing sycophants and homegrown delicacies like maguey worms, *cuitlacoche* corn fungus, hand-made tortillas, and fine tequilas for solidarity flights to Guyana, Senegal, Algeria, Iran, India, Sri Lanka, Tanzania, Saudi Arabia, Kuwait, Egypt, Israel, and Jordan amongst other far-flung venues, outposts that had rarely known a Mexican before. In his three-volume *Tragicomedia Mexicana*, which informs this narrative, José Augustín described these journeys as "sultanesque."

In Washington, the Nixonites grew increasingly apprehensive at their distant neighbor nation's swoop to the left. In 1973, after Kissinger orchestrated the coup that toppled socialist Salvador Allende, Echeverría threw open the doors of Mexico's embassy in Santiago to fleeing Allendistas. Ambassador Gonzalo Martínez Corbalá (who as a young PRI deputy had conspired with Díaz Ordaz to sandbag Uruchurtu at Santa Úrsula) packed the rooms with refugees. Many Chileans were given safe passage to Mexico, where President Echeverría welcomed them into the government bureaucracy.

But Kissinger and Nixon need not have fretted about the flamboyant president. Indeed, Echeverría subjugated those hard-core Mexican leftists who refused his favors with the same brutal hand with which Pinochet now ruled Chile.

LOS HALCONES

On June 10, 1971, Thursday of Corpus Christi on the ecclesiastical calendar and six months into Echeverría's bizarre regime, students gathered at the Instituto Politécnico for their first substantial action since October 2, 1968. Several thousand brave young people set out from the Casco de Santo Tomás in the north of the city on a march to the National Pedagogical School in solidarity with striking students up in Monterrey. Most of those who were so rudely taken three years earlier had been released from Lecumberri, and others forced into exile in Chile and Cuba had returned, but the student movement maintained a low profile. The march that day stayed away from the Centro. It had not been authorized by the regime—the military remained in control of the capital. There were still tanks in the Zócalo.

Ten blocks farther west, as the marchers spilled out onto broad México-Tacuba Avenue, they were set upon by dozens of kendo stick–wielding Halcones (hawks) with closely clipped military haircuts. Snipers on nearby rooftops opened up with long guns.

One of the first to fall was Edmundo Martín del Campo, brother of Frank and Jesús, well-traveled compañeros on the Left. Seven or 11 or 21 or 40 were murdered by the Halcones on Thursday of Corpus—the numbers are still uncertain. Sirens keened all afternoon in the north of the city and the emergency room floors at local hospitals were once again bathed in student blood.

Echeverría washed his hands of the massacre, insinuating that the plot had been hatched by General Martínez Domínguez to embarrass him and remind the nation of his responsibility for Tlatelolco. Although Guayabera Man later blamed the killings on "foreign interests and reactionaries," there was little doubt that General Martínez was determined to undermine Echeverría. The new president quickly fired the regent and his police chief, Rogelio Flores.

Who were the Halcones, the hired thugs who had conjured up the nightmare of Tlatelolco? Although time has obscured their names, one of them is certainly "El Fish," Sergio Romero, an UNAM-based provocateur. Romero denies his participation despite eyewitness I.D.

El Fish was part of a paramilitary squad on the city payroll that protected construction sites during the digging of the Metro and reported to Captain Manuel Díaz Escobar, another Díaz Ordaz holdover from Tlatelolco. No member of the Halcones has ever been brought to justice for the crimes of Corpus. Fidel Velázquez publicly debunked the Halcones' existence. "They don't exist," he bluntly told the press at one of his indecipherable Monday morning press conferences, "because I didn't see them."

AN ALPHABET SOUP OF FOCOS

Inspired by both the Cuban and the Vietnamese resistance, the *guerra de guerrillero* was already a fact of life in Mexico in the years leading up to Dos de Octubre. Arturo Gámiz had led the Moncada-like assault on a military barracks in Ciudad Madera, Chihuahua, in 1965, and both Genaro Vázquez and Lucio Cabañas roamed the sierras of Guerrero by 1967–1968. After Tlatelolco, dissatisfied students and freelance Marxists cooked up an alphabet soup of *focos*, the label assigned by Che's French collaborator Régis Debray to such guerrilla bands. The FUZ, the MAR, the FRAP, the CER, the CAP, the FMNR, and the FLN were active principally in the urban centers of Guadalajara and Monterrey. The FLN (Forces of National Liberation) would evolve into the Zapatista Army of National Liberation (EZLN) a decade later.

But the most febrile of these *focos* was the September 23rd Communist League, also rooted in Monterrey, which took its title from the date of Gámiz's failed attack. Working separately and rarely in unison, the guerrilla armies held up banks and payroll trucks, extorted industrialists, and kidnapped and zapped the class enemy.

Vázquez's ACNAR put the snatch on the rector of the Guerrero state autonomous university and eventually exchanged him for the freedom of Mario Menéndez to return to Mexico. (Menéndez, the editor of the weekly *Por Esto!* that had diligently reported on the '68 student movement, had fled to Havana to escape arrest.) The FRAP (Armed Forces of the Revolutionary People) grabbed Terrance Leonhardy, the U.S. consul in Guadalajara, and Rubén Zuno Arce, President Echeverría's father-in-law, later identified by the U.S. as an important Mexican *narcotraficante*. Just as spectacular was Cabañas's kidnapping of transportation tycoon Rubén "El Tigre" Figueroa, the power behind Mexico City's Alianza de Camioneros, which had bankrolled Uruchurtu, and an announced candidate for the governor of Guerrero.

Figueroa had publicly dared Cabañas's Party of the Poor to take him, and Lucio got his chance at a secret meeting with the candidate in the Sierra of Atoyac above Guerrero's Costa Grande. Echeverría responded to the kidnapping by pouring in 25,000 federal troops, reportedly accompanied by CIA advisers, to rescue Figueroa, a tough-as-nails political boss with a head the size and density of an Olmec monolith.

Cabañas, whose own grandfather had been a general in Zapata's Liberating Army of the South and who, like Zapata, had been reported killed many times, was finally cornered and executed in the sierra in December 1974—today, Lucio remains an icon of Mexico's hard left.

Up in Monterrey, the September 23rd Communist League was young and audacious and prone to fatal mistakes. On September 8, 1973, a handful of guerrilleros intercepted the motorcade of Eugenio Garza Sada, the kingpin of the Monterrey group, Mexico's most powerful clique of industrialists. In the firefight that ensued, the impresario was shot dead reaching for his gun, along with two bodyguards.

Garza Sada's elevated status earned him a state funeral attended by 200,000 indignant mourners and broadcast live nationwide on Televisa. Echeverría was accused of coddling the Liga and excoriated by the leaders of commerce and industry. Jacobo Zabludovsky, Televisa's toxic anchor, charged the president's leftist politics had encouraged the killers. In a spasm of contrition, Luis Echeverría pledged an unrelenting war on the subversives, the so-called Dirty War.

LAS DOÑAS

The uprising led by Cabañas and his Party of the Poor signaled massive repression along the Costa Grande. Under the command of General Mario Arturo Acosta Chaparro, troops invaded fishing villages north of the deluxe resort of Acapulco and hundreds of campesinos "disappeared" into secret prisons and torture chambers—hundreds are still missing. Many years later, Acosta was charged in the deaths of 143 local campesinos whose torture-wracked corpses were taken up in air force planes based on Acapulco's gold coast and dumped into the Pacific Ocean, the first *vuelos del muerte* (death flights) in a dirty war that by the mid-1970s had grown continental. But witnesses kept disappearing and Acosta Chaparro, although convicted by a military court, was freed on appeal.

The disappeared were catalogued as *marineros* ("sailors," i.e., those thrown in the sea), *aviadores* ("aviators," those thrown alive from helicopters), and *mineros* ("miners," those buried alive).

Besides Acosta Chaparro, some of those who managed Echeverría's *guerra sucia* were Miguel Nazar Haro, commandant of the White Brigade, which operated under the aegis of the dreadful Federal

Security Directorate (DFS) and its boss, Fidel Castro's old interrogator Fernando Gutiérrez Barrios.

The DFS offices facing the Monument of the Revolution thundered with recorded music to mask the insufferable cries of the tortured. Suspected subversives were beaten to death to the stentorian strains of Wagnerian operas. Within the Mexico City police, the agency for Delinquency Prevention (DIPD), administered by Francisco Sahagún Baca, did the president's dirty work.

Many political prisoners were held by the army at Military Camp #1 on the western edge of the Monster, where those arrested at Tlatelolco were penned up while the corpses of their comrades were incinerated. The disappeared were thought to be housed in underground cells at the installation.

When her son, Jesús Piedra, a suspected member of the September 23rd Communist League, was kidnapped by Nazar Haro in Monterrey in 1975, Rosario Ibarra would not take no for an answer. She hounded the jails and the offices of police agencies and when she got no satisfaction, she showed up at the gates of Military Camp #1 with a portrait of Jesús and demanded his "presentation with life."

Although the Generals denied culpability, the testimony of Zacarías Osorio, an army deserter seeking political asylum in Canada, would seem to question the military's protestations of innocence. Osorio, a Totonaco Indian sharpshooter with the paratrooper-fusiliers unit, operated out of Camp #1 from 1976 to 1981 before fleeing Mexico. During that period, he would often travel to guerrilla zones to transport hooded prisoners up to Mexico City. At least twice a year, Osorio would be detailed to escort political prisoners from Military Camp #1 to two bases just outside the city in Hidalgo and Mexico states, where he and other hand-picked sharpshooters formed firing squads. The bullet-riddled bodies of the victims were then reduced to ash at nearby incinerators. Although Osorio would never put a number to those he executed, he estimated that he made as many as 12 trips to the killing fields with groups of 10 to 15 prisoners each, a total of around 140 victims.

Rosario Ibarra never gave up her search for Jesús. In 1978, she and a dozen *doñas* whose sons and daughters had vanished in the dirty war staged a series of seven hunger strikes in front of the Metropolitan Cathedral, and Echeverría's successor López Portillo issued a blanket amnesty for political prisoners. When 148 were released, Jesús was not one of them. According to a list kept by Rosario and her Eureka group of the Mothers of the Disappeared, 572 political prisoners remain unaccounted for. Thirty years after Jesús was taken, she is still searching for her son.

Now a senator representing Mexico City, Doña Rosario, 81, is a fixture at demonstrations here in the capital. When I run into her, as I did last Friday in front of the U.S. Embassy on Reforma protesting the whiff of genocide in Bolivia, we embrace in the Mexican way with a peck on the cheek. I always feel blessed.

And Echeverría? Despite repeated attempts to bring him to justice for his crimes, the octogenarian ex-president continues to evade prosecution. Today he pads around his mansion in San Jerónimo in the ritzy south of the city just blocks away from the National Commission on Human Rights in total impunity, secure that he will never be called to account for the torture sessions and extrajudicial executions conducted in his name.

THE BLOB

When one compares population density maps of the Monstruo between 1970 and 1980, the difference is clearly in the upper body. If the northwest quadrant of the city (Azcapotzalco) is seen as the Monster's head, the shambling black blob that represents the urbanized sections of the city thrusts limbs in all directions but bulks up like the Hulk in the northeast (Gustavo Madero) quadrant, where its shoulders spill over into Mexico state. The blob's belly (the Centro) remains distended and it stands solidly on thick thighs and stumps extending to the southeast (Iztapalapa and Iztacalco). Slender tentacles trail into the southwest (Álvaro Obregón and Cuajimalpa) where the *ricos* were building their mansions. The *jodidos* were just beginning to settle the barrancas and abandoned sand mines that seam the zone.

Between 1970 and 1980, the population of Mexico City grew by 2,000,000, from 6.8 million to 8.8 million—the maximum decade of Mexico City growth. When the 27 surrounding municipalities that form the Metropolitan Zone were added in, the population doubled to 16 million. The city and its environs were vying for the dubious distinction of the world's most overcrowded urban monster.

The misery belt that transcends municipal boundaries girdles the dense blob on all its flanks. "Everything outside of Mexico City is Cuautitlán" was the way *capitalinos* used to arrogantly describe the rest of the country, but Cuautitlán, some 20 kilometers west of the city, was now immersed in the urban blob.

One footnote to this unruliness: The number of vehicles seeking to transit the clogged arteries of El Monstruo grew even faster than the two-legged population—from 650,000 in 1971 to a million plus in 1975, with the consequent ecological blight such proliferation would bestow on the capital.

Three decades later, we Chilangos are on doomsday watch.

DEMOCRACY PRI-STYLE

Much like his role model, Luis Echeverría, as the self-appointed avatar of Lázaro Cárdenas, did not have a close relationship with the city. Obsessed with replicating Tata Lázaro's heroic accomplishments in the *campo* and selling third world solidarity against Yanqui Imperialism everywhere else but in Mexico, Echeverría delegated administration of the world's soon-to-be-largest urban stain to Octavio Sentíes, the cunning Martínez Domínguez's replacement as regent. Don Luis signed off on urban improvements and basked in the media spotlight at the inauguration of projects, but Sentíes, a creature of the PRI mafia forever lurking over at Insurgentes #59, did the heavy lifting.

The 1970 revision of the Organic Law that governed Mexico City gave the regent, himself appointed by the president, the power to designate the chiefs of the 16 delegations. (The president had previously reserved this right.) The change strengthened the PRI's stranglehold on the political life of Mexico City. The 16 delegation headquarters where the sale of licenses and permits for just about everything from automobiles to public toilets were transacted at the *ventanillas* (little windows) were urban gold mines. Eager-to-help fixers lounged on the steps of the delegation buildings to guide the solicitor of services through the intricacies of the *ventanillas*. The *mordidas* kept the wheels of city government humming.

Echeverría and his regent boasted of "humanizing social services" for their electoral clientele and "democratizing" the Monster in pure PRI style. Neighborhood councils were established—the Juntas Vecinales—that were empowered to present local demands to the city fathers. At first the pashas on Insurgentes were fearful the councils would alter power quotients, but the juntas were soon absorbed into the party's electoral machinery and rendered toothless.

HOME IMPROVEMENTS

During the Echeverría-Sentíes regnum, the city had to borrow heavily just to stay abreast of the population crunch—Mexico City debt accounted for nearly half of Mexico's ballooning $20 billion foreign debt. The president and his regent kowtowed to the car boom, suspending expansion of the Metro and facilitating surface transportation that was already making the air unbreathable. The Circuito Interior, the Monster's first elevated roadway, distributed downtown traffic north and west into chic Polanco and the wealthy colonies beyond.

The downtown clog was caused in part by the volume of commercial traffic and the masters of the metropolis diverted food distribution from the ancient La Merced just behind the National Palace—where 5,000 trucks a day dumped their loads for the *diableros* (hand-truck boys) to trundle into the market—out into the eastern hinterlands of the city. The resistance of the vendors was outspokenly stubborn, and it took a decade for the Centro de Abastos—Metropolitan Food Distribution Center—to take shape. Today, the crumbling Centro de Abastos, a city within a city, feeds a megalopolis that consumes a fifth of the nation's food supply. Swanky Las Lomas is said to devour more meat than the entire threadbare, largely indigenous southern state of Oaxaca.

In addition to the relocation food distribution to the periphery, long-haul bus terminals were moved out of the city center to the edge of town and spaced at the four cardinal points of the compass to welcome even more newcomers to the Monstruo.

DOWN IN THE SEWERS

Psychiatrists might attribute Echeverría's enthusiasm for expanding the Monster's historically inadequate sewage system to a guilty conscience. The president had made his bones in the sewers of the repression and perhaps wanted to make amends.

Since the Porfirian-age Drenaje General (General Drain), the Grand Canal had carried off the black waters of the Monstruo north to Hidalgo state, but the canal, which lay five meters above the level of the Zócalo floor, often overflowed its banks in the rainy season and was the unfragrant source of periodic submersion of the central city.

Echeverría's version, the Drenaje Profundo or Deep Drain, unveiled in 1975, was a wonder of metropolitan plumbing with seven-square-meter water tunnels that dwarfed hard-hatted workers and their heavy equipment in construction photos. The 112-kilometer system (later expanded to 148) includes collectors at strategic points on the Monstruo's anatomy and runs downhill on gravity, diving to a depth of 217 meters before emerging from the mountains north of the city and dumping its load in the Salto River, which in turn pushes into the Tula, where, rather than just sending the shit into the Panuco and eventually the Gulf of Mexico, as did the Porfirian vision of this project, the untreated wastewater is diverted into irrigating vegetable crops in Hidalgo, the fruits of which are returned to be marketed to the famished Chilangos, a perfect circle—except that endemic E. coli epidemics amongst the poorest of the populace increases the fecal befoulment of the air we are forced to breathe.

TRUE BLUE URUS

The first Metro convoy pulled out of Chapultepec Park September 5, 1969, and traveled west to east, pausing at 16 stations en route, each demarcated by a pictograph that would enable those riders who could not read to identify their stop—Chapultepec was distinguished by a grasshopper, a translation of its Aztec name. Zaragoza Avenue out by the airport was the Metro's final destination.

Juan Cano Cortes, who piloted the first convoy, recalled that there were Mariachis in all the stations to celebrate this historic passage that would forever change how Chilangos moved around their city. Like other drivers, Cano Cortes had received his training at the Isabel la Católica station, my local stop. When the first training cars roared into Isabel la Católica at 100 kilometers an hour, Cano Cortes felt the breath being sucked out of him. "I thought it was a monster," he confessed to Díaz Ordaz, who was standing by his side. The Chango was overwhelmed with emotion.

By the time Díaz Ordaz was done, three Metro lines were nearing completion and the Monstruo's transportation future looked rosy. But Echeverría and Sentíes were true blue Urus. The Chango's successor opposed expansion of the Metro as obdurately as the Iron Regent had battled its installation. Diane Davis, in her valuable *Urban Leviathan*, surmises that Echeverría's hostility to the subway at least partially grew from his need to distinguish himself from the terminally pro-Metro Díaz Ordaz.

The president's opposition certainly was influenced by the billions he would be forced to borrow from foreign banks to complete the Metropolitan Collective Transportation System and pay for the shiny, streamlined trains, all of which were imported at lavish expense from France. To Echeverría's way of reckoning, expansion of the Metro only magnified the city's self-importance and ate up vast amounts of a federal budget that could otherwise be devoted to his pet projects in the *campo*.

By the end of Guayabera Man's regime, the three lines begun by his predecessor would be up and running—the Pink Line (Line 1), which ran east to west through the heart of the city; the Blue Line (2), running from the northwest corner to the southeast; and the Green Line (3), routed from Tlatelolco to the Centro Médico and out to University City. But in their six years of trying to tame the Monstruo, Echeverría-Sentíes added just 12 new kilometers of track, extending the Línea Rosa from Zaragoza out to Pantitlán on the eastern limits of Nezahualcóyotl, where millions of minimum-wage workers now bunked.

Echeverría's obstinate rejection of the Metro as the capital's main transportation mode had as much to do with cronyism as it did with foreign debt and limited resources for the countryside. Rubén Figueroa, the power broker in the Alianza de Camioneros who had been rescued from Cabañas by Echeverría, was a close associate of the president, and Octavio Sentíes had come to his job as regent after serving as chief corporate council for the bus owners. Privately owned buses continued to move 6,000,000 Chilangos a day.

The three Metro lines were saturated with the overflow. The platforms were so packed that travelers risked being shoved onto the tracks. At rush hour, Chilangos crushed against each other cheek by jowl and buttock to buttock and disembodied male hands groped the señoritas and not-so-señoritas. Segregated cars had to be decreed to keep the *machos* off the *hembras*. A monstrous Metro crash at the Blue Line's Chabacano station crushed 36 in 1975.

But if the service was shoddy, fares were kept artificially cheap: 50 centavos, about a half-penny fare Americano. Actually, the real price of the ticket was 16 times that, but to keep social peace, the government has always heavily subsidized Metro fares.

The Metro as an incentive to get cars off the street was and is a failed concept. The middle class and uppers wouldn't be caught dead "down there" mixing it up with the insalubrious Great Unwashed, and indeed, by the end of the 1970s there were more cars on the road then there were when Díaz Ordaz had first begun to dig.

WHERE DID THE MONEY GO?

Luis Echeverría hopscotched the globe in his spotless guayaberas preaching third world solidarity against dependence on the evil Norte. But back home, he borrowed money like it was going out of style from the two institutions that were the fulcrums of global domination, the World Bank and the International Monetary Fund.

Addicted to big government, bloated bureaucracies, and profligate spending, Echeverría found no project too grand or too tiny to be absorbed into the labyrinth of administration. In his six years as the Great Helmsman, Echeverría nationalized more than 600 floundering enterprises—from the Churubusco movie studios to chains of movie theaters, bus manufacturers in Ciudad Sahagún, Hidalgo (which became a government-run industrial park), failed resorts, hotels, publishing houses, and ballet troupes. The $20 billion USD foreign debt that Echeverría left when he abandoned public office was triple the amount when he was sworn in.

Where did it all go? The money Mexico sucked in seemed to have disappeared into a metaphorical Drenaje Profundo as budget deficits swelled 600 percent. By 1976, Mexico City alone owed nearly $10 billion USD to foreign banks and was borrowing at a much more avaricious rate than the national average. Soon to be declared the largest city in the world, the Monstruo was disappearing into a financial black hole.

THE BEST THING THAT EVER HAPPENED TO
MEXICAN JOURNALISM

By the back end of his six-year presidential cycle, Luis Echeverría was not the people's idol. Double-digit inflation (22 percent) disaffected a working class that had lost considerable buying power, and the proletarians sought relief with their feet. Electricity workers mobilized, threatening to shut down power plants much as they had back in the teens of the century if their wage demands were not met. Labor czar Fidel Velázquez threatened to squish the proletarian upstarts who were led by Rafael Galván and the ex–political prisoner Demetrio Vallejo if the workers didn't back off.

The business class was equally distressed at runaway inflation and Echeverría's leftist bombast. Nor had students buried their rancor at the butcher of Tlatelolco.

When the President, deluded by hubris, scheduled a public talk at the UNAM in March 1975, the SRO crowd inside the auditorium drowned him out with chants of *"¡Cu-leeee-ro!"* (asshole). The confrontation quickly breached academic decorum and the Estado Mayor hustled Guayabera Man out of the faculty, but several thousand irate students outside pelted him with rocks and bottles and the President's bald pate was split open by an incoming missile. The press saw blood and the Speed Graphics flashed.

Hours later, Echeverría rang up Julio Scherer, editor of *Excelsior*. Under Scherer's guidance, *Excelsior* had become Mexico's most left-leaning daily with such all-star collaborators as Carlos Monsiváis, Miguel Ángel Granados Chapa, and the maestro of mordant Mexican irony, Jorge Ibargüengoitia, aboard. The president bluntly warned Scherer not to run the photo of his wounding, which Scherer of course did, first thing the next morning on the front page.

Julio Scherer's defiance spiked Echeverría's thirst for revenge. *Excelsior* was denied all government advertising, the lifeblood for an industry with chronically anemic sales (even the scandal-stained *La Prensa* doesn't sell 100,000 copies daily). PRI *paracaidistas* landed on a site the *Excelsior* workers' cooperative had bought to build low-cost housing in Tasqueña at the end of the Blue Line and settled in under the protection of the Granaderos. An Echeverría-engineered putsch ousted Julio Scherer and his colleagues from the *Excelsior* coop.

The President's ham-handed assault proved to be the best thing that ever happened to Mexican journalism. Scherer went out and rented office space, assembled a crackerjack staff of investigative reporters, and founded the critical weekly *Proceso* (it too received no paid government publicity), which ever since has slapped around every Mexican president from Don Luis to the current stooge in Los Pinos, Felipe Calderón. Granados Chapa and other rebel pens started up *Uno*

Más Uno (One Plus One), the first left daily published in the capital since the Revolution, and when, in the early '80s, the De la Madrid government purchased publisher Manuel Becerra's allegiances, they packed up their typewriters and transferred their talents to Balderas Street to incubate *La Jornada*, today a candle in the darkness not just in Mexico but throughout this devastated continent, and perhaps the most pertinent perpetrator in the ongoing crusade for a democratic Mexico City.

DARK RUMORS TAKE FLIGHT

José López Portillo, the tall, staid finance minister who had failed to brake Echeverría's wild spending sprees, seemed an unlikely antidote to the flamboyant Guayabera Man, but, sensing the darkening economic prospects, Don Luis designated JLP heir to the throne of Mocuhtezuma—although, like Díaz Ordaz before him, he later displayed second thoughts about his choice and deliberately mined the field to succession.

When he bade adieu in his final Informe in September 1976, Luis Echeverría, citing economic stress, devalued the peso for the first time since Ruiz Cortines 24 years before him, and the currency plummeted to half its value. Prices skyrocketed. Capital flight hemorrhaged $2 billion USD in a few short weeks. More Mexican money was being banked outside of the country than in Mexican banks.

Dark rumors took flight: Mexico had run out of oil. A military coup was being plotted. The right wing and the Catholic Church cried that Echeverría's program to immunize schoolchildren was a foil for a mass sterilization campaign mandated by United Nations population control doctrine. In August, there were nighttime bombings in the city. On the 11th in San Ángel, the all-but-forgotten September 23rd Communist League tried to kidnap Margarita López Portillo, the poet sister of the president-elect—Liga chieftain David Jiménez was gunned down by her bodyguards.

Echeverría's reluctance to give up power was patent and public, and the shadow of the Caudillo clung to the city as closely as it had back in 1926 when Calles came down on the Obregonistas. In late November, military movement was reported in the streets of the Centro. A sister of one of the waitresses working tables at La Blanca called from the phone company where she was an operator and reported that Echeverría had been assassinated. Then military caissons that seemed to be transporting the remains of some important personage appeared on traffic-snarled Cinco de Mayo Street and all the waitresses put down their trays and ran to the window to gawk. This was the jittery city that José López Portillo was about to inherit.

ADMINISTRATING THE ABUNDANCE

By 1976, Mexico, once upon a time the biggest petroleum exporter, was importing 100,000 barrels daily from Venezuela—in spite of the reported discovery of new fields around Reforma on the Tabasco-Chiapas state line in 1972 at the height of the OPEC boycott of the West. Echeverría, suspicious of Yanqui intentions, did not want to break solidarity with his third world brethren and kept the finds close to his chest. But according to the *New York Times'* Alan Riding, who kept a close watch on these machinations, the word was out in Washington. By 1973, a single-sheet memo with no letterhead was distributed in U.S. oil circles alerting interested parties to the discovery of deposits totaling "20 billion barrels, the equivalent of the Persian Gulf" in Mexico's southeast.

Even after PEMEX began perforating wells in the region and the black gold was gushing, the new deposits remained unregistered. The only evidence of the new wealth, Riding notes in his exemplary *Distant Neighbors*, was the hotel boom in Villahermosa, Tabasco's state capital.

It wasn't until 1977, with López Portillo in charge and his schoolboy chum Jorge Díaz Serrano operating PEMEX, that Mexico confirmed the land-based deposit and announced gigantic finds offshore in the Sound of Campeche that dwarfed even Tabasco's gushers—60 billion barrels in proven reserves. The catch was that Mexico hardly had the technology to get at the new offshore fields.

In an unfortunate aside during his September 1978 Informe, President López Portillo embellished the bonanza: "We must now accustom ourselves to administrating the abundance." The remark would come back to haunt JLP to his grave.

By 1979, Akil 1 (wells in the Campeche field all had Mayan names) was bringing in 1.5 million barrels a day and Mexico was off to the races. Proven and probable reserves escalated to 40 billion and 200 billion respectively in 1981, and by '82 the numbers were bumped up to 72 and 250 billion. PEMEX was pumping out 3,000,000 barrels a day and sending 50 percent of it to El Norte—no single customer could buy more back then. As is the way of Washington, the U.S. wanted it all.

ORLANDO'S BONES (An interview with "Orlando")

I miss Orlando. Every Sunday morning on my way to La Blanca, he would be huddled up against the wall of La Profesa church reading from torn scraps of newspapers he had rescued from trash cans here in the Centro. He seemed particularly interested in the futbol *league. On Sundays, Don Vicente who runs the newspaper kiosk in front of the café would slip Orlando* Esto, *the sports tabloid that he would study intensely all week. Vicente thinks he rooted for Toluca.*

I called Orlando my lector, *my reader, and when he saw me coming on Sunday morning, a wide smile that warmed my morning coffee would break across his filth-caked features.*

Orlando couldn't walk and he had a hard time saying words in a way that others could understand him. He dragged himself around the Centro Histórico eating out of garbage bins outside the MacDonald's and the Burger King and the Kentucky Fried Chicken that do land-office business down here. Once when Orlando had taken up residence in the little landscaped garden outside the Telmex offices on the next block, he showed me what he had scavenged that day—two mostly eaten Big Macs, a gnawed chicken leg, a handful of stiff, ketchup-flecked French fries—and rubbed his greasy belly in delight. Telmex is owned by Carlos Slim, the richest man in the world. "Orlando" was one of the poorest.

He lasted only a couple of nights in Carlos Slim's garden. When I went by there the next day to check on him, the Telmex security guards were cleaning up the mess he'd left behind and cussing him out.

Most passersby stepped around the filthy crippled man as he sprawled on the public sidewalk. Some good souls on their way to work or Mass or morning coffee dropped coins near him but were reluctant to put them in his blackened hands. He stank ferociously.

"Orlando" was probably not even his name. I once asked him what he was called and the word that came out sort of sounded like "Orlando," so I always greeted him that way and he would grunt happily in return.

Then one Sunday, "Orlando" spoke. Andrés Manuel López Obrador had just been robbed of the Mexican presidency in July 2006 and there was a huge protest in the Zócalo. On the way back to the hotel, I ran into him crawling up Isabel la Católica on his hands and we saluted each other. I handed him a coin and he smiled beatifically and to my total amazement stated very clearly that he was the president of Mexico. "¡Yo soy el Presidente!" I never heard him talk again.

"Orlando" had no fixed address. Sometimes I would see him lying on the sidewalk outside the busy Paris Pharmacy on El Salvador Street or soaking up the morning sun on a chilly winter day against the wall of the ex–National Library across from my rooms. I worried about him a lot and was always finding old sweaters for him.

One Sunday a few months ago, he didn't show up at La Profesa. Vicente said "Orlando" hadn't come in for his newspaper. There are always a handful of beggars hanging around outside the church—I think the priest feeds them on Sunday morning, and churchgoers are always good for a few coins. But they hadn't seen him either.

The next Sunday morning, "Orlando" wasn't there either. Ramón, the old guy who parks cars for Mass hadn't seen him all week. Neither had the priest.

The third Sunday morning, it was raining hard and there was no one outside La Profesa to ask so I went looking for "Orlando." I searched out his old haunts on Salvador and Cinco de Febrero streets. Nada. I checked the alley by La Risa Pulquería where the homeless sometimes encamp. Nada. The trail grew cold.

Fearing the worst, I stopped asking for "Orlando." He had simply vanished into the maw of El Monstruo, and the Monster hadn't even bothered to spit back his bones.

"A POOR POLITICIAN IS A BAD POLITICIAN"

José López Portillo ran virtually unopposed in 1976. The PAN abstained from running a candidate because of internal scrapes, and the only competition was the Mexican Communist Party—which was proscribed, but still its unregistered standard bearer, the long-imprisoned Valentín Campa, won 5 percent of the national vote. The PRI took 80 percent nationally (Cantinflas must have gotten the rest) but only 55 percent in Mexico City.

JLP rid himself of the treacherous Echeverría as quickly as he could. Don Luis, who had eyes on the United Nations Secretary General post, was appointed ambassador to Australia, New Zealand, and the Fiji Islands, the most distant outpost on the face of the globe Mexican diplomacy afforded.

López Portillo's new boss of all bosses in the Federal District, Carlos Hank González, was a well-traveled PRI honcho. Credited with the Alemanesque maxim that "a poor politician is a bad politician," Hank was determined to be neither. The son of an unsuccessful German immigrant, he had scratched his way up from the bottom of the PRI heap. As a grade school teacher (hence his title of "Profe," or professor) in the backwater Mexico state town of Atlacomulco, he had ingratiated himself with Governor Isidro Fabela, a native of that place, and the Atlacomulco group proposed the Profe for municipal president of the state capital of Toluca.

After that it was all gravy—Hank served one term as a PRI deputy in the lower house of Congress before Díaz Ordaz appointed him director of the state grain distribution agency—the Profe immortalized his stay at CONASUPO by the installation of curious conical, orange-colored silos by the rural Mexico roadside that suggested drivers were approaching a zone inhabited by elves.

Under Echeverría's odd governance, Carlos Hank served as governor of Mexico state, the most populated and powerful entity in the Mexican union that surrounds the Monster on all sides. During six years in the state house, Hank presided over the thickening of the misery belt that edges the capital.

Invited to step across the state line into the city proper by López Portillo, Carlos Hank was appointed regent in 1976, a job that presented new horizons for his many and varied enterprises. El Profe had prospered since he taught grade school, having parlayed a humble candy factory in Atlacomulco into a fleet of trucks and then multiple PEMEX hauling contracts under the guidance of the national oil consortium's director Ramón Beteta, a revolutionary general and patron of the Atlacomulco group.

From owning trucks, Carlos Hank stepped up to manufacturing them—his Hermes Group hooked up with International Harvester in 1978. During the oil boom, Carlos Hank's *pipas* (tanker trucks) won juicy no-bid contracts to transport the precious fluid. Hank grew richer than rich. His estate in Santiago Tianguistenco featured a private zoo with hippos, zebras, tigers, cheetahs, and reportedly a giraffe.

Greased up by the oil boom, public works projects in Mexico City presented fresh opportunities to enhance the Hank fortune. Genghis Hank, as he was aptly tagged, was a go-getter regent, putting the finishing touches on the humongous Centro de Abastos in Iztapalapa that forever after bore his name. The Profe added five new Metro lines, quintupling its daily capacity.

Genghis Hank's truck fleets hauled materials and spread tons of cement during construction of 19 *ejes* or axes, 11 running east-west and 8 north-south, a grid of broad avenues with timed lights that ran one way save for a single trolley bus lane routed in the opposite direction, where pedestrians are pancaked every day. The Eje project, designed to speed traffic through the city, actually stalled the flow to a standstill during years of construction.

THE GARBAGE KINGS

Another enterprise from which the Hank machine profited handsomely was that of the Monster's chief commodity—garbage. The city then had seven open pits receiving 20,000 tons of *basura* a day. Garbage was big business, and Genghis Hank and his associates leased out the franchises to the garbage kings for a cut of the daily take.

Each dump was run like a feudal estate—*pepenadores* (garbage pickers) sifted through the incoming rubbish for valuable recyclables. Because they were paid by the weight of what they retrieved, the pickers jockeyed for position in a mad scrum under a shower of broken glass, dead animals, rancid grease, rags, paper, and rotten vegetables whenever the dump trucks came in. One payoff for franchises: The garbage kings would round up the *pepenadores*, freshen them up, and carry them off to pad out Hank rallies, the PRI's perpetual *acarreados* (trucked-in ones).

Perhaps the most celebrated of the garbage kings was Rafael Gutiérrez, who ran the Santa Cruz Meyehualco dump out in Iztapalapa like a sovereign nation. Given to sporting gold chains and gangster suits, Rafael, whose operation pulled in $15,000 USD a day, every day for 20 years, enjoyed a harem of hundreds of "wives" and is said to have sired a thousand children.

Rafael also enjoyed absolute immunity from prosecution under the Monstruo's notorious police chief Arturo "El Negro" Durazo despite dozens of reports of homicides and rapes committed in his name. Although his power was absolute out in Meyehualco, Rafael's reputation was so shady that even the PRI refused to post him for deputy. The garbage king finally ran afoul of a jealous husband whose wife he had abused, and that was the end of Rafael. Today, one of his many sons has achieved what Rafael in his lifetime could not and is the president of the Mexico City PRI.

WHAT LIES BENEATH

From the first incision, digging out the Metro lines yielded treasure troves. Every shovelful turned over priceless artifacts, shards of temple walls, offerings, likenesses of the *tochtlis* or small gods and the big ones too. The Temple of the wind god Ehécatl, around which the Pino Suárez station (Pink Line) is built, is emblematic of these discoveries, but good stuff was found on every line. For centuries, the gods of Tenochtitlán had lain there in the lake strata waiting patiently to be found again. When I sleep on the Zócalo floor with Indians camped out there to protest the theft of their lands, I feel as if I am floating on the brim of countless Aztec dynasties, and my dreams are filled with Quetzal feathers and the cries of Jaguar warriors.

In 1978, two Luz y Fuerza workers laying cables for the Mexico City electricity company under the sinking Metropolitan Cathedral stumbled onto the Coyolxauhqui stone, an eight-ton wheel that depicted the trajectory of the Aztec goddess of the moon, Coatlicue's daughter and Huitzilopochtli's jealous sister. The accidental find was the most important piece to emerge from the underground since Lady Coatlicue herself, way back in 1790.

Coyolxauhqui lay at the entrance to the Templo Mayor, which Manuel Gamio, the father of Mexican archeologists, had partially excavated in 1913 while the Mexican Revolution raged all around him. Eduardo Matos Moctezuma (no relation to the emperors) was put in charge of digging out the gore-splattered temples and turning them into a tourism moneymaker.

Since Coyolxauhqui was unearthed, major new finds have been located just about every year, the most recent being the 12-ton Diosa or Tlaltecuhtli, an ambisexual giant clawed, frog-like deity dug up at the foot of the Tláloc altar on the Ajacaracas site across the alley from the Templo Mayor, where a boisterous cantina once served up cervezas to the local riffraff—the property had been expropriated by the city to build a palace for the first left-wing mayor of El Monstruo, synchronistically named Cuauhtémoc, but the money ran out. Cárdenas's successor López Obrador was not a palace kind of guy, and he turned the Ajacaracas over to the National Anthropology Institute (INAH), whose diggers excavated La Diosa.

The discovery of the Coyolxauhqui wheel and the restoration of the Templo Mayor, the umbilicus of the Mexica universe, set the wheels in motion for a revival of pride in the Aztec past. *Conchero* dance troops sprang up on the Zócalo floor like feathered mushrooms, whirling the route of the sun across the sky and burning copal to the four directions. Prophecy was provoked—the imminent birth of the Sixth Sun, a new cycle of Mexica dominance in which the urban perversions of what once had been Tenochtitlán would be banished from the Monstruo. The founding of the city on March 12, 1325, and its fall with the capture of Emperor Cuauhtémoc on August 13, 1521, are commemorated by hundreds of dancers each year. Miguel León Portilla restored the old language in his honed translations of the verses of the hungry coyote king Nezahualcóyotl.

This outpouring of Aztec nostalgia pleased the big tlatoani López Portillo. The President had long aggrandized his reign as the return of Quetzalcóatl, the White God (JLP was very white) who rose each dawn with the morning star. López Portillo even wrote a book and commissioned a film financed by petrobucks to further this twisted hypothesis.

CITY OF INDIANS

Despite the nostalgia for their empire, the Aztec/Mexicas had never really disappeared from the city. Nahuat (modern-day Aztec) remains a living language in the rural delegations of Xochimilco and Milpa Alta and the forest villages of the Ajusco (Tlalpan) and is spoken on the streets of the Centro Histórico too. Nahuas from surrounding states driven off the land by the impoverishment of agrarian policies augment the number of speakers.

Indian cultures flourish in the city. Mazahuas have moved into La Merced and the Centro de Abastos. A hundred Otomí families reside in the Roma. Triquis and Huicholes congregate around the Ciudadela artisan market. Purépechas have put down roots in the Gustavo Madero delegation. So many Zapotecs and Mixtecos migrated to Ciudad Nezahualcóyotl that candidates running for office in Oaxaca are obligated to campaign there. All 57 of Mexico's Indian peoples and their 63 languages are represented in the Zona Metropolitana.

Although census takers from the INEGI (Instituto Nacional de Estadísticas y Geografía) count only 212,000 Indians in and around the capital, the institute's parameters are stingy—it recognizes only indigenous people who speak Indian tongues and live on Indian land. But depending on how one defines Indian and Indian land, at least 2 million and as many as 10 million indigenous people live here in El Monstruo, the largest Indian city in the world.

EL CHUECO

No habitué of López Portillo's inner circle embodied the concepts of rapine, corruption, and impunity quite so well as the incomparable Arturo "El Negro" Durazo, Mexico City's police chief from 1976 to 1982. A childhood sidekick of the well-born JLP from his Sonora school days, Durazo parlayed his connection to the soon-to-be-president into an undistinguished career in the military and police. But what El Negro lacked in talent, he more than made up for with his taste for *el chueco* (the crooked side of life).

With López Portillo's endorsement, Echeverría had appointed Durazo police commander at the capital's Benito Juárez International Airport, already a key transshipment point for Colombian cartel cocaine, and El Negro was under indictment in Los Angeles for converting the airport into a safe haven for the narcos when the new Quetzalcóatl appointed him chief of the federal district police, a force that had been in ill repute since Don Porfirio recruited criminals to catch criminals at the turn of the 20th century.

Cocaine was the signature drug of Durazo's regime. He himself was grievously addicted to the *polvo* and suffered debilitating nosebleeds for which he was treated at a Zona Rosa clinic, according to his longtime bodyguard José González González, whose tell-all book *The Negro of Negro Durazo* is the all-time best-selling Mexican paperback. Each week, noted González González, Durazo would hand out $60,000,000 (old pesos) "*tamales*"—a pound of cocaine packaged in the shape of a *tamal*—to his brigade commanders. After taking their share, the commanders would then sell the coke to their underlings. Half the profits were returned to El Negro, and the commanders split the rest.

The blow was so pure that it could withstand four cuts, quadrupling the weight—and the profits—of each *tamal*. In effect, Durazo transformed the city's police force (28,000 members at the time) into a giant drug distribution agency. Although the *polvo* was retailed on the street, the cops themselves were Durazo's best customers.

Arturo Durazo personified *prepotencia*—the brutish, bullying exercise of power so endemic to Mexican police forces. Torture was a special avocation. Not only did Durazo boast that he had made "the wax run from their ears" when Che and Fidel fell into his hands but he avowed he had sodomized Fidel with a broomstick à la Abner Louima's ordeal at the hands of New York City's Finest, and bragged that he had "waterboarded" the two revolutionaries to boot. Whether or not the Cubans were really so victimized, the police chief certainly practiced such malevolent techniques on many of the victims he "interrogated" with sadistic glee. In addition to torture, González González served as El Negro's personal *pistolero* and attests that he whacked at least 50 victims at Durazo's behest.

"El Negro" Durazo was an early enthusiast of neoliberalism, converting the Mexico City police force into a private enterprise. Cops had to buy their own uniforms and guns and badges (*charolas*) from his suppliers. Once the officers pinned on the badge, though, they were given carte blanche to extort and plunder the public, so long as a percentage was returned to the boss. The *charolas* were available to any and all citizens regardless of criminal records. Promotions also had their price—moving up from captain to major could cost a cool half-million old pesos.

Plazas or work areas were also sold to the highest bidder. The traffic division was much in demand—jacking up motorists for bogus infractions produced a hefty daily boodle. Threatened with being hauled down to the delegation where one could rot for days, drivers forked over the *mordidas* on the spot. Another excellent skam was the *grúas* or tow trucks. Durazo rented them out to *parejas*—teams of two per truck—but without the winches. Installation of the winches so that the *parejas* could go to "work" elevated the daily take.

The parked cars snatched by the *grúas* were held hostage at one of seven *corralones* or corrals. With a daily average of 1,200 cars each, the ransoms came to $31.5 million old pesos a month. Extortion of prostitutes, *padrotes* (pimps), and *hoteles de paso* in La Merced pulled in a million a day, 30 million a month. Durazo accumulated another 8 million a month from extortion by so-called "environmental" inspectors. The sale of license plates yielded a whopping $3.2 billion old pesos a month; shorting police cars five gallons a day on department vouchers, another 6.8 million. Each day, González González figures, Arturo Durazo took in about $87 million pesos from his various *chueco* enterprises.

Among Durazo's top-drawer projects was the construction of three Xanadu-like mansions. One home, "23.5" (located on kilometer 23.5 of the back road to Cuernavaca), had its own dog track, a lake, and a discothèque modeled on Manhattan's Studio 54. Police helicopters flew in food and drink for the hundreds of elite guests who flocked to El Negro's weekend pachangas. Another, a Swiss chalet high in the Ajusco with the city at its feet, was built entirely by police labor—because the chalet was off the road, all materials had to be carried in on the backs of the slave-labor cops. When El Negro was confronted on this score, he insisted that he had constructed it with his own hands—his poor wife had pushed the wheelbarrow. "El Partenón," on an island in the bay of Zihuatanejo, was the centerpiece of this orgy of bad taste. Replete with marble floors, gold toilets, and faux Grecian statuary, Durazo's Parthenon was a sorry knock-off of its Athenian namesake.

Durazo's building spree appears to have been financed by embezzling police pension funds—57 pesos were deducted from the checks of 28,000 cops every *quincena* (15-day pay period) for burial plots that did not exist. Additional revenues were raised by selling tickets to nonexistent police benefit shows for a nonexistent police retirement home.

The president and his earnest regent could not have been oblivious to what El Negro Durazo was up to. Carlos Hank and Arturo Durazo were frequently photographed dedicating fleets of new patrol cars or cutting the ribbon at sports complexes—Hank and El Negro were purported business partners in Reino Aventura, the new theme park in the Ajusco.

Durazo often dropped by Los Pinos without an appointment to visit his old schoolyard chum, whom he endearingly addressed as "Pepe," according to González González's black bio. Pepe rewarded El Negro's peccadilloes by bumping him up to Division General in the Mexican army. Fidel Velázquez presented Arturo Durazo with the annual Fidel Velázquez award, bestowed annually on public servants who had best serviced Fidel Velázquez. Durazo even entertained delusions of succeeding JLP on the throne of Mocuhtezuma.

By 1981, the penultimate year of López Portillo's kleptocracy, often dubbed the "Year of Hidalgo" on the Mexican political calendar

("*Ojalá que dejan algo*"—Here's hoping they will leave something), Arturo Durazo suddenly realized that he was about to lose presidential protection and took a powder (he took some powder with him too), finding sanctuary in Brazil, where he lay as low as he could for a few years. El Negro was eventually busted by the U.S. FBI in Puerto Rico, flown to Los Angeles to face charges there, and then returned to Mexico City, where he spent eight years in a luxury cell at the capital's eastern *reclusorio*. His health, undermined by decades of diligent drug abuse, collapsed soon after his release and he chuped his final Faro in 1992.

Durazo's palatial mansions were seized by the government—"23.5" became the Museum of Corruption under JLP's successor, Miguel De la Madrid's "Moral Renovation" crusade. But the black saga of El Negro did not end there. Any number of comandantes on the Monstruo's now 70,000-member police forces made their bones under Arturo Durazo and today proudly carry on El Negro's grand tradition of *el chueco*.

BURN ON BIG RIVER

Pumped up by the oil boom, the overheated economy was churning out 8 percent annual growth and runaway inflation. Foreign debt rose precipitously. In the south, the boom excited whole Indian communities to pack up and head for the Gulf Coast gold fields, destroying the fabric of indigenous life. Up in the capital, the most visible excrescence of the abundance was the 54-story PEMEX Towers, topped off in 1980, which outsoared by nearly 10 floors the beloved Torre Latinoamericana, the most prominent edifice on the Monster's skyline.

The agents of the oil giants and major lending institutions carrying portfolios stuffed with greenbacks milled about the courtyard of the skyscraper out on Marina Nacional in a colonia where every street is mysteriously named after a lake, trying to talk their way into an appointment with the *licenciados* upstairs. How much moolah changed hands in the upper reaches of the PEMEX Towers may never be known—a suspected arson fire in September 1982 wiped out the paperwork.

But there wasn't all that much paperwork anyway. No-bid non-contracts were let to transnational equipment purveyors, among them the first George Bush, whose secret partner in Zapata Offshore Oil Inc. was none other than López Portillo's chum Jorge Díaz Serrano. Under the pretext of moving the oil to market quickly to cover the escalating short-term debt, deals were sealed with a secret handshake and an embrace. Díaz Serrano's people placed millions of barrels on the Rotterdam spot market with no accounting whatsoever.

The oil boom transformed Coatzalcoalcos, once Don Porfirio's bustling Puerto México in tropical southern Veracruz, into the most polluted paradise on earth as wildcatters and drillers and contract workers and whores poured in to service the petrochemical plants, the effluvia from which would sometimes set the once crystalline Coatzalcoalcos river on fire.

THE BOTTOM FALLS OUT

In the spring of 1981, with consumption in decline and an oil glut looming, OPEC cut prices and Mexican light crude began to slip precipitously. In 1981–1982, Mexican oil lost half its value, dropping from $78 to $32 a barrel—it would sink beneath $10 by the middle of the decade. When Díaz Serrano offered his U.S. buyers a four-buck-a-barrel discount to keep Mexico competitive, López Portillo blew his stack and evicted him from his offices high atop the PEMEX towers.

It was too late. The oil boom had gone bust and Mexico was caught holding the bag—petroleum accounted for 75 percent of the nation's exports. In their mad mania to extract, JLP and his PEMEX director nearly quadrupled the record-breaking $22 billion USD foreign debt Echeverría had run up. Two years after López Portillo had left office and fled to Italy (Díaz Serrano went to federal prison, where he gave tennis lessons), Mexico's foreign debt accumulated to a whopping $76 billion Yanqui dollars, much of it in short-term loans borrowed at extravagant interest rates. Just servicing this inconceivable sum would cost the country $8 to $10 billion each year.

With the wolf at the door, the president dispatched Finance Minister Jesús Silva Herzog to Washington in the spring of 1982 to try and convince the Reaganites to cut Mexico some slack. Payments were coming due almost daily, and U.S. banks were dunning Los Pinos to cough up what was owed them. Foreign reserves had dwindled dangerously due to monstrous capital flight and López Portillo grew nervous. Washington offered a multibillion-dollar bailout, collateral for which would be 10,000,000 barrels of oil annually for the next five years, sold at a discount to top off the U.S. Strategic Reserve in Louisiana, take it or leave it. JLP freaked at the Americanos' chutzpah and summoned Silva Herzog home to Mexico City.

The economy was bleeding profusely. Mexican Treasury officials calculated that by August 15 the cash drawer would be bare. Washington got even more *prepotente*—13 U.S. banks stood to lose 60 billion bucks, 48 percent of their combined capital, if Mexico defaulted. Silva Herzog returned to Washington and signed on the dotted line.

The World Bank and the International Monetary fund were called in to kill the patient with shock therapy. "Structural adjustment" is the euphemism for such triage—the public sector was to be stripped down to its skeletal remains and an obese bureaucracy (1.5 million federal bureaucrats occupied 3,500 separate buildings in the capital alone) was cauterized. Massive layoffs were mandated and government subsidies slashed, particularly in the agrarian sector, which was instructed to adopt an export agricultural model. Farmers would no longer grow food crops to feed Mexicans but rather to pay off the foreign debt.

Within months, López Portillo's successor, Miguel De la Madrid, would sign a letter of intent with the IMF locking in Mexico to abide by these draconian strictures, one of five such documents that would ultimately annex the Mexican economy—and, for that matter, the country itself, to Washington forever.

THE SHAME OF IT ALL

In February 1982, having sworn to defend the peso "like a dog," López Portillo devalued the currency from 28 to 46 to the dollar. Within days, the peso had fallen to 70 and from 70 to 150, a 500 percent plunge. When the President attended public functions in Mexico City, protesters would bark at him rudely—whole restaurants would join the collective arfing, and JLP, anticipating assassination, reportedly contracted a body double.

The ostentatious complex (110,000 square meters, four houses, tennis court, and an Olympic-size pool) he built in tony Bosques de las Lomas out in Cuajimalpa became universally known as "La Colina de los Perros"—Dog Hill. Angry citizens would park at the front gate and howl.

Genghis Hank was also preparing his getaway. His final public work would be his own 20-room mansion far away from the scene of the crime in New Canaan, Connecticut, an estate plush enough to be featured in a *Town & Country* magazine spread, where for the next six years he would sit out the crisis he had helped induce.

Hank González led the voracious pack of *sacadólares* (dollar sackers) who reamed Mexico's reserves and brought the nation to default. Fully $12 billion USD fled the country between January and June 1982, an average of $150 million a day. An additional $4 billion was pulled in June.

JLP correctly held Mexico's banking system complicit in this hemorrhage. On September 1 in his final Informe, a furious López Portillo took his revenge and nationalized the banks. "They will never sack us again!" the president's voice cracked, and he broke down in tears.

Mexican flags were strung across the windows of bank buildings to indicate they were under new management. But despite their bleating, the banking class retained 34 percent ownership of their institutions and were encouraged to open *casas de cambio* (currency exchange houses) and brokerage firms. The bankers made out like bandits, as they always do. But the rest of the *pueblo* got flushed down Durazo's gold toilet. La Crisis had, in fact, become the Mexican way of life.

XIII

CITY IN CRISIS

La Crisis kicked in the door of every working-class home in Mexico City. It was like a quintuple whammy tsunami, five of them one right after another in 1983, '84, '85, '86, and '87. The economy was like a drowning sailor—every time it tried to pull itself back into the boat, the skiff would capsize all over again.

Upon his swearing-in, De la Madrid's regent Ramón Aguirre's first order of business was to inform his fellow Chilangos that the city was broke. A year earlier Carlos Hank González had averred that he was leaving City Hall with the Monstruo's financial future assured. Unlike Genghis Hank, Chilangos had no hideaway in Connecticut to flee to.

The job market collapsed—unemployment rose 15 percent in the "formal" sector in 1983. Every morning, tradesmen carrying their work tools and with their professions neatly lettered on their lunch pails—PLUMBER, CARPENTER, MASON—lined up on one flank of the Metropolitan Cathedral waiting for someone to hire them. The "informal" sector, i.e., the *jodidos* who sold in the street, now accounted for 45 percent of all jobs in the capital, according to INEGI stats. Real wages dropped 60 percent as inflation zoomed to 80 percent in 1983–1984 and topped 100 percent in the subsequent three years. Milk leapt 340 percent, eggs 480 percent, tortillas—the staff of life—280 percent. Some household products like toothpaste just disappeared from the shelves.

Under Uruchurtu's tightfisted fiscal policies, property taxes and water fees accounted for 61 percent of the city's budget—now they covered only 18 percent. The De la Madrid government was incapable of filling in the gap. City services declined accordingly—the transportation budget was reduced by 12 percent, potable water 25 percent, health services 18 percent, property regularization 56 percent. If this was happening in the capital, which received half of the total government allocations to the nation's 2,000-plus municipalities, you can imagine how hard hard times were in the Sierra of Zongolica or the jungles of Chiapas.

With the Monstruo going to hell in a handbasket, out-of-work Chilangos headed for El Norte, the first economic refugees of La Crisis. But at the same time, farmers were deserting the ravished countryside in droves and descending on the Monstruo—by the 1980s, 50 million out of the nation's 78 million citizens were living in cities, 28 percent of them in the Mexico City Metropolitan Zone. Despite the severity of the downturn, the Monster managed to grow its population 4 percent a year, about 1,100 newcomers arriving in Jodido City every day.

The impoverishment was evident everywhere. The "Marías," their nursing babies wrapped up on their backs in ragged rebozos, hunkered down against the walls and beseeched passersby for coins. Five-year-old kids and their baby sisters played at playing accordions on street corners—both the kids and the accordions were rented out by Chilango Fagans. *Tragafuegos*, fire-eaters, were emblematic of La Crisis, gulping mouthfuls of gasoline and blowing fireballs in traffic. One particularly grisly note in *Uno Más Uno* reported how two of Durazo's disciples had poured gasoline on a *tragafuego* who would not or could not cough up the mordida and set him ablaze.

THE JODIDOS GET ORGANIZED

The desperation of the jodidos did not immobilize them; they got organized. The east side of the city was a flashpoint—empty lots out in delegations like Iztapalapa and Iztacalco, swollen with newcomers where housing was at a premium, were overrun by *paracaidistas*. Under the leadership of Francisco de la Cruz, who had come to the Monstruo from the backwaters of Oaxaca to find his fortune, the Dos de Octubre encampment flourished from 1979 to 1981. A cooperative factory was established and the squatters moved from their hovels into block houses. A clinic and a kindergarten were set up. The PRI *caciques* at Insurgentes #59 did not like the looks of it, and Carlos Hank sent in the Granaderos. De la Cruz was dragged off to the penitentiary but the *colono* movement grew like kudzu.

A post-Tlatelolco generation of leftist students organized squatter communities—the CONAMUP (The National Coordinating Body of Urban Popular Movements) viewed the housing crunch as the linch-pin of class struggle. Formulated in 1981, the CONAMUP linked up *colonos* in Mexico City with their cousins in northern cities like Mon-terrey and Torreón with rich histories of organizing the poor, to form a radical front. Ruta 100 bus drivers and the Independent Proletarian Movement (MPI) organized the colonias around the terminals of the bus lines to demand extension of the routes—the MPI could turn out tens of thousands for noisy City Hall rallies. Left splinter parties like the PST (Party of Socialist Workers) and the PRT (Party of Revolution-ary Workers) and a split-off from Lombardo Toledano's moribund PPS (Popular Socialist Party) organized tenant fronts in inner-city colonias like the Guerrero.

Because La Crisis put a crimp on city budgets, the PRI, which had once owned the urban struggle organizations through the CNOP, its so-called "popular" sector, could no longer service its electoral clien-tele. Diane Davis estimates that in the early 1980s, at least 200,000 Chi-langos were active participants in the push for housing and city ser-vices. Five marches a day further complicated downtown traffic and Televisa's obnoxious Zabludovsky got grumpier and grumpier, urg-ing *la gente decente* to honk their horns and turn on their high beams to protest the protesters.

SELLING IT ON THE STREET

The first Chilangos sold their wares on the streets of Tenochtitlán and Tlatelolco before there were streets. During five centuries of periodic economic nosedives, the volume of *ambulantes* selling in the public way increased with each new crisis, and in the 1980s they became a focal point for social agitation.

At first glance, the *ambulantaje* or street commerce appears to be chaotic—but the chaos is fine-tuned. Associations of street vendors impose their own order: The juice vendors come out early to catch the predawn breakfast crowd, *taqueros* with their big baskets of *tacos de canasta* are on the streets in time to feed those rushing to work. General merchandise, *fayuca* (domestic appliances and other pirated goods), set up by mid-morning and carry on until dark. *Merengue* (homemade candy) vendors appear in the afternoon, and the *camoteros*—sweet potato people with their peculiar whistling carts—take over in the evening.

The sellers are organized into associations whose leaders stake claims on the sidewalks and portion them off to their members for a daily rental fee—the more meters you "rent," the more you pay. Collectors make the rounds each day to pick up the fees for garbage removal and bribing the police. The *lideresas*—most of the leaders are women—cut deals with PRI politicos to protect their turf and in return provide *acarreados* for their rallies and other exigencies.

In the early 1980s, the unquestioned Queen of the Ambulantes was a tough old bird named Guillermina Rico. When still a young woman in the late '50s, Rico had been denied an inside stall in Uruchurtu's remodeled "new" Merced and formed the Union of Merchants of the Old Merced, which controlled tens of thousands of vendors on downtown streets. Each year on Queen Guille's birthday, politicians and priests would make a beeline for the association's compound at Roldán #12 in the Merced for the traditional *besamanos* (kissing of hands).

But as La Crisis drove more and more workers onto the sidewalks, new associations sprang up. Alejandra Barrios, whose family controlled the streets just south of Tepito and Lagunilla market—her warehouses of dubious goods were located on Bolivia Street—chartered "The Legitimate Civic Association of Merchants," a wholly owned family enterprise, and challenged Doña Guille for the right to vend in the center of the city. The bottles flew on downtown streets. Aguirre's Granaderos often had to separate the warring associations.

TECNOS VS. DINOS

Miguel De la Madrid was a newfangled breed of PRIista. The first of three straight Mexican presidents to have taken their postdocs at either Harvard or Yale, De la Madrid represented the *tecno* or neoliberal wing of the ruling party, and he often came into conflict with the *dinos* (dinosaurs) at Insurgentes #59.

The PRI had taken 75 percent of the national vote in 1982—14 percent went to the PAN and the rest was split by five left parties that had been granted provisional registration under an electoral reform measure pushed through while López Portillo was still in a good mood. But in Chilangolandia, the PRI had barely racked up 51 percent of the vote, and it would be all downhill from there—in the 1985 midterms, the Institutionals took 71 percent nationally but the opposition's combined totals were 57 percent in the capital.

Unable to provide jobs and housing for the denizens of El Monstruo, De la Madrid offered PRI-style democracy. Home rule had been a latent demand in Mexico City since 1928, when the municipalities had been suppressed and the city placed under the thumb of the Federal District Department, whose chief was handpicked by the president and the PRI. But De la Madrid's proposal for an elected mayor and local legislative assembly was stonewalled by Aguirre, a baby *dino* and surrogate of the big boys on north Insurgentes, who correctly calculated that the PRI's majorities in the city were a thing of the past. The Institutionals were determined to hang onto control of the capital at any price. It would be another decade before the dinosaurs were voted out of City Hall.

VOTIVE CANDLES

Miguel De la Madrid lit votive candles to the moral renovation of Mexico. The previous administration's sins would be cleansed by political human sacrifice. With the citizenry barking him down whenever he descended from the Hill of the Canines, López Portillo fled to Italy and joined the Untouchables. Díaz Serrano was selected to be the official scapegoat for the many crimes committed in JLP's name. A number of underlings were sent up the river with Mr. Díaz Serrano, who was convicted of accepting kickbacks on a PEMEX tanker fleet contract.

In other excesses of moral renovation, Durazo's replacement, General Ramón Mota Sánchez, opted to redeem the souls of the unruly children of La Crisis, the *chavos banda* or youth gangs of the slums. Police repression cranked up the crackdown into a generational war. Mota Sánchez also sent in his Zorros, an elite police unit, to vamp the Chopo *tianguis*, a weekly gathering of the countercultural melting pot that is still held on Saturday mornings near the old Buenavista railroad station.

But De la Madrid's moral renovation crusade was sabotaged by the murder of Manuel Buendía, the influential *Excelsior* columnist whose daily exposés of corruption in high places ran under the rubric of Red Pública (Public Network) in more than 200 papers around the country.

On April 9, 1984, when Buendía went to claim his car at a parking garage just across Insurgentes Avenue from the Zona Rosa, an unidentified hit man put three slugs in his back and sped off into traffic on a monster motorcycle. Whodunnit?

WHAT MANUEL BUENDÍA KNEW AND WHEN

Manuel Buendía was always shaded from public view by deeply smoked glasses. He had many enemies. Among the prime suspects: a neo-Nazi arms dealer with mysterious mining claims in the north; the Tecos, an extreme right student gang based around the University of Guadalajara; the CIA, whose undercover activities in Mexico City Buendía had repeatedly exposed. Buendía was also thought to have tipped off the *Washington Post*'s Jack Anderson about Swiss bank accounts held in the name of certain De la Madrid relatives suspected of engaging in drug running—the revelations appeared in the *Post* on the same day the Mexican president was visiting the U.S. capital scouting up fresh funds to beat back La Crisis.

President De la Madrid's first response to the killing was to place the highly suspect Federal Security director José Zorrilla Pérez in charge of the investigation. In fact, Zorilla was first on the crime scene, cordoning off the parking garage and sealing Buendía's offices around the corner on London Street, where he would spend the next week sifting through the journalist's files and presumably destroying incriminating evidence.

José Antonio Zorrilla Pérez and Manuel Buendía were old friends, you see. They took target practice together at the Mexico City police firing range; the DFS capo had gifted the columnist with a new .45 and a bulletproof vest, and had pressed a DFS credential on him. Buendía pumped Zorrilla for scuttlebutt of scandal in the De la Madrid administration and in the process accumulated plenty of dirt on his pal.

Zorrilla Pérez's house was jam-packed with skeleton-filled closets. Other recipients of the prized DFS credential or *charola* included a brash Sinaloa drug kingpin, Rafael Caro Quintero. Caro Quintero, who was then managing a mind-boggling marijuana operation at the

Buffalo Ranch in northern Chihuahua, which allegedly employed 8,000 peons and turned out a preposterous 50,000,000 tons of pot a year for the nearby North American market.

Despite the immensity of the Buffalo spread, no one could seem to find it—least of all De la Madrid's secretary of defense Juan Arévalo Gardoqui, who ran Mexico's "War" on Drugs. In December 1984, at the height of the harvest, a U.S. Drug Enforcement Administration contract pilot, Alfredo Zavala, did a freelance flyover of Buffalo and reported his discovery to his boss, DEA agent Enrique "Kiki" Camarena. Both men were snatched off a Guadalajara street two months later and delivered to Caro Quintero's mansion—the house had been formerly owned by Echeverría's father-in-law, Rubén Zuno Arce— where they were tortured under the supervision of a medical doctor until they expired. Their decomposing remains were later found in a shallow grave on a Michoacán pig farm.

The killing of Kiki Camarena propelled the Reagan administration to the brink of war. Missile-rattling rhetoric bombarded Los Pinos. Reagan's ambassador to Mexico John Gavin, another Grade D actor, pulled a Henry Lane Wilson and implied invasion was at hand. With U.S. agents in hot pursuit, Caro Quintero made a dash to Costa Rica. Stopped by Mexican judicial police at the Guadalajara airport, where he was about to board a private flight, the kingpin pulled out his DFS charola and was allowed to take off.

Caro's possession of the badge cost Zorrilla Pérez his job and his agency—the Federal Security Directorate was gutted and 437 agents transferred to the federal judicial police and the Center for National Security and Investigation (CISAN) to continue their dirty war activities. Despite the accumulation of evidence, José Antonio Zorrilla Pérez was not arrested until April 1989, five years and 14 days after he had ordered the hit on Manuel Buendía. Miguel De la Madrid had just left office.

ANTIHEROES OF LA CRISIS

Rafael Caro Quintero was eventually extradited from Costa Rica and lodged at the Northern Reclusorio, where he bought himself a three-cell suite (living room, bedroom, and discothèque) and did not want for such creature comforts as drugs, alcohol, and female companionship. A staff of penniless prisoners attended to his every need.

Help wasn't hard to find in prison. La Crisis had goosed the Mexico City crime rate by 37 percent and so many *jodidos* had been rounded up that the Monster's 11 prisons and jails were coming apart at the seams. The crime waves of the 1980s were so dramatic that the U.S. State Department regularly issued travelers' advisories warning tourists that they were in harm's way if they lingered in the Mexican capital.

La Crisis generated a bevy of antiheroes. Caro Quintero's exploits became synonymous with the *narco-corrido*, Norteño border ballads that celebrated the adventurous lives of the nation's drug lords. A comedy tape cut by Caro Quintero or a reasonable facsimile of same in which the Narco pledges to pay off Mexico's ballooning foreign debt was a hot seller for the *ambulantes* clustered around the Pino Suárez Metro stop in the Centro.

Another antihero of La Crisis was the flamboyant bank robber Alfredo Ríos Galeana, a sort of Mexican Pretty Boy Floyd, whose three spectacular escapes from leaky Mexico City penitentiaries garnered headlines. Ríos Galeana, whose gang may have held up as many as 500 banks during the 1980s, had started his criminal career as a police commander in Mexico state when Carlos Hank González was governor and often made surprise live appearances at *palenques* (cockfighting arenas) in full Mariachi regalia to croon his favorite *rancheros*. How much he actually stole is uncertain, since copycat bandits identified themselves as the Maestro. After a final escape from Santa Marta Acatitla prison in 1987, Ríos Galeana had extensive plastic surgery and disappeared off the face of the earth. He was finally run to ground 18 years later when he tried to renew his visa at the Mexican consulate in Los Angeles. He had become a born-again Christian.

"SOME OTHER PENDEJO" (An interview with Isidro Zúñiga)

Isidro Zúñiga is the mozo or porter at the Hotel Isabel. His strength amazes me. In his 70s, he is six years older than I am and can still haul 100 pounds on his back without breathing hard. I can hardly lift a Kleenex.

We call Isidro campeón *because he was a national boxing champion and also a professional baseball player. A sturdy white-haired stud at 76, Isidro spends a good deal of his day chasing the* camaristas *(chamber maids) around. He revels in his past glories, and one day he brought a box of photographs of his boxing days to work and we adjourned to La Blanca to review them.*

"This is my manager, Ignacio Ayala. He was my teacher about everything—boxing, women, money, how to survive in this pendejo of a world.

"This is when I won the Golden Gloves featherweight championship at the Coliseo arena on Perú Street in 1953.

"Here I am with José 'Huitlacoche' Medel. He was a smooth little fighter from Tepito—he runs a boxing gym there now.

"And this is me when I won the national championship in Culiacán in '55. I look really young here. I got paid 3,200 pesos for that fight. It was more money than I had ever seen in my life. The kid I knocked out was a big pendejo from Sinaloa and I ran him all around the ring, hammering him with my jabs. He started bleeding bad from his nose and his manager threw in the towel. I think I must have broken it.

"I had 22 fights and 22 victories and no defeats. I knocked out 20 of my opponents. My last fight was at the Coliseo against a smooth kid from Tulpancingo and I put him down in the second round. I could have kept fighting but my mujer kept begging me to quit before I got hurt. I already had a regular job so I didn't need the money.

"Here's my baseball team, the Parrots of Puebla. I was the shortstop and third baseman and their clean-up hitter. I don't know how many home runs I hit. Un chingo. I played 12 seasons with the Parrots of Puebla and we won the championship in 1959. We played on Sundays at the Deportivo in the Carranza delegation and in Puebla during the week.

"My favorite team in the Mexican league was the Red Devils, and my favorite player was the great Beto Ávila, the first Mexican ever to play in the World Series, with the Cleveland Indians in 1948. He was their second baseman. Beto was from Veracruz where the best Mexican ballplayers come from. He tried to form a union but the owners kicked them out of the league. Beto Ávila was my idol.

"This is Udela, my mujer. I met her in her father's store in the Colonia Maza and we've been together for 53 years.

Here's my oldest son Ulises—he's a boot maker. He buys crocodile skins and ostrich skins. There's a big demand for his boots, and he makes good money.

"Here is my youngest daughter Linda—she's a financial secretary. We're all sitting in the kitchen. The kitchen is my favorite room. I own my own home—it cost me 17,000 pesos 20 years ago.

"We live in the Colonia Rastro behind the airport, on the east side where I grew up. My father worked in the slaughterhouse out there. I went to work when I was 14 at a printing plant near the Canal del Norte and I worked there for 37 years until the pinche crisis shut them down.

"The money they gave me when they shut down the plant was just about gone and I went looking for a job. I was walking past the Hotel Isabel and I saw a sign that said they wanted a mozo. Well, I figured that they could use me and I came in and applied.

"Being the mozo at the Isabel is like I'm working out. I'm in better shape than the kids who work at the hotel. I don't drink. I don't smoke. I go to sleep at eight when it gets dark and I'm up by four. I go to the Isabel and carry their stuff around all day. I can still put 50 kilos on my back. Pretty good for a broken-down old boxer, don't you think?

"My mujer wants me to retire but I'm going to keep working at the Isabel until they run me out and find some other pendejo to carry their shit around."

MAY DAY! MAY DAY!

Social turmoil came to a boil May 1, 1984, when 600,000 unusually irritated union members turned out on International Workers Day in the Zócalo to salute Señor Presidente. At Fidel Velázquez's invitation, they were encouraged to express their gratification for everything Miguel De la Madrid was doing to alleviate the afflictions of the working class. "¡Ojo por Ojo, Diente por Diente!" they chorused: An Eye for an Eye, A Tooth for a Tooth! "Chinga Su Madre Señor Presidente" (no translation needed). Some workers stripped naked to more graphically illustrate their condition—Paloma Cordero, the chaste, God-fearing First Lady, averted her eyes as the bare butts of the laboring class mooned her down below.

One contingent from the Prepa Popular Tacuba, a high school system created after 1968 to accommodate those rejected by the UNAM, took the protest one step up by flinging a Molotov cocktail onto the Presidential balcony, singeing the suits and eyebrows of panic-stricken secretaries of state. The military was ordered on red alert to deal with this recrudescence of Soviet subversion and the student perps were salted away for 10 years in the slammer.

THE GODS MUST BE ANGRY

The gods were not happy. On September 7, 1984, Tláloc let loose a downpour of biblical proportions that inundated the Viaduct, marooning cars and drowning drivers. It took weeks for the capital to dry out.

But if water did not end the world, fire almost did. Before dawn on November 29, the PEMEX liquid gas complex at San Juan Ixhuatepec ("Hill of Doves") wedged next to Tlalnepantla on the north end of town, blew sky high in a chain reaction of three mind-numbing explosions. Ten million cubic feet of liquid natural gas roared out of control.

The jodidos of San Juanico had built their hovels around the perimeter of the plants, which provided propane gas cylinders to Mexico City homes. (The leaky cylinders were a major source of the city's terrifying air pollution.) The setup resembled Bhopal, India—indeed, Union Carbide was one of 38 corporations with storage facilities in San Juanico. In the blasts, 462 *colonos* were incinerated, 4,258 injured, and 2,000 more never accounted for.

San Juan Ixhuatepec looked like Mordor on steroids from the city— exploding fireballs could be seen from the Centro Histórico—and the urban popular movement mobilized in solidarity, collecting blankets and food and medications for the survivors. San Juanico would prove to be a trial run for another more earth-shaking tragedy.

How did the regent Aguirre and his boss De la Madrid respond to the solidarity of the CONAMUP and affiliated bands of activists? When, on February 28, 1985, the Committee of Residents of San Juan Ixhuatepec AC marched on the interior secretary's offices on Bucareli to protest government negligence, leader Marcelo Moreno was manhandled, had his nose broken by the Granaderos, and was hustled off to gaol to join the Tacuba Popular Prepas and Francisco de la Cruz as urban political prisoners.

SEPTEMBER 19—7:19 A.M.

Lalo Miranda dangled his feet over the side of the unmade bed, rubbed his eyes, and stared at his shoes. How many customers would he have today in his living room barbershop?

Nieves was out in the kitchen, preparing breakfast for the three boys and contemplating the *comida corrida* menu for the off-the-books lunchtime restaurant she ran out of the cramped dining nook.

Lalo picked up his watch. It was exactly 7:19 a.m., September 19, 1985. Suddenly Lalo's shoes began to dance of their own volition.

The bedroom swooned off its axis and pogoed up and down for a full, terrifying minute. There was a loud, almost human groan, and the old *vecindad* at Regina #39 in the Centro Histórico settled back on its haunches three meters south. The ceiling dropped nearly a foot, and the walls webbed with cracks through which the sunlight shone in.

Lalo grabbed his shoes, Nieves swooped up the three boys and Perla, the toy cinnamon poodle cowering under the sink, and they dashed out into the patio as tiles smashed to earth all around them. Things were never the same after that, Nieves remembers.

Once safely outside on the crunched-up sidewalk, Lalo counted noses. There were 14 apartments in the *vecinidad*, which due to its 100-year longevity had earned the title of a "historic monument." Some of the tenants were missing. Maybe they hadn't come home last night. Maybe they were trapped in their rooms. Lalo dashed back into Regina #39, frantically knocking on doors. Doña Epifania, the upstairs neighbor in the front, was balled up under her sewing table moaning softly, and he helped the old woman to her feet. Together they inched down the collapsed hallway, crept down the stairs which seemed to be anchored to nothing, and pushed through the front gate just as a loud crack broke from the back of the building.

The 8.1 quake was the most devastating ever to rip through the Monstruo's innards. The Terremoto or Ollín (earth movement in Na-huat) or Sismo or Temblor—as people call it without any other iden-tifying features—began with the crunching of tectonic plates in the Cocos subduction zone out in the Pacific Ocean off Playa Azul, Mi-choacán. Shock waves zigzagged through that large western state toppling church towers (the ancient 1530 country church where my godchild had just been baptized was a victim), before barging into the capital at exactly 7:19. Workers were just punching in for the day. Oth-ers were on the way.

The Centro is the heart of Mexico City's garment industry, and a four-story structure that housed several sweatshops a block east on Regina had fallen into a bank. Lalo rushed over to the pile and poked in the rubble for signs of life. He thought he heard a groan and put his ear to the broken walls, then ran back to #39 and bor-rowed a shovel. He would walk the Centro for days with that shovel, pitching in where he could to dig in the rubble of fallen buildings for survivors.

DEATH TRAPS

A block away, across from my current room at the Isabel (I would not be in residence for another week), a large stone final slipped from the roof of the National Library and flattened a passing *combi* van. Mario García was squeezed into his tin kiosk on the corner assembling the morning papers. He lumbered over to help out but couldn't move the fallen slab by himself. It didn't much matter. Everyone inside—five passengers and the driver—was already dead.

Two blocks farther west out on San Juan de Letrán—now the Eje Central Lázaro Cárdenas thanks to Carlos Hank González's road building—the Torre Latinoamericana had been whipped around like a weed in a windstorm but survived the earthquake intact. The Super Leche across the Eje on the corner of Victoria was not so lucky. Two four-story apartment buildings had fallen through the roof of the packed breakfast restaurant—like La Blanca (which survived without a scratch), the Super Leche was Gachupín-owned, with large murals of cows on the walls. Between the customers and the 20 apartments upstairs, maybe 300 people were killed. There is no precise count.

At the foot of Isabel la Católica Street, a dozen blocks north on the other side of Reforma, a billowing cloud of grit and black smoke filled the horizon like a premonition of 9/11. The towers of Tlatelolco had been knocked askew, 103 of its 148 buildings seriously damaged. The Nuevo León, 13 stories tall and holding 3,000 tenants, had fallen off its foundations and lurched precariously to the right. One floor had pancaked into the next. Once again, Tlatelolco was the stage set for a massacre.

THE DEAD DOCTORS

In the Alamos colony a mile south down Isabel la Católica, my compadre Hermann Bellinghausen, a doctor who doubles as a writer for *La Jornada*, walked the damaged streets in the direction of the Medical Center. Sirens wailed in the distance. Trees had been dislodged from front lawns. At the Centro Médico, Oncology and Traumatology had come down. Seventy doctors had been crushed to death in their residence hall and hundreds of mothers and their newborns were buried under the ruins of the Hospital Juárez—six miracle babies, some still in incubators, would be discovered alive a week later. Hermann watched a doctor still in his bathrobe and slippers put a stethoscope to the chest of a dead man splayed out in a squalid little garden.

Hermann crossed over into the Colonia Roma. A 10-story building at Tamaulipas #12 had been shaken apart like it was made out of cards. The smell of gas was pungent. Hermann sat down on a ledge, ignoring the danger, and lit a cigarette. He held his breath. This monstrous city that he both hated and loved had become an assassin. He felt like an orphan.

"*Mamá, Mamá,*" a girl in a Catholic school uniform stood whimpering in the street, clutching her book bag. Neighbors knelt on the busted sidewalks in front of their collapsed homes and prayed. Later, Hare Krishnas would come out and dance on the dead in the ruins and Jesus freaks passed out leaflets saying the Chilangos had gotten what they deserved because they were sinners.

By noon, life was stirring. Hermann watched families setting up camp under sheets like Bedouins on the median strips where Uruchurtu had once planted his flowers. A whole population had suddenly mobilized itself—doctors, nurses, *taxistas,* the *vecinos* of the Roma—without anyone giving an order. What Hermann was witnessing, the birth of the civil society, would alter power balances and change Mexico in the weeks and years to come.

7:19 FOREVER

Nikito Nipongo (his comic nom de plume) ambled down Bucareli Street toward the Alameda. Government buildings spilled all over the street. The Commerce Secretariat and the Navy building were in ruins. The government itself seemed to have vanished. Bureaucrats had jumped into their sedans and hightailed it for the safety of Cuernavaca. Terrible secrets were revealed. When supervisors ordered their workers into the ruins of the Mexico City prosecutor's office to retrieve files and typewriters, they found six bodies stuffed into the trunk of an agent's car in the flattened parking garage. The bodies, reputedly Colombian drug dealers, had been wrapped in tape and were covered with cigarette burns.

The telecommunications tower near the Ciudadela had keeled over. Televisa's Chapultepec Avenue studios burst apart, killing dozens and knocking the station off the air. The hotels around the Alameda were shredded by the Sismo—Diego's "Dream of Sunday on the

Alameda" was saved only because attentive waiters stashed it in the Del Prado kitchen.

Across Juárez, the Regis Hotel had blown up. Shaken off a foundation damaged by Metro construction, the boilers exploded, igniting a pyre that burnt for 50 hours. No one knows how many were incinerated. Down in the Metro, hundreds of thousands of passengers who had been trapped for hours in the dark trains and on the crowded platforms groped their way back to the surface and into the light. The time on every clock still read 7:19.

GOVERNMENT AGAINST PEOPLE

The first response of Regent Aguirre and the De la Madrid government was stunned silence. In the neighborhoods, burglar alarms whooped but no cops showed up to investigate. You couldn't call an ambulance because the phone lines had collapsed. With no help on the way, the neighbors dug with their own bleeding hands to reach the survivors. Shovels and picks thudded against the ground in desperate unison.

Finally, 36 hours after it had all come down, the police and the military put in an appearance on Regina Street and the blocks south of the Zócalo, ordered the neighbors to stop digging and forced them away from their busted homes at bayonet point. The soldiers cordoned off the blocks or *manzanas* under the pretext of protecting private property and looted the apartments of what valuables they could put their hands on—Alma Guillermoprieto, who grew up on Calle 57 in the Centro, has documented the looting of a Mariachi-occupied apartment building east of Garibaldi Square. Fingers were chopped off to steal the gold wedding bands of dead spouses.

"The soldiers blocked off the streets and we couldn't get out to find food and water," Lalo Miranda who was the *jefe de manzana* or block captain on Regina recalls bitterly. "We fought the soldiers with rocks and our bare hands so we could rescue our neighbors," remembers Raúl Bautista, an ex-wrestler and street vendor who would soon become the scarlet-and-canary-caped Superbarrio, protector of *damnificados* (earthquake victims).

Others had easier access to their property. More than 800 sweatshops in the Centro had been demolished, the corpses of the seamstresses rotting in the ruins. Many owners were far more interested in saving their sewing machines and their inventories than their workers, and they bribed the cops to let them poke around in the rubble to remove their merchandise. There were thought to be 40,000 garment workers in the center of the city. No one knows how many thousands did not come home from work that night.

The dead were concentrated at the Social Security baseball park on Cuauhtémoc Avenue, wrapped tightly in plastic and laid out in rows all over the outfield. The stench was insufferable. Survivors looking for their family members puked all over the grass. Rescue workers sprayed the cadavers with pesticide and priests plied the corpse field giving belated last rites.

How many perished September 19? At first the De la Madrid government minimized the toll and said 4,000, and then in the face of the mounting tragedy conceded it might be 7,000. The damnificados' estimates ranged from 10,000 to a high of 25,000. How many? *Un chingo*. A lot. Who will ever know? Hospital records show the Sismo left 14,268 injured, and 2,000 were never accounted for. As in the aftermath of 9/11, pictures of the missing were slapped up on the walls of the Centro: "Alondra Terán. Nuevo León. 10,000 pesos reward."

The Temblor left 954 buildings damaged beyond repair. Another 150 came down after a second smaller quake the next afternoon. When the earth began to shake again, thousands rushed into the open Zócalo for salvation and camped there for days. Some 2,500 structures were rendered uninhabitable. It all came to about $5 billion USD in material damages. But the damage was more than material.

At first, the President refused all outside aid but later relented as the enormity of the tragedy dawned on him. As much as $30 billion is thought to have been eventually received in relief aid. People are still asking where it could have gone to.

SLEEPING THROUGH CALAMITY

Not every neighborhood of the Monstruo was kissed by the Terremoto. Hardly. Only 1.3 percent of the city's total 2.65 million units were affected. Many Chilangos slept right through the earthquake. Polanco, Perisur—the posh new shopping mall in the south of the city—Lomas, and the upscale residential areas in the west didn't feel a thing.

The Temblor had torn its way erratically through the city, touching a building here, a building there, seemingly at random. But the neighborhoods the quake selected for special attention were the most combative colonias, the ones where the residents had heroic records of resistance: Roma, Guerrero, La Merced and Tepito, the Centro Histórico where the Mexicans had confronted the Gachupines in 1810 and the greengos in 1846, and endured the depredations of one revolutionary army after another.

"NO PLACE ELSE FEELS LIKE HOME"

Earthquakes are mythic events. They have the power to transform whatever and whomever they touch. The great 1969 quake in the highlands of Peru drove the Quechuas down to the coast, set the stage for a short-lived democratic revolution, and altered the demographics of the country forever. The 1976 Nicaraguan earthquake lit the fuse for the Sandinista revolution when the dictator Somoza pocketed all the relief money. Mexico City would be no different. Yes, of course, many Chilangos perished September 19, 1985, but something really big was being born.

The *vecinos* had moved swiftly to save their own. The government wasn't doing it, so it was up to them. Dr. Cuauhtémoc Abarca, a driving force behind the damnificado organizing movement in Tlatelolco, testifies that within a half an hour of the Sismo, an organization came together. The neighbors formed human chains passing buckets of rubble from hand to hand to clear the way to get at the victims, and their many hands tied them together.

The *topos* or moles, small, wiry men like Marcos Efrén Zariñana, "La Pulga" (The Flea), burrowed into the slabs of broken concrete and packed earth to rescue the wounded. They worked night and day, gouging their way toward where they thought they had heard a hint of life. It rained hard on the third and fourth day and they were immersed in mud. But 4,016 damnificados were pulled from the ruins alive.

Thousands of volunteers, many of them *universitarios* who had not forgotten Dos de Octubre, poured into the afflicted colonias in solidarity. Along with the survivors, they fed the hungry, clothed the nearly naked, directed traffic, delivered babies, did what the government should have been doing and did not. The military ordered them to go home and they said We are home.

Damnificados. That's what the victims called themselves now— only they didn't quite see themselves as victims. "Damnificados because we were condemned by the earthquake," Lalo explains, "only we survived and are alive to tell about it."

The first meeting was pulled together on San Jerónimo in the courtyard of the cloister where the poet and feminist Sor Juana Inés de la Cruz had once shut herself up. The organization would call itself the Popular Union of New Tenochtitlán (UPNT), since Tenochtitlán was where they had always lived.

Dr. Abarca organized those who had dwelt on the roofs of Tlatelolco, the *azoteas*. Hundreds of tenants had been dislocated from their rooftop homes. The Vecinos and Damnificados of the Roma took over rubble-strewn lots and staged cultural events to mitigate the loss—a movie club and even a philharmonic of damnificados evolved. The garment workers organized an independent union and demanded reparations from their former bosses.

Women were often the leaders of the damnificado movement— Evangelina Corona amongst the seamstresses, Leslie Serna and Dolores Padierna in the Centro, Yolanda Tello in the Guerrero, Magdalena Trejo out in Valle Gómez near the airport. The longer-lived urban activists grouped around the CONAMUP provided structure and valuable life experiences in dealing with the Monstruo from the street up.

But the nucleus of damnificado organization was really the *vecindades* and apartment buildings. Each building was an organization in itself—neighbors were often cousins or members of extended families. Unlike Gringolandia, where folks who live on one side of the sheetrock never know who lives on the other, the damnificados were, as Lalo describes it, "very much in each other's lives." Their kids went to school together. They were *padrinos* at each other's weddings and graduations. They lent each other money and buried their dead together.

They had all lived in these buildings for generations, and they were determined not to be moved to the periphery of the Monstruo, out there in the misery belt far from home where the *mal gobierno* had plans to relocate them. "We will build up our colonia with our own hands," Magda Trejo told me one day as she and a group of women from the Victory of Valle Gómez collective passed bricks from hand to hand. "No place else feels like home."

"¡LUCHA, LUCHA, LUCHA! ¡NO DEJAN DE LUCHAR!"

Forty-eight hours after the Terremoto, regent Ramón Aguirre promised the press that all the damaged buildings would be torn down and the damnificados moved elsewhere, and thus the terms of engagement were defined.

The first march took place September 27, when 30,000 damnificados took to the street in hard hats and *tapabocas* (sterile masks), the accessories of the *rescatistas* (rescuers), marching from Tlatelolco to the Zócalo to serve notice on Aguirre and De la Madrid that they were not going anywhere. A second mobilization was scheduled for October 12, then still the Day of the Raza Cósmica. On the 11th, De la Madrid tried to preempt the march by expropriating 5,500 properties that landlords who never even picked up the rent anymore, because rent control had rendered the amount meaningless, would never repair. Lalo Miranda had been invited to join the neighborhood expropriation commission, inspecting suspect buildings to determine which could be rehabilitated and expropriating properties from landlords who had walked away.

"*¡Lucha, Lucha, Lucha! ¡No Dejan de Luchar! Por una Vivienda Digna, Barata y Popular,*" 50,000 damnificados chanted as they made their way through Chapultepec Park to Los Pinos on the 12th. Again Lalo was chosen to be a member of the commission that would be escorted into the presidential palace to present the damnificados' demands to the President himself. It was a moment of empowerment not only for Lalo, a former flyweight boxer whose sole 15 seconds of fame up until now had come when he was invited to the Hair Stylists Olympics in New York during the American Bicentennial, but also for the damnificado movement born from the ashes of the Temblor just 23 days earlier.

Two weeks later Dr. Abarca called 50 freshly minted damnificado groups plus the veterans of the CONAMUP to Tlatelolco to constitute the CUD, The Coordinating Union of the Damnificados, which would negotiate with De la Madrid the terms of replacement housing.

A GREAT CRIME

A great crime had been committed here, "in this place that we have been touched to live," as *cronista* (chronicler) Cristina Pacheco called the Monstruo. In her weekly public television show she told the damnificados' stories in heartbreaking detail. What happened at 7:19 a.m. on September 19, 1985, had not been a natural disaster or an act of God.

The buildings that had come down had been built badly, out of greed and negligence. Older structures, like the "historical monuments" dating back to the Colonia and the Porfiriato, had in many instances stood their ground, but jerry-built apartment buildings came down like houses of cards. Contractors had shorted the rebar, the walls were unreinforced to cut costs, the flimsy foundations fell apart. Fly-by-night construction companies had bought off the inspectors, bribed City Hall, and used their juice with the PRI to pull off the scam. It was not just God(s)' will that these structures had come down. It was a great fraud on the people.

Musicians and writers like Cristina Pacheco created an instant culture from the movement of the damnificados. Elena Poniatowska, the Polish-Mexican feminist writer, collected their stories in *Nada, Nadie*, a chronicle every bit as moving as her *Nights of Tlatelolco*, about another significant tragedy, and Carlos Monsiváis recorded the gestation of what everyone was now calling "the civil society," those without a party who demanded to be taken into account when decisions were made in their name by the politicos.

Maldita Vecindad y Los Hijos del Quinto Patio was the quintessential band of the damnificado movement, playing benefits every weekend and accompanying the marches to public ministries. "We weren't really *músicos*—we learned to play in the street," considers Roco, MV's still exceptionally solidarity-minded leader.

One voice that got lost in the maelstrom was Rockdrigo—the "Prophet of the Nopal," who had gained a following among the chavos of the metropolis singing car to car down in the Metro—crushed to death in a Tlatelolco apartment. QDEP Rockdrigo.

THE PRI WRESTLES FOR THE HEARTS AND MINDS OF THE DAMNIFICADOS

Despite the hullabaloo down below, the PRI government (*mal gobierno*) carried on its dirty business as usual. Death certificates could be bought for 8,000 pesos at the *ventanillas* in the PRI-controlled delegations and Guillermina Rico's flower vendors tripled their rates at the gates of the PRI-controlled cemeteries. But the boys up in Insurgentes #59 had been unnerved by the rapid mobilization of the damnificados and tried their damnedest to domesticate them.

Helicopters buzzed the marches dropping leaflets that warned, "Bad Mexicans are trying to disorient us. Report them to the police." The PRI sent teams to "assess" damages and identify those unfriendly to the party. Damnificados aligned with the PRI received portable heaters in the cold winter months; those that didn't got thin blankets. Aguirre and De la Madrid never missed a chance to take credit for the Public Housing Renovation program (RHP), but Lalo and his gang knew differently. "Before the earthquake, we let the PRI do everything for us—now we do it for ourselves."

Christmastime came round and the damnificados were still encamped in front of their broken homes, cooking meager meals of nopales on their tin charcoal stoves. Suddenly, a PRI van swung around the corner on Regina Street and out stepped a posse of unctuous officials bearing roast turkeys. Televisa and the *prensa vendida* magically materialized to record the charitable event. "We told them no thanks, to just go away and leave us alone," remembered the late Mario Becerra of the UPNT. "Our meal was a humble one, but truly, I think they were the best nopales I've ever eaten."

IN THE CAMPS

Since the beginning of his administration, De la Madrid had paid lip service to the increasing severity of environmental degradation in both the country and the cities of Mexico by creating the Secretariat of Urban Development and the Environment or SEDUE, which became the lead agency for the reconstruction of the Monster.

There was immediate friction between SEDUE Secretary Guillermo Carrillo Arena and the damnificados. Carrillo, an architect, had built much of the Medical Center where so many had died, and the activists demanded he be held to account. When bulldozers were sent to clear the ruins, protesters stood in front of them screaming that their loved ones were still buried in the rubble. Daily marches to SEDUE demanding Carrillo's head frequently got out of hand.

To the architect, the damnificados were like so many head lice, "subversives" bent on the overthrow of the government he represented, which was not all that far off the mark. When the SEDUE chief was threatened with prosecution for his cheesy medical buildings, De la Madrid opted out of the confrontation and replaced him with the savvy Manuel Camacho Solís, a young PRI Turk attached to the *camarilla* (power group) of budget secretary Carlos Salinas de Gortari. Both had been UNAM law school mates and had flirted with the Maoist factions on campus during 1968 before embarking on their political careers.

Camacho had a deft touch in dealing with the damnificados and convinced them to allow the clearing of lots to begin. Eight billion cubic meters of rubble were hauled off to the dumps in a record three months' time, effectively erasing the fingerprints of those who had committed this crime. "It was like watching our homes being carried off to a common grave," Hermann Bellinghausen wrote.

Two hundred thousand damnificados were moved into temporary camps during the winter of 1986–1987. Lalo and Nieves and the kids took up residence in a tin shed on a side street off the Eje Central. The winter was cold and rainy and water stood an inch deep on the cement floor. We huddled there on our folding chairs watching the Oscars on the little black-and-white screen (Lalo is a movie buff), passing Perla the poodle from lap to lap because she didn't like to get her paws wet.

Every afternoon, the tenants of Regina #39 would visit their once and future home to check up on the progress. The building was one of 179 residential "historical monuments" in the barrio that the law mandated must be restored as it was originally configured, and the tenants offered their expertise to the workmen: A wall had been here, the steps were over there. The niche for the Virgin was at the top of the stairs. Alejandro, Lalo's middle son, watched the goings-on intently and told his pop he wanted to be an architect when he grew up.

In July 1987, the Mirandas and their 13 neighbors moved back into Regina #39. The "historical monument" now belonged to the Popular Housing bureaucracy, and the apartments were sold as individual condominiums to the old tenants for surprisingly affordable monthly payments. The Guadalupana was back in her niche at the head of the stairs, and even if the *farol* (cast-iron lampshade) in the front hallway was not quite right, the neighbors were thankful. A priest said Mass. Lalo made a little speech. "We could never have done this without each other."

Some 70 percent of the damnificados were rehoused within 18 months beginning January 1, 1987, and most of the new housing passed muster. The former damnificados complained loudly when it didn't. The remaining 30 percent were not so lucky. There were still five rusting camps in and around the Centro when the new millennium dawned 13 years later.

Two years ago (2007), Alejandro Miranda graduated from the UNAM with a degree in architecture. He performed his obligatory social service in Chiapas, building a meeting hall up at Oventic, the Zapatista Army of National Liberation's *caracol* or cultural center in the highlands.

"THE PRESIDENT IS AFRAID OF US"

Nineteen eighty-eight was a presidential election year and the PRI Government was determined to deactivate the civil society before the new year was ushered in. In an excess of *desmemorización* (dixit Monsiváis), the ruling party took credit for the success of the RHP program. De la Madrid traveled to the neighbors, handing out certificates to the ex-damnificados. Mariachis tootled. The *prensa vendida* took copious notes.

The Victory of Valle Gómez collective had built its own replacement housing with funds from European foundations instead of waiting around for the government to do it for them—45,000 units were financed with NGO money. One spring morning, Lalo and I and Magda Trejo from the collective ventured out to Plutarco Elías Calles park in the Carranza delegation on the east side of the Monstruo to watch the President do his act. Soldiers had scrubbed the walls clean of antigovernment slogans, and wire mesh barricades were erected to keep the grateful ex-damnificados at bay. Magda was startled to see the people caged up like that. "Hey John," she tugged on my arm, grinning, "see how afraid the President is of us."

THE SAGA OF AN URBAN SUPERHERO

"Now we must work for those who are damnificados for life," Magdalena insisted during the founding convention of the Assembly of Barrios in April 1987. With the battle for housing en route to a successful conclusion, the damnificado movement consolidated around broader class issues.

The roots of the Asemblea had been planted in the Colonia Guerrero long before the earthquake. "Our roofs were falling in and the women had to learn to become carpenters," explained Yolanda Tello, recalling the genesis of a project undertaken by the denizens of that lively, heroic barrio to deal with deteriorating housing, much of which came down in the Sismo anyway. Young activists like Marco Rascón who had split the stodgy Popular Socialist Party to form Punto Crítico were soon involved in the organizing.

The idea of the Assembly of Barrios was to create a common front from the many barrios in the center city that would continue to work on housing issues once the RHP went out of business. The founding assembly also marked the debut of a singular personage dubbed Superbarrio. An urban superhero dreamt up by the rotund Rascón, "Super" was at first one yellow-and-scarlet suit shared by three activists of varying sizes and shapes but eventually came to be wholly occupied by Raúl Bautista, a former wrestler who sold trinkets in front of the Coliseo arena on Perú Street.

Mexican wrestling, with its good guy/bad guy duality, was a perfect metaphor for the urban movement, and Superbarrio regularly tussled with an assortment of evil stereotypes. His much ballyhooed match with the sinister "Super Landlord," scheduled for the esplanade of the Templo Mayor that summer, had to be abruptly cancelled when Aguirre's cops kidnapped the ring, declaring the sacred site unsuitable for such class war hijinks.

Superbarrio, the defender of the Centro's tenants, was ever ready to take action when evictions were threatened. Bottle rockets would be launched to summon the masked crusader, a sort of low-tech Bat signal, and Super would speed to the scene in his Barriomobile, a made-over bread truck, to help the tenants carry their furniture back inside the building which they had just been thrown out of. Although he captured the popular imagination, the PRI rulers detested Superbarrio—the governor of Jalisco once tried to rip his mask off, and Super was barred from visiting the PRI-dominated Chamber of Deputies unless he first removed it.

Superbarrio inspired the creation of other people's superheroes like Super Ecologista, who fought for a livable urban environment, and Super Animal, who defended all animals—once I invaded a slaughterhouse out in Ecatepec with Super Animal, a muscular ex-wrestler, to halt the torture of swine. The PRI even fielded their own superhero—Super Pueblo—but he vanished when Superbarrio challenged him to a match in the Zócalo.

In the autumn of 1987, Superbarrio tossed his mask into the ring and declared himself a candidate for the presidency of Mexico.

THE VIRUS OF DEMOCRACY

The Great Sismo that swept through the Monstruo September 19, 1985, was both urban cataclysm and civic redemption. The Sismo reaffirmed the primacy of the earth over a city that was arrogant enough to think it could vanquish nature. The quake was an instance of purification, clearing away the clutter and the cobwebs. It was like an egg passed across the belly of the city in the *limpias* that *curanderos* perform, cleansing the detritus of the Monstruo's soul. Although the twin towers on North Insurgentes Avenue survived the Temblor pretty much intact, the party that it housed would not.

The virus of democracy had taken up residence inside the belly of the beast, and differences within the Institutional Revolutionary Party as to how to deal with this dangerous germ caused internal bleeding.

With the 1988 *presidenciales* just months away, De la Madrid was playing coy about who would be on the receiving end of the imperial Dedazo. Political cartoonists drew the unnamed candidates, or *tapados*, with hoods over their heads like Casper the Friendly Ghosts or partisans of the Ku Klux Klan.

Those in the know signified that the *bueno* was the balding, big-eared budget secretary, Carlos Salinas de Gortari, who had been industriously shredding the social budget for the past six years. The hyper Salinas, dubbed "The Atomic Ant" by his compinches, had taken his postdoc at Harvard, where he attached himself to Zapata scholar John Womack, an alliance the Maestro probably cringes at today.

Carlos Salinas was a member of a prominent political clan—his father had been López Mateos's commerce secretary and a senator from his home state of Nuevo León, and his ne'er-do-well older brother Raúl directed CONASUPO, the state grain distribution agency formerly managed by Carlos Hank, where he soon would be accused of importing a whole shipload of Chernobyl-contaminated powdered milk to augment the meager diets of indigent children. As kids, Raúl and Carlos had murdered a 12-year-old Indian servant girl during a game of cowboys & Indians, an incident retold in the suppressed volume *A Killer in Los Pinos*, the author of which had to flee Mexico. The matter was subsequently erased from public records—when I sought to locate the article in *Excelsior* upon which the book was based, the page on which it appeared had been torn from the binder.

Carlos Salinas was not a popular choice. Fidel Velázquez thought he was punk. Other tapados felt slighted. Those PRIistas who identified with the Democratic Current founded years before by the mysteriously demised Carlos Madrazo demanded an open primary to determine De la Madrid's successor. The Democratic Current's reluctant leader was Cuauhtémoc Cárdenas, the dour son of Don Lázaro and the former PRI governor of Michoacán, where he had incited much *mala leche* by closing down cantinas and whorehouses on Sundays.

The real sparkplug behind the Democratic Current, the polemical Porfirio Muñoz Ledo, had been Echeverría's labor secretary and López Portillo's ambassador to the United Nations (he was removed after a scrape with New York City's parking cops). When Cárdenas and Muñoz Ledo challenged the occupants of Insurgentes #59 at a national PRI conclave in mid-1987, they were expelled amidst much rancorous name-calling from the party that Cuauhtémoc's father had founded.

THE SON OF THE TATA

The PARM (Authentic Mexican Revolutionary Party), a gaggle of Henriquistas and old cronies of the Tata, who up until then had always blindly backed up the PRI, proposed that Cuauhtémoc Cárdenas run on their ticket, and Cuauhtémoc, whom I had known as a much younger man in the short-lived National Liberation Movement (MLN) founded by Lázaro and Heberto Castillo in 1961, invited me to the nomination ceremony.

The soiree took place on a rain-soaked evening that September at Lázaro's widow Doña Amalia Solórzano's big house on Andes Street in Lomas de Chapultepec. Cárdenas climbed up in the bed of a pickup truck and took the pledge. Fifty witnesses huddled under awnings in the patio while the rain poured down in buckets.

Cárdenas's candidacy attracted a rainbow of left opportunists such as the militants of the Party of Socialist Workers (PST), specialists in mobilizing bedraggled colonos to mau-mau PRI authorities into delivering services; Rafael Aguilar Talamantes, an expulsee from the PST who had invented his own ersatz "Cardenista Front"—popularly known as "The Railroad"—and who gave opportunism a bad name; Lombardo Toledano's moribund Popular Socialist Party (PPS); and its

activist schism Punto Crítico. Together these and other grouplets coagulated into the National Democratic Front (FDN).

Others on the Left stayed aloof. Heberto Castillo, the nominee of
the Mexican Socialist Party (PMS) née the Mexican Communist Party
(PCM) by way of the Mexican Unified Socialist Party (PSUM), remained outside of the FDN, as did Rosario Ibarra de Piedra, the missing Jesús's mom, of the Trotskyist PRT, who had been the first woman
ever to run for the presidency back in '82. The damnificado movement
split.

Superbarrio remained in the race, a gadfly candidate insisting upon
unity on the Left. Super and his colleagues in the Assembly of Barrios
and the MUP (Urban Popular Movement) advocated full citizens'
rights long denied to Chilangos and statehood for the Federal District.
"Anáhuac," the Aztec true heart of the world, would have an elected
mayor and legislative assembly as opposed to a "representative" one—
in post-earthquake 1987, De la Madrid had prevailed over the regent
Aguirre to establish an assembly of representatives with purely consul-
tative powers in which all 66 seats were controlled by the PRI.

As expected, Carlos Salinas de Gortari, the PRI's bald-headed
wonder boy, would carry the water for the Institutionals, and burly
Manuel Clouthier, a business titan from Sinaloa whose pragmatic approach to politics defined "neo-PANismo," was designated the National Action's standard-bearer. With Cárdenas and Clouthier in the
race, for once the PRI did not have a free ride, and the stage was set for
unprecedented electoral drama.

TRAVELS WITH CUAUHTÉMOC

Cuauhtémoc Cárdenas launched his campaign for the presidency
of Mexico November 25 in Morelia, Michoacán, his home state. We
didn't even have hammers to tack the campaign signs to the sticks
and used rocks instead. The campaign itself would be as austere as its
candidate.

I would travel with Cuauhtémoc through the July 1988 elections
and for another year after the election was stolen. By my calculations, I
filed stories (mostly for Will Hearst's now defunct *San Francisco Examiner*, the "Monarch of the Dailies") from 31 states and 10 out of the 16
delegations in Mexico City. I learned the contours of México Profundo
every day of the way. Lázaro's aura enveloped his son, and the people

reached out to touch him as if he were a talisman or a saint. He shook hands with everyone. Everywhere we went, campesinos would show us the weathered papers with which the Tata had guaranteed their land. Cuauhtémoc could not turn down an invitation, and we spent whole days climbing through the sierras, pressing the flesh and dining on country *barbacoa*.

Ten fearful supporters turned out in country town plazas when we visited in January, and when we returned in April, there were 500, and they were not so afraid. By June, thousands were filling the squares, openly defying the all-powerful PRI. Indeed, most of the citizens who came out as the campaign snowballed through central Mexico were not on the Left at all but PRIistas driven to dissent by the continuing Crisis.

Cuauhtémoc Cárdenas displayed about as much charisma as a clam, but inflation in 1987 had soared 159 percent—prices had risen 4,400 times since De la Madrid and the PRI had placed Mexico in receivership and service on the foreign debt alone between 1983 and 1988 totaled $88,000,000,000 USD.

The PRI, blissed out by hubris and *prepotencia*, seemed oblivious to the *coyuntura*, the coming-together, down below. In May, Heberto Castillo cashed in his sagging candidacy and offered Cárdenas the PMS's electoral registration, guaranteeing the FDN four spots on the ballot. He also turned over his campaign buses—we had been traveling in convoys of borrowed junkers for months.

Heberto's withdrawal and the unification of the Left around Cárdenas convinced Superbarrio to drop his candidacy, and Cuauhtémoc pledged to adopt the urban popular movement's platform for Mexico City statehood. On Election Day, Cárdenas would reciprocate by casting his ballot for Superbarrio.

In June, 50,000 turned out when Cuauhtémoc was invited to speak at the UNAM by the leaders of the 1986–1987 strike against proposed tuition hikes. The *huelga* had galvanized Mexico City for months—Carlos Imaz, Imanol Ordorika, and Antonio Santos would all play pivotal roles in Cárdenas's government when he became Mexico City's first elected mayor 10 years later.

The June 30 campaign-closer in the Zócalo doubled the throng at the UNAM, then the largest crowd to turn out for a Mexican opposition candidate in recent memory. Nonetheless, news of the gathering was blacked out by Televisa, although the noxious Zabludovsky did do an interview with two of Lázaro's alleged illegitimate sons who said they were voting for Carlos Salinas and labeled their brother a traitor to the PRI and their purported father's good name. The prensa vendida pounded the son of the Tata from pillar to post every day of the campaign—only *La Jornada* kept the public informed on the daily perambulations of El Ingeniero (Cárdenas was a civil engineer).

KILLER PRIs

Although a Salinas landslide was widely predicted by the prensa vendida, the shadowy figures behind the tinted windows at Insurgentes #59 were taking no chances. The Institutionals had achieved an international reputation for electoral fraud during the De la Madrid years. The PAN had won local elections in 1983 in the northern states of Durango, Coahuila, and San Luis Potosí but lost them to the PRI in crooked vote counts. In 1985, PANista Pancho Barrio won Chihuahua to become the first opposition governor since the Mexican Revolution, only to have victory snatched from him by the PRI-controlled state election commission. Incensed right-wingers blocked international bridges in Ciudad Juárez, and PAN elder Luis H. Álvarez sat down in front of the state capital to conduct an 85-day hunger strike.

Three nights before the July 6 election, Francisco Xavier Ovando, Cuauhtémoc's go-to guy on election logistics, his assistant Román Gil, and an unidentified campaign worker closed up the office out in the Nápoles Colony hard by the Plaza México bullring off South Insurgentes and headed home. All week, men with binoculars had been spying on them from a nearby building where government textbooks were printed.

Ovando dropped the campaign worker off on the corner of Isabel la Católica and Fray Servando in front of Mexico City police headquarters six blocks south of the Hotel Isabel and continued east in the direction of the Legislative Palace—Ovando and Gil's destination was not clear. The next morning, their bullet-riddled bodies were spotted parked on the corner of Zoquipa and Rosario Streets in the grimy, industrial Colonia Tránsito less than a kilometer from the Mexican Congress.

Whodunnit? I keep asking this question. Twenty years later, how Ovando and Gil wound up dead remains a mystery, although it has often been speculated the two were lured to the Palacio Legislativo by the promise of learning the password to the computers at Insurgentes #59—the 1988 presidenciales were the first to be cybernetically tabulated, and it was projected that the fraud would be systematically fabricated on the PRI computers.

The PRI vehemently protested its innocence. Fidel Velázquez theorized that Ovando and Gil had been slain in a barroom brawl. Years later, ex–judicial police commander and paid DEA informant Guillermo González Calderoni would confess that Raúl Salinas had hired him to contract hit men for the job—Calderoni himself was later taken out in a gangland hit.

"SE CAYÓ EL SISTEMA"

We buried Xavier Ovando in a muddy cemetery plot on the outskirts of Morelia on election eve, and I stayed out in Michoacán to watch the vote come in from Cárdenas's home state. By 6:00 a.m. the next morning, hundreds were lined up outside polling places in the Indian towns around Lake Pátzcuaro. Up in the Meseta, Santiago Bravo assured me that the Purépechas would all be voting for El Ingeniero. In a railroad workers' colony down by the tracks in Morelia where the PRI had won every election 10 to 1 for years, Cárdenas had 894 votes, Salinas 16. "¡Hemos chingado el pinche PRI!" grinned one voter—"We really fucked the damn PRI!"

Just after 9:00 p.m. up in El Monstruo, a handful of PANistas had been admitted by prior arrangement into the windowless bunker on Barranca del Muerto in the south of the city, where the voter registration lists were kept and where they would be allowed to observe the results as they came in on the government computers. They seated themselves at the consoles, and the numbers started flashing across the screens. Cárdenas was running far ahead in every district they got to view before the screens went blank. Technicians rushed in from the back of the room and reported the system had gone down, then promptly escorted the PANistas from the building.

I drove back from Morelia and headed straight for the Interior Secretariat on Bucareli, where the Federal Election Commission was in recess. It was nearly dawn. Hours before, Cárdenas and Rosario Ibarra and the PANista Clouthier had paid their famous visit to accuse Interior Secretary Manuel Bartlett, who headed up the commission, of facilitating a great fraud on the Mexican electorate.

At 11:00 p.m., Bartlett had appeared before reporters to announce that "the system has crashed" (*se cayó el sistema*)—presumably he was referring to the vote-counting computers and not neoliberal rule—and that there would be no results for the next six days, traditionally the period in which the PRI cooks the vote. For months, Bartlett had been bragging that he would have results within hours of poll closing, and the reporters received this latest notice with much skepticism. Bartlett would take no questions.

The absence of hard numbers did not seem to trouble the PRI. Out at Insurgentes #59, party president Jorge de la Vega declared the Institutionals had won by an insurmountable margin—but Salinas did not put in an appearance to have his arm raised in victory. Guillermina Rico's *acarreados* blew plastic horns and clacked wooden *matracas*, but the celebration seemed less than enthusiastic. Indeed, many of the acarreados probably voted for Cárdenas.

Five years later, I had an opportunity to quiz Carlos Salinas about the highly dubious results. It was September 19, 1993. The President had come to the Zócalo for the annual homage to the damnificados who had perished in the Sismo and was breakfasting with his *camarilla* at La Blanca. The Atomic Ant polished off his *huevos con machaca* and, in a gesture of egalitarian goodwill, stepped off into the kitchen to salute the cooks. As he strode out I whirled from my stool at the counter and extended a hand. "*Señor Presidente*," I beamed, and we shook. With his little hand firmly in my grasp, I drew him to me until we were eye to eye. "Señor Presidente," I inquired, "did the system really crash?" Salinas had never been asked this question before in five years as president, and he grew rigid, pulled his paw from my grip, signaled his *guaruras* to come save him from this gringo madman, and stalked out of the restaurant. The encounter has since become a legend around the counter at La Blanca.

THE DANCE OF THE NUMBERS

With the system purportedly down, the votes were first counted by hand in the *casillas* (polling places) and then transported to the nation's 300 electoral district offices by the military. Many ballots disappeared in transit. Tens of thousands of them were discovered floating in rivers or smoldering in garbage dumps all over the country during those tense days.

Here in the Centro, the ballot boxes were concentrated at District 5 headquarters on Tacuba Street, where the results from the casillas would be tabulated and fed into the computers. Election "technicians," muscular young men with Fu Manchu mustaches, ripped open the *urnas* and extracted the bagged ballots. When the *sábana* or tally sheet attached to each bag was called out, the numbers did not coincide with those that had been posted outside the casillas on election night. The wrangling between the PRIistas and Cárdenas's people grew heated and the count was suspended.

Down in the street one floor below, a chant went up: "*¡Cárdenas Arrasó y el Pueblo Ganó!*" (Cárdenas Cleaned Up and the People Won!). When I scurried downstairs to investigate the origin of this clamor, there was Lalo and Mario Becerra and Leslie Serna and the rest of the UPNT. They had gone from casilla to casilla on the night of the election collecting the totals posted outside and they knew very well who had won.

In fact, Cuauhtémoc Cárdenas won 37 out of the capital's 40 electoral districts—the PAN took the other three, and the PRI, which could muster up only 27 percent of the vote in the city, lost them all. From July 6, 1988, through this writing, the Left has never lost a Mexico City election.

But the Democratic Front of the Earthquake had won few federal deputies July 6—the parties in Cárdenas's coalition had run their own candidates against each other, and the PRI retained its lopsided majority in the lower house. On the other hand, Porfirio Muñoz Ledo and the economist Ifigenia Martínez won both of Mexico City's senate seats to become the first members of the opposition ever to serve in what up until July 6, 1988, had been an exclusive PRI club.

The dance of the numbers galvanized the republic for the next 10 days. Cárdenas set up a command center out on Andes Street and held packed press conferences under a tent in the patio every afternoon to update the results. According to his count, he had bested Salinas by a nose, 39 percent to 37 percent with 40,000 out of the nation's 56,000 casillas reporting.

Six days later, Bartlett's numbers began to run again and Carlos Salinas was awarded the presidency with a shade over 50 percent of the popular vote. Cárdenas was assigned 31 percent and Clouthier's PAN 17 percent. The missing 16,000 polling places to this day have never been heard from.

U.S. President Ronald Reagan tendered his congratulations to the new president even before the official vote count was announced. The *New York Times*, over the objections of its own correspondents (Alan Riding had returned to Mexico to report on the fraud) called the balloting the cleanest election in Mexican history and lauded Carlos Salinas as a defender of the free market.

On July 16, ten days after this debacle, hundreds of thousands of Cárdenas supporters crushed into the Zócalo. They were so tightly jammed together that they couldn't even raise their arms to clap and cheer and they did not agree with the *New York Times'* published assessment.

The gathering was unruly and Cuauhtémoc could not control it. Firebombs were hurled at the great portals of the National Palace and there are those who still think that given the great numbers and the fury of the people, Cárdenas could have taken power that day. Instead, the son of the Tata pleaded with his people to go home and cool off. His supporters inside the military had told him that the army was preparing a bloodbath. Instead, he would fight the fraud in Congress and in the courts. Unbeknownst to his diehards, he had already met twice with Carlos Salinas at the Lomas home of the usurper's new regent, Manuel Camacho Solís.

FRAUD GOES TO COLLEGE

The Chamber of Deputies sitting as the Electoral College convened August 20. The front steps of the Legislative Palace teemed with Cárdenas's people, who would camp there for weeks. The upstairs gallery was cleared almost instantly when the leftists took to tossing the heavy coinage of the country at the PRIistas down below.

On the morning the Electoral College was seated, the blood-splattered bodies of four young men stuffed into a VW bug were found under the struts of the Interior Circuit. The Vochito belonged to Luis Del Arco, whose son Ernesto was among those slain. A '68er who had made his stand at the Politécnico and survived Tlatelolco, Luis had volunteered the car for the Cárdenas campaign in the Azcapotzalco delegation and it was plastered with Cuauhtémoc stickers. The boys had borrowed the VW to go to the movies.

Two tin workers from La Merced were framed for the crime and sent up the river for 16 years—*fabricando culpables*, manufacturing guilty ones, is the real business of the Mexican justice system. "They hurt us most when they hurt our children," Cárdenas mourned that noon on the steps of the Palacio Legislativo. Tears rolled down my stubbly cheeks.

The Electoral College was a *desmadre* from start to finish. Félix Salgado Macedonio, a wild man from Guerrero, earned his nickname "Costales" when he dumped burlap bags (*costales*) of burnt ballots from the podium. The *boletas* floated down upon the Chamber like giant confetti and the press scrambled for the souvenirs—I still have one somewhere. Cárdenas's people repeatedly tried to seize the tribune, stimulating fistfights and shoving matches. Noses were bloodied and at least one heart attack recorded.

When the Institutionals refused to open the *urnas* and count out the ballots one by one, the chant of "*¡Que Se Abran los Paquetes!*" (Open the Packages!) resounded in the strewn chamber. Phalanxes of riot police lurked in the building basement. But in the end, the PRI owned the Electoral College and Salinas was confirmed.

On September 1, Miguel De la Madrid delivered his final Informe to a joint session of Congress. When Porfirio Muñoz Ledo stood on the steps below the podium and harangued the outgoing president, he was blindsided by a rat pack of PRI governors and senators who proceeded to kick the shit out of him. Salinas was sworn in December 1 under heavy military protection. Rioters rampaged in the Zócalo.

UP IN SMOKE

For the next six months, Cuauhtémoc Cárdenas drifted aimlessly around the landscape like a part-time ghost trying to explain to those who still listened why he had not sustained the postelectoral struggle. Sometimes I hopped on the bus to take the pulse of the country where we had campaigned so assiduously in the heady days before July 6.

Cuauhtémoc hunkered in the back with his compinches, slamming down dominoes and whispering conspirationally. The task now was to consolidate, to pull together those elements of the FDN who had not already been co-opted by Salinas and the PRI and build a political party from the ruins of the campaign.

On May 5, 1989, the day marking the short-lived Zacapoaxtla victory at the Battle of Puebla, Cuauhtémoc Cárdenas paid a return visit to the Zócalo to announce the formation of the Party of the Democratic Revolution, the PRD. Fire engine sirens obliterated his droning cadences and we could hardly hear what he was telling us. By accident or design, the Legislative Palace had been set ablaze, literally melting the Chamber of Deputies—the lower house would session at an auditorium at the Centro Médico for the next two years.

Mercifully, the fire did not spread to the basement of the Palace where the ballot boxes were now consolidated under military protection. But although they were saved for the moment, that December the PRI canoodled with the PAN and voted to have the ballots incinerated, and the evidence of the Great Fraud went up in smoke.

XIV

CITY OF NEOLIBERAL NIGHTMARES

A s Salinas's regent, Manuel Camacho Solís's mission was to bring El Monstruo back into the PRI fold, exterminate the germ of the damnificado movement once and for all, and blunt the city's turn to the left.

I had an excellent opportunity to observe the new regent in action just days after he was installed at City Hall when, on the eve of the feast day of the Virgin of Guadalupe (December 12), a storehouse of *cohetones* (bottle rockets) blew up in a back alley at La Merced market, setting off propane tanks at streetside taco stands and burning the Ampudia candy market to the ground. Sixty-eight merchants and shoppers were immolated in the huge fire. The caramelized limbs of the charred victims were strewn among the ashes—it may have been the most horrific story I ever covered.

The surviving candy merchants were out of control. They had repeatedly warned the market inspectors of the danger, but the inspectors had been peaced off by the fireworks kings. When Camacho showed up on the scene with no bodyguards, the crowd turned threatening. The new regent was unfazed. Were there more *cohetones* stored in La Merced, he demanded to know? The merchants showed him the storehouses out back, and Camacho began kicking down the steel curtains that served as doors. Someone brought a crowbar and pried them open. Camacho dived inside and began flinging the rockets out in the street.

The merchants of La Merced looked on in disbelief. Then Camacho marched them down Circunvalación, the wide avenue that borders the market, to La Soledad, where a Mass was said for the dead. It was quite a show—sort of governance as performance art.

Camacho's opening act had been equally instructive. Scheduled to be the first regent ever to address the newly convened but largely decorative Mexico City all-PRI Representative Assembly on Donceles Street, in the former quarters of the Chamber of Deputies, Camacho was attacked en route by a mob of colonos whom the military had just evicted from an ecological reserve in the Ajusco. The Granaderos and the militants scuffled up and down the back streets of the Centro Histórico all afternoon, and plenty of blood was spilled. The founders of the Francisco Villa Popular Front, AKA "Los Panchos," date their organization's birth from that confrontation.

The original Panchos, like Eli Aguilar, an enigmatic figure in the 1986–1987 UNAM strike, and "El Grandote" (The Big One) Alejandro López Villanueva, had won their scars in CONAMUP mobilizations out in Iztapalapa, and they would rule the urban popular movement for years to come. After the face-off on Donceles Street, Camacho sued for peace and became the Panchos' chief benefactor when Aguilar and El Grandote led their cadre onto unoccupied tracts in the eastern delegations and set up camp. The go-between in this unlikely arrangement was Camacho Solís's young protégé and secretary of government Marcelo Ebrard, at this writing mayor of Mexico City.

EXODUS FROM THE CENTRO

With their housing demands serviced, the glue that held the CUD together came undone, and the regent's scheme to co-opt the urban popular movement was facilitated by dissension in the former damnificados' ranks.

The Popular Union of New Tenochtitlán split in two and the UPNT, at least on the blocks south of the Zócalo, went off on its own. Two of its founders, Dolores Padierna and her husband René Bejarano, both by now burgeoning PRD bigshots, bought land in the misery belt and started selling off lots for a 200-peso down payment.

Although the damnificados had fought a brave battle to stay in the Centro, many were now abandoning ship. Small businesses, weary of fighting off the *ambulantes*, pulled up stakes and relocated. Those *vecindades* that had not been rehabilitated fell into disrepair. Damaged buildings came down in heavy rainstorms and the crime rate in the Centro Histórico went up.

Out of a pre-earthquake live-in population of 300,000, only 73,000 remained—Lalo and Nieves and the kids and Perla and her puppies and myself were 10 of them. During the day, the Cuauhtémoc delegation of which the Centro Histórico is the centerpiece had a transient population of 3.6 million government workers, protesters, tourists, shoppers, and ambulantes, but at night when everyone went home it was a ghost town.

One of the more positive aspects of the Sismo was that it stanched the rush of humanity to Mexico City at last. The Federal District population stood at 8,832,067 in 1980, and the Monstruo was still growing up until September 19, 1985, at the rate of 700,000 newcomers a year. But by the 1990 census the numbers had dropped to 8,235,744. Population density thinned in eight out of 16 delegations. The Cuauhtémoc shrank from 1.2 million in 1980 to 940,000 in 1990 and 515,000 by 2000.

Where did everyone go? De la Madrid pushed for the relocation of government agencies to provincial cities, but only the INEGI, the National Statistics & Geography Institute, moved to Aguascalientes—and most of its workers elected to stay behind to keep the Monstruo company. But others were leaving.

Antolina García was leaving. The teenage mother, a Mazahua Indian originally from Mexico state, who supported herself and her baby daughter scavenging bruised fruit from the debris out back of La Merced, had had enough. "This is no kind of place to raise my child," she complained when I poked around in the skeletal remains of the candle factory where she had been living until the Sismo had taken it down. "Where I was raised, yes we were poor, but you could drink the water and the air wasn't full of bad things like here. Now I've had enough. I'm going home," she frowned, her squalling daughter trussed up in a faded rebozo on her back.

Dr. Sergio Lana was leaving. He had dug for four days and four nights to rescue his comrades buried under the residence hall in the Centro Médico. But he was disgusted by the disappearance of vast sums of the international relief money and the way the PRI had used the disaster to feather its own nest. "This city is a pigsty of corruption!" the exasperated *médico* complained. Now Dr. Lana was headed out to Michoacán to offer his services to a leper colony. "Anything is better than this."

BAD BREATH

Others were leaving because they could no longer breathe.

"The mortal breath of 3,000,000 motors vomiting their filthy mouthfuls of pure poison black halitosis, trucks and taxis and family cars all contributing their flatulence to the extinction of trees and lungs, throats and eyes. . . . What will my son breathe? Chopped-up shit? Carbonic gas? Metal dust? What will he see? The mountains of garbage choking the city? It would take just one match to set afire this vicious mass of hair, cardboard, plastic, rags, paper, chicken feet, and pig intestines, and trigger a chain reaction, a generalized combustion, a sacrificial fire consuming in just one moment all the oxygen that is left to breathe," Carlos Fuentes ranted in *Cristóbal Nonato* (Christopher Unborn *en inglés*), published in 1987 in a fit of post-earthquake apocalypse. Although the book is set five years in the future, a Tristram Shandy–like ordeal of a child who prefers not to abandon his mother's womb despite the fact that his parents have bet all their marbles on him being the first baby born on October 12, 1992, the 500th anniversary of the Conquest, *Cristóbal Nonato* was an accurate if feverish account of the environmental hell that confronted Camacho Solís in the later 1980s.

Cristóbal Nonato translated the disasters of life in contemporary "Make Sicko Seedy." "My genes are like a garbage dump," Cristóbal cries out from inside. "The city is changing my DNA into that of a cockroach! The environment is trying to kill me and I haven't even been born yet!"

Fuentes was by then living in London and Madrid.

THE MONSTRUOUS REALITY

Crude reality was just as monstrous as Fuentes's fiction. Eleven thousand tons of heavy metals hung over the heads of Chilangos every minute of the day. Seventy percent of all babies born in El Monstruo contained measurable deposits of lead in their bloodstream. Ten thousand tons of dried feces blew through Make Sicko Seedy in the spring winds. The consequent gastrointestinal disturbances that this caused only increased the shit storm. Twenty thousand tons of garbage befouled the "air" 24/7. The Metropolitan Zone's 60,000 factories spewed their effluvia without constraint. Black particulate drizzled from the smudged heavens. The ozone clung closer to the ground, searing lungs and eyes.

Because Mexico City was 7,500 feet above sea level, oxygen was cut by a third. Vehicles produce twice as much carbon dioxide as they do at sea level. The capital was sited in a bowl-like basin, and during the winter months the warm air got trapped under the cold in killer thermal inversions that converted El Monstruo into a gas chamber.

By 1985, visibility from the Torre Latinoamericana had shrunk from 12 kilometers to three. On a clear day, you could see your fingers. Each year 35,000 die of respiratory diseases caused by inhaling all this gunk. Tooth decay, rickets, schizophrenia, and depression are attributable to this venomous mix.

Lalo says that Chilangolandia has more bald people that anywhere else on the planet due to acid rain concentrations that also eat off the noses of statues and the colonial façades of the old quarter's churches. In 1998, acid rain rose to the level of having a glass of red wine poured over your scalp all day long.

When Karol Wojtyla, Pope John Paul II, came to Mexico City on his first visit in 1979, those posted along the route to hail his coming wore gas masks and *tapabocas*. "Breathing" the air was said to be the equivalent of smoking two packs of Pall Malls a day. When the Pope returned in 1990, he wore a *tapaboca* himself and never left his hermetically sealed Papamobile. By then, breathing Mexico City air was equivalent to smoking three packs of Big Reds a day.

I often identify myself as a Chilango, although I am an outlander from a place as distant as another planet, but what binds me to my neighbors is not the geography of my birth. The lung damage inflicted upon all who share the poison air of El Monstruo has made us brethren beneath the skin. Together, we have mutated into Chilangos.

THE ATTACK OF THE IMECAS

In January 1988, hundreds of Canadian starlings plopped from the sky, bopping unsuspecting pedestrians as they crashed to earth. Jorge González Torres, who would later conjure up the Mexican Green Ecological Party (now, the only green this party is really interested in is the color of money) invited me to accompany him to Parque México, an art deco enclave off south Insurgentes where the poor birds had come to rest. We filled two burlap sacks with their little carcasses and González Torres called a press conference and swore eternal vengeance on Camacho Solís if he did not halt this holocaust.

The regent took up the challenge. He installed monitoring stations to measure the Imecas—named for the Metropolitan Index of Air Quality. Cartoonists drew the Imecas as a tribe of Aztec warriors descending from the sky with their spears pointed at the Valley of Mexico.

When the Imecas hit 240, a Phase 1 emergency kicked in and schools and gas stations and some factories were closed. Phase 2—300 Imecas—closed all factories and forced drivers to leave their cars at home. The trouble was that the monitoring stations were mounted so high up, they misread levels down on the ground. Actual levels were closer to 500 Imecas, González Torres protested. "This is a matter of life and death," kvetched poet Homero Aridjis, spokesperson for the prestigious Group of 100 famous authors that purportedly included Fuentes and Gabriel García Márquez, an adopted Chilango, but was really only a Group of One: Homero.

The Imecas were just the messengers. Public Enemy Número Uno was of course the gasoline-powered engine. By 1988, the city's vehicle census was up to 3,000,000, not one of which was yet equipped with any sort of smog-eating device. Five percent of all vehicles operated in the public transportation sector, moving 84 percent of the traveling public. But 95 percent of the vehicle census, moving just 16 percent of the population, was privately owned automobiles. Each month since 1980, an average of 9,800 more cars debuted in Mexico City traffic.

Two hundred thousand vehicles choked the narrow streets of the Centro Histórico each day, puking up their noxious fumes while strikers and colonos, damnificados and campesinos, ambulantes, Cárdenas supporters, teachers, gays and lesbians, and yes, ecologists marched on the Zócalo to protest their social condition, sometimes four marches a day. Between 1989 and 1993, roughly Camacho's stay in office, the Centro Histórico was host to more than 4,000 marches. The Imecas drilled down from the unsparing heavens.

Camacho's solution: The One Day a Week Without Cars program, a scheme designed to remove 400,000 cars from circulation each day. But the program was regulated by the last three digits of one's license plate and the cops made out like little Durazos, pocketing the mordidas. Moreover, those who could afford them went out and bought new cars, one for every day of the week, and at the end of *Un Día Sin Auto*'s two-year trial period, there were 600,000 more cars idling in the city's madly snarled traffic.

A MAN AND HIS TREE

The lungs of the Monster were dangerously occluded. Deforestation had been the subtext of how the capital had grown ever since the Gachupines denuded the neighboring hillsides. The city's forested lands— the Ajusco to the south and the Desert of the Lions on the western fringe—were invaded by squatters and tree poachers, although taking down a tree without government permission was forbidden by any number of federal laws.

The regent enlisted the military to plant 100 million trees—about a quarter succumbed immediately, and arborists worried that the lethal air quality was mutating the cells of the survivors.

Manolo Muñoz, who ran an offtrack betting booth around the corner on República de El Salvador, enrolled in Camacho Solís's "Each Family a Tree" program and received a frail acacia sapling that he planted in a box on the sidewalk in front of his business. The bespectacled little bookie diligently watered and weeded and worried about his tree. He hung signs on it—LET ME LIVE! and I DON'T EAT GARBAGE— for those who took the box to be a trash bin.

In December 1990, Mexico City was visited by one of the worst bouts of air pollution ever inflicted on an urban population—virtually every day was a life-threatening experience. Manolo's tree started to dry out and shrivel up. He was frantic. He took to sleeping in his betting booth to care for it. At the end of the month, after two Phase 2 days in a row, the dying acacia chuped its final Faro and gave up the ghost. Manolo buried it in its box, closed down his betting store, and moved to Morelia, Michoacán.

COSMETIC BAMBOOZLEMENT

Camacho Solís's most futile gesture was a cosmetic one. Pollution-slobbering Vochitos were painted green and rechristened "ecological" taxis. Artists were hired to airbrush bucolic scenes of alpine meadows on the back windows of Ruta 100 buses that continued to belch black gusts of diesel smoke.

Carlos Salinas closed down the PEMEX 18th of March Refinery in Azcapotzalco in 1989, but the Imecas only attacked with increased ferocity. In 1989, readings for ozone were unacceptable on 300 out of 365 days. March 16, 1992, when the Imecas soared to 398, was perhaps the most lethal day on Camacho's calendar. A pair of pandas, the offspring of the couple Echeverría had brought home from China, expired at the Chapultepec Park Zoo. Flags were flown at half-mast throughout the city.

POLITICAL POLLUTION IS EVEN MORE DEADLY

Having stolen high office in the most egregious act of 20th-century Mexican electoral fraud, Carlos Salinas was already an extremely unpopular president at the outset of his six years in Los Pinos. Once more, the consolidation of the PRD severely stressed out the PRI bosses at Insurgentes #59. The Party of the Aztec Sun, as the PRD had taken to calling itself, had two senators in that never-before-sullied precinct, and Cuauhtémoc's people had 40 deputies in the lower house. With the threat of further gains in local elections in Michoacán and Guerrero during 1989 and '90, Salinas sent in the military.

Tanks rolled through provincial cities to intimidate potential voters and reporters were bayoneted when we tried to audit a vote count in Morelia. Militants were jailed and slaughtered in large numbers during Salinas's reign of terror—from 1988, beginning with Ovando and Gil, through 1994, fully 538 members and sympathizers of the Party of the Democratic Revolution were murdered in instances of political violence, according to a Party survey of member mortality.

The poor had voted for Cuauhtémoc Cárdenas in great numbers and Salinas plagiarized Lech Walesa, launching his own "Solidarity" program to buy off the underclass with crumbs. His protégé, Luis Donaldo Colosio, who was running the PRI operation on Insurgentes and who was so cloned to his boss that reporters tagged him "Salinas with hair," was charged with making Solidarity tick.

Chalco, a dust-choked misery belt city hard by Nezahualcóyotl with a population of 2,000,000, had been won by Cárdenas in 1988. Its ragtag residents referred to their hometown as "Death Valley." Salinas and Colosio designated Chalco as the "Cradle of Solidarity," and it was so blessed by Polish Pope Wojtyla during his 1990 junket.

To beat back the Left, Salinas and the PRI joined forces with the Right, embracing the hated PAN as a comrade in arms. After the PANistas' charismatic former presidential candidate Manuel Clouthier was killed in a highly suspect Sinaloa car crash in 1989, Carlos Salinas wooed his successor, Diego Fernández de Cevallos, a bristly, bewhiskered upper-crust attorney known variously as "El Jefe" and "La Coyota." That summer, Colosio gained the permanent enmity of the PRI's Baja California section by conceding the governorship of that border state to a PANista, Ernesto Ruffo, the first non-PRI governor anywhere on the Mexican map—Colosio would later be assassinated in Baja California.

Having bludgeoned and co-opted the opposition, the PRI was back in the driver's seat, and the Party of Salinas swept 1991 midterm elections everywhere in the land—except Mexico City.

THE HOLY SPIRIT OF HOUSTON

Carlos Salinas was a devotee of the Free Market (although he now seems to deny this perception), whose miracles he was commended by his higher power to impose upon the Mexican people whether they wanted them or not.

Salinas and the first George Bush had been elected within months of each other and enjoyed a "special relationship." Even before the two moved into their respective presidential palaces, they met in Houston, Texas, at the Lyndon B. Johnson Space Center to plot the North American Free Trade Agreement, and the "Spirit of Houston" would pervade bilateral back-and-forth for the next four years.

Miguel De la Madrid had gotten his GATT (General Agreement on Trade and Tariffs) in 1986, a door opener to the corporate globalization of the planet; Salinas was hell-bent on taking free trade up another notch. The big-eared Mexican president envisioned NAFTA (in Mexican, the TLCAN—the Treaty of Free Trade with North America) as his crowning achievement, one that would establish his place in history—although from the very beginning, the idea of getting hitched to an economy 25 times the size of Mexico's seemed as perverse as letting a 10-ton American gorilla have its way with a skeletal Mexican burro. In Salinas's feverish vision, the Free Trade Treaty would "lift all boats" and springboard Mexico from the third world to the first. Many drowned in the flood.

To prepare the ground, Salinas lured the *sacadólares* man, Carlos Hank González, home from Connecticut to serve as agricultural secretary. Genghis Hank went right to work emasculating Article 27, the section of the Constitution that was based on Emiliano Zapata's agrarian Plan of Ayala, in order to make Mexico's agricultural sector more attractive to North American Agribusiness, a deal that never quite worked out the way it was anticipated.

The *reparto*, the handing out of surplus land to the landless with which Lázaro Cárdenas had won the nation's heart, was abolished, and the *ejido* (communal farmland), which was deemed an inefficient production unit, could now be put up for sale or for rent or for "association" with transnational capital. Four years later, the evisceration of Article 27 would become the motor of the Zapatista rebellion.

FOR SALE: THE COUNTRY ONCE CALLED MEXICO

Carlos Salinas faithfully followed the instructions handed down by his neoliberal masters on Wall Street and in the White House. He never once missed a payment on Mexico's renegotiated but still $102,000,000,000 foreign debt. Salinas exported billions in debt service each year to El Norte, while all over Latin America beleaguered workers and farmers were demanding a moratorium on such payments and up-and-coming leaders like Luis Inácio da Silva (Lula) of Brazil's Workers' Party were prodding their governments to form a debtor's club and cut Washington, the World Bank, and the International Monetary Fund off without a dime.

The "usurper," as Cárdenas's people jeered him, abided by the monstrous dictates of so-called "structural adjustment," privatizing whatever De la Madrid had left him. Now 238 government enterprises were sold off to Salinas's cronies for a cool $23,000,000,000 USD. Salinas sent troops into the great Cananea copper pit in Sonora, the birthplace of the Mexican labor movement, to break a strike, and then sold the pit, the eighth-largest copper mine on Planet Earth, to his pal Jorge Larrea for a pittance.

The banks that López Portillo had nationalized in a moment of pique back in 1982 were returned to their former owners, who would loot them and sell them off to the transnational banking industry. The tepid government television network, run by the Interior Secretariat to toot the PRI's horn, was sold to Carlos's *tocayo* Ricardo Salinas Pliego, who renamed it TV Azteca after brother Raúl lent him $29 million to complete the purchase. In global financial circles, Raúl came to be known as "Senor 10%," because that's what he stiffed his clients for to get in on the ground floor of the giveaways.

The biggest steal was Telmex, the Mexican phone company, raffled off at a bargain basement price to Carlos Slim, soon to become the richest man on earth. Although Telmex charged the highest phone rates in the business, the company was in fact in terrible shape. The earthquake had dismembered its trunk lines and rats were chewing up the cables. I would pick up the phone in the middle of the afternoon and someone else would be chatting—Telmex apparently rented out private lines for a few hours a day at low-use times.

Slim rehabilitated the business and parlayed the enterprise into a $40,000,000,000 USD fortune, about half of which disappeared in the 2008 financial market bloodbath. Mexican phone rates are still the highest in the world.

HOW OCTAVIO PAZ CURED THE D.T.'S

Televisa was not thrilled by its new little brother, TV Azteca, but Emilio Azcárraga could live with it. He was, after all, a self-confessed "soldier of the PRI." Often it was not clear if Televisa was a tool of Insurgentes #59 or the Institutionals a tool of Televisa. With four national networks, 61 repeater channels, and broadcasting 21,000 hours of garbage a year, Azcárraga would dominate the dial—and advertising revenues—for years to come.

In the 1980s, Televisa had grown fat on the soaps, *telenovelas* starring the curvaceous likes of Verónica Castro and Lucía Méndez that were wildly popular as far north as Moscow. In 1990, "La Canal de Las Estrellas" (The Channel of the Stars) added one more luminary to its roster of headliners: Octavio Paz, Mexico's most celebrated poet.

Paz had veered rigidly right as he dwindled into dotage. His *Vuelta* magazine virulently attacked Cárdenas and Carlos Fuentes, the "Guerrilla Dandy," and just about anything else that had a whiff of the Left about it. After the Wall came down and the Soviet Union disintegrated, Azcárraga gave The Poet a big shovel to bury socialism on national television.

An all-star festival of right-wing loonies was scheduled for Televisa's brand-new studios out in the first world enclave of Santa Fe in Cuajimalpa in June 1990. Among the blockbuster attractions was slimy Spanish-Peruvian novelist Mario Vargas Llosa. Perversely seeking to ingratiate himself with Paz and the PRI, Vargas Llosa described Mexico's ruling party as "The Perfect Dictatorship" and the envy of despotic regimes throughout the Americas—the Sandinistas and the Cubans were at the top of the list of the PRI's admirers. (There is certainly some truth in this.) The author's choice of words did not play well over at Insurgentes #59 and the next morning, Televisa sent a limousine to Vargas Llosa's hotel and put him on the next flight to Madrid.

In October, Paz was notified that he had been awarded the Nobel Prize for literature. I literally ran into Don Octavio at Benito Juárez International Airport. The Poet was strolling through the terminal, closely guarded by husky *guaruras* on his way to the VIP lounge when I spotted him from the upstairs Meridian bar where I had been sloshing down screwdrivers to drown my frustration at having missed my flight to San Francisco. In a burst of misplaced poetic ecstasy, I rushed down the stairs to congratulate Mexico's newest Nobel Laureate, and his guaruras threw me to the terminal floor and began drop-kicking me like I was an extra point in an NFL fandango. I was carried off to a cell the size of a shoebox to sober up.

Contused and confused, I caught a cab back to the hotel and hunkered down in the Isabel's claustrophobic little bar to heal my wounds and mull what savage capitalism was really all about. I swore that the first drink would be my last drink but the last drink lasted for several months and I didn't walk away until the d.t.'s finally found me convulsing on the barroom floor. I haven't had a drink since.

SEX AND DRUGS IN THE NEOLIBERAL NIGHTMARE

The sex industry in Mexico City reflects the class struggle. Young girls in sexy attire, often underage and just in from the country, are strung along Circunvalación in La Merced. Many wear their lingerie outside their miniskirts to attract customers. Like the ambulantes, their *padrotes* or pimps rent the stretch of sidewalk they stroll, trolling for clients. When they hook a john, the two adjourn to one of the many *hotelitos de paso* that line the zone, where grubby rooms are available by the half-hour. Luxury sex hotels with mirrors on the ceiling and porno on the tube are located in more affluent zones such as Tlalpan.

In the 1980s, with the AIDS epidemic in full bloom, *sexoservidores*, male and female, began carrying condoms, but many macho customers refused to don them. Prostitutes were beaten and raped when they refused to have unprotected sex, and the world's oldest profession organized for self-defense. Two rival sex workers' associations were formed in the Merced and the sexoservidoras were issued whistles to summon help if they felt threatened by a customer. Now, in the entrepreneurial ambience of the neoliberal nightmare, they turned a bad thing into a profitable one and charged johns double if they refused to wear a condom.

"Escort" services catering to the middle and upper castes caught fire in the 1980s. *Casas de cita,* elegant houses of prostitution, were largely items of nostalgia, but madams still ran strings of pricey call girls for visiting high-rollers.

So-called illicit drugs have played a lively role in the popular history of Mexico City since the founding of Tenochtitlán, when exotic hallucinogens induced the wild visions of the priestly class. Opium dens flourished around Dolores Street in Chinatown during the early part of the last century. Pancho Villa's Division del Norte marched through town to the tune of *La Cucaracha* looking for *marijuana pa' fumar*. Rivera and Siqueiros advocated cannabis as a creative stimulant to their fellow artist union members. William Burroughs scored his junk in La Merced, he tells us in his immortal *Yonqui* (Junky). *La mota* is for sale 25 hours a day in the dives of Tepito, AKA the Barrio Bravo, Sergio González Rodríguez reminds us in his *Los Bajos Fondos* (The Low-down Places).

Despite retrograde drug laws, the Monstruo offered a glittering gamut of intoxicants during the late '80s and early '90s. Marijuana (*mota, la verde, la buena, pacheco, mengambrea, chachalaca*) was the Everyman drug, available from the Chopo *tianguis* on Saturdays near the old train station in the north all the way to the "islands" of the UNAM in the south. *Jipi*-fied street jewelers who displayed ZigZag papers on their throw-down mats usually could be counted on for a *carrujo* (50 pesos of weed wrapped up in newspaper), and reggae and blues festivals were inevitably enveloped in a dense green cloud.

For the ragged underclass, the drug of choice was *activo* or *tíner*, paint thinner pushed by Sherwin-Williams, and *cemento* (glue) dealt by Resistol-Dupont. These brain cell–chomping chemical concoctions were particularly popular amongst the *niños de la calle*, abandoned street kids who bunked at the bus terminals or under the market stalls in La Merced.

For these youthful casualties of the Monstruo's indifference, huffing *activo* blocked out the sordid, neoliberal reality. "I don't have to feel anything now," a zombied-out 11-year-old who gave his name as Loco told me one afternoon when I visited him in his *coladera* (storm drain) below the street in front of the Franz Mayer Museum, across Hidalgo Avenue from the Alameda.

COCAINE—A DRUG FOR THE NEOLIBERAL NIGHTMARE

Until Durazo's cops started dealing blow at street level, cocaine was an elite drug snorted up exclusively in the salons of San Ángel from tiny silver spoons. Small quantities were smuggled in from South America, usually through the Mexico City airport. But in the early 1980s, the Colombian cartels hooked up with the Sinaloa boys who owned the brown and black tar heroin–trafficking routes to El Norte.

Mexico City is the center of just about everything in this ultra-centralized country, but the drug trade was concentrated in El Norte, principally along the border. Small planes flew the loads into remote landing strips in Sinaloa and Tamaulipas or deep in the south in Veracruz and the Isthmus of Oaxaca, from which the cocaine was transported on the ground, avoiding Mexico City and its impossibly snarled traffic like the plague to deliver the alkaloid to its destination in the border cities.

All this changed when Amado Carrillo, "The Lord of the Skies" and big boss of the Juárez cartel, started flying DC-6's loaded gunnel to gunnel with Colombian coke straight into Chihuahua. Like all innovators, The Lord of the Skies stepped on a lot of important toes, and he came to the end of the line in 1997 in a Polanco sanitarium that he had rented out, purportedly during a liposuction procedure.

The sanitarium was located not a mile from Los Pinos, and the lawyer for the spa was none other than Salinas cohort Diego Fernández de Cevallos. The two doctors who performed the liposuction were later found chopped to pieces and entombed in cement-filled drums along the highway to Acapulco. But if the Monstruo is not Cocaine Central, it is a major Latin American banking capital. Some drug watchers calculate that $10 million USD gets washed through the change houses at the International Airport each day.

The Colombianization of Mexico set a social trend. The capos from Cali and Medellín loved Mexico, dressed up like charros, and devoured Pedro Infante and María Félix flicks. José González Rodríguez Gacha, Pablo Escobar's second in command in the Medellín cartel (once listed on *Forbes* magazine's up-and-coming billionaire list), styled himself as "El Mexicano."

THE DRUG WAR COMES TO EL MONSTRUO

As U.S. president, George Bush Sr. presented Carlos Salinas with three must-do conditions for entabling NAFTA negotiations: (a) the revision of Constitutional Article 27 to give U.S. agribiz a foot up in Mexico; (b) a crackdown on Central American migrant workers transiting Mexico (the Sandinista Revolution was "only 48 hours from Harlingen, Texas"); and (c) the head of chief Sinaloa boy Miguel Ángel Félix Gallardo, who had pioneered trade relations with the South American cartels.

Salinas put the "Iron D.A.," Javier Coello Trejo, on the case. Coello, a heavy man who wore suspenders and featured a face full of stubble, kept a large-caliber pistol on his desk the whole time I interviewed him at the Attorney General's offices off north Reforma in 1989. He had just collared Félix Gallardo in his Guadalajara *escondite* (hideaway) and he grunted with optimism about future catches of *peces gordos* (fat fish).

But Coello Trejo's days as the toast of the town were short-lived. The hired help tripped him up. Two or three times a week, his agents would accompany the Iron D.A.'s Mrs. to the beauty salon or a charity luncheon or some such social amenity in the south of the city, and while she was otherwise occupied, they trolled the region for young women to gang-rape—the Tlalpan Country Club was a preferred hunting ground.

Despite Coello Trejo's forced departure (Salinas made him the Consumer Protection watchdog), the Félix Gallardo bust opened the door to NAFTA negotiations in 1990. The Free Trade Treaty, which would increase border traffic tenfold, was a godsend for the narcos, and Colombian cartels bought up trucking companies in Ciudad Juárez, according to a 1993 Tim Weiner exposé that ran on the *New York Times* front page as NAFTA negotiations neared finalization.

The rule of thumb is that taking down one *pez gordo* favors the fortunes of another fat fish. When a capo goes down, a bloody scrum to take over the business comes next. The Sinaloa boys went after each other over *la plaza* (turf) and the right to move their loads through it. One band of Sinaloa boys, Félix Gallardo's nephews, the Arellano Félix clan, staked out Tijuana, a key border *plaza* for getting the goods farther north. The Arellano Félixes were challenged by Joaquín "El Chapo" (short-guy) Guzmán and Héctor "El Güero" (paleface) Palma, now doing business as the Sinaloa or Pacific cartel. The Arellano Félixes, 11 brothers and sisters, barely escaped with their lives when El Chapo's pistoleros took out nine staff members at Cristina's, a Puerto Vallarta disco, in 1990. Months later, the Arellanos retaliated, mowing down four at the Bali Hai, a restaurant off south Insurgentes. The drug war had come to Mexico City.

But while the Sinaloa gangs were whacking each other without much mercy, the Gulf cartel, under the baton of Juan García Abrego, the nephew of the legendary *contrabandista* Juan Nepomuceno Guerra, was taking over the routes on the eastern end of the border, where the Mexican Navy turned a blind eye to the booming air traffic on Gulf coast landing strips.

Each Mexican president has his favorite narco and García Abrego was the Salinas family's man—Raúl, forever the black sheep, was reportedly a frequent guest at García Abrego's fiestas as well as private horse races in Monterrey and neighboring Tamaulipas.

THE POPE'S BLESSING

The hostilities between the Arellanos and the Sinaloa cartel went ballistic May 23, 1993, at the Guadalajara airport where Tijuana cartel hit men (actually gang members from San Diego's Barrio Logan Calle 30) lay in wait for El Chapo. When a shiny black Grand Marquis, a vehicle much favored by the narcos (Caro Quintero once owned the Guadalajara dealership) swung into the parking lot, the gunsels opened up, mortally wounding the occupants of the incoming Grand Marquis, Cardinal Juan Jesús Posada and his chauffeur, who had driven to the airport to welcome Papal Nuncio Girolamo Prigione. Once they had turned the parking lot into a killing floor—six other allegedly innocent bystanders were dispatched—the hit men calmly boarded an Aeromexico flight that had been held for them and returned to Tijuana.

Carlos Salinas's attorney general, Jorge Carpizo, divined that Cardinal Posada had been caught in a crossfire between drug gangs, and his murder was chalked up to "mistaken identity." The Guadalajara coroner was not so sure: The Cardinal, who was swathed in his priestly surplice and sporting a large pectoral cross, had been shot in the thorax from no more than six feet away.

Cardinal Juan Jesús Posada had a curious career trajectory. The former bishop of Tijuana had had his priests officiate at the Arellano clan's weddings and baptisms, and the Vatican scandal sheet *Il Giorno* suggested that the cardinal was the recipient of much narco-largesse. Indeed, his dexterity at accumulating large donations for the Guadalajara archdiocese had been fundamental in his elevation to cardinal.

From time to time, Posada performed Mass at a tiny chapel in San Javier Hills, a zealously guarded subdivision of Mexico's second-largest city where the capos built their compounds. Experienced narco-watchers surmised that the cardinal had been the victim of the cartels' inflexible code of *plata o plomo* (silver or lead).

The Church, of course, could not get down with this analysis. Rather, Juan Sandoval Íñiguez, Posada's heir to the throne of Guadalajara, has insisted for the past 15 years that his predecessor was the target of a "Jacobin" plot hatched in the dark recesses of the Salinas administration.

On the same day Cardinal Posada was wasted in Guadalajara, a confrontation between elements of the Mexican Army and an unidentified armed group left an undetermined number of troops and one civilian dead in the canyons of southeastern Chiapas, 20 kilometers from the Guatemalan border. With all the hullabaloo up north, no one paid much mind to what turned out to be the debut performance of the Zapatista Army of National Liberation.

Months after the airport shoot-out, in September, two Arellano Félix brothers whose mug shots decorated wanted posters throughout the republic traveled unrecognized and untouched up to the Monstruo to visit with Papal Nuncio Prigione at his walled-in residence in the extremely exclusive Guadalupe Inn neighborhood. The capos reportedly professed their innocence in the whacking of a Prince of the Church. They had brought with them a package for his Holiness John Paul Wojtyla, the contents of which have never been revealed. Prigione, so the story goes, contacted Carlos Salinas at once to inform him two of the most wanted men in Mexico were sitting in his living room. The President did not seem particularly interested.

HO HO HO

Carlos Salinas was focused on more pressing business than capturing the Tijuana mob. The time was drawing nigh for him to designate a successor to take over the neoliberal enterprise. There has already been some discussion of a constitutional amendment that would promote the conservation of the "Salinas Project" via reelection. The transition, as is so often the case, promised to be a thorny one.

Manuel Camacho Solís had great expectations that he would be the Chosen One. He and Carlos were old school chums, and he had been a trusted member of his *camarilla* for years, serving Salinas as regent during difficult times. Certain that he was the *bueno*, Camacho Solís began to assemble a campaign staff.

The Dedazo came down December 10. But it was not pointed at Manuel Camacho. Luis Donaldo Colosio, "Salinas with hair," was designated the PRI nominee, virtually assuring that he would be the next president of Mexico barring extracurricular shenanigans.

Rather than seeking reelection, Carlos Salinas now had his sights set on becoming the first president of the World Trade Organization (WTO), the maximum corporate body of planetary globalization. Colosio would be entrusted with promoting the Salinas Project for the next six years. Raúl would be groomed to become governor of Nuevo León and position himself for the presidency in 2000. Then Carlos would take the reins again in 2006.

Manuel Camacho was beside himself with envy and pain. He had been double-crossed by the Salinas boys, and all in a dither he tendered his resignation as regent—his second in command, Manuel Aguilera, who had headed up the RHP housing program while Camacho served at SEDUE during earthquake days, would fill out his remaining year in office.

Manuel Camacho Solís stalked off to Lomas in a snit. But although furious at his former boss, he conformed to the PRI pledge of omertà and bit his tongue at this unspeakable indignity. Days later, the outgoing President handed down the booby prizes and Camacho became Mexico's interim foreign minister.

El Monstruo shuts down for the holidays December 15. Government offices close up, leaving only a skeleton crew to handle emergencies. Bureaucrats will not return until the end of the first week in January after the Day of Los Reyes (the Three Kings) on the 6th, when Mexicans chow down on *roscas* (coffee cake) and their moppets are peaced off with plastic toys.

The *posadas* begin, and neighbors march from door to door here in the Centro accompanying surrogate Marys and Josephs and singing traditional hymns as they beg for lodging. Blindfolded children smash at piñatas filled with fruit and candy, and sugar-crazed kids fight over the goodies. Santa Claus, that roly-poly pale-faced gringo invader, sets up camp out on the Alameda or the Monument to the Revolution, terrifying toddlers with thunderous Ho Ho Hos.

Whole walls of flashing Christmas lights spell out FELIZ NAVIDAD Y UN PROSPERO AÑO NUEVO on the façades of government buildings in the Zócalo. The *paisanos* come home from El Norte loaded down with gifts and fistfuls of Yanqui dolares. Drunks are rolled for their *aguinaldos* (Christmas bonuses). In the Centro, families flock to the Metropolitan Cathedral for the Misa de Gallo ("Rooster" or midnight Mass) and then go home to dine on *romeritos* (shrimp and swamp-grass patties). Rancor dissipates and reasonable goodwill toward men and women reigns, if only for a few days.

FELIZ AÑO NUEVO, CABRONES

For Carlos Salinas, New Year's Eve was like the puffing of a fine Havana cigar, a moment to sit back and reflect on the successful conclusion of his most cherished pipe dream. On November 17, Bill Clinton had bribed and bullied the U.S. House of Representatives into passage of the North American Free Trade Agreement, and although it had carried by only 34 votes, NAFTA would sanctify the Salinas name for the rest of history. New Year's was a time for celebration.

The president, his soon-to-be-ex-wife Cecilia Ocelli, and their three children flew down to Huatulco, the new luxury resort on the

Oaxaca coast that had been illegally expropriated from Zapotec fishing families by Miguel De la Madrid eight years previous. The spectacular presidential guesthouse stood high on the bluffs overlooking shimmering Tangolunda Bay.

The Salinas siblings—Raúl, Enrique, Sergio, and Andrea—and their recently widowed father, Raúl Sr., would join the party. Luis Donaldo and his dying wife Diana Laura and their two small children would arrive later. All day, the Salinas brood swam and sunbathed on the pristine private beach below.

At the stroke of midnight, the President's sommelier opened the first magnum of Dom Pérignon and the family toasted NAFTA and the health of the Salinas Project. They took their festive dinner out on the terrace under the stars: the traditional roast turkey, *relleno de picadillo*, black olives, and of course *romeritos* (menu thanks to *El Financiero*, January 16, 1994). The presidential yacht rolled at anchor on the billowing bay below and a New Year's cruise was contemplated. By the third magnum of Dom Pérignon the mood had turned lugubrious.

Just before 2:00 a.m., a military attaché stepped out on the terrace and handed the president a card. Salinas excused himself and went inside to take an urgent call on his secure phone from Defense Secretary Antonio Riviello Bazán in Mexico City. The general had just received an encrypted message from the 31st Military Zone in San Cristóbal de las Casas, Chiapas, indicating that an armed group had shot its way into the old colonial city and six other county seats in the region and declared war on Mexico. Say what? The president pressed the defense secretary for details. He checked his watch. The attack had occurred one hour after the North American Free Trade Agreement had kicked in. The Zapatistas were often late but they were always on time.

Carlos Salinas returned to the terrace and informed his guests that he would be flying back to the capital first thing in the morning.

THE DECLARATION OF THE LACANDÓN JUNGLE

Most everyone in the little jewel-box city of San Cristóbal de las Casas, nestled in Los Altos, the impoverished Tzotzil Mayan highlands of Chiapas, had toddled off to bed by 1:00 a.m. when the dark columns of masked Indians tramped across the Puente Blanco (White Bridge) south of town, setting sleeping dogs in the patios of the San Ramón barrio to howling.

Forty rebels split off from the main contingent to neutralize the state judicial police barracks west of the Pan American highway. The rest of the ski-masked phantoms advanced on the center of the city and laid siege to the Municipal Palace in the small, well-kept plaza, breaking into the office of the county registrar and carrying off armfuls of archives and land deeds that they burnt at bum fires under the porticos to ward off the chill.

By mid-morning, the plaza was filling with tourists—there were many Italians vacationing in San Cristóbal that year. A bit after noon, the comandantes mounted to the second-story balcony of the alabaster white Palacio Municipal to pronounce the Declaration of the Lacandón Jungle.

"We are the products of 500 years of struggle" they began, leaving little doubt that this was an Indian rebellion. What did they want? "¡Trabajo! (Work), ¡Tierra! (Land), ¡Techo! (Housing), ¡Pan! (Bread), ¡Salud! (Health care), ¡Educación!, ¡Democracia!, ¡Libertad!, ¡Paz!, ¡Independencia!, ¡Justicia!" They accused the mal gobierno of treason and treachery and demanded that Salinas resign. Then they declared war on the Mexican army in the name of the Zapatista Army of National Liberation and vowed "to march on the capital of the country, defeating the federal army on the way."

"Today, we say enough! ¡Basta ya!"

Later that afternoon, the rebel with the shotgun and bandoleras spoke with a vacationing Italian writer who sometimes contributed to the leftist L'Unità. "This is not about Salinas or free trade," Comandante Marco, or Marcos, explained: "This is about the whole neoliberal project."

WHO ARE THESE MASKED MEN?

The Monstruo awoke Monday morning with a terrible hangover and stared at the headlines through blurry eyes. There had been no newspapers on January 1, and for Chilangos this was the first word of the rebel uprising to filter in from far-off Chiapas. The fuzzy photos showed armed Indians, their deep-set impervious gaze framed behind ski masks and paliacates (kerchiefs). The Salinas government was already claiming they were Guatemalans, never considering that their own inditos could take matters into their own hands. But to those gathered around the kiosks, the rebels looked perfectly Mexican.

A military spokesperson identified their leader as a green-eyed foreigner named Marco, or Marcos. The army had cornered the subversives near a military base just outside San Cristóbal, and they would soon be subdued.

Other municipal seats in southeastern Chiapas had come under similar attack and an unknown number of civilians killed. Troops were being rushed in from nearby Tabasco, and C-130 transport planes supplied by the U.S. Pentagon were flying in additional forces from the Santa Lucía air force base just outside the capital. The air force was already bombing rebel villages. The situation was "under control."

Nonetheless, the Monstruo had the jitters. Security forces were placed on high alert in the capital. Hadn't the rebels announced that they would march on the Monstruo, "defeating the federal army on the way"? Cranked up by Televisa and the prensa vendida, war psychosis was generalized. Some 37,000 police and an undetermined number of troops swarmed over Benito Juárez International Airport, surrounding Telmex and Federal Electricity Commission (CFE) installations and the PEMEX Tower.

Just to crank up the paranoia, on the 6th a large car bomb exploded in a parking garage at the Plaza Universidad shopping center near the UNAM, heavily damaging a dozen vehicles—no live casualties were reported. On the 8th, a pickup truck from which missiles were being lobbed over the fence at Military Camp #1 blew up. The assailants escaped into the night. A CFE pylon in Tehuacán, Puebla, 100 miles southwest of the capital, was taken down. A second pylon outside of Uruapan, Michoacán, keeled over when it was rammed by a truck. A third pylon closer to the city in Cuautitlán was blown up—a second dynamite charge with the potential of blacking out the entire Metropolitan Zone was deactivated. On the 9th, a massive explosion ripped through PEMEX pipelines near Salamanca, northwest of Mexico City in Guanajuato.

When the spanking-new bubble-domed Mexican Stock Exchange (bolsa) opened for business on the 10th, the Monstruo was shaky with bomb jitters. Police dogs scoured the hallways and offices of the glass-enclosed Bolsa and knife-thin skyscraper that rises above it on the corner of Reforma and Río Rhin. But the real bomb in the buildings was the market itself, which had lost 6.2 percent of its total value in the days since the rebel attack and on the 10th dove a terrifying 12 points more in the wake of the PEMEX bombing.

With financial crisis threatening the underpinnings of the neoliberal bad dream he had achieved in the past six years, Carlos Salinas flinched and appointed a "peace commissioner" to fly to San Cristóbal and consult with local officials and the controversial bishop of San Cristóbal, Samuel Ruiz, an outspoken defender of the Indians whom Televisa was already accusing of being the brains behind the Zapatista Army of National Liberation.

Manuel Camacho Solís mulled the assignment. Just 40 days ago, Salinas had turned his back on him and chosen Luis Donaldo Colosio as his handpicked successor. His advisers cautioned that the Chiapas mission was political suicide. But by January 10th, Camacho had convinced himself that only he could save Mexico from the deepest doodoo Salinas had stepped in since the '88 election and thus redeem himself in the eyes of his party and the nation.

THE ZAPATISTAS TAKE THE CAPITAL

Despite the appointment of Camacho as peace commissioner, the Mexican military continued to advance on rebel bases in the Lacandón jungle, and the civil society that had sprung from the loins of the earthquake and been sorely tested in the postelectoral struggle of '88 mobilized to demand that Salinas call off the troops.

Superbarrio was the first to hit the streets. On January 8, he led a posse from the Assembly of Barrios up Reforma calling for an immediate cease-fire. On the 12th, 125,000 activist Chilangos marched into the Zócalo behind an immense banner that shouted, STOP THE MASSACRE! Cuauhtémoc Cárdenas, about to launch his second crusade to capture the presidency, and Rosario Ibarra, mother of Jesús, were in the first line of march. So was 90-year-old former political prisoner Valentín Campa, founder of the long-defunct Mexican Communist Party.

As the huge march wended its way through the city, hand-painted slogans were sprayed on every available wall: ¡YA LLEGAMOS!—we have arrived.

Time and time again over the course of the next 10 years, whenever the president or the military put a move on the Zapatistas, the civil society would fill the Zócalo demanding that the mal gobierno back off. It was indeed the EZLN's most dependable weapon.

READ ALL ABOUT IT!

La Jornada, along with all the other Mexico City dailies, rushed a team of reporters to San Cristóbal—the paper's regular correspondent Elio Henriques was on vacation with his family in El Salvador and the Zapatista rebellion was the left paper's kind of story. The communiqués began to flow from the jungle by the second week in January. Generally, they were delivered by a short nun to the Casa Vieja hotel, where the press and Camacho were housed. At first, they were addressed to *Tiempo*, the late Amado Avendaño's local weekly; *El Financiero* (the financial paper seemed sympathetic in the early days of the rebellion); Julio Scherer's weekly *Proceso*; and *La Jornada*. The left daily would run every single one of Subcomandante Marcos's bitingly ironic jeremiads word for word for the next decade, until at long last the Sup veered into sectarian oblivion.

By the third week in January, ace *Jornada* reporter Blanche Petrich rode horseback into the jungle with a camera crew to get the first-ever interview with Marcos and the Clandestine Indigenous Revolutionary Committee (CCRI) at Guadalupe Tepeyac, a stone's throw from Guatemala. Salinas and Colosio had been helicoptered into the village months before to inaugurate a Solidarity hospital. One of the Zapatista comandantes, Tacho, had been a waiter at the ribbon cutting.

Up in Mexico City, the *Jornadas* sold like hot bread and the paper's daily circulation topped 100,000. In a stroke of synchronicity, the Internet was just entering the lives of millions and Marcos's communiqués found adoring audiences in the U.S. and Europe. The Sup's masked mug was imprinted upon trinkets ranging from ballpoint pens to condoms (dubbed Los Alzados, "the risen-up ones") and graced the front cover of every magazine in the republic. With his trademark Sherlock Holmes pipe clenched firmly between his teeth, the Zapatista mouthpiece had become an overnight idol.

MARCOS AND THE MONSTRUO

The enigmatic guerrilla leader's biography took several years to unravel. He appears to be the son of a Tampico, Tamaulipas, furniture dealer and is purportedly a post-Tlatelolco activist student who took his degree at the UNAM's Philosophy & Letters faculty—his thesis sorted out the writings of Louis Althusser, the French existential communist philosopher who gained academic notoriety by strangling his wife.

Later, "Marcos" (Rafael Sebastián Guillén Vicente is believed to be his Christian name) would teach Communication Philosophy at the Metropolitan Autonomous University (UAM) Xochimilco campus. Because some rebels were photographed wearing Ruta 100 uniforms, it is thought he once drove a bus during his days in the Monstruo.

What is more certain is that the Subcomandante arrived in Chiapas in 1984 as part of a guerrilla *foco*, the Forces of National Liberation (FLN), and though always nostalgic for the "Monstruo," his endearing name for this conflictive megalopolis, he has not lived here since.

THE CENTER OF THE UNIVERSE

Mexico City is the absolute center of an absolutely centralized country. It is the absolute power center, the axis of government and finance and culture and the nation's history, the umbilicus of the Mexican universe. Mexico City thinks that everything that is Mexico emanates from its entrails. Perhaps no other capital in Latin America and for that matter the world so lords it over the country that surrounds it. The nation, in fact, has taken its name from the city that rules it.

A paragon of arrogance and truculence, Mexico City dominates the rest of the republic even more fiercely than Tenochtitlán gripped the Aztec empire. Distant provinces virtually disappear from the map on the prime-time newscasts. Indeed, Mexico City is the only place where the news is made. And yet, for a few short months in 1994, a band of ski-masked Indian rebels encamped in the jungles and highlands of Chiapas, Mexico's southernmost state, robbed the spotlight and stole the Monstruo's thunder.

IN THE CENTER OF THE PHOTO

When in February, the EZLN comandantes came in from the cold and stepped over the threshold into Don Samuel's cathedral for negotiations with Salinas Peace Commissioner Camacho Solís, every eye, including that of Televisa, which had been slamming "Comandante Sammy" and the Zapatistas night after night since January 1, was glued to the tube.

At the opening session, tiny Comandanta Ramona, "the smallest of the small," fished a Mexican flag from her shoulder bag and extended one end to Subcomandante Marcos, but her short arms did not quite reach and Camacho Solís gallantly came to the rescue. Flashbulbs sizzled. The photo of the ex-regent and the tiny, birdlike rebel holding up the red, white, and green standard with the eagle devouring the snake in the arms of a nopal cactus bush embossed upon it was perhaps the most iconic moment of the early days of the Zapatista rebellion, and Manuel Camacho Solís was right in the middle of it.

Much as the Zapatistas had stolen the cameras from Salinas and his NAFTA, Camacho had blacked out Colosio in the daily scuffle for headlines, and Salinas with hair's campaign was listing badly. It was all Camacho all the time in newspaper kiosks and on Zabludovsky's always skewed evening news. While Luis Donaldo was out beating the boonies for votes, the Peace commissioner got the interviews.

When he did get heard, the PRI candidate was sounding more and more like his own man and not a water boy for the "Salinas Project," and scuttlebutt surged, as it invariably does, that the President was having second thoughts about the Dedazo.

Colosio's oft-vague calls to reform the PRI had the smell of old Carlos Madrazo's doomed clean-up crusade a quarter-century earlier, and the Party bigshots on Insurgentes grew uneasy. After a particularly enthusiastic performance by the candidate March 7, the PRI brain trust (so to speak) petitioned Salinas to bring his boy to heel.

A SHOT IN THE DARK

Luis Donaldo Colosio was not looking forward to campaign appearances in Baja California. He had sorely rankled the Party bosses in Tijuana when he conceded the state's governorship to a PANista after the 1989 elections, and when he subsequently flew in to make peace with disaffected PRIistas, the chant of "¡Muera Colosio!" (that Colosio should die) had gone up at the party headquarters adjacent to the border in that tawdry town's red-light district.

The candidate would work his way into Tijuana from the airport. The first stop was Lomas Taurinas, a Solidarity colony (Colosio was identified with the Solidarity program), little more than a gully 200 meters from the border fence with U.S. California. The meeting was much larger than had been expected. The colonos, refugees from Michoacán and Guerrero and Oaxaca who scrambled for work in the *maquiladoras* (U.S.-owned assembly plants) and the pestilent local garbage dumps, had been drummed out in sizable numbers. Hundreds of plainclothes cops from five separate agencies ranging from the CISEN spy bureau to the PRI TUCAN ("Everyone United Against the PAN") goon squad were on hand to keep an eye on the meeting.

Colosio mounted the bed of a pickup truck that had been rigged out as a stage and stared at the cardboard shacks and unfinished block hovels and the discolored walls with his name writ big upon them and broke into his spiel. No one seems to remember just what he said. "*¡Vamos a ganar!*" he yelled hoarsely—"We are going to win!"—as he descended from the truck to press the flesh in the traditional "public bath." The sound system was blasting a rollicking *quebradita* called *La Culebra*—"The *culebra* (snake) is going to get you!/ You better move your feet!" Germán Castillo, Colosio's lead bodyguard, slammed into the reluctant mob to open a path. From this muddle of humanity a hand emerged clutching a cocked .38 mm Taurus revolver and put a bullet into the back of Colosio's brain. As the candidate twisted forward, a second shot was fired into his abdomen.

Luis Donaldo Colosio was dead on arrival at Tijuana General Hospital although no one wanted to say so publicly until 10:00 p.m., when an ashen-faced Carlos Salinas faced the cameras at Los Pinos to announce that the candidate had croaked. Wednesday would be a national day of mourning. The Stock Market would be closed to head off massive capital flight.

Whodunnit? I am beginning to sound like a broken record.

Three men had been taken into custody at the scene of the crime. Two were ex–Tijuana judicial police agents with lamentable human rights records who represented the PRI's TUCAN at this blood-spattered clambake.

The third, a 23-year-old mechanic, Mario Aburto from La Rinconada, Michoacán, Cárdenas's home state, was fingered as the shooter. A fourth suspect, José Antonio Sánchez Ortega, a CISEN operator, was collared running away from the crime scene. He had blood all over his shirt and tested positive for having recently fired a gun. Nonetheless, he and the two TUCANs were released that evening.

Mario Aburto was presented to the press. No questions were allowed. The next morning, he was flown back to Mexico City to face the music. Photographs of the Tijuana Aburto and the Aburto who arrived in El Monstruo do not match up. Chilangos clustered around the newspaper kiosks shaking their heads.

"Mario Aburto is a Mexican Lee Harvey Oswald," a shaken Sub-comandante Marcos told *Vanity Fair*'s Ann Louise Bardach and Global Exchange gadfly Medea Benjamin when he spoke with them that night in the Zapatista village of La Garrucha.

The bullets that had cut down Luis Donaldo Colosio also cut the Zapatistas down to size. For months, they had hogged the headlines, diverting attention from the mighty capital of the Mexicans to the Indian periphery of the country.

México Profundo, the vast backwaters of the nation that no one had ever paid much attention to before, had had its 15 minutes of fame. Now the press was packing up and hightailing it back to Mexico City where the real action was about to begin. Down the years, the media would return sporadically to Chiapas whenever things got dicey between the rebels and the mal gobierno. But for now, the Monstruo was back in charge of Mexico.

WHO WILL BE NEXT?

The mob outside the fence at Insurgentes #59 was surly. *"¡Justicia!"* *"¿Quién fue?"* (Who did it?), the crowd howled when the slain candidate's coffin was carried into the compound. "Kill Camacho!"

One by one, the PRI caciques and slimeball honchos, fixers, bagmen, legislators, governors, and camarillas gathered in the Plutarco Elías Calles auditorium, named indeed for another assassin of another would-be president (some things will never change). The ceremony would be a chance for the power cliques to cash in old debts, bait their enemies, and put in their bids to replace "Salinas with hair" on the PRI ticket. The camarillas took turns standing honor guard before the bier to display their loyalty to the dearly departed and to the Party, which had probably whacked him.

Kingmaker Carlos Hank assumed his place in the first line of mourners, with Fernando Gutiérrez Barrios, the old torturer who had served as Salinas's interior secretary, right behind him. Other cabinet ministers solemnly stood watch, as did Ernesto Zedillo, the former education secretary, who had resigned his post to take over as Colosio's campaign manager. Because he had left office early, Zedillo, a colorless neoliberal bean counter, had the inside track to succeed the dead candidate—the Mexican Constitution dictates that a presidential candidate must have left office six months before election day, and unless the Constitution could be amended quickly, a move that would require PAN and PRD acquiescence, the PRI was stuck with Zedillo.

In mid-afternoon, Colosio was transported to the Gayosso funeral parlor on Félix Cuevas Street in the Colonia del Valle, the official undertaker to the Institutionals, and laid out for public viewing pending cremation. Carlos Salinas arrived to pay his respects with the three living ex-presidents, Echeverría, López Portillo, and Miguel De la Madrid. Guatemalan Nobelist Rigoberta Menchú, to whom the PRI had granted sanctuary from the death squads, spread a *huipil* over the coffin. When Cuauhtémoc Cárdenas appeared, the crowd spat on him. Diego Fernández de Cevallos, the PAN presidential candidate, was jeered and jostled.

Manuel Camacho Solís had flown up from Chiapas. When he entered the chapel, a thickset, red-faced PRIista blocked his way and shouted that he was not wanted there. Someone threw a long, loping punch that smashed into the ex-regent's jaw. His glasses fell to the floor. "Kill Camacho!" the infuriated mourners screamed, pushing around him like they meant it. The peace commissioner's guaruras snatched him away in the nick of time. When a Televisa reporter thrust her mic into his swelling mush, the ex-regent babbled that he had nothing to do with Colosio's murder. "I don't want to be president of Mexico anymore" were his exact words.

Salinas appeared to favor Finance Minister Pedro Aspe over Ernesto Zedillo. Both, like Salinas—and De la Madrid, López Portillo, and Echeverría before him—had never been elected to any public office. Unlike the aristocratic Aspe with his regal presidential bearing, Zedillo was a nebbish, a once-upon-a-time shoeshine boy who had won a full scholarship to Yale and functioned as Salinas's gofer at Budget and Planning and later as secretary of education where his most noteworthy achievement had been the shredding of a million revised text books that hinted the military had something to do with Tlatelolco.

But Ernesto Zedillo was the PRI's only option—the PAN and the PRD wouldn't even discuss a constitutional amendment that could have opened the way for Aspe. Carlos Hank's qualified endorsement was the clincher and the white puff went up March 29. The *acarreados* from Chalco, Solidarity's birthplace, were herded into the compound and taught how to pronounce the new candidate's name.

THE VOTE OF FEAR

Genghis Hank took charge of the revived campaign, stimulating the PRI's "green vote" by withholding Pro-Campo subsidy payments to farmers until campesino leaders assured a big turnout. Hank plotted to parlay public paranoia jacked up by the Colosio assassination, the hit on Cardinal Posada, and the Zapatista uprising into the so-called *voto de miedo*, i.e., the fear vote.

The voto de miedo acquired a big booster June 14 when banker Alfredo Harp Helú, Carlos Slim's cousin (as adolescents they had shared a winning lottery ticket upon which they built their respective fortunes), was snatched by kidnappers on a busy Coyoacán boulevard. The interior secretary would later display a list of 10 kidnappable billionaires alleged to have been dropped at the scene.

Then the U.S. Alcohol, Firearms, and Tobacco Bureau tipped off *El Financiero* that several containers of automatic weapons, presumably paid for with the record ransom shelled out to redeem Harp, were en route to an unidentified guerrilla group in the state of Guerrero. The emergence of the Popular Revolutionary Army (EPR) in 1996 confirmed the shipments.

By midsummer, Genghis Hank was running radio spots featuring the tremulous voices of two children. "I'm scared," whined one. "Why are you scared?" asks the other. "Because my daddy is scared."

In a desperate gambit to rally support, Cuauhtémoc Cárdenas journeyed to Guadalupe Tepeyac to plead for Subcomandante Marcos's endorsement, but the Zapatista mouthpiece was in no mood to elevate the electoral Left and scorched the PRD during a face-to-face confrontation in the rebel hideout. The candidate returned to Mexico City with his hat if not his head in his hands.

¡PUEBLO PUTO!

Election Day—August 21—was the usual anticlimax. I covered it from the central plaza in Chalco with a block-long Solidarity billboard suspended over my head. Hysterical would-be voters who had been "razored" from voting lists in their neighborhoods descended on a special polling place where they had been promised they would be allowed to exercise their suffrage, but the *casilla*'s 300 ballots had all been doled out to the military and police assigned to keep order during the vote-taking.

The women from the colonias beseeched officials for a ballot and threatened to burn down the special casilla if they didn't get one. School would begin in a week and they needed to be checked off as having voted by the PRI flunkies to secure a spot for their kids. One weeping señora squeezed my hand and begged me to help. Her husband had just died, and permission to bury him in the municipal cemetery was conditioned on casting a ballot for Zedillo. It was a defining moment in the 1994 presidential election for me. How could you hope to beat a party that obligated you to vote for its candidate in order to bury your dead?

Unlike in 1988, the PRI did not have to steal ballots and crash computers to win. Some 3,200,000,000,000 pesos in June-to-August Pro-Campo checks to 3,000,000 farmers were withheld until election eve. Zedillo's people outspent Cárdenas 400 to one to buy off voters in the provinces. The newly created "autonomous" Federal Electoral Institute (IFE) turned a *vista gorda* (fat eye) on the buying of the election, and the *New York Times* once again tagged the balloting "the cleanest in Mexican history."

The final tally had Zedillo with 47 percent, the PAN's Diego Fernández at 31 percent, and Cárdenas, who lost everywhere in the land except the Monstruo, with 15.5 percent. Walking through Coyoacán days later, then–*Financiero* columnist Jaime Avilés spotted a wall *pinta* that just about summed it up: ¡PUEBLO PUTA! (the people are whores).

CANNIBAL PIGEONS

Despite Zedillo's big win, the PRI was at war with itself. The camarillas were squabbling with each other like flocks of cannibal pigeons over the crumbs Carlos Salinas had strewn behind. Zedillo, unlike his mentor Carlos Hank, was both a poor politician and a bad one. Oblivious to the intense chafing upstairs at Insurgentes #59, the new president blithely set about picking his cabinet. José Francisco Ruiz Massieu, the former governor of Guerrero, once married to Salinas's sister Adriana, was picked to head up the PRI delegation in the Chamber of Deputies.

On September 28, José Francisco left a huddle with his congressional delegation at the Hotel Casablanca on Lafragua Street, near the Monument to the Revolution and around the corner from Fidel Velázquez's CTM, and jumped into his unbulletproof Buick. Before he could even flip on the ignition, Daniel Aguilar Treviño, a hired hit man from Tamaulipas, walked up to the side window and blew his head off.

Aguilar, a ranch hand on a federal deputy's spread in that gulf coast state, was an inexpert killer, and his .9 mm automatic pistol jammed after he got off one shot. When he dropped the gun and walked briskly off toward Reforma, a nearby bank guard hammered him to the sidewalk like an All-Pro defensive end. Nonetheless, the one shot had been sufficient, and Ruiz Massieu's brains were splattered all over the windshield.

For a long while, Daniel Aguilar Treviño could not remember who had paid him the $15,000 Americano for the hit. Once again, the PRI had killed its own.

HIS BROTHER'S KEEPER

For the fourth time in the past 18 months, Mexico was plunged into a paroxysm of fear and loathing. Carlos Salinas, who would not give up the ghost of power until December 1, made an intriguing choice for a special prosecutor to investigate the murder of his former brother-in-law: the dead man's own brother, Mario Ruiz Massieu, the president's top drug war prosecutor.

Mario put the screws on Daniel Aguilar and soon hooked him up to a puff-haired Tamaulipas federal deputy, Manuel Muñoz Rocha, who seemed to have vanished off the face of the globe. Most probably he wound up in someone's acid bath—months later, his wife had him declared legally dead.

Without the chief suspect in the plot, Mario Ruiz Massieu turned his torture squad on the deputy's compadres, and Fernando Rodríguez González, Muñoz Rocha's sergeant-at-arms, suddenly confessed he had been contracted to organize the hit. But the confession did not really get to the heart of the matter.

What Mario Ruiz Massieu failed to disclose when he distributed incriminating depositions to the press was that he had systematically deleted the name of the Mister Big in back of Muñoz Rocha: Raúl

Salinas. The president had vetoed any mention of his incommodious brother whose involvement in this lurid affair would surely have queered the "Salinas Project."

CITY OF OMENS

During the first weeks of December, Popocatépetl, the wondrous snowcapped volcano eminently visible on clear days from the eastern and southern neighborhoods of the city, began to rumble and fume. Great exhalations of gas and molten rock vomited from its innards—the *fumarola* (smoke plume) extended five miles into the heavens and diverted air traffic into the capital. Ash fell on Isabel la Católica Street (at first I thought it was snow), and lava flows forced the evacuation of villagers who lived on the flanks of the fiery mountain they called "Don Goyo."

Such ominous moments have always invoked a sense of dread and wonderment among the Monstruo's residents. For the Aztecs, the periodic eruptions of Popocatépetl fulfilled prophecy and augured imminent times of danger and change.

CARLOS'S HOUSE OF CARDS

On December 1, Carlos Salinas draped the presidential sash over Ernesto Zedillo's narrow chest at a Legislative Palace in San Lázaro that had finally been refurbished after the still unattributed arson job three years earlier. His final Informe had been redolent with braggadocio, listing the many accomplishments of his administration: NAFTA, Solidarity, Mexico's record $40 billion USD in foreign reserves. There was no need to mention Chiapas.

But the outgoing president's numbers were disingenuous: The $40 billion in reserves had flown the coop since March. He had kept his house of cards from crashing by borrowing $33 billion more in short-term loans, which wouldn't come due until he was safely out of the country.

Moreover, the peso was dangerously overvalued, but rather than risk his reputation by devaluing it as his three predecessors had been forced to do, Salinas deeded the dirty work to Zedillo. The new president got the picture when he was summoned to a bitter late-night meeting at the Salinas digs down Tlalpan.

It really didn't take very long for the chickens to come home to roost. On December 19, Zedillo's rookie finance minister, Jaime Serra Puche, a Princeton man (the new president was a Yalie), stood up before the TV lights and announced the devaluation of the peso by 20 percent. Overnight, the peso dropped from three (i.e., 3,000—Salinas had shaved three zeros off the peso) to 10 (10,000) to a dollar. When Zedillo made the fateful decision to float the currency and let the market do its job, the peso disappeared into the netherworld.

Moreover, the banks, which Salinas had handed back to their old owners just two years previous, were being stripped to the bone—the only liquidity left was said to be the $26 billion USD in narco money washed through them each year. Interest rates ratcheted up to 100 percent, and Mexico was about to dive into its deepest economic slide since the Great Depression.

INDIAN BLOOD

Like Silva Herzog 20 years before him, Serra Puche flew off to Washington to beg Bill Clinton and the U.S. Congress to bail Mexico out once again. But Wall Street was not nearly as invested in Mexico as it had been in 1982, and the Yanqui Congress was reluctant to spend its taxpayers' good gelt on saving a corrupt government from itself. Big Bubba had to dip into a currency stabilization fund he had up his sleeve to save Zedillo's ass. This time, collateral for the $30 billion bailout was all of Mexico's oil export revenues for the next three years, to be deposited in the United States Federal Reserve Bank at the foot of Wall Street.

The first payout filled Mexico's depleted coffers February 8. The next night, Ernesto Zedillo took to the airwaves to announce he was unleashing the military on the Zapatista Army of National Liberation. Paratroopers were already jumping into Guadalupe Tepeyac. The president identified Marcos to TV viewers as Rafael Sebastián Guillén Vicente, a bearded ex-professor. An assistant kept sliding an old photo of Guillén over a mock-up of the ski-masked Marcos to emphasize the point.

Subcomandante Marcos had gotten wind of the ambush early on and was long gone, pausing every few days as he headed for the deepest folds of the Lacandón jungle to fire off communiqués to *La Jornada*.

The bailout, the Sup observed, was going to be paid back in Indian blood.

Not 24 hours after Zedillo sent in the military, I stood on the top step of the gilded Angel of Independence's circular pedestal, observing the civil society assembling for one more march to the Zócalo to detain still another government outrage against the Zapatistas. A large number of UNAM students, many in *pasamontañas* (ski masks), were marching up the Paseo de La Reforma from the south waving their arms and flashing fists of defiance. I could not make out what they were chanting until they had reached the outer edges of the *glorieta* (traffic circle), and then it dawned on me: "*¡Todos Somos Marcos!*" (We Are All Marcos!).

THE REVENGE OF THE NEBBISH

Once the bailout was secured and the Zapatistas on the run, Ernesto Zedillo took his revenge on the true enemy. On Tuesday morning February 28, 1995, 70 black-clad judicial police agents converged on Costa Street #62 in the exclusive Colonia Las Águilas where Raúl Salinas was holed up at the ritzy Pedregal home of his sister Adrianna (the former Mrs. Ruiz Massieu). When Carlos learned of the raid, he dispatched 20 heavily armed military personnel, including members of the Estado Mayor, to intercept Zedillo's posse, but a hurried call from General Roberto Miranda, who had headed that elite unit during the Salinas presidency, pulled them back and avoided a bloody battle on the quiet streets of the posh Pedregal neighborhood.

Raúl, who reportedly had ordered the hit on José Francisco Ruiz Massieu because of his mistreatment of Adriana (during the messy divorce proceedings she suggested he was gay), was led from the mansion with his head bent forward by a judicial agent, *agachado* like a common criminal, and had nothing to say to the press.

Carlos went off the deep end at the spectacle of his brother's arrest. Panicked that Zedillo would complete the coup by charging him with complicity in Colosio's killing, he appealed to his well-heeled *cuates* to save his butt, and Roberto González Barrera, "The King of the Tortilla," whose Maseca Corporation had accumulated several fortunes during the Salinas years, offered his private plane to fly the ex-president to Monterrey and refuge at the Salinas family hacienda in nearby Agualeguas.

But Carlos had become unhinged and friends feared he was suicidal. Around 1:00 a.m. on March 1, the wild-eyed ex-president banged on the door of Rosa Coronado, a Solidarity leader in a Solidarity colony off Solidarity Avenue in Monterrey, and begged for sanctuary. He was jumpy and haggard and hadn't eaten for 24 hours—he had declared himself on a hunger strike to protest Zedillo's treatment of his brother. The startled Coronado gave up her bedroom, and Salinas pulled the covers over his head and awaited the press and an apology from Zedillo. The whole country was watching this absurd telenovela with a mixture of incredulity and dread.

Late on March 2, after an angry telephone exchange between Salinas and Zedillo, the Tortilla King flew his friend back to Mexico City, where, according to Andres Oppenheimer's chronicle of this absurdist horseplay, *Bordering on Chaos*, Salinas and the new president held a tense tête-à-tête at the home of labor secretary Arsenio Farrell in upscale Tecamachalco, just north of the capital, and Carlos agreed to leave Mexico, which he did for the entire Zedillo sexenio.

González Barrera first flew Salinas to Boston, where he sought out his former Harvard maestro Womack for solace, and then across the Atlantic to Dublin, Ireland, an unlikely if Joycean refuge. The deposed Mexican president settled into a wooded estate equipped with a new wife and child. For the next six years, Salinas would relentlessly pull what strings he still had in Mexico to try and clear his bad name.

Back home in the Monstruo, mocking latex heads of the rat-eared "Pelón" (Bald One) were a hot item for the *ambulantes* plying the stalled lanes of traffic on the *ejes*.

ALAS, POOR YORICK

Raul's arrest alarmed Mario Ruiz Massieu, who figured his role in diverting the investigation would soon be public knowledge and hotfooted it for Europe, but Zedillo's people blew the whistle on Salinas's former prosecutor and he was taken off a plane in transit in Newark, New Jersey, by customs agents and charged with failing to declare $20,000 USD that was in his possession when he entered U.S. air space.

The subsequent discovery of a $10 million boodle in a Houston bank account in Mario's name eroded what little credibility he had left. With an electronic ankle bracelet keeping tabs on his every step and drinking heavily, Ruiz Massieu gobbled a bottle of valium and passed on to Mictlán in his home away from home in suburban New Jersey.

Raúl Salinas's role in the Ruiz Massieu job was tangential without the corpus delecti of Manuel Muñoz Rocha, who, phone records revealed, had called him eight times on the day of the killing. Then Mario's replacement, Pablo Chapa Bezanilla, a tough-on-crime big-city D.A., got a huge break: Raúl's tempestuous Spanish ex-bimbo María Bernal, thirsting for revenge because he had dumped her for the wealthy ex-daughter-in-law of Díaz Ordaz, decided to spill the beans.

When Raúl and María had first set up light housekeeping, they had joined a spiritualist circle that centered on an Iztapalapa-based *vidente* (seer) Francisca Zetina, AKA "La Paca," a stout, indigenous-looking woman much given to turbans and spectral-looking muumuus, who had juice in the local PRI. During a séance in her Iztapalapa home, La Paca had purportedly raised the spirit of Luis Donaldo Colosio so Raúl could apologize for his role in the assassination.

Now La Paca had had a vision: Raúl had beaten the missing Muñoz Rocha to death with an aluminum baseball bat at one of Salinas's homes off Reforma and buried the body at his Cuajimalpa horse farm (both Salinases were Olympic-level equestrians) with the appropriate name of El Encanto (The Enchantment).

On October 8, 1996, with the press as his witness and the curvaceous Bernal poured into a policewoman's uniform by his side, Chapa Bezanilla signaled the earth-mover operator to begin digging behind the horse barn, and sure enough, after an hour of scraping at the earth, the Special Prosecutor was cradling a skull like it was poor Yorick all over again. The only problem was that it wasn't Muñoz Rocha's skull at all—the DNA did not match up. The mystery deepened.

One afternoon during this bizarre skein of events, I wandered over to the Sonora witchcraft market up Circunvalación from La Merced where one is offered *limpias* (spiritual cleansings with an egg), Tarot readings, your fortune read from the palm of your hand, and the future told from a coconut shell, plus a glittering array of esoteric candles and potions and powders. Doves and roosters and goats are kept out back for Santería sacrifices. La Paca had been a frequent customer of Stall 193. I asked the proprietor if he might have any human skulls for sale. "Whole or powdered?" he wanted to know.

"MY LOVER AND MY BEST FRIEND" (An interview with "Xoxi de las Flores"—not her real name)

Xoxi has her rumbo. *She moves between Tepito and La Lagunilla, the Eje Central and the cheap hotels in the Centro Histórico, dispensing her medicine to steady customers. Marijuana is her life-support system, and she spreads it around like it was religion.*

Xoxi sits by the window at La Blanca watching the street for her cuates *and sucking up a* chela. *El Vampiro strolls by and she waves at him with her bottle to invite him in, but he's on his way to play by the Caballito.*

"My people are from the Peñón de los Baños out by the airport. Growing up there was pretty cool. You get used to noise from the airplanes when you grow up with it. After a while, it becomes a natural sound. We thought we were in the country out there. We had pigs and chickens. It's mostly warehouses but people grow corn, squash, beans. There were horses.

"When we climbed up Peñón hill, you could look down on the airport— we were practically on the runways. We got to know all the different kinds of planes. On the patriotic holidays like September 16 and November 20, we were in our glory. There would be air shows and military parades. We lived for the holidays.

"My pop was from '68. He was there at Tlatelolco. He could tell you some stories all right. He had two jobs. In the day, he worked at the Social Security behind the counter. Then he would come home and drive a taxi all night. He was what you call a ruletero—*he drove on a fixed route.*

"My pop really knows the city at night. All the bad places—the bars and the giros negros [*shady enterprises*], La Merced and Tepito and La Viga. He had the Asesina Tamalera [*Tamale Murderer*] in his cab. He would pick her up and take her to where she sold her tamales. She killed her husband and her lover and chopped them up and put their meat in her tamales. She ate them herself.

"I told you about the Cannibal of the Guerrero, right? He cooked up his girlfriends and then wrote poems about them. I met him once and he said he was going to write me a poem. I was lucky he never did. They caught him and he hung himself in the Cuauhtémoc delegation lockup. Or maybe the cops did it for him.

"There was a lot of booze and drugs in the Peñón de los Baños. But I didn't know about it. All my cousins and my big brothers kept their eyes on me. I was their baby sister and they protected me. I never knew what la mota was.

"We started to go to Neza for the dances. The sonaderos played rock on these huge, big speakers. The cops would come and try and break up the street dances and there would be a bronca. Everybody got into it—even the girls. It was la neta, el máximo.

"I met this guy who did tattoos. Let's say his name was Andrés. On one hip Andrés tattooed Tlay Dley Unka, which means ¿qué pasa? or what's going on, in Nahuat. On the other hip, he put a question mark. ¡Qué chido! I still have 'em—wanna see?"

"Well, maybe not right here in the window. . . . "

"That was the first time I smoked la yerba. I loved it from the first hit. It was such a good vibe. I had terrible migraines and it wiped them out like medicine. Ever since then, Mary Juana has been my lover and my best friend—sometimes, my only friend. She helps me to resolve my problems.

"Andrés was my first boyfriend, the first person I had sex with. I was 17 and we were together until I was 20. He taught me about being an artisan. How to make necklaces and pendants with stones and natural materials, and I decided that going around selling my jewelry would be more dignified than going to work for someone else."

Guadalupe the waitress grabs the empty bottle and brings Xoxi another Victoria.

"I was selling from a stand I set up out at the university. A bunch of us artisans out there got together and we traveled around the country doing shows, selling our jewelry, and visiting different Indian communities. One day we met the actress Ofelia Medina. She was with the Zapatistas and invited us to come to Chiapas and meet them. Comandante Tacho came and talked to us. Up until then, I hadn't really thought too much about the revolution. If it came, fine. If it didn't, I had my mota. But meeting the Zapatistas really changed how I thought.

"After that, I wanted to go to all the indigenous places. I took the train to Oaxaca and Veracruz. I went as far north as Real de Catorce and harvested peyote with the Huicholes. I really fell in love with the Huasteca, and I go up there whenever I can get away. I have a little workspace in Xilitla.

"It's so far away from the city. I can get away from all my troubles up there. There's no coca and no chelas. I go down by the river and find seeds and flowers for my jewelry. I can be with myself without any interruptions.

"But here's what's funny. When I'm out there in the country in Xilitla, I really miss the city. Not so much the people or the esmog but the energy. The Monstruo like you call it is the center of the culture and it charges me up *with energy when I'm here. So I don't know. Where do I want to live? In the country or in the city? What do you think, John?"*

THE NEOLIBERAL NIGHTMARE

The gyrations of the neoliberal nightmare had welcomed La Crisis back to the streets of El Monstruo like King Kong on crack. By spring, 10,000,000 Mexicans were not working, most of them in the capital where so many had come looking for work. The lineup of unemployed tradesmen on the west flank of the Metropolitan Cathedral had multiplied tenfold by the first months of 1995.

The return of La Crisis hit Chilangos in the gut, reducing caloric intake for half the population of Mexico City, local health officials told the PANista daily *Reforma*. Marta Reyes, a nurse who had just been laid off at General Hospital, drew off her blood into a syringe and squirted it onto the Zócalo floor in protest her situation. With so many people going hungry, hunger strikes didn't get any attention anymore, she explained to *La Jornada*.

Halfway through '95, hawking those Salinas masks in traffic was one of the few moneymakers in town. Even praying to the Virgin didn't work anymore—vendors of Guadalupana knickknacks out at the Basilica were offering 50 percent discounts.

The banks, in their vampire-like avarice, had tacked on late charges and compounded interest on top of interest, and no one could possibly pay up anymore. Forty percent of all bank loans were deemed uncollectible and 200,000 small businesses went belly-up before 1995 turned a corner into an even bleaker new year. Farmers who had taken out loans hoping to cash in on a NAFTA bonanza that never was, lost everything: the family farms, their ranches, the tractors, their cows. City slickers who had fallen for the NAFTA line sank in the quicksand of bad debt, and their cars and taxis and taco stands, furniture, condominiums, and even their pet cocker spaniels were seized by bank goons. The banks hired off-duty Mexico City cops as repo men, and they broke down doors and waved their pistols around to terrorize debtors' families.

More than 3,000 debtors were illegally imprisoned by the bankers for alleged theft. In an instructive example of just how NAFTA would work, their properties were auctioned off by the U.S.-based LaSalle Associates and the National Real Estate Clearing House.

Desperation was the mood du jour. A despondent farmer in Hidalgo poured gasoline all over himself and lit a match. Others gulped pesticides to end it all. Thirty-three unhappy Chilangos leapt in front of trains down in the Metro, a one-year record, many at the Martín Carrera station hard by the Basilica. Suicide lines were saturated with many more calls than they had clocked in the weeks after the Sismo, when some had lost everything.

SEND IN THE GRANADEROS

Not everyone was ready to throw in the towel. There was plenty of fightback left in a civil society that had stood fast since the earthquake tore the Monstruo apart.

El Barzón, which took its name from a Depression-era ditty (the *barzón* is the strap that attaches the plough team to the plough), got organized overnight and tarred and feathered rural bank officials, drove their herds on major highways to bring traffic to a standstill, and burnt down toll booths.

In El Monstruo, the Metropolitan Barzón squirted superglue into the locks of bank doors, massed in front of the bubble-domed Bolsa on Reforma and refused to let the brokers do business, threw rotting fruit at NAFINSA (small business development) officials on the next block of Isabel la Católica, and melted their credit cards in smoky pyres in the Zócalo. Barzonistas marched through the narrow streets of the Centro in their underwear or less or clad only in classic Great Depression barrels. One day, El Barzón led a fleabag circus the banks had foreclosed on to the great bronze doors of the Bank of Mexico where the elephants left steaming souvenirs for the *banqueros*. CIA sources told *El Financiero*'s Dolia Estévez that the Barzón was more subversive than the Zapatista Army of National Liberation.

What with a dozen daily marches and hordes of ambulantes invading the sidewalks, Camacho's surrogate Manuel Aguilera and Zedillo's new regent Oscar Espinosa complicated the chaos by sending in the Granaderos.

The volume of ambulantes was indeed intimidating. Pedestrians were clipped by cars when they were forced into the gutter because there was no room anymore on the sidewalks to walk. Enraged store owners whose establishments were barricaded by the street commerce hired gorillas with baseball bats to beat the street sellers off. There were perhaps 30 ambulante organizations in the Centro by then, most protected by the demised Guillermina Rico's daughter, Silvia Sánchez, or Alejandra Barrios and her *golpeadores*.

Turf battles were triangulated by the *toreros* (bullfighters), freelancers who threw down a sheet of plastic, laid out their merchandise, and posted lookouts at either end of the street. At the sound of a shrill whistle that signaled the Granaderos were approaching, the toreros swept up their goods and beat it to the next block, laying down a barrage of bottles to cover their retreat. Uninformed pedestrians would swing around a corner and get creamed by a Coke bottle or worse, a Molotov cocktail. The airlines issued warnings cautioning tourists not to book rooms at the Majestic or other downtown hotels.

TIME FOR CRIME

The Monstruo has always run the highest crime numbers in the country—there are a lot more people here to commit crimes against—but between 1994 and 1997, Mexico City suffered the mother of all crime waves. Reported crimes doubled to 720 a day, but at least 50 percent of all crimes committed in the capital were never reported because no one trusted the police—97 percent of all crimes were never solved anyway.

Whereas during and immediately after the earthquake violent crime was reduced to zero, by 1996 a violent crime was being committed ever 44 minutes. That year, for the first time in record-keeping memory, Mexico City homicides exceeded New York's pre-Giuliani numbers. Each day 600 to 800 cars were being stolen in the Metropolitan Zone, many in carjackings that left drivers dead and maimed. You could pull up to a stoplight in the Colonia Buenos Aires, the hot auto parts mecca off the Eje Central, and by the time the light changed, your tires would be gone.

Strong-arm thugs like the *chineros* of La Merced, who threw a Chinese headlock on unwary pedestrians, were local villains. Using an ATM was an invitation to be assaulted, and judging by the number of police helicopters buzzing the Centro every day, bank robberies were at an all-time high. People jumped into those little green "ecological" taxis and were never seen again. Sixty percent of the crimes committed in El Monstruo were thought to be committed by cops and ex-agents, estimated ex–Mexico City D.A. Ignacio Morales Lechuga. There were

37,000 cops on the payroll, one for every 250 citizens, just enough for every Chilango to have his or her own personal *ratero*.

Kidnappings were and are class crimes—no one bothers to put the snatch on the poor. Platoons of security *guaruras* were an essential element of every upscale household in Polanco and Lomas. Kroll Associates bulletproofed your limousine overnight.

In 1995, with the *hampa* (criminal class) overrunning the Monstruo, Zedillo mandated Oscar Espinosa to militarize the police. Enrique Salgado Cordero, a dirty-war general from Guerrero, was placed in command and brought in 11 more generals to police the delegations. Three thousand troops hit the streets in crime-ridden Iztapalapa. Stop & frisk became the order of the day in the slums of the city. People disappeared. Reporters heard rumors of death squads inside the Mexico City police, the so-called "Fraternity." In September 1997, three months before Cuauhtémoc Cárdenas would be sworn in as the Monster's first elected mayor, an elite police unit, the Jaguars, opened fire on six young men in the Buenos Aires colony. Their body parts were later found distributed in the Ajusco.

MURDER ON THE BUS

Oscar Espinosa, a dapper PRI scammer, would be Mexico City's last regent. A 1987 revision of the COFIPE electoral law contemplated the transformation of the Monstruo's ornamental Representative Assembly into a legislative one in 1993. A 1993 revision ordained that the new Legislative Assembly would elect a Mexico City mayor in 1997, restricting Espinosa's term to just three years. When the PRD took control of the assembly in '94, the rules for the 1997 election changed—the new mayor would be elected by popular vote. At any rate, Espinosa had only three years to ransack the city treasury and shower shekels upon his PRI cronies.

Why Oscar Espinosa decided to make dismantling the Ruta 100 bus corporation his first order of business remains a mystery. Ruta 100 had been created back in 1981 from the ruins of the old Alianza de Camioneros octopus by Carlos Hank—Espinosa himself was a Hank disciple and operated under the auspices of the Profe's Atlacomulco group.

One theory is that as Salinas's director of NAFINSA, the new regent had bankrolled the Havre corporation, which manufactured microbuses. The Mariscal family already owned several profitable bus routes and would stand to benefit handsomely if the 6,000 Ruta 100 buses were pulled off the streets.

A second hypothesis centered on the SUTAUR, the Ruta 100 drivers' union, an independent grouping that was a perpetual *espina* in the side of city authorities. When the SUTAUR called a strike May 1, 1989, Camacho had tried to dissolve the union and convert it into a number of decentralized cooperatives—the courts nixed the plan. Meanwhile, the Monstruo was left without surface transportation, and the army had to be called out. Military transports cruised Reforma routes, ferrying office workers to the nearest Metro station.

But perhaps the simplest explanation was that like Adolf Eichmann, Espinosa was just following orders. The SUTAUR was twinned by the rough-and-tumble Independent Proletarian Movement (MPI) under the thumb of Ricardo Barco, a radical type who delighted in torching the Stars & Stripes in front of the U.S. embassy. The Zapatistas had been photographed wearing Ruta 100 uniforms in the Lacandón jungle and Ernesto Zedillo was convinced that SUTAUR was funneling federal subsidies to the EZLN.

Whatever his ulterior motive, Espinosa assembled a bevy of pensioners who charged that the union had swindled them out of their retirement funds (maybe it had), and Barco and 10 other leaders were busted. In March 1995, Zedillo's regent had the bus line (it actually covered nearly 100 routes) declared in bankruptcy. Soon, 28,000 Havre tin-can death traps were navigating the company's old routes. The bus drivers smelled a rat.

Then one night in the spring of 1995, Luis Miguel Moreno, Espinosa's transportation secretary, borrowed a gun (a Taurus .38, made famous by Mario Aburto) from a cop, locked his office doors, and shot himself twice in the heart (TWICE in the heart?), a purported suicide. A month later, the city prosecutor charged with the investigation of the SUTAUR swindle was gunned down in front of his Colonia Anzures home. In June, Judge Abraham Polo Uscanga, who had refused to issue arrest warrants for Barco and the other union leaders, was shot execution-style in Suite 912 of the spooky old office building at Insurgentes South #300—curiously, Barco's MPI had offices in the same building. I'm not going to ask whodunnit again.

Three years later, when Cuauhtémoc Cárdenas was safely established in City Hall, Alejandro López Villanueva, one of the founders of the Francisco Villa Popular Front, was charged by federal investigators with Polo Uscanga's murder, but Cárdenas's D.A., Samuel Del Villar, refused to prosecute. The Panchos had broken their golden rule never to participate in the electoral process in 1997 and helped to bring Cuauhtémoc to power, and Cárdenas, harassed from the right by the PRI and the PAN, could ill afford to offend his base. El Grandote came home to Iztapalapa a free man.

Oscar Espinosa left office when Cárdenas took over City Hall in 1997. Cuauhtémoc put his auditors on Espinosa's bookkeeping and came up with a 400,000-peso shortfall, and the last regent became the first one ever to go to jail—not in Mexico, however. Trying to outrun the law, the PRIista fled to Managua, where Interpol snapped the cuffs on him and he spent the next 11 months in a Nicaraguan hoosegow before being extradited back to Mexico, where Zedillo cut him loose and appointed him secretary of tourism.

STEALING FROM THE LORD

The spring and early summer of 1997 were dappled with little miracles. Apparitions of the Holy Virgin were popping up all over the landscape: in the notch of an oak tree in a small town in Tlaxcala; on a garage door in Orizaba, Veracruz; on the concrete floor of the Hidalgo Metro station a dozen stops southwest of the Basilica itself.

But despite the appearances of her sainted image, the Dark Madonna was in for a rough ride, having been ambushed by the very churchman entrusted with her guardianship. In an interview with a fringe Jesuit quarterly, Father Guillermo Schulemburg, who for 30 years had amassed incalculable lucre as abbot of the Basilica, confessed that he had never accepted the apparition of the Guadalupana to the Indian Juan Diego as a true and verifiable miracle.

Although belief in miracles is not a mandatory article of faith (the Church blesses any subterfuge to steal the souls of the heathen), devotees of the Virgin (about 93 percent of all Mexicans, whether they are Catholics or not) were shocked by the abbot's revelation. *Pintas* denouncing SCHULEMBURG—TRAITOR TO MEXICO! appeared on walls in the vicinity of the Basilica, and priests petitioned the Vatican to declare an odium plebis ("hatred of the people") rap against the abbot. Now over 80, Schulemburg resigned as the Guadalupana's guardian and discreetly retreated to the golf courses of Cuernavaca where he had spent much of the last three decades anyway.

The abbot's abdication was a victory for newly anointed Cardinal Norberto Rivera. The Cardinal, Mexico's top churchman, was widely thought to have orchestrated the transaction, a Machiavellian maneuver to annex the Basilica to the Mexico City diocese, with 25 million faithful the largest under the Holy Mother Church's dominion. For centuries, the Basilica and its surrounding grounds had been autonomous, and the income generated by the most visited shrine in Christendom had accrued to the prelates vested with the promulgation of the Dark Madonna's miracles.

The take was an impressive one. Each year 10,000,000 visitors to the carousel-shaped Basilica and the Guadalupana theme park on the Hill of Tepeyac where Tonantzin once held sway filled the strategically located collection boxes with tons of small coins. Masses were offered on a sliding scale, with the most sumptuous running in the double-digit thousands of pesos, according to a schedule posted in the Basilica basement. The sale of 18,000 consecrated burial crypts had padded the abbot's pockets. Indeed, the Basilica's underground holdings are a prime source of the Church's fortune: Two underground parking lots and the public toilets (1,500 customers a day at one peso fifty a pee) converted the netherworld into a cornucopia of wealth. Pan American armored trucks carried off the loot each morning and evening.

Moreover, the Basilica owned blocks of surrounding real estate, which it leased to enterprising merchants for hefty sums. Fronting the Basilica on the Calzada de Los Misterios, 50 commercial properties, many of them shoe stores ("The Shoe Store of Faith," "The Miracle"), added to the riches piled up in the name of the Holy Virgin. All of these funding sources would now be absorbed by Cardinal Rivera's ecclesiastical jurisdiction.

THE VIRGIN OF THE METRO

It was in the midst of this spiritual uproar that Luciana Castro, a young cleaner at the Hidalgo Metro station, was visited by the newest incarnation of the Mother of the Mexicans. When she was dispatched to clean up a leak near the exit stairs to San Hipólito Church, whose presiding saint San Judas Tadeo is saddled with the burden of satisfying lost causes, the more Luciana mopped, the more the 10-inch coffee-colored stain transmogrified into the image of the Guadalupana, and finally, overcome with religious fervor, she fell to her knees in prayer.

Luciana's supervisors were not persuaded by her piety and scolded the girl and threatened her job. The stationmaster, anticipating that a Virgin sighting would fill the Hidalgo stop with uninvited pilgrims, sent a five-man work crew to eradicate the stain before the word got out, but it resisted their energetic scrubbings. The press showed up to photograph the apparition. Readers debated whether or not it really was La Virgencita.

Finally, Cardinal Norberto's opinion was solicited, and he came down in favor of the smooth functioning of the Metro. The stain was only "a water filtration"—there was no evidence of "a divine presence" on the floor beneath the exit steps. The subway management posted Norberto's considerations upon a large wall sign: THIS IS NOT A MIRACLE. Cops were dispatched to keep the curious moving.

But the faith of the masses is inexhaustible. Thousands came to pray and pay their respects. Doña Juventina Cerda, 83, reaped a small bonanza selling 5-peso roses on the steps up to San Hipólito. Many came to have their lottery tickets blessed (Doña Juventina also sold lottery tickets). "La Virgen has appeared here on the floor because she is humble like us," the old woman told me. Her cousin had recently spotted Christ the King on a wall in Colima, and the apparition could not be obliterated even though the local priest had ordered it painted over. Similarly, no matter how strenuously the Metro crews mopped, Doña Juventina was convinced that Her Sainted Gloria would shine through. She was positive that the Guadalupana's appearance would mean big changes "for the common people."

It should be noted that this holy hullabaloo exploded just two weeks before balloting for the first popularly elected mayor of Mexico City would begin. This connotation was not lost upon those who came to worship. "Something is definitely going to happen," Eduardo Martínez, a candy vendor on the station's esplanade, opined. "It will be big like the earthquake only for the good." Student Ramón Santiago, 23, was more explicit: "The appearance of the Virgin means that the PRI is going to lose the election."

The polls were in synch with Ramón's premonitions. The PRI candidate, Alfredo Del Mazo, a Hank protégé and former Mexico state governor, was not favored to win. Neither was the PAN's Carlos

Castillo Peraza, a right-wing intellectual painfully out of his habitat in the no-holds-barred rough-and-tumble of Mexico City politics.

Not all the auguries were Christian ones. In the Zócalo, Itza Cuauhtli, a red-haired *conchero* drummer and dancer, was sure a change was in the wind: "Everyone is feeling that it is coming." How would we know this change? "The change will be made in Nahuat," Itza assured me. It didn't hurt that the favored candidate, Cuauhtémoc Cárdenas, shared the name of the last Aztec emperor.

A week before the July 6 election date, a singular mishap underscored Itza Cuauhtli's prediction when the military honor guard assigned to raise the Mexican flag on the monumental flagpole in the dead center of the Zócalo unaccountably hoisted the standard upside down. Although the flag was quickly reeled down, in accordance with long-standing prophecy, as Marco Rascón pointed out in his weekly *Jornada* column, reversing the position of the eagle and the snake and the nopal bush assured Cuauhtémoc of victory.

EL PETATE DEL MUERTO

Misael González was up early on election morning sweeping out his cinder-block home in the Lomas de La Era colonia of the Iztapalapa delegation. Deputized as a vote monitor by the Alianza Cívica, a prominent election watchdog organization, Misael had sent his family off to stay at his mother's for the day so he could better coordinate the crew of observers, myself included, whom he would dispatch to voting stations where trouble was anticipated. Four phone lines had been installed to handle calls from the observers. (Cell phones were not yet in vogue.)

Iztapalapa is the most populous (1.6 million) and poorest delegation within the city limits, with 70 percent of its residents living in and around the poverty line. Although the PRI expected a big vote from local garbage workers, Iztapalapa is the home base of the Francisco Villa Popular Front, which controls two enormous housing complexes in the delegation. The Panchos, who ordinarily eschewed electoral politics and in fact burnt all propaganda posted by the PRI, PAN, and PRD at great stinky bonfires, were backing Cárdenas in exchange for future favors. How the delegation voted would determine the outcome of the first election for mayor of the Monstruo.

The highlight on Iztapalapa's religious calendar is its monumental Holy Week pageant, which had been celebrated since a cholera epidemic nearly exterminated the population in the 19th century. On Good Friday, more than a million spectators gather to observe the mock Crucifixion of Jesus Christ—always an Iztapalapa homeboy—atop Estrella Hill, the local Golgotha, and enthusiastically cheer on the phalanxes of Roman centurions while they beat and whip poor Jesus, groaning under the weight of his cruciform gibbet as he and his entourage visit the Stations of the Cross. By July 1997, the centurions had been replaced by 3,000 Mexican army troops installed in this crime-ridden delegation by Espinosa and Zedillo as part of their campaign to militarize the Mexico City police.

The phones began to ring off the hook not an hour into the election. The first anguished calls were from would-be Cuauhtémoc voters out at the vast city-within-a-city Centro de Abastos, a PRI stronghold, which covers 25 hectares of Iztapalapa real estate. Cárdenas's people had tried to vote at a polling station that apparently had been moved to another location but when they tried to vote at the substitute *casilla*, it too had been moved to who knew where, a ploy known as the *ratón loco* in the PRI's arcane quiver of electoral chicanery, because would-be voters spent all day running around like "crazy mice." We jumped in a waiting car and sped over to the produce center, where we would spend the next six hours chasing crazy mice with limited success.

But the PRI's intended dirty tricks were nullified by Cuauhtémoc Cárdenas's overwhelming popularity in a city he had first won in 1988, and by the time the polls closed well after 6:00 p.m., victory was in the bag. Misael González's elation was muted: "I'm glad Cárdenas has won. After 500 years, my neighbors finally woke up. I hope I never have to do this again." But Misael knew he would. "The PRI will never give up."

By midnight, there was no way the PRI bosses at Insurgentes #59 could distort the outcome. Consulta Mitofsky, Televisa's exit pollers, put its seal of approval on Cuauhtémoc Cárdenas's big win, and Del Mazo was figuratively wrapped in "the *petate* of the *muerto*," the straw mats in which the Aztecs bound their dead for burial. The PRD had in fact won 28 of Mexico City's 30 seats in the federal Congress and 38 out of 66 in the local Legislative Assembly, in addition to Cárdenas's landslide. In most races, the PAN had outpolled the PRI, which took just 16 percent of the total vote.

Intermittent rain squalls did not dampen the party in the Zócalo. *"¡Cárdenas Arrasó y El Pueblo Ganó!"* bellowed the PRDistas, echoing the chants of a dark night nine years previous when the Institutionals still had the wherewithal to steal an election. *"¡Muere El PRI!"* the crowd rumbled, and the party that had ruled Mexico for the better part of the 20th century lay down to die. It was indeed the beginning of the end of the dynasty.

But other deaths were on my mind that night. I had brought with me a list of the 500 assassinations that the Left had endured beginning with Ovando and Gil on election eve 1988, and I circled the rain-swept plaza reading the names of the martyrs aloud like a human shroud. A former colleague caught up with me and questioned my journalistic objectivity.

For a decade, Cárdenas and the Party of the Democratic Revolution had been the long-suffering opposition. All that had changed forever with Cuauhtémoc's victory. Now the perpetual losers would be charged with administering the most crime-ridden, corruption-saturated, chaotic, and contaminated monster in the known universe. It didn't compute.

The rain spat down from the dim heavens. Pablo Moctezuma, a founding member of the CONAMUP, and I gazed at City Hall in pensive silence. In 10 years we had marched and shouted and struggled and been abused so often that we had gotten used to it. "But we have always been the opposition," I blurted, overcome at the idea of governing the Monstruo. "Don't worry John," Pablo comforted me. "So long as we stay out here on the Zócalo, we will still be the opposition."

Six months later, Cuauhtémoc designated Pablo Moctezuma the chief of the Azcapotzalco delegation as the urban popular movement took over the administration of the city, and the PRD was no longer the opposition. The party's undertakers took measurements for its own *petate del muerto.*

XV

LEFT CITY

The Left has governed the great cities of the world before. Paris, Marseilles, Madrid, London under Red Ken, have all succumbed to the siren song of the Left at odd moments in the not too distant past. Barcelona was in fact once governed by committees of anarchists. Rome, Milan, and Naples have fallen under the Red Thumb. Stalinist proxies ruled Prague and Warsaw and Budapest and the traffic flow kept moving. The Communists took the garbage out in Moscow.

I lived in Lima under a Communist mayor named Barrantes, and he was the most beloved politician in town. Montevideo and Buenos Aires have lately been run by the Left without a noticeable diminishment in public services. The Brazilian experience is instructive. Backed up by the strength of Lula's Party of Labor, the Left was repeatedly reelected in Fortaleza and Puerto Alegre until Lula himself took the presidency and his party began to lose elections. Marta Suplicy, a savvy pluralistic lawyer, won São Paolo, the continent's second-largest megalopolis, but was overwhelmed by the city's unmanageability and subsequently lost it to a right-wing multimillionaire. Even in the belly of the beast, Milwaukee, Wisconsin, once elected a string of socialist mayors.

Arguably, the Monstruo was a different animal. With its supersize physical handicaps largely provoked by Hernán Cortez's ill-fated decision to rebuild Tenochtitlán in this cursed geography, Mexico City was more a force of nature than an urban migraine to be rationally mitigated. The Monster was powered by its own internal contradictions. It could not be made to wear the bridle of the Left or the Right. El Monstruo had no political party, or perhaps it was its own political party. Those who sought to rule here had to make peace with the beast. There were certain protocols to follow. As in all 12-step programs, those who claimed to be in charge had first to admit that they had no power over El Monstruo. Once that was established, negotiations could begin.

When the Left wins cities, expectations soar. It is presumed that left governance will favor those with whom it enjoys class affiliations—the workers, women, the powerless—but the higher the expectations, the deeper the disappointments. The sheer inertia of the city as monster is daunting. Resistance to change is so stubborn that it may take years to make a dent, a span the electoral calendar does not permit. The Left wins cities and loses them right back because the election is seen as *botín*, best translated as a "prize" or better yet, the cash taken in a bank heist. The Left fills city halls with party hacks who salivate at the juicy opportunities for personal profit dangled before their greedy eyes. The Left plays ideological favorites without regard to competence, dispensing plums to the party's clientele and indulging in wild populist giveaways that break city budgets.

The Left loses cities when it regards them as stepping-stones to higher political power, even presidencies. Most of all, the Left loses when it hordes power, isolates itself from civil society, and refuses to share the responsibilities of governing with El Pueblo.

The Left loses when it prevents the popular classes from making decisions that promote their own welfare. The Left loses when it merely dispenses *chamba* (work) without creating the mechanisms to collectivize energies, whether they be block committees or neighborhood cultural centers, local soccer teams, police watchdog commissions, environmental brigades, "economic kitchens" to feed the hungry, day care co-ops, barrio radio stations, even carpooling. The Left must build power from down below, block by block, enlisting the skills of the Lalo Mirandas and Magda Trejos and creating a culture that rejects top-down dictates. The Left must combat alienation and help urban dwellers not to be strangers to the destinies of others. Finding commonalities and defending the commons are the principles that define a left city. Sadly Cuauhtémoc Cárdenas, the son of the Tata, didn't have the slightest notion about how to turn such fine words into deeds.

SNUBBING CÁRDENAS

When Elías Contreras, a long-dead Zapatista fighter turned private eye, was packing for his first visit to Mexico City to investigate the whereabouts of "El Malo" (The Bad One) and "La Maldad" (The Evil), Subcomandante Marcos took great pains to warn him about the dangers that await him in El Monstruo, the Sup's term of endearment for Mexico City. "Beware of the Chilangos. The only time they ever work together is when they are playing dominoes in pairs," the ski-masked rebel leader cautions in *Muertos Incómodos* (Incommodious Dead Guys), a novel Marcos penned jointly with the writer of noir fiction Paco Ignacio Taibo II.

On September 14, 1997, a Zapatista delegation of 1,111 arrived in the maw of the Monstruo two months after Cárdenas's victory and just in time to celebrate Mexican Independence Day. The stated purpose of this adventure was to impress upon the Mexican Congress the urgency of shaping into law the accords reached February 16, 1996, with the Zedillo government at San Andrés Larráinzar on the mal gobierno's maps and Sakamch'en de los Pobres on the Zapatistas', which guaranteed limited autonomy for Mexico's 57 distinct Indian peoples.

The congressional balance had shifted significantly in the July elections. For the first time since 1928, when the PRI first took flight, the combined representations of the opposition PAN and PRD now constituted a slim majority over the Institutionals in the lower house—although the parties would rarely vote together.

Up in the towers on Insurgentes North, behind the tinted windows, the PRI mafia fought tooth and nail to prevent the seating of the new Congress, but El PRI had one foot in the grave and could not summon the black magic to avoid the inevitable.

Subcomandante Marcos's schemes often harbored ulterior motives, and the arrival of the 1,111 was also designed to challenge the ascendancy of the electoral Left. The Zapatistas had no faith in the political parties, chastising them for dividing and corrupting indigenous communities. The PRD, which the skeptical rebels viewed as nothing more than a PRI schism, was singled out for particular venom. Cárdenas's triumph and the PRD's advances in the Congress cried out to be challenged. For the Sup, there was no room in the Mexican political moment for more than one Left.

I was privileged to accompany the 1,111 up to the capital from San Cristóbal de las Casas, a weeklong odyssey as we traversed the southern states of the Mexican union in 38 Gran Turismo buses. We entered the Monstruo from the south and encamped in the Indian delegations of Milpa Alta and Xochimilco much as General Zapata had 82 years previous, before setting out for downtown. As dusk fell on the 14th, 1,111 Zapatistas lined up at the foot of the Paseo de La Reforma on the edge of Chapultepec Park for the mandatory march to the Zócalo. The Zapatistas are short, "the smallest of the small," and they were dwarfed by the surrounding skyscrapers, luxury hotels, and blinding sheets of neon on the movie marquees that line this Porfirian boulevard. The terror in their dark eyes, framed so dramatically by ski masks and *paliacates*, was tangible as their collective gaze fixated upon the walls of the urban canyon that at any moment might crumble and crush those who moved below. I had seen such unease in the eyes of native peoples before, in the documentary film *First Contact*, which recorded the first penetration of the inner valleys of Papua New Guinea by white devils in airplanes in 1929.

Days on the road had occluded the Mayans' bowels. When the march skirted the Alameda just before entering the old city, the compas broke ranks and made a beeline for the greensward, lowered their pants and lifted their skirts, squatted down under the trees, and shat their rebel brains out in this little patch of rain forest deep inside the belly of the beast.

The highlight of the Zapatistas' agenda in the big city was the formulation of a nonmilitary political wing, the Zapatista Front of National Liberation or FZLN. Marcos had imposed stringent restrictions on membership: The Frentistas could not be members or "adherents" of any other political party—by "any other political party" the Sup meant the PRD.

The convening session of the Zapatista Front of National Liberation was staged in the venerable Salón Los Ángeles, a Colonia Guerrero dance hall with an impossibly warped floor ("You Don't Know Mexico Until You Know El Salón Los Ángeles") upon which Chilangos had mamboed and tangoed and danzóned for generations.

Despite the EZLN's anti-PRD verbalistics, Cuauhtémoc Cárdenas showed up early at the conclave to welcome the rebels to the city he would soon govern (he would not take office until December). The Son of the Tata was accompanied by his aging mother, Doña Amalia, widow of Lázaro. The two sat there in the Salón Los Ángeles awaiting the Zapatistas for several hours, from 11:00 a.m. to 2:00 p.m. on my timepiece. The 1,111 never arrived for Cárdenas to welcome. Finally, their stomachs growling, mother and son abandoned the Salón for *comida corrida*. Not 20 minutes later, 1,111 Zapatistas assembled outside and marched into the dance palace.

HIGH-MINDED WORDS

"The city is not just a geographical or spatial place. It is an essential process of our lives and our history. The city is us and where we come from. To take back the space of the city is to recover for all of us a territory that transcribes our lives."

Cuauhtémoc Cárdenas's inaugural address as mayor was full of such high-minded prose. Attended by a particularly gray-looking Ernesto Zedillo and a host of similarly somber dignitaries, the event was stamped with the embarrassing feel of history.

Because those who had ruled the Monstruo before him had never been elected to the office, even what to call Cuauhtémoc sounded awkward. "Regent" was now a politically incorrect designation. Technically, Cárdenas was the "Jefe de Gobierno"—the Chief of Government—but most Chilangos thought of him as an *alcalde* (mayor) or even *presidente municipal*, even though the capital hadn't been a municipality in 60 years. Others could not avoid the Aztec term for ruler, *tlatoani*, the last of which had also been named Cuauhtémoc.

But whatever his title, Cárdenas's time would be short—only three years before new elections, 1,100 days in which to eradicate seven decades of the PRI's perfect dictatorship, not to mention millennia of mismanagement by those who had preceded the PRI in office.

The high-mindedness of Cuauhtémoc's ascension was abruptly deflated the moment Cárdenas descended the steep steps outside the great doors of the Legislative Assembly onto Donceles Street, where milling PRI ambulantes let fly with a *tomatazo* that soiled his crisp blue suit. It was the first pitch of a three-year siege that might best be described as government by crucifixion.

The persecution of Cuauhtémoc Cárdenas by the inmates of this urban asylum often tended toward the grotesque. No wonder that when Salman Rushdie visited Mexico City in January 1999, the final year of Cuauhtémoc's martyrdom, to inaugurate the House of Sanctuary for refugee writers on a leafy street in the Condesa, Cárdenas discovered a kindred spirit. Both men had suffered grievously the fatwas of evil ayatollahs.

GOVERNMENT BY CRUCIFIXION

For starters, during his first week in office, Cuauhtémoc Cárdenas had to dismantle his own office. So many bugs were discovered under the rugs that the floorboards had to be pried up. Wires trailed everywhere. Surveillance cameras were found embedded in the walls behind the dusty portraits of dead regents, a gift from the last of them.

Espinosa and his boys and girls had cleaned out City Hall, erased the hard drives on the computers or just taken the computers home for personal use. The fleet of city vehicles had been gravely depleted, many cars and trucks cannibalized for parts.

Paco Taibo II, who was charged with setting up cultural programs in the delegations for the new government, complained that the PRIs had absconded with all the typewriters, the furniture, even the toilet paper.

A report issued by the new government in February 1998 characterized the state of the city it had received from Espinosa as "deplorable." An audit of the books revealed gross anomalies such as hundreds of "aviators," employees on the city payroll who had never been obligated to even show up for work. About $4,000,000 USD appeared to have disappeared into a "media relations" slush fund with which Oscar Espinosa, who had been quickly named Zedillo's tourism minister, had bought off the press, handing out fat weekly *chayos* or *embutes* or *sobres* to ensure uncritical coverage.

When Cuauhtémoc decreed an end to such bribery, the prensa vendida declared war. Front-page photos of the Son of the Tata more resembled Frankenstein or the Mummy than the first elected mayor of Mexico City. TV cameras captured him in the most unflattering light, his dewlaps flapping angrily as he elbowed his way through the mobs of PRIistas who blocked the doors of City Hall during working hours. TV Azteca reduced the Jefe de Gobierno to a ridiculous hand puppet named "Cuauhtémochas." When Cárdenas rescued 21 street urchins from the *coladeras*, soldered the storm drains shut, and shipped the waifs off to Cancún for rehabilitation, an Azteca "information force" assaulted the shelter where the kids were being treated and made a huge stink about "freedom of the press" after the doctors denied them access to their young patients.

No administration had ever been treated with such rudeness by the press pack. "CHAOS," the afternoon papers would scream in 30-point type. When Cuauhtémoc flew up to Monterrey on city business, Televisa Evening News led with "One Million Without Water as Cárdenas Abandons City." From his getaway in Dublin, Carlos Salinas financed an anti-Cárdenas daily, *Crónica*.

Labor hassles dogged the new mayor. During his first month at City Hall, the auxiliary police suffered a bogus bout of "blue flu" and Espinosa's microbus drivers stalled-in in rush hour traffic to back up demands for a fare hike. The PRI's last best bet to destroy the Ingeniero before he got out of the gate was the SUTDF, the city workers' union, with 112,000 members the most powerful city employees' union in Mexico.

Lifetime leaders loyal to the mummified Fidel Velázquez threatened to shut down the Metro. Cuauhtémoc Gutiérrez, one of 50 sons of Rafael the Garbage King, suspended trash collection. The PRIistas made it clear that they could drown the Monster in sewage with a mere twist of the valves if they did not get what they wanted. Cárdenas had no choice but to buy labor peace, handing the SUTDF a blanket 18 percent raise, double what Zedillo had allowed the unions. The President's inflation gurus attacked the Chief of Government as a criminal populist.

Crime did not take a holiday. Carjackings and bank jobs and kidnappings (Daniel Arizmendi, AKA "The Earchopper," was active in the near suburbs) dominated the prime-time newscasts. Televisa and Azteca promoted true crime shows like *Duro y Directo* and *Naked City* and paid thugs to snatch purses while they filmed the *gente decente* being stripped of their belongings. John Peter Zarate, a Cushman & Wakefield real estate salesman, was murdered by the gang of "Chucky," a demented *taxista* who bore a certain resemblance to the homicidal movie doll—it didn't calm matters much when a Mexico City judge cut El Chucky loose on the grounds that several witnesses had been tortured by overzealous investigators. Don King, in town to conspire with Mexican boxing czar José Suleiman, had his Rolex ripped off in traffic. King thought he got off easy—the Rolex gang, as the scandal sheets dubbed them, sometimes maimed their victims. Paco Stanley, the TV "comedian" had two of his Rolexes so snatched.

THE MARTYRDOM OF SAINT PACO

The cauldron of fear and loathing finally boiled over June 7, 1998, when the aforementioned Paco Stanley was whacked in the parking lot of a glitzy taquería, El Charco de las Ranas (The Frog Pond), off the Periférico. TV Azteca, to whom the "comic" was under contract at the moment, broke into regular programming to call for Cárdenas's resignation. "Where is the authority? Why do we pay taxes? Why do we need elections? Enough of this impunity, ineptitude, and indifference to the citizens! We have come to the limit!" Azteca owner Ricardo Salinas Pliego thundered on air 20 minutes after the slaying. TV Azteca host Jorge "The Paleface" Gil had also been wounded in the whacking.

The network's ratings, which had been in the outhouse, zoomed to World Cup levels (48 percent viewership), a number never before achieved by Azteca, which Salinas Pliego (no relation) had bought with $29,000,000 of Raúl Salinas's (no relation) ill-got gains after the government stations were privatized by Carlos Salinas (no relation) in 1989.

Paco Stanley had achieved a following at Televisa before jumping to Azteca in the midst of a vicious ratings war, and both networks proclaimed the "comedian" had been martyred and cried out for justice. Actually, labeling Stanley a comedian stretched the job description—his humor was grounded in savage attacks upon his straight man or *patiño*, Mario Bezares. Bezares was said to greatly resent his blue-eyed boss not only for making him out a fool but because Mario's own blue-eyed son was thought to have been fathered by Paco. (Conveniently, Mario the Patiño was otherwise occupied in the men's room snorting up a gram of cocaine when out in the Frog Pond parking lot, a shaven-headed hit man with a drooping Fu Manchu mustachio approached the passenger side of Stanley's black Lincoln Navigator and put four bullets in his mush.) In addition to Gil, a busboy and an insurance salesman were mowed down when the gunman sprayed the car park before escaping over a pedestrian bridge across the ring road.

The electronic lynching of Cuauhtémoc Cárdenas had just begun. Both TV Azteca and Televisa suspended regular programming the next day and offered nine straight hours of withering attack journal-

ism featuring Saint Paco's Gran Guignol funeral at the Panteón Español, which was wall to wall with weeping fans, some of whom threw
themselves into the grave in a futile endeavor to accompany their idol
across the River Styx.

But Saint Paco's martyrdom soon smelled like dead fish. The first
autopsy reports concluded that between his internal organs and his
suit coat pockets, Paco Stanley was in felonious possession of five
grams of cocaine. A grinder to mill up the blow was found in the glove
compartment of the Navigator. The evidence of drug use by its star
employee put the kibosh on TV Azteca's sanctimonious "Just Say No"
anti-drug campaign.

The Saint had clay feet. *Chisme* was soon bubbling that Paco Stanley had been in the habit of sharing his blow with the stars on Televisa, "El Canal de las Estrellas," and distributing drugs in the dressing
rooms of TV Azteca. Speculation that Stanley had been hit for welshing
on drug debts—he had been shot in the face, a telltale sign—tamped
down the adulation. Police investigators soon established that every third day, Paco Stanley had deposited $10,000 USD in a Cayman
Islands offshore account—money he appeared to be laundering for
narco kingpin Amado Carrillo, the "Lord of the Skies," whom the "comedian" called compadre.

Indeed, Stanley and Carrillo had a visceral relationship: They
shared the same plastic surgeon, who had rebuilt both their noses—
the Lord of the Skies was "accidentally" slain by the plastic surgeon
later that summer during a liposuction procedure. Just to compound
the crime, Paco Stanley was found to be illegally in possession of a Judicial Police *charola* (badge) he habitually displayed to cops to squirm
his way out of embarrassing situations.

The Tlatoani countered the calumnies by putting his cigar-
chomping bulldog D.A. Samuel Del Villar on the felons, and Del Villar,
who had once been hired (and fired) by President Miguel De la Madrid
to coordinate his "Moral Renovation" crusade, immediately slapped
the cuffs on Mario Bezares and "El Güero" Gil, eliciting further yelps
of indignation from the two-headed TV demon. A prison informer,
"El Cocinero," who prepared meals for Luis Ignacio Amezcua, the
"King of Methamphetamine," squealed that he had overheard a chat
between the King and a leggy Uruguayan *vedette* (showgirl) implicat-
ing Erasmo "El Cholo" Pérez in the hit, and an all-points bulletin was
issued for the shaven-domed, Fu Manchued gunman.

But with all the principals in the slammer, the Cocinero suddenly flipped, either because of threats on his physical well-being or a better deal from the Feds, and the suspects were ordered released by the courts. Still, the scandal had uncovered such a malodorous mess that both TV tyrants washed their hands of Paco Stanley. To what extent this spectacle had been cooked up by Cárdenas's political enemies in the PRI and the PAN to damage the Son of the Tata's campaign when he tossed his head into the ring for yet another go at the presidency in 2000, remains conjectural.

THE PIECES OF THE PIE

Cuauhtémoc Cárdenas's smooth administration of the Monstruo's affairs largely rested on his ability to corral and co-opt the urban popular movement, a strategy that met with mixed success. Although Cárdenas espoused the concept of converting Mexico City into the 32nd state, he veered away from this commitment when he realized that statehood would translate to a sharp reduction in federal subsidies.

The PRI-run Congress mandated the Last Regent to increase borrowing limits to 11,000,000,000 pesos, and the city debt zoomed by 74 percent. Now in a scheme to cripple Cuauhtémoc's governance, the Congress, in which the hated PRI and the equally odious PAN were kings, put a moratorium on city debt, barring the mayor from borrowing any more money. With his budgets hovering around $40,000,000 USD, most of which was supplied by federal subsidies, Cuauhtémoc couldn't risk biting off the fingers that kept the Monster fed, and the tlatoani chose not to go to the mattresses.

The ability to administer a megalopolis like Mexico City resides in the art of cutting up the pie. Cuauhtémoc Cárdenas doled out pieces of the prize to the constituencies that brought him to power. Under the guidance of PRD president Andrés Manuel López Obrador, who had orchestrated Cárdenas's successful mayoralty campaign, the Left was enlisted to manage the delegations. Pablo Moctezuma took over in Azcapotzalco. Salvador Martínez de la Roca, "El Pino," a '68 student strike hero, was enthroned in Tlalpan, and Arnoldo Martínez Verdugo, onetime captain of the Mexican Communist Party, was installed in Coyoacán—one of Martínez Verdugo's first stunts was to evict squatters from a lot promised to a French supermarket chain.

Contrary to the way Genesis tells the tale, women were the back-bone and not the rib of the urban popular movement, its "natural lead-ers." At least six *veteranas* of the damnificado movement, including Yolanda Tello (Assembly of Barrios) and Virginia Jaramillo (Popular Union of New Tenochtitlán), won seats in the Legislative Assembly—UPNT founder Dolores Padierna and her toxically ambitious hubby René Bejarano had moved up to the Chamber of Deputies.

Political promotion threatened to drive a wedge between the *lideresas* and their bases. Yolanda Tello debunked the possibility of rupture: "How could I abandon my base?" she argued, sitting on her living room sofa on Sol Street in the Colonia Guerrero. "They live right on the other side of the wall." But as the PRD consolidated its hold on power and the civil society was transformed into an electoral cli-entele, the distance between Congress and community could not be bridged, and the strength of the urban popular movement went into steep decline.

In truth, the civil society was confused by its role in this new equa-tion. As the urban dilemma compacted, legislative solutions rather than social activist ones were emphasized. Housing, the soil in which the urban popular movement had first germinated, had become a black hole. Cárdenas inherited an 800,000-unit shortfall from the PRIs, and instead of opting to build popular housing projects in the cen-ter of the city, cleared the earthquake-damaged blocks south of the Alameda and sold off the lots to the Canadian real estate behemoth Reichmann—the "Proyecto Alameda" was aborted when Reichmann cashed out after its London Canary Wharf development crashed in flames.

Under a scheme engineered by Salinas and put into play when the PRI still controlled the Legislative Assembly, rent control was phased out, and the year Cárdenas took office, 20,000 bereft families in the Centro Histórico faced eviction. Indeed, the first eviction of the Cárde-nas era occurred only 34 days after the Engineer was sworn in. Nine families on Donceles, the very street on which Cárdenas had taken the oath of office, were tossed from a building in which most had lived all their lives. The time bomb was ticking. A thousand evictions were car-ried out in 1997, about 90 a month, and 3,237 judgments were obtained in 1998.

In all fairness, it must be noted that the Jefe de Gobierno refused to permit Mexico City police participation in these heartbreaking confrontations, so landlords recruited *golpeadores* from the gang of goons and strikebreakers who gravitated to the steps of the Labor Conciliation Junta in the Colony of the Doctors. Ruffians ransacked apartments for which eviction orders had been obtained from the courts, tossing tenants and their furniture into the street and stealing anything of value they could put their grubby mitts on.

As might have been calculated, the Assembly of Barrios had split just after the urban political movement took over City Hall, and there were now two Superbarrios parading around in canary tights and scarlet capes, so busy accusing each other of being "impostors" that neither had any time to rescue the evictees. In one especially gruesome confrontation on Guatemala Street, in back of the Cathedral where the Spanish government had been invited to raise up a palatial cultural center, ambulantes squatting in a crumbling four-story building fought agents serving court orders with pots of scalding water and buckets of feces until the Granaderos were sent in to subdue the squatters. The violent eviction was hardly Cuauhtémoc's finest hour.

LET THEM EAT CAKE

January 6, Epiphany on the Anglo Christian calendar and Día de los Reyes (Day of the Magi) on the Hispanic one, commemorating the arrival of the Three Wise Men in Bethlehem with their gifts of gold, frankincense, and myrrh for the Christ child, is Mexico's antidote to U.S. Christmas. To honor the date and usher in his final year as Mexico City's first elected *tlatoani*, Cuauhtémoc celebrated with a Guinness Book of Records *rosca*.

The traditional rosca is a kind of oval-shaped coffee ring slathered with slivers of dried fruit. Cuauhtémoc's record-breaking rosca stretched from the Zócalo up 20 de Noviembre Street for seven blocks all the way to Izazaga near the Pink Line Metro station, 1,749 meters (more than a mile) long. The fluffy cake was confected from 9,033 kilos of flour and larded with 2,300 kilos of sugar (Mexicans have Guinness Book of Records incidence of diabetes) and fed tens of thousands—I myself, an observant diabetic, enjoyed a slice.

No stats appear to have been kept on the number of cake-eaters who chipped teeth or choked to death by swallowing the hundreds of plastic Baby Jesuses embedded in the rosca—the tradition of embedding the Baby Jesuses has roots in the Middle Ages, when a fava bean would be inserted in the dough to symbolize the hiding of the Christ child from Herod's spies.

Long-standing custom has it that those who bite down on a Baby Jesus are obligated to throw a tamale party for their friends a month hence on Candelaria (February 2), a feast that marks the day the alleged Messiah's parents brought him to the temple in Jerusalem. In a similar ritual, the Christians of Mexico City swaddle their life-size porcelain Baby Jesus dolls, the stars of family *nacimientos* (nativity scenes), in new clothes and carry them to their parish priests to be blessed.

When I board a Metro car on Candelaria Day, so many señoras are cradling their frozen-eyed Jesus dolls on their way to Mass that I can never get a seat.

DISTINGUISHED VISITORS

Salman Rushdie was not Cuauhtémoc Cárdenas's only distinguished visitor during his final year in office.

When Don Pedro Jasso, an octogenarian Huachichil Indian farmer whose fields had been invaded by two wily San Luis Potosí swindlers named Juan, decided to go up to the Big City to visit the tlatoani and explain the situation to him, he did not have a hard time convincing his pal Chaparro Sancho ("Shorty Cuckolder"), a 16-year-old doe-eyed burro with a soft white underbelly and antenna ears, to accompany him. In fact, Chaparro Sancho was already two kilometers down the road when Don Pedro and his sons caught up with him.

Don Pedro and Shorty Cuckolder arrived in El Monstruo in mid-1998 and set up a tent on the Zócalo floor facing the National Palace. Animal stories bring out the best in the press pack, and when City Hall reporters got wind of Chaparro's raucous heehawing, they drifted over to see what all the noise was about. Don Pedro and Shorty Cuckolder soon were featured on front pages around the nation, emblems of the plight of Mexico's campesinos who had suffered so grievously under NAFTA's lashings.

By 1999, Shorty Cuckolder was the most famous burro in the land. Dozens of groupies lined up each day with carrots and cabbages and *elotes*, hard candy and stale tortillas, to ingratiate themselves with the celebrated donkey and shake Don Pedro's callused hand in solidarity, proving once again that inside every Chilango heart, a campesino lurks.

But Chaparro's growing fame had a dark side. The British Donkey Protection League, a bunch of foreign do-gooders, decided Shorty Cuckolder was being exploited and mistreated, and kidnapped the noted burro "for his own good." With his partner held incommunicado at the UNAM Veterinary School (which eventually gave Chaparro Sancho a clean bill of health), Don Pedro appealed to the mayor, Cárdenas negotiated the donkey's release, and he soon rejoined the old farmer on the Zócalo. The Mayor offered his good offices to intervene on Pedro and Chaparro's behalf and spoke with the governor of San Luis Potosí, and an agreement was worked out that involved the incarceration of the evil Juanes.

We said godspeed to Don Pedro and Chaparro Sancho at a farewell gathering on the Zócalo in June 1999, and they began their long trek north. Several months later, one of Pedro's sons called with alarming news. Shorty Cuckolder had keeled over dead in a nearby field. The hero burro had never gotten used to being back home in the country after his fling with fame in the big city. Don Pedro's son thought that Chaparro was fatally homesick for El Monstruo.

FLYING THE RAINBOW FLAG

Cuauhtémoc Cárdenas demonstrated a vocation for celebrating diversity. Under his brown hand, gays and lesbians won legal recognition from the Mexico City Assembly when local lawmakers, among them the nation's first openly lesbian legislator, Patria Jiménez, passed an ordinance barring discrimination based on sexual preference.

Cardinal Norberto was livid at the prospect that the Assembly might soon pass legislation legitimizing same-sex marriage or civil union (*sociedades de conveniencia*). "Toleration of homosexuality puts our children at risk of becoming homosexuals themselves," the churchman railed at Sunday sermons in the Cathedral. Gays and lesbians responded by staging a pilgrimage to the Villa to ask the Guadalupana for benediction. Rainbow flags were unfurled inside the Basilica.

The Monstruo's gay and lesbian community had been out of the closet since Stonewall, although the first Pride March didn't go public until 1979, instigated by, among other pioneers, Luis González de Alba, a '68 strike leader who ran a gay bar in the Zona Rosa, El Taller.

Under Cárdenas's auspices, the annual Gay, Lesbian, and Transgender Parade stretched for blocks, featuring rainbow flag–draped contingents of queers and dykes and floats (*carros alegóricos*) sponsored by the gay bars, packed with disco-dancing drag divas. Even the traditional family restaurants in the Centro Histórico, homophobic by nature, flew rainbow flags to attract partygoers.

Nonetheless, homophobia was epidemic in the city and the country that takes its name. The AIDS scourge stigmatized all those infected as homosexuals, and migrants returning from El Norte with HIV were often shunned by their families and packed off to Mexico City for the meager treatment the federal government offered to victims of the plague, known as SIDA by its Mexican initials or simply the "Gringo Disease." The murder of gay SIDA doctor Francisco Estrada in Coyoacán in 1992 galvanized the capital's gays and lesbians. Between 1995 and 2000, 213 murders of homosexuals were recorded nationally, about one a month in Left City.

DON QUIJOTE LEAVES CITY HALL

Inspired by the example of his amigo Luis da Silva, who unsuccessfully ran for the presidency of Brazil three times before achieving a positive outcome, Cuauhtémoc Cárdenas, the Son of the Tata, whom destiny had doomed to follow in his father's footprints, once again declared his determination to become president of the Mexicans and turned the keys to City Hall over to his second in command, Rosario Robles, who in October 1999 became the first woman to govern the biggest city in the Western world.

As mayor, Cuauhtémoc had been a big disappointment. Expectations had far exceeded accomplishments, but his not-quite-thousand-day experiment in trying to run the Monster from the Left was not the flat-out *fracaso* Televisa and the prensa vendida made it out to be, a spin that had everything to do with undermining his presidential candidacy.

Cuauhtémoc Cárdenas committed many errors but he also committed many acts of nobility. He dedicated his administration to promoting diversity and the taking back of public spaces, and the Zócalo beneath his windows was often replete with civic activities that ranged from Festivals of Tolerancia to Chess Day, when the plaza floor became an enormous chessboard and 5,000 games were played simultaneously, another Guinness Book of Records record. Among other good works, Cárdenas shut down a notorious women's prison in Iztapalapa and transformed it into a school for adult women and a shelter for the abused.

With his long face and skeletal physique, Cuauhtémoc Cárdenas seemed more a Quijote tilting at the windmills of power than the reincarnation of his warrior namesake, but without his cautious initiatives, the Monstruo would never have become Left City. Those who followed him in this job owe him much more than the faint praise they offer.

LA JEFA MEETS THE ULTRAS

Rosario Robles would govern the city through the 2000 general elections. Behind her girlish bangs, La Jefa was a good-looking, bad-talking, backbiting, self-described "pushy woman" driven by ill-concealed ambition to rise to the pinnacles of power. She took over City Hall at a particular messy moment.

In the spring of 1999, Zedillo's technocratic UNAM rector Francisco Barnes ("El Barney") raised tuitions 3,000 percent. Granted, students had shelled out only 50 cents Americano per semester for generations, but the steep jump put a burden on middle-class families who had three or four kids in the university system.

The Left viewed Barnes's tuition hike as a naked grab to privatize public education. NAFTA had opened the floodgates to educational entrepreneurs, often U.S. derived, and the number of private *prepas* and *patito* (bogus) universities was peaking. Upping tuition at the UNAM reflexively sparks student strikes, and a strike committee was formed, classes were suspended, red and black flags were hung up, and the students moved in and took over their faculties.

The last foiled ploy by the university management to restrict enrollment by pricing education beyond the reach of the masses had come under rector Jorge Carpizo in 1986–1987 but was rolled back by leftist students, many of whom were now apparatchiks in the PRD and at City Hall. But the CEU, as the '80s strike committee initialed itself, had failed to stop Carpizo's intent to abolish the automatic pass, and a standardized exam was now mandatory for admittance to the university system, a change that drastically reduced open enrollment. Now 100,000 young people were rejected by the UNAM system each year, and the *rechazados* had become a social force to be reckoned with.

To some, like 19-year-old José Antonio Hernández, who leapt to his death at the Talismán Metro stop in 1999, rejection by the UNAM was the last straw. Others, like my young reject pals Tony, Manuel, and Carlos, just dropped out, tuned in, and turned on. "We're beatniks like you now," Tony giggled, passing me a joint in the narrow alley between the Palace of Mining and the still-gilded central post office where the three were hawking their poems off a blanket.

El Barney's initiative stirred the stench of '68, and for once Zedillo caught the drift. Tuition hikes were put on hold. Several months later, Barnes would tender his resignation, not entirely of his own accord. But the students had won their key demands much too easily. Many activists thought it must be a trick. The General Strike Committee (CGH), a freakish reincarnation of the '68 CNH, continued to push the envelope. Brigades of strikers, their nearly naked bodies smeared with red and black paint, advanced on the Periférico ring road at rush hour on October 12 and mooned the motorists. Cárdenas, about to turn power over to Robles, made the monstrous mistake of sending in the Granaderos, who ground the students into the roadway as if they were so many hamburger patties.

The perverse spectacle of a Left city government crushing student rebellion radicalized the strikers. One front-page photo highlighted a Granadero with his boot firmly planted on the neck of a demonstrator. The "revolutionaries" on the General Strike Committee joined forces and physically ousted the "reformers." Ideological diversity in the CGH was reduced to regular ultras and ultra ultras. Among the celebrated leaders of the latter were masked young men known as "El Mosh" and "El Gato" and "El Diablo." Punches were tossed and bones broken at overheated all-night meetings in the Che Guevara auditorium. Vendida or not, the press was bodily excluded from these melees. To prevent the more moderate band of ultras from seizing the microphone, barbed wire was strung up from one side of the podium to the other.

When Rosario Robles, an UNAM political science professor in real life, bumbled into this snake pit offering to mediate, she became Public Enemy #1. Determined not to repeat her predecessor's gaffe, Rosario kept the cops at bay and was threatened with impeachment by the PAN and the PRI for not doing her duty to repress the students.

The mess dragged on into the new millennium. With the 2000 *presidenciales* already under way, Zedillo designated psychiatrist Juan Ramón de la Fuente, a smooth operator, as the new rector and sent in the militarized federal police (PFP), much as had Díaz Ordaz back in 1968. On February 6, 2000, 2500 robocops invaded University City and surprised the strikers at a CGH plenary session. They hauled 745 mostly young people off to gaol (Lecumberri was no longer available), and after 321 days, the Great Strike to Defend Public Education was broken.

But 2000 was not 1968 all over again. The pent-up social pressures that reached critical mass back then were more dispersed now—one proof of which was that the Left ran Mexico City. Zedillo's crackdown turned into Tlatelolco Lite, and all the strikers save for El Mosh, El Gato, and El Diablo were released quickly. The red and black flags came down and UNAM reopened for business.

The most aggravating irony of the Great Strike of 1999–2000 to Defend Public Education was that with the National University shut down, enrollment at private schools increased more than it ever had. Phony *prepas* and *colegios* now filled 75 pages of the Mexico City yellow pages.

SUPER ROSARIO

Robles proved an agile, publicly affable advocate for women's empowerment. She sprang into action by introducing an abortion-on-demand measure in the Mexico City Legislative Assembly, where the PRD held the upper hand. Across the Zócalo, Cardinal Norberto damned Rosario from his Sunday bully pulpit and threatened any legislator who voted up her proposal with swift excommunication. Pro-*vida* fanatics under the whip of Jorge Limón Serrano knelt on the sidewalk outside City Hall to say rosaries for Rosario. One sign read HITLER IS NOT DEAD AS LONG AS ROSARIO ROBLES IS ALIVE!

In the end, because 2000 was a presidential election year and abortion on demand was still a problematic issue in the capital, the PRD withdrew the initiative but reintroduced it under López Obrador's incoming administration, where, despite Norberto's sanctimonious tantrums, it was finally ratified, and beginning in 2007 the service was offered to all women, free of charge, in the first trimester of an unwanted pregnancy.

But the right-to-lifers fought on. National Human Rights Commission ombudsman José Luis Soberanes, reportedly a member in good standing of Opus Dei, and PANista Attorney General Eduardo Medina Mora appealed the constitutionality of the Mexico City law to an unpredictable Supreme Court, and pro-choicers feared for the worst. Astoundingly, God for once came up on the side of a woman's right to control her own body, and in 2008 the 11-member court (nine males) upheld abortion on demand. Cardinal Norberto flipped out and ordered all church bells in Left City to be clanged in mourning. Despite the incessant clamor, López Obrador's successor, Marcelo Ebrard, a protégé of Manuel Camacho Solís, struck a Juárez-like pose and congratulated the Supremes for upholding the principle of separation of church and state.

NO BUSINESS LIKE SHOW BUSINESS

The privatization and transnationalization of movie theater chains and the 10-plex-ation of such venerated pleasure palaces as the Diana and the Palacio Chino had elevated ticket prices into the hundreds of pesos for the average working-class family of five, so Robles and her cultural commissar, poet Alejandro Aura, turned the Zócalo into a free open-air movie theater and filled the bleachers every Saturday night. Challenging the NAFTA-driven Hollywood garbage that was drenching the city's commercial screens with gringo drek, the management of Left City Cinema committed themselves to showing only Mexican-made movies. *Amores Perros* (Dog Loves), Alejandro González Iñárritu's internationally acclaimed raw slice of Chilango life, was first up. But when Rosario invited the masses to view *La Ley de Herodes* (Herod's Law, which loosely translated is "Screw or Be Screwed"), the first first-run Mexican movie to openly lampoon the PRI by name, the men in the tinted glasses up in the towers at Insurgentes #59 cried foul. There was only a month before the July presidential election, and the Mayor was filling a public plaza to besmirch the good name of one of the contenders. Super Rosario refused to cancel the showing and thousands swarmed the bleachers. The chant of "*¡Muera el PRI!*" once again resounded in the Zócalo night.

Rosario Robles's *espectáculos* won her many fans and admirers. As mayor, she was outspoken and outgoing and a lot spunkier than the taciturn Cárdenas. Her feistiness got her into celebrated scrapes with a lot of male authority figures. She was unafraid to step into the ring with President Zedillo. (She refused to accompany him on a tour of the city because he had notified her at the last minute.) She went one on one with Oscar Espinosa and El Barney and Cardinal Norberto and her ex-husband Julio Moguel, a Cárdenas aide-de-camp, and even threatened to throw Pablo Moctezuma in the pokey. But those who knew Rosario too well whispered that she was conniving and over-weeningly ambitious, and she was not much trusted by many on the left side of the PRD.

Nonetheless, when Rosario Robles handed over City Hall to Andrés Manuel López Obrador (AMLO) in December 2000, she had won the hearts and minds of the party rank and file. Indeed no one ever questioned how much of other people's money Robles had spent to opiate the masses until AMLO took one look at the books and blew a fuse.

THE USEFUL VOTE

The cast of characters for the 2000 Mexican presidential passion play included Francisco Labastida, a lackluster, ferret-faced PRIista who had been Zedillo's secretary of the interior and whose uninspired campaign was financed by $110,000,000 USD illicitly abstracted from PEMEX and washed through the oil workers' union into party bank accounts. The barely ruling party was teetering on its last legs and also resorted to a series of Ponzi scheme raffles to raise funds in which the prizewinners were required to return the prizes so they could be raffled off again and again.

The PRI's disintegrating hegemony was challenged by the PAN's Vicente Fox, a handsome 6´4˝ galoot and ex-governor of Guanajuato, who barnstormed the land in a 10-gallon Stetson hat, a brass belt buckle the size of a small frying pan that spelled out F-O-X, and hand-tooled leather boots (his family owned the factory that made them), stomping out the PRI "varmints and critters" and literally cloaking himself in the banner of the Virgin of Guadalupe.

For 16 years, Vicente Fox had sold Coca-Cola to the Mexicans, rising from a route driver in El Bajío to the top of the pyramid to become the Atlanta-based transnational's CEO in Mesoamerica, and he sold himself just like Coca-Cola. Mexico has the highest per capita Coke consumption rates on the planet, so Fox was an easy sell.

Cuauhtémoc Cárdenas was an also-ran from the day he decided to run again. During the course of his third losing presidential campaign, many fair-weather friends deserted the Ingeniero for Fox, who was favored in early polling to finally dislodge the PRI from power. Jorge Castañeda and Adolfo Aguilar Zinser, Cuauhtémoc's former speechwriters, coined the phrase *El Voto Útil* (The Useful Vote) to explain their defections—a vote for Cárdenas would be a vote for a loser. Porfirio Muñoz Ledo perfidiously accepted Fox's offer of an ambassadorship and endorsed him. But the cruelest blow was the desertion of much of the civil society into the PANista camp on the grounds that Fox had the best chance to beat the PRI. Meanwhile, Cárdenas droned on from one campaign stop to the next and it was déjà vu all over again. The 2000 presidential election would be the Son of the Tata's last hurrah.

THE DINOSAUR'S EXTINCTION

Behind tinted windows on the upper floors of the 12-story party bunker, the PRI bosses had grown somber as undertakers, as their paid-for exit pollers called in the numbers from precincts around the country. Early on, it became evident that Labastida was sunk and the longest-ruling political dynasty in the solar system had just lost the presidency of Mexico. The party Don Corleones had known this was coming for a long time, but now it was happening and the enormity of the travesty stunned them.

At dusk, the party bigwigs descended to the esplanade to face the music. His collaborators formed a protective ring around Labastida and marched him into the Plutarco Elías Calles Auditorium, the site of other recent funerary events. The auditorium thrummed with edgy uncertainty. How would all this play out? With a chagrined grin pasted to his thin lips, Labastida confessed that "the results do not favor us." Grown men wept. The compadres collapsed into each other's arms. Suicides and vendettas were contemplated. Around 9:00 p.m., the other shoe dropped when Ernesto Zedillo, speaking on national television from Los Pinos, conceded the PRI's defeat and Vicente Fox's unprecedented victory.

As in the Kübler-Ross model of grief, disbelief was followed by rage, and the bereaved PRIistas shouted menacing imprecations at the outgoing president up there on the big screen. Later,

Zedillo would be threatened with expulsion from the PRI for having conceded what every Mexican knew to be a fact, and he packed up his family and his household furnishings and abandoned Mexico for a sinecure at his alma mater as head of the Yale University Globalization Institute. The last PRI president has rarely returned since.

When I awoke on Monday morning July 3, the dinosaur no longer sat on Mexico's chest and one could almost breathe at last. The day was deep blue and the sun golden in the sky, and even the afternoon acid rain felt cleansing. For once, the colors of the flag belonged to the Mexicans and not the PRI. On Insurgentes, the party slugs were cleaning out their desks; the cubicles emptied out and the banks of fluorescent lights dimmed to black from floor to floor. Chilangos who never spoke to each other greeted their neighbors with high fives. But the euphoria would not last long.

EL PEJELAGARTO

The July 2 *presidenciales* coincided with the election of the Monster's first full-term mayor. The balloting was a referendum on how the Left had managed the megalopolis during its initial three years in command of City Hall, and as expected the PRD's popular mandate was extended—but not by the margin anticipated.

The PRI candidate, Jesús Silva Herzog, son of López Portillo's finance minister, garnered only 14 percent of the vote, another acute embarrassment for the once invincible former ruling party. But the PAN's Santiago Creel, grandson of Porfirio Díaz's foreign minister Luis Creel (implicated in Huerta's plot to assassinate Madero), and whose family once owned a Belgium-size swath of Chihuahua real estate, did much better. Fox's coattails were broad, and part of the civil society held its collective nose and voted for the hated PAN. Moreover, the right-wingers had aligned with the Mexican Green Ecological Party (PVEM), a wholly owned subsidiary of the González Torres family, to co-opt the environmental *voto útil*, and López Obrador edged the PANistas only 39 to 37 percent.

While the PRD nailed down 13 out of the 16 delegations (the PRI was shut out), the PANistas advanced in the Legislative Assembly, although the rightists still could not nullify the leftists' majority. López Obrador's mandate was a mixed one.

I had first met Andrés Manuel López Obrador (AMLO) soon after the '88 mega-fraud. Cárdenas had traveled to Tabasco to endorse
Andrés, who had run his campaign in that southern state and now
was a candidate for governor for the Frente Democrática Nacional.
(The PRD did not exist yet.) We traveled down the delta of broad rivers lined by majestic palm tree groves, visiting the small towns that
dotted their banks, and AMLO introduced the reporters to the local
taste sensation, deep-fried *pejelagarto,* a prehistoric-looking, gar-like
fish that inhabited the swamps and rivers of this oil-rich state. Tabasco
is just down the Gulf from Louisiana, and the two states have much in
common: a sultry climate, corrupt politicians, and a love for fried fish.
The reporters were enchanted by López Obrador's favorite fish dish,
and we dubbed him "El Pejelagarto" in our dispatches, shortened to
"El Peje" by 2006, under which title he would be universally loved or
hated throughout the land, depending upon whom you voted for.

Elected PRD president in 1996, El Peje moved his family from
Villahermosa into a small apartment in Copilco near University City,
where he still lives. As president of the left party, AMLO engineered
Cárdenas's 1997 triumph in El Monstruo and was the anointed frontrunner to succeed him, but whether or not El Peje was a real Chilango
became an issue. The PAN and the PRI argued that El Peje received his
mail in Villahermosa and was not even registered to vote in the city
he would soon govern. López Obrador showed reporters documents
indicating that he had bought the Copilco apartment years before precisely to guarantee legal residency in the city.

With or without the papers, the PRI-PAN argument was mooted
by history—just about every other Jefe de Gobierno or Regente or Tlatoani who had governed the Monstruo dating back to the Emperor
Cuauhtémoc had come from somewhere else.

¡LOS POBRES PRIMEROS!

AMLO's December 5 inauguration was fraught with turbulence, a
sign of conflicts to come. On inaugural morning, looking frighteningly
younger than he does now, Andrés Manuel herded his family—three
young boys and his ailing wife Rocío Beltrán, who would succumb to
lupus in his first year in office—into his battered Tsuru and set off for
the Legislative Assembly. A block from the Eje Central the route was
blocked by a PRI-paid demonstration of police widows who swirled

around the Tsuru, and AMLO and the family had to abandon the old car in traffic. The new mayor eventually arrived at the Assembly on the floor of a taxi.

Vicente Fox, himself freshly inaugurated five days earlier at a contentious session of Congress, was seated in the first row at the ornate old *casona* on Donceles Street and Andrés Manuel locked into his eyes: "Mine will not be a government by and for the elites," he challenged, and a frown spread across The Fox's broad face. Many elites, including Emilio Azcárraga Jean, his father's heir, and Carlos Slim stared uncomfortably into the distance. "In a relationship like ours there will be many discrepancies," the new mayor proposed to the assembled potentates.

From the first words of his administration, López Obrador offered governance grounded in one fundamental principle: "¡Los Pobres Primeros!" (The Poor First!). According to the transcript, AMLO pronounced this phrase 10 times during the ceremony, a spoken acceptance of class war as a fact and reaffirmation that he would run the Monstruo from the Left that soured Vicente Fox and the rest of the Mexican ruling class on El Peje from day one. The rift between the two men elected at the same hour on the same day would widen into a chasm, and the bad milk between them grew into visceral hatred over the next six years.

From the first settlement of mud huts on the desolate island of the Tenochas to the brand-new millennium, El Monstruo has been overwhelmingly inhabited by poor people. The impoverishment had been serial under the Tlatoanis and the Crown and the Church and the Gachupines. When Baron Von Humboldt visited this barrio, he was appalled at the poverty of my neighbors. Tens of thousands of poor slept underfoot in the public way, he notes in his diaries, yet Mexico is an immensely rich country with more than a hundred millionaires. Whether ruled by liberals or conservatives, Don Porfirio or the rebel armies of Villa and Zapata, the proletarian president Lázaro Cárdenas, the Mexican "miracles" of the Alemán era, or the neoliberals who came next, the poor of El Monstruo have always been in the majority. Decades of PRI despotism purposefully made sure that the poor stayed poor, so that they would be dependent on the mal gobierno and vote to keep the Perfect Dictatorship in power year after year. The city that Andrés Manuel López Obrador had just inherited was just as poor as it had always been.

The numbers were illuminating. Seventy percent of the Monstruo's 8,483,623 Chilangos registered in the 2000 census earned less than three minimum salaries daily, about $12 USD a day, the official poverty line—3,200,000 earned less than two. Around 5,000,000 lived in moderate poverty and another million in extreme poverty. Out of every 100,000 children born, 470 died before their fifth birthday of diseases related to malnutrition—2,000,000 poor kids were at risk. Thirteen thousand *niños de la calle* lived in the streets. Some 12,400 unhoused Chilangos packed the shelters each winter night; uncounted thousands bedded down in the back alleys. And 600,000 elderly citizens of the Monstruo had no pensions and no source of income. The hungry circled around the refuse bins outside the fast-food franchises here in the Centro Histórico scavenging for scraps.

A beleaguered middle class trapped between rampant consumerism and diminished expectations accounts for another 20 percent of El Monstruo's population. Those considered wealthy, the really *ricos*, constitute only 3 percent of the total census. The gap is unbridgeable. Less than 10 percent of the population owns 75 percent of the city real estate, eats most of its food, and drinks up most of its water (1,000 liters per household per day, as opposed to 200 in middle-class and more proletarian sectors).

From what we can see from down below, the ricos live vacuous lives in heavily protected enclaves. An aerial spread shot by *Proceso* photographer Ulises Castellanos is revealing: The tiled roofs of Taj Mahals and marble palaces set in pristine forests spread below. Lush green lawns with posh tennis courts, garages full of classic cars, and shimmering pools are encircled by tall stone walls. The frivolity of the lives of those who hide behind those walls is depicted by Daniela Rossell in her coffee-table books of absurdist photos of the rich and famous bored out of their gourds in the mansions of Pedregal and Lomas del Bosque. (Rossell herself is rich and famous, the daughter of Díaz Ordaz's regent during the 1968 massacre.)

Interviewed in a 2003 *W* magazine puff piece, "The Fabulous Families of Mexico City," Alex Hank, Carlos's grandson, complains about bodyguards that accompany him even to the toilet and confesses he is spending more time these days at the family estate in Santiago Tianguistenco (six Tudor mansions, a private zoo, and a golf course) to get away from them. He feels like a prisoner in Mexico City, he snivels.

Mónica Serrano, daughter of *Forbes* list multimillionaire José Serrano, is annoyed because she has to fly to Dallas to shop at a Nieman-Marcus or Saks Fifth Avenue. (Note: Saks is coming to El Monstruo—Carlos Slim has just bought a 16 percent slice of the company.) Monica too is upset about all the bodyguards, which have become like accessories: The more costly and ostentatious the security, the bigger the status symbol. Yet despite the armies of *guaruras* that cover her every step, Monica doesn't feel safe in Mexico, where kidnapping the rich is a multimillion-dollar industry, and her family will soon be moving to the United States.

But poor and rich share some common ground. While the ricos race their thoroughbreds and their souped-up sports cars, play polo and golf at the country club, and stay trim with personal trainers in their own private gyms, the *pobres* get their exercise too. Every day, Josué, a *chavo* of indeterminate years, disco dances on a bed of broken glass in traffic on Congress of the Union Avenue. In a spectacular finale before the light changes, he says a few Hail Marys and Our Fathers and dives into the jagged shards—his body is seamed with crusty scabs and scars, but Josué diligently gets free tetanus shots at city clinics. He sleeps each night under a bridge near the Observatorio Metro stop. Young Josué is a new breed of street fakir, the new millennium's version of the fire-eaters that were so ubiquitous during the heyday of La Crisis.

"¡PINCHE POPULARISTA!"

Andrés Manuel López Obrador did not declare class war on the *ricos*. It has been a fact of life and a powerful social force here ever since the eagle got its talons around a writhing snake in the gnarly arms of a nopal cactus bush in 1325.

The rich peer down from the silvery skyscrapers that soar above Palmas and Santa Fe and the bubble-topped Mexican Bolsa de Valores on Reforma buying and selling choice cuts of the country called Mexico. AMLO's people are built closer to the ground and are the color of it. They crowd the sidewalks and the Metro and the 200 *ciudades perdidas* (lost cities) still unconnected to the municipal sewage system. Those who live on high confuse the poor with ants and value them about as much.

All López Obrador tried to do was raise the *pobres* up an inch. One of his first steps was to provide 600 pesos a month to every *viejo* and *viejita* over 60 inside the city limits who did not have a pension. Save for retired government workers who receive a monthly stipend, the Monstruo's senior citizens worked until they dropped, and when they dropped, their families propped them up against public walls to beg coins from passing pedestrians. As a consequence of this simple act of social justice, López Obrador built a following among those of the "third age" that borders on idolatry and is always in evidence at the demonstrations El Peje calls—such as the one today, when AMLO will lead a march on the Finance Ministry at five this afternoon.

As the Chief of Government of a city that tilts to the Left, López Obrador provided monthly stipends for the disabled and single mothers and laid the groundwork for unemployment benefits eventually promulgated by Marcelo Ebrard—real unemployment in the capital weighs in around 15 percent, and new jobs are almost exclusively in the "informal" sector, i.e., selling in the street. With 250,000 young people crashing the city job market each year, the informal sector remains the only real option for survival for those living under the poverty line.

To compound the jobs crisis, the labor market is saturated with young people rejected by the UNAM and IPN. As the 1999–2000 strike against the privatization of education underscored, the *rechazados* are a force for social disconnect, and AMLO laid the cornerstone for the University of the Federal District, which is tuition free to those "who have less."

Fox and his lot did not like what El Peje was up to at all. It was as if by raising the poor up a notch, he was bringing the ricos down, and they damned AMLO as a *pinche popularista* and much worse. López Obrador cheerfully embraced the curse. If helping the poor make their meager ends meet made him a "damn populist," then El Peje was proud to be one.

OF CROOKED CONTRACTORS AND STAR-CROSSED LOVERS

"I've never even been inside City Hall yet, but that doesn't matter because I will govern from below in the streets and colonias and barrios and housing projects," the new Mayor ranted to *La Jornada* in a pre-inaugural interview. Nonetheless, the nature of the job made it incumbent upon López Obrador to administrate the business of the Monstruo from offices in the Ayuntamiento building overlooking the

Zócalo, and once embedded inside those heartless walls, AMLO's cockiness was doused with a cold bucket of reality.

The raw truth was that Rosario Robles's craving for power had bankrupted the Monster. Every last centavo of the city budget had been spent by August, and for four months afterward she had gone on a borrowing binge to keep the Monstruo afloat. Faced with a hostile Congress not disposed to increase federal subsidies or debt limit, the Mayor went into austerity mode and cut salaries across the board, including his own. AMLO demanded a full accounting from his predecessor. The depletion of public funds was sweet music to the ears of the PAN and the PRI, who were already talking prison time. Robles responded like a wronged woman. "My husband of 20 years has left me in my worst moment," she wrote her lover, the crooked Argentinean construction tycoon Carlos Ahumada, "the politician I most admired has stabbed me in the back and become my worst enemy."

An audit of the 16 delegations turned up multiple anomalies, most associated with the Quart corporation, the linchpin of Ahumada's empire, which also included two A league soccer teams and a newspaper. Quart held suspect contracts in six delegations, three of which were in the hands of the PAN. Work contracted by the delegations was found to be uncompleted or done badly or just not done at all. Ahumada had bought up choice land in the rural Tláhuac delegation for a song and won building permits on the city's shrinking farmland that were difficult to obtain without some heavy vigorish changing palms. Eighty-five percent of all public works contracts in Iztapalapa had been awarded to Quart by Robles ally Ramón Sosamontes. In the Gustavo A. Madero (GAM) delegation where Quart also had juicy contracts, 30 million pesos had disappeared from the petty cash drawer.

AMLO ordered all delegations to void contracts with Ahumada, and he was barred from bidding on projected public works. The construction magnate, who posed as a pal of the Left, even launching a pro-PRD daily *El Independiente* to counter the Salinas-tinged *Crónica*, swore revenge.

In 2003, Robles challenged Amalia García, a soft-spoken ex-Communist and soon-to-be governor of Zacatecas, for the party presidency, and Rosario appealed to her Daddy Warbucks Ahumada to underwrite her campaign. Once a week, her gofers, who included AMLO's former personal secretary, the ubiquitous René Bejarano, picked up cash payments at Quart offices. Unbeknownst to Robles and her runners, the crooked construction king was secretly videotaping these transactions and banking the evidence as insurance against prosecution for his crimes against the city. The denouement would not be pretty.

HANG 'EM HIGH

Crime doesn't really care if the Left or the Right is reaming the Monstruo. At the end of his administration, Cárdenas claimed to have reduced criminal incidents from 700 to 400 a day, but really victims had just stopped calling the cops—nine out of 10 crimes were never prosecuted, and when they were, the authorities usually got the wrong guy. Fabricating guilty parties finances the justice industry—in fact, city cops get a bonus from judicial investigators for every suspect they turn in, and whether or not the suspect had anything to do with the crime is not really the criterion.

Public insecurity continued to be Left City's Achilles' heel. In 2001, six homicides a day kept population growth in check. In 2002, some 111 bank robberies were recorded, one every three days. "Express" kidnappings were all the rage: Victims would be plucked from their cars on the Periférico and their loved ones alerted to cough up ransoms at discounted rates. Often the calls were hoaxes, but the supposed victim's family paid up anyway.

Carjackings proliferated. When people parked on the street, they caged up their cars in cumbersome wire contraptions. Parking lot attendants—*franeleros* because they wave a flannel cloth to attract customers—sometimes stole the cars they were paid to protect. Stolen cars were driven into 30-foot trailers and transported 1,000 miles south to Central America for resale.

The average José and María had just about had enough. From the earliest days of La Crisis, offended Mexicans had taken justice into their own hands. Between 1996 and 2002, according to newspaper reports, 26 lynchings were successfully carried out nationally and many more were attempted.

For all its cosmopolitan sensitivities, the Monstruo is not immune to lynch-mob law. *Rateros* who tried to strong-arm passengers on microbus routes were sometimes stomped to death by their intended vics. A shooter who identified himself as "The Armed Avenger" and claimed Bernard Goetz, the New York subway vigilante, as a role model, racked up five kills on public transportation in the late '90s.

A thief who grabbed a priceless missal from the high altar at the Santísima, the medieval church on Moneda east of the National Palace, was beaten into a coma by Alejandra Barrios's ambulantes. Six lynchings were recorded within city limits in 1999–2000 alone.

The most frightening incidents of vigilante justice seemed to occur in the more Indian suburbs. In December 2002, a mob attacked a group of taxi drivers in Milpa Alta after the body of a slain 14-year-old was discovered in a nearby *nopalera* (cactus patch), purportedly minus her internal organs. The cops were called to break it up—Raymundo Collins, the gruff top aide to Police Chief Marcelo Ebrard, tried to negotiate with the frothing locals but finally gave up. "Hurry up and kill them so we can go home," a bored cop overheard by *La Jornada* urged the mob.

A particularly savage collective killing took place July 25, 2001, in Magdalena Petlacalco, a Nahua village in the Ajusco under the jurisdiction of Mexico City's Tlalpan delegation. When 19-year-old Carlos Pacheco, stoned on mota and *chelas*, was discovered inside the local church on the fourth day of a fiesta of the Virgin with the town virgin, a two-foot-high icon draped in necklaces of precious stones, under his arm, the *fiscales* responsible for keeping order at the fete dragged the youth to the center of the plaza and chained him to the rails around the gazebo. Church bells summoned as many as 1,000 accomplices, who took turns beating the boy. Even the women and children got in their licks. The town's priest finally called off the thrashing when he perceived Carlos had stopped breathing.

No one was ever prosecuted for this act of murder. Police Chief Ebrard, whom AMLO had appointed to win points with Marcelo's political godfather Manuel Camacho Solís, promised an investigation, but none was ever begun. Andrés Manuel himself threw up his hands and attributed Carlos's murder to local "uses and customs." "We don't intervene in such things."

López Obrador's remarks infuriated his *delegado* in Tlalpan. Gilberto López y Rivas had been a top-tier adviser to the Zapatistas and played a key role in formulating the uses and customs clauses of the San Andrés Accords on Indigenous Autonomy. "Chaining a boy up to a gazebo and beating him to death has nothing to do with uses and customs," Gilberto snapped indignantly and quit both his job as AMLO's delegate in Tlalpan and the Party of the Democratic Revolution.

The killing of Carlos Pacheco was fraught with monstrous irony—just months before the killing in Magdalena Petlacalco, the comandantes of the Zapatista Army of National Liberation had campaigned for their version of uses and customs from the very same plaza where the boy was chained up and lynched.

MARCOS RETURNS TO EL MONSTRUO

Vicente Fox boasted that he would resolve the tragedy of Chiapas "in 15 minutes," and soon after he was crowned president, The Fox sent the San Andrés Accords on to Congress to be framed into legislation. In February 2001, a contingent of 23 Zapatista comandantes and Subcomandante Marcos caravaned up to the capital for the first time since snubbing Mayor Cárdenas in 1997 to demand an audience with the Legislature.

López Obrador did not present the rebels with the keys to the Monstruo. Andrés Manuel had met with Marcos twice in 1994 and 1995 to discuss the creation of contiguous rebel governments in Chiapas and Tabasco next door, but the chemistry between the two Leftists had never jelled. The comandantes won the hearts of the Chilangos despite El Peje's aloofness, and a quarter of a million turned out in the Zócalo to welcome them.

When the PAN and the PRI balked at giving the Indians an audience, Marcos deftly feinted a return to Chiapas and Fox's image-conscious advisers leaned on the parties to let the Indians speak—it would not have looked good on CNN if the *pinches inditos* had been sent home without being heard out by the Congress of their country.

In an unprecedented moment of national drama, the masked comandantes unmasked Mexican racism and defended the San Andrés Accords on Indigenous Autonomy from the highest podium in the land, then returned to their jungle to await Congress's verdict. They didn't have to wait long. At the end of April, in another unprecedented moment, this time of national shame, the senators of the PRI and the PAN and the PRD rejected the San Andrés Accords—PRD deputies in the lower house walked out rather than vote up indigenous autonomy. The Zapatistas immediately broke off all contact with the mal gobierno, and its fury at the PRD for abandoning them in their hour of need has never abated. The EZLN has never returned to Left City.

AN ODD COUPLING

Although El Peje governed for the Poor first, he was seriously strapped for cash, and so López Obrador proposed a business partnership with the richest man on earth to rescue and revitalize the crumbling Centro Histórico. Carlos Slim would invest a billion pesos (he had 40 trillion of them) to create the Centro Histórico Foundation and match the 1.5 billion in city and federal funding.

Despite its designation as the Patrimony of Humankind by UNESCO, the Centro Histórico was in raggedy shape. The nighttime streets were more deserted than ever. Many who hadn't been evicted in the purges of 1997–1998 jumped ship and moved to Ecatepec and Tlalnepantla and Chimalhuacán—the population of the Centro had reduced itself to just 73,000 by the 2000 census. *Rateros*, not a few of them in cops' clothing, lurked around every corner.

Honky-tonks and fast-food franchises had taken over. Some 146 cantinas and 108 "entertainment centers," mostly table- and lap-dance parlors, did not attract the *gente decente* to the old quarter. Family venues closed early. "The Centro Histórico has the greatest concentration of cultural offerings in the country and the greatest risks to be assaulted," warned Carlos Monsiváis.

The old quarter was literally falling apart. When in the summer of 2002 a four-story building on Donceles Street's used book row collapsed with a sudden whoosh in the first rainstorm of the season, Ana Lilia Cepeda, coordinator of the Centro Histórico trust, leaned across her desk a few blocks south at República de Chile #8 and exhaled plaintively: "John, we are racing against time to save this neighborhood."

Ana Lilia's concern was extravagant. The Centro, Tenochtitlán, whatever you wanted to call it, has been a world power spot for the past seven centuries. One more hard rain would not vanquish the power that resides here—but it could take down a few priceless colonial buildings in a state of conspicuous disrepair, which Carlos Slim coveted.

The association of El Peje with Carlos Slim, a political chameleon who had risen to Bill Gates and Warren Buffet stature thanks to the phone company he had received from Carlos Salinas, AMLO's mortal enemy and personal Moriarty, was an odd coupling. At first, Slim seemed to function as a courier between Vicente Fox and López Obrador, but as the bad blood swelled and the PANista and the Peje stopped talking to each other, the financier took a more pragmatic approach: What was good for the Centro Histórico was good for Carlos Slim.

THE PAST SMELLS REALLY BAD

The tycoon had a soft spot for the old neighborhood where he had grown up. His dad, a young Lebanese refugee fleeing the final spasms of the Ottoman empire at the end of the 19th century, had rented a pushcart on Correo Mayor Street, later expanding into a storefront, La Estrella del Oriente (Star of the East) around the corner on Capuchinas Street—Arab and Jewish merchants still sell cheek by jowl on Correo Mayor. Young Carlos's first dip in the financial swim came as a runner at the old stock market opposite the Monte Carlo Hotel. The Bolsa de Valores on Uruguay Street had "given origin to my first fortune," he told reporters when he bought the building, which for a while served as showroom for Slim's classic jalopies.

Monies were appropriated for the renovation in late 2001 but work did not get under way until mid-2002. There had been many plans to renovate the Centro Histórico in the past. The Aztecs renovated Tenochtitlán after every flood, and Cortez built it back up from scratch. Don Porfirio and Ernesto P. Uruchurtu both gave it a whirl. Under Camacho, cheap rents lured artists back to the district, but gentrification never really took off.

Actually the "Rescue of the Centro Histórico" was a bit of a hype. The AMLO-Slim scheme would rehabilitate only 34 blocks clustered around the Zócalo out of a total of the 600 that technically comprised the Centro. Cárdenas's former secretary for urban renewal, René Coulomb, critiqued the creation of an "island of bonanza in a sea of poverty."

So the street beds were dug up and the sidewalks pulverized. Wire fences were thrown up, and we had to negotiate through a combat zone every day just to get home. The roar and clang of great machines inflicted pounding migraines. We were asphyxiated by choking dust in the dry season and sank in mud up to our belly buttons when it rained.

The renovation of the Centro Histórico has been under way for six years now and is not nearly done with yet. Hundreds of small businesses went bust because they were cut off from their customers, and the transnationals moved in. The hotels emptied out and the restaurants didn't even bother to open. Lalo broke his ankle when he fell in a ditch on Regina Street, which had been turned into an urban swamp. The tuxedos and evening gowns of the *ricos* were splattered with filth when they promenaded from La Profesa to the Casino Español for the wedding feasts.

Trenches were opened and the narrow pipes laid in Porfirio's day replaced. Remnants of the shattered past were laid bare by all the digging, and evidence of an Aztec cistern no one had ever mapped uncovered on Cinco de Mayo. When 16th-century bricks turned up around the corner near Bolívar Street, the anthropologists were invited to evaluate the pieces, and all digging was halted for a month.

The more the work crews dug, the stinkier the neighborhood got. Noxious odors that smelled like the farts of the dead seeped out of the underworld. The stench of centuries of defecating Chilangos clung to the tongue. The past smelled really bad.

WELCOME TO SLIMVILLE

Carlos Slim's interest in the renovation of the Centro Histórico was not just rooted in nostalgia. You do not get to be the wealthiest billionaire on the *Forbes* magazine hit parade by dwelling on the past. Starting with the stock market building mid-block on Uruguay Street between Cinco de Febrero and Isabel la Católica, Slim bought to the corner. Telmex and Sanborn's, the crown jewels of his empire, occupy all of Isabel la Católica to Carranza. The tycoon has picked up a dozen buildings on Carranza and Uruguay between Isabel la Católica and Bolívar one block west, including the old Capuchin monastery now rented out as a Chinese buffet. I count four full-store Sanborn's in the six blocks between my room and Tacuba Street and a couple of El Globo *panaderías* (Slim who is not so slim is the *pan dulce* king of Mexico) in addition to Prodigy Internet outlets, Denny's restaurants, Inbursa banks, Mixup record stores, and American Mobile cell phone outlets, all Slim-owned.

The multibillionaire now dominates Centro Histórico real estate, having bought up and renovated between 72 and 160 buildings in the Centro, many of which have been converted into condominiums—the exact number of Slim's holdings is a closely guarded secret.

Slim's most aggressive competitor for Centro Histórico properties is what AMLO describes as "the Israelite community." Operating under the corporate logo "Centro Histórico S.A.," the Jews of Polanco reportedly hold 41 properties in the neighborhood.

At a 2007 *encuentro* (conclave) of activists from 13 *centros históricos* in Spain and Mexico held here at the glorious Grand Hotel, the common bugaboo was not the decaying core of the old cities but the rising real estate prices after the ancient barrios are renovated that drive the remaining residents out of the neighborhood. Rents in rehabilitated buildings in Mexico City's Historic Center have risen on average 500 percent—70 percent of the tenants remaining in the Centro have lived here for a generation or more.

Six years of reconstruction has transformed the old quarter into a quaint urban village, the façades gaily painted in colors named for tropical fruits and nuts—tangerine and mamey, mango and melon and pistachio. Cute green awnings and flowerpots and faux antique street lighting have been installed. It is sort of like living in one of those picture postal cards sold at Sanborn's, except that 7–11s have replaced all the old *estanquillos* or corner stores and there are Dunkin' Donuts and Burger Kings wherever one turns.

But the schlocking of Tenochtitlán must be put in perspective. Cultural resistance here is as old as the buildings themselves. Sprayed on the wall of a Kentucky Fried Chicken outlet opposite the venerable La Profesa church, I spot this *pinta*: CARLOS SLIM! GET OUT OF THE CENTRO!

RUDY TO THE RESCUE

The cross-class collaboration between Carlos Slim and AMLO had worked out so well that the two decided to renew. Having tackled the rehabilitation of the historic center of Mexico City, the dynamic duo took on crime. Slim put together a syndicate of like-minded impresarios to foot the bill for bringing none other than the World's Número Uno Crime Fighter Rudy Giuliani to the Monstruo to assess the problems and recommend solutions. "Security attracts investment" is one of Giuliani Associates' mantras, and Rudy's arrival was feverishly anticipated. Also contracted to bring a semblance of law and order to this crime-ridden megalopolis: Leoluca Orlando, the former mayor of Palermo, Sicily, who had gone head to head with the Cosa Nostra for years.

In the post-9/11 rush, Rudy was riding the rocket of fame. Giuliani was *Time* magazine's Man of the Year and a take-charge kind of guy who had allegedly cleaned up the cesspools of Gotham—in real-ity, the 57 percent decrease in violent crime that Rudy bragged on had more to do with demographics than Giuliani's much-flogged "leader-ship" qualities: 18- to 30-year-olds, who commit 90 percent of violent crimes, had just gotten older.

The *prensa vendida* ate it up.

Chilangos learned more than they ever needed to know about "quality of life" crimes and "zero tolerance" and "CompStat" opera-tions (in which cops saturate a high-crime area and push the crooks into the next neighborhood). Armando Peñalosa, the morning counter man at La Blanca who grew up in Tepito, was mystified: "What does this Rudy guy know about our reality?"

Rudolph Giuliani's white-knight status was not shared by the darker-skinned residents of the Big Apple. The 41-shot killing of Afri-can street vendor Amadou Diallo was just the tip of the iceberg. Eight years of Rudy's proactive policing in African American and Hispanic neighborhoods had cost the city a whopping $385,000,000 in lawsuits. According to the Tepeyac Center, which speaks out for an estimated 250,000 New York Mexicans, 14 of their paisanos had been victims of Rudy's zero-tolerance pogroms—one young man had been shot in the back. Giuliani did not endear himself to New York's Mexican com-munity when he took back a prize for the first baby of the new millen-nium because she was born to an undocumented Mexican mother.

The Big Man took his time coming to town. It was rumored that the Colombian Revolutionary Armed Forces (FARC) had plans to kid-nap him the moment he set foot in Mexico City, and cancellation fol-lowed cancellation. Finally, in January 2003, Giuliani touched down at the Toluca airport in a private jet and was hustled off to be wined and dined by Slim's syndicate. The next day, Rudy and Police Chief Ebrard cruised the city's hot crime spots in a bulletproof Suburban, visiting Tepito and the Buenos Aires, the stolen car parts Kasbah. Rudy sur-veyed the street action through smoked windows, never disembark-ing from the armored SUV.

During their rounds, Giuliani and Ebrard were escorted by 300 elite robocops, 30 women members of the Policía Femenil, 10 motor-cycle cops, 26 of Rudy's private guaruras, bomb-sniffing dogs, a fleet of armed vehicles (four Suburbans, two Cherokees, two Sentras, two Malibus, one Stratus, one Grand Marquis), and a helicopter gunship overhead. The police chief justified the overkill because Rudy Giuliani was "a distinguished visitor like the Pope."

When the caravan arrived in the Zócalo for the obligatory photo op with AMLO, Pope Giuliani finally emerged from the Suburban for a half-block stroll into City Hall. There were sharpshooters up on the roofs when I came out for comida corrida around two.

Giuliani pumped López Obrador's hand. The flashbulbs fizzled. Then he got back on his private jet, and flew to New York, never to return again to the Monstruo. Several weeks later he teleconferenced with Marcelo but thereafter all business with Mexico City was conducted by his Kojak look-alike sidekick Bernard Kerik, who has since been indicted for playing footsie with the mob.

Months went by and no proposals were forthcoming. "ZERO TOLERANCE FOR RUDY," *Ovaciones* headlined, complaining that the $4.1 million USD that Giuliani had received for his expertise would pay four years of salary for 1,400 front-line Mexico City officers.

Two thousand three was a mid-term election year and Rudy's failure to deliver was an issue. Then in September, 12 volumes containing 146 recommendations arrived on Ebrard's desk at last. The recommendations bore a striking resemblance to Pope Rudy's New York game plan: Go after quality-of-life crimes—the squeegee guys on Reforma, the *putas* of La Merced, drunks pissing in the street, kids tagging public buildings. Oh, and sweep the ambulantes from the streets! Such campaigns up the arrest figures and put the fear of god in career criminals. Armando chuckled so robustly at this assumption that he almost spilt my café Americano. "Give me a break!"

Marcelo Ebrard, however, appeared to take this charade seriously. The Mexico City penal code was revised, and the theft of merchandise and/or currency worth one peso (a thin U.S. dime) or more was made punishable by jail time. Shades of Jean Valjean and Les Misérables. Left City indeed.

EL PEJE'S PYRAMID

Andrés Manuel López Obrador exhibited a mania for grandiose public works on a scale that matched that of his Aztec forebears. El Peje's most pharaonic monument was the construction of a "second-story" freeway above the Periférico ring road, an 8,000,000,000-peso mega project that urbanologist Jorge Legorreta, once a Cárdenas *delegado*, described as López Obrador's pyramid.

Building pyramids requires a lot of slaves and AMLO and his contractors hired on about 10,000 wage slaves to get the Segundo Piso under way in time for the 2003 midterms. As every big-city mayor is keenly aware, public works generate votes, and with the average worker's family weighing in at three to five adults, just his workforce alone would produce as many as 50,000 votes.

The Second Story was denounced by environmentalists the day AMLO first announced his plans. Climate change in the capital is acute. Between 1998 and 2000, local temperatures had increased two degrees on the Celsius scale and four degrees on so-called "heat islands" or hot spots, according to UNAM's Center for Atmospheric Studies. More ominously, the eternal snows up on Popocatépetl and Iztaccíhuatl were melting due to one-degree warming. Melting snows from the volcanoes would cause flooding in the lowlands. Combined with a record heat wave (35 degrees C) during Holy Week, the most sweltering time of the year, you could almost hear the polar ice caps thawing.

If Al Gore was on target, the sea would soon be lapping at the Monstruo's mile-high doorstep.

DRIVE, HE SAID

The culprit was no stranger: nearly 5,000,000 vehicles guzzling 44,000,000 liters of gasoline daily. Although the installation of smog devices was now mandatory (the Verification Centers were a gold mine for shady inspectors), the internal combustion engine continued to poison the air Chilangos are condemned to breathe.

Despite improved public transit, 12 Metro lines, prohibitions on driving two days a week, cleaner gasolines, conversion of the city vehicle fleet to ethanol, and air that actually moves, the quality of what we are breathing is not healthy. The numbers tell the story. The sale of automobiles for personal use grows 6 percent each year, twice that of the human population. AMLO's Second Story would only encourage wanton proliferation of this menace.

Getting the traffic moving at a reasonable velocity was the priority for the Peje's supporters. "If you start out for a wedding, you will arrive in time for the baptism," is the maxim of frustrated Mexico

City motorists. Traffic bottlenecks—construction, marches (down to 1.4 a day), and *topes* (1,259 speed bumps) slowed the flow down to a walk and boosted pollution 23 percent. Such vehicular manslaughter accounted for 72 percent of the air-borne contamination afflicting the Monster, according to AMLO's environmental secretary Claudia Sheinbaum, a Second Story woman who argued the Segundo Piso would eliminate the combustion of 4,700,000 liters of fossil fuels a day.

Car ownership is emblematic of middle-class aspirations, but the middle class is a decidedly minority population in Mexico City—only 16 percent of the 8.4 million residents of the city—own cars. High-end Chilangos were just as reluctant as ever to use mass transportation. "People push and shove down in the Metro and everyone smells like onions," Francisco Estrada, a theater technician, told the *New York Times*. Estrada was interviewed while marooned in Mexico City traffic.

THE ARROGANCE OF THE AUTOTARIAT

The arrogance of Mexico City drivers is lethal and legendary. In 2006, more than 5,000 pedestrians were struck down crossing the street—1,241 fatally, about 3.4 pedestrian deaths a day.

The old man stepped off the curb in swanky Polanco, looked both ways, and tentatively started to cross when a Hummer swerved off busy Marina Nacional Boulevard against the light and knocked the elderly gentleman off his feet. The driver never looked back. A dozen diners at a taco stand not six feet away continued chewing as the injured party (who was me) struggled to his feet and poked for broken bones. A block later when I indignantly complained to a cop about the nonchalance of the witnesses to this near tragedy, she giggled. "Someone gets hit at that corner every day!" she explained.

The driving class has political clout. Every administration that has governed this burg since the internal combustion engine was invented, from Don Porfirio to AMLO, has bowed to its dictatorship.

El Peje's pyramid obeyed the electoral calendar. Construction began in 2002 in time for the midterms, but the Second Story would not open for business until 2004 when voters were beginning to consider their options for the presidential race two years down the highway.

The proportions of the Segundo Piso were biblical. Few seemed to question AMLO's intentions, although building so disproportionate a structure in an active earthquake zone seemed preposterous, given what happened in the 1989 Loma Prieta dust-up when an Oakland, California, second story pancaked into the first, crushing dozens.

Nonetheless, each week, gargantuan precast sections of the Segundo Piso were trucked through the Monstruo. Giant cranes lifted the *ballenas*, or whales, into place as a hard-hatted López Obrador beamed. Even when one of the "whales" slipped its moorings and crushed a worker or two, the project continued full speed ahead. *Los de abajo*, those who lived below in the shadow of the monstrous freeway, looked up and shuddered.

In synch with Left City duplicity, in December 2004, the first seven kilometers (14 kilometers were contemplated) were dedicated to the late leftist Heberto Castillo, an outspoken foe of the Monstruo's punishing air quality. Tens of thousands of happy Chilangos strode up the on-ramp (bicycles were barred) to celebrate. It was almost like a religious pilgrimage. In fact Cardinal Norberto was on hand to bless the Segundo Piso. So was Gabriel García Márquez, no doubt gathering material for a new volume of magic realist fables.

THE FRONT-RUNNER

The July 6, 2003, midterm elections to renew the lower house, the Legislative Assembly, and the delegations coincided with the 15th anniversary of the great fraud that had deprived Cuauhtémoc Cárdenas of the presidency. The 60 percent turnout was down 10 points from 2000, reflecting widespread disappointment with Vicente Fox, Mexico's first opposition president. The PAN dropped 60 seats in the Chamber of Deputies, mostly to the PRD which had been humiliated in Fox's 2000 landslide, and the PRI regained a near absolute majority in the lower house with 223 representatives. Thanks to the AMLO-Slim-Giuliani caper and the promise of the Second Story, the PRD won back two delegations (Cuajimalpa and Azcapotzalco) and an unstoppable majority in the Legislative Assembly. Polls heralded López Obrador as the frontrunner in the 2006 presidential derby. "I am not a candidate," the Peje protested.

TERROR IN TLÁHUAC

The three men parked their car at the top of the hill right by the Popol Vuh grade school in the village of San Juan Ixtayopan in the city's rural Tláhuac delegation where Nahuat is still the lingua franca. Sometimes the men would step out of the car to snap photographs. You couldn't see their faces clearly from down below on the schoolyard, and the parents were spooked. *Chisme* spread that students had been reported missing but no one could put a name to them. A handful of *padres de familia* got up enough nerve to approach the car and ask the men what they wanted. The suspected kidnappers claimed to be plainclothesmen staking out the schoolyard for dope pushers. They pulled out badges, *charolas*, but the parents were unimpressed. Cops and kidnappers often worked hand in hand.

The kidnappers were dragged out of the car and beaten bloody. More villagers came and pitched in. By the time the lynching was consummated, 2,000 howling residents of San Juan Ixtayopan would be in the street.

As had been his M.O. in the Petlacalco killing, Police Chief Ebrard refused to intervene for fear of exacerbating the public's fury. Neither did the feds, even though it would later be revealed that the three were part of a Federal Preventive Police anti-terrorism team. The TV demons got wind of the lynching early in the afternoon and started filming. The cops were pushed before the cameras and pleaded for help through swollen lips.

It was like a ghastly reality show. Televisa and Azteca were in the throes of a ratings war, and all afternoon they took turns pumping up the hysteria. Someone brought out the gasoline and doused the cops. A match was struck. Horrifying screams shattered the evening. The stench of burning flesh filled the nostrils. One crazed assailant grabbed a charred leg and hollered like a street vendor. "A peso! Only one peso for his leg!" The cameras never missed a beat.

The auto-da-fé in Tláhuac was a qualitative leap from the lynching of Carlos Pacheco in Petlacalco three years earlier. This killing could not be explained away by "uses and customs." This was pure revenge. The cops were perceived as kidnappers and the people resorted to their own brand of justice because they knew that justice would never be served any other way. "We did what we had to do to protect our children," said one mother, attempting to explain away the horror.

The dead cops were from an elite anti-terrorism team with tails that dated back to the dark ages of the dirty war. Victor Mireles was an ex–DFS torturer who had been recruited by the CISEN spy agency. The three had staked out the Popol Vuh school not to collar drug sellers, as they claimed, but in pursuit of Francisco Cerezo (not his real name), a founding member of the Popular Revolutionary Army (EPR) and a native of Ixtayopan.

The Foxites leveled a finger at drug pushers and radicals for instigating the mayhem, and 33 parents identified from the Televisa tape were jailed. The two-headed TV lynch mob flogged Ebrard's failure to act to save the cops from burning. Under the constitutional reforms that gave Chilangos the vote to elect their own mayor, the president retained the right to approve or remove the Monstruo's police chief, and Fox summarily fired Marcelo Ebrard, further irritating the festering animosity between the President and the Jefe de Gobierno.

REMEMBER TO WEAR WHITE

The politicization of crime put the PAN and the PRD at each other's throat. Crime in the capital is historically a right-wing issue, and the AMLO-Slim end-around with Rudy Giuliani carrying the football amounted to patent infringement in the eyes of the PANistas.

Despite the application of "CompStat" et al., crime had not abated. After eight years of Left City, decent people were still under siege. Such grisly incidents as Tláhuac ("What do you expect from such savages?") were further evidence of how lawless the Monster had become under the tutelage of the Left. The brutal, bungled murder of a teacher who had just won "Teacher of the Year" honors, her body tossed into the black waters of the Gran Canal, was the tipping point: Even though it took place well outside the city limits, AMLO was blamed.

A "White March" was called and a march committee formed by the right of the PANista Right: José Antonio Ortega and Guillermo Velasco were identified with El Yunque (The Anvil), a secretive, archly Catholic cabal created back in the anti-Communist '50s. In his book of the same name, *Proceso* writer Álvaro Delgado identified three members of Fox's cabinet as being members of El Yunque.

The White March was endorsed and funded by the Coordinating Council of Impresarios (CCE), the most conservative of the business federations. Incredibly, the right-wingers' march would follow the route of the 1968 student mobilizations from Chapultepec Park to the Zócalo. March organizers professed to preach urban peace, but their real target was, of course, the pinche Peje. Everyone was invited to wear white. Televisa hoopla'ed the White March like it was its own annual charity telethon. "Only 23 days until the March for Peace! Remember to wear white!" *¡Viva Paco Stanley!*

A million alleged Chilangos (police estimates 120,000), half of them actually from neighboring Mexico state, marched Sunday, June 4, 2004. Many of them flew white balloons that called for the reintroduction of the death penalty. "*¡México! ¡México!*" the crowd chanted as if they were on their way to Díaz Ordaz's Olympics. They did *la Ola* (the Wave). Boy Scouts in short pants marched in martial cadence. Fathers of families led their purebred hounds on leashes. Fabrizio Mejía, writing in *Proceso*, claimed that middle-class marchers tried to pay for Metro tickets with their credit cards.

There were few brown faces in this sea of white, most of them ragged ambulantes selling frozen fruit ices. The matrons of Polanco and Lomas came with their Indian *chachas* (servants), and factory owners obligated their dark-skinned workers to attend. When the marchers reached the Zócalo, they pushed in around City Hall and shouted up at El Peje's window demanding his resignation: "*¡Renuncia!*"

Don Juanito López, a natty tailor with a shop in the Centro and a home in Nezahualcóyotl, joined the White March with his family. Don Juanito supports El Peje and sympathizes with the PRD, which governs in Neza, but he identifies himself as a member of the civil society. "It must have felt weird to be marching with all those PANistas," I teased as we sat elbow to elbow at La Blanca's counter, me with my café con leche and he with his manzanilla tea. "*Así es*, Señor Ross, they are such *perules* [smurfs], but the crime situation is really terrible." He was right. Even La Blanca had been held up a few weeks before.

Unwisely, AMLO dismissed the White March as a Yunque trick, ignoring the Don Juanitos of the city who had joined in just because "we have to do something."

THE REVENGE OF AN UNHAPPY LOVER

A funny thing happened to René Bejarano when he visited Televisa's Chapultepec Avenue studios in March 2004. Bejarano, López Obrador's personal secretary during his first years in City Hall but now president of the Legislative Assembly, was waved into a studio by a green-haired clown named Brozo (Víctor Trujillo), "El Payaso Tenebroso" (The Scary Clown), who specializes in truculent interviews. "Sit down," Brozo invited, "I want to show you a video that someone just dropped by," and he punched in the card. There on the monitor was René in Carlos Ahumada's office, only the contractor's features were deliberately blurred. René is stuffing low-denomination bills into a portfolio. First he counts the bills and then he slips a rubber band around them—he has brought the *ligas* with him for this purpose, and they soon become his nickname. Because there are so many bills, he can't quite zip up the portfolio and begins stuffing the money into his suit coat pockets as though impersonating a greedy politico on *Saturday Night Live*.

Subsequent videos delivered to Televisa featured Rosario Robles confederate Ramón Sosamontes picking up the payola for her campaign to become party president, and former UNAM strike leader and AMLO's delegate in Tlalpan Carlos Imaz, who appears to be weighing the money. Another stars López Obrador's secretary of finances, Gustavo Ponce, at the blackjack tables of the sumptuous Hotel Bellaggio in Las Vegas, Nevada, where he is gaming courtesy of Ahumada. The two were later indicted for contriving the 30,000,000-peso shortfall in the Gustavo A. Madero delegation.

Faced with prosecution for bribery and other crimes of persuasion, and bitter at AMLO for having cut him out of city contracts, the Argentinean had struck back. The "someone" responsible for delivering the tapes to Brozo the Clown was identified as Federico Döring, a PAN attack-dog deputy and professional character assassin with a very Germanic name. Döring in return had received the videos from Diego "El Jefe" Fernández de Cevallos, onetime PANista candidate for president, who in turn had obtained them from Ahumada during a hush-hush meeting at a posh Polanco hotel attended by the director of the CISEN, who checked the tapes for authenticity. Then they were run by AMLO's Moriarty, Carlos Salinas, whom Fox had recently encouraged to return to Mexico—Ahumada's chauffeur testified that he had driven his boss to Salinas's Tlalpan delegation estate on 11 separate occasions.

Carlos Ahumada was not around to enjoy the airing of his handiwork, having fled Mexico for parts unknown weeks before. Then in April, the crooked contractor was spotted poolside in Varadero

Beach, Cuba, a traditional spa for fugitive businessmen from Al Capone to Robert Vesco. When Mexican police tipped their Cuban counterparts that Rosario Robles had just arrived to tryst with her sugar daddy, the two were placed under surveillance. "Here I am in love," Rosario had written Carlos, whose anti-AMLO treachery, she was convinced, proved the Argentinean's great love for her. In the mash note later recovered from the Quart file drawers, she reminds her lover of passion-packed rendezvous in Berlin and Madrid and Huatulco, and "our sex shop night" in Miami, "when you told me you loved me." "You are my sun and my moon, my east and my west," Super Rosario pants. Cuban authorities soon took the star-crossed lovers into custody.

The Ahumada-Robles love fest in Cuba did not come at an opportune diplomatic moment. Relations between the Cuban communist government and Mexico had been strained ever since The Fox had ordered Fidel Castro to abandon a United Nations development summit in Monterrey that March. "Comes y te vas" ("you will eat and run"), the Mexican president had ordered the Cuban strongman. George Bush was winging in from Washington for the summit, and Fox didn't want the two of them in the same country, let alone the same room. But Fidel recorded the conversation and played it for the press to shame Martita's hubby.

Now the Cuban authorities deposed Ahumada. (Robles was allowed to leave the island on her own.) The interview, during which the devious contractor is said to confess that he had turned the videos over to the Foxistas to damage López Obrador's forthcoming presidential bid and win himself a pardon, was recorded on 30 compact discs. The Cubans later returned Ahumada to El Monstruo, where he was locked down in durance vile—but they kept the CDs.

In late May, Fox's self-promoting foreign minister Jorge Castañeda, who had once trained in Cuba as a guerrillero but who now was an outspoken foe of Fidel's, recalled ambassador Roberta Lajous from that socialist paradise and broke off diplomatic relations Mexico had maintained for 45 years through thick and thin with the Cuban revolution. In Bolivia, what was left of Che Guevara must have been twirling in his secret sarcophagus.

The scandal kept the prensa vendida enthralled for much of 2004. Ahumada had his supporters. Dragging out a hoary Mexican dicho, my friend Carlos Diez, the proprietor of La Blanca and no friend of El

Peje, philosophized: "A thief who robs a thief earns a hundred years of pardon."

Despite the relentless media assault, AMLO emerged from this mud bath smelling like a rose. He had handled no money—at least on camera. Bejarano had long since left his employ. Ahumada himself had corrupted Ponce, the finance secretary, with whom he had shared the 30,000,000-peso boodle. But the payouts were entirely legitimate, destined for Rosario Robles's campaign for PRD president, an area of campaign financing not yet covered by electoral law—although they did look bad on TV. The Left is supposed to be immune from such venal behavior.

Those who had already declared for AMLO in the upcoming 2006 presidenciales—and the numbers were increasing daily as the masses became animated by El Peje's pugnacious nature—were convinced that the plot had been concocted by the Fox and the reviled Salinas to tar and feather López Obrador, who still had a double-digit lead over probable PAN candidate Santiago Creel and the PRI's unctuous Roberto Madrazo, even though the Peje had not yet declared himself a presidential candidate.

THE CRIME OF THE CENTURY

Who owned El Encino? Don Mayolo Soto, a 65-year-old native of Cuajimalpa with a thick graying mustache and tired eyes, showed reporters the papers that attested his grandfather had received the property that abutted the high-end Santa Fe development back in 1895 from Don Porfirio himself, along with a concession to exploit the sand mines that tunneled under the ranch for the city's growing construction industry. But despite the concession, the Sotos had not prospered—Don Mayolo wore the straw sombrero and wool *gaván* of a humble colono.

Others had won similar concessions from subsequent governments to tunnel out the sand on this gully-ridden 2,000,000-square-meter ranch, originally the Rancho Memetla, of which El Encino was the principal property. In 1981, Carlos Hank González, about to escape to Connecticut, granted rights to quarry the sand mines to a crony, Federico Escobedo, and years of litigation later, ownership was still turgid.

Camacho Solís's sidekick Juan Enríquez, then director of Servimet, the agency that managed city properties, cleaned up the Cuajimalpa garbage dumps in preparation for the Santa Fe development in the late

1980s, and land-shark developers moved in, selling off lots for $22–$24 USD a square meter. Escobedo and his associates chartered "Santa Fe International Promoters" and staked a claim on the bonanza.

Santa Fe was blossoming into a gleaming first world city by the mid-1990s. Transnationals like Goodyear and Hewlett Packard were establishing company headquarters, and skyscrapers filled with luxury apartments were rising from the former garbage pits—methane burners flared day and night to burn off the subterranean garbage. A decade later, Santa Fe groups together 75 buildings (each 20 stories tall), 4,000 deluxe condominiums, five five-star hotels, seven university campuses, and four distinct shopping malls.

Transnationals were soon relocating to Santa Fe and building high-rise corporate headquarters. Among the newcomers was the American British Canadian (ABC) hospital, a top-dollar medical facility that serviced Mexico City's Anglo community. In 2004, the hospital board petitioned the Jefe de Gobierno to open up an access road to the hospital grounds that would pass through the adjacent property, El Encino. The ABC had opened a clinic that provided free care for the poor of Cuajimalpa, and AMLO gave the green light to the expropriation of a narrow strip of the ranch to accommodate the *médicos*. Heavy machinery was moved in and the Department of Public Works went to work. But Escobedo and "Santa Fe International Promoters" were agile litigators and applied to the courts for an *amparo*, an order to cease all construction until ownership issues could be ironed out.

AMLO obeyed the court order reluctantly. Public Works parked its bulldozers and graders but dragged its feet on removing the equipment, and Escobedo went back to the court claiming the city was blocking the right of way to his own property and demanding that El Peje be held in contempt for failing to comply fully with the cease and desist order.

This trivial skirmish in a distant corner of the Monster came to the attention of Interior Secretary Santiago Creel, then Fox's choice to be his successor in 2006. In the rarefied ambience in which getting López Obrador at all costs was the Fox government's lead priority, the dispute over El Encino became the crime of the century.

Attorney General Rafael Macedo de la Concha, a division general in the Mexican military, appointed a special prosecutor to nail El Peje's dick to the wall. But General Macedo had a big *problema*: As long as López Obrador remained mayor of Mexico City, he enjoyed full immunity from prosecution, the time-honored *fuero* that has saved the asses of many a Mexican politician ever since the first constitution was drawn up in 1824.

There was really only one surefire way to remove AMLO's fuero, and Creel encouraged the PAN-PRI majority in the Chamber of Deputies, which oversees such deviance, to strip López Obrador of his constitutional protection, a process known as the *desafuero*, a sort of impeachment. The moment he lost his fuero, AMLO would be liable for prosecution on the contempt of court citation.

Under the Napoleonic Code that governs Mexican justice, citizens accused of such crimes are presumed guilty until they can establish their innocence. Those so charged are taken into custody and disappear behind prison bars until the process comes to a conclusion, often light-years down the line. The accused do not even get to go to court—all judicial proceedings are conducted in jailhouse courtrooms. Those who are so imprisoned, whether eventually declared innocent of wrongdoing or not, automatically lose all their political rights, i.e., they cannot vote or run for political office. The desafuero seemed the perfect political scheme for keeping El Peje off the 2006 presidential ballot—although he had not yet even declared for that high office.

MADERO RISING

Putting all their eggs in the *desafuero* basket proved a monumental miscalculation for the Foxistas and their accomplices up in the towers on Insurgentes #59. AMLO was the most popular politico in the land—no other public figure, not even Subcomandante Marcos, had his power of convocation—and while the lower house prepared the paperwork for impeachment, López Obrador appealed to his constituents to mobilize. The PRD and the civil society, the Panchos and the pensioners, the urban popular movement and all those who perceived themselves to have benefited by the left turning of the city, consolidated to prevent the Peje's arrest and defend his right to run for the presidency of Mexico when and if he chose to do so.

Some 300,000 (police estimates) gathered in the Zócalo April 8, 2005, the date the Chamber had appointed to vote up the desafuero, an impressive number of them senior citizens hobbling on canes and walkers, in wheelchairs or leaning on their grown children's arms. "¡No Está Solo!" they cried out. "You are not alone—we are with you in this until the end." Despite the adoring mob's solidarity, El Peje asked his supporters not to accompany him to Congress. He would face the PRI-PAN's ugly music alone.

Before he climbed into his battered Tsuru to drive the few blocks to San Lázaro, Andrés Manuel López Obrador finally announced his candidacy for the office of president. He would run from behind the bars of the prisons they locked him up in if it came to that, much as Madero had defied Don Porfirio back in 1910 when, barred from the ballot, he had summoned his supporters to ignite the Mexican Revolution.

¡NO ESTÁ SOLO!

Before the terms of his political execution were consummated, López Obrador was allowed to address Congress in his own defense. "You will judge me today, but all of us will be judged by history," AMLO told the solons. Before he could even sit down, the PAN and the PRI voted overwhelmingly to strip El Peje of his immunity. In a land where the government had slaughtered hundreds of students at Tlatelolco, assassinated Villa and Zapata, stolen elections, and sold off the sovereignty of Mexico for a handful of lentils, Andrés Manuel was about to be railroaded into federal prison for trying to build an access road to a hospital.

López Obrador was facing eight years in the *bote*, to be served, it was speculated, at Almoloya, Mexico's Alcatraz, where he would share a cellblock with the nation's leading drug lords, or the Matamoros super-maxi on the U.S. border, far far away from his Mexico City base. The charges were drawn up by Macedo de la Concha's special prosecutor and 45 boxes of documentation substantiating the commission of a crime were trucked over to the Public Ministry, which would issue the arrest order. All the pieces were in place for one of the most outrageous political frame-ups since the Left had taken power in the city.

AMLO turned over management of the Monstruo to his secretary of government, Alejandro Encinas, a roly-poly ex-commie. As the days narrowed down to a precious few, López Obrador's 6:00 a.m. City Hall press conferences were packed with foreign correspondents—the screwing of AMLO was attracting international attention.

But the wheels of justice grind erratically in this benighted land, and snafus are de rigueur. The public minister sorted through the 45 boxes of documentation and could not find any crime to issue an arrest warrant for. The 45 boxes were trucked back to General Macedo's offices for revision.

The legal hiatus gave López Obrador's supporters a few days' grace to organize the biggest political demonstration to date in Mexican history. On April 24, more than 1.1 million Chilangos (police estimates) marched into the Zócalo in defense of El Peje. The great plaza could hardly contain all of them, and thousands spilled into the side streets. "¡No Está Solo! ¡No Está Solo!" the monster crowd chanted obsessively.

Three days later, Vicente Fox, belatedly realizing that the persecution of AMLO was only fueling his hated rival's candidacy, bit the bullet and instructed Attorney General, General Macedo de la Concha, to shelve the case of El Encino. In doing so, Fox grudgingly recognized that "everyone has the right to run for president." Having been made to look like fools, Macedo and his special prosecutor resigned; Santiago Creel, his credibility seriously eroded, lost prestige and the PAN bigwigs replaced him as their presidential candidate in 2006 with Felipe Calderón, whom Fox had once fired as energy secretary for stridently advancing his own presidential ambitions. AMLO's vindication jacked his double-digit lead up to 14 points.

A DANGER TO MEXICO

El Peje's growing constituency was concentrated in the capital where a fifth of the nation's voters cast their ballots, but a fifth was not enough to ensure victory, and he took to the road to build his candidacy into a national movement. Over the course of the next 16 months, López Obrador would visit all 31 state capitals, every one of Mexico's 300 electoral districts, and more than half of the nation's 2,400 municipalities in quest of the presidency.

In flagrant violation of constitutional protocols that bar an outgoing president from intervening in the campaign to select his successor, Fox went on the offensive, condemning AMLO over and over again from the podiums of power and insinuating that he was "a danger for Mexico." "Shut up, *chachalaca*" (a chattering bird), an exasperated Peje barked back, and the TV demons upbraided him for denigrating the honor of the presidency.

López Obrador was "a danger to Mexico!" the attack ads screeched. They began with black-and-whites of a designated ogre—Hugo Chávez (the PAN accused him of financing the Peje's campaign) or Subcomandante Marcos (who never missed an opportunity to knock López Obrador)—or a riot or a lynching or the city physically collapsing before the viewers' eyes. Then Andrés Manuel's sinister mug would be flashed on the screen with the word ¡PELIGRO! (Danger!) stamped over it in red block letters. Calderón's handlers saturated the media with these calumnies—sometimes four 30-second spots would run back to back during a single commercial break on Televisa's prime-time news.

To complement the ubiquitous hit pieces, Fox overran the airwaves with 100,000 public service announcements bragging about the dubious accomplishments of his regime and warning that if they were not continued by his successor, Mexico would fall apart.

The three parties in López Obrador's "For the Good of All" coalition appealed to the Federal Electoral Institute (IFE), Mexico's maximum electoral authority, to reel in the Calderón slanders and impede Vicente Fox's unconstitutional intervention in the presidential campaign, but the dice were loaded against AMLO. The three parties in the coalition—the PRD, Democratic Convergence, and the Party of Labor—had no representatives on the IFE council.

In point of fact, half the members on the council, including its chairman Luis Carlos Ugalde, had been handpicked by "La Tícher," Elba Esther Gordillo, czarina of the 1.3-million-member National Education Workers Union, one of the largest in Latin America. Gordillo, a PRIista, had tiffed with Roberto Madrazo and been excommunicated from the once ruling party. Hell-bent on revenge, she snuggled up to Vicente and Martita and volunteered to use her considerable influence to beat off both AMLO and the hated Madrazo. One example of her magical powers: 22,000 polling place officials were replaced with the Maestra's minions in the months before the July 2 balloting.

THE SHADOW OF '88

Veterans of the mega-fraud against Cárdenas did not need to dice up pigeons and examine their entrails to appreciate what was coming. I bumped into Luis Cota, an old-school Communist Party member, on the eve of the June 13 presidential debate, which was about to be shown on the big screen before tens of thousands of Pejemaniacs in the Zócalo, and we compared notes. All the signs pointed to a rerun of 1988. We remembered Ovando and Gil, executed only a few blocks east, and the 500 martyrs that followed. I could feel the coming trouble in my guts, I told my old *camarada*, a constant gnawing pain eating away at my stomach wall. Luis advised Pepto-Bismol. "I hope your guts are wrong, *compañero*."

Calderón was closing in on AMLO. From a double-digit disadvantage, the nightly bashing of El Peje on the telly had Felipe Calderón in a "technical" tie with López Obrador, although the leftist still held a two-to four-point advantage in every poll including Televisa's.

El Peje was being buffeted from both ends of the political spectrum. Subcomandante Marcos, on the road with his anti-electoral "Other Campaign," never stopped sniping at López Obrador, accusing him of torpedoing the San Andrés Accords (AMLO was never a member of Congress) and, of all things, being a secret Salinista. In May, Marcos returned to El Monstruo with his "Others" to intensify his vilification of López Obrador and took up residence six blocks south at the Rincón Zapatista, a rebel safe house that was always ringed with patrol cars.

Even Ahumada emerged from the sewers to take a swipe at his old tormenter, offering Televisa new videos. On the morning the videos were to be handed over, the imprisoned contractor ordered his *mozos* (flunkies) to shoot up his own wife's van—with his wife and kids inside (they were unhurt) as she navigated a narrow alley in a San Ángel gated community. Televisa and TV Azteca ran with the cockamamie story that AMLO's people had done the job to prevent the release of the "new video." The bulletins were enhanced with spooky music. No new videos were ever released.

The 2006 Mexican *presidenciales* may have been the most important in the modern political history of the Aztec nation, if only because the issues were so sharply defined: AMLO represented the poor against Calderón's *ricos*, the brown skins vs. the PANista's palefaces, the underclass vs. the Masters of the Universe, popular democracy vs. neoliberal economics. The vote taking even had geopolitical standing: Would Mexico continue to be Washington's lackey or line up with the new social democracies of the south?

FRAUDE ELECTORAL (ALL OVER AGAIN)

The press corps washed down the canapés with free libations on election night at López Obrador's headquarters on the mezzanine of a glitzy new hotel on the Reforma corridor. Because I make it a practice to run away from the press pack, I get to see my colleagues only every six years at these soirees, and there is always plenty of catch-up.

The gab was cut short at 8:00 p.m. when we sat down on neatly arranged hotel chairs for the promised exit polls from Televisa and Azteca. But there were no exit polls, and there was no explanation as to why there were none. Later, we would learn that the interior secretary had pleaded with the TV demons not to release the results. AMLO's pollers showed him a half-million votes ahead. *¿Fraude electoral?*

At 11:00, Luis Carlos Ugalde was to announce the first cut of the PREP or preliminary tally—the first cut of the PREP had determined the past two presidential elections. There was no PREP. The election was too close to call, the tubby, sweating Ugalde explained, backing away from the mics and sounding not unlike Manuel Bartlett back in 1988.

¿¿¿Fraude electoral???

I beat López Obrador to the Zócalo for what had been billed as a victory party. The rain beat down on the partygoers as it does every election night. The mood was not amicable. "*¡Fraude electoral!*" AMLO's people growled. "*¡Fraude electoral!*" AMLO tried to reason with his supporters: "Smile! We have already won!" No one smiled.

The numbers from the PREP began to run after midnight and we followed them on the Internet. López Obrador could never get within two points of Calderón—every time he closed, the PANista would surge. By morning, Calderón appeared to have an insurmountable advantage, but El Peje's people were not swallowing it. Not quite 42,000,000 votes had been cast and only 39,000,000 were in the PREP. Appearing on a morning Televisa interview show, Ugalde suddenly remembered that 3,000,000 votes had been held out of the preliminary count because of "possible anomalies." When the missing votes were dumped back in, Calderón's lead had been reduced to a little over 0.5 percent of the total.

On Wednesday, there were more "possible anomalies" when the 300 electoral districts met to sum up the returns from the nation's 114,000 polling places. But the numbers on the *sábanas* attached to the bags of ballots did not coincide with the numbers AMLO's people had signed off on in the *casillas*. The phantom of '88 galloped through the district counts. López Obrador's people demanded that the bags be opened and the ballots counted out by hand one by one, voting place by voting place. IFE officials gaveled down their protests.

At 4:00 p.m. on Wednesday afternoon, AMLO enjoyed a four-point lead in the electronic count but by 5:00 a.m. the next morning, Calderón had closed the gap and by 11:00 he had pulled ahead by 0.57 percent of total ballots cast, about 240,000 votes. The results were statistically impossible—virtually every polling place fed into the computers from midnight on had been awarded to Calderón.

"VOTO POR VOTO, CASILLA POR CASILLA"

An indignant López Obrador summoned his people to the Zócalo for an "informative assembly" that Saturday (July 8). The Centro was plastered with BIG WANTED FOR FRAUDE ELECTORAL signs starring Luis Carlos Ugalde. A half-million militants (police estimates) shook their fists and cursed Calderón and Fox and their PANista henchmen, the IFE and Televisa. They argued at the top of their lungs that the ballots must be counted out *"Voto por Voto y Casilla por Casilla."* AMLO pledged to carry on the fight until "the last consequences." *"¡No Está Solo! ¡No Está Solo!"* the crowd roared back.

At least 1.4 million citizens (police estimates) showed up for a second informative assembly 10 days later on July 18, topping the turnout against the *desafuero* 16 months earlier and setting a new national record for attendance at a political rally. The march from Chapultepec Park was so dense that most of the marchers could not even get into the Centro Histórico. Those who stuffed the great square were pressed so tightly together they couldn't even get their hands over their heads. When AMLO spoke, the crowd turned so silent you could have heard a Kleenex drop. Then everyone doffed their *cachuchas* and intoned the National Hymn, the one about the roar of the cannon and a Son of God in every soldier. It took me an hour to worm my way through the crush to get back to my room and file a story.

The numbers at the meetings kept swelling exponentially. López Obrador was doubling the crowd size with every informative assembly. On the 30th of July, 2.1 million (police estimates) "marched" through El Monstruo. So many Pejemaniacs had congregated that the tail of the gathering never left Chapultepec Park. Television monitors were strung up on Reforma to broadcast El Peje's remarks. This time López Obrador proposed that everyone stay right where they were in the streets until the ballots were counted *"Voto por Voto y Casilla por Casilla."* Those in hearing range responded with a resoundingly sibilant *"¡Síííííííííííííí!"* Mexico was lurching into the political unknown.

THE OCCUPATION OF EL MONSTRUO

Tents were rolled out to protect the multitudes from the drenching rains in the heroic days ahead. AMLO's Great Plantón (sit-in) stretched 13 kilometers, from the Zócalo all the way to the PEMEX fountain in Polanco. Ten thousand activists from the 31 states bedded down in the plaza, periodically relieved by fresh contingents from the provinces. Each subsequent stretch of the Plantón was covered by representations from the 16 delegations of the capital. The tents snaked down Madero Street where the residents of the Cuauhtémoc encamped, and out onto Juárez Avenue where the Carranza delegation and Colonia Guerrero—one of the Superbarrios had his own tent—took over, turned left down Reforma (Azcapotzalco, Iztapalapa, Iztacalco, Coyoacán, Tlalpan, the rural delegations, plus the GAM) through Chapultepec Park (Benito Juárez and Miguel Hidalgo) to ritzy Polanco (Álvaro Obregón and Cuajimalpa). Tens of thousands slept in the streets, much as the damnificados had done after the 1985 earthquake from which the seed of civil resistance had sprung a generation ago. I ran into Alejandro, Lalo's architect son. The circle was complete.

The Super Plantón created instant community. Each camp cooked up cauldrons of vittles to ward off the hunger of the masses. Hundreds of Porta-Potties were trucked in. The tents were turned into dormitories and art galleries and pirate radio stations. Grotesque papier-mâché "Fecales" (a scatological contraction of Felipe & Calderón) proliferated, and jocular *pintas* were thrown up on the walls. Anti-Calderón buskers moved from tent to tent to enliven the spirits of the campers. UNAM professors conducted classes, and spirited roundtables were convened. Elena Poniatowska and Carlos Monsiváis and Paco Taibo II visited different camps each day. In every tent, video screens blasted political documentaries. Poets declaimed their screeds and El Vampiro tootled wild sax. Every night, a score of jarocho players would walk the Plantón from the Zócalo to Polanco, serenading the protesters with their rollicking Caribbean melodies.

And every day, brigades marched out into El Monstruo to perform acts of nonviolent resistance, blocking the doors of the Stock Market and the banks, taking over the toll booths on the Cuernavaca highway to let motorists drive into the city free of charge, bothering the IFE at its bunker down Tlalpan, booing Televisa out on Chapultepec Avenue, disrupting the sales floor at Wal-Mart, and chaining themselves to the attorney general's offices. The cry "Airport! Airport!" went up at the meetings, and the feds sent thousands of militarized police to cordon off Benito Juárez International Airport. The Plantón turned the Monstruo into a thousand Seattles.

AMLO summoned his people to the Zócalo every evening at 7:00 p.m., updating the progress of the battle for a recount and riffing history: the struggle of Juárez and Madero for a democratic Mexico; how the Constitution granted the people the right to change their government when it no longer represented them; the uses of nonviolent resistance as practiced by Mandela and Martin Luther King. Never in my strangest dreams could I have imagined I would hear the story of Gandhi and the salt march told to tens of thousands of pissed-off Mexicans on the verge of rising up against their government.

The *veteranos* gathered to swap stories. AMLO would never sell us out like that rat Cuauhtémoc, who had secretly negotiated with Salinas behind our backs back in '88. But this is not like '88, Luis Cota argued. The Plantón and occupation of the capital were unprecedented in radical annals. The railroad workers and the teachers who marched with Demetrio Vallejo and Valentín Campa and Othón Salazar in the 1950s had never assembled such crowds. The masses summoned by the students in '68 were dwarfed by AMLO's movement.

And the summer rains poured down upon us, *aguaceros* so dense you couldn't make out the camarada standing next you. We huddled under our umbrellas and yodeled, "*¡Llueve y Llueve y El Pueblo No Se Mueve!*"—It Rains and It Rains and The People Do Not Move!

The occupation did not go unnoticed. The PANs and the PRIs and their pals on Televisa and Azteca and in the prensa vendida hollered that AMLO had "kidnapped" the city and should be prosecuted with the full weight of the law. Why had The Fox backed off when he nearly had El Peje behind bars?

Seven million vehicle trips are recorded every workday on Reforma, points out the newspaper of the same name, and without the bumper-to-bumper gridlock the air got a lot cleaner. The Imecas dipped below a hundred. You could almost breath again. Nonetheless, the motoring class was severely vexed by the Plantón—AMLO lost the sympathy of all those who had applauded the construction of the Second Story. López Obrador was a "fascist" who violated the rights of *terceros* (third parties), i.e., the Monster's 5,000,000 automobile owners. Even the Mexico City Human Rights Commission got into the act, charging that López Obrador was violating the human rights of the moneyed classes to zip down Reforma in a nifty new land yacht. Carlos Monsiváis, who, like me, has never driven a car, resigned from the movement unexpectedly.

CONSTITUTIONAL CRISIS LOOMS

AMLO challenged the vote counts in court. The PRD lawyers filed to disqualify results from thousands of polling stations where more votes had been cast than ballots allocated. At length, in mid-August, the Supreme Electoral Tribunal, which was entrusted with validating the results, issued an order to recount the ballots *"voto por voto y casilla por casilla"*—but only in 9 percent of the 114,000 polling places where the anomalies were blatant and inexplicable.

No breakout of the mini-recount was ever made public, although 2,000,000 ballots were either disqualified or changed. Extrapolating from available numbers, Claudia Sheinbaum, AMLO's point woman on the count, estimated that López Obrador had won the presidency of Mexico by a million votes. Nonetheless, the Supreme Electoral Tribunal refused to order a further recount. Calderón still led El Peje by 230,000 votes.

While this titanic *lucha* surged on the streets and in the courtrooms of the Monstruo, all hell was breaking loose 500 kilometers south in Oaxaca. Striking teachers were brutally repressed by a PRI governor named Ulises Ruiz, and the Oaxaca People's Popular Assembly (APPO) filled the state capital demanding his removal. A thousand barricades were built in and around the city, and Ruiz organized death squads to hunt down the rebels. Twenty-six were murdered and the old colonial city was often ablaze with burning buses and buildings. *México bronco* ("wild Mexico") was slipping out of control.

Constitutional crisis loomed. Mexico's Magna Carta obligated Vicente Fox to deliver his final Informe to Congress September 1, but AMLO's assets inside the legislature had seized the podium in the Chamber of Deputies and locked it down to prevent the president from speechifying. Tensions tested the breaking point.

When the Hummer ferrying The Fox and his shrill, kinetic first lady Martita Sahagún pulled up in front of the embattled Legislative Palace on Informe day, worried PANistas ran to the president to warn him of the PRD's perfidy and vowed to put their bodies on the line to take back the podium if that's what he wanted them to do. Fox stood there for a while, not really getting the picture. Martita whispered in his ear and a grim frown spread across Vicente's suddenly aging features. Then the President and the First Lady turned on their heels and retreated to Los Pinos. Fox had been the first Mexican head of state ever to be denied the podium by Congress. The imperial presidency had sucked up its final Faro.

ENDGAME FOR DEMOCRACY

On September 5, the Supreme Electoral Tribunal validated the fraudulent results and Felipe Calderón was declared president-elect. There was no higher body to appeal to. Yes, the judges conceded, there had been many many "possible anomalies," but the panel could not determine whether the sum total would have changed the outcome. The Peje's people sulked in their tents. The hard rain fell even harder. But the citizens of AMLO nation were mostly the color of the earth, *los de abajo* as the revolution had cast them, the eternal *jodidos*. To them, La Lucha was an endless series of setbacks, but they were tenacious. They knew how to *aguantar*, to hang on, the most pertinent verb in Mexico's dictionary. El Pueblo had been in the streets for seven weeks now and no one was going home just yet.

Vicente Fox was scheduled to deliver the final Grito of his presidency on September 15, Independence Eve, and he was determined to shout out his "¡*Vivas!*" from the National Palace balcony in the Zócalo, as is the prerogative of the President of Mexico. But the Zócalo was otherwise occupied by AMLO's army and they had announced that they were going to throw their own Grito, and The Fox was not invited. If indeed the outgoing president succeeded in penetrating the plaza, López Obrador's people threatened to turn their backs on him and pull down their pants in a mass mooning.

In preparation for a federal police assault to wrest back the Zócalo, the Peje's people barricaded the four corners of the great square. The PFP massed on the side streets and urban slaughter was on deck.

The Fox blinked first. To preserve public peace, the president would go instead to Dolores Hidalgo, in his home state of Guanajuato, to offer his Grito and commune with the ghost of the old rebel priest himself. AMLO chose the interim mayor, Alejandro Encinas, to yell the "*¡Vivas!*" in the Zócalo. Rosario Ibarra rang the bell.

And at midnight the Plantón was declared done. The people packed up their belongings. The tents were dismantled. The traditional Independence Day military parade was scheduled to get under way the next morning at 10:00 a.m., and López Obrador had decided that a confrontation with the armed forces at this stage of the struggle would not be helpful to his movement.

But the multitudes did not return to their homes right away. In early afternoon on the 16th, after the last tanks had rolled out, hundreds of thousands of us poured back into the Zócalo for the "National Democratic Convention," invoking the shades of Zapata and Villa and yes, the pesky Zapatistas. AMLO thanked everyone and asked them if they wanted to form their own government and the people sang out "*¡¡¡Síííííííí!!!*" and yelled "*¡No Está Solo!*" and "*¡Voto por Voto! ¡Casilla por Casilla!*" and the new chant, "*Es un Honor* To Be With Obrador!" and the skies broke apart and the rain drilled down in blinding sheets. When I put up my umbrella, it just disintegrated. "*Llueve y Llueve y El Pueblo No Se Mueve.*"

INAUGURAL PANDEMONIUM

Two months later on November 20, the day Francisco Madero had selected to ignite the Mexican Revolution 96 years before, López Obrador and his people returned to the Zócalo and the Peje was elected the "legitimate" president of Mexico by a show of hands, and the legitimate president presented his cabinet.

Andrés Manuel jumped the gun on Calderón by 10 days—Fecal's inauguration was set by the Constitution for December 1. Heavy security precautions were mounted for the occasion. Twenty-five thousand

Federal Preventive Police took up positions around the Legislative Palace. Seven kilometers of three-meter-high metal barricades were erected to keep the masses at bay. Sharpshooters perched on the roofs, scouting the streets surrounding the Candelaria de los Patos Metro stop for suspicious interlopers.

Forty-eight hours before Fox was slated to pin the presidential sash on the much shorter Calderón, pandemonium broke out in the Chamber of Deputies. López Obrador's legislators once again seized the podium but were repelled by the PANistas—the two sides uncorked water bottles at each other and bonked heads with their briefcases. Hair was pulled, ties were torn, and many punches were thrown and a few even landed. One PANista unloosed a loogie at a Peje deputy. After several hours of scrimmaging, the leftists regained a foothold and soon both parties were installed on the podium, separated only by a narrow buffer zone of peacemakers. Sometimes the adversaries snarled at each other. Sometimes they sang. No one slept. Down below, the PRIistas slumped in their *curules* in deadpan silence, waiting to cut a deal with whoever prevailed.

Felipe Calderón's handlers stared at this chaos on the tube and brainstormed to circumvent it. At midnight December 1, Televisa and TV Azteca trained their cameras on the president-elect somewhere in the bowels of Los Pinos. He is surrounded by generals and admirals. A voice off camera asks him if swears to uphold the honor of Mexico. Calderón agrees. But the ceremony is bogus. The Constitution requires the new president to swear in before Congress.

Tempers flare anew the next morning. AMLOs and Calderones go for each other up on the podium and wrestle down below in the aisles. Suddenly, amidst the flailing legislators, Calderón and Fox, cocooned by a protective flying wedge of soldiers, break through the back of the stage. Fecal is pushed to the microphone but Fox is lost in the hurly-burly, and the President-elect has to pin the red, green, and white ceremonial sash on himself. Once again, Calderón pledges to defend the honor of the Patria. He is at the microphone for 30 seconds before being whisked off by his Praetorian Guard. For the time being, Mexico would have two presidents.

THE RETURN OF CAMACHO SOLÍS

Let's backtrack to July 2. AMLO has won 16 states, mostly in southern Mexico and the major metropolitan centers in that half of the country. Although López Obrador has taken El Monstruo handily, racking up nearly 60 percent of the vote, his successor as jefe de gobierno, Marcelo Ebrard, has done even better in becoming the fourth straight leftist mayor of Left City, garnering 2.2 million votes, a half-million more than the Peje had tabulated in 2000 (1.69 million) and Cárdenas in 1997 (1.86 million), a mandate.

Marcelo's big win signaled the return of Manuel Camacho Solís to power in the city where he has played a pertinent role for over 20 years. Ebrard is Camacho's political son. He has followed his mentor up and down his erratic career path through the PRI, was Camacho's second in command when he was regent, accompanied him through the tribulations of his rupture with Salinas, and partnered with him when the wily politico formed his own vanity party before both melded into the PRD when El Peje took the city in 2000.

Manuel Camacho Solís's place in the Monstruo's political pileup cannot be underplayed. As director of SEDUE, he guided the reconstruction of the city after the great '85 quake, and, save for his suicide leap as peace commissioner in Chiapas, he has remained a central figure in the drama of the capital for a generation. His protégé Ebrard had served AMLO as police chief until he was fired by Fox after the Tláhuac lynching. The selection of Marcelo Ebrard to succeed López Obrador as mayor of this monster megalopolis was widely interpreted as payback to Camacho Solís for services rendered while AMLO ran the city.

Marcelo Ebrard Casaubón is a hunk. Tall, sturdy, and earnestly forceful, he cuts a Kennedyesque figure up there on the podiums, an image he cultivated by tying the knot with the glamorous artist-actress Mariagna Prats the week after his 2006 election. Ebrard was soon being measured for presidential timber—if he can survive the next six years in the hothouse political wars of Left City. His fortunes depend on how he navigates the treacherous shoals between AMLO and his arch-nemesis Calderón and the rapidly disintegrating PRD.

FELIPE'S BLOODY CRUSADE

Marcelo received the city from interim mayor Alejandro Encinas, who had shepherded the Monstruo through the Tumult of 2006. Not a week after Ebrard took the baton, Felipe Calderón, with whom he would have a touchy relationship in the coming years, exercised the shaky authority that his contaminated election had not conferred upon him and ordered 30,000 Mexican army troops into Calderón's home state of Michoacán and other drug-riddled jurisdictions to wage the final battle with the omni-powerful cartels.

Two years later, Calderón's crusade, which many suspect was devised to curry favor with Washington, had drenched Mexico in blood—10,000 lost their lives in the first 27 months of this futile exercise to kill off the hydra-headed cartels, including nearly 1,000 police officers and soldiers, with no appreciable diminishment of the drug flow north. At this writing, more heads have been chopped off by rival drug gangs in the past 18 months than in Baghdad at its bloodiest. Dozens of civilians have been gunned down at army checkpoints or in other collateral damage inflicted by the military upon local populations. More than a thousand complaints are on file with the National Human Rights Commission alleging the trampling of individual rights guarantees by the military, and widespread corruption in the upper echelons of the anti-drug bureaucracy has Washington gagging at the stench.

Meanwhile, hard drug consumption in Mexico has expanded dramatically and the epidemic has spawned a growing legalization movement. The leader of the PRD delegation in the Legislative Assembly has introduced a bill to decriminalize marijuana use in Left City.

Just yesterday, Ms. X, my mota connection, dropped by to voice her consternation at the sorry state of affairs in Tepito. An aging *niña de la calle* with hard-core street smarts, Ms. X is not easily shocked, but she had just encountered an eight-year-old kid smoking crack in a Tepito alley. "Eight years old, John!" the veteran party girl exclaimed. "What is this world coming to?"

TROUBLE IN TEPITO

The heads were rolling out at Benito Juárez International Airport just days after Marcelo Ebrard's swearing-in in December 2006, and newly

arrived tourists had to step smartly to conserve their own. The decapitated heads of two employees of an international freight forwarder
had just been discovered on airport grounds. The international airport
has been a popular transshipment point for drugs since Durazo's day,
but the competition was getting rowdy. Loads of ephedrine, a critical
ingredient for cooking speed, were showing up every day. The freight
forwarders were moving impressive quantities of cocaine and arms
through Benito Juárez's airport and the cartels had gone to war for
control of the *plaza*.

In January, two more heads minus their bodies (the bodies are
rarely found) were discovered by schoolgirls in the adjacent Peñón
de Los Baños colonia which Marcelo's successor as Mexico City police
chief, Joel Ortega, had designated as the Monstruo's second most dangerous drug venue behind Tepito. Indeed, the two heads were identified as belonging to operators of the Tepito Cartel. I had never heard
the Barrio Bravo boys assigned cartel status before—cartels control the
action from plantations to transport to distribution.

Not to be outdone by Calderón, before dawn on February 14,
2007, Marcelo Ebrard went to war against the Tepito Cartel. Six hundred Granaderos backed up by Federal Preventive robocops attacked
the huge *vecindad* known as The Fort at Tenochtitlán #40 (the building
has a separate address around the corner on Jesús Carranza) in the
entrails of the conflicted barrio. Ortega described Tenochtitlán #40 as
a dope supermarket where drugs were retailed 25 hours a day—350
kilos of marijuana, 3.5 kilos of cocaine, and 80 tons of pirate CDs were
retrieved from the caves and tunnels deep inside The Fort. The cops
pushed 144 families into the street, assaulting the doors and walls with
sledgehammers. The bewildered tenants huddled on the sidewalk in
the chill February dawn, wondering what next. Marcelo sent the coffee wagon around. Tenochtitlán #40 had been constructed as replacement housing after the 1985 Sismo and did not resist the pounding
long. Bulldozers were brought in to complete this orgy of deconstruc-
tion and Marcelo ordered the property expropriated under the Law
of "Extinción de Dominio," i.e., the wiping out of houses. The new
Mayor promised that a neighborhood cultural center would soon be
operating on the premises. Three years later, the Tepiteños were still
wondering when.

SAN MARCELO, GUARDIAN OF THE HEALTH OF THE PEOPLE

The new mayor's concern for the health of his Chilangos was at odds with the aspirations of the motoring classes. He closed off the Centro Histórico to traffic on Sundays and designated the Sabbath as Bicycle Only Day. Now, each Sunday, thousands of devotees of the sport pedal the streets of the old city on strange contraptions. Rollerbladers zip in and out of the two-wheeler traffic. Citywide "Cyclotrons" are scheduled once a month, and city officials are obligated to bicycle to work on the first of each month. It takes the mayor exactly 22 minutes to sprint from his Condesa digs to City Hall.

Saint Marcelo has also enhanced the quality of life for us Chilangos by declaring a no-smoking ban in public establishments. Mexico City is the most populated urban monster on the right side of the planet to promulgate such a decree, a measure that has provoked considerable resistance.

The cigarette (Carlos Slim is the leading manufacturer of Mexican coffin nails) is practically an accoutrement to the national costume. El Flaco Agustín Lara always had a Delicado drooping from his thin lips and La Doña María Félix's extravagant exhales punctuated the Golden Age of Mexican Cinema. The after-dinner *sobremesa* of cigars and cognac powers the conversations of poets and politicos in the cafés of the old quarter. The no-smoking edict was a frontal assault on a pillar of Chilango culture.

Thousands of No SMOKING logos were distributed to the doubtful proprietors of restaurants and bars and hotels—one was even tacked to the door of Room 102 of the Hotel Isabel. Some recalcitrant restaurateurs, like Marco Rascón, the original Superbarrio and now the owner of an upscale fish refectory in the Condesa, lashed out at the ban as left-wing "fascism."

Patrons who refused to crush out their butts would be first warned by the waiters, and if they balked at compliance, the police were to be called. Penalties for violating the no-smoking prohibition included a mandatory 36 hours in the slammer and steep fines. The phantom of Ernesto P. Uruchurtu was spotted dragging his chains through the back rooms of City Hall.

Police Chief Ortega was not keen for confrontations with obstreperous *borrachos* and urged discretion on the part of his cops. Instead, smokers were shown the street, where they could puff to their heart's content, and the sidewalks of the Centro Histórico were converted into public ashtrays. Bar and restaurant owners like La Blanca's Carlos Diez complained that deadbeats were stepping outside for a smoke break as an excuse to walk out on the bill.

As if getting Chilangos to pedal bicycles and stop smoking was not enough to preserve the health of the harried citizens of Monstruo-landia, San Marcelo enacted the Law of "Buen Morir," a right-to-die law that now empowers the terminally ill to discontinue treatment and chugalug Brompton cocktails until they are safely parked in Mictlán.

Although Cardenal Norberto steadfastly opposed the measure, the badmouthing was muted compared to his breast-beating in April 2007 when free abortion on demand finally kicked in. Initiated by Rosario Robles, shaped into legislation by AMLO, implemented by Marcelo, and upheld by the Supreme Court, the measure enraged the Church hierarchy, and the Council of Bishops (CEM) contracted a plot in Dolores Cemetery to inter unwanted fetuses rescued from the city hospitals.

THE GUINNESS BOOK OF RECORDS RECORD

Enhanced budgets that have more than tripled in the past 10 years, from 37 billion pesos under Cárdenas in 1997 to 122 billion in 2009, have given Marcelo the extra wherewithal to entertain Left City in the style to which it has become accustomed. Ebrard's vocation for *espectáculos* out-Robleses even Robles herself. The mayor invited the Formula One road show to the Monstruo and the monster machines careened around the five *glorietas* on Reforma at 200 kilometers an hour, their 120-decibel roar deafening the Angel and triggering cardiac arrest for one old-timer who was just trying to cross the street. Like Cárdenas with his record *rosca*, Marcelo strives for inclusion in the Guinness Book. One Christmas, he rolled out the world's biggest piñata (30 meters around) and installed what he touted as the world's greatest skating rink (433 by 153 feet) in the Zócalo.

Did you say a skating rink in the ZÓCALO? Yup. In December 2007 and again in 2008, Key Entertainment of Houston, Texas, iced over the floor of the great plaza, a conversion that would bar demonstrators without skates from Mexico's Tiananmen for months. Where the Aztecs had sacrificed hundreds of thousands of captured warriors to their complicated deities, Zamboni machines now ruled. Where revolutionaries once massed to overthrow their governments, skaters now glided and stumbled. Ebrard's logic was eminently left: Ice-skating is a sport that only the wealthy can afford. Now the city's poor would get a whirl.

Snow is a class issue in this megalopolis. When the white stuff covers the heights of the Ajusco as it does every few winters, the *ricos* don snowsuits and load the kids' sleds into the family Cherokee. The very wealthy ski at Aspen and Vail. But the *jodidos* are woefully unprepared for cold weather—central heating is hardly a universal fixture—and they are even more inexpert at winter sports. For starters, how many Chilangos even owned a pair of ice skates? A sporting goods tycoon was enlisted to donate 2,500 pairs for the trainee Hans Brinkers and Sonja Henies. Many neophytes crashed to the ice at first contact, and nurses raced to cure their bruises. A fleet of ambulances was parked outside the great rink for emergencies. Because, after all, the Zócalo is still the Centro, cops were coached to patrol the ice to collar silver-skated *rateros*.

Marcelo's addiction to setting records is insatiable. During his administration, Mexico has climbed into the top 10 in the Guinness Book of Records for countries trying to set Guinness Book of Records records. Among other achievements: the world's largest *quinceañera*, or girl's sweet 15 birthday party (180 *jovencitas* and their entourages of *chambelanes*), the world's largest *danzón* competition (more than 1,000 couples), the world's most enormous fleur-de-lis—fashioned from a million recycled aluminum cans by the Boy Scouts—the biggest kiss-a-thon on Earth (Valentine's Day 2008).

The right-wingers scoff at Ebrard's extravaganzas. Such spectacles only confirm that the Left has run out of ideas, opines Professor Jeffrey Weldon of the business-oriented Technological Institute of Mexico State (ITAM). But Left City continues to set records.

The crowning glory of all this record setting was the gathering of 18,000 naked Chilangos for a Spencer Tunick portrait in April 2007—even La Blanca's watchman and his 100-year-old father stripped for the occasion. The peak point of Tunick's record-breaking orgy of flesh came when the internationally celebrated photographer had his subjects face the Metropolitan Cathedral and prostrate themselves in Muslim prayer mode—an irate Cardenal Norberto later demanded that Tunick airbrush out the Cathedral.

ANOTHER POLICE CHIEF DONE GONE

Crime has not much slackened under Marcelo Ebrard's stewardship of the Monster. The kidnapping of the very rich continues unabated in Left City. In August 2008, after the Flower Gang (they stick daisies in the mouths of their victims) had kidnapped and slain the adolescent son of the Martí sporting goods fortune, the right-wingers staged a second (but much reduced) "White March" demanding Marcelo's resignation.

While the kidnappers and *rateros* continue to make crime pay, the forces of law and order terrorize the residents of Left City. Eleven young people were trampled to death and a policewoman killed when Marcelo's cops raided the News Divine, a grubby nightclub in the Gustavo A. Madero delegation after school on a Friday afternoon, lobbing tear gas canisters into the back room where underage teenagers were downing tequila shots and dancing in their underwear. The police then stupidly blocked all the doors so the kids could not escape. Police chief Ortega was obliged to resign, much as Ebrard had been three years previous.

WUXTRA! WUXTRA! READ ALL ABOUT IT! 15,000 ANNOYING AMBULANTES DISAPPEAR OVERNIGHT FROM THE STREETS OF EL CENTRO!

At the stroke of midnight on October 12, 2007, the Day of the Cosmic Race, hordes of ambulantes who had turned the streets of the Centro Histórico into a colossal open-air bazaar for five centuries voluntarily vanished from the 192-block area designated as Periphery A, roughly extending north-south from Tepito to Fray Servando Avenue and La Merced to the Eje Central on the east-west bias.

The ambulantes' disappearance had been hashed out during months of acrimonious negotiations with 66 distinct associations, most pertinently the Rico family (a nephew now ran Doña Guille's syndicate) and the venerable Alejandra Barrios, freshly released from the Tepepan women's prison after being extradited from Cuba, where she had fled when the husband of a rival *lideresa*, María Rosette of the Tepito mafia, was gunned down during an altercation on Argentina Street in 2005. To smother expected resistance, the associations were promised 29 inside commercial plazas, large drafty warehouses where they could relocate their sellers.

But rank-and-file ambulantes hated these *plazas*, because they were inside jobs and they made their living off street traffic. On the day before the deal came down, 15,000 stood beneath Ebrard's windows at City Hall to *mentar la madre* (speak out profanely) against the agreement. "*¡Si no hay Trabajo, nos vamos al Gavacho!*" ("If there's no work, we'll go bother the gringos"). The recalcitrant street vendors were persuaded to move on by 1,500 tear gas–wielding Granaderos and the distribution of tens of thousands of flyers threatening arrest if they were not off the streets of Periphery A by midnight October 12.

Marcelo's sleight of hand was enhanced by the "cockroach effect." Vendors simply migrated across the Eje Central to Periphery B, doubling the number of ambulantes on the other side of the street. My friend Marcia, who lives on the west side of the Eje, called in panic. She was supposed to be at a wedding by 3:00 p.m., and she couldn't get out of her building because so many ambulantes were pressed up against the front door. One 15-year-old hawking soft-core porno (*Sex With Older Women, Sex With Animals*) refused to budge. Four months later, when Marcelo made good on his pledge and all the ambulantes were pushed out of Periphery B, Marcia was finally able to leave her home.

Meanwhile, the Centro Histórico has been radically altered. For the first time in living memory, the façades of the old city's colonial gems, usually draped in greasy sheets of plastic and obstructed by the stands of the vendors, are exposed to the naked eye. One no longer has to wind through catacombs of *puestos* or step off the sidewalk into life-threatening traffic to walk the streets. The din of the sellers has been silenced and the venomous tang of their *fritangas* does not invade one's gullet. Enrique Galván, who writes the "Money" column for *La Jornada*, estimates that the expulsion of the ambulantes has increased the value of Carlos Slim's properties threefold.

The downside is that the bargains are gone. Sunglasses that sold for 200 pesos at Slim's Sanborn's and 20 pesos a few steps away on the corner of Isabel la Católica and Uruguay are no longer in easy reach. But culture vultures who had returned to the Centro with the AMLO-Slim renovation are delighted by the banishment of the ambulantes. For years, the sellers had coagulated so thickly around the museum that housed José Luis Cuevas's paintings off Moneda Street that many art lovers never even realized there was a museum there.

Despite the ambulantes' displacement, there is still plenty of action on the Centro's streets. The *boleros* (shoeshine workers) and the newspaper kiosks take up impressive slices of the sidewalk. Organ grinders lug their irritatingly out-of-tune antique *cilindrinos* from bar to bar cadging coins from customers for *la música*. Five-year-old Indian kids pump accordions on the corners. Mimes and "living statues" (the city has licensed 12 of them, but there are many outlaws) stand stock-still in the public way. *Toreros* take back the sidewalks whenever they see an opening.

How long will this lull last? Recession and depression once again has the Monstruo down in the dumps, and hard times always drive the poor to sell in the streets. Marcelo's best-laid plans will not keep them away for long. After all, the ambulantes have been with us for 500 years now. History is on their side.

MARCELO VS. AMLO

Ebrard's tenure has always seemed a high-wire act. He is indebted to López Obrador and refuses to formally recognize Felipe Calderón's pretensions to the presidency, although sometimes they share the same room. What to do with AMLO, who may well be his rival for the left presidential nod in 2012, is a dilemma.

El Peje has hardly kept his lip zippered since Calderón moved into Los Pinos. In March 2008, soon after Fecal sent a PEMEX "reform"—read "privatization"—measure to Congress, López Obrador created the Movement to Defend Mexico's Oil and brigades of women donned long skirts and floppy sombreros, strung *bandoleras* of fake bullets over their breasts, and picked up plastic Carabinas 20–20 to honor the woman *soldaderas* who fought in Villa's and Zapata's peasant armies—Las Adelitas. The brigades of Adelitas were named for hero women—Leona Vicario and the Communist organizer Benita Galeana and Rosario Ibarra de Piedra—and led by activists like actress Jesusa Rodríguez and AMLO's vote counter Claudia Sheinbaum.

The Adelitas saw their first action in April 2008 when the PAN and the PRI tried to pull off a *madruguete*—an early-morning (or late-night) secret vote from which the opposition is excluded—to fast-track the privatization scam. Outside the Senate, 13,000 Adelitas surrounded the old *casona* on Xicoténcatl Street and threw themselves in front of the senators' limousines and Hummers to prevent them from voting on Calderón's bill. The PAN and the PRI demanded that Marcelo send in the Granaderos to control these *"guerrilleras"* and *"paramilitaries,"* but the Mayor refused to intervene.

Meetings and marches lasted all summer long while the bill was debated, finally coming to a boil in mid-October when a compromise reform law that seemed to eliminate the more obvious facets of privatization was to be voted up by Congress. López Obrador called his supporters together and asked for their advice. Would they accept the compromise bill even if they hadn't won all they had been struggling for? One hundred ballot boxes were lined up on Juárez Avenue, and most of the 17,000 Adelitas and Adelitos at the street meeting voted No. A week of militant if nonviolent demonstrations followed and once again Marcelo refused to send in the riot squad. Instead, the Federal Preventive Police were called out to prevent El Peje's people from crashing the solons' vote on the reforms after the final session was moved from the Senate to an off-site office building known as El Caballito because of the abstract version of the famous equestrian statue that sits on its esplanade.

Now the PRD has divided between AMLO's people and a reformist wing popularly known as Los Chuchos because many of its leaders are named Jesús, and Marcelo Ebrard walks a fine line trying not to play favorites—at least publicly. The rift widened considerably after the chief Chucho Jesús Ortega flimflammed the party presidential election from López Obrador's *gallo*, Alejandro Encinas. Whoever wins the Left presidential nomination in 2012 may very well have no party to sponsor him (or her).

"WE ARE THE MEXICANS AND WE ARE NEVER GIVING UP!" (An interview with Berta Robledo)

Berta perched at the counter, a copy of the petroleum "reform" law Fecal was trying to ram through Congress in one hand and a magnifying glass in the other. Every once in a while, Berta consulted a dictionary she pulled out of her big shopping bag. I sat down and ordered a café con leche from Manuel.

"Ay Don Ross, they are trying to pull a fast one on us again. What do you think this means? 'Incentive contracts will be authorized to encourage contractors to complete their obligations prior to the final date assigned.' "

I told Berta I thought it was a trick. "Incentive contracts are the same thing as 'risk' contracts, which are prohibited by Article 27 of the

Constitution. Risk contracts give drillers a percentage of the oil they bring in. Incentive contracts give the drillers money instead of oil, but it's the same thing."

Berta sighed. "I still don't understand this all, but I'm getting the picture." Manuel brought the café and deftly upended the espresso into the glass of hot milk. Berta was sticking with just milk. We munched on a banderilla, *a kind of* pan dulce.

It was Thursday night and she was decked out in her Adelita duds, having just come from her brigade meeting. "We are planning for the Consulta. Do you have your ballot yet?" The Consulta would be a popular vote against privatization. Anyone, even a gringo, could vote. She handed me my ballot. Each question had a space for yes and no. There were two questions. "You vote no and no," she instructed me.

Berta's brigade was #8, "Enaguas Profundas" or Deep Petticoats—it was a joke on Calderón who wanted to drill en aguas profundas or deep water out in the Gulf. "Did you go to the debate this afternoon?" I asked. Every Tuesday and Thursday, the senators invited in experts to testify about the law, and the debates were broadcast on a big screen under a tent in the Zócalo. When Berta goes to these debates, she yells and shakes her fist at the so-called "experts" who want to privatize PEMEX.

"Ay Don John, what do you think? I had to work. Here I am about to retire from the hospital and they made me come in. But I told them I'm not going to miss the debates again. We have to do everything to stop them. Andrés Manuel can't do it all by himself." Berta pulled out her donation can and plunked it down on the counter. I paid the bill and dropped in the change and walked her to the Metro—she lives out in Tacubaya. "Buenas noches, compañera." I pecked her on the cheek. She shook my hand. "Buenas noches, Don Ross. We are going to win."

Every time I saw Berta at La Blanca that summer she was studying the law. Now she had a copy of the Constitution. "We used to think that we couldn't understand these laws they pass to trick us, but now we are studying what they mean and we are getting the power."

In the fall, the Senate passed a modified bill that didn't flat-out have the word "privatization" in it. The Adelitas tried to stop the lawmakers from voting on it. Enaguas Profundas lay down in the street. They sang "We Shall Not Be Moved" in Spanish. But still the bill passed. Berta and I met up at La Blanca that night.

"Ay, Don Ross, don't tell me anything. I'm so mad. They don't listen to the Mexicans. Who are these senators anyway? I don't think they are really

Mexicans," she fumed. Manuel brought over the charola *of* pan dulce *and we shared a chocolate* concha. *"These senators think they're so smart and powerful, but you know one thing? We are not giving up. Not now, not later. We are the Mexicans and we are never going to give up."*

PIG SPRING

Spring 2009 was an insalubrious station of the year for the Monstruo. During the first week of April—Semana Santa, when Chilangos with the wherewithal flee the broiling city for increasingly polluted beaches on both coasts—the Cutzamala river system that pumps in 70 percent of the Zona Metropolitana's water was shut down to unkink its entrails. Five million Chilangos—a quarter of the population—were left without a drop to drink.

Moreover, Mayor Marcelo, with an eye to consolidating his presidential ambitions during the run-up to July mid-term elections, was industriously reordering the megalopolis's roadways. The Interior Circuit and other vital arteries were shut down or traffic squeezed into reduced lanes due to the construction. Hundreds of thousands of trapped infernal internal combustion engines sputtered and belched, upping the Imecas to near-contingency levels. Gritty particulate drizzled from the scalding sky and respiratory ailments spiked—nearly a thousand cases of flu were registered by April 13, a statistical aberration for this time of the year.

This flu behaved distinctly from the seasonal variety. Ten thousand capitalinos die of influenza every year, usually the weakest and poorest portion of the populace, which has little access to health care, but this new flu was attacking healthy 20- to 40-year-olds, much like the Spanish pandemic of 1918 that took 20,000 lives here.

Public health officials suspected a new strain that combined both porcine and avian flus, a scourge that had long been anticipated but because Mexico had no facilities for testing the vector, samples were shipped off to a laboratory in Winnipeg, Canada (post 9/11 biosecurity prohibitions barred testing in Gringolandia), and results were not confirmed for several weeks. Meanwhile, thousands of hacking, snot-flinging Chilangos were crowding the city's emergency rooms.

Where and when the Great Swine Flu Panic of 2009 germinated aroused curiosities. Accusing fingers pointed to the festering transnational pig city in the Perote Valley on the Veracruz-Puebla border a few hundred miles east. Granjas Carroll, a subsidiary of the U.S. hog-killer Smithfield Farms, had set up the pestilent facilities soon after NAFTA cleared the U.S. Congress in 1994—the agribiz titan had been heavily fined for contaminating Virginia and North Carolina water sources, and Mexico offered a safe haven from environmental enforcement.

Indeed, Mexico's first case of suspected swine flu was detected in the Perote Valley hamlet of La Gloria, a few miles from the Granjas Carroll fence, when five-year-old Edgar Hernández was felled. Four hundred locals were subsequently sickened, but health authorities shrugged them off. Even after the suspect new flu had claimed its first fatality across the isthmus in Oaxaca April 13, mum was the PAN government's word.

President Calderón was clearly more concerned with the flagging health of an economy that was spiraling beyond recession. News of the new flu would have put the kibosh on a tourist season that had already been wrecked by the president's terrifying, ill-advised drug war—hordes of U.S. spring breakers had cancelled Cancún reservations to avoid the violence.

Felipe Calderón was particularly concerned about one U.S. tourist: popular freshman president Barack Obama, who touched down in the capital April 16 and stayed the night. The PANista desperately needed his U.S. counterpart's approbation as Mexico sank deeper into social and economic morass.

Purposefully kept in the dark about the health dangers, Baracko was escorted around the Anthropology Museum by Dr. Felipe Solís, who would expire the next week after exhibiting "flu-like symptoms." A Secret Service agent in Obama's entourage also reportedly came down with the swine flu.

Another luminary whacked by the still-secret plague was Marcelo Ebrard's political papa Manuel Camacho Solís who lay at death's door in the ritzy ABC Hospital out in Santa Fe.

Once the U.S. president was safely out of town, the Mayor, ever the guardian of the people's well-being, punched up the panic button, ordering the city's schools closed down—7,000,000 bored-out-of-their-gourd kids would spend the next two weeks driving their parents to distraction. Emergency restrictions left the Centro's bars and restaurants bereft of customers. La Blanca closed for eight days and the Hotel Isabel emptied out.

Marcelo got a one-day jump on Calderón in pumping up the panic but between the two of them the curtain came down on the Monstruo's social life. Screens and stages went dark and the museums slammed down the gates. Major soccer matches were played before an empty house in the fan-less Azteca Stadium. Cardinal Norberto called off Sunday Mass at the Metropolitan Cathedral and the Mayor, his Sabbath bike-athons.

Calderón won a significant political victory when Marcelo agreed to attend an emergency meeting at Los Pinos. Despite the Mayor's reluctance to recognize the president's much-questioned 2006 "victory," the two shared the same podium, no doubt bemused behind their blue masks at this unlikely and unholy political alliance.

The masses were frustrated by the shutdown. Three thousand flights were scratched at Benito Juárez International airport, infuriating would-be travelers. The May 1 International Workers Day march to the Zócalo was cancelled, ticking off union members—the economic downturn had driven unemployment rates to their highest peak since La Crisis of 1996. Also angered by the health strictures: prisoners at Mexico City's penitentiaries—hundreds rioted at the Southern Penitentiary when conjugal visits were denied.

To demonstrate his tattered authority, Calderón went on national TV three nights running and urged his constituents not to kiss or embrace in public, as is the Mexican social norm. Chilangos were advised to stand six feet apart, a statistical impossibility. Everyone was to wear blue *tapabocas* (surgical masks). Even the *sexoservidoras* of the street brigades (Brigadas Callejeras) in La Merced donned the masks and refused the *besos* of their clients. However, the usually jam-packed Metro, a logical incubator of contagion, remained open—it was joked that you could get a seat if you blew forcefully into a wad of Kleenex while munching on a handful of *chicharrones* (fried pork rinds).

Although the crime rate purportedly dipped by 40 percent, one enterprising, blue mask–wearing hold-up artist took down a pair of downtown banks. One of the few who defied peer pressure to put on the tapaboca was Oscar the Vampire, who continued to tootle on the vacant streets of the Centro, insisting that the public couldn't catch swine flu from a saxophone.

By late April, 80 deaths had been attributed to the piggish influenza for which medication was impossible to obtain. Tamiflu, produced by the Swiss pharmaceutical titan Roche, rocketed from 400 pesos to over a thousand for a 10-capsule cycle. Exasperated sneezers stormed the Farmacia Paris on Cinco de Febrero and the gendarmes had to be summoned to keep order.

As the panic crested, the vaunted solidarity of the Monstruo's denizens crumbled. When *Proceso* magazine cronista Fabrizio Mejía was locked out of his apartment, none of his neighbors would open their door to provide him with an extra key for fear of infecting their families. The Mexican family is considered the treasure of this country but if the truth be told, the "treasure" is really "my family"—not yours.

Because most cases were recorded in the capital where facilities for keeping tabs on the numbers were more fine-tuned, the swine flu quickly transmogrified into the Mexico City flu. Cars with Day Efe license plates were stoned in Guerrero state and the old "kill-a-Chilango" psychosis rebounded out in the provinces.

But scenes from Pig Spring were almost worth the price of admission: a cleaner in hospital scrubs and blue tapaboca swabbing down a statue of an Aztec warrior at the Templo Mayor museum; pedestrians lowering their tapabocas to sneak a forbidden smoke; Oscar in a top hat and frock coat playing the threads of his heart out to invisible passersby.

When I returned to the Hotel Isabel after a hundred days wrestling with liver cancer in California, a uniformed security guard in jackboots and surgical mask insisted upon smearing my palm with goopy hand sanitizer. "I know it's all a *faramalla* [trick, farce] but that's what the boss wants."

By mid-May, the panic had subsided and alarm was replaced with disdain. AMLO's supporters had suspected a Calderón conspiracy and many had refused to wear their tapabocas, which were blue, the PAN colors. Andrés Manuel himself had been threatened with heavy fines by the IFE for holding a public meeting in his native Tabasco in violation of health strictures. Some considered the PAN-demic had been plotted by the prudish National Action Party to exterminate public lovemaking by exuberant young couples on the Alameda. Others compared the swine flu faramalla to the mythical Chupacabras, a vampire-like "goatsucker" immortalized by a Chico Che cumbia. Indeed, the "Cumbia de La Influenza" ("The best way now to commit suicide/ Is to eat *ricos tacos de pastor*") was getting ample airplay.

For a millennium and more, those who have been touched to live here have had to deal with corrupt governance, environmental devastation, preventable epidemics, and endemic poverty, but their social immune system is still healthy enough to resist the bullshit of their rulers—whether they come from the Right or the Left.

THE FUTURE IS NEXT

The PRD, a party of the opposition, has held power in Mexico City for a decade now. A whole generation is growing up having known no other government than that of the Left. What happens next?

The bicentennial of Mexico's independence and the 100-year anniversary of the Mexican Revolution are up ahead on the 2010 calendar. Not heeding the lessons of Don Porfirio's downfall due to promiscuous spending on superfluous monuments for the 1910 Centennial, both Ebrard and Calderón are trying to sell the citizenry the same bill of goods.

With extravagant fanfare that included pyrotechnics above Chapultepec Castle, the president unveiled plans for a Bicentennial Arc at the foot of Reforma (!) and the rebranding of the heavily toxic "ecological" park on the site of the old PEMEX refinery in Azcapotzalco as "El Parque Bicentenario."

But times have changed and not everyone in Left City is buying the bicentennial hogwash. A 100-story "Bicentennial Tower" that would have set a Guinness Book of Record for Latin American skyscrapers, topping even the 85-story Torre Mayor constructed on Reforma during AMLO's reign, has been rejected by neighborhood associations in the Cuauhtémoc and Miguel Hidalgo delegations. Metro Line #12—the "Bicentennial Line"—that would run from the west of the Monstruo all the way to Tláhuac in the east is being challenged by the farmers of that rural delegation. A super-size "Bicentennial Tunnel," the "Supervía" that would have sped traffic from the Insurgentes circle out to Santa Fe, has succumbed to the Great Depression.

THE FUTURE IS PAST

1810, 1910, 2010. . . . Mexico's political metabolism is measured in hundred-year cycles, with social explosions programmed for the tenth year of the century. Will El Monstruo mark 2010 with revolutionary upheaval?

The future of Left City does not rest on a new Mexican revolution, or for that matter revolutionary models anywhere else in Latin America. The Leftness of this city is predicated on the energy we Chilangos invest in it, in the involvement of civil society in decision making and the distribution of power, the salvation of habitat, and how well the lessons of the past are learned in the future management of El Monstruo. Indeed, we ourselves are the Monster—each of us, all 23,000,000 of us, are its cells.

What comes next will be what came before, and it has never been a bed of roses. I have lived here for 25 years and I still can't drink the water from the tap, and pretty soon, if current depletion levels continue apace, there will be no water for anyone to drink. These 23,000,000 sentient human beings now test the carrying capacity of the Zona Metropolitana. The class divide has grown dangerously wider. There are five rats for every Chilango among us. A quarter of the Monstruo's residents suffer some mental illness. On the 50th anniversary of the publication of Carlos Fuentes's *Where the Air Is Clear*, bad air kills 35,000 citizens of this monstrous city each year.

The Monstruo is forever on the brink of simultaneous disasters. We are surrounded by 34 volcanoes, and monster earthquakes tremble beneath our feet. It has always been that way in this dangerous geography. The Aztecs sacrificed hundreds of thousands so that the gods would be pleased and not throw them out of this place. The struggle of Chilangos against the dire conditions that their physical environment imposes upon them is the true story of this city.

Cities themselves are a kind of biblical curse. Cain slew Abel and built the first city. But urban catastrophe is our bread and butter, and even if all the walls fall down tomorrow, there will still be a city here. In the end, the Monstruo is the people who have lived in this place and built it up over and over again, millennium after millennium, each time angry gods or natural disaster or foreign conquest or revolutions have torn it down. Us Chilangos have clung to this complicated birthright as steadfastly as the stones upon which our Monstruo stands, and like the stones, we are here to stay.

ACKNOWLEDGMENTS

Mil gracias to: Carlos Diez, Manuel García, Armando Penaloza, Daniel Valencia, and all the compas at the Café La Blanca; Toño and the pandilla at the Hotel Isabel; the history buffs at the Librería Madero, La Torre de Papel, and México Viejo; the staff at the Biblioteca Miguel Lerdo de Tejada; Colombe Chappey and Hermann Bellinghausen; all the Mirandas; the Karakoleros; Berta Robledo; Don Juanito; Don Ray; Don Inocencio; Don Isidro; "Alfredo"; "Orlando"; "Samuel"; Oscar "El Vampiro" & Rocío G; Alfonso Suárez Romero ("Daniel"); Pedro and Pablo Moctezuma Barragán; Marcia Perskie; Sid Dominitz; QR Hand; Steve Hiatt; Maestro John Womack; my doctors Catherine Frenette, David Horwitz, and Mark Dondero M.M.D. for keeping me breathing; and most of all, to Carl Bromley, who continues to exhibit unreasonable faith in my work; and of course, Elizabeth Bell, without whom *El Monstruo* would still be a whim. To you all, my full-bore agradecimientos.

WRITING EL MONSTRUO

El Monstruo: Dread & Redemption in Mexico City is the bittersweet fruit of a fortuitous *coyuntura* (coming together) of time and place. I am indeed fortunate to have written this defense of place in a place where I have been touched to live for the past quarter of a century. But the place where I live and write is being gentrified and sold off to the highest bidder, so who knows how long I will continue to be able to live and write here in this once-upon-a-time island kingdom.

The old quarter of Mexico City is honeycombed with repositories of the past—the many used bookstores on Donceles Street and the narrow alley between the General Post Office and the Palace of Mining plus antiquarian booksellers such as the Librería Madero provide a rich loam of history in which to grow this narrative. Museums like the Museo de la Ciudad, the Museo del Templo Mayor, Carlos Monsiváis's Museo del Estanquillo, and the National Museum of Interventions, among others, preserve what is in perpetual danger of being lost. Lecture series at the Colegio Nacional and the National Palace deepened the text, and the invaluable newspaper archives at the Biblioteca Miguel Lerdo de Tejada of the Secretaría de Hacienda filled in the holes. But more than the old stone buildings and yellowing pages of the ledgers, it is my neighbors who have persevered here in El Centro down the years who have most vitally informed this manuscript, rolled back the dark corners of what came before, and solved some of the mysteries the past invokes. What follows is a chapter-by-chapter look at my sources and inspirations.

Introduction. Although research for *El Monstruo* is very much grounded in site specifics, the insatiable quest for information took me for wild rides on the Internet. More than any of the 10 books I have published down the years, *El Monstruo* was assembled from the vast number of specialist pages readily accessible with the flick of a finger. Javier Marías's *Negra Espalda del Tiempo*, to which "Murder at the Hotel Isabel" is indebted, would never have been available if I had not bumped into it during my cybernautic flights. Similarly, Beat history in Mexico City is amply available on the net and in the writings and recollections of local Beat historians such as José Vicente Anaya. Details of my first visit to "El Monstruo" are lifted whole from a still-unpublished memoir of the times, *Los Marijuanos de Zapicho*.

Chapter I: Birth of a Monster draws upon monographs published in several editions of the Atlas de la Ciudad de México, issued by the Colegio de México. The prehistory of human settlement in the Valley of Mexico is the subject of much anthropological controversy and necessitated repeated visits to the library at the Museo Nacional de Antropología out in Chapultepec Park. The travels of outlanders in the Valley were elucidated by various texts that have survived the tears of time, among them the Codex of Xólotl.

Chapter II: City of Flowers & Smoking Hearts. Aztec-Mexica literature abounds in the environs. Too often it begins with Bernal Díaz del Castillo's *The Discovery and Conquest of Mexico* and Fray Bernardino de Sahagún's *Historia General de las Cosas de Nueva España*, both Conquistador chronicles. The writings of Miguel León Portilla and the delvings of Eduardo Matos Moctezuma are useful antidotes to the Spanish vision of Aztec savagery, as are Jacques Soustelle's treatises on the Mexica belief system. Gary Jennings's potboiler view of Aztec hijinks flavored my research. Frequent visits to the Museum of the Templo Mayor provided visualization of what it was I was writing about.

Chapter III: City of Palaces & Ghosts. Jonathan Kandell's exemplary biography of the city, *La Capital*, led me down many streets, as did texts collected in Ricardo López Méndez's *Estampas de Historia de México*. A brace of antiquarian bookstores here in the Centro were treasure troves of pertinent information on the colonial epoch, as were 49 issues of the Carlos Slim–financed glossy magazine *Centro: Guía Para Caminantes* that detail the hidden histories of colonial structures here in *la Primera Cuadra* of Mexico City. Indeed, the streets posted with little tile plaques affixed to still-standing gems were themselves valuable informants.

Chapter IV: City of Betrayed Hopes. Historical documents archived at the National Museum of Interventions and the museum's many publications provided valuable understandings of the plethora of foreign invasions that wracked the city and the country in the years following liberation. Lorenzo Meyer and Josefina Zoraida's *The United States and Mexico* remains a definitive text, as is Daniel Cosio Villegas's four-volume *General History of Mexico*. Much of my vision of this tragic period was first developed for *The Annexation of Mexico: From the Aztecs to the IMF*. Finding the scenes of the crimes was aided and abetted by the antiquarians who helped me to pinpoint, (amongst other obscure locales) the vanished cemetery where Santa Anna's leg was disinterred (now a traffic circle).

Chapter V: City of Order & Progress. John Kenneth Turner's classic exposé of the underbelly of the Porfiriato in *México Bárbaro* remains an inspiration to this writer. The chronicles of José María Marroqui, the city's official *cronista* during most of Don Porfirio's tyrannical domination of the capital, further elucidated the class oppression of the times. Enrique Espinosa López's voluminous *La Ciudad de México: Compendio Cronológico de Su Desarrollo Urbano* was a godsend in explaining the monumental expansion of the metropolis under the dictator.

Chapter VI: City of the Cannibal Revolution. The Mexican Revolution is embedded in the city's literary subsoil and the failing memories of its oldest citizens. The daily course of the 1910–1919 Mexican revolutions is charted in the crumbling newspapers preserved in great ledgers at the Lerdo de Tejada Library around the corner from my digs. I am particularly indebted to José Ángel Aguilar's two-volume chronicle of the Ten Tragic Days and John Lear's *Workers, Neighbors, and Citizens:*

The Revolution in Mexico City for the history of labor struggles during this turbulent time. Maestros John Womack (*Zapata and the Mexican Revolution*) and Friedrich Katz (*The Life and Times of Pancho Villa*) illuminated the narrative, as did visits to the much neglected Museum of the Revolution underneath the Monument of the same name. But my most prized sources were the Chilangos whose grandparents and parents and sometimes themselves knew the story of the Mexican Revolution firsthand and still pass it around over coffee at downtown cafés like La Blanca.

Chapter VII: City of Artists & Assassins. The murals of Rivera, Orozco, Siquieros, and their contemporaries and jewel-box settings like Kahlo's Casa Azul and Diego's San Ángel studios are still at the center of Mexico's cultural offerings and exude a taste of the artistic ferment that permeated the Monstruo during the 1920s. Although I dispute Enrique Krauze's political skews, I am grateful to him for his biographies of Carranza, Obregón, and above all, Calles. The Cristero War spawned a rich literature as exemplified in the writings of Jean Meyer. The fractious history of the Mexican Left is documented in the archives at the Universidad Obrera, on the pages of *El Machete,* and in the day-to-day scribblings of the mainstream anti-Communist press. The complicated dance cards of Modotti and Julio Antonio Mella et al. are unraveled in volumes like Elena Poniatowska's *Tinísima* and Mildred Constantine's *Tina Modotti: A Fragile Life.*

Chapter VIII: City & Country. Lázaro Cárdenas's antecedents and presidency have been a source of fascination ever since I grew to political adulthood in the Michoacán outback. This chapter borrows much from the Tata's *Apuntes* taken during the 1933 election campaign. Adolfo Gilly's various volumes examining the Cárdenas years expanded my vision, as did Salvador Novo's chronicles of the Monstruo while Lázaro ran the show. Frank Tannenbaum's work and the many volumes of Carleton Beals were vital assets. Newspaper accounts, particularly those that appeared in *El Universal,* padded out the picture. My long association with Cuauhtémoc Cárdenas helped to resolve points of puzzlement.

Chapter IX: City of Miracles & Hype. The 1940s and '50s were moments of maximum growth for the Monstruo, and a handful of texts such as Humberto Muñoz's study *Migración y Desigualdad Social en la Ciudad de México* and Espinosa López's *Compendio Cronológico* supplied invaluable stats, graphs, and maps on the mass migration from the countryside. Documents supplied by the city government of Nezahualcóyotl were similarly helpful in detailing the sprawl of that squatter city. Diane Davis's *Urban Leviathan* was an essential text, and the narrative owes a special debt to José Agustín's three-volume *Tragicomedia Mexicana*, which informs much of the manuscript from 1940 to the final decade of the century.

Chapter X: Uruchurtu's City. The Iron Regent's long reign was amply recorded in the newspapers of the day. Chava Flores's *Relatos de Mi Barrio* provided musical accompaniment and the life work of Nacho López and Héctor García helped me to see the Monstruo in black and white. Paco Ignacio Taibo II's *Ernesto Guevara, También Conocido Como El Che* provided rich details of the comandantes' stay in Mexico City before they sailed out to make a revolution. Research into the life and death of Mambo king Pérez Prado offered insights into the Cuban community here in the city. Diane Davis reveals how public transportation drew a deep divide between Uruchurto and Díaz Ordaz and eventually finished off the Iron Regent.

Chapter XI: City of Dread & Redemption. *Dos de Octubre ¡No Se Olvide!* Each October 2, the massacre at Tlatelolco is reexamined in close detail. The 40th anniversary of that watershed event presented a cornucopia of remembrance. Nightly forums featured talks by those who lived those tragic days and a windfall of written materials filled in the gaps. I am particularly indebted to *La Jornada*'s day-by-day recapitulation of the events leading up to Tlatelolco. The libretto for this chapter was written first by Carlos Monsiváis in *Días de Guardar* and, of course, Poniatowska's *La Noche de Tlatelolco*.

Chapter XII: City of Denial & Shame. Perhaps because of the frequent scandals and the universal disparagement of Echeverría and López Portillo, this is one of the most fecund periods for observers of contemporary Mexican history to dig into. Alan Riding, who covered these shady dealings for the *New York Times*, put them together in his invaluable *Distant Neighbors*. Julio Scherer's weekly *Proceso* magazine continues to lay into these two cads. As always, José Agustín underwrote the narrative. For my neighbors here in the Centro Histórico, the bad old days of El Negro Durazo remain a living legend.

Chapter XIII: City in Crisis. The shared experiences of these eventful years from economic collapse to the literal collapse of central city neighborhoods and the beginning of the end of a political dynasty that ruled Mexico for a half-century is preserved in the oral histories from which this chapter is drawn. City in Crisis seeks to incorporate the stories and voices of those who survived these terrible times to change the country and the city. Written sources from which I drew these scenes were themselves the stories of others—Poniatowska's *Nada, Nadie*, and Cristina Pacheco's chronicles (*Mar de Historias*) are vivid elements in this mosaic. My own experiences blended into the mix—the story of the damnificados' impact on El Monstruo is borrowed from a long piece I did for *Fire in the Hearth*, edited by Mike Davis and Steve Hiatt, and my travels with Cuauhtémoc Cárdenas helped unmask the monstrous electoral fraud of 1988.

Chapter XIV: City of Neoliberal Nightmares. As the seam of history becomes more contemporary, the writer is presented with a colossal slagheap of materials to cull and consider. Because accounts written in the heat of the moment tend to be more about deadlines than literature, the task of assembling a coherent narrative cost me sleepless nights. I have drawn these tales largely from hundreds of articles and several books (*Rebellion From the Roots*, *The Annexation of Mexico*, and *The War Against Oblivion*) that I churned out during this feverish decade. Other writers who helped me keep the daily drama in perspective were Subcomandante Marcos, Hermann Bellinghausen, Carlos Montemayor, Luis Hernández Navarro, Yvon Le Bot, José Agustín, Carlos Monsiváis, and Paco Taibo II.

Chapter XV: Left City is a stab at trying to make sense out of 10 years of left rule of the Monstruo. The fingerprints of personal participation in these stories are unavoidable. I was here (and still am), reporting on these sea changes for a handful of marginal publications—*Noticias Aliadas* in Lima, the *San Francisco Bay Guardian*, *CounterPunch* on the net, and my own newsletter, first called *México Bárbaro* and then *Blindman's Buff*. Most often, the reportage did not offer an ample vision of just what a left city should look like. Writers like John Zerzan (*The Twilight of the Machines*) were an asset in conceptualizing urban pipedreams and realities. Reading *La Jornada*, which has been a fulcrum for democratic change in both the city and the nation for 25 years, keeps my feet on the ground every morning. I am also grateful to the various left city governments that have published a host of documentation reflecting the city's growth and history down the years, some of which (the handsome volume *Ciudad de México: Crónica de Sus Delagaciones* is one) are as self-critical as they are self-serving.

GLOSSARY

acarreados "trucked-in ones," brought from elsewhere to swell crowd counts
agachado crouched over
aguacero downpour
aguardiente homemade liquor
altiplano highlands
ambulante street vendor
atole corn gruel
Ayuntamiento City Hall

bala ciega "blind bullet," stray shot
barbudo "bearded one"
basura trash
beso smooth
bolsa stock exchange
bombero firefighter
borracho drunk
bote clink
bronca brawl

cachucha baseball-type cap
cacique rural boss

camarilla coterie
camarista chamber maid
campo countryside
casilla voting place
casona mansion
caudillo strongman
chacha an indigenous servant girl
chambelanes a sort of honor guard of adolescent boys at a girl's Sweet
     15 party (*quinceañera*)
charola tray; *slang for* badge
chela *slang*: beer
Chilango *slang*: Mexico City–ite
chingo a lot, a shitload
chisme gossip
chupar Faros smoke a last cigarette before execution: to die
Científicos an elite group under Porfiro Díaz
cilindrino hand-cranked organ
Ciudadela armory
comida corrida three-course lunch
compinche buddy
conchero conch shell trumpeter
cuate pal
curules seats for dignitaries

Day Efe D.F., the Distrito Federal: Mexico City
desagravio atonement, amends
desmadre brawl, free-for-all
diablero hand-truck porter
dicho saying

efectivo cash
ejido village functioning as a rural communal production unit
elote corn on the cob
escuadrón de fusilamiento firing squad
espina thorn

foco guerrilla grouplet
fracaso bungled mess, failure
fritanga greasy fried snack

Gachupín slang: Spaniard (literally "spur-rider")
gallo rooster. slang: whoever you're backing or betting on (think cock-
     fighting)
gaván thick wool serape
gente decente decent people
glorieta traffic circle
Grito Hidalgo's famous cry "¡*Viva México!*," repeated by presidents in
     public every Independence Day eve.
guarura bodyguard

hembra (n.) female
huapanguero singer of *huapangos*, improvised songs from the Huasteca
     region.
huevos con machaca eggs with simmered meat

Imecas units of air pollution
Informe State of the Union address

jipi hippie
jodidos "screwed ones," the powerless underclass
jovencita young lady
julia paddy wagon

licenciado lawyer
Luz y Fuerza Light and Power

macho (n.) male
maciza lean meat
mal gobierno "bad government," the establishment
milagro miracle
mordida bribe
mozo porter
mujer woman, wife
multifamiliar housing project

neta the coolest
nota roja "red note" sensational news item

obra construction project

paliacate kerchief
panadería bread shop
paracaidista squatter
patrón boss
pendejo jerk, asshole
periférico ring road
pinche *expletive*: damned
pinta spray-painted slogan
plaza turf where narcos operate
polvo powder, cocaine
prensa vendida sellout press
prepotencia arrogance
puesto stand
pulque corn beer
puta prostitute

quebradita a herky-jerky dance to banda music

ratero strong-arm crook
reclusorio hoosegow
reparto distribution of land to the landless
rosca Day of the Kings coffee cake ring
ruletero cabdriver who runs a fixed route
rumbo itinerary

Sábana tally sheet
santa madriza holy whupping
sexenio six-year term
sexoservidores sex workers
sobremesa postprandial socializing
sonadero street DJ

tapaboca sterile mask
tecpatl Aztec obsidian knife
teporocho drunk
tianguis bazaar
tilma cactus-fiber cloak
tlatoani Aztec emperor

tocayo, tocaya one who has the same name as another
tochtli a minor Aztec god; also rabbit

vecindad slum building
vecino neighbor
viejo, viejita elder

zafarrancho ruckus
zipizapi pitched battle

BOOKS & PERIODICALS CONSULTED

BOOKS

Agee, Philip. *Inside the Company: CIA Diary*. U.K.: Penguin Books, 1975.

Aguilar, José Angel. *La Decena Trágica* Vols. I and II. Mexico City: Instituto Nacional de los Estudios Históricos de La Revolución Mexicana, 1981.

Agustín, José. *La Tragicomedia Mexicana* Vol. I—*La Vida en México 1940–1970* (1990); Vol. II—*La Vida en México 1970–1982* (1994); Vol. III—*La Vida en México 1982–1994* (1998). Mexico City: Planeta.

Anaya, José Vicente. *Los Poetas Que Cayeron del Cielo: La Generación Beat Comentada y en Su Propia Voz*. Mexico: Instituto de Cultura de Baja California, 1998.

Atlas de la Ciudad de México. Mexico City: Departamento del Distrito Federal/Colegio de México, 1986.

Beals, Carleton, with Diego Rivera. *Mexican Maze*. New York: Lippincott, 1931.

Beals, Carleton. *The Coming Struggle for Latin America*. New York: Halcyon House, 1940.

Bellinghausen, Hermann. *Crónica de Multitudes*. Mexico City: Editorial Océano, 1987.

Bolaño, Roberto. *The Savage Detectives*. New York: Picador–Farrar Straus, 2007.

Bonfil Batalla, Guillermo. *México Profundo: Una Civilización Negada*. Mexico City: Grijalbo, 1967.

Brenner, Anita. *The Wind that Swept Mexico* (first published 1943). Austin, Texas: University of Texas Press, 1984.

Cárdenas del Río, Lázaro. *Apuntes: 1913–1956*, Vols. I and II. Mexico City: Universidad Nacional Autónoma de México, 1972.

Castillo, Bernal Díaz del. *La Historia Verdadera de la Conquista de Nueva España*. Mexico City: Porrúa, 1955.

Codex Boturini. Mexico City: Secretaría de Educación Pública, 1975.

Constantine, Mildred. *Tina Modotti: Una Vida Frágil*. Mexico City: Fondo de Cultura Económico, 1979.

Cosio Villegas, Daniel (ed.). *A Compact History of Mexico*. Mexico City: Colegio de México, 1973.

——*Historia General de México* Vols 1–4 (ed.). Mexico City: Colegio de México, Mexico City, 1976.

Cross, John C. *Informal Politics: Street Vendors and the State in Mexico City*. Stanford, Calif.: Stanford University Press, 1998.

Davis, Diane E. *Urban Leviathan: Mexico City in the 20th Century*. Philadelphia: Temple University Press, 1994.

Davis, Mike and Steve Hiatt (eds.). *Fire in the Hearth*, London: Verso, 1990.

Díaz, Marco (ed.). *La Ciudad: Concepto y Obra*. Mexico City: Universidad Nacional Autónoma de Mexico (UNAM), 1987.

Espinosa López, Enrique. *Ciudad de México: Compendio Cronológico de Su Desarrollo Urbano 1521–2000*. Mexico City: Instituto Politécnico Nacional (IPN), 2003.

Flores, Chava. *Relatos de Mi Barrio*. Mexico City: Ageleste, 1994.

Fuentes, Carlos. *Where the Air Is Clear*. New York: Farrar Straus, 1960.

——*Cristobal Nonato*. Mexico City: Fondo de Cultura Económico, 1987.

Gibler, John. *Mexico Unconquered*. San Francisco: City Lights, 2009.

Gilly, Adolfo. *El Cardenismo: Una Utopía Mexicana*. Mexico City: Cal y Arena, 1994.

——*La Revolución Interrumpida*. Mexico City: El Caballito, 1971.

González González, José. *Lo Negro del Negro Durazo*. Mexico City: Editorial Posada, 1987.

González Rodríguez, Sergio. *Los Bajos Fondos: El Antro, la Bohemia, y el Café*. Mexico City: Cal y Arena, 1988.

González Ruiz, José Enrique (ed.). *El Chaparro y Yo: Un Huachichil en el Corazón del Anáhuac*. Mexico City: Ediciones Unios, 1998.

Gortari Rabiela, Hira de with Regina Hernández Franyuti. *La Ciudad de México y el Distrito Federal: Una Historia Compartida*. Mexico City: Departamento del Distrito Federal, 1988.

Hart, John Mason. *Empire and Revolution: Americans in Mexico Since the Civil War*. Berkeley and Los Angeles: University of California Press, 2002.

Humboldt, Alexander von. *Political Essay on the Kingdom of New Spain*. New York: Riley, 1811 (cited in Kandell).

Jennings, Gary. *Aztec*. New York: Avon Books, 1980.

Kandell, Jonathan. *La Capital: The Biography of Mexico City*. New York: Random House, 1988.

Katz, Friedrich. *The Life and Times of Pancho Villa*. Stanford, Calif.: Stanford University Press, 1998.

——*The Secret War in Mexico*. Chicago: University of Chicago Press, 1981.

Kemper, Robert V. (trans. Poli Delano). *Campesinos en la Ciudad: Gente de Tzintzuntzan*, Mexico City: Secretaría de Educación Pública, 1976.

Krauze, Enrique. Biografías de Poder series. Mexico City: Fondo de Cultura Económico, 1987:

——*Francisco Villa: Entre el Angel y el Fierro*

——*Venustiano Carranza: Puente Entre los Siglos*

——*Álvaro Obregón: El Vértigo de la Victoria*

——*Plutarco Elías Calles: Reformar Desde el Origen*

——*Lázaro Cárdenas: General Misionero*

Lear, John. *Workers, Neighbors, and Citizens: The Revolution in Mexico City*. Lincoln, Neb.: University of Nebraska Press, 2001.

León Portilla, Miguel. *Visiones de Los Vencidos*. Mexico City: UNAM, 1973.

——*Microhistoria de la Ciudad de México*, Mexico City: Departamento del Distrito Federal, 1974.

Lewis, Oscar. *The Children of Sanchez*. New York: Vintage Books, 1961.

López Méndez, Ricardo (ed.). *Estampas de Historia de México*. Mexico City: Secretaría de Educación Pública, 2003.

López Obrador, Andrés Manuel. *Entre la Historia y la Esperanza*. Mexico City: Grijalbo, 1995.

Luna Córnea. *Nacho López*. Mexico City: Consejo Nacional Para la Cultura y el Arte, 2008.

Marías, Javier. *Negra Espalda del Tiempo*. Madrid: Alfaguara, 1998.

Marroqui, José María. *La Ciudad de México*, Vols. I–III. Mexico City: Jesús Medina,1969.

Martínez Assad, Carlos. *El Henriquismo, Una Piedra en el Camino*. Mexico City: Martin Casillas Editores, 1982.

Matos Moctezuma, Eduardo. *Vida y Muerte en el Templo Mayor*. Mexico City: Fondo de Cultura Económico, 1995.

Meyer, Jean A. *The Cristero Rebellion: The Mexican People Between Church and State 1926–1929*. U.K.: Cambridge University Press, 1976.

Monsiváis, Carlos. *Días de Guardar*. Mexico City: Ediciones Era, 1970.

——*No Sin Nosotros*, Era, 1996.

Muñoz, Humberto, Orlandina de Oliveira, Claudio Stern (eds.). *Migración y Desigualdad Social en la Ciudad de México*. Mexico City: UNAM and Colegio de Mexico, 1977.

Nipongo, Nikito. *Museo Nacional de Horrores*. Mexico City: Editorial Océano, 1988.

Novo, Salvador. *Antología 1925–1965*. Mexico City: Editorial Porrúa, 1966.

Oppenheimer, Andres. *Bordering on Chaos: Guerrillas, Stockbrokers, Politicians, and Mexico's Road To Prosperity*. New York: Little, Brown & Co., 1996.

Ota Mishima, María Elena. *Siete Migraciones Japonesas 1890–1978*. Mexico City: Colegio de México, 1982.

Pacheco, Cristina. *Mar de Historias*. Mexico City: La Jornada, 1986–2008

Paz, Octavio. *The Labyrinth of Solitude*. New York: Grove Press, 1985.

Poniatowska, Elena. *La Noche de Tlatelolco*. Mexico City: Era, 1971.

——*Nada, Nadie: Las Voces del Temblor*. Era, 1988.

——*El Tren Pasa Primero*. Madrid: Alfaguara, 2006.

——*Tinísima*, Era, 2006.

Revueltas, José. *El Apando*. Mexico City: Era, 1969.

Riding, Alan. *Vecinos Distantes: Un Retrato de los Mexicanos*. Mexico City: Joaquín Mortiz/Planeta, 1985.

Ross, John. *Rebellion From the Roots: Indian Uprising in Chiapas*. Monroe, Maine: Common Courage, 1995

——*The Annexation of Mexico: From the Aztecs to the IMF*. Common Courage, 1998.

——*The War Against Oblivion: Zapatista Chronicles 1994–2000*. Common Courage, 2000.

——*Zapatista! Making Another World Possible: Chronicles of Resistance 2000–2006*. New York: Nation Books, 2007.

——*Los Marijuanos de Zapicho*, unpublished.

Sahagún, Fray Bernardino de. *Historia General de las Cosas de Nueva España*. Mexico City: Porrúa, 1956.

Scherer, Julio García and Carlos Monsiváis. *Parte de Guerra: Tlatelolco 1968* (Documentos del General Marcelino García Barragán). Mexico City: Editorial Aguilar, 1999.

Secretaría de Educación, Ciudad de México. *México: La Ciudad y Sus Governantes*. Mexico City: 2000.

——*Ciudad de México: Crónica de Sus Delegaciones*. Mexico City: 2007.

Soustelle, Jacques. *El Universo de los Aztecas*. Mexico City: Fondo de Cultura Económico, 1979.

Subcomandante Insurgente Marcos and Paco Ignacio Taibo II. *Muertos Incómodos: Falta Lo Que Falta*. Mexico City: Joaquín Mortiz, 2005.

Taibo, Paco Ignacio II. *Ernesto Guevara, También Conocido Como El Che*. Mexico City: Grupo Editorial Planeta, 1997.

Tannenbaum, Frank. *Mexico: The Struggle for Peace and Bread*. New York: Alfred A. Knopf, 1950.

Turner, John Kenneth. *México Bárbaro*. Mexico City: Costa Amic, 1911.

Ulloa, Berta. *La Revolución Intervenida*. Mexico City: Colegio de México, 1976.

Womack, John. *Zapata and the Mexican Revolution*. New York: Vintage Books, 1968.

Zerzan, John. *The Twilight of the Machines*. Port Townsend, Wash.: Feral House, not copyrighted, 2008.

Zoraida Vázquez, Josefina and Lorenzo Meyer. *The United States and Mexico*. Chicago: University of Chicago Press, 1985.

PERIODICALS

NEWSPAPERS
1900–1920:
La Convención (Mexico City)
El Diario (Mexico City)

El Dictamen (Mexico City)
El Imparcial (Mexico City)
El Liberal (Mexico City)

1914–2009:
Excelsior (Mexico City)
La Crónica de Hoy (Mexico City)
Cuarto Poder (Chiapas)
El Día (Mexico City)
El Economista (Mexico City)
El Financiero (Mexico City)
Financial Times (London)
El Independiente (Mexico City)
La Jornada (Mexico City)
Los Angeles Times
El Machete (Mexico City)
Milenio (Mexico City)
The News (Mexico City)
New York Times
Ovaciones (Mexico City)
El País (Madrid)
Reforma (Mexico City)
San Francisco Bay Guardian
San Francisco Chronicle
San Francisco Examiner
El Sendero del Peje (Mexico City)
Tiempo (San Cristóbal de las Casas)
El Universal (Mexico City)
Uno Más Uno (Mexico City)
Wall Street Journal
Washington Post

MAGAZINES & PERIODICALS
Blindman's Buff (Mexico/USA)*
Business Week
Centro: Guía Para Caminantes (Mexico)
Contralínea (Mexico)
Counterpunch (online)
La Crisis (Mexico)

Forbes Magazine
México Bárbaro (Mexico/USA) *
Mexico Journal (Mexico)
The Nation
Nexos
The New Yorker
Noticias Aliadas (Lima)
Proceso (Mexico)
The Progressive
Punto (Mexico)
Sierra
Texas Observer
Time Magazine
La Voz del Periodista (Mexico)
W Magazine
Z Magazine
Zócalo (Mexico)

*Published electronically by the author.

INDEX